Informatik-Fachberichte
Herausgegeben von W. Brauer
im Auftrag der Gesellschaft für Informatik (GI

33

GI – 10. Jahrestagung

Saarbrücken 30. September – 2. Oktober 1980

Herausgegeben von R. Wilhelm

Springer-Verlag
Berlin Heidelberg New York 1980

Herausgeber
R. Wilhelm
Fachbereich 10 – Angewandte Mathematik und Informatik
Universität des Saarlandes
6600 Saarbrücken

AMS Subject Classifications (1979): 68 A 45, 68 A 50, 94-00, 60-00
CR Subject Classifications (1974): 2.1, 4.0, 4.33, 4.43, 6.0

ISBN-13: 978-3-540-10388-2 e-ISBN-13: 978-3-642-67838-7
DOI: 10.1007/978-3-642-67838-7

CIP-Kurztitelaufnahme der Deutschen Bibliothek
Gesellschaft für Informatik:
GI-Jahrestagung. – Berlin, Heidelberg, New York: Springer.
Bis 5. 1975 u.d.T.: Gesellschaft für Informatik: Jahrestagung / GI,
Gesellschaft für Informatik e.V.
10. 1980. Saarbrücken, 30. September – 2. Oktober 1980. – 1980.
(Informatik-Fachberichte; 33)

2145/3140 - 5 4 3 2 1 0

V o r w o r t

Für die 10. Jahrestagung der Gesellschaft für Informatik wurde die Aufteilung der Vorträge in eingeladene Hauptvorträge übersichtsartigen Charakters, Fachgesprächsvorträge zu ausgewählten Themen und Kurzvorträge aus allen Gebieten der Informatik beibehalten, wie sie sich auf den Jahrestagungen in Berlin und Bonn bewährt hatte. Aus den Fachausschüssen und Fachgruppen der GI und dem Programmkomitee kam eine Reihe von Themenvorschlägen, die sehr verschiedene Gebiete der Informatik abdecken und einen breiten Interessentenkreis ansprechen. Auf der einen Seite liegen ausgesprochene Praktiker-Themen wie "Betriebliche Anwendungen der Datenverarbeitung" und "Rechnerunterstütztes Entwerfen und Konstruieren" auf der anderen Seite die mehr hochschulbezogenen Themen wie "Künstliche Intelligenz" und "Theoretische Informatik". Dazwischen liegen die für Hochschulinformatiker, System- und Anwendungsentwickler gleichermaßen interessanten Gebiete "Datenbanken", "Software-Entwicklung, Softwarepflege" und "Schutzmechanismen in Rechensystemen".

Da die Zusammenfassung aller Fachgesprächs- und Hauptvorträge in einem Tagungsband diesen nahezu unverkäuflich gemacht hätte, beschloß das Programmkomitee eine Zweiteilung des Tagungsbandes. Da das Fachgespräch "Rechnerunterstütztes Entwerfen und Konstruieren (CAD)" den größten Einzelbeitrag zu der Tagung leistete, wurden Hauptvortrag, Fachgesprächsvorträge und ein Kurzvortrag zu diesem Thema in einem zweiten Band veröffentlicht. Wir hoffen, dadurch beiden Bänden eine größere Verbreitung zu ermöglichen.

Das Echo auf die Einladung zum Einreichen von Vorträgen war sehr groß, so daß etwa die Hälfte der eingegangenen Fachgesprächsvorträge abgelehnt werden mußte. Anzumerken ist besonders die starke Beteiligung französischer Vortragender, sicherlich resultierend aus der zentralen Lage des Tagungsortes.

Allen, die zum Gelingen der Tagung beigetragen haben, dem Programmkomitee, den Programmausschüssen für die einzelnen Fachgespräche, dem Organisationskomitee und allen, die ihr Interesse an der Jahrestagung durch Einsendung eines Beitrages bekundet haben, möchte ich hiermit herzlich danken. Besonderer Dank gebührt Frau G. Jacquinot für ihren unermüdlichen Einsatz in allen Phasen der Tagungsvorbereitung.

Saarbrücken, im Juli 1980 Reinhard WILHELM

Folgende Firmen haben die Tagung finanziell unterstützt:

Euro Data GmbH & Co. KG, Saarbrücken

IBM Deutschland GmbH

Karlsberg-Brauerei KG, Homburg

Landeszentralbank im Saarl., Saarbrücken

Gebr. Röchling Bank, Saarbrücken

Saarbergwerke AG, Saarbrücken

Saarbrücker Zeitung, Saarbrücken

Siemens AG, München

PROGRAMMKOMITEE

G. Hotz, Saarbrücken
C.H.A. Koster, Nijmegen
D. Krönig, Konstanz
K. Lagally, Stuttgart
J. Loeckx, Saarbrücken
D. Morgenstern, München
H.-H. Nagel, Hamburg
P.L. Reichertz, Hannover
H. Schecher, München
A.-W. Scheer, Saarbrücken
P.P. Spies, Bonn
W.G. Spruth, Böblingen
W. Stucky, Karlsruhe
W. Ulshöfer, Ludwigshafen

Aus dem GI-Präsidium: P. Mertens, Nürnberg
Vorsitzender: R. Wilhelm, Saarbrücken

PROGRAMMAUSSCHÜSSE

Fachgespräch Software-Entwicklung, Software-Pflege

Vorsitzender: D. Morgenstern, München

R. Duschl, München
H.-J. Eckardt, München
Ch. Haenel, München
H.-J. Hoffmann, Darmstadt
G. Leitz, München
D. Morgenstern, München
J. Nehmer, Kaiserslautern
R. Nowak, München
H. Sattler, München
P. Schlichtiger, München
D. Schütt, München
H. Wössner, München

Fachgespräch Datenbanken

Vorsitzender: W. Stucky, Karlsruhe

A. Blaser, Heidelberg
G. Hanisch, Leverkusen
J. Höhe, Köln
G. Schlageter, Hagen
W. Stucky, Karlsruhe

Fachgespräch Schutzmechanismen in Rechensystemen

Vorsitzender: G. Merbeth, München

Th. Härder, Darmstadt
P.P. Spies, Bonn

K. Lagally, Stuttgart
E. Maehle, Erlangen
G. Merbeth, München
H. Stiegler, München
H. Wettstein, Karlsruhe
P. Wüsten, München

Fachgespräch Neuere Tendenzen in der theoretischen Informatik und ihre Auswirkungen auf die Praxis

Vorsitzender: G. Hotz, Saarbrücken

G. Hotz, Saarbrücken
K. Indermark, Aachen
K. Mehlhorn, Saarbrücken

Fachgespräch Betriebliche Anwendungen der Datenverarbeitung

Vorsitzender: A.-W. Scheer, Saarbrücken

P. Mertens, Nürnberg
A.-W. Scheer, Saarbrücken
W. Ulshöfer, Ludwigshafen

Fachgespräch Künstliche Intelligenz

Vorsitzender: H.-H. Nagel, Hamburg

W. Bibel, München
J. Foith, Karlsruhe
H.-H. Nagel, Hamburg
P. Raulefs, Bonn
J. Siekmann, Karlsruhe
W. Wahlster, Hamburg

Seite

INHALTSVERZEICHNIS

H a u p t v o r t r ä g e

F a c h g e s p r ä c h e (KV = Kurzvortrag)

SOFTWARE-ENTWICKLUNG, SOFTWARE-PFLEGE

KÜNSTLICHE INTELLIGENZ/ARTIFICIAL INTELLIGENCE

BETRIEBLICHE ANWENDUNGEN DER DATENVERARBEITUNG/
BUSINESS APPLICATIONS OF ELECTRONIC DATA PROCESSING

Expert Systems: Looking Back and Looking Ahead

Edward A. Feigenbaum
Computer Science Department
Stanford University
Stanford, CA USA 94305

1.0 Introduction: Symbolic Computation and Inference

This paper will discuss the applied artificial intelligence work that is sometimes called "knowledge engineering". The work is based on computer programs that do symbolic manipulations and symbolic inference, not calculation. The programs I will discuss do essentially no numerical calculation. They discover qualitative lines-of-reasoning leading to solutions to problems stated symbolically.

1.1 Knowledge

Since in this paper I often use the term "knowledge", let me say what I mean by it. The knowledge of an area of expertise—of a field of practice--is generally of two types: a) Facts of the domain--the widely shared knowledge that is written in textbooks, and in journals of a field; that constitutes the kind of material that a professor would lecture about in a class. b) Equally as important to the practice of a field is the heuristic knowledge--knowledge which constitutes the rules of expertise, the rules of good practice, the judgmental rules of the field, the rules of plausible reasoning. These rules collectively constitute what the mathematician, George Polya, has called the "art of good guessing". In contrast to the facts of the field, its rules of expertise, its rules of good guessing, are rarely written down. This knowledge is transmitted in internships, Ph.D. programs, apprenticeships. The programs I will describe require, for expert performance on problems, heuristic knowledge to be combined with the facts of the discipline.

1.2 Expert Systems

The act of obtaining, formalizing and putting to work these kinds of rules is what we call "expertise modeling". In the modeling of expertise, we construct programs called "expert systems". The goal of an "expert system" project is to write a program that achieves a high level of performance on problems that are difficult enough to require significant human expertise for their solution. The more common strategy of AI research is to choose a highly simplified problem--sometimes called a "toy problem"--and exploit the toy problem in depth. In contrast, the problems we choose require the expertise of an M.D., or a Ph.D., or at least a very highly trained specialist in a field, to solve.

An expert system of this type consists of only two things: a knowledge base, and an inference procedure. The knowledge base contains the facts and heuristics; the inference procedure consists of the processes that work over the knowledge base to infer solutions to problems, to do analyses, to form hypotheses, etc. In principle, the knowledge base is separable from the inference procedure.

1.3 The Scientific Issues Underlying Knowledge Engineering

What are the central scientific issues of the Artificial Intelligence field from which this more applied research draws its inspiration? I'd like to categorize these under three headings.

First is the problem of knowledge representation. How shall the knowledge of the field be represented as data structures in the memory of the computer, so that they can be conveniently accessed for problem-solving?

Second is the problem of knowledge utilization. How can this knowledge be used in problem solving? Essentially, this is the question of the design of the inference engine. What designs for the inference engine are available?

Third, and most important, is the question of knowledge acquisition. How is it possible to acquire the knowledge so important for problem-solving automatically or at least semi-automatically, in a way in which the computer facilitates the transfer of expertise from humans (from practitioners or from their texts or their data) to the symbolic data structures that constitute the knowledge representation in the machine? Knowledge acquisition is a long-standing problem of Artificial Intelligence. For a long time it was cloaked under the word "learning". Now we are able to be more precise about the problem of machine learning; and with this increased precision has come a new term, "knowledge acquisition research".

This is the most important of the central problems of Artificial Intelligence research. The reason is simple: to enhance the performance of AI's programs, knowledge is power. The power does not reside in the inference procedure. The power resides in the specific knowledge of the problem domain. The most powerful systems we will be building will be those systems which contain the most knowledge.

This knowledge is currently acquired in a very painstaking way that reminds one of cottage industries, in which individual computer scientists work with individual experts in disciplines painstakingly to explicate heuristics. If applied Artificial Intelligence is to be important in the decades to come, we must have more automatic means for replacing what is currently a very tedious, time-consuming and expensive procedure. The problem of knowledge acquisition is the critical bottleneck problem in Artificial Intelligence.

2.0 A Brief Tutorial Using the MYCIN Program

As the basis of the exposition of underlying ideas, I will use a well-known program called MYCIN.(1) MYCIN is a program for medical diagnosis and therapy. It produces diagnoses of infectious diseases, particularly blood infections and meningitis infections; and advises the physician on antibiotic therapies for treating those infectious diseases. MYCIN conducts a consultation with its user, a physician. This physician is to be distinguished from another kind of doctor who works with MYCIN, the expert. The expert is the person who introduces rules into the MYCIN knowledge base. The user exploits these rules in a dialogue, an interactive consultation that finally terminates in a diagnosis and therapy. The consultation is conducted in a stylized form of English; the doctor never knows about the LISP program underneath. In the consultation the doctor is asked only for patient history and laboratory test results (exogenous data the computer couldn't possibly infer).

A program like MYCIN is using qualitative reasoning to discover a line-of-reasoning, leading to a result (in this case a diagnosis). We can expect that it should be able to explain that line-of-reasoning to the user. In fact, I believe it is necessary that expert consultative systems do so; otherwise, the systems will not be credible to their professional users.

2.1 Knowledge in MYCIN

Figure 1 shows a piece of knowledge in MYCIN. MYCIN contains about five hundred rules, about half of them for blood infections, half for meningitis infections. Each such "production rule" consists of an "if" part and a "then" part (sometimes called "situation part" and "action part"). The "if part" defines a set of conditions of relevancy such that if each of these clauses is true, then the conclusion follows.(2) The rule is shown in approximately the way the expert would enter it; and exactly the way the doctor would see the rule if it were displayed. This piece of knowledge will be evoked from the knowledge base if the conditions are true, and will be built into the line-of-reasoning.

If: 1) The infection which requires therapy is meningitis, and
2) The type of the infection is fungal, and
3) Organisms were not seen on the stain of the culture, and
4) The patient is not a compromised host, and
5) The patient has been to an area that is endemic for coccidiomycoses, and
6) The race of the patient is one of: black asian indian, and
7) The cryptococcal antigen in the csf was not positive

Then: there is suggestive evidence that cryptococcus is not one of the organisms which might be causing the infection.

Figure 1: A piece of knowledge in MYCIN

2.2 Inexact Inference

In MYCIN, there is a way for the expert to state to what extent, on a scale from Ø.1 to 1.Ø, he believes that the preconditions imply the conclusion. 1.Ø is definitional certainty; Ø.9 is "very strong evidence"; Ø.6 is "suggestive evidence"; and so on. These indices are combined in MYCIN with a very simple and easily explained function, yielding an index called a "cumulative certainty factor", an index of "strength of belief" in the line-of-reasoning.

2.3 MYCIN Diagnosis and Therapy

Figure 2 shows a typical MYCIN diagnosis. Then MYCIN proceeds to conduct a shorter consultation with the physician about such things as the patient's known sensitivities to various types of antibiotics and the resistance shown by certain organisms to various kinds of antibiotics. MYCIN then produces a therapy recommendation such as shown in Figure 3.

INFECTION-1 is MENINGITIS

+ <ITEM-1> E.COLI [from clinical evidence only]
+ <ITEM-2> PSEUDOMONAS-AERUGINOSA [from clinical evidence only]
+ <ITEM-3> KLEBSIELLA-PNEUMONIAE [from clinical evidence only]
+ <ITEM-4> DIPLOCOCCUS-PNEUMONIAE [from clinical evidence only]

Figure 2: An example of a MYCIN diagnosis

```
My preferred therapy recommendation is as follows:
   In order to cover for Items <1 2 3 4>:
      Give the following in combination:
      1) AMPICILLIN
      Dose: 3.5g (28.0 ml) q4h IV [calculated on basis of 50 mg/kg]

      2) GENTAMICIN
      Dose: 119 mg (3.0 ml, 80mg/2ml ampule) q8h IV [calculated on
            basis of 1.7 mg/kg] plus consider giving 5 mg q24h
            Intrathecal
      Comments: Monitor serum concentrations

      Since high concentrations of penicillins can inactivate
      aminoglycosides, do not mix these two antibiotics in the same
      IV bottle.
```

Figure 3: An example of a MYCIN antibiotic therapy recommendation

---

2.4 MYCIN's Line-of-Reasoning

MYCIN's line-of-reasoning is a chain of rules that concludes the (perhaps uncertain) presence of an infecting organism from laboratory test data and patient history. The line-of-reasoning is discovered by backward chaining. The search starts with the various possible organisms as "goals to be achieved" and terminates with the data.

The explanation facility can exhibit selected portions of the chain as requested by the user. It can answer a variety of queries during or after the consultation dialogue, such as: "Why (are you asking me for this information)?" or "How (was some particular conclusion reached)?"One interesting form of query is shown in Figure 4. To answer it, MYCIN must keep track of not only acceptable lines-of-reasoning, but also the invalid lines explored, along with reasons for unacceptability.

```
USER: WHY DIDN'T YOU GIVE TETRACYCLINE FOR E.COLI IN REC-1

MYCIN:  TETRACYCLINE was discounted for ITEM-1 (RECOMMENDATION-1)
because there is evidence that this e.coli is not sensitive to it.
```

Figure 4: An example of MYCIN's explanation facility

2.5 MYCIN'S Inference Procedure

We can remove the knowledge base of MYCIN and substitute a set of rules from another domain. That is equivalent to saying that the knowledge base and the inference procedure are separate things in an expert system. Removing from MYCIN its infectious disease diagnosis rules yields an inference "engine" which we call EMYCIN (for Essential Mycin or Empty Mycin or Engine Mycin).

3.0 Building a New System with the EMYCIN Tool: PUFF

Combining with EMYCIN a set of rules for pulmonary function diagnosis (diagnosis of lung diseases) produced a diagnostic program called PUFF (Osborn et al. 1979). In this diagnostic situation, a patient is breathing in and out of an instrument called a spirometer, producing measurements of flow of air in expiration and inhalation, versus lung volume. Data reduction is done by a PDP-11, and data interpretation is done by PUFF.(3) The PUFF report is reviewed by an expert physician, is signed if accurate, put into the patient record and sent to the referring physician. Currently, about 85 per cent of the PUFF outputs are signed without modification.

PUFF consists of about 100 production rules of the MYCIN-like type. It produces reports like that shown in Figure 5.

INTERPRETATION: Elevated lung volumes indicate overinflation. In addition, the rv/tlc ratio is increased, suggesting a mild degree of air trapping. Forced vital capacity is normal but the fevl/fvc ratio is reduced, suggesting airway obstruction of a mild degree. Reduced mid-expiratory flow indicates mild airway obstruction. Obstruction is indicated by curvature in the flow-volume loop of a small degree. Following bronchodilation, the expired flow shows slight improvement. This is confirmed by the lack of change in airway resistance. The low diffusing capacity indicates a loss of alveolar capillary surface, which is moderate.

CONCLUSIONS: The low diffusing capacity, in combination with obstruction and a high total lung capacity would be consistent with a diagnosis of emphysema. The patient's airway obstruction may be caused by smoking. Discontinuation of smoking should help relieve the symptoms.

PULMONARY FUNCTION DIAGNOSIS:
1. MILD OBSTRUCTIVE AIRWAYS DISEASE.
EMPHYSEMATOUS TYPE.

Figure 5: An example of the output of PUFF

4.0 Another Application of the EMYCIN Tool

A group designing airplane wings for the U.S. Air Force uses a software package, called the MARC package(4) for finite element analysis. The package is excellent but complex. Its use requires considerable expertise. The design group wanted a MYCIN-like expert system to consult with designers on the use of the MARC package. EMYCIN was used to create the expert system SACON (for Structural Analysis Consultant)(Bennett and Engelmore 1979). An engineer brings to SACON his design specifications for the structure. SACON produces for him an analysis plan, which he can then translate into subroutine calls for the MARC software.

Figure 6 shows a MYCIN-like production rule for SACON. Figure 7 exhibits a SACON output-analysis plan.

If: 1) The material composing the substructure is one of metal,
2) The analysis error (in percent) that is tolerable is between 5 and 30,
3) The nondimensional stress of the substructure is greater than .9, and
4) The number of cycles the loading is to be applied is between 1000 and 10000,

Then: It is definite that fatigue is one of the stress behavior phenomena in the substructure.

Figure 6: A piece of knowledge (production rule) in the SACON system

---

The following analysis classes are relevant to the analysis of your structure: General-inelastic

The following are specific analysis recommendations you should follow when performing the"structure analysis:

Activate incremental stress - incremental strain analysis.
Model nonlinear stress-strain relation of the material.
Solution will be based on a mix of gradient and Newton methods.
User programs to scan peak stress at each step and evaluate fatigue integrity should be used.
User programs to scan stresses, smooth, and compare with allowable stresses (with appropriate safety factors) should be used.
User programs to scan deflections, calculate relative values, and compare with code limits, should be called upon.
Cumulative strain damage should be calculated.

Figure 7: A SACON output (analysis plan)

5.Ø Concluding Remarks on MYCIN-like Systems

Before leaving the topic of MYCIN-like systems, let me just remark on two trends. The first is a trend in knowledge engineering to put in software packages what we know about building expert systems. EMYCIN represents one of the first of these packages. There are other packages, built for different types of inference procedures. The AGE system assists in the building of inference procedures of a type called "blackboard models", first developed at Carnegie-Mellon University in the HEARSAY-2 speech understanding project. Another package assists with knowledge representation. Called the UNIT package, it is similar to the packages KRL and KL-ONE.

Second, let me mention a unique package that facilitates teaching of knowledge in knowledge bases built for expert systems. This package, called GUIDON (5), is capable of teaching whatever EMYCIN can reason about. Thus, GUIDON can presently teach infectious disease diagnosis and therapy; pulmonary function disease diagnosis; and the use of the MARC structural analysis package. GUIDON consists of a set of rules for another kind of expertise, the expertise of good teachers. If you blend the rules of good teaching with the rules of good practice in a field, then you can teach well the rules of good practice in the field. This is important because the rules of good practice are almost never taught explicitly! They are usually taught informally, by apprenticeship, as I have mentioned earlier.

6.Ø Hypothesis Formation and Theory Formation: DENDRAL and META-DENDRAL

The most widely used of the expert systems of knowledge engineering is the DENDRAL system (Buchanan and Feigenbaum 1978). Initially, DENDRAL analyzed mass spectral data, and inferred a complete structural hypothesis (topology only) for the molecule. DENDRAL was subsequently generalized to produce a set of structural candidates from whatever constraints happened to be available in the problem--not only the mass spectral constraints, but constraints from nuclear magnetic resonance, from other spectral data like IR or UV, or any other information that the chemist happens to know about the problem. Given a set of constraints from various kinds of available data DENDRAL will produce a set of candidate structures that are the best explanations of the data.

6.1 DENDRAL'S Knowledge and Method

DENDRAL's knowledge sources are shown in Figure 8.

Graph Theoretic	Connectivity, Symmetry
Chemical	Atoms, Valences, Stability
Spectroscopic	Mass Spectrometric Fragmentation Rules; Nuclear Magnetic Resonance Rules
Contextual	Origin of Sample, Chemical Properties, Method of Isolation
Judgmental	Goodness-of-Fit Between Predicted and Observed Data

Figure 8: DENDRAL's Sources of Knowledge

DENDRAL uses a three-stage problem-solving process. The first stage is one in which constraints on solution are inferred from spectral data. Given those constraints, plus all other constraints the chemist has noted, the program generates all structures satisfying the problem-specific and the general chemical constraints. Finally it tests the candidates to choose and rank the best. This method is called a plan-generate-and-test strategy.

6.2 DENDRAL'S Applications

DENDRAL has been used in thousands of chemical structure analyses. It has users in universities and industries throughout the U.S., Europe and Australia. Some operate over the international TYMNET to Stanford; others use DENDRAL on their own machines. DENDRAL has been "exported" to the U.S.A. National Institutes of Health. The British recoded it for a PDP-10 in Edinburgh, Scotland. It is running at Lederle Laboratories in Pearl River, New York; and at other chemical and drug companies. Developed in LISP, it was rewritten in BCPL for efficiency. It has also been used to teach structure elucidation in the 1st-year graduate course in organic chemistry at Stanford, and also to check the correctness of published structures.

6.3 Knowledge Acquisition

The knowledge acquisition bottleneck is a critical problem. How is it that chemists arrive at their rules of mass spectrometry? They derive these rules or theories by induction from laboratory experience. The META-DENDRAL program was an attempt to model the processes of theory formation.

The "meta" level, or knowledge acquisition level, of DENDRAL, accepts as input a set of known structure-spectrum pairs. We have stored thousands of these in our computer. The output of META-DENDRAL is a set of general fragmentation rules of the form used by DENDRAL, viz. some particular subgraph of a chemical molecule gives rise to some particular fragmentation. (IF this subgraph occurs, THEN this fragmentation process will occur).

META-DENDRAL's method is also a plan-generate-and-test method. The planning process is called interpretation and summarization, interpreting each spectral data point as a fragmentation, collecting evidence for similar processes and bond environments. The generation process generates a space of plausible rules (not plausible structures ala DENDRAL, but plausible rules of mass spectrometry) constrained by the evidence and by some user-supplied context. The test phase tests the plausible rules, using all the evidence--positive and negative evidence--and generalizes or specializes the rules to improve support from the evidence, seeking a better fit between rules and evidence.

In a major knowledge acquisition experiment, META-DENDRAL inferred the rules of fragmentation for a family of complex steroidal molecules whose mass spectral theory was of interest to our chemist collaborators. A total of 33 rules (covering 3 subfamilies) were formed, all chemically plausible and of high quality (measured in terms of the amount of input data accounted for by each).

How good is META-DENDRAL? To what extent have we succeeded in forming by machine a piece of reasonable scientific theory, i.e. a set of fragmentation rules for in mass spectrometry? We chose the classical scientific route for answering that question. We wrote out the results of the experiment described above and sent the paper to a respected scientific journal, as a scientific contribution. The contribution was refereed and published in the Journal, the standard qualification for a piece of new knowledge entering the science.

7.0 Knowledge Acquisition, Discovery, Conjecturing: AM

Another attempt at modeling knowledge acquisition and discovery was the development of the AM Program.(6) AM's task is the discovery of mathematical concepts (not necessarily new to mankind, but interestingly complex for a program to have discovered).

AM begins with a set of elementary ideas in finite set theory: the idea of a set, a multi-set, set equality, etc. The program contains heuristic knowledge relevant to generating new mathematical concepts, the kinds of heuristics that an expert mathematician would have. It also has heuristics for discarding the bad ideas generated to pick out the interesting new mathematical conjectures. These are the so-called heuristics of interestingness. Thus the knowledge base contains heuristics of combination ("generate"), and heuristics of interestingness ("test").

The program searches a space of possible conjectures that can be generated from the elementary ideas, chooses the most interesting, and pursues that line-of-reasoning. As usual, the program is capable of explaining its line-of-reasoning. The user can interact with the program to give familiar labels to newly-generated concepts, such as: "call that concept 'add'"; "call that 'prime'". The program uses the label subsequently, so that the explanation trace is understandable to the human.

With its heuristics, the program searched the space discovering concepts like: list equality (a specialization of general set equality); cardinality, therefore number; add, subtract, multiply, divide; factoring and the concept of a prime; and the fundamental theorem of arithmetic (the unique factorization of numbers into primes). AM made some conjectures in number theory that were almost really new (discovered many years ago but basically unexplored).

The program eventually began exploring a bigger space than it could cope with, for reasons that are related to my earlier discussion of power and knowledge. As AM plunged deeper into number theory, its general mathematical heuristics became less powerful at controlling search. It needed more specific heuristics about number theory. But these were not given initially because of the possible claim that could be made that the program was initially biased toward discovering number theory. The program lost power as it needed the specialized knowledge that it did not have. A new project, called EURISKO, is exploring how a program can discover new heuristics, as it invents new kinds of things (e.g. as it discovers ideas in number theory, how can it invent heuristics about number theory?)

8.Ø Two Major Principles of Knowledge Engineering

These have already been mentioned earlier and will be summarized here.

The first is that the problem-solving power exhibited by an intelligent agent's performance is primarily the consequence of its knowledge base, and only secondarily a consequence of the inference method employed. Expert systems must be knowledge-rich even if they are methods-poor. This is an important result and one that has only recently become well-understood in AI. For a long time AI focused its attention almost exclusively on the development of clever inference methods. But the power of its systems does not reside in the inference method; almost any inference method will do. The power resides in the knowledge.

Second, experience has shown that this knowledge is largely heuristic knowledge: judgmental, experiential, uncertain. This knowledge is generally "private" to an expert, not because the expert is unwilling to share publicly what he knows, but because he is often unable to. ("What the masters really know is not written in the textbooks of the masters".) This knowledge can be extracted by a careful, painstaking analysis by a second party (a knowledge engineer), operating in the context of a large number of highly specific performance problems. The expertise being modeled is multi-faceted; an expert brings to bear many and varied sources of knowledge in performance.

9.Ø The Promise of Knowledge Engineering

There is presently considerable interest in the scientific, engineering, and industrial use of knowledge engineering techniques. The promise, recognized but barely realized to date, is threefold.

9.1 Cost Reductions

There is a possible enormous cost savings in computation and instrumentation by using these methods. Here I would like to make the case concretely not abstractly. In signal processing applications, involving large amounts of data with poor signal/noise ratios, it is possible to reduce computation costs by several orders-of-magnitude by the use of knowledge-based reasoning rather than brute-force statistical methods.

One of the expert systems whose construction I supervised (Nii and Feigenbaum 1977) involved the interpretation of massive amounts of signal data with very poor signal/noise ratios. The object of the program was to produce a continuously updated "situation understanding" of the objects producing the signals, their positions in space, and their velocities. Using standard signal-processing techniques of cross-correlation and auto-correlation, the computational requirements far exceeded the bounds of all computation available for the problem. In the statistical technique, no use was made of a wealth of knowledge available to interpret the signal data, for example: "textbook" information of the objects as signal-generating sources; "good guesses" available to the human controllers about the "most likely" moves of the objects over considerable periods of time; previously discerned patterns of movement; the laws of physics dictating what the objects could possibly do; what neighboring observing sites had observed; and so on. This was the true symbolic "semantics" and context of the problem. The ongoing model of the situation could be inferred almost completely from this symbolic knowledge, with only occasional reference to the massive amount of signal data for hypothesis verification and for noticing changes. The expert system we built using AI's methods of symbolic inference was able to accomplish the task using (an estimated) two orders of magnitude less computation than the statistical methods required. There is an important lesson here. It makes little sense to use enormous amounts of expensive computation to tease a little signal out of much noise, when most of the understanding can be readily inferred from the symbolic knowledge surrounding the situation.

There is an additional cost saving possible. Sensor bandwidth and sensitivity is expensive. From a symbolic model it is possible, with precision, to generate a set of signal expectations whose emergence in the data would make a difference to the verification of the ongoing model. Sensor parameters can then be "tuned" to the expected signals and signal directions; not every signal in every direction needs to be searched for.

Consider the DENDRAL program described earlier. Because the DENDRAL program knew so much about chemistry in general and mass spectrometry in particular, it could solve structure problems using low-resolution data that chemists could solve at that time only by uwing high-resolution instruments. Low-resolution instrumentation plus knowledge-based reasoning equalled the performance of high-resolution instruments. A low-resolution instrument costs only about $5,000 while a high-resolution instrument costs about $100,000. Therefore, $5,000 plus "smarts" equals a $100,000 instrument.

9.2 The Inevitability Argument

There is a certain inevitability to knowledge engineering and its applications. The cost of the computers will fall drastically during the coming two decades. As it does, many more of the practitioners of the world's professions will be persuaded to turn to economical automatic information processing for assistance in managing the increasing complexity of their daily tasks. They will find, in most of computer science, help only for those of their problems that have a mathematical or statistical core, or are of a routine data-processing nature. But such problems will be rare, except in engineering and physical science. In medicine, biology, management--indeed in most of the world's work—the daily tasks are those requiring symbolic reasoning with detailed professional knowledge. The computers that will act as "intelligent assistants" for these professionals must be endowed with such reasoning capabilities and knowledge.

9.3 The Most Important Gain: New Knowledge

The methodology that I have been describing allows a field to "get its hands on" the real knowledge of the field. The real knowledge of the field is not in the textbooks of the field. The textbooks lack the experiential, judgmental, heuristic knowledge known to the excellent practitioners of the field. When experts argue, the bases on which they argue are largely unspoken. The methodology we use gives a way of bringing heuristic knowledge to the surface and making it concrete—so that it can be discussed, so that consensus can be achieved. If consensus is not achieved, at least the alternatives to the consensus are available for examination. In the end it may be irrelevant that a computer program is available to be an "intelligent assistant". The gain to human knowledge by making explicit the heuristic rules of a discipline will perhaps be the most important contribution of the knowledge-based systems approach.

10.0 Problems of Knowledge Engineering

Though knowledge engineering has made great advances in the last ten years, and is witnessing the pressure toward industrial application, it faces persistent problems.

10.1 The Lack of Adequate and Appropriate Hardware

Artificial Intelligence is largely experimental, not theoretical, computer science. It builds and tests systems. Its laboratory is the computer, and it is suffering from lack of adequate laboratory facilities.

Currently applied AI is machine-limited. That was not the case for the first 15 years of AI. The capabilities of computers to process symbols exceeded our ability to conceive interesting ways to process them. In the last few years the field definitely has been limited by the size and power of its computers. For example, the DENDRAL program is now solving much larger and more difficult problems than we ever conceived that it would solve. System designers are always gentle to their systems: they know the computational boundaries of what is feasible; but users do not. The users have real problems that can easily exceed the computational capabilities of the systems that we provide them. Problems in the physical sciences can command any number of large computers, while an AI project is worth only a small fraction of a DEC PDP-10. The scale must be changed.

AI researchers are now discovering how to construct specialized symbol manipulation machines. These computers have not yet been built by industry because the industry does not yet perceive a wide-spread market. In the past we have adapted the classical computing machines for the symbol manipulation activities that are indeed more general activities of computing. The list processing systems, particularly LISP, in which most AI work has been done, have been pasted on top of the instruction code of conventional computers. That is a mistake. We need specialized symbol processing devices.

The silver lining on the cloud is the emergence of two kinds of facilities, neither of which is yet wide-spread, but both of which are coming. The first is the large memory machine. The era of the 18 bit address of the PDP-10 is ending. We are still using PDP-10's, but we envision machines with address spaces up to 32 bits. Of course the cost of memory is dropping dramatically. It is now possible to buy 2 million words of 36 bit memory for less than 200,000 dollars. Secondly, we see developments like the one at MIT, of a LISP machine(MIT 1979), a piece of hardware and micro-code that runs a version of the LISP language. This provides highly efficient list processing in a personal computer environment. At the moment it is still too expensive to afford as a "personal" machine, but the cost should drop by about a factor of two every few years for the next decade.

10.2 Lack of Cumulation of AI Methods and Techniques

The second problem is the lack of cumulation of AI methods and techniques. The AI field tends to reward scientifically irresponsible pseudo-innovation. That is, it tends to reward individuals for reinventing and renaming concepts and methods that are well-explored.

How does one cumulate knowledge in a science? One way is to publish papers and hope that other people read them and use the ideas. A more traditional way in computer science is to cumulate ideas in software packages, e.g. the cumulation of computational methods of statistics in the large statistical packages. The creation of software packages such as EMYCIN, AGE(Nii and Aiello 1979), ROSIE (at the Rand Corporation), and the various knowledge representation systems, is a hopeful sign that we will solve the problem of cumulation.

10.3 Shortage of Trained Knowledge Engineers

One of the problems of knowledge engineering is the shortage of trained knowledge engineers. There is a strong and growing demand for such specialists. The universities are producing very few of them, but are themselves consuming almost the entire product.

There is significant industrial demand. The Xerox Palo Alto Research Center has hired a number of artificial intelligence researchers to investigate the office automation systems of the future--electronic offices. It is envisioned that programs will help process the "paper" that will flow electronically through the system, as well as perform other office functions such as calendar management, intelligent sorting of electronic mail, and intelligent access to files.

One company servicing the oil industry, Schlumberger, is beginning work on applying knowledge engineering methods to handle the following problem: the number of interpretations that have to be done for signals (coming from physical instrumentation of oil wells) is growing much larger, and it is expensive and difficult to train new interpretation specialists. Schlumberger is interested in replication of expertise. They want to discover what the expertise consists of and then copy it for use at their outlying sites.

Texas Instruments has established an AI group to explore educational uses of AI, and also some aspects of computer-aided design. IBM has a group in Palo Alto, CA, studying the use of AI in system design, and in diagnosis of computer system failures.

There are a number of military applications of AI that are being done now. Hence the defense contract firms are also in the market for knowledge engineers.

Are there any silver linings to this cloud of shortage of people? I think there are. One is the recognition that the AI community must create for itself the equivalent of the aerospace industry to apply its skills and methods to real-world problems. Each new application cannot be done, in the future, by the few skilled technologists at the university laboratories. AI must have an industry that is capable of performing the process and producing useable devices.

10.4 The Problem of Knowledge Acquisition

Another problem of applied AI is a critical scientific problem--the problem of knowledge acquisition. Since the power of expert systems is in their knowledge bases, successful applied AI requires that knowledge move from the heads of experts into programs. This is now a largely manual process of working together with experts. If we continue in this way we could be well into the 21st century before we get generaldy powerful intelligent agents. The process is too slow. Therefore we seek more automatic methods for transferring and transforming knowledge into its computer representation.

We now have knowledge-acquisition systems that are interactive, involving semi-automatic ways of steering the expert to the right piece of knowledge to introduce into the system. We have also done experiments in automatic knowledge acquisition, extracting knowledge directly from "nature", i.e. from data, from evidence (e.g. the META-DENDRAL program described earlier).

Thus, there are silver linings with regard to knowledge acquisition, but the problem is an extremely difficult and important bottleneck problem in this field.

10.5 The Problem of Obtaining and Sustaining Funding

There is great difficulty in obtaining and sustaining sufficient funding for this kind of research. Why?

Like other empirical sciences, AI is much more expensive than its theoretic counterparts. AI projects do not fit the traditional academic model of professors and students. AI projects generally require full-time, post-doctoral professionals and programmers. Computer scientists and experts in the discipline are needed.

Knowledge engineering projects tend to be viewed as high-risk projects and off the "mainstream" of the target discipline. Hence, when these projects are reviewed, peer review is hard to obtain at all. In an era of budget stringency, these peer reviews do not provide the necessary judgments of high priority to fund such projects. When a project, is given a peer review by a group consisting of some computer scientists and some specialists in the domain of expertise, the specialists in the domain will assign high priority to the laboratory work of their own discipline and not to some off-mainstream, high-risk adventure. The same is true of the administrative judgments made by funding agencies concerning program relevance and priority. To put it another way, <u>the knowledge engineering community is not yet a well-established clientele.</u>

Historically the average knowledge engineering project has taken a long time to reach fruition. PUFF and SACON are exceptions, but generally, quick results are rare. Therefore the hit-and-run approach for funding is inappropriate at this stage of the development of knowledge engineering. But there are silver linings. The U.S. National Library of Medicine is funding five-year research programs on knowledge representation. The U.S. Defense Department support is solidifying. And Japan's Ministry of International Trade and Industry is considering large long-term support.

Adequate, long-term funding is important from the point of view of capturing the interest of experts in a domain. Intensive collaboration of experts is a key problem. These relationships between computer scientists and collaborators are very fragile. If the longevity of the grants is not sufficient, then the collaborations will evaporate, as has happened many times to applied AI projects.

10.6 The Development Gap

Finally, there is the so-called "development gap". There is a lack of an orderly bureaucratic process in the research funding agencies for handling programs afer they have achieved their first success as a research project.

Promising knowledge engineering projects, on whose success in application the future credibility of the field depends, have fallen, or will certainly fall, into the so-called "development gap". Industries, also, should be educated so that they perceive a commercial self-interest in filling the gap.

11.0 Acknowledgments

It is fitting, in conclusion, and perhaps instructive to the reader, to acknowledge the major sources of research funds for the work of my groups, the Heuristic Programming Project and SUMEX Project at Stanford University. The primary research funding has come from two agencies over the years: The Defense Advanced Research Projects Agency (ARPA); and the Biotechnology Resources Program of the US National Institutes of Health (NIH). Project support for particular programs has been granted by the US National Science Foundation. Relatively recently we have received support from the US National Library of Medicine; from the Office of Naval Research; from Schlumberger-Doll Research; and from the IBM Corporation.

The work described in this article has been programmed on the facilities of the SUMEX-AIM Computer Resource at Stanford. SUMEX-AIM is a national computer resource for research on the application of artificial intelligence to biology and medicine. The national users (the AIM community) access the computer over the national computer networks TYMNET and ARPANET. The facility consists of Digital Equipment Corporation computers, a dual PDP-10 (KI) with 0.5 megawords, and a 2060 with 0.5 megawords. The research language used is INTERLISP. We are now expanding to significant use of a DEC 2060 with 1.0 megawords and a DEC VAX 11/780 with very large main memory.

Footnotes:

1. Developed originally as the Ph.D. thesis of E.H. Shortliffe, Computer Science Department, Stanford University. Further developed by the Heuristic Programming Project at Stanford. (Shortliffe, 1976) The EMYCIN system, described later, was developed by William VanMelle as his Ph.D. thesis (VanMelle, 1980)

2. Any logical combination of the "if side" clauses can be used.

3. PUFF was developed on a PDP-10 computer at Stanford in collaboration with doctors at Pacific Medical Center in San Francisco, and now runs at the hospital on a PDP-11. (Osborn, et al. 1979)

4. For MARC Analysis Research Corporation.

5. Developed as the Ph.D. thesis of William J. Clancey at Stanford University. (Clancey, 1979)
6. Developed by Douglas B. Lenat as his Ph.D. thesis at Stanford University. (Lenat, 1976)

References:

Bennett, J. S. and Engelmore, R. S., "SACON: A Knowledge-based Consultant for Structural Analysis," Proceedings of the Sixth International Joint Conference on Artificial Intelligence, pp. 47-49, 1979.

Buchanan, B. G. and Feigenbaum, E. A., "DENDRAL and META-DENDRAL: Their Applications Dimensions," Artificial Intelligence 11, 1978.

Clancey, W. J., "Transfer of Rule-Based Expertise Through a Tutorial Dialogue", doctoral dissertation, Computer Science Department, Stanford University, September 1979. (Also Stanford University Computer Science Report 79-769)

Lenat, D., "AM: An Artificial Intelligence Approach to Discovery in Mathematics as Heuristics Search," doctoral dissertation, Computer Science Department, Stanford University, July 1976.

LISP Machine Manual, Artificial Intelligence Laboratory, M.I.T., 1979.

Nii, H. P. and Aiello, N., "AGE: A Knowledge-based Program for Building Knowledge-based Programs," Proceedings of the Sixth International Joint Conference on Artificial Intelligence, pp. 645-655, 1979.

Nii, H. P., and Feigenbaum, E. A., "Rule Based Understanding of Signals," in Waterman and Hayes-Roth (eds.), Pattern-Directed Inference Systems, Academic Press, 1978.

Osborn, J., Fagan, L., Fallat, R., McClung, D. Mitchell, R., "Managing the Data from Respiratory Measurements," Medical Instrumentation, 13:6, November,1979.

Shortliffe, E., "Computer-based Medical Consultations: MYCIN", New York, American Elsevier, 1976.

VanMelle, W. "A Domain-Independent Production Rule System for Consultation Programs", Proceedings of the Sixth International Joint Conference on Artificial Intelligence, pp.923-925, 1979.

RELATIONAL DATABASE SYSTEMS: WHERE WE STAND TODAY

W. Frank King, III

International Business Machines, Inc.

IBM Research, San Jose, California 95193 USA

ABSTRACT:

It has been ten years since E. F. Codd published the breakthrough paper [1] on the idea of a relational database. After this decade of intensive research it is appropriate to evaluate where we stand: to examine the original objectives for relational systems to see if they have been achieved, to examine where relational systems stand with respect to performance, and finally to examine where additional research is needed.

This paper will be presented at the IFIP 8th World Computer Congress in Tokyo,

1.0 ORIGINAL MOTIVATIONS

In his address to this Congress in 1974 [3], Codd outlined the objectives of relational systems.

1. to provide a high degree of data independence;
2. to provide a community view of the data of spartan simplicity, so that a wide variety of users in an enterprise (ranging from the most computer-naive to the most computer-sophisticated) can interact with a common model (while not prohibiting superimposed user views for specialized purposes);
3. to simplify the potentially formidable job of the data base administrator;
4. to introduce a theoretical foundation (albeit modest) into data base management (a field sadly lacking in solid principles and guidelines);
5. to merge the fact retrieval and file management fields in preparation for the addition at a later time of inferential services in the commercial world;
6. to lift data-based application programming to a new level -- a level in which sets (and more specifically relations) are treated as operands instead of being processed element by element.

1.1 Data Independence

Of these objectives data independence has received the most attention and has been achieved to a considerable extent.

SQL [4], QUEL [5], Query By Example [6] and other relational languages allow data accesses and updates to be expressed without mentioning or implying the existence of specific access paths or the physical layout of data. This has the advantage of making application programs simpler and also allows the data management system to choose an optimal strategy for evaluating the program. It is difficult to imagine how a system without a high level language would allow programs to adapt to new storage structures.

For example for the database of Figure 1, to determine if manager Portal has a service person in his office, one invokes the following SQL query:

```
SELECT NAME

FROM EMPLOYEE, OFFICE

WHERE EMPLOYEE.OFFICE = OFFICE.LOCATION

AND OFFICE.MANAGER = 'Portal'

AND EMPLOYEE.JOB = 'Service'.
```

Since the language specifies only what is desired, and not how to obtain it, the system has several choices. For example, one strategy is to search EMPLOYEE looking for service people and for each such entry, use the corresponding OFFICE value to enter into the OFFICE table to see if that employee works for Portal. Another strategy involves first searching OFFICE to find what LOCATIONs Portal manages and then search EMPLOYEE for service people at those locations. Other strategies involve sorting one or both tables.

In System R and other relational systems there is an optimizer[7] which is responsible for selecting the strategy which minimizes the 'cost' of carrying out the SQL statement. Cost is based on estimates of CPU and I/O requirements. Using an optimizer in this way has two benefits: First, the user need not be concerned with storage details, and thus may be more productive. Secondly the user is prohibited from 'taking advantage' of knowledge of such details. The second benefit allows the program to continue functioning as the underlying storage structures evolve with time.

To illustrate that this approach gives programs some independence from data reorganization as the system is 'tuned', suppose there are two transactions which must be run periodically against the database in Figure 1.

T1: List all employees at a given office.

T2: List all employees with a certain job.

When written in a high level language these two queries may be described without specifying the access paths to be used to locate the records which satisfy the query. The transactions will work correctly no matter how the data is organized. If the users expect to run T1 99% of the time, and T2 1% of the time, a database structure which results in high performance is: given an office name, there should be a fast way to find all employees in that office, (e.g. an index on the OFFICE field of the EMPLOYEE table), and records of employees at a given office should be clustered together in secondary storage (to minimize I/O).

Suppose, however, that these estimates are wrong or that the use of the system changes so that T2 runs 99% of the time. Performance on the above database structure will be very poor, and the database will have to restructured. Namely the OFFICE index may be dropped, and a clustering index on JOB should be created. An essential characteristic of a flexible system is that this restructuring not require that programs T1 and T2 be rewritten.

In general, because of the very high level language, most database structuring issues can be deferred until after the applications are written. This 'install now, tune later' philosophy also eases application programming by deferring many performance decisions and by separating performance decisions from application function decisions.

The data independence discussed above is related to the physical storage aspects, for example what indexes exist and how data is placed in storage. Logical data independence has been advanced somewhat but more remains to be done. Logical data independence implies that the application program is independent of the relational schema. For example suppose that initially an inventory database is designed under the assumption that a part is stored in only one warehouse. Such a database may contain one relation

INVENTORY

WAREHOUSE #	PART #	QUANTITY ON HAND

where INVENTORY contains for each part the warehouse where the part is stocked, and the quantity on hand. A program to list parts in short supply would be as follows:

```
SELECT      PART #, QUANTITY ON HAND

FROM        INVENTORY

WHERE       QUANTITY ON HAND < THRESHOLD;
```

Now suppose we change the schema so that a part can be stocked at several warehouses. The same relation suffices (now the key is part #, warehouse #) but the above query is incorrect.

The correct query would be

```
SELECT     PART #, SUM (QUANTITY ON HAND)

FROM       INVENTORY

GROUP BY   PART #

HAVING     SUM (QUANTITY ON HAND) < THRESHOLD;
```

Attribute migration is another common form of schema modification which effects existing programs.

On the other hand some changes in schema can be provided without affecting existing programs. For example the addition of a new field, say part description, can be added without impacting existing applications. This type of schema modification is supported in System R. Techniques for transforming programs in the presence of schema modification must be developed before full logical data independence can be achieved.

1.2 Common Data Model and Set Oriented Application Programming

Several relational systems (System R, Ingres [5]) have been developed where the same interface is available to both application programmers and non-programmer end users. Figure 2 illustrates how SQL [8] defines the data of interest to the program and specifies which program variables are to be used for input ($Z) and output ($X, $Y,). The OPEN statement causes the binding of input variable values and output variable addresses. Subsequently the FETCH statement causes values to be returned into the output variables.

This embedding approach uses the set-oriented facilities of SQL to specify the data of interest, but the data is treated record by record because of limitations in the host programming languages. Therefore objective 6 (set oriented programming) has been only partially achieved but objective 2 (the use of a common model between programmers and non-programmers) has been successfully demonstrated. In several studies of the usability of System R, the use of a common tabular model and the SQL language to describe the intent of an application was cited as having considerable value in enhancing the communication between application programmers and users describing desired applications.

1.3 Database Administration

The database administrators's function has been eased somewhat because of features available in relational systems. We distinguish two areas: database control, and system control.

Database control concerns the definition of the database and the authorization of users to access various subsets of the database. Data control in System R consists of facilities to define and drop relations and to extend a relation by adding a new column. Key uniqueness can be defined (and enforced by the system) by defining a unique index on the collection of key fields. Although integrity assertions and triggers have defined for SQL [9,10], these data control mechanisms have not been implemented. All the data definitions are stored in relations which makes this information accessible through the same facilities as are available to normal user data.

Flexible data control mechanisms contribute to database design by allowing the database administrator to be more experimental in his schema design. Enhanced logical database independence would also contribute to schema design in the same manner. In addition the normalization concepts [12] which have developed since 1970 also suggest guidelines for schema design.

However much research remains to be done to establish techniques for schema design.

System R uses the view mechanism to define the data which a user may be authorized to access. A view can be defined by the SQL language so that data dependent subsets may be specified. The authorization system [13] provides mechanisms for GRANTING and REVOKING users privileges to use (insert, delete, update by column, read) tables or views. The authorization system is integrated into the overall database system and the authorization information is stored in a relation as any other data. The data control environment should be contrasted with current systems where data definition and authorization are implicitly controlled by the generation of control blocks and their subsequent installation into data sets.

System control in System R is handled in an analogous way in that the system itself can be used to control its own configuration. Indexes (access paths) can be added or dropped, physical resources (disk space, control blocks) can be queried as to usage and status, etc. using on line facilities.

1.4 Theoretical Foundation

In his early papers Codd introduced two formal notions which have been the basis of additional theoretical studies: normalization [14], and relational completeness [15]. In particular normalization has been the source of much additional research and is a very useful guideline for database design, however this entire area is outside the focus of this paper.

1.5 Inferential Systems

Several inferential and natural language systems have been attemped [16,17] using a relational database manager as a base. However a discussion of progress in this area is outside the scope of this paper which is focused on relational systems per se.

2.0 RELATIONAL SYSTEM PERFORMANCE

A key question has been the performance potential of relational systems. Perhaps the key contribution of System R has been its emphasis on and approach to performance. In this section we discuss the architecture of System R from the performance viewpoint and summarize some performance statistics. The architecture has two major ideas which effect performance: precompilation (a flexible binding time mechanism), and the access path selection techniques.

2.1 Precompilation

The System R architecture is shown in Figure 3. The Relational Data System (RDS) is split into two distinct functions: (1) a precompiler, called XPREP, which is used to precompile host-language programs and install them as 'canned programs' under System R, and (2) an execution-time system, called XRDI, which controls the execution of these 'canned programs' and also executes SQL statements for ad-hoc terminal users.

When an application programmer has written a PL/I or COBOL program with imbedded SQL statements, his first step is to present the program to the System R precompiler, XPREP, Figure 4. XPREP finds the SQL statements in the program and translates them in three phases into a machine-language 'access module'.

1. Parsing: The parser checks the SQL statement for syntactic validity, and translates it into a conventional parse-tree representation. The parser also returns to the System R precompiler two lists of host program variables found in the SQL statement: a list of input variables (values to be furnished by the calling program and used in processing the statement) and a list of output variables (target locations for data to be fetched by the statement). For example, if the SQL statement being parsed were

   ```
   SELECT NAME,SALARY INTO $X, $Y
   FROM EMPLOYEE WHERE OFFICE = $A AND JOB = $B
   ```

   the input variables would be A and B, and the output variables would be X and Y.

2. Optimization: The System R optimizer is then invoked with the parse tree as input. The optimizer performs several tasks:

   a. First, using the internal catalogs of System R, it resolves all symbolic names in the SQL statement to internal database objects.

   b. A check is made that the current user is authorized to perform the indicated operation on the indicated table(s).

c. If the SQL statement operates on one or more user-defined views, the definitions of the views (stored in parse tree form) are merged with the SQL statement to form a new composite SQL parse tree which operates on real stored tables.

d. The optimizer uses the system catalogs to find the set of available indexes and certain other statistical information on the tables to be processed. This information is used to choose an access path and an algorithm for processing the SQL statement. The design of this access path selection process is given briefly below, and in more detail in [7]. The optimizer represents its chosen access path by means of an ASL (Access Specification Language) [18] specification, and by constructing the RSS control blocks to be used in processing the statement.

3. Code generation: The code generator translates the ASL structures produced by the optimizer into a 370 machine-language routine which implements the chosen access path [19] and will access the database by using the RSS control blocks which were produced by the optimizer.

Each access module contains the SQL statement from which it was originally constructed. This enables the module to be rebuilt if its original access path should become invalid at some future time. When the access module is complete, it is stored in the System R database for later use. If the user who precompiled the program passes the authorization test for all SQL statements in the program, he receives the 'RUN' privilege for the access module.

When the precompiler translates a SQL statement it must also replace the SQL statement in the user's PL/I or COBOL program by a CALL. The call invokes XRDI, the System R entry point used for executing a stored access module. The parameters of the call are the name of the access module, an operation-code, and the addresses of the input and/or output variables to be used in processing the statement.

After the System R precompiler has replaced all the SQL statements in the user's program by calls to XRDI, the program contains pure PL/I or COBOL, and it may be compiled using one of the conventional language compilers. The resulting object program is now ready to be run on System R.

When a 'canned program' is run on System R, it makes calls to XRDI, which in turn loads and invokes the access module for the program. The access module operates on the database by making calls to RSS, and delivers the result to the user's program. This process is illustrated in Figure 5.

The ad-hoc user of System R is supported by a SQL application program called the User-Friendly Interface (UFI), which controls dialog management and formatting of the display terminal. The UFI has an access module of its own, but its access module is not complete because UFI's purpose is to execute SQL statements which are not known in advance. When a user enters an ad-hoc SQL statement, UFI passes the statement to XRDI by means of special 'PREPARE' and 'EXECUTE' calls. The effect of these calls is to cause a new access module to be dynamically generated for the new statement. The dynamically generated access module contains machine-language code, and is in every way indistinguishable from one which was generated by the precompiler.

System R permits many users to be active simultaneously, performing a variety of activities. Some users may be precompiling new programs while others are running existing 'canned programs'. At the same time, other users may be using UFI, querying and updating the database and creating new tables and views. All these simultaneous activities are supported by the automatic locking subsystem [20] built into the RSS.

The advantages gained for canned programs by the precompilation step are twofold:

1. Much of the work of parsing, name-binding, access path selection, and authorization checking can be done once by the precompiler and thus removed from the process of running the canned program.

2. The access module, because it is tailored to one specific program, is much smaller and runs much more efficiently than a generalized SQL interpreter.

2.2 Access Path Selection

In this section we will outline how the access path selection portion of the optimizer works.

A <u>query block</u> is represented by a SELECT list, a FROM list, and a WHERE tree, containing, respectively the list of items to be retrieved, the table(s) referenced, and the boolean predicate specified by the user. A single SQL statement may have many query blocks because a predicate may have one operand which is itself a query. For each query block, an access path is selected by the optimizer.

The optimizer first determines the evaluation order among the query blocks in the statement. Then for each query block, the tables in the FROM list are processed. If there is more than one table in a block, permutations of the join order and of the method of joining are evaluated. The access paths that minimize total cost for the block are chosen from a tree of alternate path choices.

The optimizer examines both the predicates in the query and the access paths available on the tables referenced by the query, and formulates a cost prediction for each access plan, using the following cost formula:

COST = PAGE FETCHES + W x (RSI CALLS).

This cost is a weighted measure of I/O (pages fetched) and CPU used (instructions executed). W is an adjustable weighting factor between I/O and CPU. RSI CALLS is a predicted number of records returned from the RSS to be used in evaluating this query. Since most of System R's CPU time is spent in the RSS, the number of RSI calls is a good approximation for CPU utilization. Thus the choice of a minimum cost path to process a query involves an attempt to minimize total resources required.

Each query block's WHERE tree of predicates is examined. The WHERE tree is initially considered to be in conjunctive normal form, and every conjunct is called a <u>boolean factor (BF)</u>. Boolean factors are notable because every record returned to the user must satisfy every boolean factor. A BF may be a single predicate or a subtree headed by an OR. It is either the whole WHERE tree or is connected to the tree root only by ANDs.

The RSS has a particularly efficient implementation for checking certain combinations of <u>simple</u> predicates. SQL predicates are said to be <u>simple</u> if they can be put in the form: <column-name,scalar-comparison,literal-value>. An index is said to <u>match</u> a boolean factor if the boolean factor is a <u>simple</u> predicate whose referenced column is the index key; e.g., an index on SALARY matches the predicate 'SALARY = 20000'. If an index matches a boolean factor, an access using that index is an efficient way to satisfy the boolean factor.

A simple boolean factor is a BF composed of simple predicates. A simple BF in disjunctive normal form can be checked directly by RSS, eliminating the overhead of RSS calls to retrieve non-qualifying records. Non simple predicates must be applied by the compiled program to test each record retrieved by an RSS call.

The optimizer retrieves statistics on the tables in the query and on the access paths available on each table. The access paths considered are indexes and segment scans. Indexes retrieve records in key value order. A segment scan retrieves records in a RSS determined order but touches each data page only once. One index may be clustering, so that records having the same or adjacent key values are stored on the same data page. The statistics kept are the following:

For each table T,
- -NCARD(T), the cardinality of table T
- -TCARD(T), the number of 4K byte pages occupied by T

and for each index I on table T,
- -ICARD(I), the number of distinct keys in index I
- NINDX(I), the number of pages in index I.

These statistics are maintained in the System R catalogs, and come from several sources. Initial table loading and index creation initialize these statistics. They are then updated periodically by an UPDATE STATISTICS command, which can be run by an authorized user. System R does not update these statistics at every INSERT, DELETE, or UPDATE because of the extra database operations and the locking bottleneck this would create. Continuous maintenance of statistics would tend to serialize access to a table for users that modify the table contents.

Using these statistics, the optimizer assigns a selectivity factor for each boolean factor in the WHERE predicate. This selectivity factor is the expected fraction of records which will satisfy the predicate. The product of the selectivity factors with the table cardinalities produces QCARD, the expected cardinality of the query result.

For single table queries, the cheapest access path is obtained by evaluating the cost for each available access path. For each such access path, a cost is computed along with the ordering of the records it will produce. An order is 'interesting' with respect to a query if the query result must be grouped or sorted in that order. Scanning along the SALARY index in ascending order, for example, will produce some cost C and a record order of SALARY (ascending). To find the cheapest access plan for a single table query, we need only to examine the cheapest access path which produces records in each 'interesting' order and the cheapest 'unordered' access path. For a single table query, if there are no GROUP BY or ORDER BY clauses in the query, the cheapest access path is the one chosen. If there are GROUP BY or ORDER BY clauses, or joins, then the cost for producing that interesting ordering must be compared to the cost of the cheapest unordered path plus the cost of sorting QCARD records into the proper order. The cheapest of these alternatives is chosen as the plan for the query block.

For handling joins, the System R optimizer chooses among two methods. Reference [21] showed that for the System R context, one of these two methods is usually optimal. We first describe these methods for two way joins and then we discuss how they are extended for n-way joins. In joins involving two tables, one table is called the outer table, from which a record will be retrieved first, and the other is the inner table, from which records will be retrieved, possibly depending on the values obtained in the outer table record. A predicate which relates columns of two tables to be joined is called a join predicate. The columns referenced in a join predicate are called join columns.

The first join method, called the <u>nested loops</u> method, begins by opening a cursor on the outer table and retrieving a record. For each outer table record obtained, a cursor is opened on the inner table to retrieve, one at a time, all the records of the inner table which satisfy the join predicate. The composite records formed by the outer table record/inner table record pairs comprise the result of this join. A clustering index which matches the join predicate is a particularly good path for the inner table.

The second join method, <u>merge join</u>, begins by opening cursors on two access paths which produce outer and inner table records in the join column order. An outer table record is retrieved. As in the nested loop join, inner table records are retrieved which match the outer table record on the join column value. As before, the composite records formed by the outer table record/inner table record pairs comprise the result of this join. This method differs from the nested loop method in that for each new join column value, the position of the first matching inner table record (if any) is marked by a placeholder. Thus when the outer table cursor is advanced, if the next outer record's join column value is the same as the previous outer record's, then the inner table cursor can be continued from the placeholder position. If the next outer record's join column value is greater than that of the previous outer record, then the inner table cursor is advanced from its current position. In doing this, the inner cursor may find no matches for that outer record, and this will cause an advance of the outer table cursor. This iterates until the next match of inner and outer join column values. It should be noted that all of the inner and outer records will be scanned at least once and that those passed over will never be rescanned during the rest of the join processing.

Merge joins require the outer and inner tables to be scanned in join column order. This implies that, along with the columns mentioned in ORDER BY and GROUP BY, columns of equi-join predicates (those of the form Table1.column1 = Table2.column2) also define 'interesting' orders. If there is more than one join predicate for a pair of tables, one of them is used as the join predicate and the others are treated as ordinary predicates. The merging method is only applied to equi-joins, although in principle it could be applied to other types of joins. If one or both of the tables to be joined has no indexes on the join column, it must be sorted into a temporary list which is ordered by the join column.

The costs for joins are computed from the costs of accessing each of the tables using the cost formulas for single table access paths. Let C-outer(path1) be the cost of scanning the outer table via path1, and N be the cardinality of the outer table records which satisfy the simple predicates on the outer table. N is obtained from the product of the selectivity factors of all simple predicates on the outer table.

Let C-inner(path2) be the cost of scanning the portion of the inner table which corresponds to one join column value in the outer table, applying all simple predicates. Since the column value of the join predicate for the outer table is known, the join predicate is now <u>simple</u>. Then the cost of a join is

C-join(path1,path2)=C-outer(path1)+NxC-inner(path2)+sort cost if required

A n-way join access path consists of an ordered list of the tables to be joined, the join method used for each join, and a plan indicating how each table is to be accessed. If either the outer composite table or the inner table needs to be sorted before joining, then that is also included in the plan.

2.3 Performance

Chamberlin et al [8] have done a performance study of System R to understand the cost of precompilation and to evaluate the overall system performance. A portion of the study is summarized here. For a range of ad hoc queries (simple selection, two relation join, selection after grouping) the total cpu time to process (precompile and execute) ranged from 270 to 630 msec. on a 370/158. The execution time ranged from 27 to 175 msec. The experiment was run on a 7.4 megabyte database of three tables. For application programs containing SQL statements, the precompilation time was less than the PL/I compile time and the execution time ranged from 30 to 65 msec.

These data indicate that relational systems can be implemented with reasonable performance and that exotic hardware (associative memories, etc.) is not a prerequisite for relational systems.

3.0 FUTURE DIRECTIONS

Now that relational technology is at hand it is appropriate to look at the new directions which may shape the next generation of database research and development. For pedagogical purposes I have divided future directions into two areas: functional enhancements to database systems, and database system architecture.

3.1 Functional Enhancements

Current database system products offer considerable database accessing function and relational systems (System R, Ingres, Query By Example) have demonstrated even higher level database interfaces. In addition the use of these interfaces from several environments has been demonstrated (ad hoc query, interactive application programming, telecommunications). The next step is to provide a variety of data model types at the choice of the user with common underlying data. That is, the user could decide on a network data model for one application and a relational model for another when both applications used the same data. Date [22] has designed a Universal Data Language which supports this notion for PL/I, and it appears feasible to implement such a system as long as the various models are carefully coordinated. The support of several existing models may have certain problems where the semantics of the models do not coincide. For example suppose one application wanted a hierarchical model with the association between parent and child records controlled by procedural selection of the parent as is possible in IMS. This procedural selection has no analogue in the relational model so that it would not be possible to have a full function relational model over the same data. Of course as long as the hierarchical model is determined by value oriented positional selection, a corresponding relational model can be supported.

As discussed above additional levels of data independence will be an important future direction. Techniques must be developed to insulate applications from changes in the logical structure of the database. Earlier we illustrated this problem for a change in the relational schema. Another dimension of schema independence arises during application conversion (say converting applications from a hierarchical schema to a relational schema). Techniques must be developed to convert application logic to take advantage of the new schema capabilities.

Relational database systems automatically select the best technique for accessing the required data. Distributed systems provide additional dimensions to this process. Related to physical data independence, the location of the node performing the execution of the request will have to be determined. In addition the request may be executed at several nodes. For example a join involving tables at different sites may be partially executed at several sites.

In future distributed systems (like one being investigated in our laboratory based on System R) data may be partitioned between nodes, may be replicated for performance and availability, and may be kept in various versions (say as of a certain time). These extensions must be provided in a manner so that the application program has the illusion that the application ran at a single site, with a single database copy, with the integrity implied by a serial schedule [23].

A final area where considerable research is being focused is data semantics, or in operational terms, having the system take more responsibility for the correctness of the data itself. Current systems provide only rudimentary assistance of the following forms:

1. (Unique) value support. If a key field is declared to be unique, the system will check each insertion/update to maintain this constraint. In addition some systems allow the database definer to specify values of fields (for example marital status is either single, married, widowed, divorced; age is an integer greater than 0 and less than 137).

2. Transaction support. A related sequence of database actions can be bracketed by the application programmer to indicate that these actions are to be either completely done, or if a malfunction occurs during the course of the sequence, to be completely undone. The transaction notion is used to guarantee that _if_ a transaction preserves the correctness of the database, then partial transactions do not occur.

3. Consistency (Program Isolation). Related to transaction support is the notion of consistency which addresses the problem of multiple transactions concurrently sharing the same data. Level three consistency [24] provides that each concurrent transaction is executed so that the effect is as if the transactions were executed in some serial order. Systems which provide level three consistency do not require the application programmer to be aware of consistency problems.

More powerful semantic support has been proposed. SQL has defined both integrity constraints and triggers. Integrity constraints are any valid SQL predicate to be checked against the database contents at the end of the transaction and extend value support to subset membership (employee # in medical file must be employee # in personnel file) and to data dependent value checking (manager's salary not greater than his superior), etc. In addition constraints on transitions (age monotonically increasing) of database values have been defined. However efficient techniques for implementing these constraints have not been explored. Triggers are database transactions which can be invoked when certain events occur (on update of inventory, if quantity on hand is less than ...). In SQL these transactions are constrained in that they consist only of SQL statements and the triggering event can depend only on database contents. Several investigations have begun [25] into defining constraints and triggers using abstract data type concepts thus using the full programming language power for their description.

3.2 Database System Architecture

In this section we will outline expected new directions in the architecture of database systems. Of primary concern here are those future directions which will come about because of the need for higher performance database systems. Current full function database systems, e.g. IMS, running on a large mainframe (3033 class) can execute 10 to 15 transactions per second where a transaction causes the execution of 100K instructions and 7 to 10 input/output requests to the database (I/O's for program loading, message input and output, logging are in addition). Higher performance, lower function systems can do better. The

Airlines Control Program (ACP)[26] can execute 180 transactions per second where the transaction causes the execution of 15K instructions and 10 I/O's.

The complexity of a transaction which affects the performance of a database system, can be characterized by the following factors:

1. Number of application program instructions executed.
   Clearly this is application dependent. However in a study of a banking application (account withdraw/deposit, update teller file, update bank ledgers) on System R, we found that the application instruction execution was 3-4 % of the total number of instructions executed.

2. Number of database management system instructions executed.

   This is determined by the complexity of the facilities used by the transaction. Reductions in this number are primarily effected by reducing the complexity of the data model supported by the database management system and by reducing the function of the ancillary aspects of the database management system (level of consistency, recovery, maximum database size supported, dynamicity of definition and control aspects, etc.). The first reduction technique is illustrated by the Main Storage Data Base of the Fast Path feature of IMS [27] where the usual hierarchical data model is restricted to be a root segment only (flat file). The DL/I language can access this database using the usual search predicates. Even more extreme is ACP where the database is a collection of fixed length records accessed by relative record number.

   The second complexity reduction technique is also illustrated by Fast Path where the main storage database is virtual memory resident (no buffer pool management, etc.). As another example, System R can be run as a single user system with no locking overhead.

   Related to the complexity of the database management system is the complexity and usage of the underlying operating system. For example the input/output supervisor of ACP is considerably faster than in most contemporary operating systems (2500 instructions in VM/370). CICS - [28] does its own tasking to avoid the overhead of OS/370 task management.

3. Number (and elapsed time) of accesses to secondary storage. Current DASD technology provides 25-35 msec. access to a random disk block. DASD-cache systems such as the Memorex 3770 are available to reduce this access time if the hit ratio (locality of reference) is high enough. Alternatively intelligent disk controllers have been proposed and built [29,30,31,32,33] which can process a larger, higher level data request. The Content Addressable File System (CAFS) [29,30] can process a boolean predicate (AGE < 25 and (SALARY < 4000 or JOB = SALES MANAGER)) in the controller and return the records satisfying the predicate to the host.

   Typically these devices can search a collection of tracks (cylinder) in parallel, applying the predicate to each record as it streams past the read head. More complicated searches (relational projection and join) have also been proposed. For the case of record selection, if we assume IBM 3350 characteristics then 30 tracks are being searched in parallel, each consisting of 19.6K bytes in 16.6 msec. However the track to track seek requires another 10 msec. For comparison assume the record length is 100 bytes implying approximately 220 records searched per msec. On a 3033 class machine System R can apply a search predicate to roughly 14 records per msec. (depending on predicate complexity) if the data is in the buffer pool or to approximately 1 record per msec. if data transfer from DASD is required.

This rough analysis illustrates the applications where the intelligent controller technology is viable i.e., to applications requiring large scale searches of non indexed files. For example if the buffer hit ratio is such that System R can search 7 records per msec. then its performance using an index will be comparable to an intelligent disk controller if the index reduces the records to be searched by a factor of only 30.

Perhaps a simpler technique to reduce secondary storage access is to increase the buffer pool size of the database management system itself. If the buffer pool management is carefully designed this can have important effects in reducing the apparent transaction complexity (increasing the transactions per second). In an experiment using System R on an emulated [34] 10 mip processor with a large database, Howard [35] found that a large buffer pool (> 1 megabyte) could substantially enhance system performance (Figure 6). This figure also illustrates that with processors at expected speeds in the early 1980's, we cannot expect to get to ACP or higher levels of performance for full function database management system with only faster processors and larger buffer pools. New architectural directions are required.

From the above discussion we can draw the following conclusions:

1. The application program logic execution cost is relatively insignificant.

2. By reducing the complexity and function of the database management system one can increase performance. ACP provides an operational example at 180 transaction per second for a 5 mip processor operating at 85% utilization [26].

3. Intelligent disk controllers are not applicable to typical database management system applications.

4. Large buffer pools reduce DASD accesses and operating system path length and can be expected to increase full function database management system performance but not up to ACP levels.

From these conclusions we are left with the question of how to get ACP (or higher) performance levels with full function database capabilities. Four architectural approaches are being examined: multiprocessing, vector processing, backend database processors, and high speed connected collections of minicomputers. These last two approaches are distinguished from the first two by the degree of coupling between the processors. Both multiprocessors and vector processors assume a central shared memory whereas both the backend and the mini approaches have a teleprocessing/channel connection between the processors.

System R, IMS and other systems are designed to run in a multiprocessor environment in that all the code is reentrant and can be concurrently executed. In contrast CICS [28] is run entirely in one partition (address space) with no concurrent execution possible. However little is known about the performance implications of two or higher levels of multiprocessing.

Backend database machines were first proposed by Canaday et al [36]. More recently Hsiao [37] has proposed a database machine with properties rather like an intelligent disk controller. The main distinction is that the Database Computer (DBC) uses indexes to narrow the parallel by track search to specific cylinders of the database rather than doing a full file search as with CAFS. The performance analysis [38] which compares DBC to System R, shows very little performance advantage for DBC for typical transactions.

The analysis examined several access path selection strategies for single table queries. The two most important are option 1 (clustered index matching equality predicate) and option 3 (nonclustered index matching equality predicate).

Using the equations of the analysis [38] and the parameter values for System R in Figure 7, we get the ratio of System R cost to DBC cost shown in Figure 8 (where cost is I/O time plus normalized CPU time) for options 1 and 3.

We can observe that for reasonably selective indexes (small values of n/i) the System R technology compares well with the special purpose DBC technology.

The remainder of the discussion on future architecture directions will be focused on two new approaches, vector processor architectures and interconnected minicomputers. In certain of high transaction rate environments many of the transactions are of the same type (e.g. account balance checking, but for various accounts; cash withdrawals, etc.). This suggests that some form of inter transaction parallel processing may be possible for such data base applications.

One approach being investigated at the IBM San Jose Research Laboratory is to consider a <u>vectorized</u> cpu architecture. The vectorized architecture would extend the normal instruction set by associating with each register a vector of n registers. This would permit extension of each instruction operand (memory location, register) to a vector of operands. For example, the load instruction L R1, 0(R2) (which in normal mode places into register 1 the contents of the memory location contained in register 2) would load a vector of registers R1 = (R11, R12, ... R1n) from the memory locations contained in registers R2 = (R21, R22, ... R2n) respectively. For transactions which could be executed in parallel, each set (column) of registers is associated with a particular transaction and up to n transactions could be executed in parallel.

To illustrate this approach consider the program flow graph of Figure 9 where each box represents a linear sequence of instructions. The last instruction of the box labeled 1 is a branch instruction; some executions will proceed to box 2 and others to box 3. Now with a vector cpu as discussed above we could execute, say 5, transactions in parallel through box 1. Then perhaps three of these transactions would branch to the left and 2 to the right. Because of the single instruction mode, box 2 and 3 must be executed serially but with box 2 having 3 transactions in parallel and box 3 having 2 transactions in parallel. Now all five transactions could execute box 4 in parallel. For this approach to be feasible, we must find a way of grouping transactions so that essentially the same instruction sequence is executed, however with different data.

The highspeed connected collection of minicomputers approach is being pursued by Dewitt [39] in the DIRECT project, Figure 10, at the University of Wisconsin, and by the System D project at IBM, San Jose. DIRECT interconnects a collection of LSI 11/03 microprocessors to CCD memories via a serial cross bar switch. In addition this interconnection of microprocessors and memories is a backend to a host PDP 11/45 which handles terminal communications and executes user code. There is an intermediate PDP 11/40 which interacts with the host, controls the microprocessors (allocation) and manages the contents of the CCD memory and the associated mass storage device.

A varible number of processors can be assigned to a query where each processor can perform relational operators (restrict, project, join, etc.) on the data in the CCD memory to which it is attached. For example if relation A is M pages long and relation B is N pages long, M>N, and if M processors are assigned to the join then the join can proceed in parallel as follows: each page of A is transmitted to a processor. A page at a time of B is transmitted to each processor which does the two page join. Similarly projection and restriction can be done in parallel. Since no indexes are used by DIRECT, this system is oriented to the same application environment as intelligent disk controllers; large file searches. However, this architecture could be used to enhance the performance of typical database transactions.

System D interconnects a collection of Series 1 (40) minicomputes via a ring and is developing techniques to handle typical database transaction processing. In contrast to the data partitioning approach being studied by DIRECT (where a table is partitioned into pages and each processor has full relational function to apply to its portion of the table), System D is studying functional partitioning where separate processors do data management, access path selection, concurrency/consistency control, recovery and checkpoint processing, etc.

SUMMARY

We have examined the progress made toward the goal of a relational database system described by Codd a decade ago. Striking progress has been made in the areas of data independence, higher level application programming, a simple data model which can be used in several environments, and easing the database administrator function. On the performance side relational systèms can approach the performance of current network and hierarchic database systems. In all, the original goals of the relational approach have been fulfilled.

Much remains to be done to shape the database systems of the future. Systems are needed which support more than one data model, which have more data independence, which support distributed applications, and which know more about the data in the database.

Much higher performance systems are needed. Alternative database architectures which involve new machine hardware capabilities are being studied. I believe that multi and vector processing approaches as well as systems of interconnected minicomputers are exciting directions for the next decade.

ACKNOWLEDGEMENT

During much of this decade I have been involved with the relational research at the IBM San Jose Research Laboratory and therefore much of this paper was based on the experiences of the System R project [2]. It is my pleasure to acknowledge my colleagues on the System R team.

REFERENCES

1. E. F. Codd, A relational model for large shared data banks, Communications ACM 13, 6 June 1970, 377-387.

2. M. M. Astrahan, et al., System R: relational approach to database management, ACM Transactions on Database Systems 1,2 June 1976, 97-137.

3. E. F. Codd, Recent investigations in relational database systems, Information Processing 74, 1017-1021.

4. D. D. Chamberlin, M. M. Astrahan, K. P. Eswaran, P. P. Griffiths, R. A. Lorie, J. W. Mehl, P. Reisner, and B. W. Wade, SEQUEL2: a unified approach to data definition, manipulation, and control, IBM Journal Research & Development November 1976, 560-575.

5. M. Stonebaker, E. Wong, P. Kreps, and G. Held, The design and implementation of INGRES, ACM Transactions Database Systems 1,3 (Sept. 1976), 189-222.

6. M. M. Zloof, Query By Example, 1975 AFIPS National Computer Conference Procedures Vol. 44, AFIPS Press, Montvale, N.J., pp. 431-438.

7. P. G. Selinger, M. M. Astrahan, D. D. Chamberlin, R. A. Lorie, and T. G. Price, Access path selection in a relational database system, IBM Research Report RJ2429, San Jose, California, January, 1979; ACM 1979, SIGMOD, pp. 23-34.

8. D. D. Chamberlin, et al. Support for repetitive transactions and ad-hoc query in System R,IBM Research Report RJ2551, San Jose, California, May 1979.

9. K. P. Eswaran and D. D. Chamberlin, Functional specification of a subsystem for data base integrity, Proceedings of Very Large Databases Conference, September 1975, pp. 48-68.

10. K. P. Eswaran, Specifications, implementations and interactions of a trigger subsystem in an integrated database system, IBM Research Report RJ1814 San Jose, California, November 1976.

11. V. Lum, S. Ghosh, M. Schkolick, D. Jefferson, S. Su, J. Fry, T. Teorey, B. Yao, 1978 New Orleans Data Base Design Workshop Report, IBM Research Report RJ2554, San Jose, California, July 1979.

12. R. Fagin, Multivalued dependencies and a new normal form for relational databases, ACM Transactions Database Systems, Vol. 2, No. 3, September 1977.

13. P. G. Griffiths and B. W. Wade, An authorization mechanism for a relational database system, ACM Transactions Database Systems 1,3 September 1976 242,255.

14. E. F. Codd, Further normalization of the data base relational model, Courant Computer Science Symposia 6, Data Base Systems, New York, May 1971, Prentice-Hall, New York, 1971, pp. 33-64.

15. E. F. Codd, Relational completeness of data-base sublanguages, Courant Computer Science Symposia 6, Data Base Systems, New York, May 1971, pp. 65-98.

16. E. F. Codd, Seven steps to rendezvous with the casual user, IFIP TC-2 Working Conference Data Base Management Systems, North-Holland, Amsterdam, April 1979.

17. J. Mylopoulos, A. Borgida, P. Cohen, N. Roussopoulos, J. Tsotsos, and H. Wong, TORUS-a natural language understanding system for data management, Proceedings 4th International Joint Conference Artificial Intelligence, Tbilisi, USSR, Sept. 1975, pp. 414-421.

18. R. A. Lorie and J. F. Nilsson, An access specification language for a relational data base system, IBM Research Report RJ2218, San Jose, California, April 1978.

19. R. A. Lorie and B. Wade, The compilation of a very high level data language, IBM Research Report RJ2008, IBM Research, San Jose, California, May 1977.

20. J. N. Gray, R. A. Lorie, and G. R. Putzolu, Granularity of locks in a shared data base, Proceedings Very Large Data Bases Conference, September 1975, pp. 428-451.

21. M. W. Blasgen and K. P. Eswaran, On the evaluation of queries in a relational data base system, IBM Research Report RJ1745, San Jose, California, April 1976.

22. C. J. Date, An architecture for high level language database extensions: PL/I version, Proceedings SEAS Anniversary Meeting, Cambridge, England, September 1977.

23. K. P. Eswaran, J. N. Gray, R. A. Lorie, and I. L. Traiger, The notions of consistency and predicate locks in a data base system, Communications of ACM 19, November 1976, 624-633.

24. J. N. Gray, R. A. Lorie, G. R. Putzolu, and I. L. Traiger, Granularity of locks and degrees of consistency in a shared data base, IFIP TC-2 Working Conference Modeling in Data Base Management Systems, North-Holland, Amsterdam, January 1976.

25. M. L. Brodie, et al, What is the use of abstract data types in data bases? Proceedings Fourth International Conference on Very Large Data Bases, West Berlin, Germany, September 1978.

26. J. E. Siwiec, A high-performance DB/DC system, IBM Systems Journal Vol. 16, No. 2, 1977, pp. 169-195.

27. W. C. McGee, The information management system IMS/VS Part II: Data base facilities, IBM Systems Journal, Vol. 16, No. 2, 1977.

28. CICS General Information Manual, GC33-0066-4, Fifth Edition, September 1979, p. 6.

29. E. Babb, Implementing a relational database by means of specialized hardware, ACM Transactions on Database Systems, Vol. 4, No. 1, March 1979, pp. 1-29.

30. G. F. Coulouris, J. M. Evans, and R. W. Mitchell, Towards content addressing in data bases, Computer Journal, 15, 2 (1972), pp. 95-98.

31. C. S. Lin, D. C. P. Smith, and J. M. Smith, The design of a rotating associative memory for relational database applications, ACM Transactions on Database Systems, 1, 1 March 1976, 53-65.

32. E. A. Ozkarahan, S. A. Schuster, and K. C. Smith, RAP - an associative processor for data base management, Proceedings of 1975 NCC, Vol. 44 AFIPS Press, Montvale, N. J., pp. 379-387.

33. S. Y. W. Su and G. J. Lipovski, CASSM: A cellular system for very large data bases, Proceedings Very Large Data Base Conference Framingham, Massachusetts, September 1975, pp. 456-472.

34. J. H. Howard, Experiments with virtual memory buffering, in preparation.

35. J. H. Howard Private communication.

36. R. H. Canaday, R. D. Harrison, E. L. Evie, J. L. Ryder, and L. A. Wehr, A Back-end computer for data base management, Communications of ACM, October 1974, Vol. 17, No. 10, pp. 575-582.

37. J. Banerjee, D. K. Hsiao, and K. Kannan, DBC-A database computer for very large databases, IEEE Transactions on Computers, Vol. c-28, No. 6, June 1979, pp. 414-429.

38. J. Banerjee and D. K. Hsiao, Performance study of a database machine in supporting relational databases, Proceedings Very Large Data Bases, West Berlin, Germany, September 1978, pp. 319-329.

39. D. J. DeWitt, DIRECT-A multiprocessor Organization for supporting relational database management systems, Vol. c-28, No. 6, June 1979.

40. IBM Series/1 Manual, GA34-0035-4, Fifth Edition, January 1979.

EMPLOYEE			
NAME	OFFICE	JOB	SALARY
Smith	Paris	Sales	15000
Jones	Bonn	Sales	18000
Clark	Boise	Sales	12000
Jones	Boston	Service	17000
Kent	Paris	Service	15000
Davis	London	Service	13000
Jacob	Rio	Sales	12000
. . .			

OFFICE		
LOCATION	MANAGER	PHONE
San Jose	Biasgen	7152
Paris	Portal	9123
London	Portal	3278
Bonn	Roever	1287
. . .		

Figure 1

```
$LET PEOPLE BE
     SELECT NAME, SALARY
     INTO $X, $Y
     FROM EMPLOYEE
     WHERE JOB = $Z;

$OPEN PEOPLE; /* BINDS VALUE OF Z */

$FETCH PEOPLE; /* FETCHES ONE EMPLOYEE INTO X AND Y */

$CLOSE PEOPLE; /* AFTER ALL VALUES HAVE BEEN FETCHED */
```

Figure 2

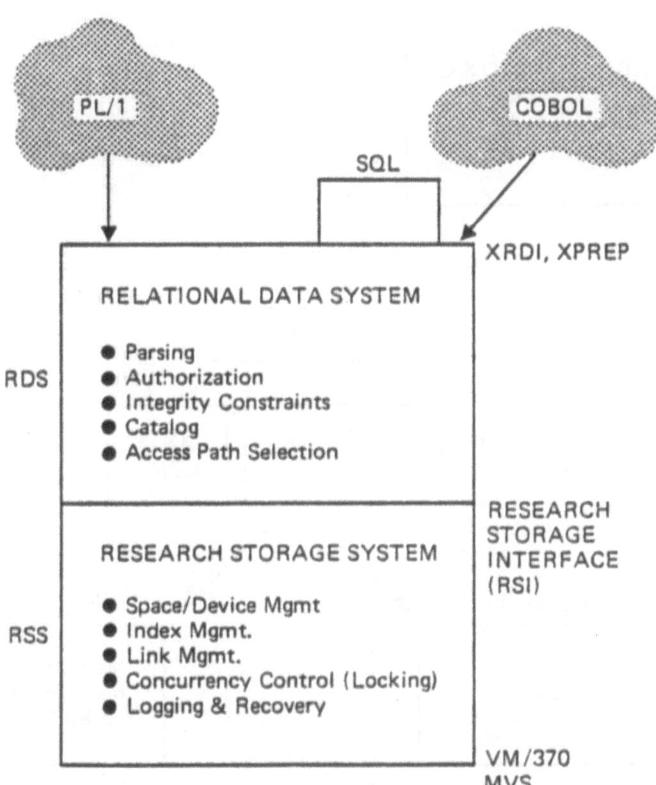
PL/1
COBOL
SQL
XRDI, XPREP
RELATIONAL DATA SYSTEM
RDS
● Parsing
● Authorization
● Integrity Constraints
● Catalog
● Access Path Selection
RESEARCH STORAGE INTERFACE (RSI)
RESEARCH STORAGE SYSTEM
RSS
● Space/Device Mgmt
● Index Mgmt.
● Link Mgmt.
● Concurrency Control (Locking)
● Logging & Recovery
VM/370
MVS

Figure 3

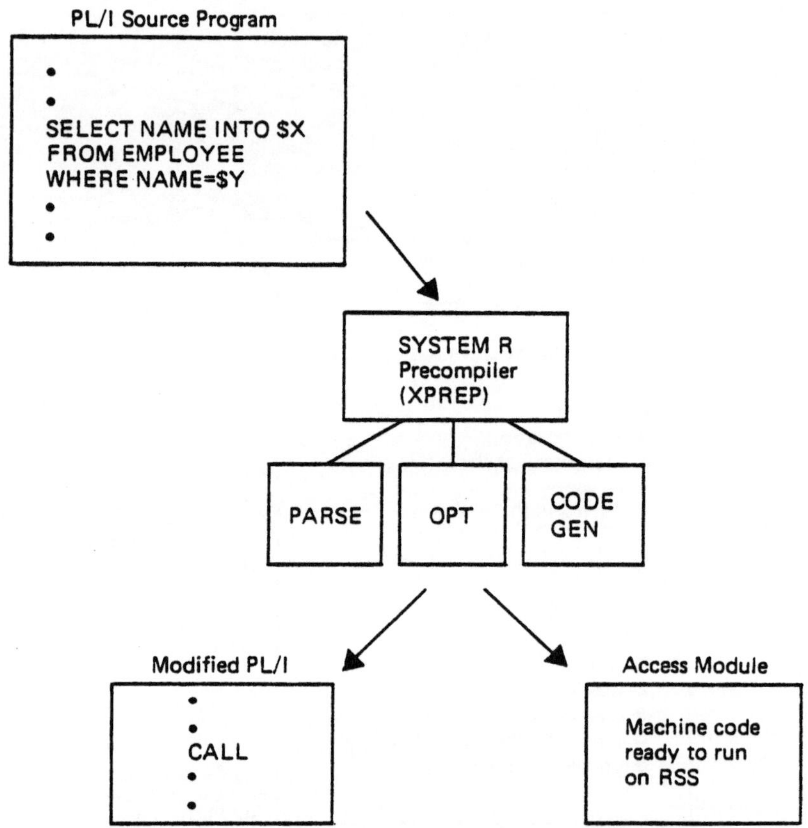
PL/I Source Program
•
•
SELECT NAME INTO $X
FROM EMPLOYEE
WHERE NAME=$Y
•
•
SYSTEM R
Precompiler
(XPREP)
PARSE
OPT
CODE
GEN
Modified PL/I
•
•
CALL
•
•
Access Module
Machine code
ready to run
on RSS

Figure 4

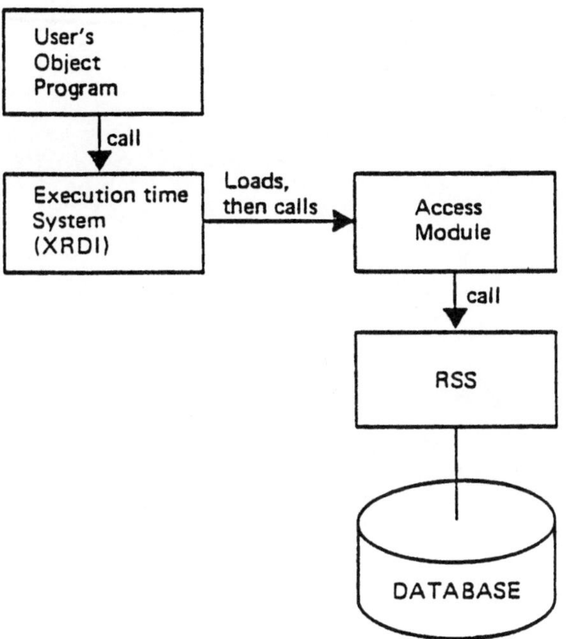
User's
Object
Program
call
Execution time
System
(XRDI)
Loads,
then calls
Access
Module
call
RSS
DATABASE

Figure 5

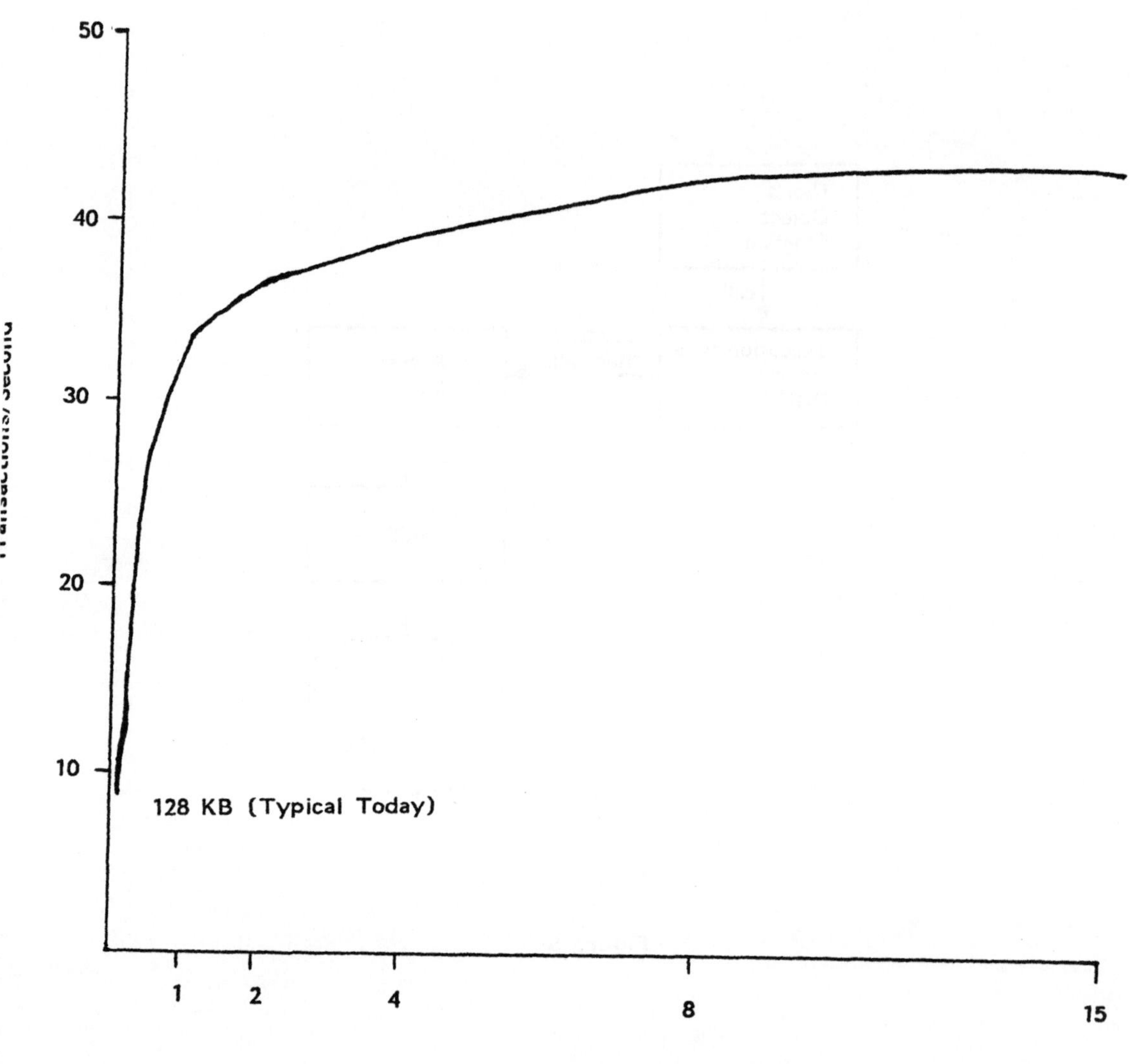

Figure 6

n	= relation cardinality. We assume 100,000 records for this comparison.
p	= number of predicates in the query as in [38] p = 2.
1/h	= number of records which can be searched in one page access if the record is in the access if the record is in the buffer pool. This is 250 for System R. The performance analysis [38] used 10
i	= image cardinality
f	= number of index accesses per index search. For System R with typical key sizes, this is
$\log_{200} n$	= i.e., for 8 million records the index is three pages deep. We have assumed f = 3.
B_g	= average number of records per data page. In System R we find this to be 40 for records of 100 bytes.
B_d	= average number of records per cyclinder. For 3350 technology for 100 byte records, this is 5880. However the assumption in the analysis was that a record in DBC is twice the length in the System R environment. Hence typically B_d is 2500.

Figure 7

	OPTION 1	OPTION 3
n/i	System R Time/ DBC Time	System R Time/ DBC Time
1	1.26	.08
2	1.27	.10
5	1.30	.16
10	1.35	.27
50	1.77	1.10
100	2.29	2.14

Figure 8

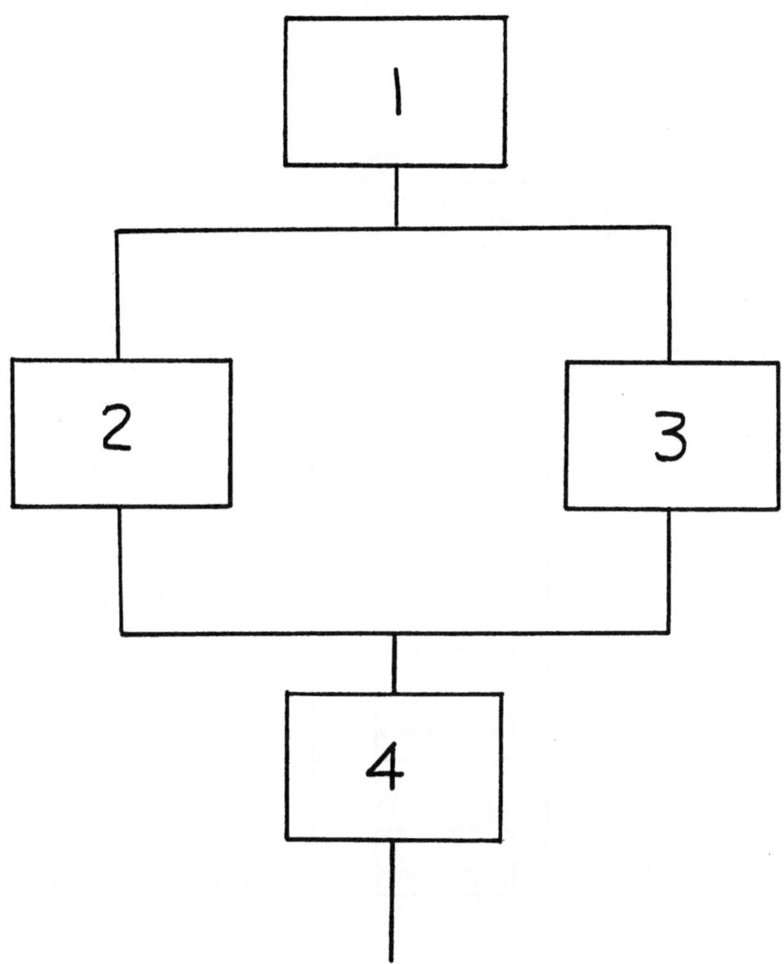

Figure 9

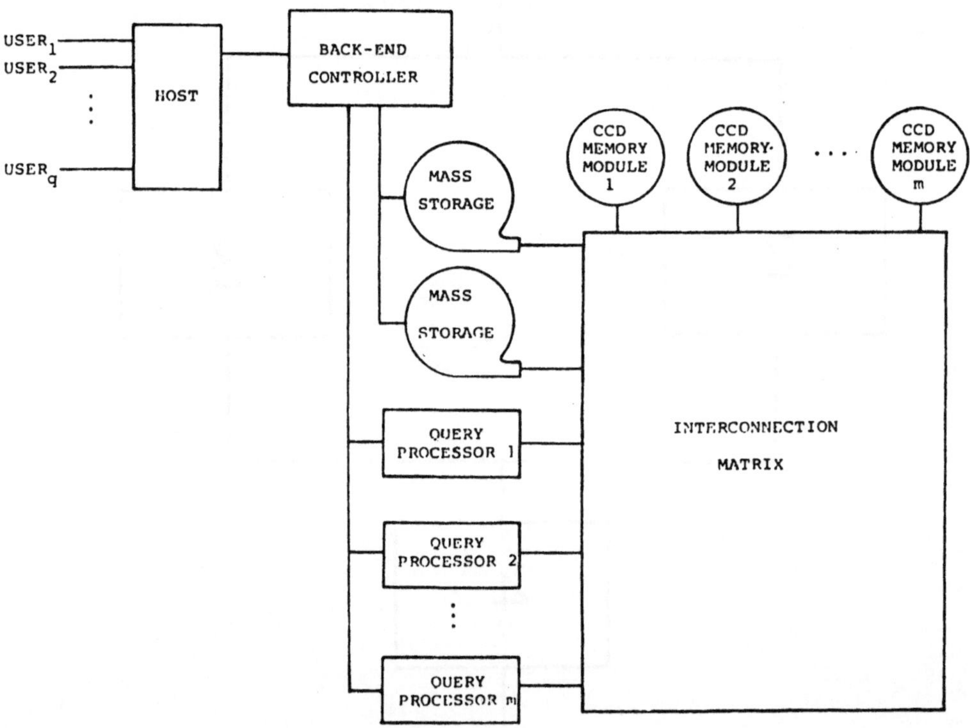
USER1
USER2
USERq
HOST
BACK-END CONTROLLER
MASS STORAGE
MASS STORAGE
CCD MEMORY MODULE 1
CCD MEMORY MODULE 2
CCD MEMORY MODULE m
QUERY PROCESSOR 1
QUERY PROCESSOR 2
QUERY PROCESSOR m
INTERCONNECTION MATRIX

Figure 10

Capabilities and Protection

R.M. Needham
University of Cambridge

Introduction

Of late years protection has been seen as a very important issue in computer system design, and one of the strands of research and development in protection has been the exploitation of the ideas of capabilities. In the present talk I shall try to gather together some of the motivations for work on protection, which motivations are various and not always compatible, as a preliminary to seeing to which of the various problems the ideas of capabilities are of practical importance.

Protection issues really came into prominence with the advent of the time-shared computer. The first manifestations concerned filing systems; when it became customary to have organised ways of naming and accessing bodies of data or program it also became necessary to have control upon who might make use of particular data. At that time access to files seemed the main worry because inside main memory the situation was simple enough not to present great difficulties. There was typically a single user program in the machine at a time, or, if there were more than one they occupied carefully delimited but simple regions. Provided that a workmanlike job had been done of keeping the user programs apart, protection in main memory did not offer a great challenge. The picture of protection as being concerned mainly with access to files did not survive very long, and it is interesting to consider some ways in which it turned out to be inadequate.

Firstly there was perhaps more than met the eye to doing the 'workmanlike job' just mentioned. Operating systems grew in complexity and it became harder and harder to ensure that they were reasonably correct. It became clear that something would be needed to keep the various parts of an operating system apart from each other, the reason not being any consideration of security or privacy but simply ruggedness, in the sense that the parts of the program stand a better chance of correctness. It became notorious about that time that operating systems failed because of unpredicted interactions between one part and another of the system; because of the real-time uncertainties one suffered from irreproducible faults a great deal. A typical example fault from a Cambridge operating system took 14 months to find. An index to a table was not being properly set up in unusual circumstances. In the result, an arbitrary word of memory had its junior bit forced to zero. The underlying event occurred every couple of hours; it resulted in a system crash about once a week. Protection between parts of the system would have detected the fault at first occurrence, not on those (very confusing) occasions where really bad consequences ensued. It became clear that developing large real-time programs, of which operating systems were a type-example, would be so much easier if one could arrange that each subprogram or program module could have access to exactly and only that workspace, data, or code which was really necessary for the proper execution of its task. There is no emphasis on privacy here at all. We just want errors to be made noticeable and indeed to force themselves on our attention.

Indeed, in principle we could consider doing away with the protection once we were satisfied that the program in question was complete and correct; in practice nobody would ever do this if only because programs of this kind never stop being improved and developed. It is worth laying some emphasis on this type of protection because it has aspects which are rather different from those sometimes held to be important. For example, questions of revocation of privilege just do not arise.

We have just sketched one line of argument which gave rise to interest in protection. There is a quite different one. Developments in system architecture made it necessary to be much more elaborate about protection of material in main memory than we had been before. In the early time-shared systems each user had what was often called a core-image, and if the core-image contained system material it had been copied there. Any access control necessary took place at the time of initial copying. Similarly if material were to be updated then permission was sought at the moment of writing. It made sense for a program to be refused permission to write to a certain file and therefore to write to another instead. All this simplicity was compromised by the development of systems of which Multics may be taken as a type example, where the basic operation was not copying but sharing. It was the Multics design which first exhibited processes with large and elaborate segmented address spaces, in which segments could be shared more or less arbitrarily with other processes, and, most importantly, different segments belonging to the same address space had vastly different access status. Indeed, it was common for many of the segments constituting an address space to be totally inaccessible except when the locus of control was suitable. To a large extent this reflected the design philosophy of processes with "the operating system in every process", i.e. the treatment of a process as a virtual machine with its own operating system. Joined to all this was the use of dynamic binding in which the names of files were used as a means to their automatic linkage to appropriate processes. We may sum up the position by saying that in the Multics type of system there was, by comparison with what had gone before, a need to eal with very complicated address space structures and with very different protection requirements at run-time. In the earlier systems once material was addressable, i.e. in the main memory, real or virtual, of the machine it was of necessity properly accessible. Only properly accessible material would ever be allowed to be copied into main memory from a filing system. In the newer type of machine material perfectly well could be, and was, in the address space of a user process but not accessible to the user's code.

It may be noticed that the protection mechanism in the newer type of system of which I have taken Multics as an example has two slightly different tasks to perform. On the one hand it is concerned with the internal protection of the operating system as discussed above: that is to say with those precautions which help with system development and maintenance and make systems rugged. On the other hand it is required to implement the access controls at the user level, preventing improper access to system material and enforcing access levels to ordinary files or segments. In the earlier type of time-sharing system a read-only file could be copied into main memory, the copy could be written to but, because the file was read-only, the changed version could not be refiled. In the Multics structure the segment as a portion of the user's address space needed to be read-only, since we were dealing with the material itself not with a copy. It is in the context of access by users and their programs that issues arise about the duration of access permission and in particular about revocation of access permission. It was remarked earlier that when considering protection within an operating system the situation was quite static and there was no interest in revocation of access permission; indeed access permission almost seemed a strange way to talk in that context. At the level of users and access to files it is different. In the earlier time-sharing systems revocation issues did not arise since permissions referred to point actions such as copying a file or parts of it. Either a copy or a write was permitted or it was not. In a system of the Multics type, where a user program was in a more permanent relationship with a segment (not a copy) it became necessary to answer questions about what should happen if a (file system) access privilege were removed while a user process were busily using the segment in question. The point I am trying to make here is that the protection requirements of the generalised system such as Multics were very much more complex than those of earlier systems, and essentially had to answer two quite different needs - the ruggedness of the operating system itself and the proper control of user activities.

When it was realised how extensive were the demands placed on protection mechanisms it was natural to look to see whether the full generality of the situation was being addressed. It at once became clear that it was not. Two further possibilities were evident. The first was mutual suspicion. It is as reasonable for the user to seek to protect his program from the operating system as it is for the operating system to protect itself from the user program. In general, any two programs should be able to behave with mutual suspicion, that is to say to be able to be sure that the integrity of the one is not compromised by the actions of the other. The second requirement was very different. All protection mechanisms devised to date had been based essentially upon the protection of addresses rather than upon the protection of data. This had been true right from the earliest days of encapsulating the single user program that was present in the main memory of a machine at a time. Saying that information should be protected in the sense that certain information although it could for example be copied or altered could not be printed out, or that nothing which depended on that information could be found in a publicly available file was quite different. The protection techniques of the time were inadequate for this, and so are those of today.

Capabilities

This has been a somewhat lengthy introduction to protection problems but is is I believe a necessary one to introduce the ideas of capabilities in order to be able to assess their scope and limits as protection tools. Fundamentally there seem to be two ways of controlling access to something. One is to have the principal requiring access be equipped with a suitable identifier, and to arrange that whenever access is needed the identifier be checked against a list of principals permitted access in the present circumstances. Note that this approach requires identification of the context as well as of the principal. The other is to issue unforgeable tickets of permission the mere possession of which indicates entitlement to have some particular access. It may be that there is some bureaucracy associated with the issue of the ticket, but once issued it may be used with little or no formality and little expense. Such tickets are known in computer circles as capabilities, and they are found in use at various levels of abstraction. I shall first give some properties that are true of capabilities however implemented and at whatever level, and then explore the use made of the various instances of the same general idea.

Generic definition of a capability

This type of definition must be rather informal because in various applications there are various detailed differences. It will be assumed that capabilities have the following rough properties:

1. Capabilities are unforgeable. They may only be manufactured or altered with suitable authorisation.
2. Capabilities are valid on presentation. No further enquiry is needed as to the authority of any principal presenting a capability to perform some action.
3. Capabilities are transferable. They may be transferred from one program or user to another without formality; in general they may not merely be transferred but copied.
4. Capabilities are self-identifying. They contain a name or something which leads to the name of the object or action which they enable.
5. Capabilities should not be misleading. A principal holding what appears to be a capability for a certain action should not find on attempting to use it that the virtue has gone out of it.

In general we shall see that the use of capabilities is convenient when the authorisation to do something is remote in space and time from the actual use, and when the authority has to be transferred from one principal or program to another. Capabilities may usually be thought of as having a name part and a control part. The name part specifies the object to which the capability refers. It may actually be the name of the object, or it may specify a path which leads in a definite manner to that name. The control part indicates which of the possible actions that can be performed on the object are enabled by the particular capability. We shall see that in some cases the distinction between the two parts cannot be maintained; it is clearly not a fundamental one since one could give an object different names according to the operation to be performed. This is not customary.

Protection in Main Memory

The earliest practical applications of capabilities were to the protection of segments of main memory. The first proposals were made by Fabry, and practical machines were built by the Plessey Company (System/250) and the Computer Laboratory of Cambridge University (CAP). It is probably fair to say that the motivation in all cases was to achieve a finer grain of protection within operating systems and within suitable application programs. It was observed by the designers that existing protection mechanisms were too coarsely grained and too inflexible. If one were to take seriously the desire that a program or program module should, for reasons of development and ruggedness, have access to exactly and only that which was logically necessary to its function, various consequences followed. Firstly it must be possible to protect material in detail. If it was necessary for a program to have access to a particular area of data of, say 29 words, it could well be necessary to give it practical access to a much larger region of memory because of the excessively coarse grain of the protection system. Secondly it must be possible to represent rapidly changing protection environments. The areas of memory to which access is really necessary do not remain constant for very long. Systems are made up of relatively small routines or modules between which control passes very rapidly. It is thus not simply necessary to be able to represent a particular protection environment in great detail but for it to be possible for control to transfer from one protection environment to another very quickly.

The systems mentioned solved this problem in rather different ways but with one outstanding common feature. A protection environment was represented by a set of capabilities which were of two sorts: capabilities for segments of memory and capabilities for protection environments. At any time exactly and only those memory segments were available for which capabilities were present in the current environment, and the use of a special instruction (ENTER) in conjunction with a capability for another environment would cause a protection domain switch. The inviolability of the capabilities themselves was ensured by segregating them into special segments called capability segments, and arranging that the ordinary data manipulation instructions of the machine would not work on any words which belonged to a capability segment. Segment capabilities in each case had a name part which directly or indirectly defined the position in memory and the size of the segment, and a control part which defined the available access (read,write, execute). Capabilities for protection environments essentially consisted of capabilities for the capability segments defining the new environments, with suitable control parts.

It was the experience of the implementors of systems built on this principle that system construction was very easy relative to comparable exercises on ordinary machines. Programming error is inevitable but it made itself manifest much more quickly than was usual. The consequence of errors was almost invariably a protection violation and one never had the classical problem of the corruption of random pieces of memory by unknown agents.

In this type of capability system the hardware support is inevitably bound up with addressing. Every memory access requires to be supported by a capability, and the manner of use is typically for some part of the address or the instruction to select a capability the name part of which leads to the absolute base of the segment in memory. Accordingly the capability hardware looks like a particular form of address translation logic. In the Cambridge CAP machine the capability unit constitutes about 15% of the processor hardware, and I believe this is typical. The use of capabilities does not have a major effect on the machine performance; that this should be so is a very important design consideration since every memory access involves a capability . There is a small effect which derives from the fine grain of protection and which concerns the use of a cache. In a fine-grained system it may well be that all the bits of an address are changed by the address translation and it is thus not possible to start cycling a cache in parallel.

As already stated, it would be perfectly possible to take a quite conventional operating system, cut it up into suitable small pieces, and arrange to protect each section by means of capabilities in the manner outlined. In practice a somewhat different attitude has been taken, perhaps stimulated by parallel developments in programming languages. If we consider the collection of capaibilities constituting a protection environment, we shall see typically three sorts. There are capabilities for segments of code, capabilities for segments of workspace, and capabilities for segments of data which persist from one use of the protection environment to the next. Furthermore we shall see that there are a number of protection environments which differ only in the values of the persistent data; the sturcture is the same and so are the code segments. This leads one to think of the protection environment as the representation of an abstract object. An abstract object is defined by the operations that can be performed on it; it is essential that only the permitted operations be able to be performed. This is just the characteristic of a protection environment. Nothing can be done to the data part other than by the code in the code part: this code defines the permitted operations. We think then of bringing into being an instance of an abstract object by constructing a protection environment suitably. How is such an environment handled and passed round as a unit? By means of a capability for it, naturally, which will be an ENTER capability, because the only use one may validly make of the object is by entering the protection environment to use the code for the permitted operations. It is literally impossible to do anything else, and the representation used in the data part is completely invisible to the user. The capability mechanism thus supports very naturally the important principles of data abstraction and information hiding. It is at first sight a little unusual to think of an open file, a terminal, or a file directory, as being procedures, but once one is familiar with the idea it seems quite natural. It is also a mode of thought which leads on in a very straightforward way to another use of capability ideas. Abstract objects may be quite long-term things and are presumably to be found in a filing system. Do the ideas of capability-based protection extend to filing systems?

Capabilities in Filing Systems

In a standard type of filing system a user takes a copy of some material (or of course perhaps the only version), arranges for it to be written to disc and for an entry to be placed in a file directory giving a suitable name and access status for the new file. One can take a different attitude and say that if any material is accessible to a program then the program must have a capability for it, and that the action of filing something consists of preserving a capability for it. If we take the latter attitude we shall have a capability-based filing system and a variety of consequences follow.

Firstly, the nature of the capabilities themselves must be re-examined. When capabilities are used to give access to segments of main memory the name parts of the capabilities are, or lead to, physical addresses of material in main memory or perhaps on a swapping disc. If capabilities are to be able to be preserved for future use the name part, as preserved, must be of altogether more long-term validity. It is necessary to devise a suitable long-term naming scheme for all objects whether simple or compound. Ideally such names should never be re-used, which means that they must be quite long. This leads to complications in the use of the same capabilities for access to material in main memory, because large capabilities may be slow and clumsy to handle. There seem to be two solutions. One is to build more hardware so that associative translation may take place from the long identifier to the physical address. The other, which is adopted in the CAP, is to recognise that capabilities for access to main memory are different, and to translate from the long-term name to a short-term name when a capability is retrieved from the filing system. The converse translation has to take place when a capability is preserved. Although more complex in principle, this approach has the attractions of economy particularly when one remembers that short-term capabilities often exist in multiple copies. Note, for example, that when the CAP operating system in an earlier version had started up and was ready to run users' work there were 28 kilobytes of capabilities: one would hesitate to make all capabilities several times bigger.

Secondly, it is necessary to arrange that an object is maintained in existence whenever any capability for it is preserved anywhere. It seems a practical necessity to have an analogous form of separation in the filing system to that between data segments and capability segments in main memory. If we know and can identify which filed objects are repositories of capabilities then it becomes practicable to perform the garbage-collection operations necessary to recover space occupied by objects which no longer have preserved capabilities. Since capabilities for capability-containing objects may themselves be preserved it is quite possible to generate detached looped structures and true garbage-collection is necessary. This fact acted as a deterrent to some designers of capability-based filing systems, who arranged that one preserved capability, typically the first to be preserved for a particular object, was marked as special. If the special capability for an object were destroyed then so was the object itself. This is undesirable since it violates the last of the requirements given in the generic definition of a capability, namely that capabilities are not misleading. Other preserved capabilities for a deleted object would be misleading. It has been demonstrated in the CAP project that asynchronous garbage collection of the filing system is not very difficult and that the possibility of detached loops need not worry us.

Thirdly, we must face the issues of revocation. It was remarked earlier that when capabilities are used for the protection of material in main memory revocation issues hardly arise. This is especially true if the purpose of the capability-based protection is to improve the ruggedness of the operating system. As soon as we extend the ideas to filing systems the matter becomes much more important. Should it be the case that whenever a particular user or other principal is given a capability for something he may preserve it and maintain his access to that object for all time? The designers of Multics (not a capability system) held the view very strongly that if the owner of an object revoked permission to use it from another principal, then that revocation should have instant effect. For example if a user's permisison to use a certain compiler were removed, then a compilation actually in progress would terminate. A good deal of discussion and design effort has been put into designing cpaability systems with this property, the work of Redell and Fabry being the best. They showed that it is possible to arrange, by putting an extra step in the evaluation of the name part of a capability, that capabilities can be revoked. Necessarily, if we do this then general property 5 will have to be abandoned, because a revoked capability is misleading. That it has been revoked will not become evident until an attempt is made to use it.

Capabilities in Networks

This is the second time we have found general property 5 to be in danger, and perhaps it is worth considering whether it is a valid property at all. A final type of application of c apability ideas suggests the contrary. It is possible to use capabilities in networks of computers, where the capabilities are passed from one machine to another in order to transfer privileges. In this context, however, there is no direct analogue to the hardware segregation of capabilities which is used when using capabilities for protection of main memory. Accordingly some other means has to be found to make capaiblities unforgeable, which was done in main memory be disabling the regular data manipulation orders of the machine from working on the contents of a capability segment. The only available technique appears to be sparseness. That is to say, capabilities are bit-patterns chosen from such a sparsely-populated space that unforgeability is in the practice guaranteed. It is almost necessary to this scheme that when a capability is presented as a sign of authority it be checked to see whether it is a good capability rather than an arbitrary bit-pattern. Again property 5 has disappeared. It thus seems that there is some doubt about its validity and perhaps one should drop it from the catalogue.

The ideas of capabilities date from the middle 1960's. The time is thus about ripe for industrial exploitation and there are indeed signs of this happening. The IBM System/38 is a capability machine of a kind, and capability ideas for memory management have recently been attracting much interest from microprocessor manufacturers One hears rumours from other parts of the industry but as yet few concrete announcements Beyond that it is the author's opinion that more will be heard of capabilities in the context of control and authorisation in networks. To date little has been done but workers with a background in the capability approach have been quick to recognise the opportunities of local networks in particular. This should not be surprising, since the problems of local networks are essentially the same as those of large shared computers; they just arise in a different technology.

References

England, D. (1974) Capability concept mechanism and structure. IRIA Int. Workshop on Protection in Operating Systems. Rocquencourt, pp63-82 (Plessey System 250)

Fabry, R. (1968) Preliminary Description of a Supervsor for a Machine oriented around Capabilities, ICR Quarterly Report 18, 1B. University of Chicago.

Wilkes, M.V. & Needham, R.M. (1979) The Cambridge CAP Computer and its Operating System. New York, Elsevier/North-Holland.

Redell, D.D. & Fabry, R.S. Selective Revocation of Capabilities. IRIA Int. Worshop on Protection in Operating Systems, Rocquencourt, pp197-209.

EFFIZIENZ PARALLELER RECHNER

Z. Galil und W. Paul

Dieser Aufsatz gibt einen informalen und gerafften Überblick über einige Ergebnisse aus [PV 79] und [GP 80]. Er beschäftigt sich mit der Frage, wie man einen Computer mit sehr vielen Prozessen verdrahten soll.

Wir beginnen mit einigen historischen Bemerkungen. Mit der Turingmaschine hatte man bereits Anfang der 30er Jahre ein Konzept für Rechenanlagen, das einerseits technisch realisierbar war und es andererseits zumindest prinzipiell gestattet, jede überhaupt algorithmisch lösbare Aufgabe zu lösen. Dafür, daß sich diese Maschinen in der Praxis nicht durchgesetzt haben, scheinen zwei Schwächen des Modells verantwortlich zu sein:

(1) das verallgemeinerte Tonbandgerät-Design ist technisch unattraktiv und schwerfällig

(2) auf den ersten Blick scheint es, als ob man für jede Funktion, die man berechnen will, eine eigene Maschine bauen müßte. Solange man das glaubt, wird man eine Maschine für eine spezielle Aufgabe nur dann bauen, wenn man ein sehr großes Interesse an der Lösung gerade dieser Aufgabe hat. Zumindest muß man vorher wissen, welche Aufgabe man später mit der Maschine lösen will.

Wie wir wissen ist die zweite Schwäche behebbar, aber das Programmieren universeller Turingmaschinen ist natürlich denkbar umständlich.

Der von-Neumann-Maschine haften diese Schwächen nicht mehr an. Ihre hervorragenden Merkmale sind

(3) technisch die 2-Teilung der Maschine in eine kleine aktive Komponente (den Prozessor) und eine große passive Komponente (den Speicher).

(4) logisch die Universalität: die Maschine kann relativ komfortabel so programmiert werden, daß sie jede andere Maschine simuliert.

Man kann sich also einen von-Neumann-Rechner kaufen, ohne im voraus eine genaue Vorstellung davon zu haben, was man später damit ausrechnen will. Besser noch, man weiß sogar, daß man (wenn man von der Beschränkung des Speichers absieht) zur Lösung jeder überhaupt algorithmisch lösbaren Aufgabe gewappnet sein wird.

Universalität ist unabhängig von der verfügbaren Technologie eine höchst wünschenswerte Eigenschaft von Rechenanlagen. Die Teilung der von-Neumann-Maschine in eine kleine aktive und eine große passive Komponente scheint hingegen auf eine Technologie zugeschnitten, wo logische Bausteine (Röhren, Transistoren) teuer sind. Inzwischen sind logische Bausteine sehr billig geworden. Man kann Taschenrechner und Armbanduhren, die zu den erstaunlichsten Kunststücken fähig sind, für ein Spottgeld kaufen... und ein Rechner mit 1 Million Prozessoren ist wohl bald technisch realisierbar. Was kann man durch den Bau eines solchen Rechners gewinnen, und wie soll man überhaupt so viele Prozessoren verdrahten?

Es ist klar, daß man mit N Prozessoren nicht mehr Aufgaben lösen kann, als mit einem einzigen. Man könnte aber hoffen, gewisse Aufgaben bis zu N mal schneller lösen zu können, was für die praktische Lösbarkeit einer Aufgabe natürlich von entscheidender Bedeutung wäre. Das folgende Beispiel zeigt, daß dieser Effekt in der Tat auftritt.

Die Verteilung der Temperatur T auf dem Rand eines Stücks Blech wird von außen konstant gehalten. Wir interessieren uns für die Verteilung der Temperatur für sämtliche Punkte des Blechs. Die Verteilung der Temperatur auf dem Blech wird durch eine unter Physikern wohlbekannte Differentialgleichung beschrieben. Um die Verteilung der Temperatur auf dem Blech zu finden, muß man eine Randwertaufgabe lösen, was analytisch höchstens dann gelingt, wenn sowohl die Form des Blechs als auch die Verteilung der Temperatur auf dem Rand einfach sind. Numerisch weiß man sich jedoch zu helfen, indem man die Aufgabe diskretisiert:

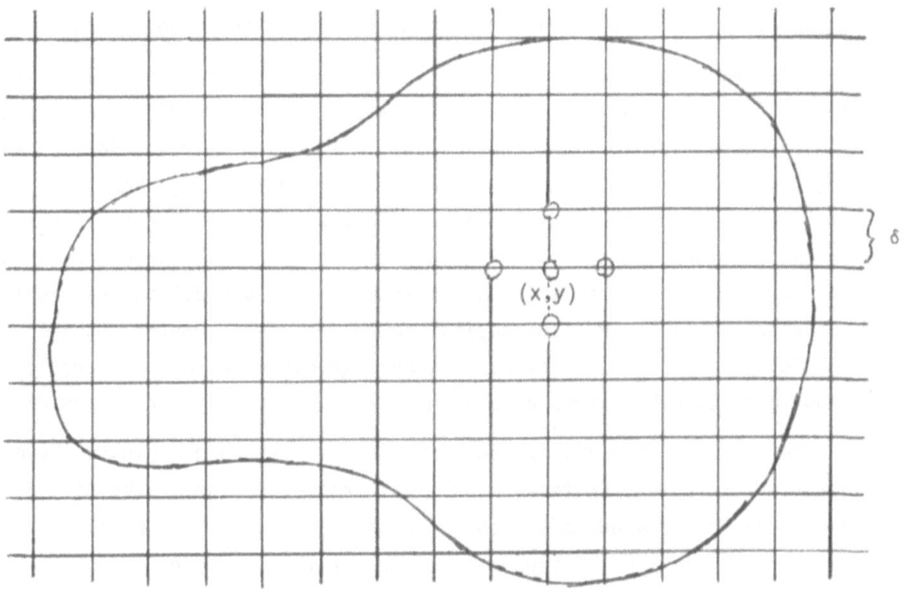

Bild 1

Man legt ein Gitter mit Maschenweite δ über das Blech und löst die Aufgabe iterativ. $t_i(x,y)$ bezeichne die Näherung der Temperatur $T(x,y)$ im Gitterpunkt (x,y) nach dem i-ten Iterationschritt. Man beginnt mit

$$t_0(x,y) = \begin{cases} T(x,y) & \text{für } (x,y) \text{ auf dem Rand} \\ \text{mehr oder weniger beliebig sonst} \end{cases}$$

Aus der Differentialgleichung erhält man eine Regel zum iterieren, indem man Differentialquotienten (etwa $\frac{\partial t(x,y)}{\partial x}$) durch Differenzenquotienten ($\frac{t(x+\delta,y) - t(x,y)}{\delta}$) ersetzt und beispielsweise nach einem Vorkommen von $t(x,y)$ auflöst. Man erhält so mit einer passenden Funktion f zum Beispiel

(5) $t(x,y) = f(t(x,y), t(x-\delta,y), t(x+\delta,y), t(x,y-\delta), t(x,y+\delta))$.

Indiziert man das t auf der linken Seite der Gleichung (5) mit i und die t 's auf der rechten Seite mit $i-1$, so erhält man eine Iterationsregel, und man kann in vielen Fällen zeigen, daß die Folgen $t_i(x,y)$, $i \in \mathbb{N}$ gegen einen Wert konvergieren, der in Abhängigkeit von der Maschenweite δ mehr oder weniger nahe bei der gesuchten Lösung $T(x,y)$ liegt.

Ist N die Anzahl der Gitterpunkte, so muß ein von-Neumann-Rechner für eine Iteration N mal die Funktion f auswerten. Säße hingegen auf jedem Gitterpunkt (x,y) ein Prozessor $P(x,y)$, der die Aufgabe hat, die Folge $t_i(x,y)$, $i \in \mathbb{N}$ zu berechnen, so könnte für jedes i die i-te Iteration wie folgt durchgeführt werden: jeder Prozessor $P(x,y)$ konsultiert seine Nachbarn um die Daten $t_{i-1}(x-\delta,y)$, $t_{i-1}(x+\delta,y)$, $t_{i-1}(x,y-\delta)$, $t_{i-1}(x,y+\delta)$ zu beziehen und wertet dann die Funktion f aus. Da die Prozessoren $P(x,y)$ gleichzeitig arbeiten, vergeht für eine Iteration jetzt im wesentlichen nur die Zeit, die gebraucht wird um 1 mal die Funktion f auszuwerten.

Durch paralleles Rechnen kann man also manche Aufgaben sehr viel schneller lösen, als sequentiell. Durch Kombination von Techniken aus [PR 78], [PR 79] und [GP 80] kann man sogar zeigen, daß man t Schritte auf dem von-Neumann-Rechner (formal: RAM[+,-] mit logarithmischem Kostenmaß [AHU 74]) in $O(t \log\log t/\log t)$ Schritten durch einen vollständigen binären Baum der Tiefe $O(t \log\log t/\log t)$ von endlichen Automaten simulieren kann (sofern $t \geq n \log n/\log\log n$, wobei n die Länge der Eingabe ist). Das heißt, daß kein Problem so inhärent sequentiell ist, als daß man es nicht durch massiven Einsatz paralleler Rechenkapazität schneller lösen könnte, als auf einer sequentiellen Maschine. Praktisch ist das Ergebnis in dieser Form bedeutungslos, da man für $t = 400$ bereits mehr Automaten braucht, als Elektronen im Universum Platz haben.

Nun mögen immerhin N = ca 1 Million in Form eines vollständigen binären Baums der Tiefe $\log N-1$ verdrahtete Prozessoren als attraktives Design erscheinen. Es gibt jedoch sehr einfache Aufgaben, die sich auf einem Baum von Prozessoren nur sehr mühsam und auf anderen einfachen Netzen sehr effizient lösen lassen:

Nehmen wir an, der Baum ist mit endlichen Automaten besetzt, jeder Automat hat z Zustände, und die Eingabe erfolgt bitweise auf den Blättern $b_1 \ldots b_{N/2}$.

Bild 2

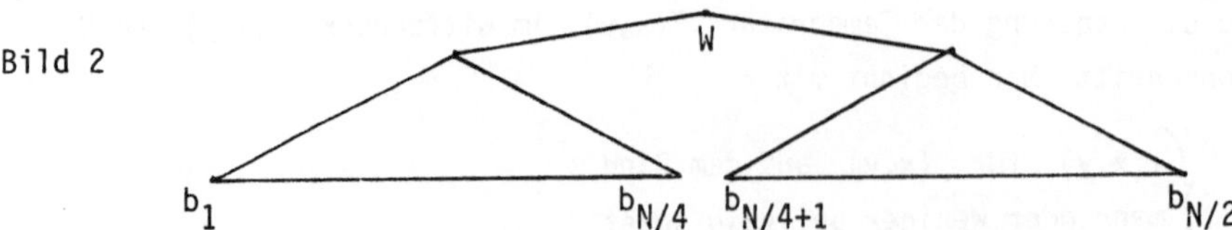

Falls das Rechnernetz entscheidet, ob die Eingabe ein Palindrom ist, d.h. vorwärts wie rückwärts gelesen werden kann, so kann man sich leicht überzeugen, daß der Automat an der Wurzel W des Baums für verschiedene Palindrome der Länge N/2 verschiedene Folgen von Zuständen durchlaufen muß. Ist t die längste Zeit, die beim Erkennen von Palindromen der Länge N/2 auftritt, so folgt

(6) $(z+1)^t \geq 2^{N/4}$ bzw.
$t \geq N/4 \log(z+1)$.

Erweitert man das Netz für $i \in \{0,\dots,N/4-1\}$ um die Verbindungen $(b_{N/4}-i,\ \delta_{N/4}+i+1)$, so läßt sich die gleiche Aufgabe in $O(\log N)$ Schritten lösen.

Ein ähnlicher Effekt tritt auch auf, wenn wir N Automaten in einem $\sqrt{N} \times \sqrt{N}$ -Gitter verdrahten.

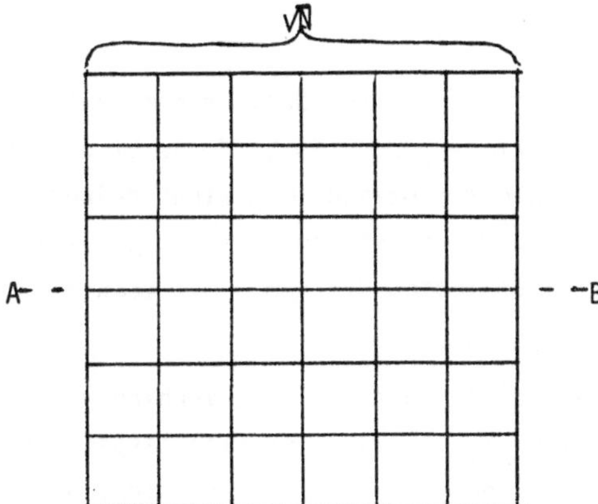

Bild 3

Besteht die Eingabe aus N Bits, von denen die Automaten der ersten Zeile die ersten $\sqrt{N}$ Bits lesen, die Automaten der zweiten Zeile die zweiten $\sqrt{N}$ Bits etc., und es soll entschieden werden, ob die Eingabe ein Palindrom der Länge N ist, so bilden die Automaten auf dem Schnitt A...B in Bild 3 einen Flaschenhals für den Informationsfluß; es folgt

(7) $(z+1)^{t\sqrt{N}} \geq 2^{N/2}$ bzw.
$t \geq \sqrt{N}/2 \log(z+1)$.

Hier drängt sich die Vermutung auf, daß es für jedes Netz G eine Aufgabe A und ein Netz G' gibt, so daß A auf G' erheblich schneller als auf G gelöst werden kann. Modelliert man Netze aus sehr vielen Prozessoren durch unendliche Netze (ebenso wie man große endliche von-Neumann-Rechner durch unendliche Registermaschinen modelliert), so läßt sich das auch durch ein einfaches Diagonalargument zeigen [GP 80]. Im endlichen Fall tritt keines der obigen Probleme auf, wenn wir einfach jedes Paar von Prozessoren direkt verbinden, aber das scheint schon für relativ kleine Prozessorzahlen N technisch nicht machbar zu sein.

All dies liefert Evidenz dafür, daß man mit keinem Netz sämtliche Aufgaben optimal lösen kann. Wird man deshalb parallele Rechner nur für ganz spezielle Aufgaben bauen? Und selbst falls man im voraus weiß, daß man numerisch die Temperaturverteilung auf Blechstücken ausrechnen will: welche Form soll man dem Gitter von Prozessoren geben? Ein quadratisches Gitter ist sicher gut für mehr oder weniger quadratische Blechstücke, aber schon viel weniger gut für sehr lange dünne. Ganz zu schweigen davon, daß man mit der gleichen Anlage vielleicht auch gerne Eigenschaften von Kristallen ausrechnen würde, wozu ein dreidimensionales Gitter von Prozessoren viel angebrachter wäre.

Das Hauptergebnis von [GP 80] besagt, daß es einen Ausweg über universelle "programmierbare" Netze gibt, die jedes andere Netz mit gleich vielen Prozessoren wenigstens einigermaßen effizient simulieren können. Wir skizzieren die entsprechenden Konstruktionen.

Sei ein beliebiges Netz G von P Prozessoren gegeben, in dem jeder Prozessor mit höchstens d anderen Prozessoren direkt verbunden ist; d heißt der Grad von G. In einem Schritt des Netzes G kann jeder Prozessor mit einem seiner Nachbarn Daten austauschen. Diese Kommunikation zwischen Prozessoren in einem beliebigen Netz G muß ohne zu großen Zeitverlust von einem festen Netz G_o mit ebenfalls P Prozessoren hergestellt werden.

Mit Hilfe des Heiratssatzes kann man zeigen, daß sich die Verbindungen eines beliebigen Netzes vom Grad d in d Klassen $E_1,\ldots,E_d$ einteilen lassen, so daß für jedes i das Netz G_i, in dem nur die Verbindungen aus E_i vorkommen, Grad 1 hat. Ein Schritt im Netz G wird simuliert, indem für $i = 1,\ldots,d$ nacheinander Kommunikation entlang den Verbindungen aus E_i simuliert wird. Es genügt also, Netze F vom Grad 1 zu simulieren. Numerieren wir die Prozessoren eines Netzes von 1 bis P, so definiert ein Netz vom Grad 1 eine Permutation Π_F auf $(1,\ldots,P)$ nämlich

$$\Pi_F(i) = \begin{cases} i & \text{falls Prozessor } i \text{ mit keinem anderen Prozessor verbunden ist} \\ \text{die Nummer des Prozessors, mit dem Prozessor } i \text{ verbunden ist} & \text{sonst.} \end{cases}$$

Die Waksman-Permutationsnetze W_P sind induktiv durch Bild 4 definiert [W 68]. Man kann zeigen, daß es in W_P zu jeder Permutation Π auf $(1,\ldots,P)$ P Wege $w_1(\Pi),\ldots,w_P(\Pi)$ gibt, wobei jeweils $w_i(\Pi)$ am Eingang i beginnt und am Ausgang $\Pi(i)$ endet.

Verdrahten wir P Prozessoren, indem wir sie auf die Eingänge von W_P setzen, die inneren Knoten von W_P mit zusätzlichen einfachen Prozessoren bestücken und die Ausgänge von W_P mit den Eingängen identifizieren, so erhalten wir ein Netz, das einen Schritt in einem beliebigen Netz F von Grad 1 in $2 \log P$ Schritten simulieren kann: man stellt für jedes i die Kommunikation zwischen Prozessor i und Prozessor $\Pi(i)$ entlang dem Pfad $w_i(\Pi_F)$ her; diese Pfade haben ungefähr Länge $2 \log P$.

In dieser Konstruktion werden allerdings P Prozessoren von $2P \log P$ Prozessoren simuliert, von denen jeder nur alle $2 \log P$ Schritte wirklich etwas tut. Preparata

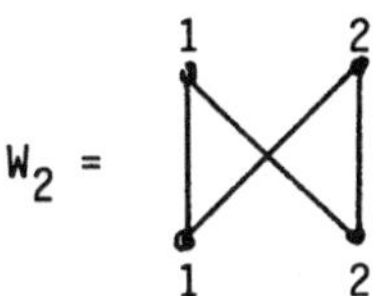

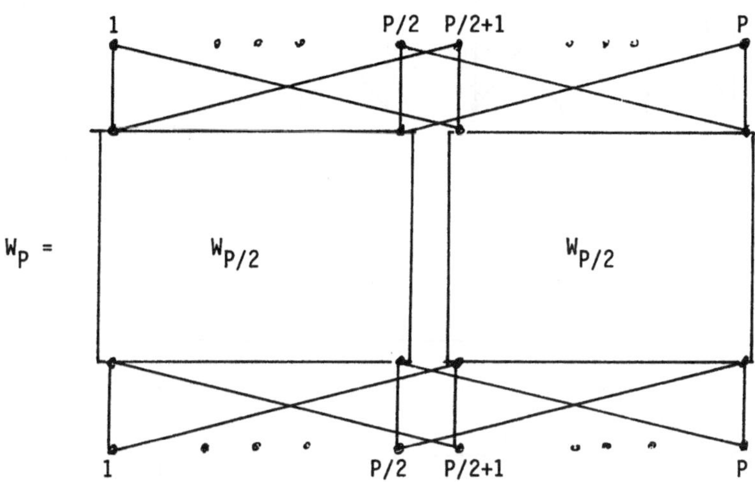

Bild 4

und Vuillemin haben erkannt, daß man in dieser und vielen ähnlichen Situationen bei geringem Zeitverlust bereits mit P Prozessoren auskommt. Betrachten wir als Beispiel die obere Hälfte von W_8 (Bild 5). Identifiziert man für alle i die Prozessoren auf dem senkrechten Weg vom Eingang i zum Ausgang i , so stellt man fest, daß zunächst die Prozessorenpaare

(1,5) (2,6) (3,7) (4,8)

kommunizieren; dann

(1,3) (2,4) (5,7) (6,8)

und schließlich

(1,2) (3,4) (5,6) (7,8) .

Danach finden die gleichen Kommunikationen in umgekehrter Reihenfolge statt. Ordnet man die Prozessoren wie in Bild 6 auf einen Würfel an, so finden die ersten Kommunikationen entlang den Verbindungen in z-Richtung statt, die zweiten in x-Richtung und die dritten in y-Richtung.

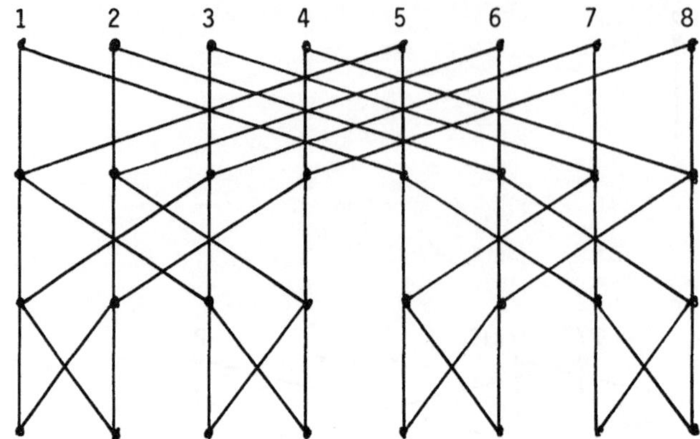

Bild 5

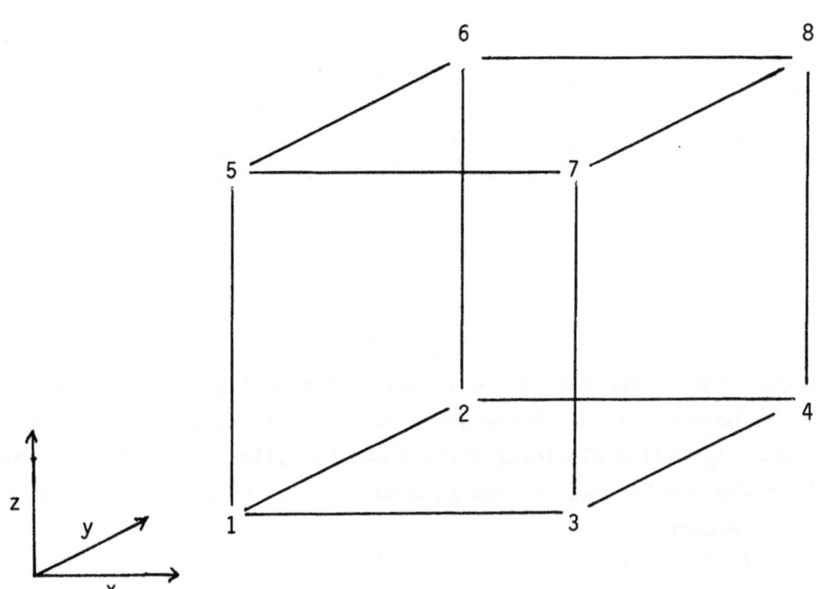

Bild 6

Allgemein können P auf einen log P dimensionalen Würfel angeordnete Prozessoren das Netz W_P ohne Zeitverlust simulieren.

Unglücklicherweise hat das resultierende Netz Grad log P , was für große Prozessorzahlen P zu groß wird. Dies kann behoben werden, indem man jede Würfelecke durch log P Knoten ersetzt, die auf einem Kreis angeordnet sind (Bild 7) .

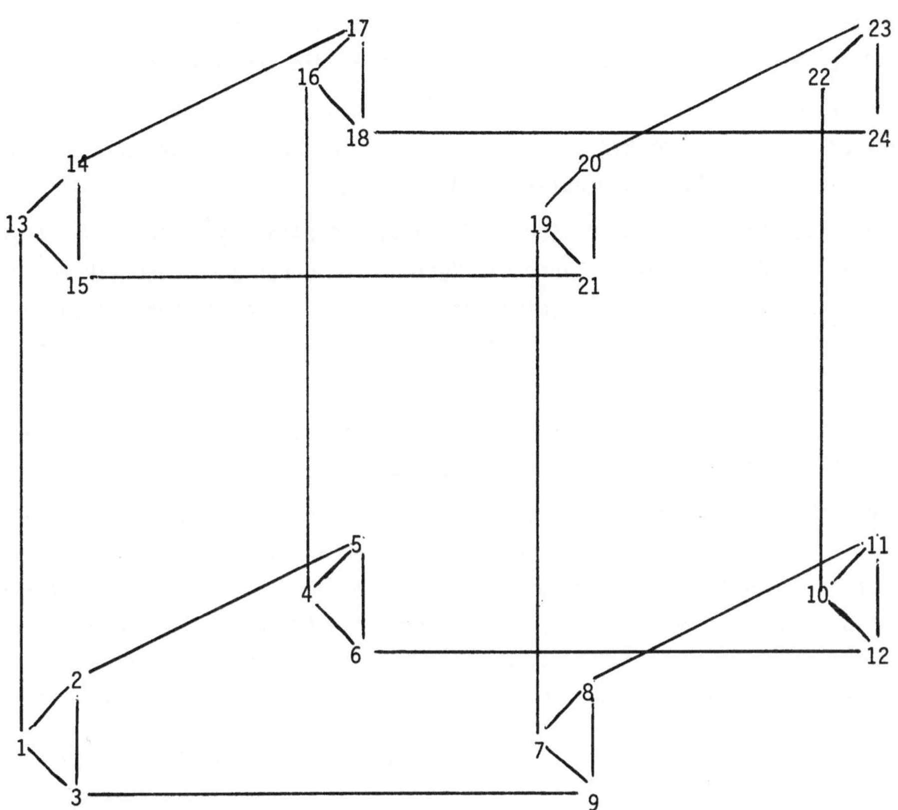

Bild 7

Man erhält so die cube-connected cycles (CCC) aus [PV 79]. Der Graph, den man so erhält, hat wieder P log P Prozessoren, aber Preparata und Vuillemin beobachten, daß die P-dimensionalen CCC bereits $W_{P \log P}$ simulieren können:

Durch 2-maliges Rotieren der Daten auf den Zyklen können in 4 log P Schritten die Kommunikationen zwischen Prozessoren auf verschiedenen Zyklen hergestellt werden, in weiteren 2 log P Schritten die Kommunikation zwischen Prozessoren auf den gleichen Zyklen. Die obere Hälfte des Permutationsnetzes W_P kann also in 6 log P Schritten von CCC simuliert werden; die gleiche Zeit genügt zur Simulation der unteren Hälfte von W_P . Insgesamt kann damit ein Schritt eines beliebigen Netzes vom Grad d in 12 d log P Schritten simuliert werden. Durch Einfügen von O(P) zusätzlichen Kanten in CCC kann diese Schrittzahl in die Nähe von 2 d log P gebracht werden.

Eine zweite Simulation - ebenfalls mit P Prozessoren, die durch CCC verbunden sind - erlaubt es sogar, ein System von P Prozessoren zu simulieren, die miteinander kommunizieren, ohne an feste Verbindungen gebunden zu sein. Dies ist eine Simulation durch Sortieren:

Die Bausteine von Sortiernetzen sind Vergleichsboxen. Sie haben 2 Eingänge und 2 Ausgänge min und max . Legt man an die Eingänge 2 Zahlen a und b an, so erscheint am Ausgang min die kleinere und am Ausgang max die größere der beiden Zahlen.

Ein P-Sortiernetz ist ein Netz von Vergleichsboxen mit P Eingängen und P Ausgängen, so daß gilt: legt man an die Eingänge P beliebige Zahlen an, so erscheinen diese Zahlen an den Ausgängen aufsteigend sortiert.

Batcher [B 68] konstruierte P Sortiernetze mit $O(P(\log P)^2)$ Boxen und Tiefe $O((\log P)^2)$. Dabei werden 2 Typen von Netzen, von denen jedes dem Waksman-Permutationsnetz ähnlich ist, rekursiv geschachtelt. Analog zu der früheren Argumentation kann gezeigt werden, daß CCC mit P Prozessoren Batchers P-Sortiernetz in $O((\log P)^2)$ Schritten simulieren können.

Wir zeigen, wie man durch 2-maliges Sortieren einen Schritt von P Prozessoren 1,...,P simuliert, die wie folgt kommunizieren:

In jedem Schritt t kommuniziert Prozessor i mit genau einem Prozessor q(i,t) . Kommuniziert Prozessor i mit keinem anderen Prozessor, so sei q(i,t) = i . Die Prozessoren i und q(i,t) kommunizieren, indem sie die Inhalte von speziellen Kommunikationsregistern C_i und $C_{q(i,t)}$ austauschen (in [GP 80] wird gezeigt, wie man allgemeinere Situationen handhabt). Wir betrachten im folgenden einen festen Schritt t und lassen den Index t weg. Die Simulation wird durch ein Beispiel mit P = 6 illustriert.

i =	1	2	3	4	5	6
q(i) =	5	3	2	6	1	4

Zunächst gibt jeder Prozessor i das Paar [q(i),i] ins Sortierwerk. Man kann sich dieses Paar als eine Postkarte mit Adresse q(i) und Absender i vorstellen. Der Text der Postkarten ist stets der gleiche:

"Lieber Adressat! Ich, der Absender, wüßte gerne den Inhalt Deines Kommunikationsregisters"

und braucht deshalb nicht hingeschrieben zu werden. Im Beispiel werden die Paare

[5,1] [3,2] [2,3] [6,4] [1,5] [4,6]

ins Sortierwerk gegeben. Nun wird nach der 1. Komponente sortiert, und die Adressaten erhalten die Postkarten

[1,5] [2,3] [3,2] [4,6] [5,1] [6,4] .

Die Adressaten überschreiben die Adresse mit dem Inhalt ihres Kommunikationsregisters

$[C_1,5]$ $[C_2,3]$ $[C_3,2]$ $[C_4,6]$ $[C_5,1]$ $[C_6,4]$

und schicken die Karten zurück an die Absender (sortieren nach der 2. Komponente)

$[C_5,1]$ $[C_3,2]$ $[C_2,3]$ $[C_6,4]$ $[C_1,5]$ $[C_4,6]$.

Damit kann auf CCC mit P Prozessoren ein Schritt einer Menge von P frei kommunizierenden Prozessoren in $O((\log P)^2)$ Schritten simuliert werden.

Ähnliche Ergebnisse gelten natürlich auch für jedes andere Netz von P Prozessoren, auf dem man in $O(\log P)$ Schritten Permutationen realisieren und in $O((\log P)^2)$ Schritten sortieren kann, z.B. das Shuffle-Exchange-Netz [K 73] mit P Prozessoren 1,...,P mit den folgenden Verbindungen

$(i, 2i-1)$ für $i \leq P/2$
$(i, 2(i-P/2))$ für $i \geq P$
$(i, i+1)$ für $i < P$
$(P,1)$

Bild 8 zeigt das Shuffle-Exchange-Netz mit 8 Prozessoren.

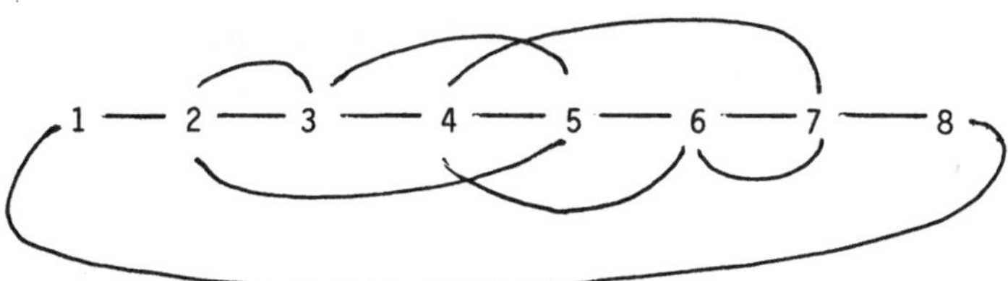

Bild 8

Die obigen Überlegungen lassen es denkbar erscheinen, daß der Benutzer eines künftigen general purpose parallel computers U neben Daten und Programm auch noch sein eigenes Netz G spezifiziert, das dann von U simuliert wird. Dazu braucht man Sprachen, um sehr große Netze zu beschreiben und für die Simulation durch Permutationsnetze auch "Compilationstechniken", die einem aus der Beschreibung eines Netzes G die Dekomposition in Netze G_i vom Grad 1 und deren Einbettung auf das Permutationsnetz liefert.

Die Dekomposition eines Netzes vom Grad d in $\binom{d}{2}$ Netze vom Grad 1 ist einfach. Die besten bekannten Algorithmen zur Dekomposition in d Netze suchen perfekte matchings in gewissen bipartiten Graphen, wofür auch auf parallelen Rechnern keine besonders schnellen Verfahren bekannt sind. Andererseits sieht man für viele Netze wie binäre Bäume und Gitter die Dekomposition mit bloßem Auge. Für kompliziertere aber häufig benutzte Netze kann man sie ein für allemal ausrechnen und abspeichern.

Die Einbettung eines Netzes vom Grad 1 auf das Permutationsnetz W_P erfordert im wesentlichen $\log P$ mal das Finden von Zusammenhangskomponenten von Graphen, die aus disjunkten Kreisen bestehen und P Knoten haben. Diese Zusammenhangskomponenten kann man z.B. durch O(log P)-maliges Sortieren finden, so daß die Einbettung mit Hilfe von CCC insgesamt in $O((\log P)^4)$ Schritten gefunden werden kann [LPV, GP 80].

Literatur.

[AHU 74] Aho, Hopcraft and Ullman: the design and analysis of computer algorithms, Addison-Wesley 1974

[B 68] Batcher: sorting networks and their applications, proc. AFIPS spring joint computer conference,vol. 32, 307-314, 1968

[GP 80] Galil and Paul: a theory of complexity of parallel computation, preprint Tel Aviv University und Universität Bielefeld, 1980

[K 73] Knuth: sorting and searching, Addison-Wesley 1973

[PR 78] Paul and Reischuk: a graph theoretic approach to determinism versas nondeterminism, erscheint in ACTA INFORMATICA

[PR 79] Paul and Reischuk: on time versas space II, proc. 20th IEEE-FOCS, 298-306, 1979

[PV 79] Preparata and Vuillemin: the cube-connected-cycles: a versatile network for parallel computation, proc. 20th IEEE-FOCS, 140-147, 1979

[W 68] Waksman: a permutation network, J. ACM 15, 159-163, 1968

[LPV] Lev, Pippenger and Valiant: a fast parallel algorithm for routing in permutation networks, erscheint in IEEE-TC.

Die Rezeption des Buches "Die Macht der Computer und die Ohnmacht der Vernunft"

J. Weizenbaum (MIT, z.Z. Hamburg)

Kurzfassung

Mir wurde die Aufgabe gegeben über verschiedene Folgen der Veröffentlichung meines Buches

"Die Macht der Computer"

zu berichten. In diesem Vortrag werde ich die folgenden Punkte besprechen:

1. Inwiefern war der Boden bereit solch ein Buch zu empfangen? Ich werde behaupten, daß die im Buch erwähnten strittigen Fragen schon das Bewußtsein vieler Informatiker, und auch das anderer Techniker, belastete.

2. Was war die Hauptkritik des Buches und wie hat sich diese Kritik im Laufe der Zeit erhalten? In diesem Zusammenhang müssen die folgenden Punkte erwähnt werden:

   2.1 Daß das Buch nicht ernst zu nehmen ist weil:

      2.1.1. Der Autor links orientiert ist

      2.1.2. Das Buch nur ein Zug in einem innenpolitischen Kampf zwischen dem Computer Science und den Linguistics Departments im M.I.T. ist.

      2.1.3. Der Autor hat seine Wissenschaftsfähigkeit verloren und hat sich nur deswegen zur Kritik seiner früheren Kollegen gewendet.

      2.1.4. Die Schwierigkeiten, besonders im Bereich der Künstlichen Intelligenz, die im Buch besprochen wurden, waren nur Kinderkrankheiten die, schon lange bevor das Buch erschien, überwunden waren.

   2.2 Daß das Buch, obwohl es kritisch gegenüber der Künstlichen Intelligenz ist, immerhin doch die irreführenden Hauptthesen der Künstlichen Intelligenz, z.B. daß künstliche Intelligenz überhaupt möglich ist, verteidigt.

   2.3 Daß das Buch unwissenschaftliche "Unmöglichkeitssätze" ausspricht.

   2.4 Daß das Buch keine politische Belehrung oder Führung anbietet.

3. Was ich seitdem gelernt habe.

APPLICATION OF META-COMPILATION METHODS IN THE ADA TEST TRANSLATOR DEVELOPMENT *)

Knut Ripken **)

Summary

This paper is written to show that the application of a special software development method which is normally only supported by tools can also be beneficial in the absence of these tools. It describes how effort was saved in the Ada Test Translator development by structuring the translator in the same modular way as if it had been generated by the advanced Munich Compiler-generating System MUG2 and by coding several semantic attribute evaluation passes in a form very closely resembling the corresponding input language to MUG2.

1. Introduction

An important phase in the Ada development program of the US DOD was the test and evaluation phase of preliminary Ada [Ada 79] in the fall of 1979. As a supporting tool for this phase, the final competing contractors for the language design had to develop a test translator for their language.

In this paper, we present some methodological aspects of the test translator development for the successful language design which are considered to be of general interest as they provide an example of a software development project where it has proven beneficial to apply a normally tool-based methodology, even without the tool support.

The method referred to is that of semantic attribute evaluation, which is extensively employed in compiler generating systems (for an overview, see [Räi 77]).

We thus adopt here the practical point of view of compiler writers equipped only with a parser generator, but borrowing methods from more complete compiler generating systems in order to implement a quite complex language fully and in a non-academic environment.

The test translator project took place under rather special conditions :

(1) There was a very severe time constraint.

(2) The language to be implemented was under development, and changed substantially until very late in the project (two and a half months before the initial delivery date).

(3) It was not required that the test translator be efficient in time or storage space.

Hence, it would have been an ideal project to employ a compiler generating system, assuming that such a system would have :

(1) speeded up the implementation

(2) facilitated modifications, and

(3) perhaps introduced some overhead in time and space.

Unfortunately, no such system was available on the host machine, a Honeywell Series 60 (Level 68) Computer with a Multics system installed at MIT, Cambridge, Massachusetts

---

*) The work reported was performed as part of the CII HONEYWELL BULL development of an Ada Test Translator. It was sponsored by DARPA under contract number MDA 903-77-C-0331, and monitored by William Carlson, Information Processing Techniques Office.

**) Author's address : TECSI-SOFTWARE
29, rue des Pyramides
F - 75001 PARIS

(chosen as a Honeywell computer on the ARPAnet). In particular, we regretted the fact that the authors of the Munich Compiler-generating Systems MUG1 [GRW 76, WRC 76, Gan 76] and MUG2 [GRW 77, Gie 79, Wil 79/section 2] did not develop portable systems but rather chose a machine-dependent implementation language in order to satisfy their goal of demonstrating that efficient compilers could be generated efficiently.

With no such advanced system on hand, we decided that we would even save effort by organizing the translator in the same way as the compilers which are generated by MUG2, and by coding the attribute evaluation in a form very much resembling the input language for that part of MUG2 which generates the attribute evaluation.

The subject of our paper is this methodical approach of mimicking a compiler generating system while starting out only with a parser generator.

In Section 2, we attempt to introduce and motivate the structure of this test translator

In Section 3, we describe the abstract syntax tree and its construction. This tree is the suitable intermediate form of a source program.

In Section 4, the attribute evaluation is discussed, i.e., how the nodes of the abstract syntax tree are decorated with semantic information during different compiler phases.

We end the paper with a discussion of the approach in Section 5.

2. The Structure of the Ada Test Translator

In MUG2, an abstract syntax tree (program tree) is used as the intermediate program form which serves as the basis for the description of the compiler subtasks. In a MUG2-generated compiler, the program tree is traversed in different compiler passes which perform semantic analysis, optimizations and code generation. The advantage of a program tree over a concrete syntax tree as constructed by a parser is that it no longer contains structure which is irrelevant after parsing, and hence occupies less storage space.

In a compiler-generating system such as MUG2, the choice of one suitable universal intermediate program form with its set of operations primarily reduces the number of notational and conceptual difficulties for the user. But, as a secondary effect, in compilers generated or built following such a model, the amount of code which is source-language independent and implements the manipulation of the compiler-internal data structures is also reduced.

In the test translator project, the goals both of avoiding notational and conceptual cluttering and of avoiding the writing of any unnecessary code were imperative. They led us to structure the Ada test translator in the same way as MUG2-generated compilers, i.e., the main translator mechanism is traversing the program tree and decorating it with semantic information in the form of attributes.

There are six passes over a tree before its interpretation, which also basically consists of a traversal of the tree resulting from this analysis, with, to be sure, occasional jumps and iterations.

As Ada is rather complex to compile, traversal and attribute evaluation only account for a small percentage of all the compiler code as well as lexical and syntactic analysis do (Figure 1). The bulk of the code is accounted for by the semantic actions. It is, however, important to note that the latter are directed and structured by the attribute evaluation in an (abstract-)syntax-directed top-down way.

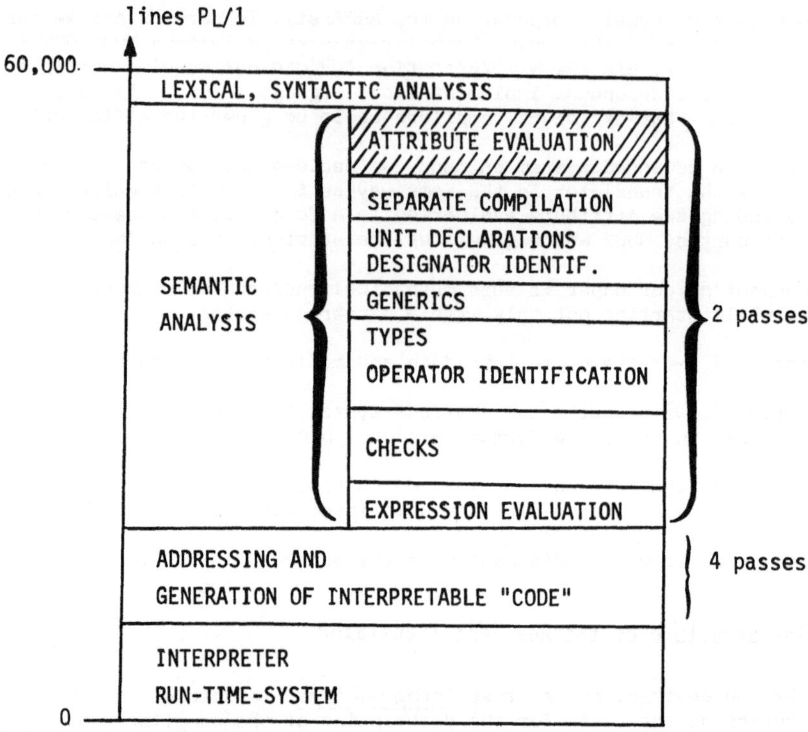

Figure 1 Code distribution among the different test translator phases. The shaded section corresponds to traversal and attribute evaluation during the two passes of semantic analysis.
(The number of passes was determined by aspects of project organization.)

3. The Program Tree and its Construction

For the generation of a syntactic analyzer, the system SYNTAX [Bou 80] was available which had been developed within the DELTA-project at INRIA [Bla 73, Lor 74], SYNTAX received as input an LALR(1)-grammar for Ada in BNF-notation and produced parser tables for a fixed parser skeleton. Now, lacking a system such as MUG2 which generates a program tree constructor from a string-to-tree grammar, one way to build a tree constructor could have been to exploit SYNTAX' capability to generate calls to semantic actions within the generated parser according to the connection of semantic action identifiers with the production rules of the input grammar : the semantic actions would have been the tree-constructor actions.

We chose a different solution which required less time and effort. Instead of coding grammar-dependent tree building actions we incorporated a grammar-independent tree constructor in the fixed parser skeleton.

3.1 The Grammar-Independent Built-in Tree Constructor

This constructor can be viewed as one semantic action which is called by the parser upon each reduction. It works in a standard way described by the following rules (T1) through (T7).

(T1) The roots of the trees which correspond to the nonterminals of the right-hand side are made the sons of a new node representing the nonterminal of the left-hand side to which the parser has reduced.

In order to keep the possibility of giving meaningful names to the nodes of the tree thus constructed, SYNTAX was modified to accept the specification of a node name for each production.

(T2) The name associated with a production is given to the node created for the left-hand side nonterminal.

(T3) The omission of a node name for a production with one right-hand side nonterminal is then used to signal the tree constructor to avoid any action upon a chain reduction.

(T4) A reduction of the empty string always causes the tree constructor to generate a leaf EMPTY.

(T5) A right-hand side terminal denoting a class of lexical symbols, e.g."IDENTIFIER", always causes the tree constructor to generate a leaf with the same name.

Example 3.1. :

Given the following productions : ("=" and ";" are the separator of left-hand and right-hand sides and the terminator of a production, respectively. Nonterminals are enclosed by angle brackets. "≠" serves as escape character.)

```
<OBJECT_DECLARATION>       = IDENTIFIER : <CONSTANT_OPTION> <TYPE>
                                          <INITIALIZATION_OPTION> ; "OBJECT"
<CONSTANT_OPTION>          = ;
<CONSTANT_OPTION>          = CONSTANT ; "CONSTANT"
<INITIALIZATION_OPTION>    = ;
<INITIALIZATION_OPTION>    = <EXPRESSION> ;
```

and a source program segment corresponding to the following parse tree :

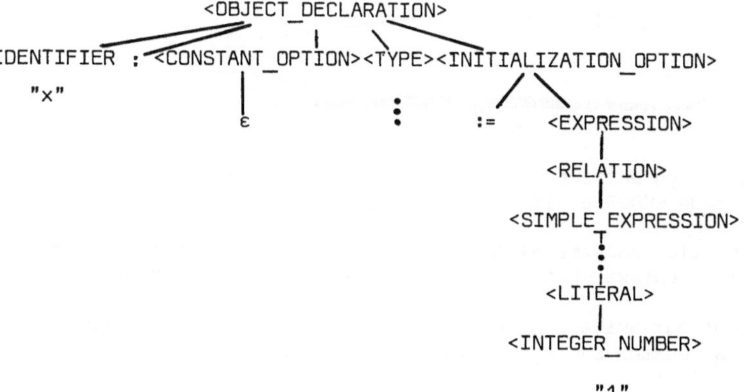

Then the corresponding abstract tree will be :

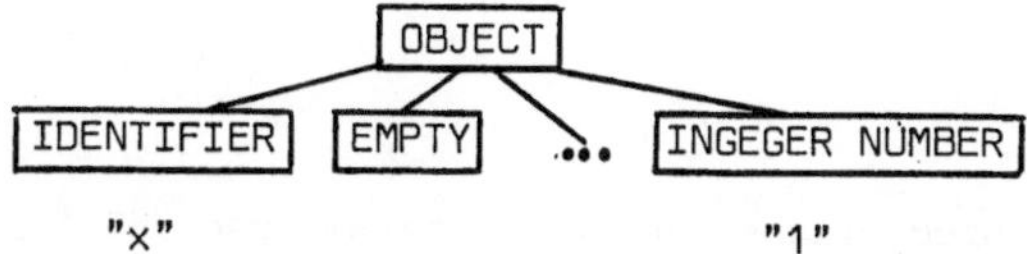

(T6) Left-or right-recursive lists are constructed as one family in the abstract tree if the name of the nonterminal representing the list ends in "_list".

Example 3.2. :

Given the productions :

<OBJECT_DECLARATION_LIST> = <OBJECT_DECLARATION>≠; ;

<OBJECT_DECLARATION_LIST> = <OBJECT_DECLARATION_LIST><OBJECT_DECLARATION>≠; ;

and a parse tree

<OBJECT_DECLARATION_LIST>

n-fold <OBJECT_DECLARATION_LIST><OBJECT_DECLARATION> ;

<OBJECT_DECLARATION> ;

<OBJECT_DECLARATION_LIST>

;

<OBJECT_DECLARATION>

Then the corresponding abstract tree will be :

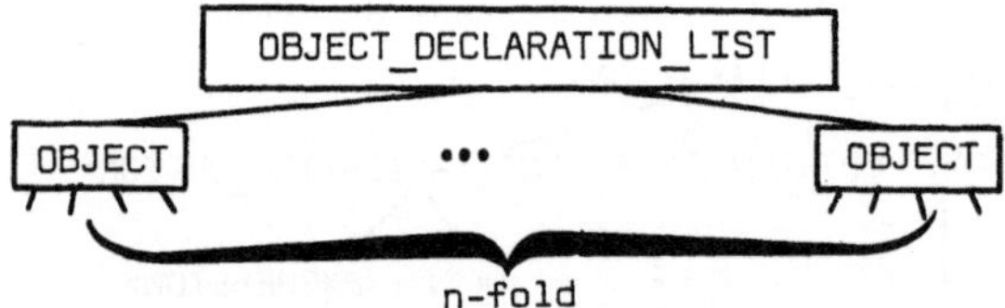

(T7) In case of syntactic errors, the tree constructor collects all dangling subtrees under a node ERROR as if they were list elements.

Therefore, semantic analysis always works on consistently built trees and may decide depending on the context whether to analyze within such error-subtrees.

It is clear that our built-in tree constructor builds only a "condensed" parse tree with node names renamed and syntactic structure removed where it is unnecessary for the semantic analysis.

But the program tree constructed this way turned out to be completely adequate as the intermediate form for the semantic analysis.

3.2. The Program Tree Nodes

Our Ada-LALR(1)-grammar had 361 productions, and the program tree 163 "operators", i.e. differently named nodes.

As our implementation language PL/1 (the natural choice on Multics) does not know record variants and we had to avoid coding too many tests for operator types, we used the same based PL/1-structure to represent the different operators :

```
   dcl 01  node based
       ,02  name fixed bin            /* operator identification */
       ,02  father like node_locator
       ,02  brother like node_locator
       ,02  son like node_locator     /* node-locator is a generalized "pointer"
                                         consisting of an offset and a segment number.
                                         (We provided for multi-segment program trees).
                                      */
            /* Follow further attributes related to the program tree structure
               which ease the program tree traversal. */
       ,02  degree fixed bin          /* number of sons */
       ,02  position fixed bin        /* position of the node as son */
       ,02  is_list bit
       ,02  first_list_element bit
       ,02  last_list_element bit
            /* lexical attributes */
       ,02  symbol
            ,03  table_index ...
            ,03  head ...             /* text position */
            ,03  tail ...
            ,03 hash_code ...
       ...;
```

Each node references its father, first son and right brother in the program tree which can thus be easily traversed in a top-down left-to-right fashion (cf. the next section).

The lexical attributes of terminal operators are evaluated in parallel with parsing and tree construction. In order to be able to associate error messages with meaningful text positions, the attributes "head" and "tail" are evaluated for nonterminal operators so that they indicate the exact beginning and end of the corresponding source program portion.

It remains to be said that SYNTAX was modified to render two more useful services. The first service is a listing indicating for each operator the possible operators for all its son positions. This is useful for checking the cases to be considered in the semantic analysis. The second service is the generation of code skeletons for the analysis which is discussed in the following section.

4. Attribute Evaluation

The main advantage of attribute grammars for compiler writing lies in the principle of expressing syntax-directed semantic analysis in the local context of production rules. Therefore, an implementation based on an attribute grammar is highly structured in the sense that it is always transparent, indicating :

- which attributes characterize which entity
- where these attributes are evaluated
- on which other attributes they depend
- where these attributes are used.

4.1. Local Evaluation Context

Since in the Ada test translator the attributes are associated with the nodes of the program tree, the attribute evaluation rules are not based on the context-free LALR(1)-grammar but on the abstract syntax. Here we followed the MUG2-aproach of a "modified attribute grammar" [Gan 74], suitable for multipass attribute evaluation. Attribute evaluation is subdivided into passes which are realized as left-to-right depth-first tree traversals. Hence each node is visited twice, once upon the entry of its subtree (entry-visit), once upon the exit from its subtree (exit-visit). Attributes are single-assignment variables and hence can be divided into categories of inherited and derived attributes, which are only evaluated at entry-visits and exit-visits, respectively.

In our implementation, we allow the following local attribute dependency at a node n : an inherited attribute may depend on :

- the inherited attributes of the father and of the left brothers of n
- the derived attributes of the left brothers of n
- any attributes of the father, the brothers and n itself which have been evaluated in a previous pass ;

a derived attribute may depend on

- the inherited attributes of n, its sons and its father
- the derived attributes of the sons of n
- any attributes of the father, the sons and n itself which have been evaluated in a previous pass.

Note that we allow a derived attribute at n to depend on inherited attributes of the father of n. By doing so, we are violating the principle of restricting the attribute dependency to one production rule of the context-free grammar underlying the attribute grammar, but we ease the determination of the analysis context in many cases where abstract syntax tree nodes are overloaded due to a strong syntactic overloading in Ada (e.g. the construct 'indexed-component'). (In fact, the only attributes of the father of n inspected at an exit-visit of n are in our implementation the attributes "name" and "i_context", indicating a context-case).

The local attribute dependency is more restricted at entry-visits of nodes which are list-elements and at exit-visits of nodes which are list-heads because of the variable number of brothers and sons, respectively. In these cases, only the direct brothers and the last son, respectively, count as brothers and sons, respectively, of the evaluation context.

4.2. Implementation

The basic idea of our implementation is the separation of the tree traversal activity from the analysis activity. Since the order of the traversal is fixed, a procedure called the "tree traverser" steers each evaluation pass by only inspecting the structural attributes of the program tree nodes. At each visit, it establishes the local evaluation context by setting pointers to the nodes of the context. For each pass k, the attribute evaluation statements to be executed at entry-visits and exit-visits are contained in procedures "pass_k_inherited" and "pass_k_derived", respectively. These procedures basically consist of case-statements with the cases corresponding to the possible evaluation contexts. Their evaluation statements reference attributes using the pointers established by the tree traverser, e.g. "father → node.name".

We illustrate the interface between the tree traverser and "pass_k_inherited" and "pass_k_derived", respectively, by associating the pointers with the nodes of the context.

entry-visit/pass_k_inherited :

a) father→node.is_list = false

father

brother(1) visited brother(n)

b) father→node.is_list = true

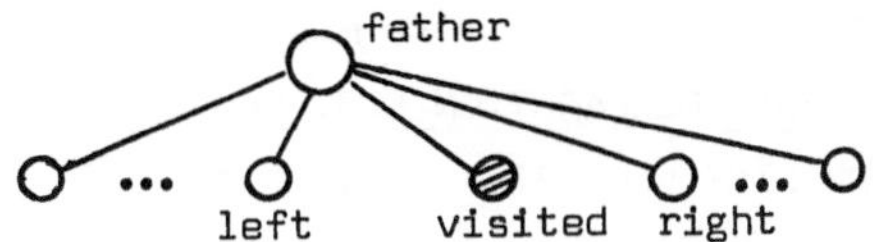

exit-visit/pass_l_derived :

a) visited→node.is_list = false

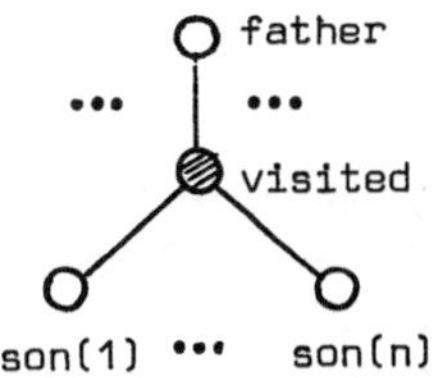

b) visited→node.is_list = true

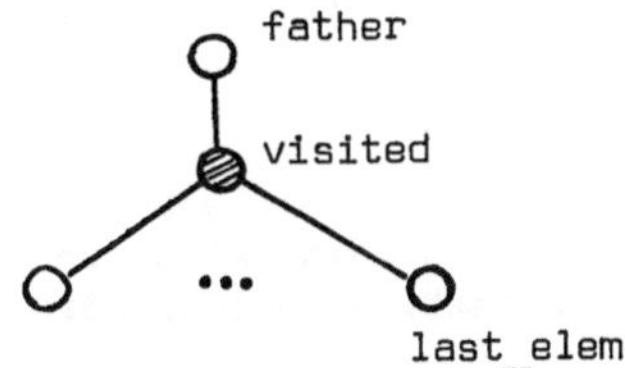

A parameter "visit_position" gives the position of a node as a son if it is not a list element and indicates for the node which is a list element whether it is the first, first_and_last, last or an element in the middle having left and right brother.

For each pass k, pass_k_inherited has the following form :

```
pass_k_inherited : procedure ;
        /* declarations */
goto father_kind (father → node.name) ;
/* ABORT_STATEMENT */  father_kind(1) :
     1)
        goto father_kind_end ;
⋮
/* ASSIGNMENT_STATEMENT */  father_kind (14) :
        goto ASSIGNMENT_STATEMENT_SON  (visit_position) ;
ASSIGNMENT_STATEMENT_son(1) :
     2)
        goto ASSIGNMENT_STATEMENT_son_end ;
ASSIGNMENT_STATEMENT-son(2) :
     2)
ASSIGNMENT_STATEMENT_son_end :
        goto father_kind_end ;
⋮
/* DECLARATION_LIST */  father_kind(30) :
        goto DECLARATION_LIST_son (visit_position) ;
DECLARATION_LIST_son(11) :  /* first_and_last */
     3)
```

```
            goto DECLARATION_LIST_son_end ;
 DECLARATION_LIST_son(12) : /* first */
         3)
            goto DECLARATION_LIST_son_end ;
 DECLARATION_LIST_son(13) : /* middle */
         3)
            goto DECLARATION_LIST_son end ;
 DECLARATION_LIST_son(14) : /* last */
         3)
 DECLARATION_LIST_son_end :
         4)
            goto father_kind_end ;

  :

 father_kind_end :
 end pass_k_inherited ;
```

In the positions 1), 2), and 3), statements may appear evaluating any inherited attributes of "visited→node" or calling semantic actions with attributes, accessible in the local context, as actual parameters.

In position 1), "visited" points to the only son of a node labelled "ABORT_STATEMENT" ; in positions 2), "visited" points to the first and second son, respectively, of an operator "ASSIGNMENT_STATEMENT", etc.

Analogously, for each pass k, pass_k_derived has the following form :

```
 pass_k_derived : procedure ;
       /* declarations */
 goto visited_node_kind (visited→node.name) ;
 /* ABORT_STATEMENT */  visited_node_kind(1) :
           5)
                                              goto visited_node_kind_end ;
  :
 /* ASSIGNMENT_STATEMENT */  visited_node_kind(14) :
           5)
                                              goto visited_node_kind_end ;
  :
 /* DECLARATION_LIST */  visited_node_kind(30) :
           5)
                                              goto visited_node_kind_end ;
  :
 visited_node_kind_end :
 end pass_k_derived ;
```

Here, in the positions 5), statements may appear evaluating any derived attributes of "visited →node", e.g. of the operators "ABORT_STATEMENT", "ASSIGNMENT_STATEMENT", and "DECLARATION_LIST", or calls to semantic actions may appear, again with attributes, accessible in the local context, passed as actual parameters.

We have deliberately used the PL/1 form (and not a much nicer Ada form) in order to show that even in PL/1 a case-statement, simulated with the help of a label array, can be made readable. Since PL/1 does not allow the definition of enumeration types, node names are explicitly declared as named constants. Their values, however, must be used as label array indices. Fortunately, this does not bother us at all for we have made the parser generator generate the above skeletal forms for the pass procedures. It has all the necessary information collected from the grammar input and can well edit the above forms. Hence, the parser generator is the only one ever to use the values of the node name constants.

On the other hand, this means - and this is the most important advantage - that the only coding which must be done by hand for the attribute evaluation is that of coding assignments to attributes and calls to semantic actions together with some case discriminating code for the different contexts to be considered for the operator visited. Hence the coding is reduced to a readable minimum resembling in principle the input to a compiler generating system such as MUG2.

Of course, a compiler generating system may do much checking on the input thus protecting the compiler writer from errors, and it may do optimizations in the attribute evaluation thus reducing time and storage requirements of the compiler. As for the protection, we did at least the following :

- the declarations of pass_k_inherited and pass_k_derived do not include the declaration of the pointers son(1), son(2) .... last_elem and brother(1), brother(2), ... left, right, respectively, so that references beyond the allowed context are detected when the pass procedures are compiled ;

- the inherited and derived attributes have names with the prefix "i_" and "d_", respectively, so that a rapid visual scan allows the detection of illegal attribute evaluations at exit- and entry-visits, respectively.

As for the optimization, not much can be done without violating the principles of methodological cleanliness and readability which was out of the question for us. In some cases, the code size of the evaluation may be reduced, e.g., common code in the positions 3) of pass_k_inherited could be placed in position 4).

5. Conclusion

In implementing the Ada test translator, we followed the method of attribute evaluation upon which most of the actual compiler generating systems are based. With a negligible effort compared to the total effort of the project, we extended the available parser generator and set up a compiler structure supporting the method. We are convinced that by employing this method we were able to write important complex central parts of the test translator in a clear, readable, well-structured top-down and self-documenting fashion while at the same time having a minimum of protection and reducing the manually written code considerably.

The intermediate form of an attributed program tree seems to become a standard intermediate form for Ada-compilers [Sto 80], especially as the interface of a common front-end with exchangeable code generators for a variety of target machines [Rip 78, BNL 80].

Our experience with the test translator has convinced us that an attributed program tree is a convenient intermediate representation even without a compiler generating system.

However, the two-fold transformation from the Ada representation grammar over the LALR(1)-grammar to the abstract syntax is a big step in abstraction, especially because of the overloading of some constructs, e.g., "name", "indexed component". The formulation of the semantic analysis on the program tree must therefore be preceded by a careful case analysis. Unfortunately, during a compilation, the applicable case can often not be detected and "signalled" by the syntactic analysis before the semantic analysis, but can only be determined after declaration analysis and name identification.

Of course, we could not follow the attribute method as dogmatically as a generating system with storage optimization capabilities [Gan 79, Räi 79] could permit it. We had to take a more pragmatic standpoint by implementing, for instance, much of the scope information and the symbol table as global attributes. They are pointed to by local attributes as well as the type and operator sets to be manipulated for operator identification [GaR 80].

On the other hand, viewing, for instance, the symbol table as a global attribute and therefore implementing it together with its operations as an abstract data type, contributes to the modularity and hence modifiability of the translator, as we experienced when we had to modify the translator as the language design changed.

In the test translator situation, perhaps the most important advantage of our approach was that it rendered the translator easily modifiable by having the attribute evaluation play a "buffer" role between syntactic and semantic analysis. Due to the fact that the tree traversal is done in a standard way and separated from the semantic analysis, i.e. that in the attribute evaluation only nodes of the local context are accessible and that nodes may not be accessed in the semantic actions at all, most syntactic changes only had a local effect on the attribute evaluation and no effect on the semantic actions. After writing a one-page program which inserts the old attribute evaluation statements in the proper places in the new skeletons generated for attribute evaluation by the parser generator, we could implement syntax changes several times in a few minutes real-time without doing any manual changes to the translator.

Acknowledgement

The development and application of the methods reported here owes much to Pierre Boullier, INRIA, whose suggestions and invaluable discussions as well as his implementation of the tools mentioned contributed so much to the project. I am also grateful to Jean D. Ichbiah and to all Ada project members for stimulating discussions.

References

[Ada 79] Preliminary Ada Reference Manual. ACM Sigplan Notices 14,6 (June 1979) part A.

[Bla 73] Blaizot, L., DELTA Système de description de Langages et de traducteurs par attributs. Rapport de Recherche 20, IRIA Laboria, Le Chesnay, June 1973. (French)

[BNL 80] Brosgol, B.M., Newcomer, J.M., Lamb, D.A., Levine, D.R., Van Deusen, M.S., Wulf, W.A., TCOL-Ada : Revised report on an intermediate representation for the preliminary Ada Language. Computer Science Department, Carnegie-Mellon University, 15 February 1980.

[Bou 80] Boullier, P., Génération automatique d'analyseurs syntaxiques avec rattrapage d'erreurs, Acte des journées Francophones sur la production assistée de logiciel, Genève, Janvier, 1980. (French)

[Gan 74] Ganzinger, H., Modifizierte attributierte Grammatiken, Report No. 7420, Abt. Mathematik, Technische Universität München, 1974 (German).

[Gan 79] Ganzinger, H., On storage optimization for automatically generated compilers. Theoretical Computer Science, 4th GI Conference, K. Weihrauch (ed.), Springer-Verlag, Berlin-Heidelberg - New York, March 1973, 132-141.

[GaR 80] Ganzinger, H., Ripken, K., Operator Identification in Ada : formal specification, complexity and concrete implementation, Sigplan Notices 15, No. 2 (1980), 30-42.

[Gie 79] Giegerich, R., Introduction to the Compiler generating system MUG2, Report TUM-INFO 7913, Institut für Informatik, Technische Universität München, May 1979.

[GRW 76] Ganzinger, H., Ripken, K., Wilhelm, R., MUG1 - an incremental compiler-compiler, Proceedings of ACM'76, 1976, 415-418.

[GRW 77] Ganzinger, H., MUG1 Manual, Report No. 7608, FB Mathematik, Technische Universität München, 1976 (German).

[Lor 74] Lorho, B., De la définition à la traduction des langages de programmation : Méthode des attributs sémantiques, Thèse d'Etat, Université Paul Sabatier, Toulouse, Novembre 1974 (French).

[Räi 77] Räihä, K.-J., On attribute grammars and their use in a compiler writing system. Report A-1977-4, Dept. of Computer Science, University of Helsinki 1977.

[Räi 79] Räihä, K.-J., Dynamic allocation of space for attribute instances in multi-pass evaluators of attribute grammars, Proc. of the Sigplan Symposium on Compiler Construction, Sigplan Notices 14, No. 8 (1979), 26-38.

[Rip 78] Ripken, K., A formal method for describing machine code generation with local optimizations, Lecture Notes of the EEC-CREST-Course on "State of the Art and Future Trends in Compilation", IRIA, 1978, 247-306.

[Sto 80] "Stoneman", Requirements for Ada programming support environments, U.S. Department of Defense, February 1980.

[Wil 79] Wilhelm, R., Computation and use of data flow information in optimizing compilers, Acta Informatica 12 (1979), 209-225.

[WRC 76] Wilhelm, R., Ripken, K., Ciesinger, J., Ganzinger, H., Lahner, W., and Nollmann, R-D., Design evaluation of the compiler generating system MUG1, Proc. of the 2nd International Conference on Software Engineering, 1976, 571-676.

ABSTRACTION AND REFINEMENT PRINCIPLES APPLIED TO THE CONCEPTION OF FUNCTIONALLY DISTRIBUTED SYSTEMS

Alain TARABOUT, Bernard MAILLOT, Irène VATTON

Laboratoire IMAG, B.P. 53X
38041 GRENOBLE Cedex, France

ABSTRACT

This paper deals with the construction of functionaly distributed computing systems by stepwise refinement. We implemented some new connection mechanisms between "units", defined as being both modules and processes. Units exchange messages through a general communication mechanism supported by the WAIT/SEND instructions and using transition automaton. Our model can be used for the development of systems which have to be distributed on several physical machines and for the evaluation of such systems.

1. PRELIMINARIES

1.1. Systems and machines

Let us first consider two major aspects which are common to all operating systems :

- an Operating System can be seen as the interpreter of a specific language which is the user level language, thus hiding to the user some constraining characteristics of the hardware. This language defines an abstract machine which is supposed to be easier programmed than the existing hardware ;
- an Operating System is also a resource allocator or scheduler whose work is both to guarantee a good usage of the physical resources and to share those resources among the user programs and service programs. For that work, all existing or proposed schedulers must be efficient (at least their authors generally pretend they are).

  An Operating System thus contains access functions to the resources which are used through the language of the abstract machine it defines.

Not only in operating systems do these two aspects exist. The idea that we are going to point out in this paper should apply to most computer applications, provided they are multiusers, and not only to those which are explicitly named "operating system". From now on, we shall use the generic word "system" to designate those computer applications which are both an interpreter and a scheduler as defined above.

The access functions of an abstract machine defined by a system appear as typed objects (LIS), called logical resources. It is possible to handle logical resources and abstract machines in the same way as physical resources and real machines. In other words, one can build new abstract machines on previously existing machines (abstract or physical). The new machine can be viewed as an interface between its users and the machines on which it is built.

At any level, this interface must be done by the interpreter part of the new machine. In every new machine there should also be a resource allocator to schedule the processes and share the logical resources of the machine. In the HYDRA project (WUL) for instance, this work is done by policy modules written by the users.

1.2. Modules and processes

We suggest to build a system by combining the abstraction and refinement principles (DAH, WIR). In practice this consists in defining machine levels built one upon another (DIJ).

Each one of these machines should provide logical resources (i.e. typed objects) and primitive operations (i.e. access functions) to use them. Speaking from the programmer's point of view, every logical resource should be clustered in a piece of code and data called a module, or in a hardware module (PAR). Making modules is now commonly considered as a good practice when decomposing systems.

We do join this point of view ; moreover, in our model every machine involved in the decomposition of a system is itself composed of modules. The user level of a system corresponds to the highest machine level of its decomposition. When a user program is executed by the system, it is in fact first interpreted by this top-level machine. The execution of every instruction of the program is accomplished by invoking one or several access functions associated with modules of this machine.

These access functions are themselves programs which are interpreted by lower level machines.

As a matter of fact the execution of a program by a machine of a given level leads to executions of other programs belonging to modules of lower level machines. Based on the same system structure (stepwise refinement leading to abstract machines composed of modules), two execution schemes may be developed. They differ essentially in the definition of what is called a process.

The first scheme corresponds to the procedure call mechanism : all the programs involved in the execution of a given program are executed under control of the same process. A few processes exist in such a scheme.

A stack is associated with each process and a whole module context is pushed every time a new module is called, and pulled when it is left. One important drawback of this execution scheme is that it needs quite a lot of memory for the processes stacks : whole module contexts are saved in the stack though only small contexts associated with the access functions would be sufficient.

Another drawback is that it does not take full advantage of the decomposition of a system in modules. Effectively pipelining and parallel processing cannot be used for modules which call one another : because every calling module is supposed to be busy even if the only work it still has to do for the process is to return control.

Finally, using such an execution scheme makes it difficult to replace any module, or set of modules, by a piece of hardware (microprocessor and memory for instance).

The execution scheme that we suggest is based on message transfers. Each module has one (or several) particular process associated with it ; we call it a cyclic process. These processes communicate with each other by sending (SEND) and receiving (WAIT) messages. This scheme is quite similar to the one used in the HYDRA project (WUL), but it differs slightly from Hoare's CSP (HOA), as in our case the messages are not transmitted upon "rendez-vous". We give the name units to those modules which can communicate with each other. Then the unit notion both covers the static notion of module, and the dynamic notion of process. The notion of unit will be starting point of our structuring model.

The following example illustrates what a unit may be.

Example :

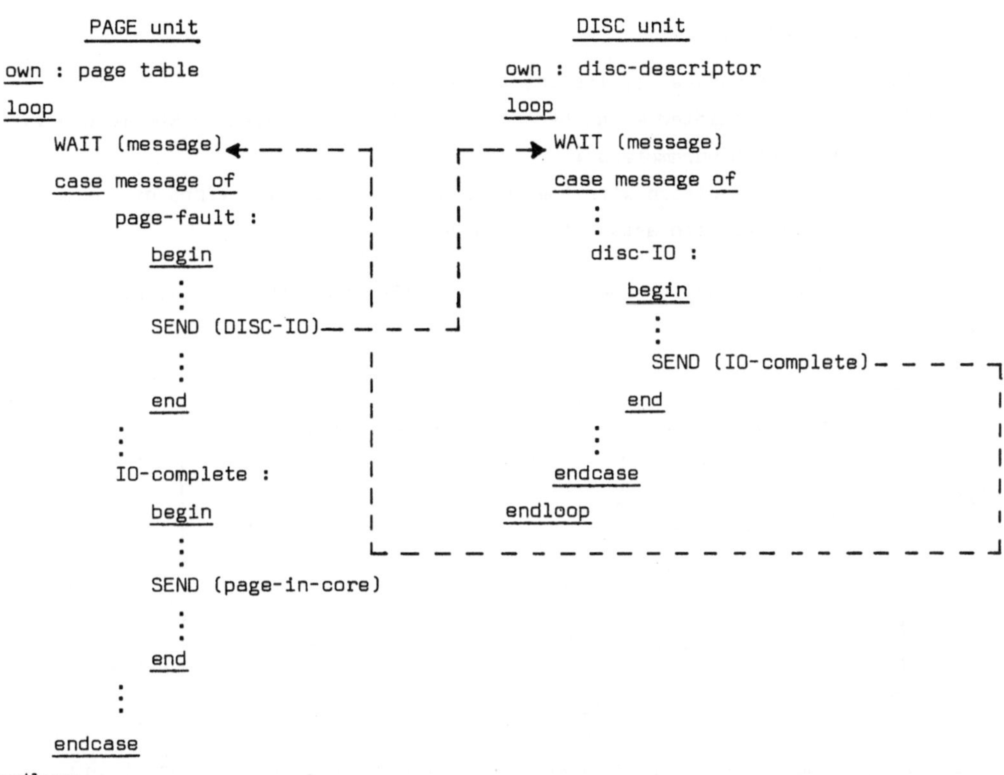

The PAGE and DISC units contain a paging mechanism. Each one of these units could eventually be implemented on different physical processor communicating by any physical mean (bus, wire, ...). Two access functions have been figured in the PAGE unit : "Page fault" and "IO-complete". One access function has been figured in the DISC unit : "DISC-IO". In this example, each message is supposed to contain an access function name with associated parameters. Messages are buffered at the entry (input) of every unit.

2. MACHINE STRUCTURES AND HIERARCHIES

We shall now examine how units can be assembled to make machines and what relations exist between units which belong to machines of different levels. This will constitute an original point in our presentation.

2.1. How to connect units

Functionally, a unit is defined by its inputs and outputs :

- the inputs are associated with the access functions enclosed in the module : function calls with parameters ;
- the outputs are associated with the exits of the access functions of the module : return codes with associated messages.

In the above example, the units named "PAGE" and "DISC" have the following inputs and outputs.

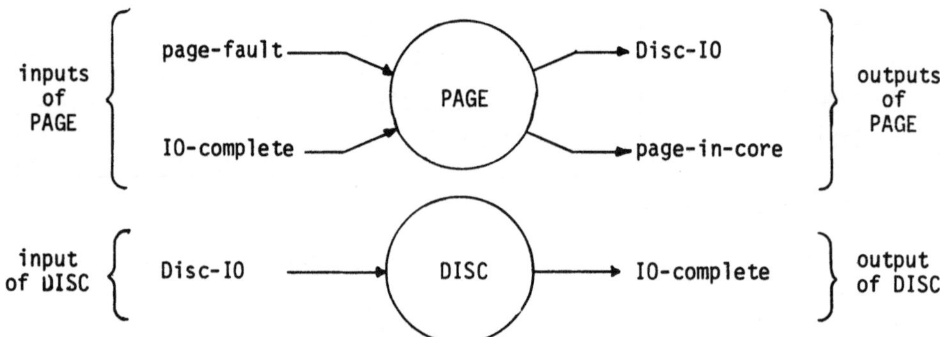

At first sight it seems very easy to connect units : one has just to associate inputs with outputs. In fact there are several ways of making such associations. We will classify them in three groups :

a) Static connections

As for hardware modules, each output of a unit can be connected to only one input of another (or the same) unit.

Such connections have a major drawback with is to prevent a unit from being called as a subroutine, unless duplicate inputs and outputs have been defined to provide multiple connections for the same function. Anyway this solution involves both overhead within the unit for additional message switching, and permanent accounting for the available inputs and outputs.

b) Dynamic connections

Connections can also be postponed to run-time. Each message must then contain routing information used by a connection kernel.

This information can be for instance the name of the called unit with the number of the input and it can be set up by the calling unit before sending the message. In this case much of the connections are inside the units and are therefore very difficult to be controlled. Moreover every unit should know at compile time all the other units to which it will be connected. This makes later usage of every unit very difficult, thus preventing actual modularity.

c) Semi-static connections

We have tried to gather the advantages of both static and dynamic connections :

- connections can be defined after the programming of the units ;
- modularity : a unit must not depend on the other units to which it is connected ;
- no limitation on the number of later connections to a unit (this limitation does exist on hardware modules) ;
- ability to have procedure calls between units.

All this can be obtained in combining static and dynamic connection :

- static connection graphs are first defined between units as in case a)
- routing information contained in every message is interpreted at run time to determine first which connection graph must be used and then to which unit the message must be routed.

A solution of that type has been developped in the HYDRA project but it has still one of the drawbacks that we have mentioned. In order to provide their units with a procedure call mechanism they have defined two extra commands named "CALL" and "RETURN" in addition to the SEND command. As a result, the connections are partly contained in each unit : whether the SEND or CALL or RETURN command is issued by a unit depends upon the way it must be connected to the other units. We think that the way a unit processes a message should depend only upon the command and parameters contained in the message and not upon how this message has been routed to the unit or must be returned to the caller.

What we suggest in order to allow procedure calls between units is to define static connections with finite-state automata rather than with graphs and we call them transition automata. Of course, to use a finite state automaton implies that every message is associated with a sequential process. This is a choice we decided to make ; besides, it makes it possible to control pirate messages as far as a new message can only be created by creating a new process.

2.2. Machine definition

A machine can then be constructed from units by defining a transition automaton. Functionally a machine is defined exactly like a unit, i.e. by its inputs and outputs :

- inputs are a subset of the inputs of its components ;
- outputs are a subset of the outputs of its components.

A machine can then be used exactly like a unit to construct a new machine. In other words, a machine can contain units and included machines. When a message comes into an included machine the identification of the outer machine automaton is pushed into a stack associated with the process (message) together with its current state for that process. The inner machine automaton is then used for the routing of the message in the inner machine. Reverse operations take place when the process goes out of the included machine.

This decomposition of a machine in units connected by an automaton and communicating with messages does easily fit to hardware implementation. For instance units can be realized on microprocessors. Moreover a specialized processor can be built to serve as a connection kernel like the one we have just described. The operations performed would be the following :

- machines and units creation and control,
- transition handling,
- message creation, destruction and switching.

2.3. Usage and extension

Let us come back to our primary goal which is to build a system gradually by defining intermediate abstract machines and machine levels.

2.3.1. Abstract machine definition and usage

As we have said at the beginning of this paper, an abstract machine defines both a language and logical resources. We shall now point out briefly some advantages that can be derived from our structuring method in both interpreting a language (MAI2) and allocating logical resources (MAI3).

a) The interpretation of an instruction of the language of a machine M may be done by one or several units. In the second case, we suggest to group the units in an intermediate machine M' corresponding to the interpretation of the instruction. Additions or suppressions of instructions in the language can then be achieved very easily by adding or suppressing components (i.e. units or intermediate machines) in the machine M : see (MAI2) for details.

Example

In the previous example, the DISC unit serves only as a subroutine to the PAGE unit when a page fault is processed. If we consider a "page fault" as an instruction a PAGING machine could be created to process this instruction.

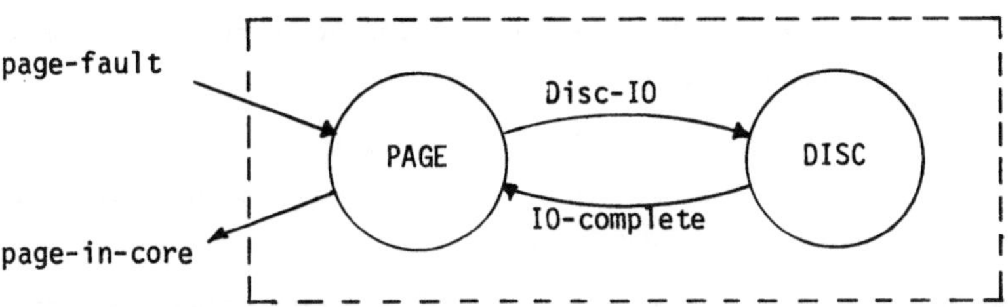

PAGING machine

b) The components of a machine (i.e. units or included machines) handle the logical resources of this machine. But they may also be logical resources themselves. For instance, in the previous example, the DISC unit can be seen as one resource if there is only one disk drive.
In such a case, where a unit is a resource, an allocation occurs at the time a message is taken by the unit, and the resource becomes free when the message is sent back by the unit.

A scheduler could then be created as a unit and be placed in the automaton both before and after every unit that has to be scheduled :

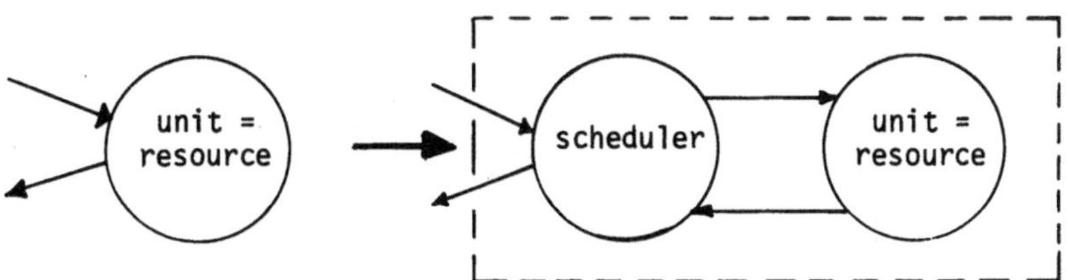

As figured above one could create an intermediate machine for every scheduled unit.

2.3.2. Extension

The model we have described so far allows the definition of machines from units and also, by inclusion, from previously defined machines.

We have implicitly supposed that the units did preexist, or at least could be created from programs written in one specific language : the language defined by the physical machine plus a few commands interpreted by the connection kernel. In fact, we have implicitly distinguished the cyclic processes associated with the units from the processes associated with the messages.

Now we define two units called WAIT and SEND and let the user use them ; then he can create machines which contain these units. In other words these machines can define languages which include the WAIT and SEND commands. Thus processes executed by these machines receive, process and send messages in the same way as cyclic processes do, so they can be cyclic processes too.

Finally units can be created on every machine which contains at least the WAIT and SEND units whatever level this machine is.

It should be noted that the inclusion of the WAIT and SEND units in any machine is possible because WAIT and SEND are connection instructions which are not related to any language. They are instructions of every level.

Nevertheless, because the interpretation of WAIT and SEND involves access to a message, the level of data representation must be unique for all messages, at whatever level the associated cyclic process may work.

The WAIT and SEND units lead to a powerful extension mechanism called refinement. As a matter of fact, refinement is associated with top down specification of a system. Once a language has been defined and programs have been written in that language to solve a given problem, an interpreter must be written for that language. In our model, this interpreter is a machine : i.e. a set of units. Each one of these units can itself be built on a lower level machine ; the interpreter is a set of programs which are themselves interpreted. At the bottom of the refinement scheme there are physical units which execute the programs of the last programmed units.

3. DISTRIBUTED SYSTEMS

Units can be defined on any machine - either abstract or physical - which is able to interpret or execute the WAIT and SEND instructions, these instructions being eventually made with hardware or microprogrammed or interpreted by software units. Generally speaking, any unit of our model may be a hard - or firm - or software unit.

By assembling such units it is then possible

- to build systems distributed on multiprocessor architectures, each component of the system being realized by software as well as hardware ;
- to evaluate the future performances of a system designed to run on a distributed architecture, by using a centralized realization of the connection kernel.

Let us examine these two points.

3.1. Building systems distributed on multiprocessor architectures

There are two different kinds of processors in any machine (MAZ) :

- specialized processors corresponding to the units of our model,
- general purpose processors corresponding to the included machines of our model.

As a result, our model is able to take into account different kinds of decentralized architectures : centralized machines with satellite computers, multi-microprocessors and network-machines. It allows any possible degree of distributed communication control among components, because the control mechanisms of the WAIT and SEND units can be decentralized in any possible way. For instance, the PAGE and DISC units of our previous example can be implemented on two different computers, the PAGE one managing a core memory and the DISC one being charged of the disc drives. We shall call site a set of machines for which the communication control is done by the same couple of WAIT/SEND units.

The transition automata used to connect the units in a given site are defined by a specialized unit, called connector. A particular connector may be implemented on each site, but it is also necessary to have one connector common to all sites as far as sites are also connected via transition automaton and WAIT/SEND units : each one of these units must receive a copy of these automata when the connections are set up. The routing information associated with the transition automata are part of the control information included in the messages. They are interpreted by the WAIT and SEND units of the site, which transfer the messages among the components of the site according to the local sub-automaton. This local automaton may itself include sub-automata if some components of the site are included machines (see § 2.2.).

3.2. Evaluating functionally distributed systems

The connection and communication kernel that we did implement runs on a centralized computer (the IRIS 80 of the Grenoble University Computing Center). A feature which is proper to our implementation concerns the communications among units : the transfer of a message is done by copying the associated part of the virtual space, not through bus or wire.

If we want to evaluate the time performances of a system which has to be realized on a distributed multiprocessor, we have to integrate our kernel as part of a measurement system. Let us illustrate this point with an example.

Let S be a functionally defined system ; we want to evaluate an eventual implementation of S on a multi-microprocessor :

- we first write a simplified version of S, defining a unit for each processor and grouping units having a common memory ;
- we observe and measure the behavior of S, i.e. how separate commands are executed in the processors network of S, and then measure the activity of the communication kernel (WAIT and SEND units) when S is running with a global load. We can then assign probabilistic coefficients to the transitions between units of S, and obtain the probabilistic automaton of the processors network ;
- this probabilistic automaton is used as an input to a simulator of queuing networks (MER). Other parameters of the simulator are the durations of message transfers between units and service times of the units. It is then possible to measure and analyze the performances of S when giving different values to the parameters of the simulator and different input laws.

This approach gives a powerful means of defining systems which have to be distributed on multiprocessor architectures. By adjusting parameters, it would be possible to evaluate the best communication techniques for a given architecture : units communicating via a common memory, bus-like transfers among components, transmissions through synchronous/asynchronous lines. It would be also possible to evaluate what units should be microprogrammed for global efficiency.

4. CONCLUSION

We have combined the classical structured programming concepts (DAH) and the stepwise refinement methodology (WIR) into a universal system structuring model.

A notion of unit has been defined as being both a module and a process.

Communication between units is done by message switching which is directed by automata associated with abstract machines.

A standard extension mechanism based on the creation of units onto abstract machines allows stepwise refinement in system development.

We have used this model to build the kernel of a real system (MAI1), thus proving its validity.

It is especially suitable for the development of systems which have to be distributed on several physical machines, for example on a multi-microprocessor architecture, as well as for defining the best suitable architectures of a given distributed system.

It can also be used of course for the development of a centralized system.

ACKNOWLEDGEMENT

This paper is based on the work of the OURS team in Grenoble : J. BRIAT, J. ESTUBLIER, P. LAFORGUE, B. MAILLOT, J. RAYMOND, S. ROUVEYROL, X. ROUSSET de PINA, A. TARABOUT, I. VATTON.

5. BIBLIOGRAPHY

(DAH) O.J. DAHL, E.W. DIJKSTRA, C.A.R. HOARE
"Structured programming", Academic Press, 1972.

(DIJ) E.W. DIJKSTRA
"Hierarchical ordering of sequential processes".
Acta Informatica, Vol.1, Fasc.2, 1971.

(HOA) C.A.R. HOARE
"Communicating sequential processes".
CACM Vol.21, n° 8, 1978.

(JAM) A.J. JAMMEL, H.G. STIEGLER
"Structural decomposition and distributed systems".
Leibniz Rechenzentrum, München, November 1977.

(LIS) B. LISKOV, S. ZILLES
"Programming with abstract data type".
SIGPLAN notices, Vol.9, 4, 1974.

(MAI1) B. MAILLOT, A. TARABOUT, I. VATTON
"Un outil de recherche en systèmes informatiques".
Thèses Docteur-Ingénieur et 3ème Cycle, Institut National Polytechnique de Grenoble, December 1978.

(MAI2) B. MAILLOT, A. TARABOUT, I. VATTON
"Application du principe d'abstraction-raffinement à la conception de systèmes répartis. Un exemple de mini-SGBD réparti".
International Seminar on Distributed Data Sharing Systems, Aix-en-Provence, INRIA ed., March 1979.

(MAI3) B. MAILLOT, A. TARABOUT, I. VATTON
"Allocation de ressources dans un système réparti".
Rapport de Recherche INRIA n° 6, January 1980.

(MAZ) G. MAZARE
"Systèmes multi-microprocesseurs : problèmes de parallélisme, définition et évaluation d'un système particulier".
Thèse d'Etat, Grenoble, June 1978.

(MER) D. MERLE, D. POTIER, M. VERAN
"A tool for computer system performance analysis".
In "Performance of Computer Installations", D. FERRARI editor,

North Holland Publishing Co., 1978.

(PAR) D.L. PARNAS
"On the criteria to be used in decomposing systems into modules".
CACM Vol. 15, n° 12, 1972.

(WIR) N. WIRTH
"Program development by stepwise refinement".
CACM Vol. 14, n° 4, 1971.

(WUL) W.A. WULF editor
"The HYDRA operating system".
Carnegie Mellon University.

DARTS
Ein Softwareentwurfswerkzeug für Echtzeitprogramme

Dipl.-Math. Hans Keutgen
Dipl.-Inform. Hans Meyer
GEI-GESELLSCHAFT FÜR ELEKTRONISCHE
INFORMATIONSVERARBEITUNG M.B.H.
Albert-Einstein-Straße 61
5100 Aachen

1 Überblick

DARTS (Design Aid for Real-Time Systems) ist ein Werkzeug für den Entwurf, das Elemente zur Beschreibung der Modularisierung, des Echtzeitverhaltens und der Datenstrukturen enthält. Die Entwicklung von DARTS wird durch Mittel des 3. DV-Programms der Bundesregierung unterstützt.

DARTS deckt zwei Aufgabenstellungen der Entwicklung von Software ab:

- Entwurfsunterstützung von Softwaresystemen in den Phasen Grob- und Feinentwurf,
- Entwicklungsbegleitende Dokumentation von der Grobentwurfs- bis hin zur Wartungsphase.

1.1 DARTS-Entwurfsansatz

Der DARTS-Entwurfsansatz unterstützt die Techniken der Modularisierung und der schrittweisen Verfeinerung.
Beide Techniken ermöglichen den strukturierten Entwurf von Systemen im 'top-down' Verfahren. Der methodische Ansatz hört nicht bei der Schaffung der Grobstruktur auf (das ist im übrigen der größte kreative Akt des Entwurfes), sondern die Beschreibung der internen Algorithmen ist ein wesentlicher Teil. Damit leistet die Methode deutlich mehr als der Ansatz des strukturierten Entwurfs, der die Module als Ganzes betrachtet - also nichts über deren Innenleben aussagt - und nur die Schnittstellen beschreibt. Erst die Verwendung von Pseudocode (darauf basiert die DARTS-Sprache) zur Beschreibung des algorithmischen Ablaufs zeigt an, wie eine einmal getroffene Entwurfsentscheidung die Lesbarkeit und damit die Test- und Wartbarkeit des später entstehenden Codes beeinflußt. Darüberhinaus zwingt die Verwendung der Grundkonstrukte der strukturierten Programmierung zu einem klaren, leicht nachvollziehbaren 'straight forward' Kontrollfluß.

Neben der Beschreibung des Kontrollflusses erlaubt die gewählte Datenbeschreibungsform eine Strukturierung der Daten nach der Methode der schrittweisen Verfeinerung. Durch ein Regelsystem ist eine Überprüfung des Datenzugriffs durch verschiedene Module möglich.

Die zur Festlegung des Echtzeitverhaltens verwendeten Schlüsselwörter erlauben die Überprüfung der Programmstruktur auf Zusammenhang, Synchronisation und Deadlockfreiheit. Diese Analysen basieren auf einem statischen Kontrollverfahren.

DARTS erstellt ein aufbereitetes Entwurfsdokument, das umfangreiche Querverweislisten, statische Analysereports und eine ausgewählte Metrik enthält.

1.2 DARTS-Dokumentationsansatz

Der DARTS-Dokumentationsansatz forciert darüberhinaus wesentliche Faktoren, die die Transparenz des Entwicklungsprozesses deutlich erhöhen. Bei richtiger Verwendung des Hilfsmittels liegt die gesamte Interndokumentation - Strukturbaum, strukturierter Entwurf und strukturierte Codevorgabe - vor, ehe eine einzige Zeile Code entstanden ist. Diese Dokumentation wird als Kommentar in den zu erstellenden Code übernommen, so daß bei ggfs. erforderlichen Änderungen im Entwurf nur ein Dokument gepflegt werden muß.

DARTS wird unter den Randbedingungen

- leicht zu erlernen
- gut zu verstehen
- verarbeitbar auf 'Mini'-Rechnern

entwickelt und befindet sich z.Z. mit einem Subset (realisiert auf PDP 11/03 und PDP 11/34) bereits im industriellen Einsatz.

2 Erstellen eines DARTS-Entwurfes

Nachdem in einer Definitionsphase die Anforderungen an ein zu entwickelndes System festgelegt worden sind und eine Gliederung in grobe Funktionsblöcke erfolgt ist, wird diese Aufteilung festgeschrieben und bildet die Grundlage für den Grobentwurf, der mit den sprachlichen Mitteln des DARTS-Entwurfssystems beschreibbar ist.

Dieser Grobentwurf wird im 'top-down' Verfahren je nach Größe und Komplexität des Problems über mehrere Stufen schrittweise verfeinert. Die untersten Verfeinerungsstufen bilden dann einen vollständigen Programmentwurf, der ohne Schwierigkeiten in eine Programmiersprache umgesetzt werden kann.

- Der Grobentwurf umreißt die Lösung des Problems. Er ist daher kurz und prägnant und kann somit schnell erstellt werden. Dieser Grobentwurf wird so lange geprüft und verbessert (Walkthroughs), bis er die Zustimmung aller Beteiligten findet. Der globale Lösungsansatz ist dadurch festgelegt.

- Jede weitere Stufe des Entwurfes entsteht durch Verfeinerung der Vorhergehenden, wobei die globale Struktur und Auffteilung des Grobentwurfes beibehalten wird. Anzustreben ist bei der Verfeinerung eine Struktur, die einer Baumstruktur 'möglichst nahe' kommt.

3 Struktur eines DARTS-Entwurfes

Ein DARTS-Entwurf besteht aus einer Anzahl von Segmenten, wobei zwischen zwei Arten unterschieden wird:

- Informationssegmente
  Sie enthalten größere Kommentare und Informationen, die zur Überprüfung des Entwurfes, insbesondere des Datenflusses, und zur Erzeugung von Querverweislisten dienen.

- Ablaufsegmente
  Sie bilden die Elemente der Verfeinerungsstruktur und enthalten die Beschreibung des algorithmischen Ablaufs.

3.1 DARTS-Informationssegmente

Folgende Informationssegmente können in einem DARTS-Entwurf verwendet werden:

- Systemdatensegmente
  Sie beschreiben das Input-/Outputverhalten des Gesamtsystems, sowie Daten, die für das Gesamtsystem von Bedeutung sind, und Resourcen.

- Environmentsegmente
  Sie dienen der Beschreibung des Input-/Outputverhaltens von eigenständigen Systemteilen, denen sie zugeordnet sind.

- Datensegmente
  Sie dienen zur Beschreibung von 'langlebigen' Daten und den diesen Daten zugeordneten Zugriffsrechten und zur Definition von Resourcen. Resourcen im DARTS-Entwurfssystem sind Objekte, die exclusiv benutzt werden sollen. Dieser verallgemeinerte Resourcenbegriff beinhaltet sowohl Datenbereiche, zu entwerfende 'Zugriffsprozeduren' als auch zu beschreibende Hardwareeinheiten.

- Externalsegmente
  Sie erlauben es, Querbezüge zu Entwurfsteilen herzustellen, die nicht Bestandteil des vorliegenden Dokumentes sind.

- Textsegmente
  Sie beinhalten größere Kommentare, die zum Verständnis des Entwurfes vom Ersteller eingefügt werden können.

- Indexsegmente
  Sie enthalten die Definition von Begriffen, deren Auftreten im Dokument referiert werden soll (z.B. zur Erzeugung von Querbezügen auf das Pflichtenheft).

- Indexzeichensegmente
  Sie ermöglichen die Definition von Sonderzeichen, aufgrund derer auf alle Wörter, die mit diesen Zeichen beginnen, eine Referenz erzeugt wird (z.B. zur Kenntlichmachung von Revisionen, Bearbeitern etc.).

3.2 DARTS-Ablaufsegmente

Dem Benutzer stehen zwei unterschiedliche Ablaufsegmente zur Verfügung:

- Aktivitäten
  Sie dienen der Beschreibung von parallel ablauffähigen Teilen des Gesamtsystems.

- Module
  Sie erlauben die Beschreibung von zeitlich unabhängigen Teilen und dienen zusätzlich der schrittweisen Verfeinerung von Ablaufsegmenten.

Jedes Ablaufsegment besteht aus zwei Teilen:

- Datenbeschreibung
  Sie ermöglicht die Beschreibung und Verwendungsspezifikation von Daten

- Ablaufbeschreibung
  Sie enthält die Beschreibung des algorithmischen Ablaufs.

Beide Teile beruhen auf der Methode der schrittweisen Verfeinerung, d.h. in jeder Stufe des Entwurfs ist sowohl von der Daten- als auch von der Ablaufbeschreibung nur soviel sichtbar, wie es für das Verständnis dieser jeweiligen Stufe erforderlich ist. So ist es z.B. auf einem hohen Entwurfsniveau nicht sinnvoll, die letzten Einzelheiten einer Datei bereits zu kennen.

3.2.1 DARTS-Datenbeschreibung im Ablaufsegment

Die DARTS-Datenbeschreibung gliedert sich in mehrere Komponenten

- Beschreibung des Ein-/Ausgabeverhaltens
  In zwei Listen werden die Größen angegeben, die in dieses Ablaufsegment importiert bzw. aus diesem Ablaufsegment exportiert werden.

- Definition von Daten
  Es besteht die Möglichkeit, Datenelemente zusammen mit ihrem Typ und ihrer Struktur zu definieren.

- Strukturierung von Daten
  Datenstrukturen können in hierarchischer Form Schritt für Schritt aufgebaut werden, d.h. es können nur vorher definierte Daten weiter verfeinert werden.

Auf der Grundlage dieses Datenansatzes lassen sich durch mengentheoretische Betrachtungen und durch ein definiertes Regelwerk Prüfungen über den jeweiligen Entwurf ausführen.

3.2.2 DARTS-Ablaufbeschreibung

Die Beschreibung des algorithmischen Ablaufs, also der Kontrollstruktur, innerhalb eines Ablaufsegmentes lehnt sich in ihren Grundelementen an die Konzepte der strukturierten Programmierung an. Die Entwurfssprache stellt Hilfsmittel zur Verfügung, die folgende Beschreibungen erlauben:

- strukturierte Konstrukte: Sequenz, Iteration und Selektion,
- Bearbeitung von Interrupts,
- Synchronisation paralleler Aktivitäten,
- Steuerung paralleler Aktivitäten.

Neben den dafür verwendeten Schlüsselwörtern unterliegt die Beschreibung innerhalb eines Ablaufsegmentes keinerlei syntaktischen Einschränkungen. Der Benutzer kann die Sprachmittel und den Stil der Beschreibung frei wählen und somit den Entwurf für alle an der Entwicklung Interessierten - Angehörige des Entwicklungsteams, Kunden, Implementierer - lesbar und verständlich gestalten. Da somit eine für das zu entwickelnde System relevante Terminologie verwendet werden kann, ist es sichergestellt, daß der Entwurf für alle Beteiligten leicht zu verifizieren ist und die Entwicklung die geforderten Spezifikationen trifft.

4 Datenbeschreibungsmöglichkeiten im DARTS-Entwurfssystem

Die Beschreibungsmöglichkeit von Daten im DARTS-Entwurfssystem gliedert sich in mehreren Komponenten, die sowohl das Ein-/Ausgabeverhalten von Daten in Bezug auf eine betrachtete Einheit des Entwurfs - also den Datenfluß, als auch die Zugriffsrechte auf bestimmte Datenbereiche darstellbar machen.

Wie schon oben angeführt (Pkt. 3.1 und 3.2), werden dem zu entwerfenden Softwaresystem Systemdatensegmente, den Aktivitäten Environmentsegmente und den Modulen eigenständige Datenbereiche zugeordnet.

Die folgende Beschreibung zeigt, wie zum einen der Datenfluß durch ein zu entwerfendes System dargestellt werden und zum anderen die Modellierung verschiedener Datenkonzepte mittels der vorgegebenen Möglichkeiten der Entwurfssprache erfolgen kann.

4.1 Beschreibung des Datenflusses

Die Beschreibung des Datenflusses erfolgt in mehreren Ebenen. Zuerst werden die Ein-/Ausgabegrößen des Gesamtsystems beschrieben.

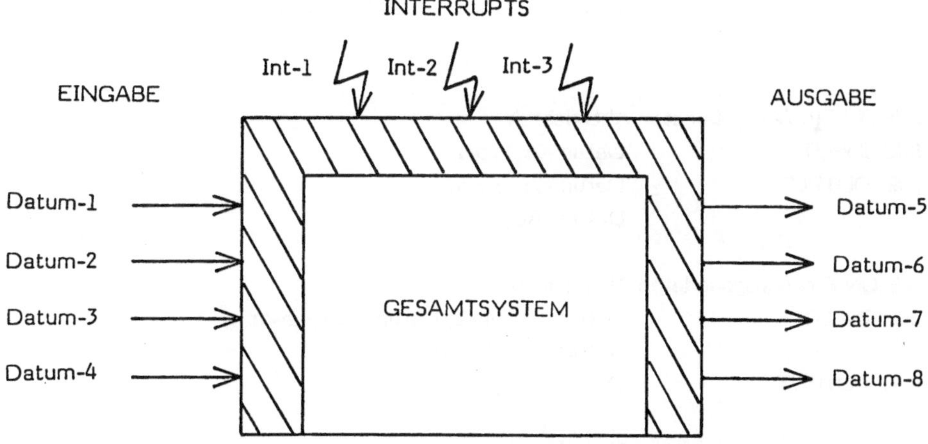

Beschreibungsform:

```
%SYSTEMDATA System Ein-Ausgabeverhalten
DEFINE INPUT        Datum-1, Datum-2: Typ-1; Datum-3: Typ-2;
                    Datum-4: Typ-3;
                    Int-1, Int-2, Int-3: IRPT.
DEFINE OUTPUT       Datum-5, Datum-6: Typ-1;
                    Datum-7, Datum-8: Typ-4.
```

Nach der Aufteilung in parallel ablauffähige Teile des Gesamtsystems (Aktivitäten) wird der für die jeweilige Aktivität relevante Teil der Systemeingabe bzw. -ausgabe in den Environmentsegmenten beschrieben.

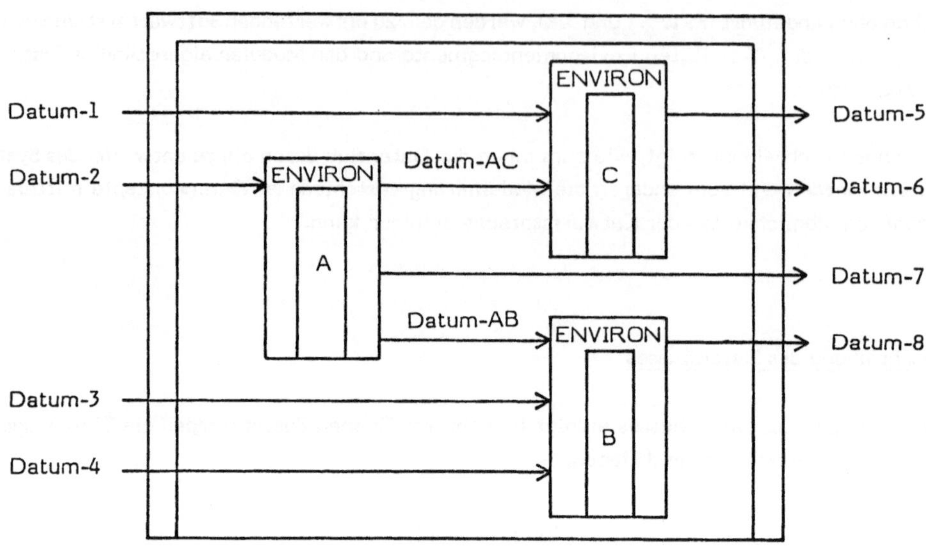

Beschreibungsform:

%ENVIRON Ein-/Ausgabedaten Aktivität A
DEFINE INPUT Datum-2: Typ-1
DEFINE OUTPUT Datum-7: Typ-4;
Datum-AB, Datum-AC: Typ-n

%ENVIRON Ein-/Ausgabedaten Aktivität B
DEFINE INPUT Datum-3: Typ-2; Datum-4: Type-4;
Datum-AB: Typ-n
DEFINE OUTPUT Datum-8; Typ-4

%ENVIRON Ein-/Ausgabedaten Aktivität C
DEFINE INPUT Datum-1: Typ-1; Datum-AC: Typ-n
DEFINE OUTPUT Datum-5, Datum-6: Typ-1

Die Zuordnung zwischen den Aktivitäten und den Environmentsegmenten erfolgt in der Beschreibung der Aktivität.

%ACTIVITY A
USING Ein-/Ausgabedaten Aktivität A
⋮

%ACTIVITY B
USING Ein-/Ausgabedaten Aktivität B
⋮

%ACTIVITY C
USING Ein-/Ausgabedaten Aktivität C
⋮

Neben den Systemein-/-ausgabedaten, die somit auf die einzelnen Aktivitäten verteilt werden,

werden alle Daten beschrieben, die die Aktivität verlassen bzw. in die Aktivität eingehen. Erfolgt also ein Datentransport zwischen zwei oder mehreren Aktivitäten, der nicht über gemeinsam benutzte Datenbereiche abgewickelt wird, so müssen auch diese Daten in dem entsprechenden Environmentsegment angegeben werden.

Innerhalb einer Aktivität wird der Datenfluß durch die diese Aktivität bildenden Module angegeben.

Das geschieht durch die in den Modulen zur Verfügung stehenden Datenbereiche. Die Teile der Eingabe bzw. Ausgabe der Aktivität, die von einzelnen Modulen verwendet werden, sind gemäß ihres Ein-/Ausgabeverhalten in IN bzw. OUT-Listen anzugeben.

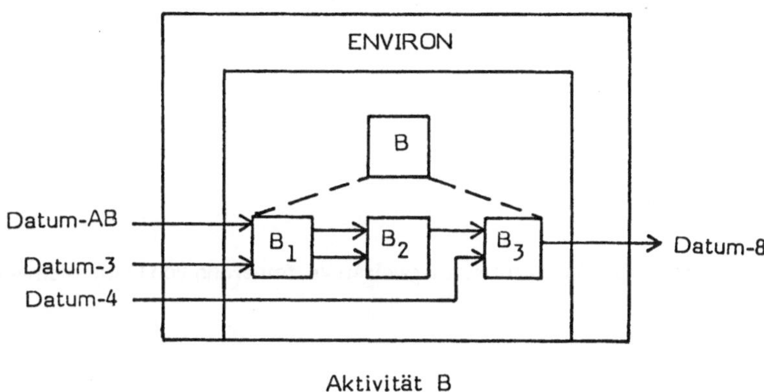

Aktivität B

Die Aktivität B, die die Eingabegrößen Datum-3, Datum-4 und Datum-AB und die Ausgabegrößen Datum-8 hat, verwendet weiterhin intern die drei Größen Lokal-1, Lokal-2 und Lokal-3.

Der Datenfluß wird dann folgendermaßen angegeben:

```
%ACTIVITY B
USING   Ein-/Ausgabedatei Aktivität B
DATA
DEFINE LOCAL                Lokal-1, Lokal-2: Typ-i;
                            Lokal-3: Typ-j

ENDDATA
     :

%Module  B1
DATA
IN       Datum-3: Typ-2; Datum-4: Typ-3; Datum-AB: Typ-n
OUT      Lokal-1, Lokal-2: Typ-i
ENDDATA
     :
```

Durch diese Möglichkeiten kann der gesamte Datenfluß durch ein System dargestellt und überprüft werden.

Neben diesen Datenbeschreibungen können in allen Datendefinitionsbereichen bereits definierte Daten strukturiert werden, z.B. kann das Datum Datum-1 durch die folgende Beschreibung strukturiert werden:

```
REFINE   Datum-1 CONSIST OF Datum-11, Datum-12
REFINE   Datum-11, Datum-12 CONSIST OF Datum-13, Datum-14
```

Die Struktur hat dann folgendes Aussehen:

```
Datum-1
    Datum-11
        Datum-13
        Datum-14
    Datum-12
        Datum-13
        Datum-14
```

Diese Art der Strukturierung kann auch zur schrittweisen Verfeinerung von Datenelementen benutzt werden.

4.2 Kommunikation zwischen Aktivitäten

Zur Kommunikation zwischen Aktivitäten werden keine fest vorgegebenen Konzepte gefordert, sondern die zugrundegelegten Beschreibungsformen ermöglichen die Modellierung verschiedener Konzepte und geben dem Benutzer somit einen hohen Grad an Entwurfsfreiheit. Weiterhin wird dadurch erreicht, daß die DARTS-Entwurfssprache nicht nur in eine bestimmte Programmiersprache abbildbar ist, die fest vorgegebene Konzepte unterstützt, sondern in mehrere wie z.B. FORTRAN, PEARL, MODULA und Concurrent PASCAL.

Die Definition von gemeinsam benutzbaren Datenbereichen erfolgt im Systemdatensegment oder auch in eigenständigen Datensegmenten durch die Angabe von PERMANENT-Daten. Durch die zusätzliche Angabe von den Systemteilen, die auf diese Datenbereiche zugriffsberechtigt sind, wird festgelegt, welche Systemteile (Aktivitäten oder auch Teile von Aktivitäten) mittels dieses Datenbereiches kommunizieren.

Sollen diese Datenbereiche weiterhin mit exclusivem Zugriff belegt werden, so werden sie zu Resourcen erklärt.

Im folgenden werden die Beschreibungsmöglichkeiten einiger Konzepte angegeben.

- Kommunikation über gemeinsame Datenbereiche ohne exclusiven Zugriff (Common-Bereiche)

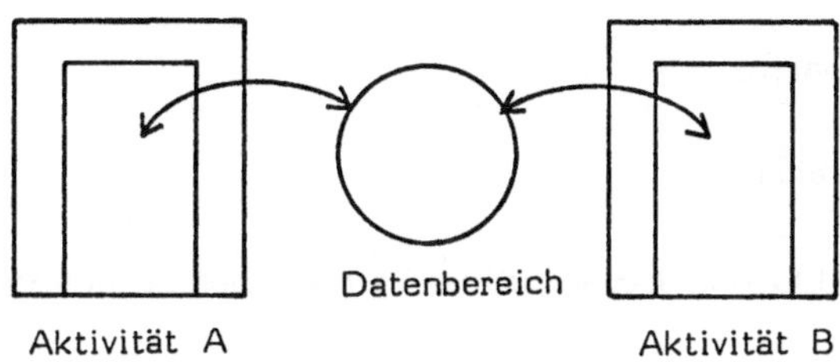

Beschreibungsform:

```
%DATA Commonbereich
DEFINE PERMANENT     Datenbereich
        ACCESS BY    A,B: ACTIVITY
REFINE Datenbereich CONSIST OF Datum-1, . . ., Datum-n
```

Die Verwendung dieser Daten in den Aktivitäten wird anhand der angegebenen Namen erkannt und die entsprechenden Stellen werden referiert.

- Kommunikation über gemeinsamen Datenbereich mit exclusivem Zugriff

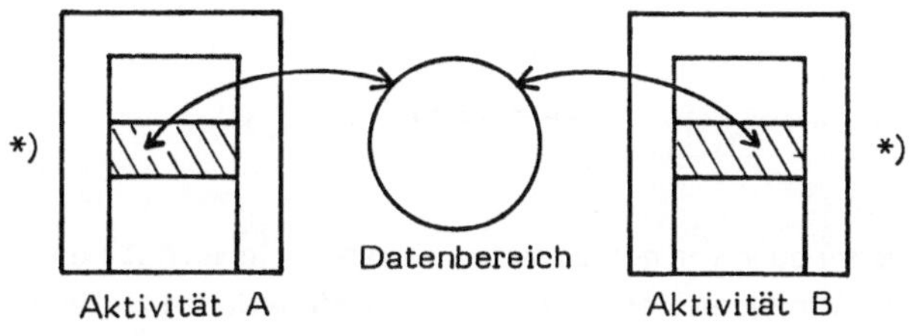

*) critical regions

Beschreibungsform:

```
%DATA Exclusiver Zugriff
DEFINE PERMANENT     Datenbereich
        ACCESS BY    Zugriffsfunktion-A, Zugriffsfunktion-B: MODULE
REFINE Datenbereich CONSIST OF Datum-1, . . .,Datum-n
DEFINE RESOURCE    Datenbereich: DATA
```

Bei der Verwendung von Daten aus dem Datenbereich muß dieser oder der verwendete Teilbaum von den Zugriffsfunktionen belegt werden. Das geschieht durch eine REQUEST und RELEASE Klammerung.

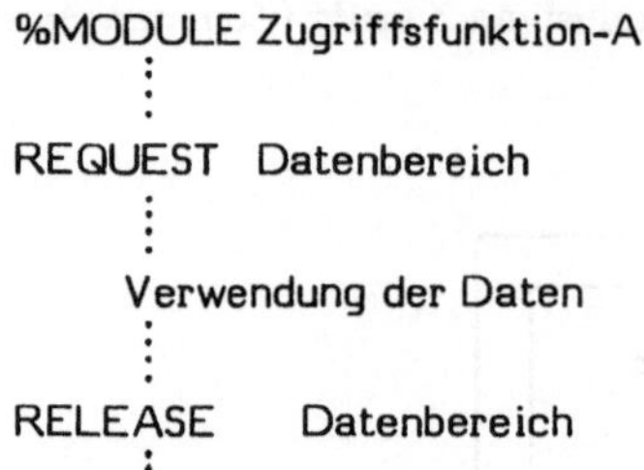

```
%MODULE Zugriffsfunktion-A
      :
REQUEST   Datenbereich
      :
      Verwendung der Daten
      :
RELEASE     Datenbereich
      :
```

Während der REQUEST-RELEASE Sequenz ist der Datenbereich für weitere Zugriffe geschützt.

Das Sperren des Zugriffs bei der Verwendung von Resourcen geht auch in die Überprüfung des Echtzeitverhaltens ein. Diese Überprüfung ist ein weiterer Bestandteil des DARTS-Entwurfssystems.

- Kommunikation über Monitore

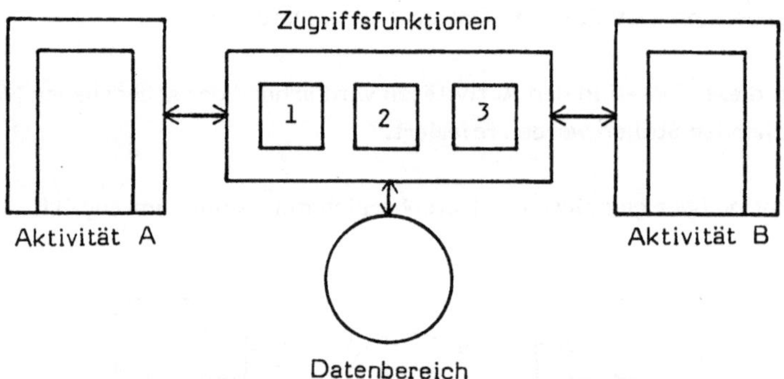

In Erweiterung zur Beschreibung von gemeinsamen Datenbereichen mit exclusivem Zugriff müssen bei der Modellierung von Monitoren auch die Zugriffsfunktionen zu Resourcen erklärt werden.

Beschreibungsform:

```
%DATA Monitor
DEFINE  PERMANENT    Datenbereich
        ACCESS BY    Zugriffsfunktion-1, Zugriffsfunktion-2,
                     Zugriffsfunktion-3: MODULE
        INIT BY      Initialisierungsfunktion: MODULE

REFINE Datenbereich  CONSIST OF Element-1,Element-2,Element-3
DEFINE RESOURCE      Zugriffsfunktion-1,Zugriffsfunktion-2,
                     Zugriffsfunktion-3, Initialisierungsfunktion: MODULE;
                     Datenbereich: DATA
```

Bei der Verwendung muß dann sowohl eine REQUEST-RELEASE Operation beim Aufruf der Zugriffsfunktion als auch in der Zugriffsfunktion bei der Verwendung des Datenbereiches erfolgen.

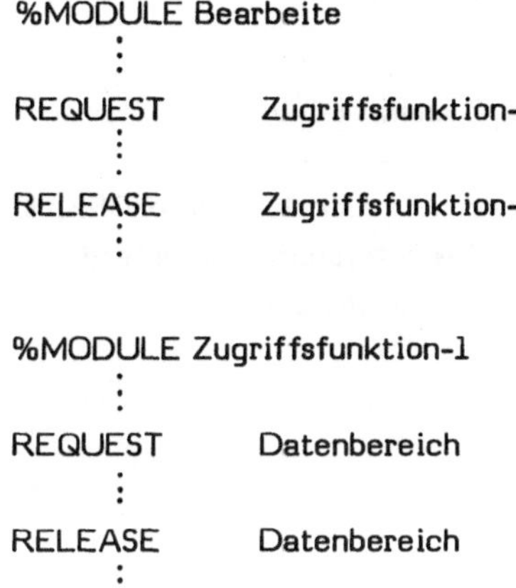

```
%MODULE Bearbeite
    :
REQUEST      Zugriffsfunktion-1
    :
RELEASE      Zugriffsfunktion-1
    :

%MODULE Zugriffsfunktion-1
    :
REQUEST      Datenbereich
    :
RELEASE      Datenbereich
    :
```

Durch diese Art der Modellierung wird gewährleistet, daß Überholvorgänge beim Zugriff auf den Datenbereich ausgeschlossen sind.

Neben der Verwendungg von PERMANENT-Daten zur Kommunikation zwischen Aktivitäten, können diese Daten aber auch zur Beschreibung von Konzepten dienen, die das Prinzip von 'hidden data' innerhalb einer Aktivität beschreiben.

Zu diesem Zweck reicht es, die entsprechenden zugriffsberechtigten Module in der dem Datenbereich zugeordneten ACCESS-Liste anzugeben.

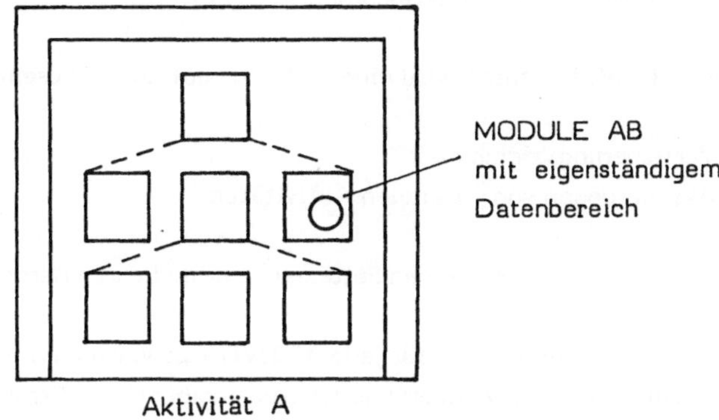

Beschreibungsform:

```
%DATA    hidden data
DEFINE   PERMANENT     Datenbereich
         ACCESS BY     AB: MODULE
REFINE   Datenbereich  CONSIST OF Element-1,Element-2,Element-3
```

Im Gegensatz zu den in der Beschreibung des Datenflusses verwendeten lokalen Daten (DEFINE LOCAL), haben die PERMANENT-Daten die Lebensdauer des Gesamtsystems und unterliegen nicht den Scope-Regeln, die für die Definition von lokalen Daten relevant sind.

5 DARTS-Prozessor

Der DARTS-Prozessor

- bringt die mit Hilfe eines üblichen Texteditors erstellte formatfreie Eingabe in ein übersichtliches Layout,
- erzeugt Querverweislisten des Kontroll- und Datenflusses, sowie der angegebenen Indizes,
- erstellt eine Metrik,
- überprüft die Datenkonsistenz sowie das zu erwartende Echtzeitverhalten.

Das Ausgabeformat erlaubt es, sofort zu erkennen, welcher Ausgabeteil auf der jeweiligen Seite ausgegeben ist (z.B. welcher Segmenttyps, welche Querverweisliste etc.) und wie sich die betrachtete Seite zum betrachteten Ausgabeteil verhält.
Die Ablaufsegmente werden so formatiert, daß die Kontrollstruktur direkt ersichtlich ist. Für Iteration und Selektion werden entsprechende Einrückungen vorgenommen. Echtzeitsprachelemente werden aufgrund ihrer Funktion kenntlich gemacht.

Innerhalb von Ablaufsegmenten wird eine Referenz auf die in diesem Segment enthaltenen

- Verfeinerungssegmente
- Aktivierungen von parallelen Aktivitäten

durch die Angabe der entsprechenden Seitennummer und durch besondere Visualisierung kenntlich gemacht.
Neben den Querverweislisten wird für jede ACTIVITY bzw. isolierte Modulverfeinerung ein Aufrufbaum erzeugt, der die Verfeinerungsstruktur angibt. Diese Struktur wird mit einer reinen Baumstruktur verglichen und aus dem Ergebnis eine Metrik abgeleitet, die den Grad der Abweichung von der Baumstruktur angibt.

Bei der Überprüfung des zu erwartenden Echtzeitverhaltens wird der Systementwurf auf korrekte Synchronisation, Interruptverhalten, Resourcenverwendung, Deadlockfreiheit und isolierte

Teile untersucht.

Das Verfahren beruht auf einer statischen Analyse des in der DARTS-Sprache beschriebenen Entwurfes. Zu diesem Zweck werden alle echtzeitrelevanten Sprachelemente aus dem Entwurf extrahiert und auf Activity-Vektoren abgebildet. Diese Activity-Vektoren repräsentieren die parallel ablauffähigen Teile des zu realisierenden Systems.

6 DARTS-Ausblick

Die DARTS-Methode wird weiterentwickelt in Bezug auf

- die Ausweitung auf ein Spezifikationssystem,
- die Durchführung von Simulationen,
- den Anschluß an ein Projektmanagementsystem.

THE USE OF NESTED SCHEME PARAMETERS IN THE SYSTEM CIP*)

R. Steinbrüggen
Technical University of Munich

CIP - a system for interactive program development - operates on arbitrary context-free languages. At the moment it is running on the wide spectrum language CIP-L and on the language of relational algebra. The efficiency depends on the transformation catalogues. In the system CIP, complex transformations can be defined which (1) cover wider classes of special cases and (2) summarize frequently used chains of transformations.

Definitions: Regard words in which certain syntactical subwords are named (by capital letters). A <u>bare scheme</u> is the relation tree (in a linearized form) of the named subwords of a word (for example A[B[C, D]] and B[A[C], A[D]]). A <u>context</u> is a fragmentary word in which all named subwords are regarded as gaps. A <u>bare context</u> is a fragmentary bare scheme in which the branches are viewed as gaps (for instance A[.] and B[.,.]). <u>Abstraction</u> of a word: Replacement of some named subwords x_i by the corresponding bare contexts the gaps of which are consistently filled with the named subwords of the x_i. The resulting expression is called a (generalized program-) <u>scheme</u>. Under abstraction, the names of subexpressions become parameters for purposes of substitution and unification ("context-parameters"). Nested occurrences are possible. (Program-) <u>transformations</u> are tuples of three schemes, an "input template", an "output template", and an "applicability condition".

Context parameters are introduced into the system for two reasons: (1) They enable transformations (e.g. distributive laws) to be defined for variable contexts. (2) They serve to expand the input and output templates of transformations which are to be applied successively to nested subwords so that the locations of applications become the whole word. In expanded form, transformations can be composed into one single transformation, for instance

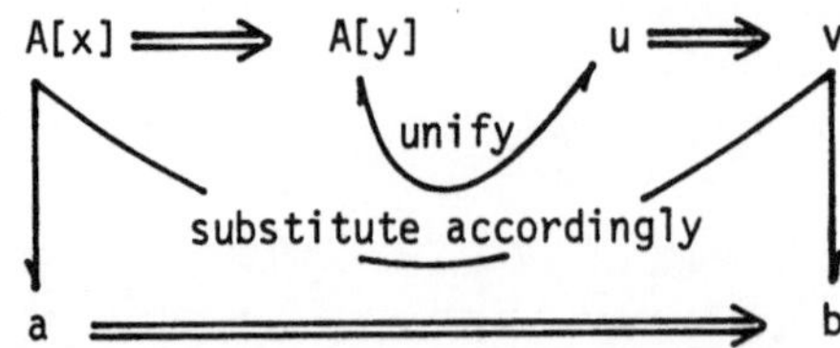

Cf. R. Steinbrüggen: Pre Algorithmic Specifications of the System CIP. Part 1.
- : Parameters at Dependent Tree Positions. TUM-INFO, 1980.

*) This research was carried out within the Sonderforschungsbereich 49, Programmiertechnik, Munich.

Das Projektmodell - eine Grundlage für die ingenieurmäßige Software-Entwicklung

Wolfgang Hesse
SOFTLAB GmbH
Arabellastr. 13
D-8000 München 81

Zusammenfassung: Auf der Grundlage eines einheitlichen, systematisch aufgebauten Begriffssystems wird ein Projektmodell entwickelt, das die Phasen, Tätigkeiten, Produkte und Projektführungsmaßnahmen von Software-Projekten benennt, beschreibt und miteinander in Beziehung setzt. Das Projektmodell umspannt alle Projektphasen von der Analyse bis zum Betrieb und zur Wartung des fertigen Systems und wird in Software-Projekten verschiedener Größenordnungen eingesetzt.

Abstract: A project model for software projects is established on a uniform, systematic terminological basis. In this model, the phases, activities, products and management actions of software projects are identified, described and related to one another. The project model spans all project phases from analysis to operations and maintenance and is used for software projects of various size.

Inhalt

1 Einleitung

"Denn eben wo Begriffe fehlen,
da stellt ein Wort zur rechten Zeit sich ein".

(Goethe, Faust)

Gut 10 Jahre nach Einführung des Begriffs "Software Engineering" wird noch vielerorts das Fehlen einer Methodologie für diese Disziplin beklagt (vgl. z.B. /WED 79/). Grundlage jeder Methodologie ist eine einheitliche, umfassende, allgemein anerkannte Begriffswelt. Die Stellung des Software-Ingenieurs zu seiner Begriffswelt läßt sich aber vielfach noch am ehesten durch das einleitende Zitat charakterisieren: Fehlende oder vermeintlich fehlende Begriffe werden durch Worte ersetzt, die sich mehr oder weniger zufällig "einstellen", wo und wann immer sie gebraucht werden.

Die Folge ist ein wild wucherndes, selbst von Eingehweihten oft schwer zu durchdringendes Begriffsdickicht.

Als beredtes Zeugnis für die z.Z. noch herrschende Begriffs-Unsicherheit seien einige Beispiele aufgeführt:

- eine Fülle von sogenannten "software life cycles",
- eine Vielzahl von Dokumentations-Vorschriften ("Rahmen-Spezifikation", "Entwicklungs-Dokumentation", "Prozeß-Organisation") bei DV-Herstellern, -Entwicklern und -Anwendern, häufig mehrfach unter dem gleichen Dach miteinander koexistierend und konkurrierend,
- unterschiedliche Interpretationen von Begriffen wie "System", "Prozeß", "Spezifikation", "Implementierung", "Verifikation", "Validation", "Planung", "Organisation" etc.

Versuche, die Durchführung von Software-Projekten auf eine einheitliche begriffliche Grundlage zu stellen, gibt es genügend. Meistens beruhen sie auf einem sogenannten "software life cycle", d.h. einer Aufzählung von Projektphasen und den dabei entstehenden Ergebnissen. Bekannte Beispiele sind die Zyklen von BOEHM (/BOE 76/ und /BOE 79/), METZGER (/MET 73/ und /SUR 78/) und KIMM et al. (/KIM 79/). Eine illustrative, aber keineswegs erschöpfende Übersicht geben PETERS und TRIPP in /P-T 78/.

Den meisten Zyklen und sonstigen Dokumentations-Vorschriften sind in mehr oder weniger ausgeprägtem Maße die folgenden Eigenschaften gemeinsam:

- Sie sind zu grob und häufig unvollständig, d.h. decken nicht den gesamten "Lebenszyklus" eines Software-Projektes ab.
- Die Begriffsbildung ist unsystematisch und daher wenig einprägsam und schwer rekonstruierbar.

- Die Begriffe sind nichtssagend ("Realisierung I", "Realisierung II"), pleonastisch ("Design specification") oder unsinning ("Spezifikation der System-Konstruktion").
- Anerkannte Prinzipien des "Software Engineering", wie z.B. das "Geheimnisprinzip" bzw. die "Daten-Abstraktion" werden nicht berücksichtigt.
- Aspekte der Projektführung ("Projekt-Management") werden zu wenig oder gar nicht betrachtet.
- Es gibt keine (rechnergestützten) Werkzeuge, die die Richtlinien durch Vorgaben von Mustern, Aufbereitung und Verwaltung von Dokumenten unterstützen.
- Es gibt keine Technologie, die den Produktions- und Projektführungs-Tätigkeiten eine ausgewählte und abgestimmte Sammlung von Techniken gegenüberstellt.

Im folgenden wird ein Modell vorgestellt, das in den genannten Punkten über die meisten "life cycles" hinausgeht und deshalb "Projektmodell" genannt wird. Es unterstützt den gesamten Software-Lebenszyklus mit ausführlichen Beschreibungen aller Phasen, Tätigkeiten, Produkte und Projektführungsmaßnahmen. Es bildet die methodische Grundlage für eine "Software-Technologie", die bestehende Software-Entwicklungsmethoden, -techniken und -werkzeuge in einem gemeinsamen Rahmen - mit weitgehender automatischer Unterstützung - zur Verfügung stellt.

In diesem Papier bilden die Phasen- und Produktstruktur und die dafür relevante Begriffsbildung den Schwerpunkt. Damit wird der Bezug zu den zahlreichen, zu diesem Thema vorliegenden Arbeiten hergestellt. Wenn Fragen der Projektführung und der technologischen Unterstützung hier aus Platzgründen weniger ausführlich behandelt bzw. nur gestreift werden, so soll das über ihre Bedeutung nichts aussagen. Für eine ausführliche Darstellung des gesamten Themenkomplexes wird auf /HES 80/ verwiesen. Einen Statusbericht über Methoden der Programm- und Systemkonstruktion liefert /END 78/.

2 Projektphasen

Grundlage des Projektmodells ist die Einteilung eines Projektablaufes in *Phasen*. Phasen haben bestimmte Teilziele des Projekts zum Gegenstand, die sich in (Teil-) *Produkten* niederschlagen und bestimmte phasentypische *Tätigkeiten* erfordern. Normalerweise wird eine Tätigkeit über eine Phase hinweg vom gleichen Bearbeiter wahrgenommen.

Es ist eine bekannte Tatsache, daß Tätigkeiten, die verschiedenen Phasen zugeordnet sind, sich gegenseitig überlappen können und daß daher eine minutiöse Abgrenzung der Phasen gegeneinander nicht möglich ist. Manche "software life cycles" bringen diese Tatsache graphisch deutlich zum Ausdruck (siehe z.B. METZGER's Zyklus in /SUR 78/). Wir definieren ein Phasenende (und damit den Beginn der Nachfolgephase - selbst wenn Vorarbeiten für diese bereits laufen -) durch die (erfolgreich überprüfte)

Fertigstellung des Produkts bzw. der Produkte, die Gegenstand der Phase sind.

Kennzeichnend für die Phaseneinteilung (wie auch für das gesamte Projektmodell) ist die Symmetrie (vgl. auch Abb. 2): Auf einen vorbereitenden Projektabschnitt, bestehend aus der Analyse- und der Definitionsphase, folgt die Entwicklung des eigentlichen "Systems" (hier immer im Sinne von Software-System verstanden, ohne dessen Umgebung mit hinzuzurechnen) und ein abschließender Abschnitt, bestehend aus der Installations- und der Betriebs- und Wartungsphase.

Der mittlere Abschnitt (System-Entwicklung) ist dreigeteilt in die Unterabschnitte Entwurf, Implementierung und Integration. Entwurf und Integration erfolgen normalerweise in jeweils zwei Phasen,die verschiedenen Entwicklungsebenen zugeordnet sind. Im Falle von kleineren Projekten kann sich diese Unterteilung erübrigen.

Ein Projekt läuft also in neun (im verkürzten Falle in sieben) Phasen ab, die folgendermaßen benannt sind:

- Analyse
- Definition
- Entwurf (1 oder 2 Phasen)
- Implementierung
- Integration (1 oder 2 Phasen)
- Installation
- Betrieb und Wartung

3 Tätigkeiten und Produkte

3.1 Analysephase

Gegenstand der Analysephase ist das wissenschaftliche, technische, organisatorische, kommerzielle oder sonstwie geartete Problem, das im Laufe der späteren Phasen durch ein EDV-System (oder womöglich auf andere Weise) gelöst werden soll. Die Analysephase startet häufig mit nicht mehr als einigen vagen, mündlich geäußerten Ideen, in günstigeren Fällen mit einer irgendwie gearteten (schriftlichen) Problembeschreibung.

Aufgrund dieser Vorgaben wird der Ist-Zustand der Organisationsstruktur untersucht, in die das künftige System eingebettet werden soll. Dazu gehört die Untersuchung bestehender Einrichtungen, die Beschreibung gegenwärtiger Verfahrensabläufe, Aufnahme von Vorstellungen beteiligter Personen und künftiger Benutzer des Systems sowie das Aufzeigen und Bewerten von Schwachstellen.

Dieser Ist-Analyse wird ein Soll-Konzept gegenübergestellt, in dem Vorstellungen über die künftigen technischen Einrichtungen und Verfahrensabläufe entwickelt werden. Darin enthalten ist der *Aufgaben-Katalog*, in dem die Aufgaben aufgezählt sind, die das künftige System übernehmen soll. Ist-Zustand und Soll-Konzept bilden zusammen die *Problem-Analyse*, das Produkt der Analysephase.

3.2 Definitionsphase

Der Aufgaben-Katalog dient als Vorgabe für die *Definitionsphase*, die der Analysephase nachfolgt. Wird während der Analysephase der Blick nach "außen" gerichtet (vom Standpunkt des Entwicklers aus gesehen, d.h. also in Richtung auf die Umwelt des künftigen Systems), so ist die vorherrschende Blickrichtung der Definitionsphase die nach "innen", d.h. auf die Funktionen und Leistungen des zu entwickelnden Systems. Diese werden in der *Aufgaben-Definition* zusammengestellt und unter dem Gesichtspunkt der angestrebten Systemlösung gruppiert. Eine wichtige Rolle spielt in vielen Fällen die Auswahl des Basissystems (Hardware und/oder Software), auf dem das geplante System aufsetzen soll und die Vorgehensweise, nach der es in die bestehende Umwelt eingebettet werden soll.

Als Synonyme für die Aufgaben-Definition finden sich an anderer Stelle die Begriffe "Problem-Spezifikation" (/MET 73/) und "Anforderungs-Definition" (/KIM 79/).

Einen wesentlichen Teil der Aufgaben-Definition bilden die *System-Anforderungen*, die den folgenden Entwurfsphasen als Vorgabe dienen. Für diese ist mancherorts der Begriff "Pflichtenheft" in Gebrauch. Eine mögliche Untergliederung teilt die System-Anforderungen in funktionale Anforderungen (Benutzer-Anforderungen, Anforderungen des Basissystems, Anforderungen von Nachbarsystemen) und leistungsmäßige Anforderungen (wie Datendurchsatz, Antwortszeiten, Mengengerüst, Fehlertoleranz, Verfügbarkeit etc.) auf.

3.3 Entwurfsphasen

Eine der wesentlichen Tätigkeiten beim Entwurf ist die *Modularisierung*, d. h. die Zerlegung des Systems in kleinere Arbeitseinheiten. Die Zerlegung erfolgt baumartig. Die Knoten des Baumes heißen *Bausteine*. Spezielle Bausteine sind (vgl. Abb. 1):

- das *System*: Wurzel des Baumes
- die *Moduln*: Blätter des Baumes
- die *Komponenten*: alle übrigen Knoten des Baumes

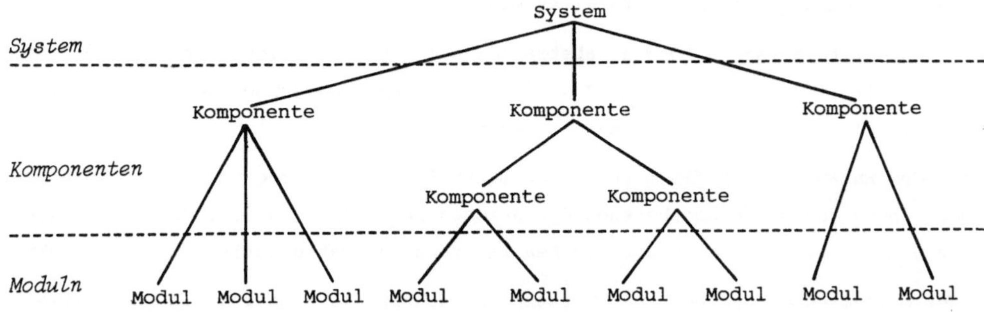

Abb. 1: Zerlegungsbaum eines Systems

Selbstverständlich ist auch der Spezialfall der Baumtiefe 2 zugelassen, d.h. es gibt keine Komponenten und das System wird direkt in Moduln zerlegt.

Unser Modulbegriff orientiert sich an den "klassischen" PARNAS'schen Vorstellungen (vgl. /PAR 72/) sowie am Begriff und an der Methode der Daten-Abstraktion (/L-Z 75/). Übersichten über mögliche Modularisierungskriterien geben ALTMANN und DENERT (/ALT 78/, /DEN 79b/).

Eine hervorstechende Eigenschaft des Projektmodells ist es, daß sich die drei Entwurfsebenen System, Komponente, Modul in der Phaseneinteilung widerspiegeln. Die entsprechenden Phasen heißen System-Entwurfsphase, Komponenten-Entwurfsphase und Modul-Implementierungsphase. Die Komponenten-Entwurfsphase entfällt, falls der Sonderfall des direkt in Moduln zerlegten Systems vorliegt. Der Begriff "Modul-Implementierungsphase" zeigt an, daß sie neben der Entwurfstätigkeit weitere Aktivitäten einschließt (siehe unten).

Die grundsätzlich analoge Vorgehensweise bei allen Entwürfen (unabhängig von der Entwurfsebene) war ausschlaggebend für die analoge Begriffsbildung für diese Phasen.

Jeder Entwurf eines Bausteines B (d.h. des Systems, einer Komponente oder eines Moduls) geht von gewissen *Anforderungen* an diesen Baustein aus, die sich aus der Konstruktion des nächstübergeordneten Bausteines bzw. im Falle des Systems aus der Aufgaben-Definition ergeben.

Der Entwurf für B erfolgt in zwei Schritten: Spezifikation und Konstruktion. Dabei gibt die Spezifikation Auskunft darüber, *was* von dem Baustein B erwartet wird, während die Konstruktion Aussagen darüber macht, *wie* er realisiert werden kann (/B-G 79/).

Die *Spezifikation* ist also eine Präzisierung und Detaillierung der Anforderungen. Wenn entsprechende formale Hilfsmittel ("Spezifikationssprachen") zur Verfügung stehen, läßt sich - mit gewissen Einschränkungen - eine Formalisierung erreichen. Die Spezifikation nimmt noch keinerlei Bezug auf Realisierungsentscheidungen und läßt damit den Weg für verschiedene technische Lösungen offen. Eine wichtige Stelle in der Spezifikation eines Bausteines nimmt dessen Einbettung in seine Umgebung, d.h. die Beschreibung seiner *Schnittstellen* ein.

Der (von der technischen Lösung) abstrahierenden Spezifikation steht die konkretisierende *Konstruktion* gegenüber. Hier werden Lösungsentscheidungen getroffen und (möglicherweise alternative) Lösungswege erarbeitet.

Liegt dem Entwurf von B die Methode der Daten-Abstraktion zugrunde, so gehört die Beschreibung der von B angebotenen Operationen zur Spezifikation, die Repräsentation der von B verwalteten Daten und die Realisierung der Datenzugriffe zur Konstruktion.

In der System- und Komponentenentwurfsphase enthält die Konstruktion normalerweise eine Zerlegung des vorgegebenen Bausteins B in Teilbausteine B1, ... Bn und die speziellen Anforderungen an Bi, die dann wieder für den Entwurf von Bi maßgebend sind (i = 1, ...n). Hier schließt sich der Kreis der Entwurfstätigkeiten, die im Zyklus Anforderungen - Spezifikation - Konstruktion zu immer detaillierteren Entwürfen führen.

Aufgrund der Spezifikation (und - in eingeschränktem Maße - der Konstruktion) eines Bausteins B wird der *Testentwurf* für B erstellt, der die Grundlage für seine spätere Validation bildet (vgl. unten).

Das Gesamtprodukt der Systementwurfsphase ist der *Systementwurf*, das Gesamtprodukt der Komponenten-Entwurfsphase ist die Gesamtheit der *Komponentenentwürfe* für alle Komponenten, in die das System zerlegt ist.

3.4 Modul-Implementierungsphase

Die Modul-Implementierungsphase nimmt eine Mittelstellung zwischen den Entwurfs- und den Integrationsphasen ein. Sie beginnt wie eine Entwurfsphase: Vorgabe für die Implementierung eines Moduls M sind die *Modul-Anforderungen*, die bei der Konstruktion der M übergeordneten Komponente in der Komponenten-Entwurfsphase festgelegt wurden. Ziel der *Modul-Spezifikation* ist es, diese Anforderungen zu detaillieren und so weit wie möglich zu formalisieren. Insoweit gelten die Aussagen des vorigen Abschnitts zum Thema "Spezifikation".

Die *Konstruktion* eines Moduls besteht in dessen *Programmierung*, d.h. der Umsetzung der spezifizierten Anforderungen in ein Programm. Ergebnis dieses Schrittes ist der *programmierte Modul*. Muß die Programmierung auf einem sehr niedrigen sprachlichen Niveau, etwa in Assemblersprache, erfolgen, so empfiehlt sich die Anfertigung einer Konstruktions-Beschreibung (oft mißverständlich "Spezifikation" genannt) in einer geeigneten höheren Programmiersprache mit möglichen Text-Einschüben ("Pseudo-Code") oder mit einem ähnlich gearteten, adäquaten Beschreibungsmittel.

Der Abschluß der Implementierungsphase für M bildet die Validation von M. Unter *Validation* verstehen wir Tests, Programmdurchsichten ("code reading") und Beweise.

(Manche Autoren, z.B. BOEHM in /BOE 79/, benutzen dafür den Begriff "Verifikation", den wir jedoch den formalen, auf Beweisen gegründeten Methoden vorbehalten möchten).

In der Praxis steht unter den genannten Möglichkeiten natürlich der Test im Vordergrund. Die Validation eines Moduls M erfolgt gegenüber der Spezifikation von M aufgrund des *Modul-Testentwurfs*, in dem der Modul-Bearbeiter Teststrategie, Testfälle und Testdaten aus der Spezifikation heraus festgelegt hat.

Die *validierten Moduln* werden der Folgephase mit dem Ziel der Integration zu Subsystemen bzw. zum Gesamtsystem übergeben.

3.5 Integrationsphasen

Erfolgte beim Entwurf eine Aufteilung des Systems in Komponenten und Moduln, so besteht die Integration aus dem Zusammenfügen von Moduln zu Subsystemen und schließlich zum Gesamtsystem.

Ebenso wie auf der Entwurfsseite den Entwurfsebenen System und Komponenten je eine Entwurfsphase zugeordnet war, entsprechen den Integrationsstufen der Subsysteme und des Gesamtsystems die *Subsystem-Integrationsphase* bzw. *System-Integrationsphase*.

In den beiden Integrationsphasen unterscheiden wir wieder jeweils zwei Hauptaktivitäten, die spiegelbildlich den Entwurfsaktivitäten entsprechen:

- *Montage*, d.h. das Zusammenfügen von Bausteinen zu Subsystemen bzw. zum Gesamtsystem (als Gegenstück zur Konstruktion durch Zerlegung) und

- *Validation*, d.h. Überprüfung eines Produkts gegenüber den Festlegungen des Testentwurfs (als Gegenstück zur Spezifikation).

Subsysteme nehmen bei der Integration eine analoge Stellung ein wie Komponenten beim Entwurf. In bestimmten Fällen werden sie sogar identisch sein. Dann hat man den Vorteil, daß die Validation der Subsysteme (= Komponenten) direkt gegenüber der entsprechenden Komponenten-Spezifikation erfolgen kann. Es können aber auch gewichtige Gründe gegen eine solche Subsystem-Struktur sprechen, z.B. die Anforderung, ein Subsystem, das Teile mehrerer Komponenten benutzt, vorzeitig fertigzustellen. In diesem Fall wird die Validation von S durch einen gesonderten Subsystem-Testentwurf vorbereitet, der auf Grund der Spezifikation für die in S eingehenden Systemfunktionen erstellt wird.

Analog zur oben beschriebenen Zerlegungsstruktur des Systems bilden das integrierte Gesamtsystem, Subsysteme und implementierte Moduln eine Baumstruktur (die "Integrationsstruktur"), wobei im Falle der Baumtiefe 2 alle Subsysteme und damit die Subsystem-Integrationsphase entfallen können.

3.6 Installationsphase, Betrieb und Wartung

Nach erfolgter Validation wird das System in seiner Ziel-Umgebung *installiert*, dort einer weiteren Validation unterzogen ("Abnahmetest") und schließlich formell an den Auftraggeber übergeben.

In die System-Integrations- bzw. Installationsphase fallen auch mögliche Tuning-Maßnahmen. Dabei werden noch nicht erreichte Leistungs-Anforderungen an das System durch gezielte Verbesserung ("Optimierung") leistungssensibler Systemteile erfüllt.

Nach erfolgter Abnahme geht das installierte System in die Betriebs- und Wartungsphase über, damit ist im allgemeinen das Projektende erreicht.

4 Überblick über die Phasen, Tätigkeiten und Produkte

In diesem Abschnitt wird ein zusammenfassender Überblick über die oben eingeführte Begriffsbildung gegeben.

Alle Begriffe für Phasen, Teilprodukte und Produkte werden in systematischer Weise aus zwei Bestandteilen zusammengesetzt. Bis zum Programmierungsschritt geschieht dies nach dem Schema «Präfix» - «Suffix». Dabei stehen die Präfixe für den jeweiligen Phasengegenstand, die Suffixe für Vorgaben, Produkte und Teilprodukte (vgl. Tabelle).

Präfix	Suffix
Problem-	Katalog
Aufgaben-	Anforderungen
System-	Analyse
Komponenten-	Definition
Modul-	Entwurf
	Spezifikation
	Konstruktion

Ab dem Programmierungsschritt, d.h. vom Auftreten der ersten Software-Bausteine an, werden die Begriffe nach dem Schema «Adjektiv» «Substantiv» gebildet. Dabei stehen die Substantive für den behandelten Baustein, die Adjektive für den Produktzustand (vgl. Tabelle).

Adjektiv	Substantiv
programmierter	Modul
montierter(s)	Subsystem
validierter(s)	System
implementierter	
integrierter(s)	
installiertes	

Abb. 2 gibt eine zusammenfassende Darstellung der Phasen, Tätigkeiten, Teilprodukte und Produkte des Projektmodells. Diese Darstellung zeigt besonders deutlich die Systematik und Symmetrie: Vorbereitenden Phasen (Analyse, Definition) stehen abschließende Phasen (Installation, Betrieb und Wartung) gegenüber, Entwurfsphasen (für System und Komponenten) entsprechen Integrationsphasen (für System und Subsysteme), Spezifikationen (für System, Komponenten und Moduln) dienen als Vorgabe für die Validation entsprechender Bausteine, und die Konstruktion (Aufteilung in kleinere Bausteine) findet ihr Spiegelbild in der Montage (Zusammenbau zu größeren Einheiten). Symmetrieachse des gesamten Modells ist die Modul-Implementierungsphase und innerhalb dieser die Tätigkeit des Programmierens, womit die nach wie vor zentrale Bedeutung dieses Schrittes unterstrichen wird.

Phasen	Tätigkeiten und Teilprodukte	Halbfabrikate/Produkte
Analyse	analysieren Problem-Analyse Aufgaben-Katalog	Problem-Analyse
Definition	definieren Aufgaben-Definition System-Anforderungen	Aufgaben-Definition
System-Entwurf	spezifizieren System-Spezifikation konstruieren System-Konstruktion Komponenten-Anforderungen	System-Entwurf
Komponenten-Entwurf	spezifizieren Komponenten-Spezifikationen konstruieren Komponenten-Konstruktionen Modul-Anforderungen	Komponenten-Entwürfe
Modul-Implementierung	spezifizieren Modul-Spezifikationen programmieren programmierte Moduln validieren validierte Moduln	implementierte Moduln
Subsystem-Integration	montieren montierte Subsysteme validieren validierte Subsysteme	integrierte Subsysteme
System-Integration	montieren montiertes System validieren validiertes System	integriertes System
Installation	installieren installiertes System	installiertes System
Betrieb, Wartung	betreiben	laufendes System

Abb. 2: Das Projektmodell: Phasen, Tätigkeiten und Produkte

5 Projektführung

Neben den rein produktionsbezogenen Tätigkeiten erfordert die Abwicklung eines Software-Projektes eine Reihe von Management-bezogenen Aktivitäten, die wir als *Projektführungs-Maßnahmen* bezeichnen wollen.

Auch für die Projektführung ist die phasenorientierte Betrachtungsweise hilfreich. Dabei wird jede Produktionsphase von Projektführungstätigkeiten eingerahmt. Einer Produktionsphase geht die Planung voraus, sie wird begleitet von Anleitungs-, Steuerungs- und Qualitätssicherungs-Maßnahmen und durch ein formal festgelegtes Fertigstellungsverfahren abgeschlossen (vgl. Abb. 3).

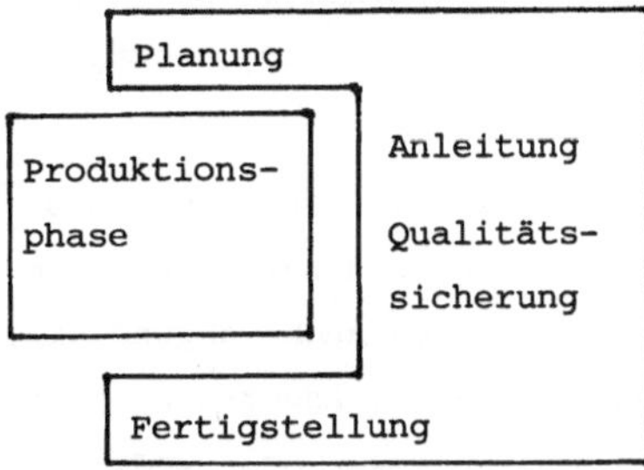

Abb. 3: Projektführungstätigkeiten für eine Produktionsphase

In ähnlicher Weise bilden die Projekt-Initialisierung und der Projekt-Abschluß eine Klammer um das Gesamtprojekt (vgl. Abb. 4)

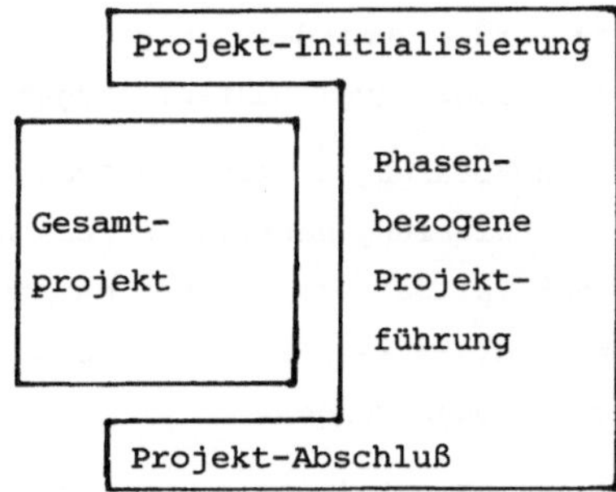

Abb. 4: Projektführungstätigkeiten für das Gesamtprojekt

Bei der Projekt-*Initialisierung* steht der Vertragsabschluß zwischen Projekt-Auftraggeber und -Auftragnehmer im Mittelpunkt. Eine *Projektvereinbarung* ergänzt die vertraglichen Abmachungen, regelt den Einsatz technischer und methodischer Hilfsmittel, die Übergabe der Produkte, eine mögliche Übergangsstratgie etc.

Durch die *Projektplanung* wird zu Projektbeginn verbindlich festgelegt, in welcher

Form bzw. mit welchen (begründeten) Abweichungen das Projektmodell auf das vorgegebene spezifische Projekt angewendet werden soll.

Sie umfaßt also Phaseneinteilung, Festlegung der Tätigkeiten, (Teil-)Produkte, Überprüfungen, Einsatz von Werkzeugen und Hilfsmitteln, sowie die Aufgabenverteilung an die einzelnen Projekt-Mitarbeiter bzw. -Teams. Hierhin gehört auch eine mögliche Aufteilung des Projektes in Teilprojekte, die dann jeweils eine eigene Projektplanung erfordern.

Für alle geplanten Tätigkeiten sind der Bearbeitungszeitraum, der Personaleinsatz und die Kosten festzulegen und phasenbezogen aufzuschlüsseln.

Aufgrund dieser Gesamtplanung werden die einzelnen Phasen sukzessive im Detail geplant. Die Vorausplanung erfolgt mit nach zeitlichem Abstand abnehmendem Detaillierungsgrad. Die einzelnen Phasenpläne werden im Laufe des Projekts ständig fortgeschrieben und dem neuesten Stand angepaßt.

Die Planung ist damit das wesentliche Mittel für das Management zur Steuerung des Produktionsprozesses. Die jeweiligen Phasenabschlußtermine bieten dabei natürliche Eingriffspunkte. In Ausnahmefällen muß der Projekt-Manager jedoch auch während eines Phasenverlaufs steuernd in den Produktionsprozeß eingreifen, um veränderte Projektziele zu verfolgen, Krisen zu beheben, Resourcenprobleme zu lösen oder andere Schwierigkeiten zu beseitigen.

Die *Anleitung* des Projektteams erfolgt laufend im Rahmen von Projektbesprechungen und Schulungsveranstaltungen. Schriftliche Unterlage dafür ist das *Projekthandbuch*. Dieses enthält alle für die Projektdurchführung notwendigen technischen Unterlagen, Methoden- und Werkzeugbeschreibungen, Sprachmanuale, Literaturauszüge etc. Es ist eine projektspezifische Zusammenstellung von Technologie und wird - zumindest in großen Teilen - durch Auswahl aus der allgemeinen Software-Technologie (vgl. unten) aufgebaut.

Die *Qualitätssicherung* besteht aus einer oder mehreren Überprüfungen aller im Projektverlauf anfallenden Produkte durch nicht direkt an der Entwicklung beteiligte Personen. Dadurch unterscheidet sich die Qualitätssicherung von der Validation, die von dem jeweiligen Bearbeiter eines Produkts selbst durchgeführt wird. Es kann also auch die Validation eines Bausteines einer Qualitätssicherung unterzogen werden.

Qualitätssicherung bezieht sich einerseits auf Entwürfe von Bausteinen, zum zweiten auf validierte Software-Produkte. Für die erste Art von Überprüfungen benutzen wir den Begriff "Review", für die zweite Art "Inspektion".

So betrifft ein System-Review einen Systementwurf, ein Komponenten-Review einen Komponenten-Entwurf und ein Modul-Review eine Modul-Spezifikation. Von letzterem zu unterscheiden ist die Modul-Inspektion, die einen validierten Modul zum Gegenstand hat. Analog sind validierte Subsysteme und das validierte System Gegenstand von Subsystem- bzw. System-Inspektionen.

Eine Inspektion kann entweder in einem nochmaligen, vom Validations-Test unabhängigen Test erfolgen. Bei automatischen oder halbautomatischen Testverfahren ist allerdings eine Überprüfung des entsprechenden Test-Entwurfs am wirkungsvollsten. In diesem Falle könnte man also die Inspektion auch als Testentwurfs-Review bezeichnen.

Erfolgreiche Überprüfungen durch Reviews bzw. Inspektionen sind die Voraussetzung für die *Fertigstellung* von Produkten. Das bedeutet, daß die Arbeitsergebnisse (Entwürfe oder Software-Bausteine) freigegeben werden und von allen beteiligten Mitarbeitern als Arbeitsgrundlage herangezogen werden können. Die Fertigstellung eines Produkts wird häufig auch als das Erreichen eines *Meilensteines* bezeichnet. Ist das Produkt zur direkten Übergabe an den Auftraggeber bestimmt, so kann nach erfolgter Fertigstellung die Installation beginnen. Sollte ein fertiggestelltes Produkt geändert werden müssen, so hat der Produkt-Verantwortliche stets dafür zu sorgen, daß eine lauffähige freigegebene Version zur Verfügung steht.

Nach erfolgreicher Installation beim Auftraggeber wird mit den *abschließenden* Tätigkeiten der Projektführung das Projektende erreicht.

Dazu können gehören: Benutzerschulung, Organisation der Betriebs- und Wartungsphase, Abfassung von Projektabschluß- und Erfahrungsberichten, Erfassung von statistischen Daten über das Projekt etc.

6 Zusammenhänge zur Technologie

Wie schon eingangs angedeutet, gehört zu einem Projektmodell, das die Phasen, Tätigkeiten, Produkte und Projektführungsmaßnahmen eines Software-Projekts beschreibt, eine Technologie, die sowohl die Produktion als auch die Projektführung in allen Phasen unterstützt. Wir verstehen unter einer *Software-Technologie* eine Sammlung von Prinzipien, Methoden, Verfahren, Werkzeugen und Hilfsmitteln (zusammengefaßt unter dem Sammelbegriff "Techniken"), die dem Software-Ingenieur in möglichst handlicher und leicht verwertbarer Form zur Verfügung steht. Eine solche Technologie ist gegenwärtig im Aufbau und wird an anderer Stelle beschrieben werden.

Wesentlich ist der enge Zusammenhang zwischen Projektmodell und Technologie. Jeder Bestandteil der Technologie wird auf seine Eignung für die im Projektmodell beschriebenen Tätigkeiten hin untersucht, und umgekehrt wird dem Entwickler bzw. Projekt-Manager für jede Tätigkeit eine Auswahl geeigneter Techniken angeboten.

Aus der Menge der Techniken soll an dieser Stelle nur ein Werkzeug hervorgehoben werden, das in besonders enger Verbindung zum Projektmodell steht: die Projektbibliothek. Dabei handelt es sich um ein umfangreiches Projektführungs- und Dokumentationssystem, das die Produktion in allen Phasen durch Vorgaben ("Produktmuster") unterstützt, alle im Projektverlauf anfallenden Dokumente, Entwürfe und Software-Bausteine im Rechner verwaltet,und damit eine jederzeit aktuelle Gesamtdokumentation des Projekts zur Verfügung hält.

Die Struktur der Projektbibliothek, die sich eng an die Struktur und die Begriffswelt des Projektmodells anlehnt, ist in /DEN 79a/ beschrieben, die Implementierung einer ersten Version ist abgeschlossen.

7 Konklusion und Erfahrungen

Zum Abschluß werden die wichtigsten Eigenschaften des Projektmodells zusammengefaßt, und es wird kurz über seinen Einsatz in aktuellen Software-Projekten berichtet.

Gegenüber den eingangs erwähnten Unzulänglichkeiten existierender Modelle und "software life cycles" weist das Projektmodell folgende Eigenschaften auf:

- Vollständigkeit: Das Projektmodell überspannt alle Phasen der Produktion von der Analyse bis zur Wartung und die Projektführungsmaßnahmen von der Initialisierung bis zum Projektabschluß.
- Modularität: Der Projektablauf ist in überschaubare, separat zu behandelnde Arbeitsabschnitte gegliedert, die wohldefinierte Vorgaben und Ergebnisse haben und mit Hilfe dieser genormten "Schnittstellen" flexibel miteinander kombiniert werden können.
- Systematik: Alle Begriffe sind nach einem einheitlichen, zugrundeliegenden Schema gebildet. Analogien sind bei der Begriffsbildung so weit wie möglich berücksichtigt.
- Übersichtlichkeit: Die systematische Begriffsbildung ist eine wesentliche Voraussetzung für die Übersichtlichkeit, Einprägsamkeit und Rekonstruierbarkeit des Modells. Einen weiteren wesentlichen Beitrag dazu leistet die oben näher erklärte Symmetrie (vgl. Abschnitt 4), die sich nur in wenigen bekannten Modellen in Ansätzen findet (vgl. z.B. /BOE 79/).
- Allgemeinheit: Das Modell ist so allgemein gehalten, daß es in gleicher Weise auf "große" und "kleine" Projekte (möglicher Fortfall ganzer Phasen!), auf Stapel-, Prozeß- oder Dialog-orientierte Systeme, kommerzielle, Anwender- und Systemprogramme etc. anwendbar ist.
- Kompatibilität: Das Projektmodell ist mit anderen Modellen gleicher Zielsetzung verträglich; die wesentlichen Begriffe sind auf adäquate Begriffe anderer Modelle abbildbar.
- Unterstützung durch Technologie: Das Projektmodell steht in engem Zusammenhang mit einer Technologie, die die Produktion, Dokumentation und Projektführung in allen Phasen - zum Teil maschinell - unterstützt.

Das Projektmodell ist einerseits aus Erfahrungen heraus entstanden, die man in einem Software-Haus in den letzten Jahren mit Software-Projekten aller Größenordnungen gesammelt hat.

Auf der anderen Seite dient es als methodische Grundlage für aktuell laufende Projekte, aus denen heraus das Begleitmaterial zum Projektmodell ständig ergänzt und überarbeitet wird.

Aus der Reihe von Projekten, in denen das Projektmodell erfolgreich eingesetzt wird, bzw. in Vorversionen erfolgreich erprobt wurde, seien als Beispiele die folgenden Großprojekte genannt:

- Software-Entwicklung für ein Rechnernetz der Reise- und Touristik-Branche
- Automatisierung einer Leitzentrale eines Energieversorgungs-Unternehmens
- Neukonzeption des Informationssystems für einen Großflughafen

Weiterhin werden im Rahmen von "Technologie-Transfers" zur Zeit wesentliche Elemente des Projektmodells von einem Hersteller und von Anwendern als Grundlage für die eigene Methoden-Unterstützung und Technologie übernommen.

Bei allen Projekten, in denen das Projektmodell eingesetzt wurde, berichteten Projekt-Manager, Entwickler und Anwender über vorwiegend positive Erfahrungen. Es wurde allgemein anerkannt, daß hier ein gangbarer Kompromiß zwischen den möglichen Extremen (zu geringe Unterstützung der Projektarbeit einerseits - zu starre Reglementierung andererseits) gefunden wurde. Selbstverständlich muß mit der Verwendung eines solchen Modells eine ständige Schulung von Mitarbeitern und Anwendern einhergehen. Gerade aber für die hausinterne Schulung, die vom Autor dieses Beitrages seit über einem Jahr turnusmäßig für neue Mitarbeiter durchgeführt wird, hat sich das Projektmodell als solide Grundlage erwiesen.

Berichte über Mängel und Lücken bei der Arbeit mit dem Projektmodell betreffen in erster Linie die noch unvollständige Technologie und die noch verbesserungsfähige maschinelle Unterstützung. Hier wird ein Schwerpunkt zukünftiger Arbeiten liegen.

Die vorliegende Arbeit wurde mit Mitteln des Bundesministeriums für Forschung und Technologie (Förderkennzeichen 081 5054 A) und der SOFTLAB GmbH gefördert. Für die Unterstützung dieser Arbeit, für Anregungen und Diskussionen zum Thema "Projektmodell" sowie für die kritische Durchsicht des Manuskripts danke ich meinen Kollegen H. Becker, C.H. Correll, E. Denert, R. Franck, G. Heldmann, B. Losbichler, U. Maiborn und P. Schnupp.

Literatur

/ALT 78/ ALTMANN, W.: Beschreibung von Programm-Moduln zum Entwurf zuverlässiger Softwaresysteme, Dissertation, Arbeitsberichte 11,16 des IMMD der Univ. Erlangen-Nürnberg (1978)

/B-G 79/ BALZER, R., GOLDMANN, N.: Principles of good software specification and their implications for specification language, Proc. IEEE Conf. on Specification of Reliable Software, Cambridge/Mass., pp.58-67 (1979)

/BOE 76/ BOEHM, B.W.: Software Engineering, IEEE Transact. on Computers, C-25, 12, pp. 1216-1241 (1976)

/BOE 79/ BOEHM, B.W.: Guidelines for verifying and validating software requirements and design specifications, EURO IFIP 79, pp. 711-719, North Holland 1979

/DEN 79a/ DENERT, E.: The project library - a tool for software development, Proc. 4th Int. Conf. on Software Engineering, München, IEEE Cat. 79CH1479-5C, S. 153-163 (1979)

/DEN 79b/ DENERT, E.: Software-Modularisierung, Informatik-Spektrum 2.4, November 1979

/END 78/ ENDRES, A.: Methoden der Programm- und Systemkonstruktion: ein Statusbericht, Proc. GI - 8. Jahrestagung, Inf.-Fachberichte 16, S. 29-73, Springer 1978

/HES 80/ HESSE, W.: Software-Projekttechnik, Interner Bericht, SOFTLAB GmbH, München (1980), Veröffentlichung als Bericht der GMD Bonn-Birlinghoven geplant

/KIM 79/ KIMM, R., KOCH, W., SIMONSMEIER, W., TONTSCH, F.: Einführung in Software Engineering, de Gruyter 1979

/L-Z 75/ LISKOV, B., ZILLES, S.: Specification techniques for data abstraction, IEEE Trans. on Software Engineering 1,1, pp. 7-18 (1975)

/MET 73/ METZGER, P.W.: Managing a programming project, Prentice Hall 1973

/PAR 72/ PARNAS, D.L.: A technique for software module specification with examples, CACM 15,5 pp. 330-336 (1972)

/P-T 78/ PETERS, L.J., TRIPP, L.L.: A model of software engineering, Proc. 3rd Int. Conf. on Software Engineering, Atlanta, IEEE Cat. 78-CH1317-7C, pp. 63-70 (1978)

/SUR 78/ SURBÖCK, E.: Management von EDV-Projekten, de Gruyter (1978)

/WED 79/ WEDEKIND, H.: Eine Methodologie zur Konstruktion des Konzeptionellen Schemas, in: Datenbanktechnologie, Bericht Nr. 2 des German Chapter of the ACM, Teubner 1979

PRAXISBEZOGENE SYSTEMENTWICKLUNG AUS GANZHEITLICHER SICHT

Hans-Joachim Habermann
Jürgen Kirbach
GMO - Gesellschaft für moderne Organisationsverfahren
Alsterufer 36
D 2000 Hamburg 36

1. SYSTEMENTWICKLUNG

Der Begriff Systementwicklung hat mindestens vier verschiedene Bedeutungen:

- **AUFGABE:**
  Systementwicklung (Anwendungssystementwicklung) ist die Aufgabe der Entwicklung, Produktion von Anwendungssystemen, die verkürzt als 'Systeme' bezeichnet werden.
- **BEREICH:**
  Systementwicklung ist eine aufbauorganisatorische Einheit, wie z.B. Abteilung, deren Aufgabe die Systementwicklung ist.
- **AUFTRAG:**
  Systementwicklung ist ein Auftrag an die Organisationseinheit Systementwicklung, für Anwender ein Anwendungssystem zu entwickeln.
- **PROZESS:**
  Systementwicklung ist der Prozeß der Entwicklung eines Anwendungssystems von der Idee bis zum Produkt.

Entsprechend viele Fachgebiete steuern zur Systementwicklung etwas bei:

Requirements Engineering:	Leistungsspezifikationsverfahren,
Software Engineering:	Software-Ersrtellungsmethoden,
Systemtheorie:	Modellbildung,
Organisationslehre:	Organisationsmethoden,
Managementlehre:	Managementtechniken,
Projektmanagement:	Projektplanungs-, -steuerungs- und -nachbereitungsverfahren,
Anwendungsfach:	projektbezogen: Methoden der Anwendung.

Die Aufgaben der Systementwicklung reichen von der Initialisierung eines

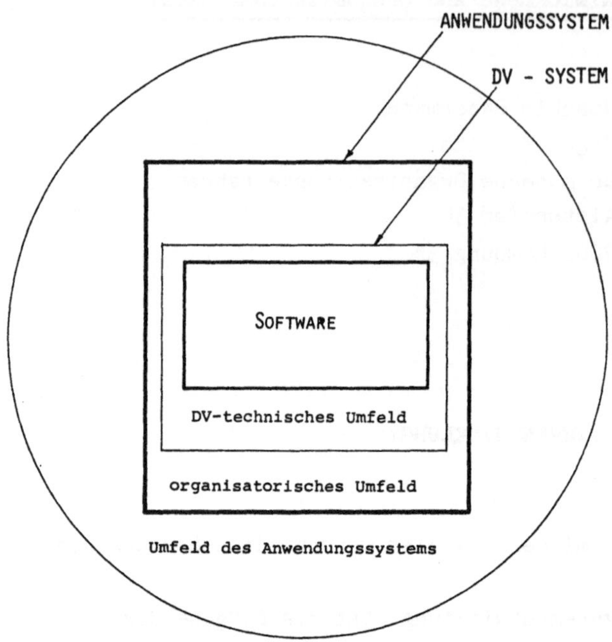

Projektes bis zur Inbetriebnahme des produzierten Anwendungssystems, das während der anschließenden Betriebsphase von der Systembetreuung gewartet und sich verändernden Anforderungen angepaßt wird.

Häufig wird unter 'System' in diesem Zusammenhang nur das Software-System, allenfalls das DV-System verstanden. Der Begriff Anwendungssystem ist umfassender, wie Abb. 1-1 zeigt.

Der automatisierte Kern ist in Umfelder eingebettet. Erst das Zusammenarbeiten aller Systemteile sichert die Aufgabenerfüllung der Anwendung.

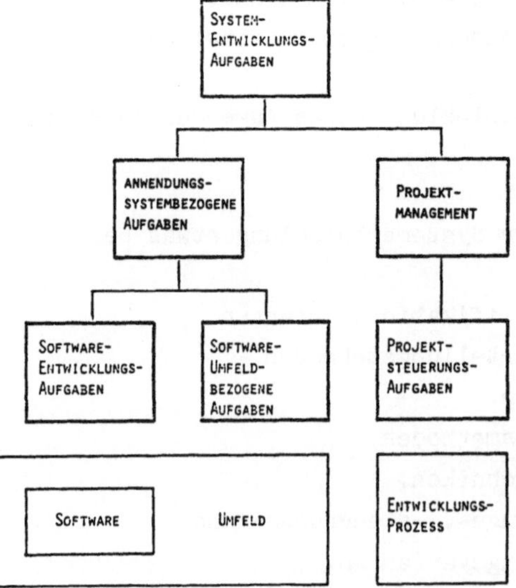

Die praktische Bedeutung dieser Unterscheidung liegt in der bewußten Einbeziehung der Umfeldgestaltung und deren Schnittstellen in Systementwicklungsaufträge. So werden beispielsweise die Arbeitsgestaltung unter Mitwirkung der Benutzer (Menschen) und die Mitverantwortung der Anwender (Bereich) mit Hilfe eines Arbeitsteilungs- und Vorgehenskonzepts für Systementwicklungen zum gestaltenden Entwicklungsfaktor.

Unter Einbeziehung des Projektmanagements ergibt sich die in Abb. 1-2 dargestellte Aufgabengliederung.

2. PRAXISBEZUG

Die Systementwicklung spielt eine Sonderrolle im Unternehmen wie in den Fachdisziplinen. An Hand von drei Modellen werden Ähnlichkeiten mit anderen Fachgebieten aufgezeigt, die uns für das Verständnis der Systementwicklung hilfreich und übernehmbar erscheinen.

- Systementwicklung ist Textverarbeitung.
- Systementwicklung ist Konstruktion und Fertigung.
- Systementwicklung ist Anwendung.

2.1 SYSTEMENTWICKLUNG IST TEXTVERARBEITUNG

In der Systementwicklung wird Software produziert. Es werden Umfelder gestaltet. Hardware wird gekauft. Die Software besteht ausschließlich, die Umfelder weitgehend aus Texten: formalisierte Texte für Maschinen sowie verbale Beschreibungen für Menschen.

Je arbeitsteiliger die Systementwicklungsprojekte werden und je stärker Mitverantwortung und Mitwirkung von Anwendern und Benutzern integriert werden, desto wichtiger werden schriftliche Unterlagen für erarbeitete Zwischenergebnisse und Vorschläge, über die diskutiert und abgestimmt wird.

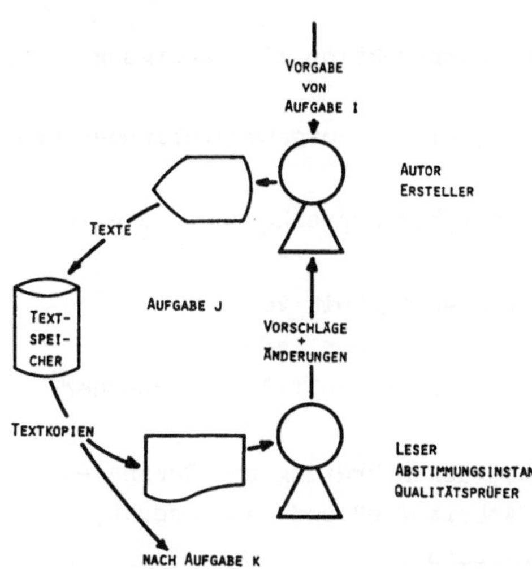

Zwischenergebnisse werden zu späteren Zeitpunkten Grundlage weiterer Entwicklungsaufgaben sein. Texte dienen der Kommunikation, Abstimmung und als Arbeitsvorgabe, wie durch den Autor-Leser-Zyklus nach Dr. Reinhold Thurner (THU 79) in Abb. 2-1 dargestellt.

Zusätzlich zu den Benutzern beziehen wir noch einen weiteren Adressatenkreis in die Textverarbeitung der Systementwicklung ein: die Systembetreuer.

Das grundlegende Textverarbeitungswerkzeug, der Editor, bestand in der Systementwicklung lange aus spaltengerechten Formularen, Bleistift und Radiergummi. Heute gehen wir davon aus, daß ein Rechner ohne die Verfügbarkeit komfortabler und effizienter Textverarbeitungswerkzeuge kein geeigneter Entwicklungscomputer ist. Nur wenige Rechner kommen dadurch in die engere Wahl (KRA 80, THU 80). Zu den notwendigen Werkzeugen für einen Entwicklungscomputer zählen wir:

- Bibliothekssysteme mit Texteditor,
- Dienstprogramme zum Kopieren, Formatieren, Vergleichen, Sortieren, Montieren,
- Compiler zur statischen Analyse und Codeerzeugung,
- Dokumentationssysteme einschließlich Datenlexikon,
- Analyse- und Entwurfswerkzeuge mit logischen Prüfungen,
- Programmgeneratoren wie DELTA mit parametrisierbaren Montagefunktionen,
- Diagnose- und Testhilfen,
- Projektmanagementsysteme.

2.2 KONSTRUKTION UND FERTIGUNG

In der Systementwicklung geht es in erster Linie um die Gestaltung und Erstellung eines Produktes. Sie kann mit Einzelfertigung oder Prototypenbau verglichen werden. Beide beginnen mit der Konstruktion.

Die Analogien zwischen Systementwicklung und Konstruktion mit Fertigung beziehen sich auf

- den Projektcharakter der Vorhaben, mit den gleichen Aufgabenstellungen des Projektmanagements,
- die hierarchischen Produktstrukturen nach dem Baugruppenkonzept, die in Stücklisten dokumentiert werden,
- die phasenbezogene Vorgehensweise und Verfahrenstechnik von der Leistungsspezifikation des Produktes bis zu dessen Auslieferung,
- die an Berufsbildern orientierte Arbeitsteilung einschließlich externer Qualitätsprüfung,
- die Qualitätsmerkmale technischer Produkte, deren Prüfung und Garantie,
- die Integration der Dokumentation in den Arbeitsfluß und das Produkt,
- die Einführung und der Stellenwert von Standards,
- die Verwendung von Normteilen nach Normteilkatalogen,
- die zunehmend automatische Unterstützung von Konstruktion und Fertigung.

Greifen wir einige Highlights heraus: Die Konstruktion erarbeitet die Spezifikationen des Produkts. Nach der Konstruktionslehre wird der Konstruktionsprozeß in drei Phasen gegliedert, die nacheinander ablaufen und deren Ergebnisse zunehmend detailliert sind, wie Abb. 2-2 zeigt:

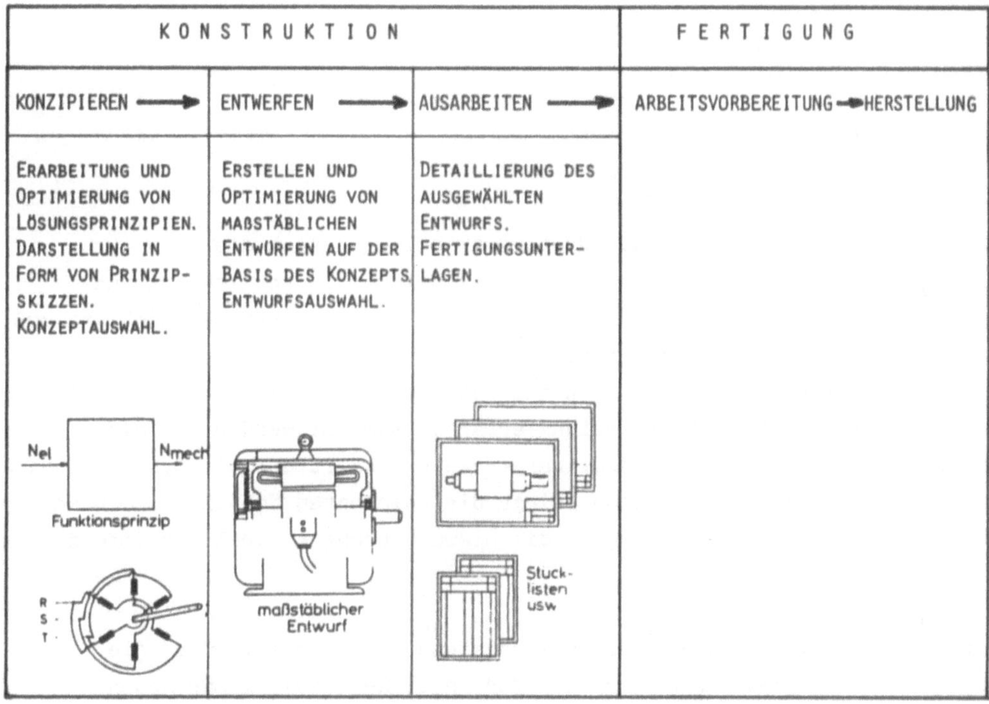

In der Konstruktion ist eine hierarchische Produktstruktur selbstverständlich. Sie wird in Stücklisten dokumentiert. Sogenannte Strukturlisten besitzen eine Einrückstruktur, wie wir sie auch aus der strukturierten Programmierung kennen. Zwischen beiden gibt es jedoch einen gravierenden Unterschied: Stücklisten zeigen die hierarchische Montagestruktur bei der Herstellung der Produkte. Strukturierte Programmlisten zeigen die hierarchische Kontrollstruktur des Ablaufes der fertigen Programme nach deren Montage. Die Stücklisten der Systementwicklung enthalten Bausteine, die funktions- , programm- und dokumentationsorientiert, aber nicht kontrollflußorientiert sind. Die Montage geschieht parametrisiert mit Generatorsystemen wie DELTA. Eine wesentliche Forderung an derartige Werkzeuge ist die Abdeckung der gesamten Produktbreite in allen Entwicklungsphasen.

Wir wissen heute aus der Konstruktion, daß Normteile nicht durch rückschauende Analyse, sondern durch vorausschauende Gestaltung entstehen. Die Verwendung von Normteilen muß vorgeschrieben werden und gültige Normteile müssen in einem Katalog dokumentiert sein. Mit Datenlexika beginnt dieser Prozeß in der Systementwicklung. Die automatische Einschleusung von Normteilen ist eine wichtige Funktion von Generatorsystemen.

2.3 ANWENDUNG

Anwendungen sind Gegenstand der Systementwicklung. Auch die Systementwicklung ist eine Anwendung. Das heißt, die Entwicklung und Implementation von Datenverarbeitungssystemen für die Systementwicklung muß nach den gleichen Regeln erfolgen, wie die Entwicklung von Systemen für andere Anwendungen. Da Texte auch als Daten behandelt werden können, ist damit ein Kern der Systementwicklung erfaßt. Zumeist werden für die Systementwicklung nur Standardsoftware-Pakete gekauft und wie Systemsoftware installiert. Erst eine Revision bringt die ungeahnten Schätze an Schrankware ans Tageslicht. Das ist Software, die niemand benutzt, weil das Umfeld nicht mitgestaltet wurde.

In der Systementwicklung kostet es mindestens genau soviel Mühe, die Mitarbeiter zu fördern und zu motivieren, neue Werkzeuge gemäß neuen Verfahren einzusetzen, wie die Benutzer anderer Fachabteilungen mit neuen Anwendungssystemen vertraut zu machen.

In den Designphasen einer Systementwicklung arbeiten heute Anwendungsspezialisten der Datenverarbeitung. Die Analogie zwischen Anwendung und Systementwicklung erlaubt den Schluß, daß es den Anwendungsorganisatoren im Qualifikationsprofil vergleichbare Systementwicklungs-Organisatoren geben wird, deren Aufgabe das verfahrenstechnische und DV-organisatorische Design von 'Systementwicklungs-Systemen' ist.

3. GANZHEITLICHES SYSTEM-ENTWICKLUNGSKONZEPT - MODULARE ORGANISATION

Mit dem Systementwicklungskonzept (SEK) haben wir uns die Aufgabe gestellt, eine durchgängige Organisationsgrundlage für die Systementwicklung zu schaffen, die auf den vorgenannten Modellen aufbaut und eine ingenieurmäßige Systementwicklung hochwertiger Systeme ermöglicht. Die Zielsetzung zeigt Bild 3-1.

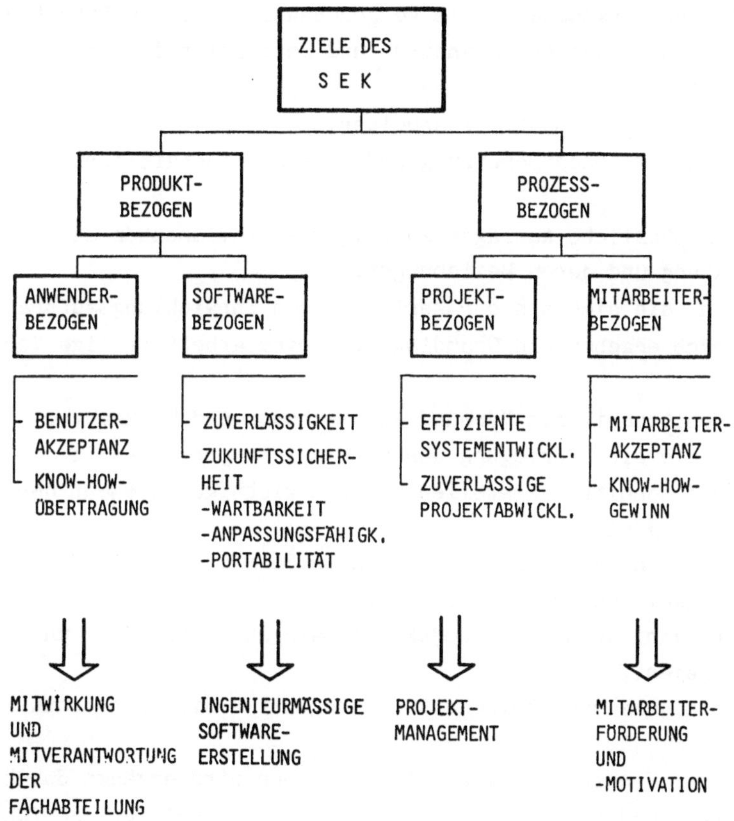

SEK bildet das Skelett, auf dessen Grundlage eine Verfahrenstechnik und Projektmanagement in die Systementwicklung eingeführt werden kann. Anwender- und Anwendungsunabhängingkeit sichert die Einsatzbarkeit in der Systementwicklung unterschiedlicher Unternehmen. Natürlich bedeutet die Unabhängigkeit als Designkriterium, daß viele Variablen enthalten sind, die der individuellen Ausformung bedürfen. SEK ist daher kein Systementwicklungshandbuch. Es ist vielmehr eine Grundlage, mit einem Angebot an Bausteinen, mit dem zukunftsgerichtet, aber individuell, eine

Systementwicklung organisiert werden kann. Die Systementwicklung ist ständig im Fluß und der Umfang organisatorischer Maßnahmen groß. Es ist deshalb gar nicht so wichtig, welcher Baustein der nächste sein wird, als das Bewußtsein, sich immer zielgerichtet in einem Konzept zu bewegen und zusammenhängende Moduln einzuführen. Darunter verstehen wir ein Bündel organisatorischer Maßnahmen mit starker innerer Verflechtung, aber überschaubaren Schnittstellen nach außen. Beispielsweise kann ein Modul für die Einführung einer neuen Methode aus folgendem Maßnahmenbündel bestehen:

- Kauf von unterstützenden Werkzeugen (soweit notwendig).
- Integration der Werkzeuge in die Vorgehensweise und den Datenfluß.
- Entwicklung von Kriterien, Standards und Beispielen für den Methodeneinsatz.
- Schulung und Motivation der Mitarbeiter.
- Überwachung der Methodenbenutzung und deren Wirtschaftlichkeit.

SEK macht grundsätzliche Aussagen zu folgenden Komponenten der Systementwicklung und deren Beziehungen.

- die Aufgaben, die sich aus der Zerlegung des Entwicklungsauftrages in Einzelaufträge ergeben und Grundlage für eine arbeitsteilige Vorgehensweise sind,
- die Verfahrenstechnik als Verbund der Methoden und Werkzeuge,
- die Phasen, die eine Zerlegung des Entwicklungsprozesses in Entwicklungsabschnitte darstellen und ein wichtiges Element der Projektsteuerung sind,
- die Ergebnisse, deren Standardisierung in Form und Inhalt Grundlage für Übergabefähigkeit und Prüfbarkeit ist,
- die Projektorganisation mit Projektteam als Aufgabenträger und Projektmanagement,
- die Standards, als verbindliche Anweisungen für die Systementwicklung,

Die Stellung der Fachabteilung als Auftraggeber wird ergänzt durch ihre Mitverantwortung und Mitwirkung bei der Systementwicklung. So führt die bereits in Bild 1-2 angedeutete Aufgabenstrukturierung zu einem anwendungsbezogenen Aufgabenbündel, das die Fachabteilung im Rahmen des Projektteams in eigener Verantwortung durchzuführen hat. Häufige Abstimmungen erarbeiteter Zwischenergebnisse mit Beteiligten im Rahmen eines Phasen- und Meilensteinkonzeptes ermöglicht die Übernahme von Verantwortung.

4. VERFAHRENSTECHNIK

Unzureichend vorbereitete Umfelder und zu hohe Versprechungen von Verkäufern einzelner 'Methoden' haben in vielen Unternehmen aufgrund der Nichterfüllung von Erwartungen eher zu einer Skepsis gegenüber diesem Angebotsbereich geführt.

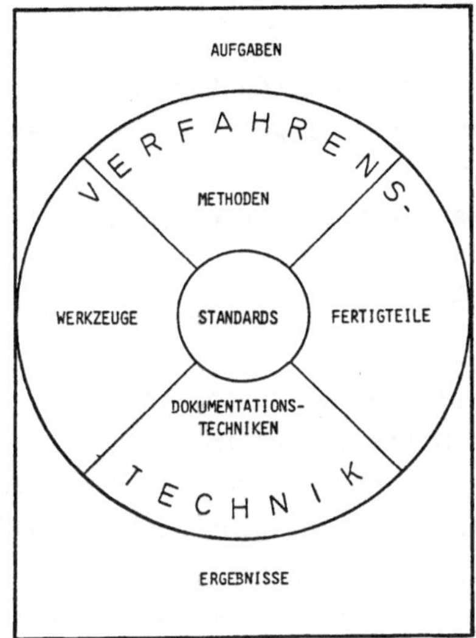

Wir übernehmen für die praktische Systementwicklung den Begriff der Verfahrenstechnik aus der Fertigung und meinen damit eine theoretisch und praktisch fundierte, ganzheitlich durchorganisierte Vorgehensweise mit koordiniertem Einsatz der in Bild 4-1 dargestellten Mittel.

Verfahren und Dokumentationstechniken stellen die auf die Praxis zugeschnittenen Methoden dar, auf die die Konstruktion un Anwendung der Werkzeuge aufbaut.

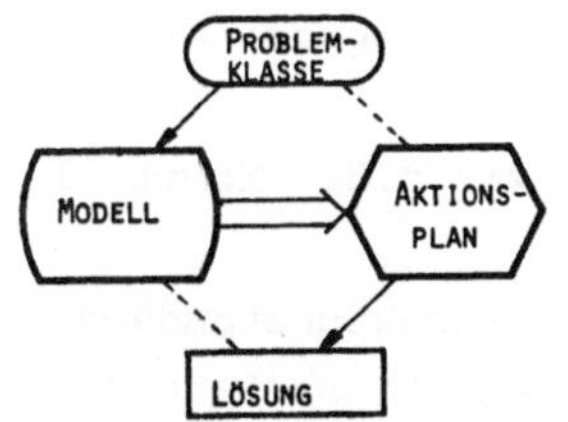

Nach dem Diebold-Bericht DV 7603 bezieht sich eine Methode auf eine Problemklasse und enthält als charakteristisches Element einen Aktionsplan wie im Bild 4-2 dargestellt.

Daraus folgt, daß es nicht **die** beste Methode für die Lösung aller Aufgaben gibt, sondern daß Methodenauswahl aufgabenbezogen erfolgen muß.

Dokumentationstechniken unterscheiden sich von Methoden durch den fehlenden Aktionsplan. Sie haben den Charakter von Sprachen und bestimmen die Form der Ergebnisse, nicht den Weg dorthin. Ihre Anwendung ist Voraussetzung einer Qualitätskontrolle.

Werkzeuge sind Hilfsmittel zur verfahrensgerechten Unterstützung bzw. der Automatisierung von Verfahren und Dokumentationstechniken. Der Begriff Werkzeug umfaßt alle Hilfsmittel zur Unterstützung, vom einfachen Formular bis hin zu Generatoren.

Ein Methodenverbund, wie er heute gefordert wird, läßt sich durch einen Werkzeugkasten in Form einer Methodenbank mit kompatiblen Werkzeugen (Generatorbank) errreichen, die unter einem koordinierenden Standardisierungskonzept eingesetzt werden. Zu den Vorteilen des Werkzeugeinsatzes gehören insbesondere:

- Qualitätssteigerung,
- Produktivitätssteigerung,
- Automatisierung der Einhaltung von Standards.

In diesem Zusammenhang ist die zentrale Rolle der Standards für die industrielle Praxis zu erwähnen. Diese verbindlichen Regelungen erfüllen folgende Aufgaben:

- Vereinheitlichung der Produktform einschließlich Zwischenergebnissen,
- Wiederverwendbarkeit von Normteilen,
- Orientierungs- und Kommunikationsgrundlage für die beteiligten Mitarbeiter.

Standards sind die grammatischen Regeln spezialisierter sprachlicher Ausdrücke. Kenntnis der Standards ermöglicht Mitteilungen in stenographischer Kürze (z.B. 4711) in einer bekannten Schablone, die sofort wiedererkannt wird und mittels derer eine Einordnung und Zuordnung ermöglicht wird. Damit werden durch das Produkt selbst wichtige Informationen in direkter Form übertragen (Selbstdokumnetation). Dieser Übertragungsprozeß ist insbesondere für die Wartbarkeit eines Systems ausschlaggebend. Standards müssen langlebig konzipiert werden und einprägsam sein.

Für die (automatische) Montage von Fertigteilen, wie z.B. Normteilen werden u.a. folgende Standards wirksam:

- Katalogierungsstandards
  - Entwicklungsbibliotheksstandards
  - Namensstandards
  - Parametrisierungsstandards
- Programmstrukturstandards
  - Dokumentationsstandards
  - Versionskennzeichenstandars

Der konsequente Ausbau von Fertigteilen und der Einsatz einer einheitlichen Generatorbank ermöglicht die Verwendung von Moduln aus der Entwicklungsbibliothek analog einer Methodenbank. Die Entwicklung der Programmiersprachen und Compiler geht hin zu größerem Leistungsvermögen. Was heute noch in Form explizierter Werkzeuge, wie Generatoren, in der Verfahrenstechnik enthalten ist, kann morgen im Compiler integriert sein. Die Verwendung leistungsfähiger Programmiersprachen leert jedoch keineswegs den verfahrenstechnischen Werkzeugkasten, sie räumt ihn auf. Das liegt daran, daß Programmiersprachen nach anderen Kriterien designed werden als generierende Werkzeuge. Beispiel: ADA-Texte enthalten absichtlich ca. 30

Prozent mehr Redundanz als PASCAL-Texte. Eine Generatoreingabe soll möglichst wenig Redundanz enthalten und Schreibarbeit sparen. Entsprechend unterschiedlich sind die Leistungserwartungen in der Praxis für Werkzeugsysteme und Compiler wie die folgende Aufstellung zeigt:

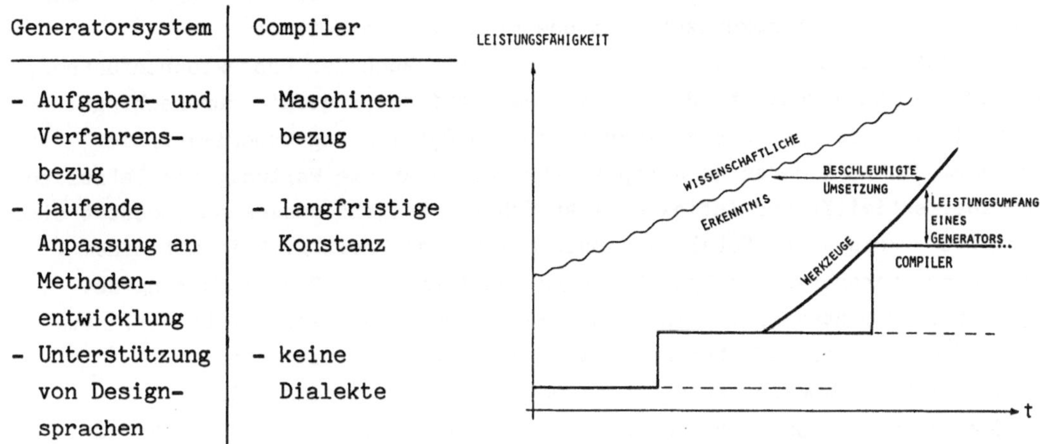

Generatorsystem	Compiler
- Aufgaben- und Verfahrens-bezug	- Maschinen-bezug
- Laufende Anpassung an Methoden-entwicklung	- langfristige Konstanz
- Unterstützung von Design-sprachen	- keine Dialekte

Auf einem Markt konkurrierender Werkzeugsysteme stellt sich für die Praxis die Frage nach Auswahlkriterien:

- Einbettung in das verfahrenstechnische Konzept,
- Kompatibilität mit bestehenden Standards
- Kompatibilität aller benutzten Werkzeuge (Garantie eines durchgängigen Datenflusses)
- Arbeitsmittel in Form handlich strukturierter Lexika und Kataloge
- Wirkung auf Produktqualität,
- Effizienzerhöhung
- Integration der Dokumentation,
- Einführungsaufwand,
- Erweiterung und Anpaßung an zukünftige Entwicklungen.

Die Einführung der Verfahrenstechnik ist nicht mit einer Entscheidung abgeschlossen. Wir empfehlen dazu stufenweises Vorgehen:

- Erarbeiten eines langfristigen Konzeptes (s. Abschnitt 3).
- Pilotprojekte mit aufgeschlossenen Mitarbeitern und späterem Multiplikationseffekt durch Verteilung der erfahrenen Mitarbeiter auf mehrere Projekte.
- Qualifikationsgruppenorientierter Methoden- und Werkzeugeinsatz mit zugehörigen Standards in allmählich zunehmendem Umfang.
- Entwicklung von Normteilen.

5. PROJEKTMANAGEMENT

Projekte sind temporäre Organisationsformen zur Erreichung eines bestimmten, vorher festgelegten Zieles, des Auftragsergebnisses. Die Freizügigkeit der Projektumgebung ist gekennzeichnet sowohl durch Freiheit der Projektinitialiserung, etwa durch 'Zuruf', als auch der Projektdurchführung, in der die Individualität des Projektteams auf das Ergebnis durchschlägt. Vorteil einer solchen Freizügigkeit ist die Entwicklung experimenteller Systeme, Nachteil deren hohe Kapazitätsbindung an die Wartung, die letztlich zur Ineffektivität und Inflexibilität führt. Projektmanagement bedeutet eine gezielte - keineswegs totale - Einschränkung der Freizügigkeit mit einem Gewinn an Transparenz bezüglich Kosten und Terminen. Die Einführung des Projektmanagements stellt einen Umdenkungsprozeß des Managements dar, nach dem Projekte in verstärktem Maße nach ihrer Effektivität unter Kosten-/Nutzen-Aspekten ausgewählt und abgewickelt werden. Das Projektmanagement hat dabei keinen direkten Einfluß auf die Qualität der Auftragsergebnisse. Die dazu eingesetzte Verfahrenstechnik, führt aber zu einer verstärkten Arbeitsteilung, die wiederum einen höheren Bedarf an Projektmanagement weckt. Schnittstelle zwischen Projektmanagement und Ergebnisqualität ist die Qualitätskontrolle, wenn sie zur Voraussetzung der Freigabe für weitere Projektteile und der Entlastung des Projektteams gemacht wird.

Die Verfahrenstechnik des Projektmanagements hat eine Erhöhung der Verläßlichkeit bezüglich der Termine und Kosten der Projekte sowie der Ergebnisqualitäten zum Ziel. Verläßlichkeit bedeutet die Möglichkeit zur Prognose und die spätere Einhaltung der prognostizierten Größen innerhalb von Toleranzen durch die Projekte. Dies wird nur erzielbar sein durch Informationsgewinnung über diejenigen Faktoren und Ereignisse, welche Termine und Kosten beeinflussen sowie die aktuelle Informationsweitergabe über deren Auftreten.

Es werden folglich drei Grundphasen des Projektmanagements, unterschieden:

1. **PLANUNG:**
   Aufgabe der Planung ist die Prognose der Planungsgrößen, z.B. Termine und Kosten, und die Vorbereitung der Projektsteuerung im Einklang mit der Prognose. Dem Auftraggeber werden bereits hier verbindlichen Zusagen gemacht.
2. **STEUERUNG:**
   Aufgabe der Steuerung ist das Überwachen der Projektabwicklung um frühzeitige Abweichungen der prognostizierten Planungsgrößen erkennen zu

können und aufgrund dieser Erkenntnisse in die Abwicklung und Planung von Projekten einzugreifen.

3. **NACHBEREITUNG:**
Eine quantitative Projektdokumentation während der Projektdurchführung ist Voraussetzung für eine systematische Auswertung von Störungen der Planungsfaktoren und die Umsetzung dieser Erkenntnisse in die Praxis der Planung mit dem Ziel besserer Vorhersagen.

Projektmanagement kann manuell durchgeführt werden. Es gibt Software-Werkzeuge, die dem Projektmanagement Fleißarbeit abnehmen und ihm so ermöglichen, sich auf Entscheidungen zu konzentrieren.

Die Wahl eines Werkzeuges wird man abhängig machen von der Menge der zu verarbeitenden Informationen, von dem Aktualitätsanspruch des Projektmanagements aber auch von der geforderten Qualität der Projektdaten:

Die heutigen Werkzeuge unterstützen in den administrativen Aufgaben, indem sie umfangreiche Rechnungen aufgrund aktueller Daten vornehmen und unterschiedlich ausgewählte Ergebnisse verdichtet und sortiert den verschiedenen Empfängern bereitstellen Die Entscheidungen bleiben bei den Verantwortlichen. Unterschiede zwischen den verschiedenen Werkzeugen liegen in der Menge der gleichzeitig zu behandelnden Projekte, in deren Strukturierungsmöglichkeiten Grundlasten, Ausfallzeiten, Personalkapazitäten, Sachmittel, in der Existenz und Leistungsfähigkeit von Netzplan- und Kostenrechnung, in der Flexibilität und Empfängerfreundlichkeit der Berichte sowie in der Dialogfähigkeit. Grndsätzlich basieren alle Systeme auf einem Betriebskalender, der in Perioden (meist Wochen) eingeteilt ist. Die Länge der günstigsten Periode bestimmt sich aus der Veränderungsrate der Planungsdaten. Die Verarbeitung ist periodenorientiert, d. h. Aktualisierungen der Verarbeitungsdaten durch Rückmeldungen aus laufenden Projekten, deren Verarbeitung und das Erstellen der Berichte erfolgt einmal pro Periode. Innerhalb der Perioden gibt es eine Aktualitätsunschärfe. Diese läßt sich auch nicht durch Dialogfühigkeit ausräumen, sondern nur durch Organisation der Rückmeldungen in noch kleineren Intervallen, was einen entsprechend höheren Kontrollaufwand und Freizügigkeitsverlust der Projektmitarbeiter bedeuten würde. In der Praxis ist die Aktualitätsunschärfe von viel geringerer Bedeutung als sie aus theoretischer Sicht erscheint. Es genügt, wenn Mitteilungen über wesentliche Veränderungen die Verranwortlichen unverzüglich erreichen.

6. FORDERUNGEN DER PRAXIS

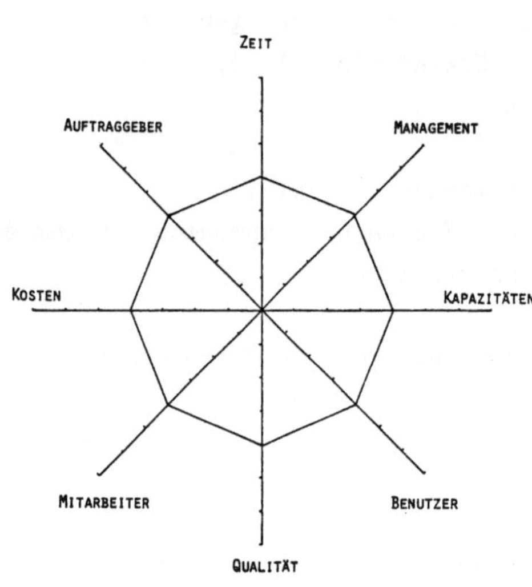

Zur Einordnung der in der Praxis erhobenen Forderungen an die Systementwicklung wird in Abb. 6-1 beispielhaft das Spannungsfeld gegenläufiger Interessen (Zielen) gezeigt, dem die Systementwicklung unterliegt (hier als Kiviat-Graph dargestellt):

Die Fläche innerhalb des "Prioritätensterns" ist ein Modell des begrenzt zur Verfügung stehenden Gesamtaufwandes. In der hier aufgezeigten, idealiserten Form macht man es jedem ein bißchen recht, daraus folgt, daß man es allen nicht recht macht.

Man sollte in Zukunft bewußt entscheiden:

1. welches Ziel die höchste Priorität hat,
2. welchem Ziele Aufwand entzogen werden soll.

Durch bewußt getroffene Entscheidungen wird eine Offenheit erzielt, die einen großen Teil der Emotionen aus den oft hitzig geführten 'Sachdebatten' nimmt. Die quantitative Forderung nach Balance zwischen Terminen, Kapazitäten, Kosten, wird durch den Einsatz von Verfahrenstechnik im Projektmanagement unterstützt. Die qualitative Balance zu halten wird wichtiger werden, wenn man sich z.B. die Dimensionen Wartungskosten bzw. Systemakzeptanz vor Augen hält. Gerade der Einsatz von Verfahrenstechnik birgt die Gefahr zunehmender Bürokratiserung. Die Entwicklung eines Systems, das dem Menschen gerecht werden soll, muß die Balance auf vielen Ebenen halten:

- Für den Menschen, aber wirtschaftlich vertretbar.
- Strukturiert, transparent, aber nicht starr zerbrechlich.
- Verwaltet, geordnet, aber nicht bürokratisch.
- Umfassend in den Grundfunktionen, aber nicht kleinlich detailliert.
- Dezentral, aber nicht zerplittert.
- z.B. Kennzahlen auf Zentralrechner).
- Schutz der Privatsphäre, ohne Schaden für die Allgemeinheit.

7. ERFAHRUNGEN UND AUSBLICK

Der Ansatz einer ganzheitlichen Organisation der Verfahrenstechnik steht noch am Anfang. Bezüglich des Einsatzes von Werkzeugen und deren Einfluß auf die Produktivität liegen schon mehrjährige Erfahrungen vor. Die folgenden Vergleiche beziehen sich auf das seit 5 Jahren im Einsatz befindliche Generatorsystem DELTA von Dr. R. Thurner, SODECON AG, Zürich, das von der GMO in der BRD vertrieben wird.

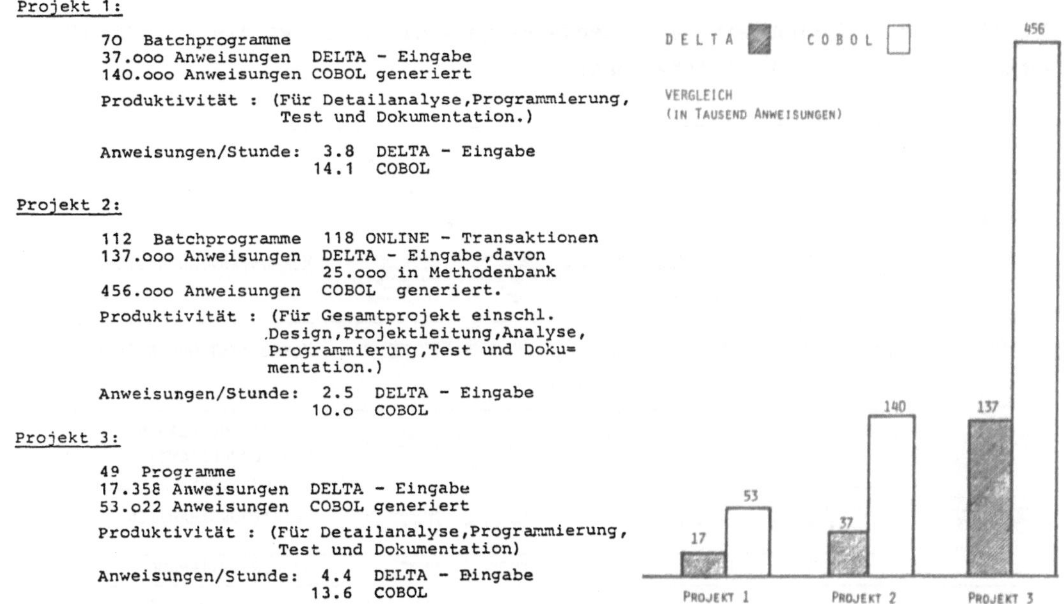

Projekt 1:

70 Batchprogramme
37.ooo Anweisungen DELTA - Eingabe
140.ooo Anweisungen COBOL generiert

Produktivität : (Für Detailanalyse,Programmierung, Test und Dokumentation.)

Anweisungen/Stunde: 3.8 DELTA - Eingabe
14.1 COBOL

Projekt 2:

112 Batchprogramme 118 ONLINE - Transaktionen
137.ooo Anweisungen DELTA - Eingabe,davon 25.ooo in Methodenbank
456.ooo Anweisungen COBOL generiert.

Produktivität : (Für Gesamtprojekt einschl. Design,Projektleitung,Analyse, Programmierung,Test und Doku= mentation.)

Anweisungen/Stunde: 2.5 DELTA - Eingabe
10.o COBOL

Projekt 3:

49 Programme
17.358 Anweisungen DELTA - Eingabe
53.o22 Anweisungen COBOL generiert

Produktivität : (Für Detailanalyse,Programmierung, Test und Dokumentation)

Anweisungen/Stunde: 4.4 DELTA - Eingabe
13.6 COBOL

Bei aller Vorsicht in der Interpretation der vorliegenden Daten, spiegeln sie den Eindruck derjenigen Anwender wider, die über erste Anlaufschwirigkeiten hinweg, dem verfahrenstechnischen Vorgehen treu geblieben sind.

Da nach Aussagen der Anwender die von DELTA generierten COBOL-Programme bei vergleichbarer Leistung nicht wesentlich länger sind als von Hand geschriebene, zeigen die Zahlen einen tatsächlichen Produktivitätsgewinn um den Faktor 3. Dieser Gewinn wird nach ersten Aussagen noch gesteigert in der Phase Wartung und Betreuung.

Dennoch liegt nicht in der Produktivität der größte Vorteil, denn sie hat bei einem EDV-Budget von 1 - 3 Prozent des Unternehmensumsatzes nur geringen Einfluß im Sinne einer Sensitivitätsanalyse. Entscheidendes wird mit der Qualitätsverbesserung erreicht.

Zur Zeit sind viele Anwender noch dabei, die immer größer werdende Flut von Angeboten zu ordnen und zu bewerten. Es wird deutlich, daß es erst wenige Ansätze aus ganzheitlicher Sicht gibt. Dabei bildet die Auswahl und der Einsatz einer einzelnen Methode, mit unterstützenden Werkzeugen sicher den wichtigsten, aber nur einen ersten Schritt. Es ist gar nicht so wichtig, mit welcher der anerkannten Methoden man beginnt. Viel bedeutender ist der lange Atem, um die notwendigen nächsten Schritte zu einer ganzheitlichen Verfahrenstechnik zu machen. Erst ein in dieser Weise geordnetes Bewußtsein ist in der Lage, die adäquaten Methoden einzusetzen.

Wie sich dieses Bewußtsein typischerweise entwickelt, zeigt die aus NOL 79 entnommene und ergänzte Aufstellung:

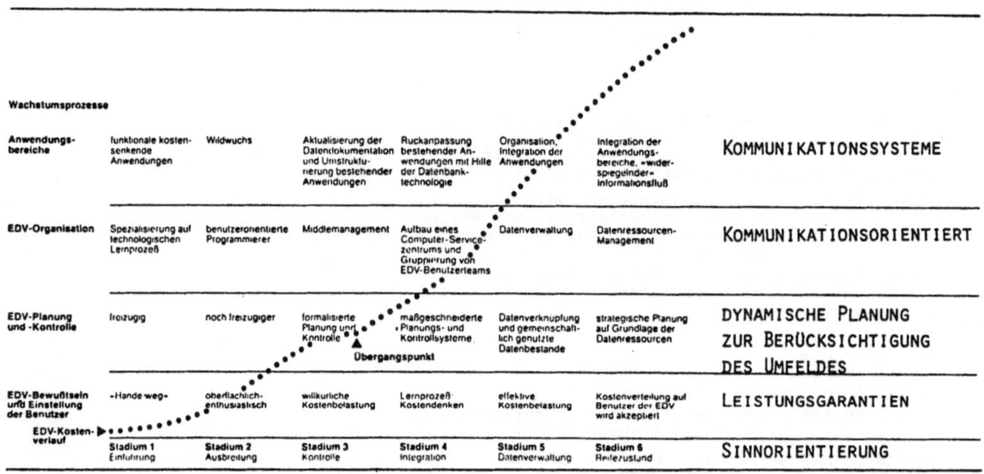

Die Lösung des Bewußtseins von der Technik wird erst möglich, wenn deren Beherrschung sicher ist. Die Frage nach zukünftigen Anwendungssystemen stellt sich nicht als Frage nach den vertretbaren Kosten, sondern nach der zu verantwortenden Qualität.

/KRA 80/ Dietrich Kracht: DELTA - interaktive Systementwicklung mit einem dedizierten Entwicklungscomputer, IKD 1980

/NOL 79/ Richard L. Nolan: Krisenmanagement in der Datenverarbeitung, HARVARD MANAGER 3/1979.

/THU 79/ Reinhold Thurner: DELTA-Manual 116, SODECON AG, Zürich.

/THU 80/ Reinhold Thurner: Der Entwicklungsrechner - ein Werkzeug für den Systementwickler, ONLINE-adi-Nachrichten 6/1980.

Die Einführung der Strukturierten-Software-Dekompositions-Methode bei GOLEM

Horst Biller
Volker Schmidt-Ramsin

SIEMENS AG
Dv ST DB 2
Otto-Hahn-Ring 6
8000 München 83

1. Einleitung

In den letzten Jahren wurden zahlreiche Methoden entwickelt, die ein strukturiertes Entwerfen und Entwickeln von Software-Systemen unterstützen (/Gewald/).

Bei Anwendung dieser Methoden entsteht schrittweise parallel zur Entwicklung eine technische Dokumentation des Systems, die nach Abschluß der Entwicklung die Grundlage für die Betreuung, d.h. Fehlerbehebung und Weiterentwicklung bildet. Wie wichtig eine solche Dokumentation ist, braucht wohl nach der bitteren Erfahrung, die in der Vergangenheit oftmals mit großen Systemen gemacht wurde, nicht besonders betont zu werden.

Der Einsatz von Techniken des Software Engineering bei der Neuentwicklung von Systemen ist heute allgemein üblich. Etwas andere Anforderungen an solche Techniken entstehen allerdings dann, wenn diese für ein bereits bestehendes Produkt eingeführt werden sollen, das unter anderen Gesichtspunkten entwickelt wurde. In diesem Fall ist es z.B. ganz wesentlich, die bereits bestehende Dokumentation so weit wie möglich zu berücksichtigen und auch eine Nachdokumentation der vorhandenen Programme zu ermöglichen.

In dieser Arbeit wird die Einführung einer Entwicklungsmethodik am Beispiel des Informations Retrieval Systems GOLEM beschrieben. Nach einer Schilderung der Ausgangssituation wird die im letzten Jahr eingeführte Entwicklungs- und Dokumentationsmethode, die Strukturierte Software Dekompositions-Methode (SSD-Methode), beschrieben. Insbesondere wird gezeigt, wie bei der Nachdokumentation vorgegangen wurde.

Abschließend werden die bisherigen Erfahrungen zusammengefaßt. Zweck dieser Arbeit ist es nicht, neue Verfahren darzustellen, sondern vielmehr einen Bericht aus der Praxis der Einführung bewährter Verfahren bei einem bestehenden Produkt zu geben.

2. Die Ausgangssituation

1978 war das Information Retrieval System GOLEM bereits 10 Jahre im Einsatz. Während dieser Zeit wurde es erheblich erweitert und insbesondere bei der Umstellung vom Betriebssystem BS1000 auf das BS2000 intern restrukturiert. GOLEM ist überwiegend im Assembler codiert und besteht zur Zeit aus 75 Moduln mit insgesamt ca. 150.000 Befehlen. Das System ist bis zur Modulebene gut strukturiert, innerhalb der Moduln allerdings sind die Regeln der strukturierten Programmierung (/Dijkstra/) manchmal nicht eingehalten. Der Code ist teilweise sehr komplex, da höchste Anforderungen an die Performance des Systems gestellt werden.

Da die Entwicklung des Systems nicht von Anfang an streng nach den

Phasen Projektierung, Design, Feinspezifikation und Codierung durchgeführt wurde, war auch eine diesen Phasen jeweils entsprechende Dokumentation nicht vorhanden. Die vorhandene Dokumentation beschrieb recht gut die global verwendeten Datenstrukturen, sie war jedoch ungenau und lückenhaft in der Beschreibung der Funktionen.

Seit 1976 wurden für die Weiterentwicklung von der Phase Design an Nassi-Shneidermann Struktugramme (/Nassi/) verwendet. Zu diesem Zweck wurden COLUMBUS-Anweisungen (/COLUMBUS/) geschrieben, aus denen durch die Programme COLLIST bzw. COLNASS Blockstrukturlisten bzw. Struktogramme auf dem Schnelldrucker erzeugt werden können.

Es bestand und besteht ein Marktdruck zur laufenden Weiterentwicklung des Systems. Als Konsequenz daraus und aus der zur Verfügung stehenden Personalkapazität für das Produkt GOLEM kann eine Nachdokumentation und unter Umständen erforderliche Restrukturierung nur schrittweise neben der laufenden Weiterentwicklung erfolgen.

An die für GOLEM einzuführenden Entwicklungs- und Dokumentationsverfahren wurden außerdem folgende Forderungen gestellt:

- Die Methode muß sowohl zur Nachdokumentation als auch zur Neuentwicklung geeignet sein.
- Eine Nachdokumentation des bestehenden Codes sollte sich ohne großen Aufwand erstellen lassen.
- Die vorhandene Dokumentation sollte soweit als möglich genutzt werden, um den Aufwand in Grenzen zu halten.
- Bei den Programmanalyse-Hilfsmitteln darf nicht vorausgesetzt werden, daß der Code den Regeln der strukturierten Programmierung entspricht.
- Andererseits sollen sehr wohl strukturelle Schwächen erkannt und Restrukturierungshinweise gegeben werden.
- Bei der Neuentwicklung von Programmteilen muß eine den Entwicklungsphasen angepaßte, abgestufte Dokumentation erzeugt werden. Als Ergebnis der Phase Projektierung soll die Leistungsbeschreibung, d.h. eine präzise funktionale Beschreibung des Systems, seine Grobstruktur sowie die Beschreibung der Benutzerschnittstelle vorliegen; als Ergebnis der Phase Design die Modulstruktur mit einer Beschreibung der Schnittstellen und des funktionalen Ablaufs der Moduln; als Ergebnis der Phase Feinspezifikation eine Beschreibung der Verarbeitungsalgorithmen entsprechend den Regeln der strukturierten Programmierung unter Verwendung von COLUMBUS Anweisungen.
- Sowohl bei der Neuentwicklung als auch bei der Nachdokumentation muß die Unterstützung durch maschinelle Hilfsmittel möglich sein. Bei der ersten Erprobung sollte zwar kein Aufwand für die Erstellung von Hilfsmitteln erbracht werden. Bei einer Bewährung der Methode allerdings sollte eine maschinelle Unterstützung möglich sein.
- Mit der Entwicklungsmethodik für funktionale Erweiterungen zusammen sollte eine Strategie zur Einarbeitung (und Nachdokumentation) in unbekannten Code gegeben werden.
- Die Methode muß leicht erlernbar sein und von den Entwicklern akzeptiert werden. Insbesondere darf sie keine zu hohen Anforderungen an die theoretischen Kenntnisse stellen.
- Die Dokumentation sollte in den Code integriert werden.

3. Die Strukturierte-Software-Dekomposition (SSD)

Die Strukturierte-Software-Dekompositionsmethode (SSD) stellt die Verbindung mehrerer bekannter und bewährter Techniken dar, die entsprechend den spezifischen Anforderungen angepaßt wurden. Im einzelnen stützt sich diese Methode auf Zustandsdiagramm, HIPO-Technik (/Stays/, /HIPO/), Nassi-Shneidermann Struktogramme und COLUMBUS (/COLUMBUS/).

Drei logische Beschreibungsebenen wurden gewählt, um das Programm möglichst durchschaubar und doch detailliert darzustellen. Entsprechend den verschiedenen Entwicklungsphasen kann jede Beschreibungsebene einer Phase zugeordnet werden. Großer Wert wurde auf den Übergang von einer Ebene auf die nächste gelegt, damit keine Darstellungsweise in der Luft hängt. Um möglichst viele Aspekte des Programmes erfassen zu können, wurde nicht eine einzige Darstellungsmethode gewählt, sondern mehrere, jedoch eine für jede logische Beschreibungsebene. Prinzipiell wäre mit jeder der vorzustellenden Techniken eine Beschreibung aller Stufen möglich.

Auf der obersten Ebene wird das Programm mit Hilfe von Zustandsdiagrammen (State-Diagram) beschrieben. Hier steht die Beschreibung der Benutzerschnittstelle im Vordergrund. Wir begnügen uns mit der Darstellung und verbalen Beschreibung aller für die Benutzer sichtbaren Funktionen, deren Verkettung und den Ereignissen, aufgrund derer sie ablaufen.

Ein Zustandsdiagramm besteht aus folgenden Elementen:

- dem Graphen, der optisch die logische Stuktur des Systems aus Benutzersicht widerspiegelt
- und den erläuterden "Wöterbüchern" der Zustände, der Funktionen und der Ergebnisse, unter denen die einzelnen Funktionen ablaufen.

Zustände sind Ausgangs- und Endpunkte von Funktionen. Sie bilden die Knoten des Graphen. Auf oberster Darstellungsebene bildet oft das "Wörterbuch" der Funktionen und das der Ereignisse eine redundante Information, (z.B. das Ereignis zu Funktion A besteht nur darin, daß Funktion A ablaufen soll). Aus diesem Grunde ist es zweckmäßig, das Wörterbuch der Ereignisse in diesem Falle wegzulassen.
Bild 1 zeigt ein Beispiel für ein Zustandsdiagramm.
Es beschreibt ein Programm, das eine Datei von Sätzen fester Länge verwaltet und diese Sätze

- auf die Datei schreibt,
- von der Datei liest,
- auf der Datei löscht.

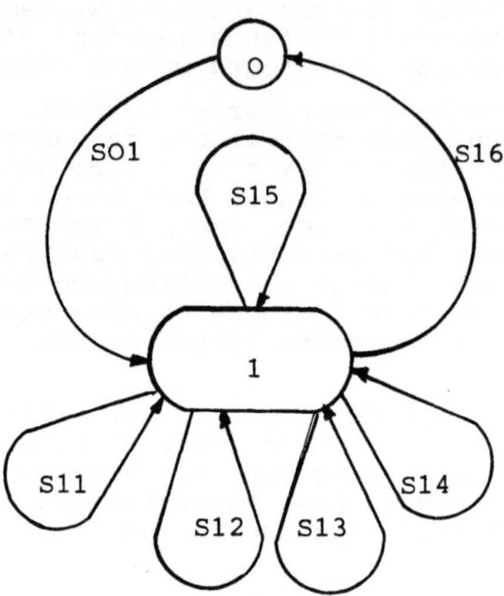

ZUSTÄNDE:

O: PROGRAMMAUFRUF
1: PROGRAMMSTEUERUNG

FUNKTIONEN:

SO1: IF DATEIWECHSEL
THEN ALTE DATENBEREICHE SICHERN
NEUE DATEN INITIALISIEREN
S11: SATZ BEREITSTELLEN
S12: SATZ BESCHREIBEN
S13: SATZ LESEN
S14: SATZ FREIGEBEN
S15: LESEN/SCHREIBEN DATEI
S16: ENDEROUTINE

Bild 1: Zustandsdiagramm

Zusätzlich zum Zustandsdiagramm wird während der Entwicklungsphase Leistungsbeschreibung eine hierarchische Darstellung der Funktionen in einer H-Karte erstellt.
In einer H-Karte (Hierachie-Karte /Stays/,/HIPO/) werden die Funktionen in Ebenen nach folgenden Regeln angeordnet:

- Funktionen der verschiedenen Ebenen werden durch Kästen dargestellt.
- Funktionen werden in ihre Subfunktionen zerlegt, diese bilden die Funktionen der nächst tieferen Ebene.
- Die Zuordnung Funktion-Subfunktion wird durch Kanten dargestellt.
- Ist eine Funktion Subfunktion mehrerer Funktionen, so werden die Kanten durch eine Liste dieser Funktionen ersetzt.

Die Funktionen des Zustandsgraphen bilden die zweitoberste Ebene in der H-Karte. Im Unterschied zum Zustandsgraphen erhält man aus der H-Karte keine Aussage über den möglichen dynamischen Ablauf eines Systems, sondern sie beschreibt nur die statische Untergliederung von Funktionen in Subfunktionen, d.h. die Systemstruktur.

Zustandsdiagramm, die H-Karte der oberen funktionalen Ebene und die syntaktische Beschreibung der Benutzerschnittstelle ergeben die Leistungsbeschreibung. Die Leistungsbeschreibung erfüllt drei Funktionen:

- Sie bildet für den Anwender die Beschreibung des Systems.
- Sie ist für den Entwickler die Definition des Entwicklungsauftrages.
- Sie ist Grundlage für die Benutzerdokumentation.

Es hat sich gezeigt, daß die Diskussion mit dem Anwender über die Funktionen des Systems anhand der Graphen leichter zu führen ist als vergleichsweise anhand einer verbalen Beschreibung oder einer Beschreibung mit Pseudocode. Die Wahl der Zustandsdiagramme ist zusätzlich auch durch die Integration der Nachdokumentation begründet. Dies wird in Kapitel 4 näher erklärt.

Aufgabe in der nächsten Phase, dem Design, ist es, jede der in der H-Karte aufgeführte Funktion durch ein IPO (Input-Prozess-Output- Diagram,/Stays/) zu beschreiben.

Das IPO besteht aus 3 Teilen,

- der Beschreibung der Input- und Outputschnittstelle der Funktion (Beschreibung der Datenfelder und deren Bedeutung),
- der Prozessbeschreibung in einer Pseudosprache,
- den Querverweislisten.

Als Prozessbeschreibungssprache wurde eine relativ freie pseudoprozedurale Sprache gewählt, die sich an den Kontrollstukturelementen der Programmiersprache PASCAL orientiert. Die Routinen bzw. Subroutinen werden verbal in verkürzter "Objekt-Verb" Form bezeichnet.
In den Querverweislisten werden alle Funktionen aufgeführt, die diese Funktionen benutzen bzw. die von ihr benutzt werden.

Diese Beschreibung wird später in den Code übernommen. Aus diesem Grund haben wir in Abweichung von der ursprünglichen HIPO-Technik auf die graphische Darstellung des "Datenflusses" verzichtet. Mit Abschluß der Design-Phase liegt erstmals eine vollständige Beschreibung des Programmes vor.

Die Umsetzung der einzelnen Funktionen in die nächste (dritte) Beschreibungsstufe erfolgt in der Phase Feinspezifikation mittels Columbusbefehlen. Columbusbefehle sind Makrobefehle des Precompilers "COLUMBUS", die das Codieren nach Regeln der Strukturierten Programmierung im Sinne von Dijkstra voraussetzen und überwachen. Diese unterste Ebene ist die Inline-Code Dokumentation.

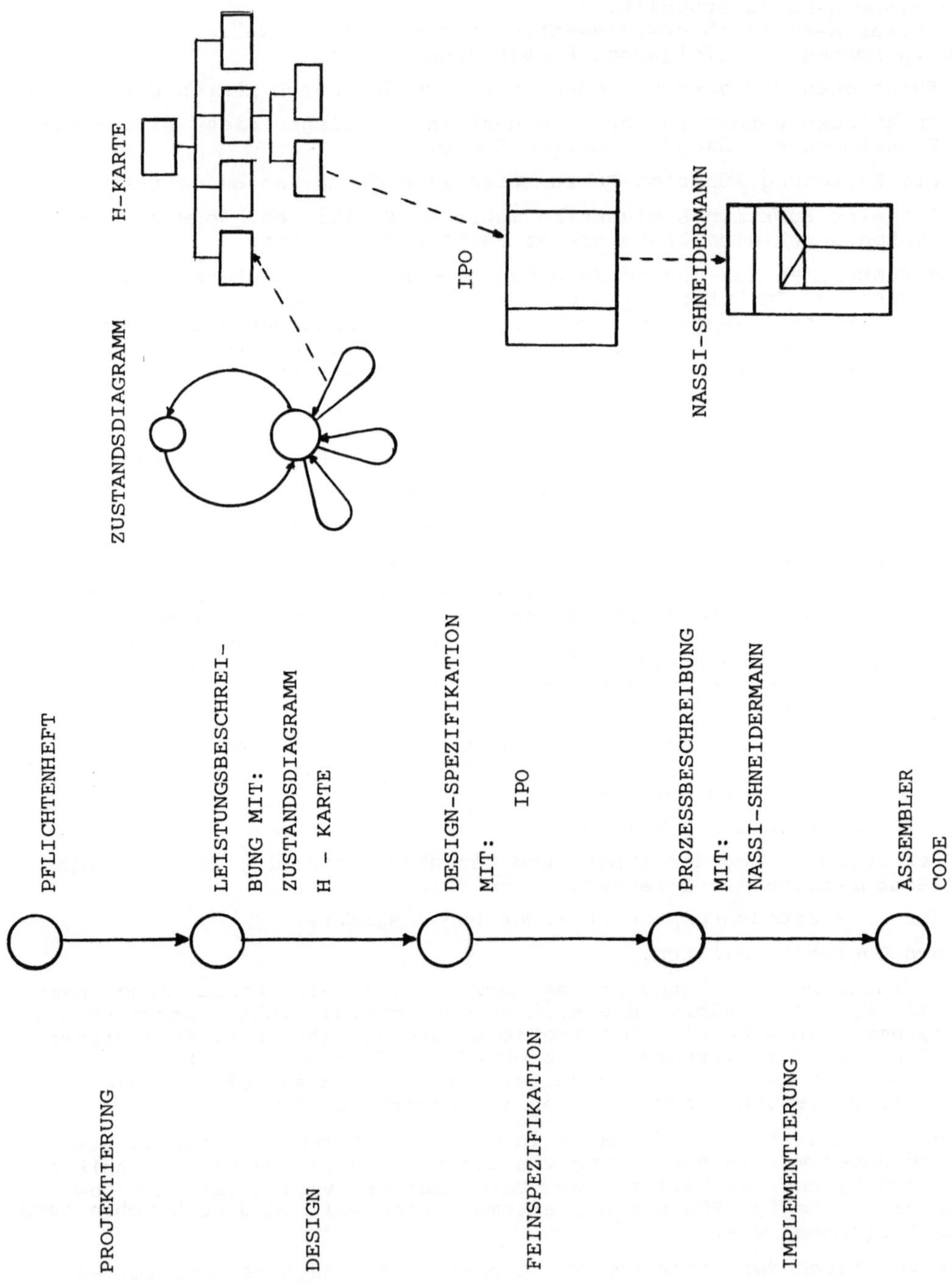

Bild 2: Vorgehensweise beim Entwurf

Zusammenfassend gibt das Bild 2 nochmals einen Überblick über die Entwurfsmethodik.

4. Nachdokumentation

Ziel der Nachdokumentation ist es, durch einen iterativen Prozess die logische Struktur eines Programmes herauszukristallisieren und das Zustandsdiagramm und die HIPO's zu erstellen. Dabei sollen strukturelle Schwächen des Programmes als Hinweis für einen eventuell erforderlichen Redesign aufgezeigt werden.

Die einzige sichere Unterlage eines Programmes, von der ausgegangen werden kann, stellt der Code mit der vom Assembler erzeugten Crossreferenzliste dar. Eventuell vorhandene alte Dokumentation kann nur als Anhalt, nicht aber als zuverlässig angesehen werden, da nicht sicher gestellt ist, das jede Änderung des Codes sich auch in der Dokumentation niedergeschlagen hat.

Der erste Schritt besteht darin, das Programm in zusammengehörige Teile zu untergliedern. Eine mögliche Vorgehensweise besteht darin, das Programm von hinten nach vorn durchzugehen und alle RETURN-Sprünge und Branchregisterbefehle (BR, BCR) zu markieren. Diese können Endpunkte von operativen Einheiten sein. Gewöhnliche Sprungbefehle hingegen stellen keinen Hinweis dieser Art dar, vielmehr sind bei alten Codes oft operative Einheiten durch Branchbefehle (BC) scheinbar willkürlich zerstückelt, die während der Fehlerbehebung eingeführt werden.

Einen weiteren Einblick in die Programmstruktur vermittelt eine Analyse des Programmes unter drei Gesichtspunkten:

- Herausfinden "wichtiger" Entscheidungen.
- Auflisten der Kontrollelemente und deren Bedeutung.
- Zusammenfassen zusammengehöriger Codeteile zu Verarbeitungsschritten und Benennen dieser Teile.

Alle Abfragen, die sich

- direkt oder indirekt auf externe, vom Benutzer eingegebene Steuerparameter beziehen,
- auf Bedingungen beziehen, die außerhalb der zu untersuchenden Routine gesetzt werden und so für die Routine die gleichen Eigenschaften haben wie externe Steuerparameter,

haben im obigen Sinne wichtige Entscheidungen zur Folge. Das Prädikat "wichtig" soll auf die Schlüsselrolle hinweisen, die solchen Entscheidungen bei der Funktions- bzw. Subfunktionsauswahl zufällt.

Ein ähnliches Gewicht kommt den Entscheidungen zu,

- die Teile einer Case-Konstruktion sind,
- bzw. deren nachfolgende Verarbeitungszweige groß sind.

Der Entscheidungsgraph (Flow Graph/Aho/) bietet die Möglichkeit, alle so erhaltene Information über das Programm zu sammeln und graphisch darzustellen. Der Entscheidungsgraph besteht aus drei Elementen, den

- Zuständen
- Kanten
- Verzweigungen.

Zustände werden durchnummeriert, Kanten mit Buchstaben und Ziffern unterschieden und die Bedingungen der Verzweigungen direkt in den Graphen geschrieben.

Der Beginn des Programmes ist der Ausgangszustand Ø des Graphen. Von hier führt eine Kante A bis zu ersten "wichtigen" Entscheidung. Unmittelbar vor der Entscheidung wird ein Zustand 1 eingeführt. Jeder Ast der Verzweigung wird nun wie oben dokumentiert. Die Kante B führt vom Zustand 1 bis zur nächsten "wichtigen" Entscheidung des einen Astes und die Kante C vom Zustand 1 bis zur nächsten "wichtigen" Entscheidung des anderen Astes. usw.

Die Kante A,B, usw. werden in "Objekt-Verb'-Form" beschrieben (z.B. DATEN INTIALISIEREN, DATEI OEFFNEN). Die Zustände 1,2 usw., erhalten Programm-Label als Namen. Bild 3 ist ein Entscheidungsgraph der Steuerungsroutine in Bild 1 dargestellten Programmes.

Ist dieser Entscneidungsgraph erstellt worden, enthält er in der Regel noch sehr viele Implementierungsdetails. Im schlimmsten Fall ist es sogar eine 1:1 Abbildung des Codes. Dieser Graph ist eine Beschreibung der ersten Abstraktionsstufe (Stufe Ø). Um ein Zustandsdiagramm zu erreichen, müssen meist durch eine stufenweise Vergrößerung (/PAIGE/) mehrere Entscheidungsgraphen verschiedener Abstraktionsstufen (Stufe 1,...n,) erstellt werden, mit dem Ziel, daß jede Kante eine klar definierte Funktion entspricht. Dabei werden jeweils Teile des Entscheidungsgraphen, die einen Eingang und Ausgang besitzen, durch eine Kante ersetzt.
Aus jedem Abstraktionsschritt, der unter Umständen recht schwierig sein kann, erhält man sehr viele Restrukturierungshinweise. Denn oft werden nur aus Gründen der "Codeersparnis" Routineteile von außen angesprungen, was zur Folge hat, daß man diese Routine nicht mehr so einfach mit einer Objekt-Verb-Beziehung beschreiben kann. Dies bedeutet aber auch eine Einschränkung unseres Ziels, in der Abstraktion soweit fortzufahren, daß nur noch die logische Struktur des Programmes wiedergespiegelt wird. Denn solange diese Schwäche im Code nicht behoben ist, darf eine Dokumentation nichts anderes vorgaukeln. So wird man bei der Nachdokumentation selten einen idealen Zustandsgraphen erhalten, sondern meist einen Zwitter zwischen Zustandsdiagramm und Entscheidungsgraphen. Damit ist die Dokumentation der obersten Ebene erstellt.

Zur Erstellung der H-Karte und der dazugehörigen IPO wird nun wie beim Programmneuentwurf vom Zustandsdiagramm ausgegangen. Dabei sind die oben erstellten Entscheidungsgraphen ein wichtiges Hilfsmittel, vor allem bei der IPO-Erstellung.

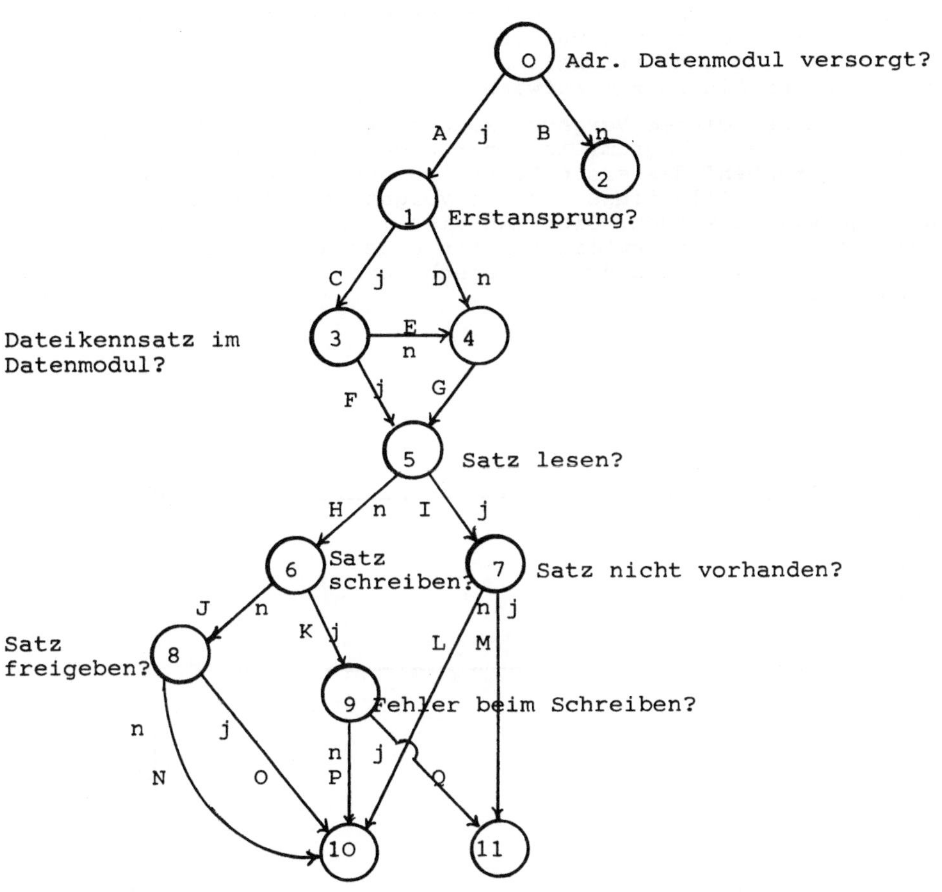

Zustände:

O: UIZNL: Programmaufruf

1: UIZNL1:

2: UIZNLF1: Programmabbruch mit Dump

3: UIZST5:

4: UIZST4:

5: UIZST6:

6: UIZNL2:

7: UIZLES:

8: UIZNL6:

9: UIZSR:

10: UIZSRR: Programmende

11: UIZNLF2: Programmabruch mit Dump

Funktionen:

A: Daten initialisieren

B: Melden Fehler

D: Sichern alter Datenbereich

E: Laden neuen Datenbereich

I: Satz lesen

K: Satz schreiben

M: Fehler melden

N: Satz bereitstellen

O: Satz freigeben

Q: Fehler melden

C,F,G,H,J,L,P: Nulloperationen

Bild 3: Entscheidungsgraph

Im Falle der Nachdokumentation wird der letzte Schritt, die Inline-Dokumentation im Pseudocode, soweit es sich nicht um einen restrukturierten Programmteil handelt, nicht durchgeführt. Dies würde erfahrungsgemäß einen hohen Aufwand bedeuten und, da der Code oft nicht strukturiert ist, auf Schwierigkeiten stoßen. Der Informationsgewinn steht in keinem Verhältnis zum Aufwand.

Gewisse Schritte bei diesem Vorgehen können maschinell unterstützt werden. Z.B. wurde ein Programm in einer anderen Abteilung entwickelt, das weitgehend das erste Erstellen des Entscheidungsgraphen abnimmt (/AUTODOK/). Allerdings muß der Vorgang der Abstraktion intellektuell geleistet werden. Gibt man diesem Programm die Routinengrenzen an, so liefert es sämtliche Datenfelder auf die in dieser Routine zugegriffen wird und zwar unterschieden in Lesezugriff und Schreibezugriff.

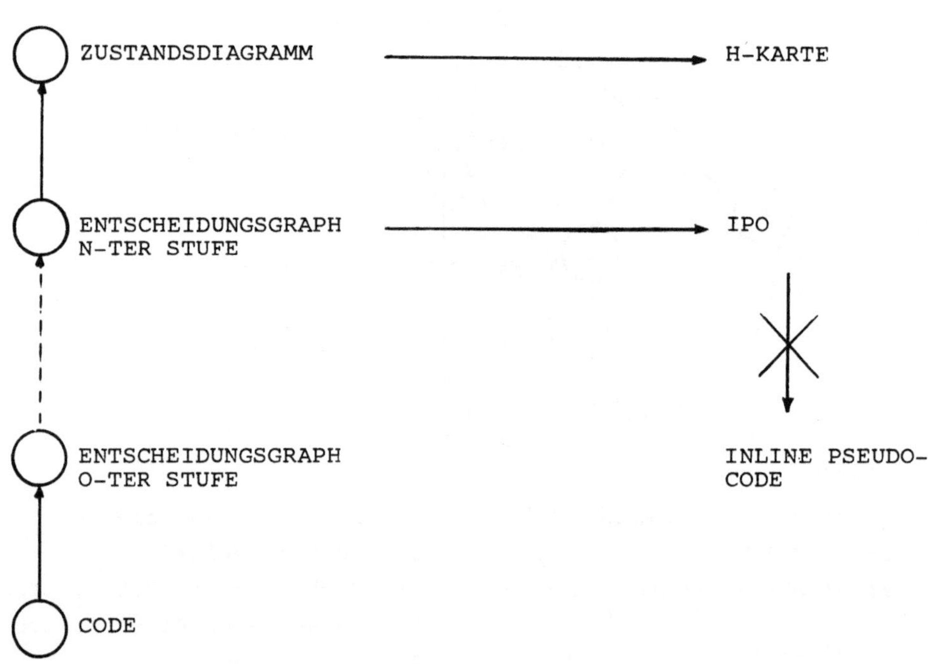

Bild 4: Vorgehensweise bei der Nachdokumentation

5. Erfahrungen im Einsatz

Diese Methoden wurden im Rahmen eines Pilotprojektes zur Nachdokumentation einer besonders fehleranfälligen GOLEM-Komponente erprobt. Neben der dabei erstellten Dokumentation der Komponente zeigen sich weitere Ergebnisse:

- Die strukturellen Schwächen dieser Komponente wurden deutlich aufgezeigt.
- Gleichzeitig erfolgte eine gründliche Einarbeitung eines neuen, in der Entwicklung unerfahrenen Mitarbeiters in diese Komponente. Diesem wurde durch das gezielte Vorgehen eine wesentliche Hilfe geboten, die die mangelnde Erfahrung bei weitem ausglich.
- Aufgrund der erstellten Dokumentation konnten in einem späteren Projekt funktionale Erweiterungen dieser Komponente mit wesentlich geringerem Aufwand und größerer Sicherheit als bei vergleichbaren früheren Projekten durchgeführt werden.
- Als gewisser Nachteil der SSD-Methode bei der Neuentwicklung hat sich gezeigt, daß die Beschreibung der Datenstrukturen gegenüber der Beschreibung der Funktionen zurücktritt. Deshalb wird die SSD-Methode um Konventionen zur Darstellung von Datenstrukturen und die Beschreibung von Datenzugriffen im Pseudocode erweitert werden.

Die insgesamt positiven Erfahrungen führen dazu, diese Methode für die gesamte GOLEM-Entwicklung einzuführen.

6. Literatur

Aho: Aho, Alfred V., Principles of Compiler Design; Addison-Wesley Publishing Company, Reading, Massachusetts 1977

AUTODOK: AUTODOK Bedienungsanleitung, SIEMENS AG UB D AP GE

COLUMBUS: Softwareprodukt COLUMBUS (ASSEMBLER)-System zur Unterstützung der Strukturierten Programmierung, SIEMENS AG Bestell-Nr. D15/5228-01

Dijkstra: Dijkstra E., A Discipline of Programming, Prentice Hall Inc. Engelwood Cliffs, NJ (1976)
Dijkstra E., Notes on Structured Programming, T.H.E. Report Nr. EWD-248, 70-WSK-03, second edition (April 70)

Gewald: Gewald K., Software Engineering, R. Oldenburg Verlag München (1977)

GOLEM: GOLEM BS2000, Ein System zum Speichern und Wiedergewinnen von Informationen, SIEMENS AG DATA PRAXIS Bestell-Nr. D15/5817-01

HIPO: HIPO - A Design Aid and Documentation Technique, GC 20-1851, IBM Corp., New York

Mc Cabe: Mc Cabe T., A Complexity Measure, IEEE Transaction of Software Engineering Vol. SE-2 Nr. 4 (Dec. 76)

Nassi: Nassi J. and Shneidermann B., Flowchart Techniques of Structured Programming, SIGPLAN Notices Vol. 8 (Aug. 73)

Paige: Paige M., On Partitioning Program Graphs, IEEE Transactions on Software Engineering, Vol. SE-3 Nr.6 (Nov. 77)

Stays: Stays J., HIPO and integrated program design, IBM System Journal Vol. 15, Nr.2, 1976

Eine Methode zum Entwurf betrieblicher Informationssysteme

Hubert Österle, Lehrstuhl für Betriebsinformatik, Universität Dortmund

1. Betriebliches Informationssystem

Systeme zur Finanzbuchführung, Lagerhaltung, Fertigungsplanung und Vertriebsplanung sind typische Beispiele für betriebliche Informationssysteme. Sie bestehen aus Informationen, Prozessoren und Methoden sowie den Beziehungen zwischen diesen Komponenten. Informationen bedeuten hier - im Gegensatz zur Informationstheorie - das Wissen um oder die Kenntnis über Sachverhalte [DIN 44300, Schmitz und Seibt S. 18 f.]. Prozessoren sind Menschen (die Mitarbeiter der Fachabteilungen, in der Folge auch Benutzer genannt) und Maschinen (isolierte Kleinrechner, intelligente Terminals und Zentralrechner). Methoden sind Algorithmen und nicht formalisierte Verfahren der maschinellen und manuellen Informationsverarbeitung. Betriebliche Informationssysteme sind demnach soziotechnische Systeme. Programme und Rechner repräsentieren nur einen Teil aus dem gesamten System.

2. Komplexität und Abstraktion

Folgende Charakteristika kennzeichnen die Entwicklung betrieblicher Informationssysteme:

. Der Rechner übernimmt einen immer größeren Teil der betrieblichen Informationsverarbeitung, insbesondere der Massendatenverarbeitung.

. Nachdem zunächst die einfachen Routinetätigkeiten automatisiert worden sind, werden zunehmend anspruchsvollere Aufgaben angegangen.

. Die Integration der Teilsysteme eines Betriebes setzt sich durch.

. Die Anzahl maschineller Prozessoren, die in einem Informationssystem enthalten sind, wächst im Zuge der Verteilung der Intelligenz.

. Die permanente Weiterentwicklung der Betriebe als organischer Gebilde erzwingt eine laufende Anpassung der Informationssysteme.

Die Entwicklung der Informationssysteme ist den an sie gestellten Anforderungen nicht gewachsen. Kennzeichen dafür sind:

. Termin- und Kostenüberschreitung in der Entwicklung von Informationssystemen.

. Unzufriedenheit bei den Benutzern.

. Hohe Wartungskosten als Folge von Qualitätsmängeln
(im Durchschnitt ca. 60 - 70 % der gesamten Personalkapazität der

Softwareentwicklung [vgl. Black, Central Computer Agency (Hrsg.), Diebold]).

Die Probleme gehen überwiegend auf die hohe Komplexität der Systeme zurück. Diese ergibt sich aus der Diskrepanz zwischen dem Informationsumfang, der in der Entwicklung eines Informationssystems zu bewältigen ist, und der Informationsverarbeitungskapazität des Menschen. Elshoff [S. 115 f.] hat für betriebliche Anwendungsprogramme (in PL/I) empirisch erhoben, daß ein Programm im Schnitt

. 384 Bezeichner enthält,

. von denen 277 in Operationen benutzt werden, und

. daß jeder Bezeichner durchschnittlich viermal verwendet wird.

Dem steht eine simultane Verarbeitungskapazität des bewußten Kurzzeitgedächtnisses des Menschen von ungefähr fünf Begriffen gegenüber [vgl. Cooke und Bunt, Weinberg, Tracz]. Dies bedeutet, daß der Mensch die Systementwicklung nur durch Segmentierung und Sequentialisierung bewältigt, d.h., daß er die Aufgabenstellung in kleine Teilaufgaben zerlegt, die er nacheinander bearbeitet. Die größte Schwierigkeit sind dabei die Schnittstellen zwischen den Teilaufgaben, also ihre Interdependenzen.

Zur Bewältigung der Komplexität benutzt der Mensch die Abstraktion. Man unterscheidet dabei die klassenbildende und die komplexbildende Superierung [vgl. Frank S. 106, Weltner S. 27 f.]. In der <u>klassenbildenden Superierung</u> ersetzt man eine Menge von Begriffen durch einen Oberbegriff, indem man Merkmale der Begriffe wegläßt (z.B. Ballspiel für Fuß-Ballspiel, Hand-Ballspiel etc.). Von <u>komplexbildender Superierung</u> spricht man, wenn man mehrere Begriffe durch einen Oberbegriff ersetzt, der eine Zusammenfassung darstellt (z.B. Fußballmannschaft für die Elemente Tormann, Libero etc.).

Im rein intuitiven Vorgehen sucht der Mensch ohne von außen vorgegebene Regeln Abstraktionen. Die Schwierigkeit dabei ist, günstige Abstraktionen zu finden und so dafür zu sorgen, daß alle Elemente und Beziehungen eines Informationssystems für sich und in ihren Interdependenzen überblickt werden. Da dies intuitiv nur mangelhaft gelingt, wie die Erfahrung zeigt, sind seit längerem intensive Bemühungen zu erkennen, Entwurfsmethoden zu entwickeln, welche die Abstraktion strukturieren, also Hilfen anzubieten, um günstige Abstraktionen zu finden. Bild 1 zeigt eine Zusammenstellung der bekanntesten Ansätze.

1	Entwurfsmethoden
Methode	**Autor(en)**
Top-down/Schrittweise Verfeinerung	Conway und Gries, Dijkstra, Mills, Wirth
Bottom up	
HIPO (Hierarchy plus Input-Process-Output)	IBM (Hrsg.)
Composite Design	Stevens e.a., Yourdon und Constantine
LITOS (Linzer Technique of Software Design)	Schulz
SADT (Structured Analysis and Design Technique)	Softech (Hrsg.), Ross und Schoman
IA (Information Analysis)	Lundeberg
Transitionsnetze	Peterson, Petri
LOGOS	Rose
SREM (Software Requirements Engineering Methodology)	Alford und Burns
JSP (Jackson Structured Programming)	Jackson
ISDS/HOS (Integrated Software Development System / Higher Order Software)	Hamilton und Zeldin
Entscheidungstabelle	Dreßler e.a., Erbesdobler e.a., Strunz
Abstrakte Datentypen	Ehrich, Guttag, Liskov und Zilles

3. Methode des mehrdimensional abgestuften Entwurfs

Eine Analyse der Methoden aus Bild 1 hat gezeigt, daß deren Strukturierung auch nicht annähernd bis zu einer Algorithmisierung reicht. Die Verfahren enthalten aber einige Hinweise, welche die Beherrschung komplexer Informationssysteme vereinfachen. Die hier vorzustellende Methode versucht, diese Abstraktionshilfen in einem geschlossenen Ansatz verfügbar zu machen.

Die Grundlagen der Methode sind:

. Mehrdimensionale Betrachtung

Zwischen den Elementen eines Informationssystems sind verschiedene Beziehungstypen zu betrachten. Die wichtigsten sind die der hierarchischen Ordnung von Begriffen, der Präzedenz und der Kontrolle.

. Abgestufte Dimensionseinführung

Die Methode beginnt mit jener Systemdarstellung, welche die einfachste Form der Beziehungen berücksichtigt, und nimmt nach und nach zusätzliche Dimensionen (Beziehungstypen) in die Betrachtung auf, bis schließlich eine vollständige Formulierung des Informationssystems vorliegt.

Im folgenden geben wir einen groben Überblick über die Bestandteile und die Arbeitsweise der Methode [zur detaillierten Darstellung s. Österle S. 185 ff.].

3.1. Bestandteile

3.1.1. Komponentenliste

Die Komponentenliste ist eine ungeordnete Aufzählung aller zu einem bestimmten Zeitpunkt bekannten Funktionen und Datentypen eines Subsystems des zu entwerfenden Informationssystems. Sie zeigt die einfachste Beziehung auf: Komponente K ist enthalten im Informationssystem.

3.1.2. Komponentenhierarchie

Die Komponentenhierarchie ordnet die Elemente der Komponentenliste nach den im Anwendungsbereich gängigen Begriffshierarchien. So würde etwa folgende Zerlegung festgehalten:

Lohnabrechnung
  Bruttolohnermittlung
  Nettolohnermittlung
    Steuern berechnen
    Krankenkassenbeitrag ermitteln

Die Komponentenhierarchie differenziert den Beziehungstyp der Komponentenliste zur Aussage: Komponente k ist Teil der Komponente K.

3.1.3. Schnittstellenentwurf

Der Schnittstellenentwurf legt die Schnittstelle zwischen den Prozessoren eines Informationssystems, vornehmlich aber die zwischen Mensch und Maschine fest. Die wichtigsten Formen sind

. grobe Druckbildentwürfe,

. Skizzen von Erfassungsformularen und

. eine grobe Darstellung von Bildern eines Bildschirmdialoges zusammen mit dem Dialogablauf.

Der Beziehungstyp des Schnittstellenentwurfs heißt: Prozessor A gibt den Datentyp D lt. Format F an Prozessor B. Die Elemente des Datentyps sind weit detailliert.

3.1.4. Präzedenzgraph

Der Präzedenzgraph zeigt den Fluß der Daten durch ein IS, d.h., aus welchen Datentypen über welche Funktionen welche Datentypen entstehen. Die einfache Form des hier verwendeten Präzedenzgraphen ist in Bild 2 erklärt.

2	Symbolik der Präzedenzgraphen
SYMBOL	BEDEUTUNG
(d)	Datentyp d.
[f / p]	Funktion f auf Prozessor p.
(d) → [f / p]	Datentyp d ist Eingabe für Funktion f.
[f / p] → (d)	Funktion f erzeugt den Datentyp d.
(d) ↔ [f / p]	Funktion f verwendet und erzeugt Datentyp d.

Die gerichteten Kanten drücken die Präzedenzbeziehungen aus. Sie besagen, daß die Ausführung einer Funktion f die Existenz eines Exemplars eines Datentyps d_e voraussetzt und daß die Existenz eines Exemplars eines Datentyps d_a die Ausführung einer Funktion f voraussetzt (Die Bestellung Nr. 3133 ist ein Exemplar des Datentyps Bestellung.) Die Einschränkung auf ein Exemplar eines Datentyps ist nötig, da beim Fortschreiben aus einem Datentyp zum Zeitpunkt t ein Datentyp zum Zeitpunkt t + 1, also aus einem Exemplar das nächste, entsteht. Diese Interpretation des Präzedenzgraphen entspricht der Verwendungsform in Literatur und Praxis [vgl. eine ähnliche Form bei Wedekind S. 178 ff.]. Die sich daraus ergebende Bedeutung einiger zusammengesetzter Konstrukte im Präzedenzgraph ist in Bild 3 dargestellt.

3	Zusammengesetzte Konstrukte im Präzedenzgraph

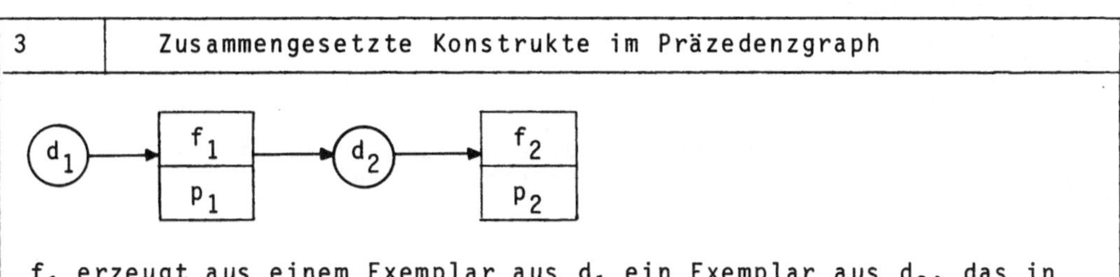

f_1 erzeugt aus einem Exemplar aus d_1 ein Exemplar aus d_2, das in f_2 eingeht. f_1 und f_2 laufen also bezüglich eines Exemplars aus d_1 und d_2 sequentiell ab. Das heißt nicht, daß f_1 und f_2 bezüglich unterschiedlicher Exemplare nicht nebeneinander ablaufen können.

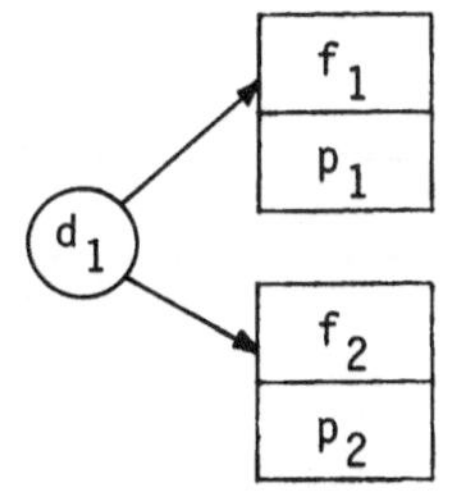

- Bei Existenz eines Exemplares aus d_1 läuft entweder f_1 oder f_2 ab (Selektion) oder
- bei Existenz eines Exemplares aus d_1 laufen f_1 und f_2 nebeneinander ab oder
- f_1 und f_2 laufen für unterschiedliche Exemplare aus d_1 nebeneinander ab.

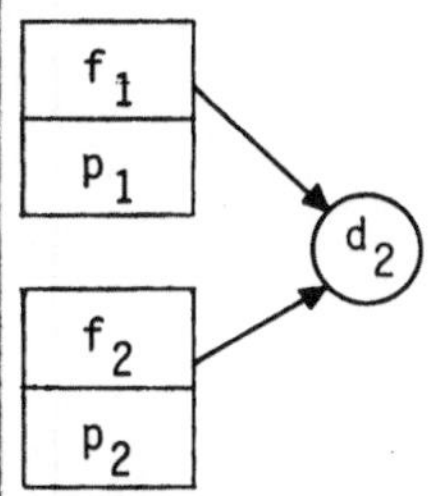

Ein Exemplar aus d_2 entsteht aus der Ausführung von f_1 und/oder f_2.

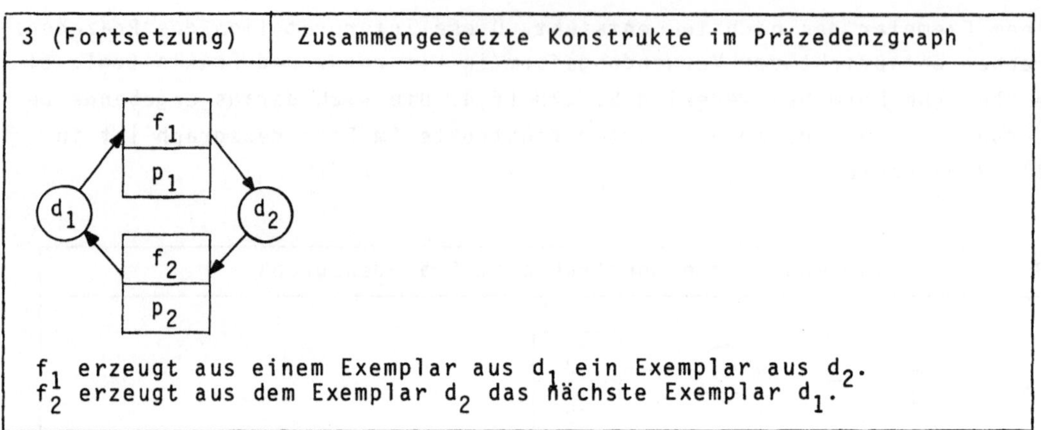

f_1 erzeugt aus einem Exemplar aus d_1 ein Exemplar aus d_2.
f_2 erzeugt aus dem Exemplar d_2 das nächste Exemplar d_1.

3.1.5. Kontrollbaum

Der Kontrollbaum beschreibt die Kontrollstruktur. Er benutzt die im Bild 4 gezeigten Komponenten.

4	Konstrukte des Kontrollbaumes
Kontrollbaum	**Entsprechung in Entwurfssprache**
. Sequenz F f_1 . . . f_n	<u>PROCEDURE</u> F Funktion f_1 ... Funktion f_n <u>END</u>
. Iteration F f(i)	<u>FOR ALL</u> i <u>DO</u> Funktion f(i) <u>END</u>
. Nebenläufigkeit F f_1 . . . f_n	<u>PARALLELY DO</u> Funktion f_1 ... Funktion f_n <u>END</u>

4 (Fortsetzung)	Konstrukte des Kontrollbaumes

Kontrollbaum	Entsprechung in Entwurfssprache

. Synchronität

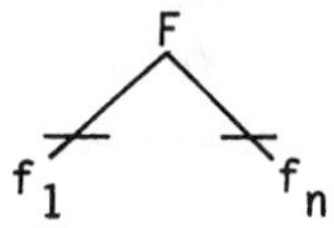


```
SYNCHRONOUSLY DO
  PROCEDURE p1
  ...
  PROCEDURE pn
END
PROCEDURE pi
  ...
  RESUME pj
  ...
END
PROCEDURE pj
  ...
  DETACH
  ...
  DETACH
  ...
END
```

. Selektion

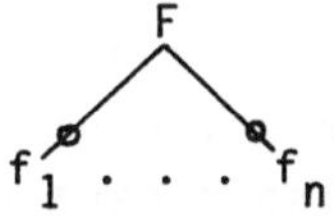


```
CASE Bedingung OF
  Typ 1: Funktion f1
  ...
  Typ n: Funktion fn
END
```

. Entscheidungstabelle

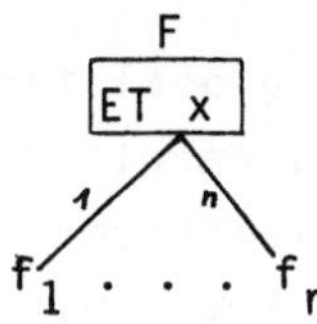

ET x:

Bedingung 1	a_{11}	...	a_{1n}
...	...	...	...
Bedingung c	a_{c1}	...	a_{cn}
AKTION	1	...	n

Anmerkung:

ET x ist der Bezeichner der Entscheidungstabelle.
ak_i steht für den Aktionsanzeiger der k-ten Bedingung und i-ten Regel.

. Unbestimmtheit

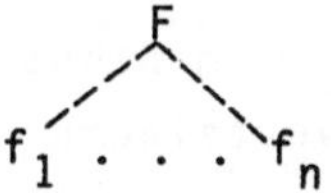

Die Koordination nebenläufiger Funktionen geschieht ähnlich wie in Transitionsnetzen über Stellen, wenngleich nur Teilaspekte eines Netzes in der Baumdarstellung wiedergegeben werden können.

Die Synchronität entspricht grob dem Coroutinen-Konzept in SIMULA. Die Koordination der quasiparallelen Teilfunktionen erfolgt über Konnektoren und Konnektorreferenzen. In diesem Rahmen kann auf dieses Konstrukt nicht näher eingegangen werden.

Die Entscheidungstabelle hilft, komplexe Entscheidungssituationen, die mit der Selektion nur aufwendig beschreibbar sind, kompakt darzustellen.

Die Unbestimmtheit wurde aus der Erfahrung heraus aufgenommen, daß es insbesondere im Grobentwurf häufig schwer fällt, sich zwischen Sequenz und Nebenläufigkeit zu entscheiden. Die Festlegung kann damit auf einen späteren Zeitpunkt verschoben werden.

Der Beziehungstyp des Kontrollbaumes gibt an, ob eine Funktion f_i nach, neben, synchron mit oder alternativ zu einer Funktion f_j bzw. wiederholt ausgeführt wird.

3.1.6. Markiertes Instanzennetz

Das markierte Instanzennetz [vgl. Lockemann und Mayr S. 74 ff.] dient der Untersuchung von Problemen der Nebenläufigkeit, die im Kontrollbaum unzureichend transparent gemacht werden können. Es greift also diesen Aspekt aus der Kontrollstrukturbetrachtung heraus und macht ihn einer isolierten Analyse zugänglich. Hier wird nicht näher darauf eingegangen.

3.1.7. Moduldefinition

Der Kontrollbaum beschreibt ein Informationssystem von der globalsten Ebene bis auf die Stufe elementarer Operationen wie etwa Statements der Zielsprache. Aus Gründen der Obersichtlichkeit wird er in Teilbäume zerlegt, von denen jeder als Modul betrachtet wird. Für jeden Modul wird die Ein- und Ausgabe als Liste der entsprechenden Datentypen beschrieben. Damit wird auch auf globaler Ebene der Definitions- und Wertebereich von Funktionen angegeben.

3.2. Prozedere

Der grundsätzliche Ansatz dieser Entwurfsmethode ist es, unter Verwendung der eben besprochenen Hilfsmittel ein IS nach und nach im Sinne der komplexbildenden und der klassenbildenden Abstraktion zu verfeinern. Das

IS wird also einerseits in Teilsysteme zerlegt; andererseits werden die Aspekte (Dimensionen) eines IS stufenweise aufgenommen.

Bild 5 zeigt, wie der Entwerfer ein Informationssystem in Abschnitten entwickelt und welche Schritte er pro Abschnitt durchläuft.

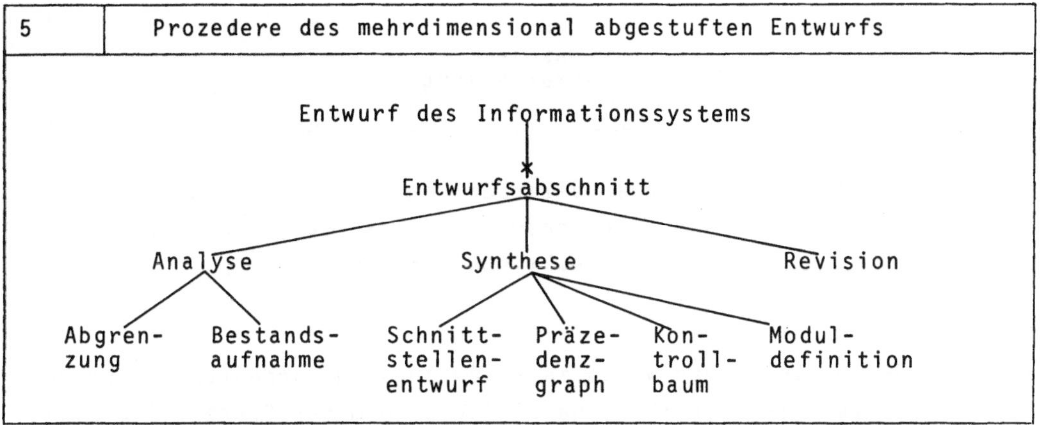

In der Analyse grenzt der Entwerfer das im aktuellen Entwurfsabschnitt zu behandelnde Teilsystem von seiner Umgebung ab, indem er dessen Funktion sowie Ein- und Ausgabe grob festlegt. Danach sammelt er in Komponentenlisten und Komponentenhierarchien alle Bestandteile des Teilsystems, die zu diesem Zeitpunkt bekannt sind. Er geht in der Analyse vom Transaktionsbestand aus. Das ist die Menge jener Datentypen, welche die Ausführung des Teilsystems auslösen.

Die Synthese kombiniert die in der Analyse gefundenen Komponenten zu einem Teilsystem. Sie konkretisiert zunächst die Schnittstellen zwischen den Prozessoren, sofern dies für das Teilsystem relevant ist. Damit ist beispielsweise in Form des Formularentwurfs eine anschauliche Basis für die Festlegung des Datenflusses im Präzedenzgraph und die der Kontrollstruktur im Kontrollbaum gegeben. Für die Synthese gibt es Regeln wie beispielsweise:

- Das Teilsystem ist erst für die "Normalverarbeitung" und danach für die Fehlerbehandlung zu konzipieren.
- Für jede iterative Komponente muß eine Anfangs-, Einzel- und Endeverarbeitung vorgesehen werden (s. Bild 6).
- Für jede Eingabe im Dialog ist ein Korrekturzyklus mit Abbruchmöglichkeiten vorzusehen.

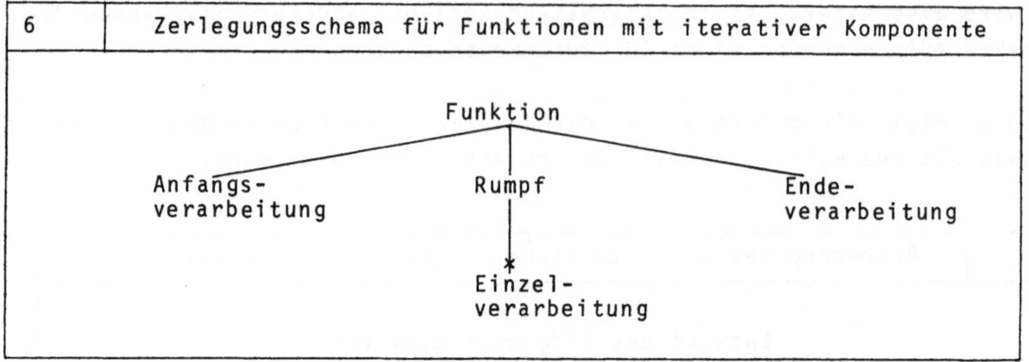

Die Revision ist eine kritische Überarbeitung des zuvor entworfenen Teilsystems und seiner Umgebung. Auch dazu sind Hinweise für ein zweckmäßiges Vorgehen und außerdem eine Checkliste vorhanden.

3.3. Beispiel

Praktische Beispiele können wegen ihres Umfangs nur andeutungsweise gezeigt werden. Es wird hier für eine einfache Form der Bestelldisposition versucht.

In einer Artikelstammdatei wird auf Veranlassung des Benutzers für jeden Artikel geprüft, ob der Mindest-Lagerbestand unterschritten ist. Alle zu bestellenden Artikel werden zu Bestellungen an Lieferanten zusammengefaßt und in einer Bestellvorschlagsliste ausgedruckt. Der Benutzer prüft, ob die Bestellvorschläge akzeptiert werden können, korrigiert sie ggfs. im Dialog und veranlaßt den Druck der Bestellungen.

Der Entwurf dieses Systems könnte im ersten Entwurfsabschnitt wie folgt ablaufen:

. Analyse
- Abgrenzung
  Teilsystem: Bestellwesen
  Eingabe: Artikelstammsätze
  Kreditorenstammsätze
  Ausgabe: Bestellung
  Aufgabe: Maschinelle Bestellvorschläge, manuelle Korrektur, maschinelle Bestellschreibung

- Bestandsaufnahme
  Funktionen: Bestellungen ermitteln
  Bestellung pro Lieferant drucken

Bestellung prüfen
Bestellung korrigieren
Bestellung drucken

Datentypen: Artikelstammsatz
Kreditorenstammsatz
Bestellung
Bestellvorschlagsliste
Bestellkorrektur

. Synthese
- Schnittstellenentwurf

Auf dieser globalen Ebene genügt folgende Festlegung bezüglich der Mensch-Maschine-Schnittstelle:

-- Die Bestellvorschläge werden in einer Liste ausgedruckt.
-- Die Korrekturen werden am Bildschirm ausgeführt.
-- Die Bestellungen werden auf Papier ausgedruckt.

- Präzedenzgraph (s. Bild 7)

7 Präzedenzgraph für die Bestelldisposition

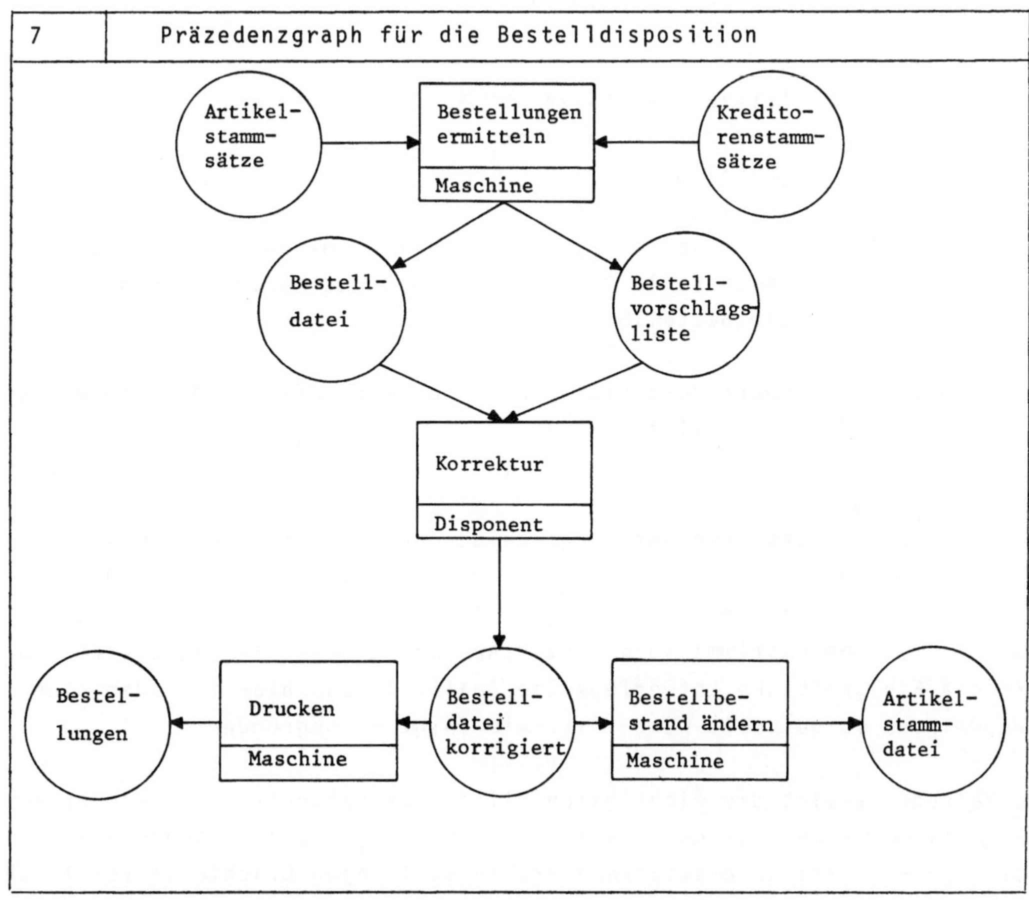

- Kontrollbaum (s. Bild 8)

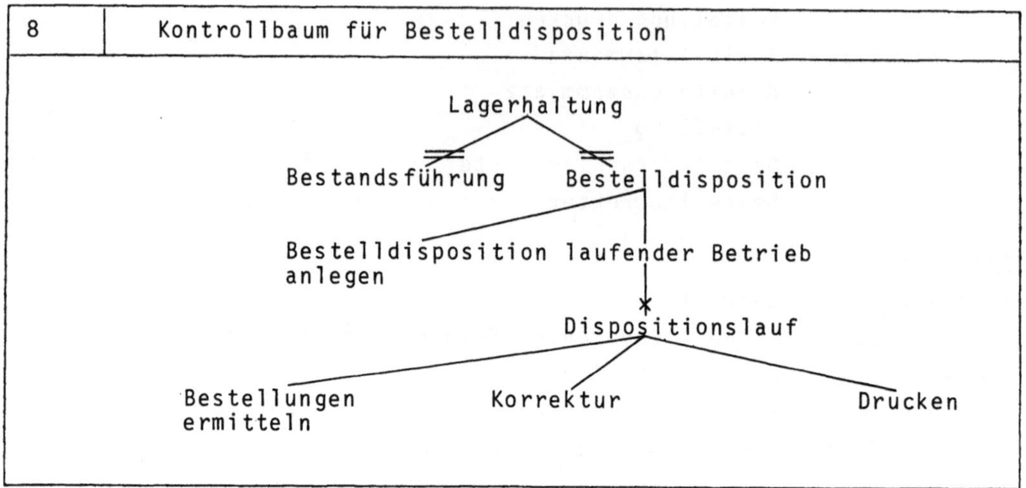

Bestelldisposition anlegen heißt, bezogen auf die Bestelldisposition den Initialzustand aller Dateien zu schaffen.

- Moduldefinition

Eingabe:	Artikelstammsätze Kreditorenstammsätze
Ausgabe:	Bestellungen Artikelstammsätze
Aufgabe:	Maschinelle Bestellvorschläge, manuelle Korrektur, maschinelle Bestellschreibung und Fortschreibung der Bestellbestände

In den nächsten Entwurfsabschnitten wird der nun vorliegende Entwurf verfeinert und ggfs. umgestaltet.

3.4. Bewertung

Die Strukturierungsstärke der vorgeschlagenen Entwurfsmethode bleibt weit hinter dem wünschenswerten Grad der Formalisierung zurück. Dies hängt nicht nur mit der hier sehr gerafften Darstellung der Methode zusammen. Vielmehr bestimmt auch unter Anwendung aller Regeln des Verfahrens die Fähigkeit des Entwerfers die Qualität. Daß hier trotzdem eine neue Methode vorgestellt wurde, ist wie folgt zu begründen:

Die Methode vereint die wichtigsten Hilfen der bekannten Entwurfsverfahren in einem geschlossenen Ansatz. Die Erprobung des mehrdimensional abgestuften Entwurfs an praktischen Problemstellungen brachte im Vergleich zu den eingangs erwähnten Entwurfsverfahren durchweg zufriedenstellende Ergebnisse.

Folgende Faktoren sind dafür verantwortlich:

. Die von Entwurfsschritt zu Entwurfsschritt variierende Sichtweise (Mehrdimensionalität) stellt immmer andere Aspekte in den Vordergrund. Wie die Erprobung zeigt und auch im Beispiel aus Punkt 3.3. sichtbar wurde, kommen dadurch immer wieder zusätzlich Komponenten und Beziehungen zum Vorschein, die in der eindimensionalen Betrachtung der meisten bekannten Verfahren u.U. nicht sichtbar werden.

. Die Entwicklung von einer äußerst einfachen Darstellung (Komponentenliste) zu einer schließlich umfassenden Beschreibung (Kontrollbaum und Moduldefinition) geschieht durch stufenweises Hinzunehmen neuer Beziehungen und ist dadurch pro Schritt einfach durchzuführen.

. Das Kontrollkonstrukt Nebenläufigkeit, das nur in wenigen Entwurfsmethoden zugelassen ist, gestattet Mehr-Prozessor-Systeme zu entwerfen. Dies sind alle Informationssysteme, an denen Menschen und Maschinen beteiligt sind [s. dazu Griese und Mühlbacher].

. Die Entwurfsmethode beschränkt sich nicht auf die maschinelle Informationsverarbeitung, sondern bezieht auch die menschliche ein. Dadurch werden Informationssysteme nicht mit Programmen, sondern mit betrieblichen Organisationen gleichgesetzt.

. Zerlegungsschemata wie das der Anfangs-, Einzel- und Endeverarbeitung helfen, alle Komponenten zu berücksichtigen.

. Die Methode ist vom Grobentwurf bis auf die Ebene der Programmstatements ohne Bruch in der Darstellung oder im Vorgehen verwendbar.

. Die Arbeitsweise wird vom Entwerfer nach einer gewissen Einübung als natürlich empfunden.

Literaturverzeichnis

AFIPS 72, AFIPS Conference Proceedings, Vol. 41, Montvale 1972.

Alford, M.W., Burns, F., R-Nets: A Graph Model for Real-Time Software Requirements, IEEE Transactions on Software Engineering 3 (1977) 1, S. 97-108.

Black, R.K.E., Effects of Modern Programming Practice on Software Development Costs, in: COMPCON '77, a.a.O., S. 250-253.

Central Computer Agency (Hrsg.), Evaluation of Programming and Systems Techniques. Implications of Using Modular Programming, Central Computer Agency, Civil Service Department, Her Majesty's Stationery Office, London 1973.

COMPCON '77, Fifteenth IEEE Computer Society International Conference, IEEE Catalogue No. 77CH1258-3C, Long Beach 1977.

Conway, R., Gries, D., An Introduction to Programming, Cambridge 1975 (2. Auflage).

Cooke, J.E., Bunt, R.B., Human Error in Programming: The Need to Study the Individual Programmer, INFOR 13 (1975) 3, S. 296-307.

Diebold Deutschland GmbH (Hrsg.), Einsatz softwaretechnologischer Methoden mit Normungseffekt, Frankfurt/Main 1976.

DIN 44300, Informationsverarbeitung Begriffe, Berlin und Köln 1972.

Dreßler, H., Hammelmann, I., Wilhelm, H.A., Entscheidungstabellen, München und Wien 1972.

Ehrich, H.-D., Algebraische Spezifikation von Datenstrukturen, in: Mühlbacher, J. (Hrsg.), a.a.O., S. 47-61.

Elshoff, J.L., A Numerical Profile of Commercial PL/I Programs, Software - Practice and Experience 6 (1976) 4, S. 505-525.

Erbesdobler, R., Heinemann, J., Mey, P., Entscheidungstabellentechnik, Berlin u.a. 1976.

Frank, H., Kybernetische Grundlagen der Pädagogik, Band 1: Allgemeine Kybernetik, Baden-Baden 1969 (2. Auflage).

Griese, J., Mühlbacher, J., Konstruktionsprinzipien und Problembereiche für Mensch-Maschine-Kommunikationssysteme, in: Noltemeier, H. (Hrsg.), a.a.O., S. 315-332.

Guttag, J.V., The Specification and Application to Programming of Abstract Data Types, Technical Report CSRG-59 der University of Toronto 1975.

Hamilton, M., Zeldin, S., Higher Order Software - A Methodology for Defining Software, IEEE Transactions on Software Engineering SE-2 (1976) 1, S. 9-32.

IBM (Hrsg.), HIPO - A Design Aid and Documentation Technique, IBM Form GC20-1851-0, White Plains 1974.

Jackson, M.A., Principles of Program Design, London e.a. 1975.

Liskov, B., Zilles, S., Programming with Abstract Data Types, SIGPLAN Notices 9 (1974) 4, S. 50-59.

Lockemann, P.C., Mayr, H.C., Rechnergestützte Informationssysteme, Berlin e.a. 1978.

Lundeberg, M., Information Analysis, ISAC-Report 1971.11.15-4401, The Royal Institute of Technology, Stockholm 1971.

Mühlbacher, J. (Hrsg.), Datenstrukturen, Graphen, Algorithmen, München und Wien 1978.

Noltemeier, H. (Hrsg.), Computergestützte Planungssysteme, Würzburg und Wien 1976.

Österle, H., Entwurf betrieblicher Informationssysteme, Habilitationsschrift, Dortmund 1980.

Peterson, J.L., Petri-Nets, Computing Surveys 9 (1977) 3, S. 223-252.

Petri, C.A., Kommunikation mit Automaten, Schriften des Rheinisch-Westfälischen Instituts für Instrumentelle Mathematik an der Universität Bonn, Heft 2, Bonn 1962.

Rose, C.W., LOGOS and the Software Engineer, in: AFIPS 27, a.a.O., S. 311-323.

Ross, D.T., Schoman, K.E., Structured Analysis for Requirements Definition, IEEE Transactions on Software Engineering 3 (1977) 1, S. 6-15.

Schmitz, P., Seibt, D., Einführung in die anwendungsorientierte Informatik, München 1975.

Schulz, A., Methoden des Softwareentwurfs und Strukturierte Programmierung, Berlin und New York 1978.

SofTech (Hrsg.), An Introduction to SADT. Structured Analysis and Design Technique, Bericht der SofTech, Inc., Waltham 1976.

Stevens, W.P., Myers, G.J., Constantine, L.L., Structured Design, IBM Systems Journal 13 (1974) 2, S. 115-139.

Strunz, H., Entscheidungstabellen und ihre Anwendung bei der Systemplanung, -implementierung und -dokumentation, Köln 1969.

Tracz, W.J., Computer Programming and the Human Thought Process, Software - Practice and Experience 9 (1979) 2, S. 127-137.

Weinberg, G.M., The Psychology of Computer Programming, New York u.a. 1971.

Weltner, K., Informationstheorie und Erziehungswissenschaft, Quickborn 1970.

Yourdon, E., Constantine, L.L., Structured Design, Bericht der Yourdon, Inc., New York 1975.

Konstrukte zur Darstellung und Prüfung semantischer Regeln

Bernd Breutmann und Rosmarie Mauer
Siemens AG - ZT ZFE FL INF
Otto-Hahn-Ring 6
8000 München 83

1. Einleitung

Eine wesentliche Aufgabe einer Datenbank besteht darin, einen Informationsbereich (das ist eine Sammlung von Informationen aus einem abgegrenzten Teil der realen Welt) zu repräsentieren. Um diese Aufgabe zu erfüllen, muß sichergestellt werden, daß die in der Datenbank dargestellten Informationen bezüglich ihrer Struktur und ihrer Beziehungen untereinander den semantischen Regeln gehorchen, die den Informationsbereich festlegen. Dazu sind folgende Teilaufgaben zu lösen:

1. Während des Datenbankentwurfs sind alle den Informationsbereich definierenden semantischen Regeln zu formulieren.
2. Innerhalb des Datenbanksystems sind die beim Datenbankentwurf formulierten Regeln formal darzustellen.
3. Vom Datenbankmanagementsystem (kurz DBMS) ist zu prüfen, ob die gespeicherten Daten den dargestellten Regeln genügen.

Das Problem der semantischen Integrität besteht in der Lösung der Teilaufgaben 2 und 3.

Heute eingesetzte Datenbankmanagementsysteme behandeln diese beiden Aufgaben nur unzureichend. Üblicherweise sind Darstellung und Prüfung semantischer Regeln über ein Paket von Anwendungsprogrammen verstreut. Es fehlt eine einheitliche Methodologie zur Darstellung semantischer Regeln, so daß Prüfroutinen von den Anwendungsprogrammierern ad hoc konstruiert werden. Oft sind semantische Regeln impliziter Bestandteil eines Anwendungsprogramms, d.h., als solche nicht erkennbar. Diese Vorgehensweise bei der Darstellung semantischer Regeln bewirkt einen hohen Grad von Datenabhängigkeit. Sie verursacht Schwierigkeiten, wenn Anwendungsprogramme, die Datenstruktur oder das semantische Regelwerk geändert werden sollen. Die Prüfung des Datenbestands auf semantische Integrität erfolgt oft nur periodisch. Innerhalb der Zeitperioden kann die Datenbank falsche Daten enthalten. Eine solche Datenbank ist jedoch keine brauchbare Grundlage für Entscheidungen, die innerhalb einer Organisation mit Hilfe der Datenbank getroffen werden müssen.

Um das Problem der semantischen Integrität lösen zu können, ist es notwendig, die semantischen Regeln innerhalb des Datenbanksystems zentral mit Hilfe eines geeigneten Datenmodells darzustellen und jeweils bei Änderungen eines Datenbankzustandes zu prüfen, ob die gespeicherten Daten den semantischen Regeln genügen. An ein Datenmodell zur Darstellung semantischer Regeln stellen wir folgende Anforderungen:

1. Alle semantischen Regeln müssen explizit und formal dargestellt werden. Diese Forderung impliziert unserer Meinung nach:
   - daß atomare Fakten, d.h. die kleinsten informationstragenden Einheiten eines Informationsbereichs, modelliert werden. Insbesondere vermeidet man dadurch Aggregationen (z.B. Tabellen), die Beziehungen zwischen atomaren Fakten implizit enthalten.
   - daß explizit unterschieden wird zwischen Objekten des Informationsbereichs und ihrer Identifikation in der Datenbank.
   - daß nicht nur statische Aspekte sondern auch das dynamische Verhalten eines Informationsbereichs dargestellt werden.
2. Bei der Darstellung semantischer Regeln muß abstrahiert werden von benutzerspezifischen Aspekten (z.B. Art der Aggregation von Information) und von effizienz-orientierten Aspekten (z.B. Zugriffsart, Darstellung von Daten im Speicher etc.)

In /8/ und /13/ wird gezeigt, daß das ursprüngliche Relationenmodell bzw. record-orientierte Datenmodelle nicht allen genannten Anforderungen genügen. Besser geeignet für die Darstellung semantischer Regeln sind sog. konzeptionelle Datenmodelle. Sie wurden entwickelt zur Darstellung der Typen von Informationen eines Informationsbereichs sowie der zwischen ihnen bestehenden Gesetzmäßigkeiten. Eine formale Darstellung dieser Art heißt konzeptionelles Schema. (Eine Übersicht und ein Vergleich konzeptioneller Datenmodelle findet sich in /1/.)

Dieses Papier befaßt sich mit solchen Konstrukten zur Darstellung semantischer Regeln, die bisher nur in wenigen Vorschlägen für konzeptionelle Datenmodelle behandelt werden. Sie basieren auf dem Object-Rollen-Modell von Falkenberg (/11/). Eine Typisierung semantischer Regeln und Vorschläge zu dieser Darstellung findet man in /3/. Nach einer kurzen Einführung in das Objekt-Rollen-Modell (Kap. 2.1.1) wird ein generalisiertes Identifikationskonzept vorgestellt (Kap.2.1.2).

Es erlaubt die explizite Unterscheidung von Objekten der realen Welt (z.B. Personen) und der Namen, die diese Objekte identifizieren (z.B. Personalnummer). Die Konstrukte zur Darstellung des dynamischen Verhaltens eines Informationsbereichs (Kap. 2.2) basieren auf dem Begriff des atomaren Ereignisses (Kap. 2.2.1). Zur Darstellung von Abhängigkeiten zwischen atomaren Ereignissen dient der Ereignisgraph (Kap. 2.2.2). Um semantische Regeln darstellen zu können, die sich explizit auf die Zeitdimension beziehen, wird eine Methode zur Definition anwendungsspezifischer Kalendersysteme vorgestellt (Kap. 2.2.3), die es erlaubt, "Zeit" implementierungsunabhängig zu modellieren. Kap. 3 enthält ein Verfahren zur Aufrechterhaltung semantischer Integrität. Es basiert auf dem Begriff des Ereignisgraphen und erlaubt die interaktive Konstruktion von Datenbanktransaktionen. Verwendungsmöglichkeiten für konzeptionelle Schemata sowie weiterführende Überlegungen zu den beschriebenen Konstrukten werden in Kap. 4 skizziert.
Die in diesem Papier beschriebenen Konstrukte und Verfahren sind Bestandteil der Sprachen CSL (Conceptual Schema Language) und CML (Conceptual Manipulation Language), deren Syntax und Semantik in /5/ beschrieben ist. Beide Sprachen werden zur Zeit implementiert.

2. Konstrukte zur Darstellung semantischer Regeln

Die Konstrukte des Objekt-Rollen-Modells werden erweitert um ein generalisiertes Identifikationskonzept und um Konstrukte zur Darstellung des dynamischen Verhaltens eines Informationsbereichs. Der dabei vorgestellte Ereignisgraph und die Objekt-Rollen-Struktur sind Bestandteil des konzeptionellen Schemas. Die Objekt-Rollen-Struktur repräsentiert gültige Datenbankzustände. Der Ereignisgraph repräsentiert erlaubte Zustandsübergänge (sog. Datenbanktransaktionen).

2.1 Darstellung statischer Aspekte

2.1.1 Das Objekt-Rollen-Modell

Das Objekt-Rollen-Modell (/11/) ist eine Methode zur Darstellung der atomaren Fakten eines Informationsbereichs. Grundkonzepte sind Objekte, Rollen und Assoziationen. Objekte sind atomare, wohlunterscheidbare Elemente des Informationsbereichs. Assoziationen sind Darstellungen von atomaren Fakten. Sie geben an, welche Objekte miteinander in Beziehung stehen und welche Rollen sie dabei spielen (siehe Fig. 1).

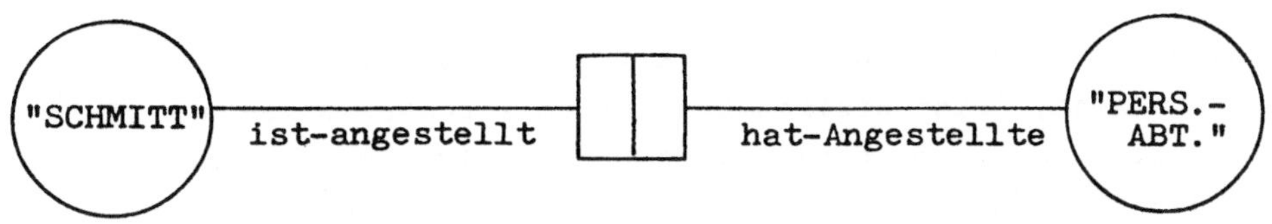

Fig. 1: Assoziation zur Darstellung des Faktums:
"Schmitt ist in der Personalabteilung angestellt".

Objekte, die gewisse Eigenschaften gemeinsam haben, werden zu Objekttypen zusammengefaßt. (Z.B. lassen sich Objekte, die die Rolle "ist angestellt" spielen, zum Objekttyp PERSON zusammenfassen; siehe Fig. 2.) Ein Assoziationstyp ist definiert durch die Typen der assoziierten Objekte und die Rollen, die diese Objekte in Assoziationen dieses Typs spielen. Die Menge der zu einem beliebigen, aber festen Zeitpunkt t in der Datenbank existierenden Objekte bzw. Assoziationen eines Typs heißt Population dieses Typs zum Zeitpunkt t. Fig. 2 zeigt die Darstellung eines Informationsbereichs mit Hilfe einer Objekt-Rollen-Struktur.

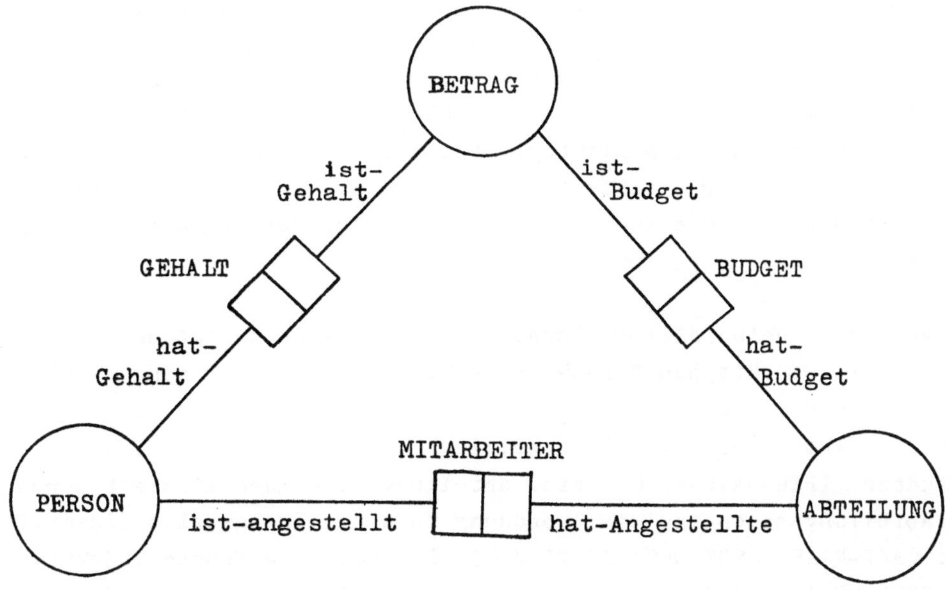

Fig. 2: Ein Beispielinformationsbereich

2.1.2 Objekte, Namen und Identifikatoren

In nahezu jedem Informationsbereich gibt es Objekte, die nicht die Eigenschaft haben, Zeichenfolgen über einem Alphabet zu sein (z.B. Personen, Abteilungen, Städte). Diese Objekte (wir nennen sie "non-string"-Objekte) können in einer Datenbank nicht direkt, sondern nur mit Hilfe von Namen ("string"-Objekte) gespeichert und identifiziert werden. In der Praxis ist die Beziehung zwischen einem "non-string"-Objekt und seinem Namen nicht immer eindeutig. So kann ein "non-string"-Objekt durch mehrere Namen identifiziert werden - und zwar gemeinsam (z.B. Vor- und Nachname einer Person) oder alternativ (z.B. Personal- oder Sozialversicherungsnummer einer Person) - oder ein Name dient zur Identifikation mehrerer "non-string"-Objekte (z.B. kann "Herrmann" Vorname der einen und Nachname einer anderen Person sein). Darüberhinaus kann sich die Identifikation eines Objekts im Laufe der Zeit ändern (z.B. wenn eine Person heiratet).

Das folgende Identifikationskonzept erlaubt es, auch komplexe Identifikationsstrukturen im konzeptionellen Schema explizit darzustellen:

1. Es wird zwischen "string"-Objekten und "non-string"-Objekten unterschieden. Dies geschieht durch eine Klassifizierung der Objekttypen: Selbstidentifizierte Objekttypen enthalten ausschließlich "string"-Objekte (z.B. Personalnummer). Nichtselbstidentifizierte Objekttypen enthalten ausschließlich "non-string"-Objekte.
2. Die Identifikationsstrukturen von "non-string"-Objekten werden dargestellt durch Assoziationen zwischen "non-string" Objekten und ihren Namen: Zu jedem nichtselbstidentifizierten Objekttyp O wird ein Identifikator definiert. Er besteht aus der Menge von Assoziationstypen, die die Identifikationsstruktur der Objekte in O repräsentiert.

Ein Anwendungsbeispiel für dieses Identifikationskonzept enthält Fig. 3: Die Objekttypen PERSON und ABTEILUNG in Fig. 2 sind nichtselbstidentifizierend. Folgende Identifikationsstrukturen seien vorausgesetzt: Eine Person wird identifiziert durch ihre Personalnummer (Identifikator: {PERSONAL-NR}). Eine Abteilung wird identifiziert durch den Abteilungsnamen und die Zuordnung zu einer Zweigstelle (Identifikator: {ABT-NAME-ASSOZ,ORGANISATION}). Der neu eingeführte Objekttyp ZWEIGSTELLE ist wiederum nicht selbstidentifizierend. Es werde identifiziert durch den Zweigstellennamen (Identifikator: {ZWEIGST-NAME-ASSOZ}).

Bemerkungen:

1. Eine ausführliche Beschreibung dieses Konzepts und eine formale Definition des Identifikators findet man in /3/. Ein ähnliches Identifikationskonzept enthält /2/.

2. Das Identifikationskonzept erleichtert die Änderung von Namenskonventionen. Bei einer Frage nach "non-string"-Objekten in einem Anwendungsprogramm muß der Identifikator nicht explizit angesprochen werden. Er kann vom DBMS implizit erstellt werden. Fragen dieser Art müssen nicht neu programmiert werden, wenn sich die Identifikationskonventionen ändern.

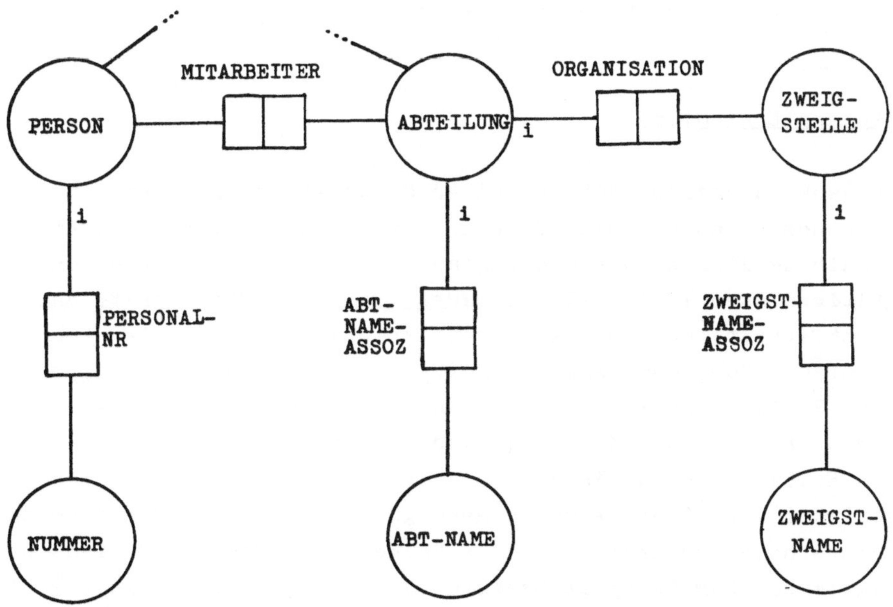

Fig. 3: Identifikation von Objekttypen aus Fig. 2

2.2 Darstellung dynamischer Aspekte

Normalerweise ist ein Informationsbereich durch die Objekt-Rollen-Struktur allein nicht ausreichend definiert. Zum Informationsbereich aus Fig. 2 existieren beispielsweise eine Reihe weiterer semantischer Regeln, die in Fig. 4 aufgelistet sind. Sie sind mit den bisher vorgestellten Konstrukten nicht formulierbar. Um sie darstellen zu können, werden in den folgenden Kapiteln Konstrukte zur Modellierung von Ereignissen, von Ereignisabhängigkeiten und von Kalendersystemen vorgestellt.

(R1) Jeder Angestellte hat ein Gehalt.

(R2) Jede Person, die ein Gehalt verdient, ist in einer Abteilung angestellt.

(R3) Jede Abteilung hat ein Budget.

(R4) Das Budget der Abteilung ist größer als die Summe der Gehälter der Mitarbeiter der Abteilung.

(R5) Gehälter dürfen nicht größer als 10 000 DM sein.

(R6) Wenn eine Person die Abteilung wechselt, darf sich das Gehalt nicht innerhalb der nächsten 6 Monate ändern.

Fig. 4: Zusätzliche semantische Regeln für den Beispielinformationsbereich (siehe Fig. 2)

2.2.1 Atomare Ereignisse

Ein Datenbankzustand besteht aus einer Menge atomarer Fakten (Assoziationen). Einen Datenbankzustand ändern heißt Ändern von atomaren Fakten. Deshalb bezeichnen wir den Beginn, das Ende und die Änderung einer gültigen Assoziation als atomares Ereignis. Der Begriff "atomar" ist gerechtfertigt, weil ein atomares Ereignis sich auf die atomaren Fakten bezieht. Zu jedem Assoziationstyp unterscheiden wir 3 Ereignistypen: Den Beginn, das Ende und die Änderung von Assoziationen dieses Typs. Wir betrachten die Änderung einer Assoziation als atomar und nicht als Kombination von Ende einer Assoziation und Beginn einer anderen Assoziation, weil ein Änderungsereignis oft einen anderen semantischen Sachverhalt beschreibt als die Folge eines Ende- und eines Beginnereignisses. Zum Beispiel bedeutet die Änderung einer Assoziation des Typs MITARBEITER (siehe Fig. 2) für eine Person etwas grundsätzlich anderes als die Aufeinanderfolge von Ende und Beginn von Assoziationen desselben Typs. Das erste Ereignis bezeichnet eine Versetzung, das zweite und dritte, daß ein Beschäftigungsverhältnis zunächst beendet und dann wieder begonnen wurde.

2.2.2 Abhängigkeiten zwischen Ereignissen

Ereignisse treten in einem Informationsbereich meistens nicht isoliert auf. In Fig. 4 impliziert ein Ereignis des Typs "BEGINN MITARBEITER" ein Ereignis des Typs "BEGINN GEHALT" (Regel R1). Um Ereignisabhängigkeiten explizit darstellen zu können, führen wir den Begriff eines

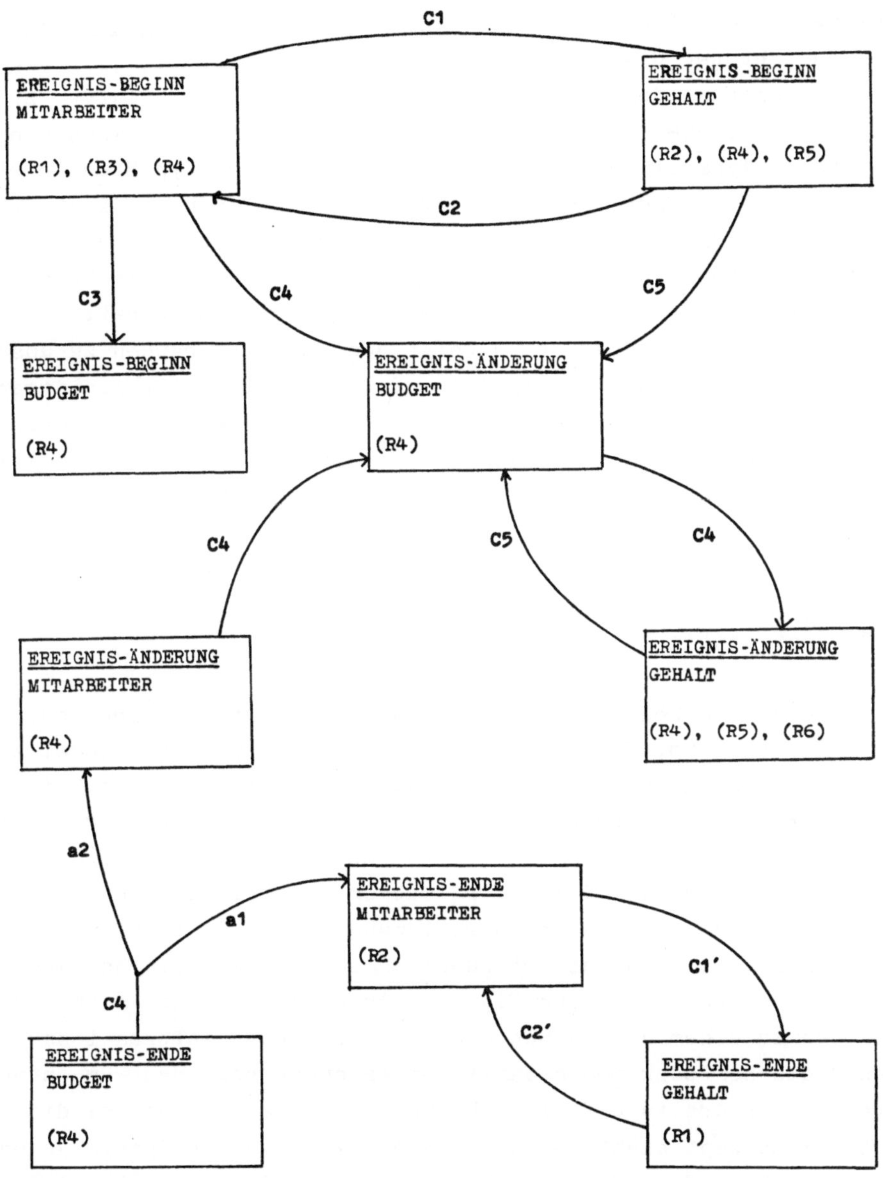

BEDINGUNGEN:
C1: Person hat kein Gehalt(Regel R1)
C2: Person ist nicht in einer Abteilung angestellt(Regel R2)
C3: Abteilung hat kein Budget(Regel R3)
C4: Budget der Abteilung < Summe der Gehälter ihrer Mitarbeiter (Regel R4)
C5: Budget der Abt. der Person < Summe der Gehälter ihrer Mitarbeiter(R4)
C1': Person hat ein Gehalt (Regel R2)
C2': Person ist in einer Abteilung angestellt(Regel R1)
ALTERNATIVEN:
a1: Mitarbeiter müssen entlassen werden
a2: Mitarbeiter müssen versetzt werden

Fig.5:Ereignisgraph für den Beispielinformationsbereich(Fig.2, Fig.4)

Ereignistypgraphen (Abkürzung: Ereignisgraph) ein. Ein Ereignisgraph ist ein gerichteter Graph. Zu jedem Ereignistyp enthält der Ereignisgraph einen Knoten, der bezeichnet wird durch den Ereignistyp. Er enthält die semantischen Regeln, die geprüft werden müssen, wenn ein Ereignis dieses Typs eintritt. Falls ein Ereignis vom Typ N unter einer Bedingung C das Auftreten eines Ereignisses vom Typ N′ bedingt, enthält der Ereignisgraph eine gerichtete Kante von N zu N′, die mit C markiert ist. (Neben Ereignisknoten kann ein Ereignisgraph Schaltknoten enthalten, an denen eine Kante verzweigt, wenn alternative Folgeereignisse möglich sind.) Fig. 5 zeigt den Ereignisgraphen zu unserem Beispielinformationsbereich (Fig. 2, Fig. 4). Ein Ereignisgraph repräsentiert Datenbanktransaktionen. Ein und dasselbe atomare Ereignis kann, bezogen auf den Ereignisgraphen zu verschiedenen Transaktionen führen - je nach dem auf welchen Datenbankzustand das Ereignis trifft.

2.2.3 Konzeptionelle Zeit

Semantische Regeln können sich direkt auf die Zeitdimension beziehen (siehe z.B. Regel R6, Fig. 4). Um solche Regeln im konzeptionellen Schema ausdrücken zu können, ist es notwendig, Begriffe wie Zeitpunkt und Zeitintervall einzuführen. Bisherige Ansätze in dieser Richtung (/6/, /7/, /10/) leiten diese Begriffe implizit aus dem Gregorianischen Kalendersystem ab. Diese Implikation entspricht nicht den Anforderungen aller denkbaren Informationsbereiche. In Simulationssystemen kann es zum Beispiel erforderlich sein, die Zeitachse anders als üblich einzuteilen (siehe Fig. 6). Andererseits kann sich ein in Israel oder in einem arabischen Land installiertes Informationssystem auf den jüdischen oder mohamedanischen Kalender beziehen. Um Anforderungen dieser Art zu erfüllen, bieten wir eine Methode an, die es erlaubt, im konzeptionellen Schema unabhängig von der Systemuhr oder einem festen Kalendersystem ein anwendungsspezifisches Kalendersystem zu definieren (/3/, /4/). Die Methode basiert auf der Annahme, daß ein Kalendersystem aus einer beliebig tiefen Hierarchie von Zeitsegmenttypen besteht. Ein Zeitsegmenttyp ist eine Zeiteinheit, die benutzt wird, um die Zeitachse zu segmentieren (z.B. Tage, Monate, Dekaden). Jeder Zeitsegmenttyp besteht aus Zeitsegmenten (z.B. ist Januar ein Zeitsegment vom Typ Monat). Für jedes Zeitsegment T, das zu einer Stufe i innerhalb der Hierarchie gehört, muß spezifiziert werden, mit welchen Zeitsegmenten der Stufe i-1 T beginnt und endet (siehe Fig. 6). Schließlich müssen die Zeitsegmente, die zur Spitze der Hierarchie gehören, sich auf einen Punkt auf der Zeitachse beziehen. Dieser Punkt markiert den Nullpunkt in der anwendungsspezifischen Zeitrechnung. Basierend auf der Definition eines Kalendersystems wird ein Zeitpunkt definiert als Tupel von verschiedenen Zeitsegmenten. (25, 2, 1, 5) bezeichnet zum Beispiel den 25. Tag des zweiten Monats im ersten Jahr der Dekade 5, bezogen auf das Kalendersystem in Fig. 6. Ein Zeitintervall wird dargestellt durch ein Paar von Zeitpunkten.

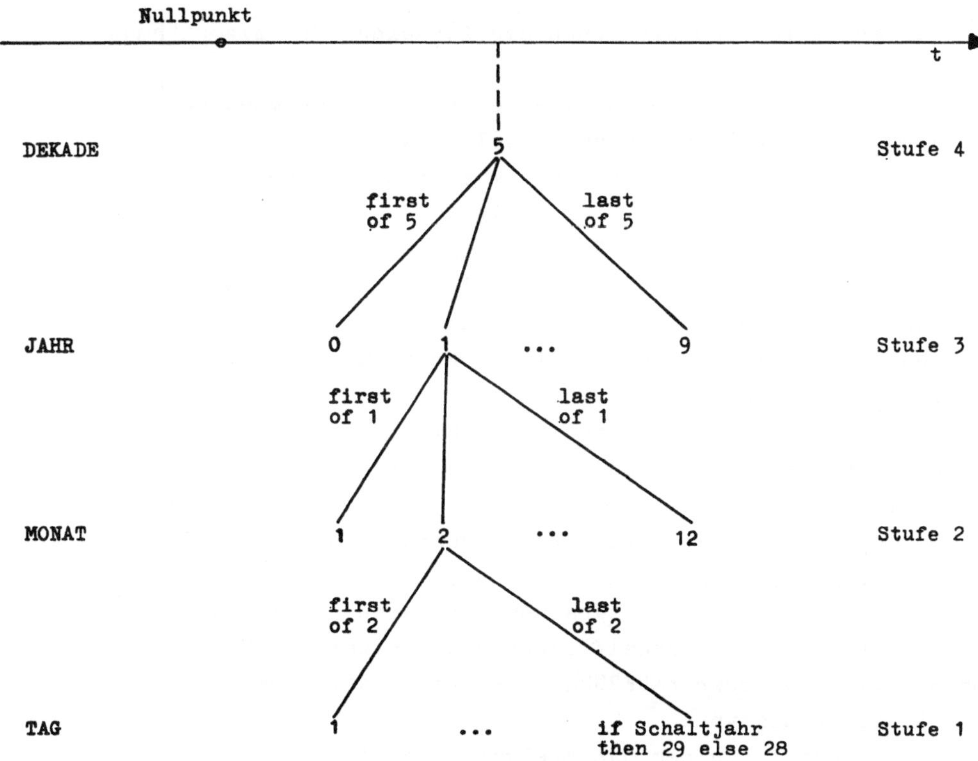

Fig. 6: Ausschnitt aus einem anwendungsspezifischen Kalendersystem

3. Aufrechterhaltung der semantischen Integrität

Im wesentlichen sind drei Teilprobleme zu lösen, um die semantische Integrität der in einer Datenbank gespeicherten Information zu gewährleisten (/12/, /9/, /17/):

(P1) Es sind Folgen von Update-Anweisungen zu konstruieren, um eine Datenbank von einem konsistenten Zustand in einen konsistenten Folgezustand zu überführen (d.h. es ist eine konzeptionelle Transaktion im Sinne von /17/ zu konstruieren; unter einer Update-Anweisung verstehen wir eine Anweisung, die ein atomares Ereignis eingibt).

(P2) Den Update-Anweisungen sind diejenigen semantischen Regeln zuzuordnen, die geprüft werden müssen, wenn das entsprechende atomare Ereignis eintrifft.

(P3) Um den Benutzer gegebenfalls umfassend über die Verletzung einer semantischen Regel informieren zu können, müssen Fehlersituationen frühzeitig erkannt werden.

3.1 Der Ereignisgraph als Grundlage für einen Prüfalgorithmus

Zwei Eigenschaften des Ereignisgraphen sind im Zusammenhang mit der Entwicklung eines Prüfverfahrens von Interesse:

1. Die semantischen Regeln sind im Ereignisgraphen nach Ereignissen strukturiert: Zu jedem Ereignis E existiert ein Knoten, der die von E verletzbaren Regeln enthält.
2. Der Ereignisgraph repräsentiert Transaktionen: Zu jedem Ereignis E wird (durch markierte, gerichtete, von E wegführende Kanten) spezifiziert, unter welcher Bedingung welches Folgeereignis einzutreten hat.

Aufgrund der ersten Eigenschaft ist Problem P2 bereits zur Spezifikationszeit des konzeptionellen Schemas gelöst. Die zweite Eigenschaft erlaubt die Lösung von P1 derart, daß Transaktionen interaktiv vom Benutzer und DBMS konstruiert werden können. Dies geschieht mit Hilfe sog. Ereignisprozeduren (siehe /3/, /4/):
Zu jedem Knoten E im Ereignisgraphen wird eine Ereignisprozedur definiert. Der Prozedurkopf spezifiziert den Ereignistyp E, d.h.,

- ob BEGINN, ENDE oder ÄNDERUNG einer Assoziation vorliegt
- den Assoziationstyp A
- den Zeitpunkt T, zu dem das Ereignis eintritt.

Formale Parameter sind die bezüglich A assoziierten Objekte und der Zeitpunkt T. Im Prozedurrumpf werden diejenigen semantischen Regeln formuliert, die von Ereignissen des Typs E verletzt werden können. Eine vom Knoten E zu einem Knoten E´ führende Kante K wird im Rumpf der Prozedur E durch einen bedingten Aufruf der Prozedur E´ dargestellt. Die Bedingung entspricht der Markierung der Kante K. Fig. 7 zeigt ein Beispiel für eine Ereignisprozedur. Der Aufruf der Prozedur EVENT-BEGIN MITARBEITER im Rumpf der Prozedur EVENT-BEGIN GEHALT (Fig. 7) ist nicht vollständig spezifiziert: ´?´ bezeichnet einen fehlenden Parameter. In diesem Fall wird der Bildschirmbenutzer aufgefordert, den fehlenden Parameter einzugeben (bzw. wird - bei Stapelbetrieb - in der Transaktion nach dem entsprechenden, vollständig spezifizierten Ereignis gesucht). Falls der Benutzer (bzw. das Anwendungsprogramm) die Forderung des DBMS erfüllt, wird ´?´ durch den aktuellen Parameter ersetzt und der Prozeduraufruf wird ausgeführt.

```
EVENT-BEGIN GEHALT
    WITH PERSON X, BETRAG Y
    AT T

BEGIN
    * R5 * Y ≤ 10 000;
    * R2 * IF X NOT OBJECT-IN MITARBEITER
           THEN CALL EVENT-BEGIN MITARBEITER
                     WITH PERSON X, ABTEILUNG ?
                     AT T;
    * R4:  Budget der Abteilung der Person größer als Summe
           der Gehälter ihrer Mitarbeiter *
                     ⋮
END;
```

Fig. 7: Skizze der Ereignisprozedur zum Ereignistyp "BEGINN GEHALT"

3.2 Integritätsprüfung

Die im konzeptionellen Schema festgelegten Regeln können nur dann verletzt werden, wenn ein Datenbankzustand durch das Eintreffen von Ereignissen verändert wird. Es sei $F = (E_1,\ldots,E_m)$, $m \geq 1$, eine Folge von atomaren Ereignissen, die vom Benutzer oder Anwendungsprogramm durch eine von TRANSBEGIN und TRANSEND geklammerte Folge von Update-Anweisungen der DBMS bekannt gemacht wird. F ist eine möglicherweise unvollständige Transaktion. Unter Verwendung der Ereignisprozeduren wird wie folgt geprüft, ob F eine zulässige Transaktion ist:

1. Es wird geprüft, ob $E_1,\ldots E_m$ gültige Ereignisse darstellen, d.h., ob
   - die aktuellen Objekte der Objekttypdefinition genügen
   - "non-string"-Objekte richtig identifiziert sind
   - die Rollennamen, Objektypnamen und Assoziationstypnamen den Festlegungen des konzeptionellen Schemas entsprechen.

   Diese Prüfung bezieht sich nur auf das konzeptionelle Schema und nicht auf den aktuellen Zustand der Datenbank.

2. Falls F die Prüfungen von Schritt 1 besteht, werden die Ereignisse $E_1, \ldots E_m$ provisorisch ausgeführt. Schritt 3 wird damit auf einer vorläufig geänderten Datenbank ausgeführt.
3. Für jedes Ereignis in F wird die entsprechende Ereignisprozedur aufgerufen. Die im Prozedurrumpf spezifizierten Regeln werden der Reihe nach überprüft. Falls ein Folgeereignis verlangt wird, muß der Benutzer das verlangte Ereignis eingeben. Das Folgeereignis wird der Folge F angegliedert und die entsprechende Ereignisprozedur wird aufgerufen. Falls eine semantische Regel verletzt wird, bzw. wenn die Forderung nach einem Folgeereignis nicht erfüllt wird, wird die Prüfung abgebrochen, die Ereignisfolge F zurückgewiesen, und werden die provisorischen Änderungen in der Datenbank zurückgenommen.
4. Falls Schritt 3 nicht zum Abbruch führt, werden die provisorischen Änderungen (Schritt 2) als gültig betrachtet. In diesem Fall heißt F eine Transaktion.

4. Abschließende Bemerkungen

Nicht alle Fragen der Darstellung und Prüfung semantischer Regeln konnten in diesem Papier vollständig beantwortet werden. So ist zum Beispiel die Behandlung verzögert oder fehlerhaft eingegebener Ereignisse noch Gegenstand laufender Untersuchungen.
Die Verwendungsmöglichkeiten der vorgestellten Konstrukte zur Darstellung semantischer Regeln sind unter zwei Aspekten zu sehen:
Kurzfristig lassen sie sich einsetzen während des Datenbankentwurfs oder der Umstrukturierung von Datenstrukturen. Beim Entwurf von Datenbanken ist es zweckmäßig, zunächst die semantischen Regeln eines Informationsbereichs mit Hilfe eines konzeptionellen Schemas zu modellieren. Erst im zweiten Schritt sollte das konzeptionelle Schema durch Hinzufügen semantisch irrelevanter Aspekte (Aggregation, Zugriffspfade, Zuordnung semantischer Regeln zu Änderungsprogrammen) auf das zur Verfügung stehende Datenbanksystem transformiert werden. Beim Umstrukturieren einer Datenstruktur ist es sinnvoll, zunächst die bestehende, nichtkonzeptionelle Datenstruktur zu konzeptionalisieren, d.h. die semantisch relevanten Aspekte von den Aspekten zu trennen, die im Lauf der Entwicklung der Datenstruktur aus Effizienzgründen oder wegen spezifischer Eigenschaften des Datenmodells modelliert wurden (z.B. Doppelbelegung von Records, Auflösung von m:n - Beziehungen über Dummy-Records etc.). Im zweiten Schritt kann das konzeptionelle Schema in die beabsichtigte Datenstruktur transformiert werden.

Langfristig kann ein konzeptionelles Schema Bestandteil eines praktisch verwendeten DBMS sein, sei es als Benutzerschnittstelle oder als zentrale Schnittstelle innerhalb einer Drei-Schichten-Architektur (siehe z.B. /15/, /16/).
Die in diesem Papier vorgestellten Konzepte werden derzeit im Rahmen der Implementierung eines Modells der Drei-Schichten-Architektur realisiert. Die zentrale Schnittstelle, repräsentiert durch CSL- und CML-Programme (/3/, /5/), wird dabei auf eine interne relationale Schnittstelle (/14/) abgebildet. Ein Ziel der Implementierung ist es, aus der Sicht sowohl des Implementierers als auch des Benutzers Aussagen über die Verwendbarkeit der beschriebenen Konstrukte in der Praxis zu erhalten.

Anmerkung

Die Autoren danken den Herren Dr. Eckhard Falkenberg, Theodor Fink, Klaus Hahne und Johann Lemke, Siemens AG, für ihre Zusammenarbeit und hilfreiche Diskussionen beim Entwurf der Sprachen, deren Grundkonzepte in diesem Papier beschrieben sind.

Literatur

/1/ Biller H., Neuhold E.J., "Concepts for the Conceptual Schema" in Nijssen G.M. (ed.), Architecture and Models in Data Base Management Systems, North-Holland, Amsterdam, 1977

/2/ Biller H., Neuhold E.J., "Semantics of Data Bases: The Semantics of Data Models", Information Systems, Vol.3, No.1, 1978

/3/ Breutmann B., Falkenberg E., Mauer R., "CSL: A Language for Defining Conceptual Schemas", in: Bracchi G., Nijssen G.M. (eds), Data Base Architecture, North-Holland, Amsterdam, 1979

/4/ Breutmann B., "The Temporal Dimension of Conceptual Schemas", Working Paper, IFIP WG 2.6, Munich, March 1979

/5/ Breutmann B., Mauer R., "CSL and CML: Languages for Defining, Retrieving and Updating Conceptual Data, Part I: Overview, Part II: Specification of Syntax and Semantics", Siemens AG, Zentralbereich Technik, April 1980

/6/ Bubenko jr. J.A., "The Temporal Dimension in Information Modelling", in: Nijssen G.M. (ed), Architecture and Models in Data Base Management Systems, North-Holland, Amsterdam, 1977

/7/ Bubenko jr. J.A., "On the Role of ´Understandig Models´ in Conceptual Schema Design", Proc. 5th International Conference on Very Large Data Bases, Rio de Janeiro, Oct. 1979

/8/ Codd E.F., "Extending the Data Base Relational Model to Capture More Meaning", IBM-Report RJ 2472 (32359), IBM Research Lab., San Jose´, California, Jan. 1979

/9/ Eswaran K.P., Chamberlin D.D., "Functional Specifications of a Subsystem for Data Base Integrity", Proc. Int. Conf. on VLDB, Framingham, Mass., Sept. 75

/10/ Falkenberg E., "Time Handling in Data Base Management Systems" University of Stuttgart, Report 07/1974, 1974

/11/ Falkenberg E., "Concepts for Modelling Information" in: Nijssen G.M. (ed.): Modelling in Data Base Management Systems, North-Holland, Amsterdam 1976

/12/ Hammer M.M., McLeod D.J., "Semantic Integrity in a Relational Data Base System" in: Kerr D.S., Joffeman K.L. (eds.), Data Base Management, IFIP 74, 1974

/13/ Kent W., "Limitations of record-oriented Information Models", Technical Report TR 03.028, IBM, Santa Teresa Lab., San Jose, California, May 1977

/14/ Navathe S.B., Lemke J., "Mapping in the Three Level DBMS Architexture: From a Conceptual Model to a Relational Internal Model", Central Research an Development Laboratory, Siemens AG, Munich 1979

/15/ Nijssen G.M., "A Gross Architecture for the Next Generation Data Base Management Systems", in: Nijssen G.M. (ed.), Modelling in Data Base Management Systems, North-Holland, Amsterdam 1976

/16/ Nijssen G.M., "On the Gross Architecture for the Next Generation Data Base Management Systems" in: Gilchrist B. (ed.), Information processing 77, North-Holland, Amsterdam 1977

/17/ Nijssen G.M., "Framework for Evaluating ANSI, CODASYL and other Data Base Approaches", Advanced Course on Data Management Systems, Milano, Course Notes, June 1978

DYNAMIC CONSISTENCY CONSTRAINTS IN THE CONCEPTUAL SCHEMA AND THEIR CONNECTIONS WITH THE EXTERNAL SCHEMA

Carl August Zehnder and Bertram Thurnherr
Institut für Informatik
Eidgenössische Technische Hochschule (ETH) Zürich

Abstract:

To include consistency constraints in a data base system we need special tools, languages to describe them and software to enforce them. In this paper a language concept (which extends the classical relational model) is presented for the logical design of a data base on the conceptual and the external schema level. The application of this concept has shown, that the use of its extensive consistency constraints can even improve the performance of a data base. However, in every case it improves the maintainability.

1. Where should Consistency Constraints be placed?

From a conceptual point of view it is obvious that consistency constraints in a data base environment (fig. 1) must be integrated in the data base system and not distributed over the application programs, for different reasons:

- Consistency can only be maintained if all entrances to the data base are protected always and by the entire set of valid rules.

- The maintenance of the set of consistency rules is easier if it is concentrated.

- The application programs can be simplified considerably.

Figure 1: The data base concept

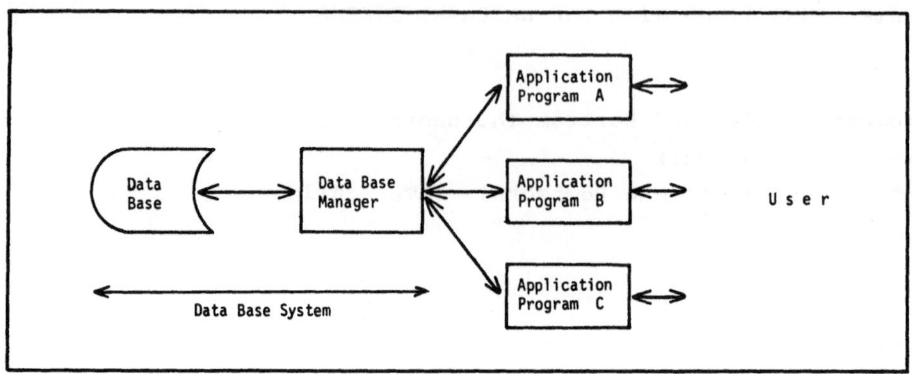

In practice, however, consistency constraints are not yet concentrated in the data base system very often. The main reasons are:

- Only for simple constraint types the corresponding protection features can be standardized and are available in present day data base systems (e.g. unique identification keys, some value range/-domain checks).

- Non-static consistency constraints (which often have to be represented by programs and not by data type declarations) are not always included in the "data" base.

- The use of consistency protecting routines for each data access is considered expensive.

- Analysts and programmers do not know about integrated consistency constraints.

In this paper we argue for a consequent integration of consistency constraints in a data base system. And, even more relevant from the point of view of a designer, the maximum amount of consistency rules shall be included in the classical data description, the schema, even some of the dynamic consistency constraints (e.g. dependencies from the actual content of the data base). Only the remaining constraints then have to be formulated as programs and included into the data base seperately. (Other data checks can still exist in application programs, e.g. for unusual but tolerable cases; they are not part of a closed and enforced data base consistency concept, however.)

This integration brings a lot of advantages, even more than those mentionned above. Applications of the concepts and languages presented in the next paragraphs have shown that a consequent integration of consistency constraints in the conceptual and external schemas, i.e. on a very high level, can even simplify and therefore improve the access mechanisms.

Many readers remember the discussions about programming languages some years ago. Should the programmer be separated from hardware and machine language features by high-level, PASCAL-type languages? Shall the freedom of the programmer be limited? And how about efficiency? - But history has proven, that efficiency can be maintained, even improved, since only logical cleanness provides easily maintainable programs over years.

But this comparison with programming languages indicates also that an adequate language is a prerequisite for the integration of consistency anywhere, here in the data description language (DDL). Such a language shall be presented shortly to give an impression of its features for the conceptual and the external schema [ANSI/SPARC 75]. The internal schema is of minor importance in this conceptual discussion, but an implementation of these concepts includes the internal part as well [MARTI/REBSAMEN/THURNHERR 80].

2. The Conceptual Schema in the Extended Relational Model

For the design of a data base, i.e. for the formulation of the global logical data structure, we use the extended relational model [THURNHERR/ZEHNDER 79]. Therefore a brief introduction of the extended relational model will be given with respect to its effects on the conceptual schema rather than discussing all its concepts at length.

The designer of a data base, i.e. of its logical data structure, has to group the objects of the real world (entities) which are of interest to the applications into a finite number of classes called entity sets (ES). This representation of a part of the real world is by no means unique, however.

The analysis of a simple example which will be used throughout this paper results in the following data structure, presented in a graphical form (block diagram):

Figure 2: Block diagram for a production plan data base

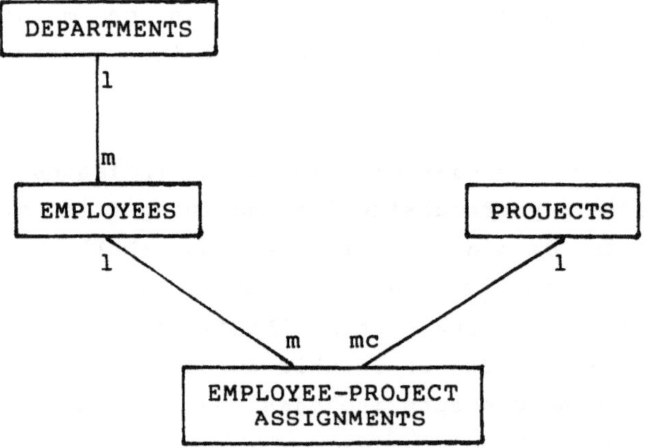

In this chart, boxes represent entity sets and lines are the connections between those entity sets.

Each connection between two entity sets (ES) is based on two directed associations. The association (ES1,ES2) indicates the number of potential entities in ES2 which can be associated with one entity in ES1. For the data base design it is important to distinguish between four types of associations (figure 3).

Figure 3: Association types

association (ES1,ES2)	number of entities of ES2 which are associated to a single entity of ES1
1: (simple association)	one and only one
c: (conditional association)	either Ø or 1 (c = Ø/1)
m: (multiple association)	at least 1 (m >= 1)
mc: (conditional-multiple ass.)	either Ø or more (mc >= Ø)

Together with the inverse associations (ES2,ES1), 16 types of connections are possible between two entity sets. These connections are also referred to as relationships (cf. [THURNHERR/ZEHNDER 79]).

The entity sets themselves can easily be represented by the relations of Codd's relational model (cf. [CODD 7Ø]) so that the tuples correspond to entities. In the relational data model, attibutes must not be structured (i.e. must be scalars) and redundancies threatening the data consistency must be removed. As a result, m-m-relationships must be described explicitly in a new relation and two entity sets cannot be represented in the same relation, if there is a 1-m- or a 1-mc-relationship between them (see figure 2).

Unfortunately, the classical relational model lacks some global concepts: The normalization process removes only redundancies due to local considerations (transitive dependence) within one relation. The extended relational model incorporates therefore global concepts between all relations of a data base to formulate existing connections between the corresponding entity sets in order to assure data consistency. As in Codd's model, these connections are expressed using common attributes in the related relations, but in the extended relational model these connections must be explicitly declared on the conceptual level.

Figure 4 shows the association of relations using common attributes. Since there is an m-m-relationship between the entity sets EMPLOYEES and PROJECTS, an additional entity set describing the association has to be introduced.

Figure 4: Association of relations using common attributes

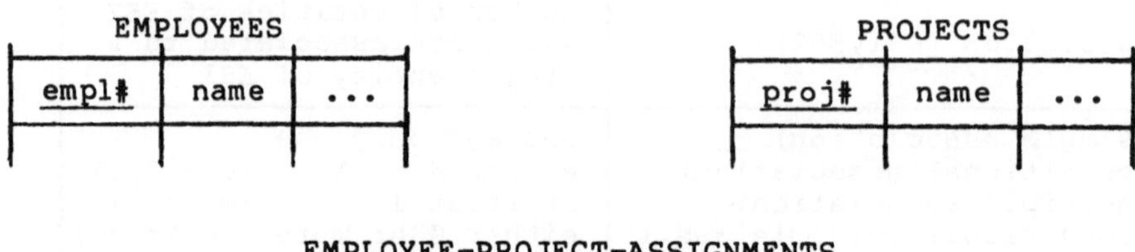

A tuple of the relation EMPLOYEE-PROJECT-ASSIGNMENTS with a given attribute combination (empl#,proj#) is only meaningful and allowed, if there are both an employee with number empl# and a project with number proj#.

Attribute values are selected from well defined domains. For the above reason, two types of domains have to be distinguished:

- A static domain is a set of (scalar) values, known at the time of definition of the data base and invariant over time.
- A dynamic domain is a set of values or value combinations, which are used as identification key values in one specific, the defining relation. (Each value or value combination of a dynamic domain corresponds to exactly one tuple in the defining relation.)

A dynamic domain defined over an identification key of a relation contains exactly as many members as the corresponding relation has tuples at any time. This concept is used to express connections between relations in the extended relational model:

A relation R2 is based on a relation R1 if and only if R2 uses a dynamic domain generated by an identification key of R1.

Now all relationships between entity sets can be specified explicitly in the schema of a relational-type DBMS, and as a result it is possible to check data consistency. In our example of figure 2, the identification key empl# in EMPLOYEES generates a dynamic domain from which the attribute empl# of relation EMPLOYEE-PROJECT-ASSIGNMENTS takes its values.
The above definition allows only hierarchical relationships, i.e. relationships where at least one of the associations is of type 1 (1-1, 1-c, 1-m, 1-mc), between two entity sets using dynamic domains. On the conceptual level, all other relationships (namely c-c, c-m, c-mc, m-m, m-mc, mc-mc) must be handled by introducing explicitly a new relation based on both of the two related relations. This concept is an extension to the classical relational model where only network-type relationships (m-m, m-mc, mc-mc) are described that way (cf. [CODD 70] and [THURNHERR/ZEHNDER 79]).

Therefore, the attributes of the relations in the conceptual schema can have either a global or a local significance, depending on whether they are used to describe not only the properties of an entity but also to describe relationships:

- An attribute is called global, if it is a key attribute in at least one relation of the data base.

- An attribute is called local, if it occurs in only one relation and is not a key attribute.

Attributes which are neither global nor local are possible in the relational model, but are prohibited in our extended relational model. Such attributes could occur if a property of an entity is described in two different relations (overlapping entity sets).

Both the concept of the dynamic domain and the distinction between global and local attributes now can be used as a tool to formulate strict consistency constraints. In [THURNHERR 80], rules for the formulation of such constraints are described in some detail. Here, we present only the most important steps in the design process.

1. The entity sets which shall be described in a data base and their

relationships are drawn as block diagram.

2. Overlapping entity sets have to be found and represented by an additional comprehensive entity set.

3. Now normalization takes place (third normal form, only 1-... relationships).

4. All attributes have to be separated: local or global.

5. Local attributes are defined over static domains. (The scope of local attributes is restricted to a single relation.)

6. Global attributes carry the relationships between the different entity sets. A global attribute is defined in exactly one relation over a static domain where it must be part of the identification key of that relation. Wherever else this global attribute occurs, it must be based on a dynamic domain built by other relations. (This base construction may not be circular.)

The idea behind such construction rules is to provide a tool for data base design. Using this methodology, a designer of a conceptual schema is able to develop his schema in a way similar to stepwise refinement in program design.

The practical construction of a conceptual schema using the above methods needs a language for conceptual schemas. Such a Conceptual Schema Language (CSL) with a MODULA-similar syntax is presented in [THURNHERR 80], an example is given below. The corresponding data base management system must provide the consistency checks.

Figure 5: Example of a conceptual schema:

```
define conceptual~schema mini~production~plan privacy~lock abcd

  static~domain int3 = 1..999;
                int5 = 1..99999;
                work = (concepts,production);
                nametype = char(3Ø);
                dat6 = Ø1Ø1Ø1..311299;

  global~attribute dept#: int3;    {department-number}
                   empl#,          {employee-number}
                   proj#: int5;    {project-number}

  relation DEPARTMENTS
    export dept~dom;
    attribute
      dept#;
      name:          nametype
    ident dept# define dept~dom
    unique name
  end DEPARTMENTS;

  relation EMPLOYEES
    import dept~dom;
    export empl~dom;
    attribute
      empl#;
      dept#:         all dept~dom;
      name:          nametype;
      birthdate:     dat6
    ident empl# define empl~dom
  end EMPLOYEES;

  relation PROJECTS
    export proj~dom;
    attribute
      proj#;
      name:          nametype;
    ident proj# define proj~dom
  end PROJECTS;

  relation PROJECT~EMPLOYEE~ASSIGNMENTS
    import empl~dom, proj~dom;
    attribute
      empl#:         all empl~dom;
      proj#:         some proj~dom;
      kind~of~work:  work
    ident (empl#,proj#)
  end PROJECT~EMPLOYEE~ASSIGNMENTS

end mini~production~plan.
```

3. External Views of the Data

Relational data base thinking traditionally starts with a set of tables - relations in first normal form - which describe a portion of the real world. These relations are usually split up into quite a number of smaller relations, free of redundancy, easy to update. This process is called normalization (cf. [CODD 70]). In the extended relational model, the number of relations is even larger, since we are forced to introduce new relations, e.g. to describe comprehensive entity sets in the case of overlapping entity sets and to handle non-hierarchical relationships between two entity sets (cf. [THURNHERR/ZEHNDER 79]). Therefore, a consistent data base is composed of numerous small component relations whose direct relationships determine a partially ordered data structure (figures 2, 5).
The user generally prefers to look at relations or tables in first or second normal form, since those relations are easy to read and provide an overview including relationships between different relations. As a result, it is desirable to join several conceptual relations into a (single) external relation. Since such external relations are not stored physically, the element of redundancy brought in by the join has no drawbacks at all.

We do not want to discuss the full set of relational algebra operators here; the rest of this section deals with only a few simple operations, able to provide the desired external view. In conjunction with such a transformation from conceptual to external schema, only the two operators natural join and projection are required for the construction of external relations.

An important aspect of the transformation is that in the case of the natural join additional restrictions are introduced: In the relational algebra, joins must only be based on attributes over the same (static) domain but nobody asks whether the result actually has some sort of meaning. This is the reason why the word "join" shall be omitted. Instead, the term composition (or "to compose") tries to capture the concept of "joining" conceptual relations together under stronger restrictions to form a larger unit.

Composition rule 1 (R1):

Two conceptual relations may be composed to build an external relation, if one relation is based on the other. The composition must be defined by a natural join over the (global) attributes of a dynamic domain exported in the base relation and imported in the other one.

This rule effectively prohibits "meaningless joins": only relationships inherent in the system as defined in the conceptual schema can be exploited for the composition. In a sense, the dynamic domains are not only the media for data consistency but also the guidelines for data base queries.

In order to illustrate the reasons for the second rule we assume a data structure which is only slightly more complex than that of our previous example: There is an additional relationship between the entity sets DEPARTMENTS and PROJECTS, expressing the responsability for a project by a certain department, for instance. This additional "direct" relationship leads to a cyclic data structure as shown in figure 6.

Figure 6: Cyclic data structure in the production plan data base

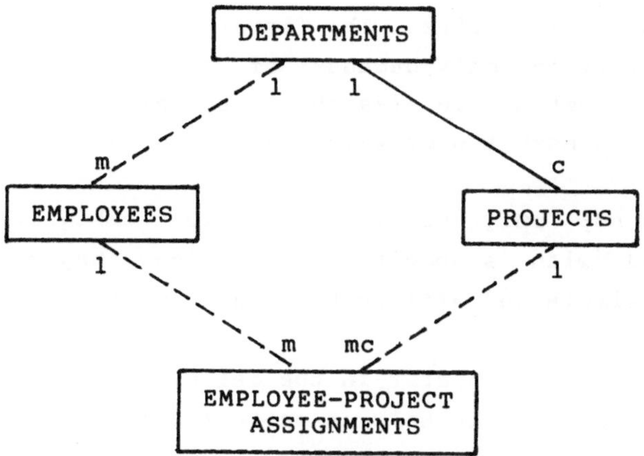

Obviously, the meaning of the direct relationship DEPARTMENTS-PROJECTS

differs considerably from the relationship expressed by the three other relationships indicated by the dashed connecting lines. If the user wishes to form an external relation comprising both elements of DEPARTMENTS and PROJECTS, three distinct possibilities arise from the cyclic data structure: either he wants to know which department has employees working on a project or he wants to know which department is responsible for a project. Finally, the display of both relationships may be desired. In the last case, each external tuple could contain two different conceptual tuples from the DEPARTMENTS relation. According to our policy, namely to revoke normalization, we rule such a possibility out.
As a result we demand that a sector of the conceptual schema to be composed to one external relation must have a tree structure, "growing up" from the lowest included conceptual relation (e.g. EMPLOYEE-PROJECT-ASSIGNMENT). This is formulated more precisely in composition rule 2.

Composition rule 2 (R2):
Defining an external relation, from each conceptual relation at most one dynamic domain may be used as a base for other relations.

For the construction of an external relation from conceptual relations following the above rules (R1) and (R2), the specification becomes quite simple: only a list of the participating conceptual relations and dynamic domains is required. The (imported) dynamic domains must be declared explicitly not only because of possible cycles in the graph of the data structure (as above) but also because there may exist more than one connection between two entity sets.

These two rules do not only serve to resolve ambiguities in the meaning associated with a specific composition, they also allow the implementation of simple and efficient access algorithms.

The use of the projection operator in the definition of an external relation is explained with the help of another composition rule.

Composition rule 3 (R3):
Building an external relation from conceptual relations, an arbitrary number of attributes may be omitted by projection, and

the number of tuples may be restricted by set operations on the (static) domains of local attributes.

The feature of restricting external domains to a subset of a corresponding conceptual domain provides a data protection tool: The user can only access data tuples whose attribute values lie within the domains defined in his external schema.

The following example demonstrates how the concepts discussed above can be formulated in an external schema language (ESL).

Example: Defining an external schema

```
define external~schema production~plan~table privacy~lock wxyz
   of conceptual~schema mini~production~plan privacy~key abcd

   static~domain short~name = char(2Ø);

   relation WHOLE~ENTERPRISE
      ( DEPARTMENTS, EMPLOYEES [dept~dom], PROJECTS,
        EMPLOYEE~PROJECT~ASSIGNMENTS [empl~dom,pjt~dom] )
      item
         from DEPARTMENTS use
            name => dept~name:          short~name
         from EMPLOYEES use
            empl# => employee~number:  transferred;
            name  => employee~name:    transferred
         from PROJECTS use
            name => proj~name:          short~name
         from EMPLOYEE~PROJECT~ASSIGNMENTS use
            kind~of~work:              transferred
      searchkey empl := employee~name
      permission find, obtain
   end WHOLE~ENTERPRISE;

end production~plan~table.
```

In this example, some domains are identical to the domains declared in the conceptual schema (transferred), others are newly defined domains (short~name).

The example also shows additional data protection concepts: access rights (find, obtain, insert, delete, modify) can be granted selectively (permission). These considerations must be made at the time when the external schema is defined. In order to grant new permissions or to revoke existing ones, a modification facility for external schemas is desirable.

4. Meta Data Base Design

The description concepts of chapters 2 and 3 cannot only help to design a data base in a smart but theoretical manner, they are implemented in a small data base management system called RDBETH, which is completed in its main components.

An important feature of RDBETH is the fact, that the description of RDBETH itself is done in the same mode as the user data within any of the user data bases managed by RDBETH. The description of RDBETH is therefore a data base, called meta data base, and RDBETH includes schema compilers, a DML-precompiler and a Data Base Manager which handles the meta data base and the user data bases as well interpretatively.

Since it is a major purpose of the present paper to show the suitability of the above CSL and ESL languages for the practical data base design, some figures about the size of the meta data base shall be presented here. (A meta data base is complex enough to prove the practicability of a data description method for nontrivial applications.)

Relations of the conceptual meta schema describing
- the conceptual schema: 14 relations
- the internal schema : 8 relations
- the external schemas : 13 relations

External relations to the meta schema:
- For each type of the schema compilers (CSL-compiler, ESL-compiler, ISL-compiler) an external meta schema is described; it resembles the three parts of the conceptual meta schema.
- Beside this run time organization the initialization process needs an additional set of tables (relations) and programs.

For all details see reference [MARTI/REBSAMEN/THURNHERR 8Ø].

5. Conclusions

The above CSL and ESL languages were used in different fields of applications (university administration, geographic data bases). As the main results the following summary can be presented:

- The block diagram allows already a concise presentation of the data structure which can be understood and discussed by the users.

- The CSL and ESL languages are not only able to describe data structures (schemas) at all, but also to include consistency constraints in the schema which until now in most cases are treated by programs outside the schema in its proper sense.

- The restriction of accesses to external schemas in ESL language avoids complicated (costly!) access mechanism implicitely.

- The schema concept presented here consists of a very limited number of language elements and is easy to learn and to maintain in applications.

References:

[ANSI/SPARC 75]
ANSI/X3/SPARC Study group on Data Base Management Systems. Interim Report 75-02-08. FDT (Bulletin of ACM SIGMOD)7, 1975.

[CODD 70]
Codd, E.F.: A Relational Model for Large Shared Data Banks. Comm. ACM, Vol. 13, No. 6, June 1970. Codd, E.F.: Further Normalization of the Data Base Relational Model, Courant Computer Science Symposium "Data Base Systems" (Rustin ed.), Prentice Hall, New York 1971.

[MARTI/REBSAMEN/THURNHERR 80]
Meta Data Base Design - Consistent Description of a Data Base Management System. Berichte des Instituts für Informatik der ETH Zürich, No. 34, Zürich 1980.

[THURNHERR 80]
Thurnherr, B.: Konzepte und Sprachen für den Entwurf konsistenter Datenbanken. Diss. ETH 6526, Zürich 1980.

[THURNHERR/ZEHNDER 79]
Thurnherr, B. and Zehnder, C.A.: Global Data Base Aspects, Consequences for the Relational Model and a Conceptual Schema Language. Berichte des Instituts für Informatik der ETH Zürich, No. 30, Zürich, März 1979.

DYNAMICS IN INFORMATION SYSTEM DESIGN AND MANAGEMENT

C. ROLLAND, C. RICHARD

C.R.I.N.

UNIVERSITE PARIS I Panthéon Sorbonne
Centre de Calcul
12 Place du Panthéon
75231 PARIS CEDEX 05

ABSTRACT : Our research goal is in information system (IS) design and management (the REMORA project). In the first instance, we were interested in the definition of a model of IS design. This model allows a complete representation of real world phenomena. It integrates at the conceptual level data, processes and dynamics in the design of IS. We set forth this model in the first part of this paper. In the second instance, we try to define a system of tools allowing IS definition, creation and functionning compatible with the general model previously defined. We present the dynamics automaton which manages the IS evolving in the course of time in the second part of this paper.

I - INTRODUCTION

For large and integrated information systems consistency and completeness become today operational objectives for designers. But we notice that they strongly disconnect the design of the data systems and the design of the programs systems. Therefore, they do not consider the time interrelations among data, among programs and among data and programs. Consequently, the IS synchronization situations are not correctly presented and solved.

We believe that consistency and completeness require the integration of the three aspects : data, programs, synchronization, and our work is a contribution for this.

We developed a relational type model to define, at the conceptual level, the integrated design of data, programs and synchronization and a language to describe the IS conceptual definition.
In the same way, we now develop a system of tools that from IS conceptual specification provides IS physical definition, IS creation, IS functionning and IS use compatible with our general model. The goal of these tools is to create an IS evolving as the dynamic reality it represents.
We insist in this paper on model and dynamics automaton for IS evolving.

II - A CONCEPTUAL MODEL FOR IS DESIGN

21 : The conceptual design step

In all computer fields searchers came to the same conclusion : in order to obtain a correctly implemented system an abstract definition must previously be done.
In the data base fields designers define a conceptual schema, at the first step of the design process (they named conceptual design level) as a formal representation of facts perceived in their static dimensions (2), (16), (17). This schema is used for the implementation of stored data.
In the programming field designers define the functional specifications of a problem (14), (12), (20). These specifications are used for programs writing.
In operating field searchers use also formal specifications associated or to high level languages (9), (13) or to models and features in order to express synchronization situations (11), (21), (22).

22 : The Information system conceptual schema

For information system design we adopt the same approach. We define, at the conceptual design step, a conceptual information system schema.
But we make the hypothesis that the complete aspects of real phenomena must be represented in IS design. Not only must static aspects of the organization (as in data base) be represented but also the evolution of the items in time. The transformations and the time interrelations of the organization components must complete their static structure expressed by the data schema.
In our point of view, the information system conceptual schema is a unique schema where the static structure (the organization components structure) and the dynamic structure (the transformations rules and the time interrelations) must be represented.
Our IS conceptual schema is the integration of these three aspects. It is analogous to the data schema for the data part and to the problem formal specification for the

programs and time interrelations parts.
For the definition of the IS conceptual schema, we need a model. This model must provide elements for the construction of the conceptual set of data, the conceptual set of programs and the conceptual control of the time relations between programs.

23 . The model

231. What do we need to represent ?

i) We showed (24), (25) that in a dynamic perspective we have to represent three categories of phenomena described by their properties : OBJECTS, EVENTS, OPERATIONS and that the dynamic dimension is completely represented by three types of interconnections between the three categories of phenomena : MODIFY, ASCERTAIN, TRIGGER.

ii) It results in the following definitions :
An OBJECT is a durable, concrete or abstract component of the organization that can be particularized (5), (16).
Examples : the customer Durand, the product number 33.

An OPERATION is an action that can be executed alone, at a given time in the organization and that modifies the state of one or more objects.
Example : the "order analysis" number 312 creates the object "accepted order" number 202.

An EVENT is anything that can happen at a given time that ascertains the state change of one or more objects and that triggers one or more operations.
Example : the event "order arrival" number 615 triggers the operation "order analysis" number 312.

iii) We propose a causal type definition for the organization dynamics : the events cause the execution of operations which produces state changes of objects that could become events.
These definitions are founded on the distinction from objects states (a state can be durable), from object state changes (a state change is instantaneous) and from events (an event is a noteworthy state change ; not all state changes are events).

232. How do we represent ?

The conceptual model must satisfy two main requirements : to be formal and to represent easily and homogeneously the classes of facts previously defined.

i) We choose the relational formalism (7).
ii) We include time.
iii) We introduce relation types in order to represent different categories. There are three relation types : C-OBJECT type, C-OPERATION type, C-EVENT type (respectively written C-OB, C-OP, C-EV).
The correspondance between reality and conceptual representation is :
Each class of phenomena is represented by one or several relations.
Each property of a phenomenon class is represented by an attribute of one of the previous relations.
The category of the class of phenomena is represented by the relation type.

We give here the formal definition of the three relation types in their normlized form (corresponding to an elementary representation of phenomena).

233. The model concepts definitions

These definitions use a new kind of functional dependency (FD) (4), we name permanent functional dependency (PFD) (18).

Definition : Let A and B be attributes of a relation R.
Let Dom (A) be the domain of A and Dom (B) the domain of B
Let f be a time varying function such that f : Dom (A) $\rightarrow$ Dom (B)
f is a permanent functional dependency denoted A $\div\!\!\rightarrow$ B if, at every point in time, since its creation date, for a given value a $\in$ Dom (A) there will be a unique value b $\in$ Dom (B).
A PFD is a stronger dependence than a FD : if A $\div\!\!\rightarrow$ B, at every point in time the value b is the same and never can be undefined.

2331. The C-OB type operation

Definition : Let OB be the set of the attributes representing the properties of phenomena of the OBJECT category.
Let F be the set of the elementary, direct, canonical (4) and permanent dependencies over OB.
A subset R of OB is a C-OB relation type if :
1 $\exists$ a subset I $\subset$ R key of R
2 $\forall$ K $\in$ (R-I) I $\div\!\!\rightarrow$ K $\in$ F
3 $\nexists$ in (OB-R) L such (I $\div\!\!\rightarrow$ L) $\in$ F

Examples : customer - description (ncustomer, name, custcreatdate)
customer - situation (ncustomer, custmodsitdate, situation)

customer - income (ncustomer, custmodindate, income)

custcreatedate : the date of the customer creation
custmodsitdate : the date of the customer situation modification
custmodindate : the date of the customer income modification

The three relations define a customer in the loan management example we give in the next paragraph. Each relation C-OB describes a particular temporal aspect of the customer : customer description identifies the customer, customer-income define his income (used to a loan acceptation) ; customer-situation defines his situation with the bank.

Meaning : a relation C-OB represents a time consistent aspect of a real world object class. It brings together all the properties of the class having an identical dynamic behavior ; that is to say properties created, modified or suppressed at the same time. The elementary form of the C-OBJECT concept is ensured by properties 1 and 2 . The C-OBJECT relations can be considered as those obtained by the decomposition of 3NF (18) object relation. The C-OB represents the elementary state of the IS.

2332. The C-OP relation

Definition : Let OP be the set of the attributes representing the static and temporal properties of the phenomena of the OPERATION category.
Let IOB be the set of the keys of the relation C-OB
Let $P = OP \cup IOB$
Let F be the set of the elementary, direct canonical and permanent dependencies on P.
A subset R of P is a relation C-OP if
1 $\exists$ $I \subset R$ key of R
2 $\forall$ K (R-I) $\exists$ $(I \dot{\rightarrow} K) \in F$
3 $\exists$ in R at most one attribute $\in$ IOB
4 $\nexists$ in (P-R) L such $(I \dot{\rightarrow} L) \in F$

Examples : Monthly-loan-evaluation-oper (nmonthleval, datecrea)
monthly-loan-evaluation-text (nmonthleval, datemoevte, loan-monthly-eval)
monthly-loan-evaluation-exec (nmonthleval, nmontdatexe, nloan-molosi)

In the loan management example these three relations define the monthly evaluation of the accumulated debit due by each customer. Each relation C-OP describes a particular aspect of this operation class. The first relation identifies the "monthly evaluation" operation class. The second relation defines the management rule used to calculate the new debit of the loans : the attribute loan-monthly-eval is the designation of this rule that will be describedas an integrity constraint in the conceptual language. The third relation defines the executions of the C-operation and the

C-object "loan-monthly-situation" (identified by nloan-molosi) modified by these executions.

Meaning : A relation C-OP represents a time consistent aspect of a real world operations class. It describes an elementary aspect of a class of real operations having a specific dynamic behavior. Notice that we define the C-OP by reference to the C-OB concept. The 1 and 2 properties of the C-OP type ensure the elementarity of the C-OPERATION concept. The operations corresponding to a c-operation create objects corresponding to a unique c-object. Thus, a C-operation can be interpreted as the representation of the smallest transformation that can happen to a C-object. In the previous example, the monthly-evaluation operation modifies the "loan-monthly-situation" object. The C-OP represents the elementary transformation of the IS.

2333. The C-EV type relation

Definition : Let EV be the set of the attributes representing the properties of the EVENT category.

Let IOB be the set of the keys of the relations C-OB and IOP the set of the keys of the relations C-OP.

Let $U \doteq EV \cup IOB \cup IOP$

Let F the set of the elementary, direct, canonical, permanent, functional dependencies over U.

A subset R of U is a relation C-EV if

1 $\exists$ $I \subset R$ key of R,

2 $\forall$ $K \in (R-I)$ $\exists$ $(I \div\!\!\rightarrow K) \in F$

3 $\exists$ in R at most one attribute $\in$ IOB

4 $\nexists$ in (U-R) L such $(I \div\!\!\rightarrow L) \in F$

Examples : repaying-delay-ev (ndelrep, datecreav)
repaying-delay-pred (ndelrep, date-del-reppre, pinit-delrep, pfin-delrep)
repaying-delay-arr (ndelrep, date-delrepar, nloan-molosi)
repaying-delay-trigg (ndelrep, date-delrepri, npencre, date-npencre)

These four relations define the real world event class "repaying-delay". Each relation describes a particular aspect of this event class. The first relation identifies the class. The second relation defines the event as the particular state change of the object and the third relation defines the object whose state change is the event. The state change of the object is defined by two predicates : pinit-delrep describes the initial state of the object (debit $<$ 3 monthly-rate) and pfin-delrep describes the final state of the object (debit $\geq$ 3 montly-rate). The object is identified by the key (nloan-molosi) of the C-object concerned "loan-monthly-situation". The fourth relation defines the penality operation triggered by the event. The event is identified by its key (ndelrep, date-delrepri) ; the operation is identified by by its key (npencre,date-npecre). A relation C-OP describes this operation of penality.

Meaning : A relation C-EV represents a time consistent aspect of a real world event class. It describes an elementary aspect of a class of real events having a determined dynamic behavior. Notice that we define the C-EV by reference to the C-OB and C-OP concepts. Notice that the 1 and 2 properties of the type C-EV induce the elementarity of the concept : a C-event can be interpreted as the representation of a noteworthy state change of one C-object which triggers operations corresponding to one or more operations. In the previous example the delayed-repaying event is defined by a particular state change of a "loan-monthly-situation" object and triggers an operation of penality.

The C-EV represents the noteworthy elementary state change of the IS which induces elementary transformations.

Notice that the triggering can be conditional. If a condition is associated to an event definition it expresses that the operation is triggered only if the condition is true. The triggering can also be iterative. Then the operation is triggered at several times for each C-OB occurence defined in the c-op factor.

234. The conceptual schema

The IS conceptual schema is a collection of relations belonging to the three types previously defined. It can be split into sub-schemas which describe respectively the static and dynamic aspects represented.

- The static schema is the set of the type C-OB relations. It corresponds to the conceptual data structure and represents the static structure of the organization components.
- The dynamics schema is the set of the types C-OP and C-EV relations. It describes the interrelations among C-objects, C-operations, C-events. It represents the organization dynamics in terms of causal interconnections among the phenomena categories of the organization.

For easier understanding, we use in this paper a graphic notation to describe the two sub-schemas corresponding to an example of customer loans management in a bank.

3. EXAMPLE AND EVALUATION

31. The problem

It is an extension of an example presented in (1). It concerns the management of loans granted to customers under the following conditions :

Loan grant : a customer can not have more than one loan not yet repayed. Loans are

granted to customers that have an annual income greater than US 4 000 and have never been suspended in previous loans. The final agreement is done by the loans director and the amount of the loan and its duration are established.
Repaying : it is done in a monthly basis. The monthly rate to be repayed is calculated either when the loan is granted or when loan conditions are revised. In this calculation the loan total amount, its duration and the interest rate are calculated. Customers have a certain freedom to repay the loan. Every month, at the date it specifies, the customer payment may be greater or lower than the monthly rate. These customers may then be in advance or late in relation to their repaying. The control of customer situation is done every first day of the month by a comparison between the accumulated rates repayed (its credit) and the accumulated monthly rates dues (its debit).
Repayment in advance, whenever a customer has repayed in advance at least the equivalent to three months rates, his loan is revised and the monthly rate, the loan duration and the total amount due are recalculated as if a new loan was granted to him and the last one refused.
Repayment delayed, whenever a customer has a delay that is at least equivalent to three monthly rates, a penality (a tax) is applied to his loan (a % over the total amount due). This penality is increased every month if the delay is not eliminated and when the customer in delay refunds, the payment should first of all refunds the accumulated credit.
Customer situation, a customer that has a loan and has no delay is an active customer. A customer that has a loan and is submitted to a penality is suspended. A customer that has already got a loan but does not have one at the moment is non-active.

Loan refund, a loan is refunded when the customer ends repaying. In other words, when the accumulated credit is equal to the total amount due.

32. The static schema

It is represented on figure 1.
Comments : We introduce the C-CLASS notion. A C-CLASS is a subset of relations belonging to a type. It represents a real world class of phenomena. Each relation of a same class describes a particular aspect of the real class.
We define in this problem three C-objects C-CLASS : loan C-class, customer C-class, day C-class. The loan C-Class connects three C-OB relations which correspond to the four different states of a loan in course of time : required (C9), refused(02), waiting for agreement (03), granted (04) and the five different aspects of a loan : the monthly rate (05), the payment (06), the delay penality(07), the repaying (08), the monthly loan-situation (01) and the payment-penality (014). The customer C-CLASS is described by three C-OB relations : the customer-description (010), the customer-situation (011), the customer-income (012). The dependence between C-class keys define the data structure and represents the real association classes between pahenomena.

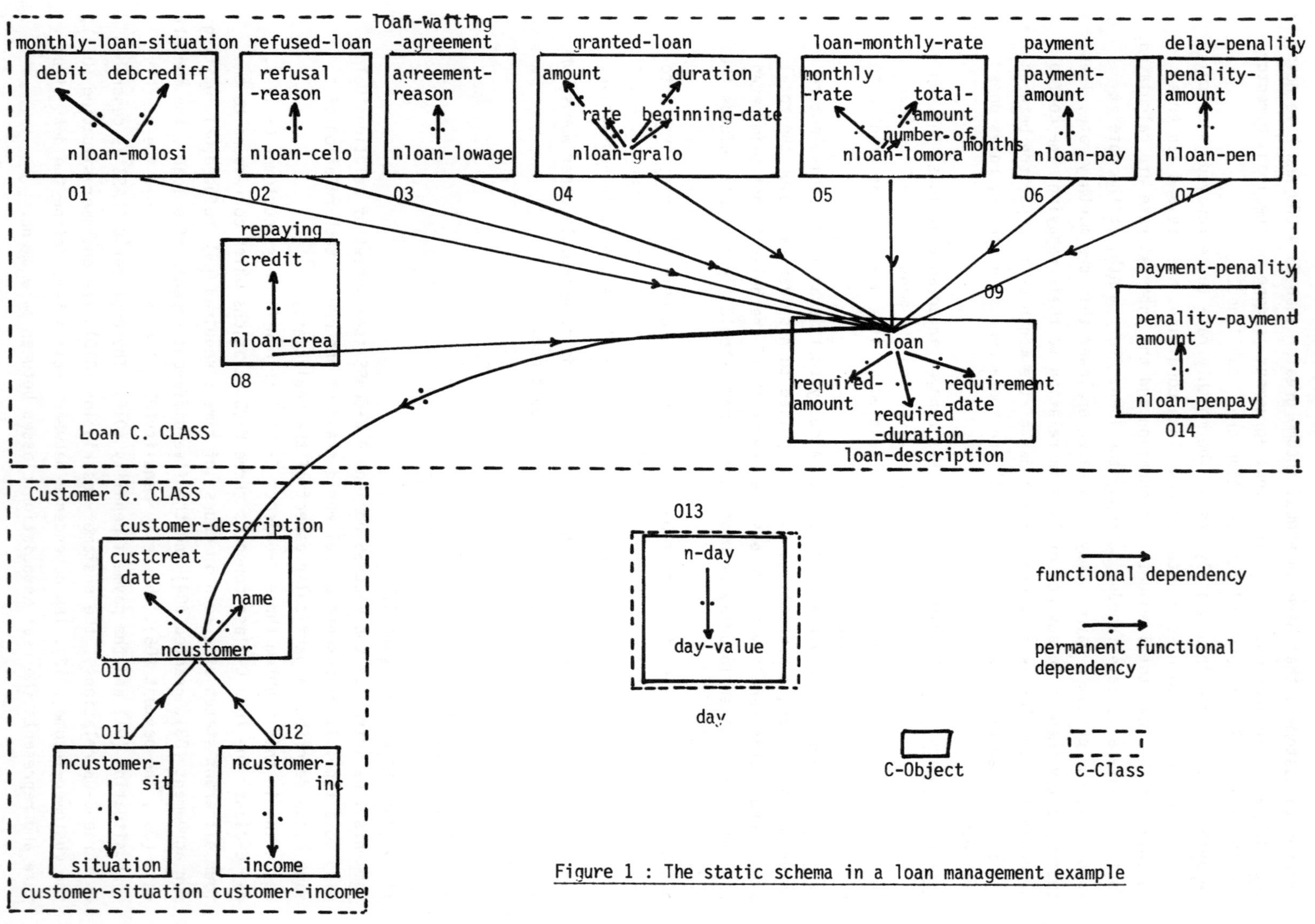

Figure 1 : The static schema in a loan management example

33. The dynamics schema

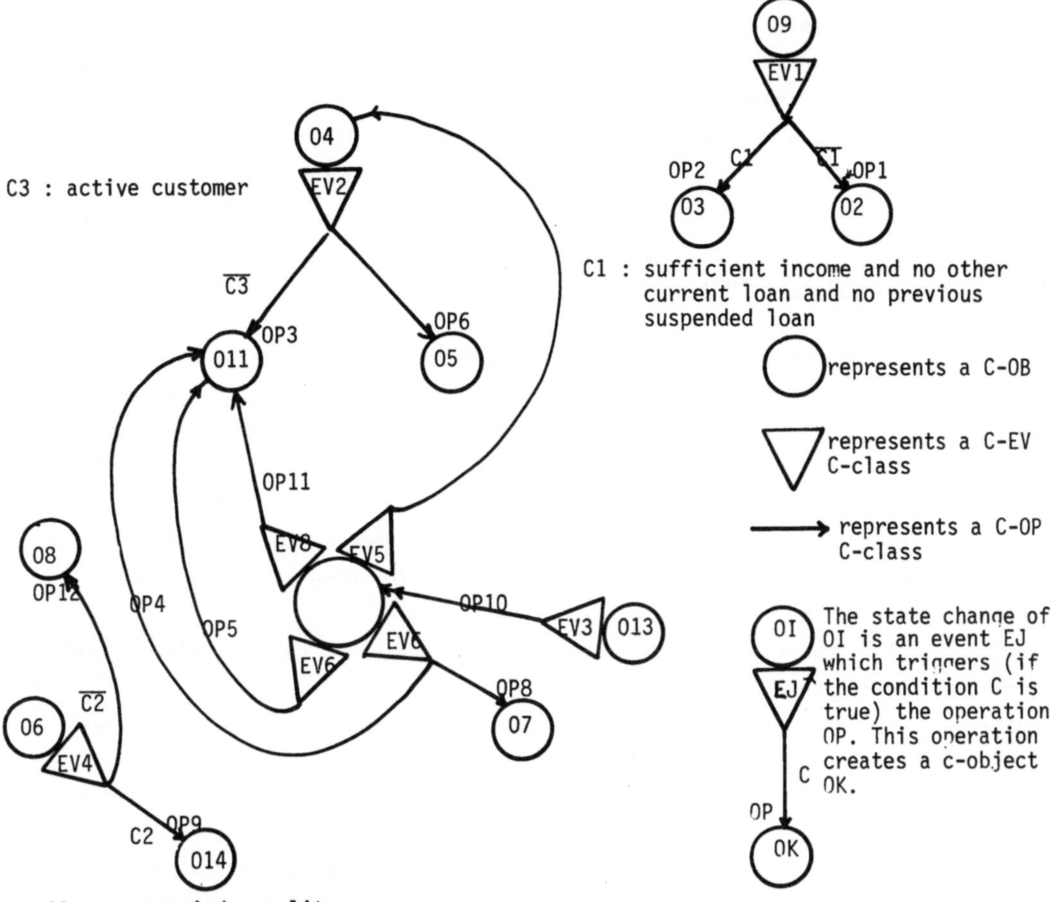

C2 : an unpaied penality

Figure 2 : the dynamics schema in a loan management example

C-EV C-CLASS

EV1 : arrival of a loan requirement
EV2 : arrival of a granted loan
EV3 : loan exigibility day
EV4 : arrival of a payment
EV5 : repaying advance
EV6 : repaying day
EV7 : end of a loan
EV8 : end of the repaying delay

C-OP C-CLASS

OP1 : refusal of a loan requirement
OP2 : acceptation of a loan requirement
OP3 : customer activation
OP4 : customer suspension
OP5 : customer disactivation
OP6 : monthly rate computation
OP7 : loan modification
OP8 : penality creation
OP9 : penality payment
OP10 : monthly loan evaluation
OP11 : customer re-activation
OP12 : credit increase

Comments : the dynamics schema highlights all the noteworthy state changes (events) and all their consequences (operations triggering and object state changes). For example it clearly appears that there are four types of state change of the object loan-monthly-situation (01) : the event EV5 induces an operation of loan modification (OP7) ; the event EV6 triggers the operations of customer suspension (OP4) and penality creation (OP8) ; event EV7 induces the operation of customer disactivation (OP5) and event EV8 triggers the operation of customer activation (OP11).

34. Evaluation about synchronization's representation

A lot of paper (17) intend to introduce programs modelization connected with data modelization and a few of them try to introduce time and synchronization aspects in IS design. The dynamics schema expresses the synchronization between processes.
Let us examine shortly how the conceptual model allows the synchronization problems representation.
The analysis of the current notions of synchronization lead us to settle that the three following conditions must be satisfied in order to solve a synchronization problem :
Condition 1 : to precisely define the set of the synchronized system processes and the set of system resources.
Condition 2 : to define the interrelations among these processes (i.e. their dependence ou independence)
Condition 3 : to define their temporal co-operation rules, according to those defining the considered problem logic, that is to say to define an order over the processes execution that respects these rules therefore insuring the system consistency.
These three conditions will be our reference to analyze how our conceptual approach of modelling takes into account the synchronization. So we will intuitively demonstrate that the conceptual model allows to satisfy these three conditions by means of the C-EVENT concept. One can find in (23) a more strict and formal presentation of this demonstration. It consists in extracting from the set of chronological functional dependencies of a conceptual schema those useful to determine the synchronization rules.

Condition 1 : In our conceptual approach of the synchronization, the processes set is the set of the operations described by the C-OPERATIONS, and the set of system resources is the set of the objects described by the C-OBJECTS. Such an approach corresponds to a reasoning in terms of elementary processes, that is to say in terms of processes triggered consequently to the state change of one and only one object and acting upon one and only one object.

Condition 2 : Every operation (that constitutes a process in our approach) described by a C-OPERATION is necessarily triggered by an event described by a C-EVENT. Therefore the dependence or independence among the C-EVENTS that trigger those C-OPERATIONS expresses the interrelations among the C-OPERATIONS.
If we refer to the loan-management example previously presented it appears clearly that an event of EV2 type (arrival of a granted loan) can occur if an event of EV5 type has occured because the modification of a loan can only be the consequence of a repaying advance. So we can say that the C-EVENT EV2 is dependent of the C-EVENT EV5. As the C-OPERATION OP6 (monthly rate computation) is triggered by the C-EVENT EV2 and as the C-OPERATION OP7 (loan modification) is triggered by the C-EVENT EV5, we can say that the C-OPERATION OP6 is dependent of the C-OPERATION OP7. Thus, we have pointed out that the relations of dependence or independence among C-EVENTS express the dependence or independence of the C-OPERATIONS they trigger.

Condition 3 : Each state change of the system is due to an operation execution issuing the modification of an object of the system. Moreover, every event is a state change and it triggers one or more operations. Then, the ordering of the C-OPERATIONS according to their dependence or independence relations represents their temporal cooperation rules, that is to say that it permits to define an order over their executions. This ordering is defined by the concatenation of dynamic cycles (a dynamic cycle is the sequence C-EVENT, C-OPERATION, C-OBJECT) by means of the C-EVENT concept.
Thus, the creation of a C-OBJECT 13 (day) is a C-EVENT EV3 that triggers the C-OPERATION OP10 (monthly loan evaluation). The C-OPERATION OP10 induces the C-OBJECT 01 state change. This state change does not always constitute a C-EVENT EV5 (repaying advance). When it constitutes a C-EVENT EV5, this C-EVENT triggers the C-OPERATION OP7 (loan modification) that modifies the C-OBJECT 04 (granted loan).
As showed above, the C-EVENT concept allows to define an ordering over the C-OPERATIONS executions : the arrival order of the C-EVENTS occurences permits to define an ordering over the execution of the occurences of the C-OPERATIONS they trigger. For instance, the arrival of an EV3 occurence followed by the arrival of an EV5 occurence allows to define the ordering of the executions of the corresponding occurences of OP10 and OP7 : execution of the occurence of OP10 and afterwards execution of the occurence of OP7.
The interest of such an approach relies mainly on the following features (26)(23).

1) The qualities of the conceptual modelling and particularly :
11) its semantic character
12) its simplicity related to the semantic evidence of the concepts, to the causality of the model and to the elementary aspect of the concepts
13) its rigour, related to the structuralistic aspect of this approach (its consists in analyzing a problem in terms of structure and not in terms of functions to carry out) and to the acuracy of the concepts defined in a normalized form.

Let us illustrate these remarks on the loan example by discussion of the subgraph corresponding to the repayment advances and delay management. Let us recall that the monthly situation of a loan (occurence of the c-object 01) induced by the execution of an operation of the OP10 type might constitute an event belonging to one of the four classes EV5, EV6, EV7, EV8 according to the state change nature of 01. The state change is defined by the initial and final predicates associated to each one of these four classes.

Let M be the attribute "monthly-rate" and D the attribute "debcrediff". We recall that "debcrediff" is, for a given loan, in a given month, the difference between the accumulated credit and the accumulated debit.

The initial and final predicates associated to these four C-EVENTS are expressed by the following table.

C-EVENT	INITIAL PREDICATE	FINAL PREDICATE
EV5	TRUE	$D \geq 3 * M$
EV6	$D < 3 * M$	$D \geq 3 * M$
EV7	TRUE	$D = 0 \wedge DT = T$
EV8	$D \geq 3 * M$	$D < 3 * M$

DT= debit
T= total amount

The conceptual modelling qualities are well illustrated by the given example, particularly :

- the conceptual description constitutes a semantical approach of a problem : the advance and delay in payments descriptions of the example are the modelling of the problem itself, through the model three concepts, and these descriptions are not the modelling of a technical solution to this problem ; neither technical considerations nor any implementation or optimization choice are considered in these descriptions.
- description simplicity is made evident by the comparison of the conceptual description and the Petri nets with inhibitory arcs description. As a matter of fact, the functioning description (of the system given as an example) by the Petri nets representation could be :

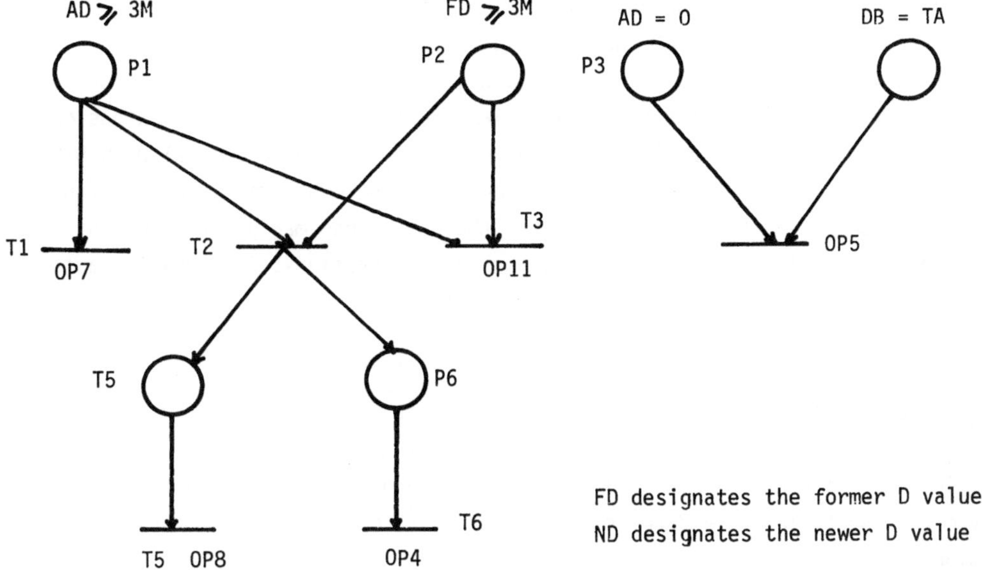

We notice that this description is more complex thanthe conceptual description. In particular, we have to describe both conditions and their evaluation mechanisms and also to distinguish D ocaurences (the former D value and the actual D value). Moreover, when a combination of two conditions triggers many operations we have to introduce as many intermediate places as there are operations to trigger (as in T2, and P6, P5). Finally, in contradistinction to the conceptual approach that is of structuralist type, this kind of approach induces the designer to a less rigourous attitude in the modelling process because functions to be ensured by the system and their concatenation are not as clearly expressed that the components structure of the system.

III. THE DYNAMICS AUTOMATON FOR THE IS EVOLUTION CONTROL

31. Information system management system

The conceptual model allows a more complete representation of the reality than a data base. The more complex the reality the designers want to represent completely the more difficult the IS design and use without an automatic aid. So we propose (27),(19) to realize an information system management system (ISMS) analogous to a DBMS. The ISMS will assume several functions :

- At the design time it chooses the physical implementation, it generates the physical structureand controls the creation of the IS. This generation implies the creation of the algorithms corresponding to the operations classes and to the events predicates.
- At the use time, it controls the dynamic evolution of the IS by means of a particular tool called dynamics automaton that selects and executes the operations related

to any object state change recognized as a real event.
We have retained to develop an ISMS working with the conceptual description of the IS. Consequently, the designer using such ISMS will only provide a semantic description without any reference to the physical implementation. The ISMS is an extension of a relational type DBMS. We realize it as an extension of the relational DBMS SYNTEX. In the scope of the ISMS is the same than for any DBMS one must admit that its functions are more complete. They include not only the consistent manipulation of the data and the control of the events that trigger these operations. The dynamics automaton achieves by this way the permanent IS consistency.

32. Dynamics automaton functioning

The dynamics automaton has to manage a dynamic reality or more precisely it has to manage the representation of a dynamic reality given through the IS conceptual description.
At a conceptual level of specification, the dynamics automaton is an abstract machine composed by a set of abstract and general mechanisms under the control of a scheduler that activates them at the right time. The scheduler works according to its own rules, with its own informations according to the automaton functioning structure i.e. the IS conceptual description.
-The local information we call c-references managed by the automaton are references to the objects, operations, events states in the IS. The C-OB-reference indicates the creation of a C-OB instance ; the C-EV-reference indicates that an IS event was produced ; the C-OP-1-reference indicates that an operation must be executed on the IS ; the C-OP-2- reference indicates that an operation has been executed on the IS.
- The functioning rules of the scheduler express how the dynamics automaton takes the decisions concerning the actions that are executed on the IS after every produced state change. We describe them with our conceptual model though the conceptual schema of the automaton functioning.

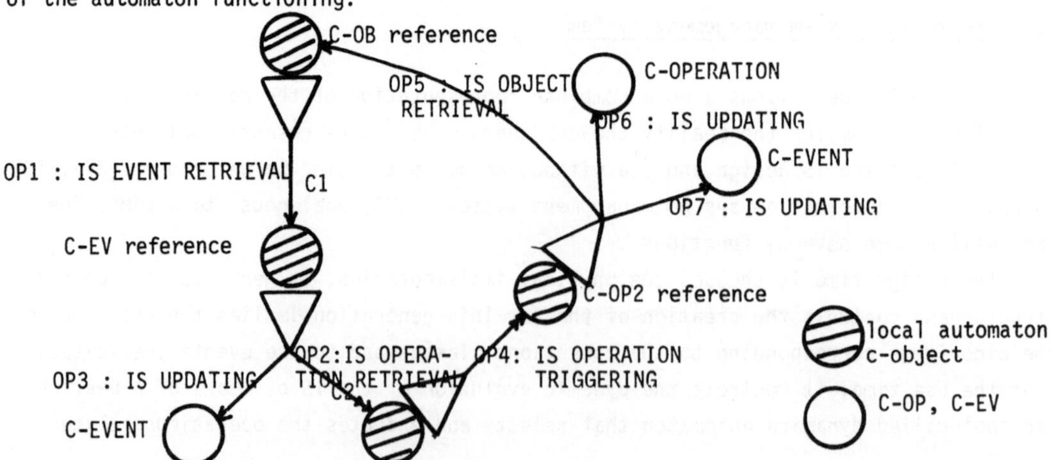

The c-operations of this schema express the mechanisms of the automaton. We can notice two kinds of mechanisms : the control mechanisms and the operating mechanisms.
The scope of the control mechanism is :

- to recognize an object state change as an event belonging to a c-event (OP1)
- to identify the operations belonging to c-operations to trigger and to control if those operations can be triggered (OP2)
- to identify the operations executions consequences (OP5)
- to update the IS (OP3, OP6, OP7).

The scope of the operating mechanisms is to start and to control the execution of the operations communicated to it by the control mechanisms (OP4).
According to the former comments on synchronization problems, we notice that the mechanisms are the primitives of the synchronization machine associated to our modelization type.

IV. CONCLUSION

We think that a complete representation including objects, operations and events allows a more consistent and useful IS management.
The IS consistency results to the dynamics automaton. This tool controls all the state changes of the IS objects and automatically triggers and synchronizes all the actions working on objects. So, the error risks in IS updating are minimized.
The extension of the objects representation by operations and events increases the IS usefulness for the end users. They find in the IS a complete and faithful representation of the reality they have to manage.

V. REFERENCES

1 - ABRIAL, RJ : "A specification language" - IFIP Congress - Tokyo, Japon - 1978

2 - ANSI-SPARC : "Report on data base management system" - Final report - 1977

3 - BANON D :"Projet Remora : un outil pour la gestion des systèmes d'information" Thèse de 3è cycle - Nancy - France - 1979

4 - BEERI C., BERNSTEIN A., GOODMAN N. : "A sophisticate's introduction to data base normalization theory" - Proceedings of 4th International Conference on VLDB, Berlin, Allemagne - 1978

5 - CHEN PPS : "The entity relationship model towards a unified view of data" - ACM/TODS - Vol 1, N° 1 - 1976

6 - CHESSERON M : "Modèle de représentation et méthode de construction des composantes dynamiques d'un système d'information dans le projet Remora" Thèse de 3è cycle - Nancy - France - 1978

7 - CODD E.F. : "A relational model of data for large shared data bank"
Communications ACM - Vol 13, N° 6 - 1970

8 - CODD E.F. : " Further normalization of the data base relational model"
Data base systems - Prentice Hall - Englewood Cliffs - 1972

9 - DAHL J, NYGAARD K : "SIMULA : an algol based simulation language"
CACM - Vol 19 - N° 9 - 1966

10 - DEMOLOMBE R and all : "SYNTEX 2" - Rapport DRME n° 74 227 - Vol 3 - 1975

11 - DENNIS JB : "Record of the project MAC" - Conference on concurrent systems and parallel computation - ACM - New York - 1970

12 - DIJKSTRA EW : "Hierarchical ordering of sequential processes" - Acta Informatica Vol 1 - N°1 - 1971

13 - DIJKSTRA EW : "Guarded command - non determinacy and formal derivation of programs" CACM - Vol 18 - N° 8 - 1975

14 - GUTTAG J : "Abstract data types and the development of data structures"
Communication ACM - Vol 20 - N° 6 - 1977

15 - Institut Notre Dame de la Paix : "Workshop on data structure for information system" - Namur - Belgique - 1974

16 - IFIP working conference on "Modelling in data base management systems"
Freudenstadt - Allemagne - 1976

17 - IFIP working conference on "Formal models and practical tools for information system design" - Oxford - Angleterre - 1979

18 - KRIEGUER M :"Projet Remora : modèle de représentation et méthode de construction des composantes statiques d'un SI" - thèse de 3è cycle Nancy France 78

19 - LEIFERT S : "Un langage de spécification de système d'information. Un outil pour leur gestion", Thèse de 3è cycle - Nancy - 1980

20 - LISKOV B, ZILLES S : "Programing with abstract data types" - Very high level languages symposium - Santa Monica - 1974

21 - PATIL SS : "Circuit implementation of Petri Nets" - Computation structures group, Memo 73 - Projet PAC - MIT Cambridge - 1971

22 - PETERSON JL : "Petri Nets" - Computing surveys - Vol 9 - N° 3 - 1977

23 - RICHARD C. : "Une approche conceptuelle des problèmes de synchronisation : Projet Remora" - Thèse de 3è cycle - Nancy - 1979

24 - ROLLAND C, FOUCAUT O : "Concepts for design of information system conceptual schema and its utilization in the Remora Project" Proceedings in the 4th International Conference on VLDB - Berlin - Allemagne - 1978

25 - ROLLAND C and all : "Le projet Remora" - Rapport final de contrat - Publication IRIA - France - 1979

26 - ROLLAND C, RICHARD C : "Concepts for a distributed computing system design" Seminar on distributed data sharing system -IRIA/IGDD, Aix en Provence - 1979

27 - ROLLAND C, RICHARD C.,LEIFERT S : "Tools for information system dynamics management" Proceedings of the 5th International conference on VLDB, RIO DE JANEIRO-BRESIL,1979

28 - ROLLAND C, LEIFERT S, RICHARD C : "Le pilotage de l'évolution des systèmes d'information" Séminaire INFORSID sur les méthodes et outils pour la conception des systèmes d'information" - Aix en Provence - France - 1980

KONSTRUKTIVE ABSTRAKTE DATENTYPEN

Prof. Dr. H. Wedekind
Universität Erlangen-Nürnberg
Informatik VI
Martensstraße 3, 852 Erlangen

1. Die Unzulänglichkeit der herkömmlichen Konzeption für die Anwendungsprogrammierung

Der in dieser Arbeit unterbreitete Vorschlag, Konstruktive Abstrakte Datentypen (KAD) zur Programmspezifikation einzuführen, beruht auf der Beobachtung, daß die herkömmliche Konzeption zumindest für die Anwendungsprogrammierung keinerlei Bedeutung erlangt hat. Unter herkömmlicher Konzeption sollen die Spezifikationsmethoden verstanden werden, wie sie von Liskov und Zilles [11], Guttag und Horning [5], aber auch von Parnas [16], [17] entwickelt wurden. Diese Darstellungen beschränken sich auf die Spezifikation operativer Begriffe, wie z.B. STACK, QUEUE oder TREE, die vornehmlich in der Systemprogrammierung Anwendung finden. Ein Abstrakter Datentyp ist aus herkömmlicher Sicht eine Menge von Datenobjekten, zu der nur über Operationen zugegriffen werden kann, die in ihrer Wirkung auf den Zustand der Objekte genau festgelegt wurden. Die Objekte selbst treten nach "außen" nicht in Erscheinung, da von den vielen logischen und physischen Details, die die Objekte unterscheiden, abstrahiert wird. Diese Abstraktion wurde von Parnas als Grundsatz formuliert und ist in der Literatur unter der Bezeichnung "Geheimnisprinzip" bekannt geworden [18]. Die Kritik an den herkömmlichen Abstrakten Datentypen soll in drei Punkte untergliedert werden.

a) Die Unabhängigkeit des impliziten Definierens von lebensweltlichen Begriffen
Die prägenden Arbeiten über Abstrakte Datentypen sind dadurch gekennzeichnet, daß sie den axiomatischen Ansatz verfolgen oder, wie im Falle von Parnas, den Gedanken einer Zustandsmaschine umsetzen. In beiden Vorgehensweisen werden zur Begriffseinführung implizite Definitionen benutzt, die es erlauben, Begriffe beliebig auszutauschen, ohne den Wahrheitsgehalt einer Aussage zu verändern. Man spricht von Eigenbegriffen des Axiomensystems [19, S. 377] , die mit Bezug zur Lebenswelt absichtlich unkontrolliert eingeführt werden, um sich von unsicheren Ontologien zu befreien. Seit dem Streit zwischen Frege und Hilbert [4] ist das implizite Definieren immer wieder heftig diskutiert worden (siehe z.B. Lorenzen [15, S. 190], Hempel [8, S. 81] und Stegmüller [19, S. 376] etc. Die Auseinandersetzung endete mit einer "Arbeitsteilung", die zum Inhalt hat, daß derjenige, der lebensweltliche Begriffe kontrolliert einführen will, implizite Definitionen allein schon wegen der möglichen Begriffsinvarianz meiden muß, und daß all jene, die auf der Grundlage eines Axiomensystems folgern wollen, dieser Beschränkung nicht unterliegen. Die herkömmlichen Ansätzes für Abstrakte Datentypen heben diese Arbeitsteilung wieder auf mit der Konsequenz, daß sie für Anwendungen untauglich sind. Artefakte wie RECHNUNG, KONDIGUNG etc., die im

Gegensatz zu STACK, QUEUE etc. in der Dingwelt keine Entsprechung haben, können herkömmlich nicht einwandfrei spezifiziert werden, da nicht gezeigt werden kann, wie diese Begriffe für praktische Zwecke implizit festzulegen sind.

b) Das Abstraktionsprinzip als Präzisierung des Geheimnisprinzips

Das von Parnas in die Diskussion gebrachte Geheimnisprinzip ist nur eine metaphorische Redewendung, die den Prozeß des Abstrahierens nur undeutlich wiedergibt. Bei einer expliziten Theorie über Abstrakte Datentypen sollte auf die klassische Abstraktionstheorie von Frege/Lorenzen [14], [21] zurückgegriffen werden, um so den Vorgang der Typenbildung unmittelbar darstellen zu können.
Seien $c_1, c_2, \ldots, c_n$ konkrete Objekte, die in einem Beispiel etwa auch durch die Eigennamen Müller, Mayer, etc. bezeichnet werden. $A(c_1), \ldots, A(c_n)$ seien Aussagen über $c_1 \ldots c_n$. Allgemein führt man die Aussageform A(x) ein. A könnte z.B. für PERSONAL stehen, wenn über $c_1 \ldots c_n$ z.B. Aussagen über eine Personalzugehörigkeit gemacht werden sollen. Das Abstraktionsprinzip verlangt, daß erst die logische Gleichheit von Objekten konstatiert wird, um dann die Menge dieser gleichen Objekte als neues abstraktes Objekt $\epsilon_x A(x)$ einzuführen.

1) Logische Gleichheit $\sim$

$$c_1 \sim c_2 \sim \ldots c_n =_{DF} A(c_1) \leftrightarrow A(c_2) \leftrightarrow \ldots \leftrightarrow A(c_n)$$

2) Abstraktion

$$A^*[\epsilon_x A(x)] =_{DF} \bigwedge_x (\bigvee_{1 \leq i \leq n} c_i \sim x \rightarrow A(x))$$

Das neue abstrakte Objekt $\epsilon_x A(x)$ wird durch die Aussage $A^*[\epsilon_x A(x)]$ dargestellt. A* kann im Unterschied zu A in diesem Fall keine konkreten Objekte als Argument aufnehmen. Der Prozeß kann für schon eingeführte Abstrakte Objekte verallgemeinert werden.

1) Logische Gleichheit $\underset{x}{\sim}$

$$A(x) \underset{x}{\sim} B(x) =_{DF} \bigwedge_x A(x) \leftrightarrow B(x)$$

2) Abstraktion

$$\left.\begin{matrix} C^*[\epsilon_x A(x)] \\ = \\ C^*[\epsilon_x B(x)] \end{matrix}\right\} =_{DF} [A(x) \underset{x}{\sim} B(x)] \quad \rightarrow \quad \left\{\begin{matrix} C(A(x)) \\ C(B(x)) \end{matrix}\right.$$

Die geschweifte Klammer bedeutet, daß die Erzeugung eines abstrakten Objektes, nämlich $\epsilon A(x)$ oder $\epsilon B(x)$, jeweils über die logisch gleichen Aussagen A(x) oder B(x) geschieht, über die wegen ihrer Gleichheit in einer gemeinsamen Formel mit dem Zeichen C gesprochen werden kann.

Für eine weitere Stufe gilt:

$$C(x) \underset{x}{\sim} D(x) =_{DF} \bigwedge_x C(x) \leftrightarrow D(x)$$

$$\left.\begin{array}{l} E^* \; [\epsilon_x C(x)] \\ = \\ E^* \; [\epsilon_x D(x)] \end{array}\right\} =_{DF} [C(x) \underset{x}{\sim} D(x)] \quad \rightarrow \quad \left\{\begin{array}{l} E(C(x)) \\ E(D(x)) \end{array}\right.$$

Konstruktiv bedeutet, daß nur solche Mengenzeichen auftreten dürfen, die vorher durch Abstraktion gewonnen wurden. Bild 1 verdeutlicht den Abstraktionsprozeß.

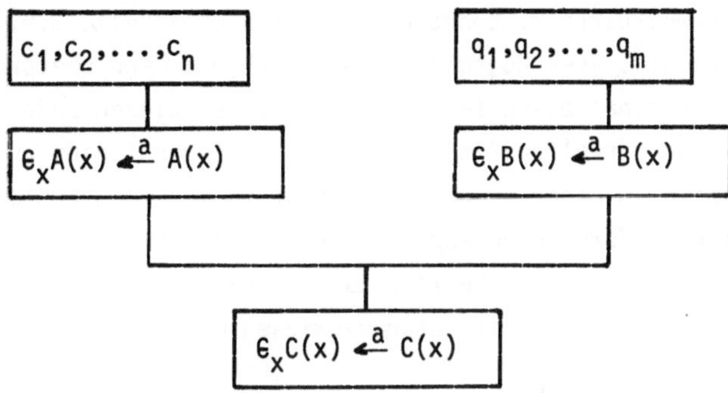

Bild 1: Abstraktionsprozeß ($\overset{a}{\leftarrow}$ bedeutet: durch Abstraktion von einer Aussageform in eine Menge (abstraktes Objekt) überführt)

c) Kritik an der Methodologie

Der unter Punkt a) vorgetragene Einwand hat natürlich Konsequenzen für die gesamte Entwicklungsmethodologie von Programmen. Bild 2 zeigt die herkömmliche Methodologie und die Methodologie für KAD.

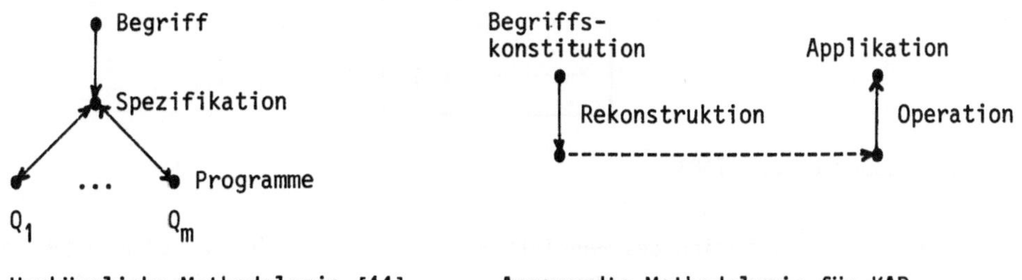

Bild 2: Zwei unterschiedliche Methodologien

Herkömmlich bleibt der Übergang vom Begriff zur Spezifikation ungeklärt. Er ist mit der Hoffnung verbunden, daß die Spezifikation den Begriff erfaßt. Ziel der Methodologie ist, die Spezifikation so zu formulieren, daß die Korrektheit der Programme relativ zu den Spezifikationen bewiesen werden kann. Eine Angewandte Methodologie hingegen geht von der Konstitution der Begriffe in der Lebenswelt aus und rekonstruiert zunächst diese Begriffe. Begriffe fallen schließlich nicht vom Himmel, sondern müssen vor ihrem Gebrauch auch logisch "hergestellt" werden. Eine Rekonstruktion ersetzt das Original. Die Adäquanz mit dem Original wird behauptet, sie ist aber nicht beweisbar, da mit Bezug zu dem Wissen einer Konstitution nichts zu beweisen ist. Entscheidend ist auch nicht die Beweisbarkeit, sondern die Kritisierbarkeit, d.h., jeder methodische Einzelschritt nebst seiner Begründung kann von jedermann überprüft und eine Übereinstimmung mit dem Original bezweifelt werden. Rekonstruieren bedeutet, daß die Begriffe schrittweise und zirkelfrei in einen logisch einwandfreien Zustand gebracht werden, bevor mit ihnen in einer anschließenden Operation programmtechnisch gearbeitet werden kann, um dann durch eine Applikation in die Lebenswelt zurückzufinden. Wegen des hier geforderten knappen Rahmens kann im Hinblick auf die Einzelheiten einer Rekonstruktion nur auf die Literatur verwiesen werden [12], [13], [14], [15], [20], [22],[23].

Um die Unterschiede zur herkömmlichen Spezifikation aufzeigen zu können und um eine Rekonstruktion zu exemplifizieren, wählen wir das bekannte Beispiel STACK aus, wohl wissend, daß die lebensweltliche Bedeutung dieses einfachen Begriffs über eine Dingwelt nur gering ist. Wir gehen von der in Bild 3 gezeigten Anschauung eines STACK ganzer Zahlen aus.

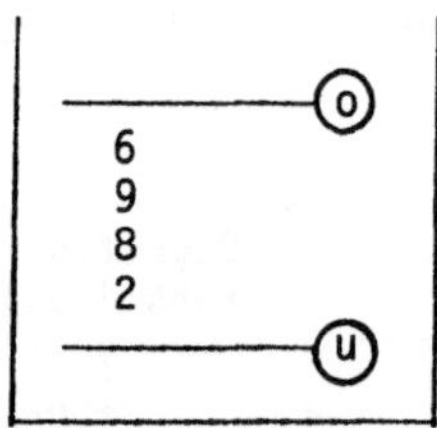

Bild 3: Anschauung eines STACK.

Zur vollständigen Konstitution des Begriffs STACK gehören noch die Bedingungen, daß nur "oben" ein Zeichen hinzugefügt (PUSH-Operation) oder entfernt (POP-Operation) werden darf. Wenn die Bedingungen nicht eingehalten werden, so handelt es sich um einen anderen Begriff, nicht aber um ein STACK. Das Original in Bild 3 wird in Bild 4 rekonstruiert.

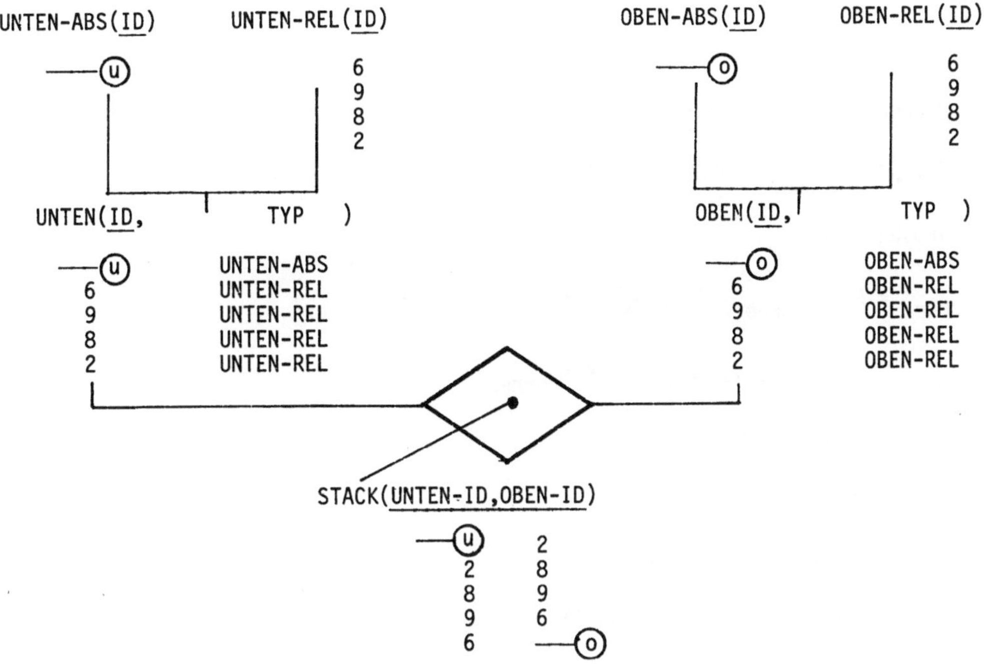

Bild 4: Rekonstruktion des Begriffs STACK. (ID=Identifikation ist ein Prädikat, das ein Objekt eindeutig identifiziert)

Wie Frege beginnen wir mit dem Zeichen. Es werden die Begrenzungszeichen —(u) und —(o) unter den Begriff UNTEN-ABS(OLUT) bzw. OBEN-ABS(OLUT) gebracht. Die anderen Objekte fallen je nach ihrer Rolle sowohl unter die Begriffe UNTEN-REL(ATIV) und OBEN-REL(ATIV). Durch weiteres Abstrahieren gelangen wir zu den Begriffen UNTEN und OBEN. Eine Komposition (Raute), ein zweites Mittel, um Begriffe zu rekonstruieren [23], führt dann zum rekonstruierten Begriff STACK, in dem selbstverständlich Zugriffspfade (Sortierfolge, physische Nachbarschaft) nicht implizit enthalten sein dürfen. Die aufgeführten Bedingungen, daß Hinzufügen und Entfernen nur bei OBEN-ABS erfolgen dürfen, werden in der Datenbankliteratur Integritätsbedingung genannt. Es kann zwischen Zustandsbedingungen und Übergangsbedingungen unterschieden werden [7, S. 170], [3]. Zustandsbedingungen sind solche, die in jedem Zustand der Datenbank erfüllt sein müssen. Übergangsbedingungen dagegen sagen nur etwas über erlaubte Änderungen aus. In einer geeigneten Sprache müssen auch beliebige komplexe Übergangsbedingungen formulierbar sein. Wir wollen an dieser Stelle nicht die Datenmanipulationssprache SEQUEL [2] heranziehen, sondern die Übergangsbedingungen zur Erhaltung der Integrität bei PUSH- und POP-Operationen mengenalgebraisch formulieren, um so von konkreten Produktsprachen unabhängig zu sein.

Integritätsbedingungen:

Für PUSH

a) Vorbedingung: Eindeutigkeit

$\langle x, -\textcircled{o} \rangle \notin STACK_{vorher}$ {PUSH(STACK,x)};

b) Übergangsbedingung

$$STACK_{nachher} = STACK_{vorher} - \{\langle v, -\textcircled{o} \rangle \mid \langle v, -\textcircled{o} \rangle \in STACK_{vorher}\}$$

$$\cup \{\langle v,x \rangle \mid \langle v, -\textcircled{o} \rangle \in STACK_{vorher}\}$$

$$\cup \{\langle x, -\textcircled{o} \rangle\};$$

Für POP

a) Vorbedingung: Nichtleerer STACK

$\langle -\textcircled{u}, -\textcircled{o} \rangle \notin STACK_{vorher}$ {POP(STACK)};

b) Übergangsbedingung

$$STACK_{nachher} = STACK_{vorher} - \{\langle v, -\textcircled{o} \rangle \mid \langle v, -\textcircled{o} \rangle \in STACK_{vorher}\}$$

$$\cup \{\langle u, -\textcircled{o} \rangle \mid \langle u,v \rangle \in STACK_{vorher} \quad \langle v, -\textcircled{o} \rangle \in STACK_{vorher}\};$$

Die Notation der Vorbedingungen wurde in Anlehnung an Hoare [9] gewählt. P{Q}R bedeutet allgemein, daß die Operation Q im Hinblick auf die Präkondition P das Ergebnis R liefert. R besteht in unserem Falle aus den Booleschen Prädikaten "true", "false". Integritätsbedingung und Rekonstruktion machen den Begriff STACK aus. Die Darstellung mag im Vergleich zur axiomatischen Methode unelegant wirken. Sie kann aber auf beliebige lebensweltliche Bedingungen angewandt werden; und Eleganz sollte man, nach Hilberts eigenen Worten, den Schneidern überlassen, die davon mehr verstehen.

2. Die Definition Konstruktiver Abstrakter Datentypen

2.1 Der Aufbau

Es ist das Ziel dieser Arbeit, KAD mit der Absicht einer Programmspezifikation einzuführen. Es soll der Begriff KÜNDIGUNG als Beispiel dienen. Der Begriff läßt sich erstellen, wenn PERSONAL und KONTO bereits konstruiert wurden. Im wesentlichen besteht der Prozeß darin, ein Restgehalt zu berechnen und eine Löschung in PERSONAL und KONTO vorzunehmen. Die dreistufige Abstraktion wird in Bild 5 gezeigt.

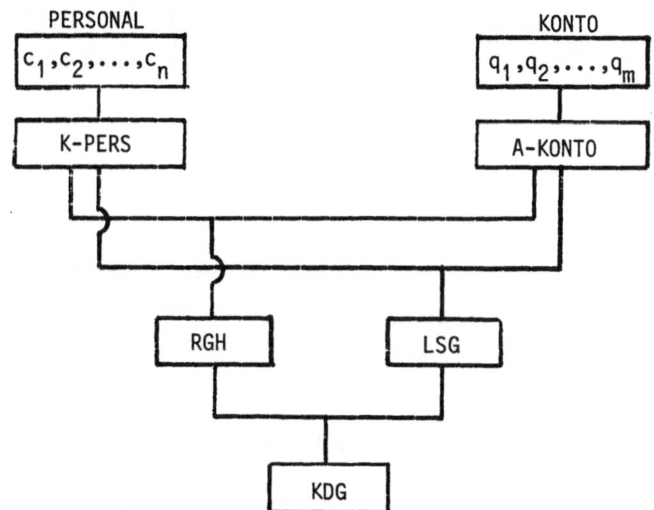

Bild 5: Schematische Darstellung des KAD KÜNDIGUNG
Abkürzungen: K-PERS=KÜNDIGENDES PERSONAL; A-KONTO=AUFZULÖSENDE KONTEN; RGH=RESTGEHALT; LSG=LÖSCHUNG; KDG=KÜNDIGUNG.

Explizite Definitionen:

A) Festlegung des "domain of discourse", d.h., des kündigenden Personals und der aufzulösenden Konten.

I) K-PERS*

$$c_i \sim c_j =_{DF} \text{K-PERS}(c_i) \leftrightarrow \text{K-PERS}(c_j) \text{ für } i \neq j$$

$$\text{K-PERS*}[\epsilon_x \text{K-PERS}(x)] =_{DF} \bigwedge_x (c_i \sim x) \rightarrow \text{K-PERS}(x)$$

Effekt: Keiner.
Der Effekt einer Abstraktion wird ähnlich wie bei Parnas (16) separat notiert.

II) A-KONTO*

$$q_i \sim q_j =_{DF} \text{A-KONTO}(q_i) \leftrightarrow \text{A-KONTO}(q_j) \text{ für } \neq j$$

$$\text{A-KONTO*}[\epsilon_x \text{A-KONTO}] =_{DF} \bigwedge_x (q_i \sim x) \rightarrow \text{A-KONTO}(x)$$

Effekt: Keiner.

B) Prädikatisierung

I) RGH*

$$\text{K-PERS}(x) \underset{x}{\sim} \text{A-KONTO}(x) =_{DF} \bigwedge_x \text{K-PERS}(x) \leftrightarrow \text{A-KONTO}(x)$$

$$\left.\begin{matrix} \text{RGH*}[\epsilon_x \text{K-PERS}(x)] \\ = \\ \text{RGH*}[\epsilon_x \text{A-KONTO}(x)] \end{matrix}\right\} =_{DF} \text{K-PERS}(x) \underset{x}{\sim} \text{A-KONTO}(x) \rightarrow \left\{\begin{matrix} \text{RGH}(\text{K-PERS}(x)) \\ \text{RGH}(\text{A-KONTO}(x)) \end{matrix}\right.$$

Effekt: $c_i,\ c_j \ \varepsilon$ RGH

$q_i,\ q_j \ \varepsilon$ RGH

Bemerkung:

"ε" wird Kopula genannt und besagt in der Form $a\varepsilon N$, daß dem Objekt a die Eigenschaft N zugesprochen wird. Den Objekten c_i, c_j, q_i, q_j wird somit ein Restgehalt zugewiesen. Wie das Restgehalt berechnet wird, ist "Implementierungsdetail".

II) LSG*

$$\text{K-PERS}(x) \underset{x}{\sim} \text{A-KONTO}(x) =_{DF} \bigwedge_x \text{K-PERS}(x) \leftrightarrow \text{A-KONTO}(x)$$

$$\left.\begin{matrix} \text{LSG*}[\epsilon_x \text{K-PERS}(x)] \\ = \\ \text{LSG*}[\epsilon_x \text{A-KONTO}(x)] \end{matrix}\right\} =_{DF} \text{K-PERS}(x) \underset{x}{\sim} \text{A-KONTO}(x) \rightarrow \left\{\begin{matrix} \text{LSG}(\text{K-PERS}(x)) \\ \text{LSG}(\text{A-KONTO}(x)) \end{matrix}\right.$$

Effekt: $c_i,\ c_j \ \varepsilon$ LSG

$q_i,\ q_j \ \varepsilon$ LSG

Bemerkung:

Die Objekte c_i, c_j, q_i, q_j werden gelöscht, d.h., sie sind nicht mehr zugänglich.

III) KDG*

$$\text{RGH}(x) \underset{x}{\sim} \text{LSG}(x) =_{DF} \bigwedge_x (\text{RGH}(x) \rightarrow \text{LSG}(x)$$

$$\left.\begin{matrix} \text{KDG*}[\epsilon_x \text{RGH}(x)] \\ = \\ \text{KDG*}[\epsilon_x \text{LSG}(x)] \end{matrix}\right\} =_{DF} \text{RGH}(x) \underset{x}{\sim} \text{LSG}(x) \rightarrow \left\{\begin{matrix} \text{KDG}(\text{RGH}(x)) \\ \text{KDG}(\text{LSG}(x)) \end{matrix}\right.$$

Effekt: $c_i, c_j \in$ KDG

$q_i, q_j \in$ KDG

Bemerkung:
Zugewiesenes Restgehalt und Löschung zusammen führen über Abstraktion zur Kündigung.

Auf die besondere Bedeutung der KAD für die Datensicherung im Rahmen des Datenschutzes soll nur kurz hingewiesen werden. Es dürfte einleuchtend sein, daß ein KAD ohne Schwierigkeiten als ein Datenobjekt im Sinne der gesetzlich geforderten Zugriffskontrolle aufgefaßt werden kann. Bull [1] fordert z.B., daß Persönlichkeitsprofile, in denen von diversen personenbezogenen Dateien abstrahiert wird, unter besonderen Sicherheitsvorkehrungen stehen oder ganz verboten werden müssen. Ein geordneter Zugriff zu Persönlichkeitsprofilen ohne dogmatisches Verbot ist nach unserer Erkenntnis nur über die Formulierung eines entsprechenden KAD möglich. Das Abstrakte Objekt ersetzt dann die konkreten Objekte in der Sicherheitsmatrix und weiter dann auch in der Capability-Liste.

2.2 Synchronisation (Ablaufintegrität)

So wie Begriffskonstruktionen durch Integritätsbedingungen intensional (inhaltlich) präzisiert werden, so sind für die KAD im Übergang "Operation" Ablaufbedingungen zu stellen, die ebenfalls analytisch sind. Im Begriff KÜNDIGUNG ist schon enthalten, daß RGH vor LSG erfolgt. Die Abstimmung von Prozessen wird Synchronisation genannt. Der Terminus "Bedingungen der Ablaufintegrität" ist deutlicher. Jones [10, S. 12] führt aus, daß für Abstrakte Datentypen die Synchronisation, neben der Bezeichnung (naming) und der Sicherung (protection), eine dritte, wesentliche Komponente ist. Habermann [6] hat mit seinen "path expressions" eine recht brauchbare Form vorgeschlagen, um operationale Integritätsbedingungen zu formulieren. In seiner Notation würde

<u>PATH</u> RGH; LSG <u>END</u>

bedeuten, daß RGH und LSG strikt hintereinander ausgeführt werden. Das Zeichen ";" erzwingt somit die Ausführung des linken KAD-Teils vor dem rechten. "+" bedeutet nach Habermann, daß nur hintereinander ohne feste Reihenfolge ausgeführt werden muß. Weitere Relationen, die eine Überlappung der Ausführungen zulassen, werden in der Habermannschen Arbeit erläutert.

Im Zuge der Einführung Relationaler Datenbanksysteme hat man im Hinblick auf die operationale Integrität eine neue Sicht auf die Problemstellung eingeführt, die man selbstbewußt mit der von Kuhn eingeführten Bezeichnung "Paradigmawechsel" hervorhebt. Es wird das Denken in Transaktionen als Integritätseinheiten und darüber hinaus als Wiederherstelleinheiten (recovery units) empfohlen. In der Tat bedeutet Abkehr von der bloßen Speicherkonsistenz und Hinwendung zur "logischen Konsistenz" einen Bruch mit der Vergangenheit, der vom Standpunkt der KAD notwendigerweise vollzogen werden mußte. Eine Transaktion in der neuen Lesart "sieht" zu Beginn eine Datenbank im konsistenten (integeren) Zustand. Während ihres Ablaufs können diverse, nicht konsistente Zustände angenommen werden. Nach ihrem Abschluß muß aber die Konsistenz der Datenbankzustände gewährleistet sein. Nur Veränderungsoperationen, nicht aber Leseoperationen gefährden die Konsistenz. Eine Transaktion $T(T_1; T_2; \ldots; T_n)$ besteht je nach dem Grad der mikroskopischen Betrachtung seitens der Datenbankbenutzer aus einzelnen Transaktionsschritten T_i, von denen einige atomaren Charakter haben. Das Semikolon in der Klammer von T wird im Habermannschen Sinne benutzt. Eine Unzerlegbarkeit bedeutet, daß ein Schritt aus Konsistenzgründen vollständig ausgeführt werden muß und daß im Fehlerfalle unvollständige Teilschritte vernichtet werden müssen. Die Festlegung der Transaktionsschritte, insbesondere der atomaren Transaktionsschritte, ist nach der Definition von KAD möglich. Denn ein KAD kann ablauforientiert als Transaktion aufgefaßt werden. Eine KAD enthält die Aufbauanweisung einer "nachparadigmatischen" Transaktion. So enthält z.B. die Transaktion KÜNDIGUNG (KDG) als eine Ausprägung den atomaren Schritt $[RGH(c_i,q_i);LSG(c_i,q_i)]$. Es macht nämlich aus der Sicht der Kündigung keinen Sinn, für eine Person das Restgehalt zu berechnen, um dann keine Löschung des Personalstammsatzes und des Personalkontos vorzunehmen.

```
TRANSAKTION KDG
    BEGIN .
          :
          READ PERSONAL(c_i),
          READ KONTO(q_i),
          [RGH(c_i,q_i);LSG(c_i,q_i)]
    END
```

Wie das vieldiskutierte Thema "Methodenbanken" mit Bezug auf den Gegenstand dieser Arbeit einzuordnen ist, müßte einer gesonderten Untersuchung überlassen bleiben.

Literatur:

[1] Bull, P.: Zur verfassungsrechtlichen Verankerung des Datenschutzes, in ÖVD-Online, (1979), Heft 11, S. 3-8.

[2] Chamberlin, D.D. et al.: SEQUEL2: A unified approach to data definition, manipulation and control, in IBM Journal of Research and Development, Vol. 20, No. 6, Nov. 1976, S. 560-575.

[3] Eswaran, K.P. and Chamberlin, D.D.: Functional specification of a subsystem for database integrity, in: Proc. of the Ing. Conference on VLDB 1975, Framingham, Ma, Sept. 22-24, 1975, S. 48-68.

[4] Frege, G.: Über die Grundlagen der Geometrie, in Jahresberichte der Deutschen Mathematiker-Vereinigung (DMV), Band 12 (1903), S. 319-323, S. 368-375, Band 15 (1906), S. 293-309, S. 377-403, S. 423-430.

[5] Guttag, J.V. und Horning, H.H.: The algebraic specification of abstract data types, in: Acta Informatica, Vol. 10 (1978), S. 27-52.

[6] Habermann, A.N.: On the concurrency of parallel processes, in: Jones, A.K. (Hrsg.): Perspectives in computer science, Academic Press, New York, S. 77-90.

[7] Härder, Th.: Die Implementierung von Datenbanksystemen, Carl Hanser Verlag, München, 1978.

[8] Hempel, C.G.: Grundzüge der Begriffsbildung in der empirischen Wissenschaft, Bertelsmann Universitätsverlag, Düsseldorf, 1974.

[9] Hoare, C.A.R.: An axiomatic basis for programming, in: Comm. of the ACM, Vol. 12 (1969), No. 10, S. 576-583.

[10] Jones, A.K.: The object model - A conceptual tool for structuring software, in: Bayer, R. e.a. (Hrsg.): Operating Systems, Lecture Notes in Computer Science, Springer-Verlag, Berlin-Heidelberg-New York, 1978, S. 8-16.

[11] Liskov, B.H. und Zilles, S.N.: Specification techniques for data abstraction, in: IEEE Transactions on Software Engineering, SE-1, (1975), S. 7-19.

[12] Lorenzen, P.: Konstruktivismus und Hermeneutik,in: Lorenzen, P.: Konstruktive Wissenschaftstheorie, Suhrkamp Verlag, Frankfurt, 1974, S. 113-119.

[13] Lorenzen, P.: Konstruktive und axiomatische Methode, in: Lorenzen, P.: Konstruktive Wissenschaftstheorie, Suhrkamp Verlag, Frankfurt, 1974, S. 219-233.

[14] Lorenzen, P.: Gleichheit und Abstraktion, in: Lorenzen, P.: Konstruktive Wissenschaftstheorie, Suhrkamp Verlag, Frankfurt, 1974, S. 190-198.

[15] Lorenzen, P. und Schwemmer, O.: Konstruktive Logik, Ethik und Wissenschaftstheorie, Bibliographisches Institut, Mannheim, 1975.

[16] Parnas, D.L.: A technique for software module specification with examples, in: Comm. of the ACM, Vol. 15 (1972), Nr. 5, S. 330-336.

[17] Parnas, D.L.: On the criteria to be used in decomposing systems into modules, in: Comm. of the ACM, Vol. 15 (1972), No. 12, S. 1053-1058.

[18] Parnas, D.L.: Information distribution aspects of design methodology, in: Proc. of 1971 IFIP Congress in Lublijana, Vol. 1, North-Holland, Amsterdam, 1972, S. 339-344.

[19] Stegmüller, W.: Hauptströmungen der Gegenwartsphilosophie, Band I, Kröner-Verlag, Stuttgart, 1976.

[20] Thiel, Chr.: Grundlagenkrise und Grundlagenstreit. Studien über das normative Fundament der Wissenschaften am Beispiel von Mathematik und Sozialwissenschaften, Meisenheim, 1974.

[21] Thiel, Chr.: Gottlob Frege - Die Abstraktion, in: Grundprobleme der großen Philosophen, Philosophie der Gegenwart I, S. 9 - 44, UTB-Taschenbuch 147, Vandenhoeck & Rupprecht, Göttingen, 1972.

[22] Wedekind, H.: Eine Methodologie zur Konstruktion des Konzeptionellen Schemas, in: Niedereichholz, J. (Hrsg.): Datenbanktechnologie, Teubner-Verlag, Stuttgart, 1979.

[23] Wedekind, H. und Ortner, E.: Systematisches Konstruieren von Datenbankanwendungen - Zur Methodologie der Angewandten Informatik, Carl Hanser Verlag, München, 1980.

MODULARER DATENBANK ENTWURF FÜR KLEINRECHNER

Hermann Bense, Universität Dortmund, Abt. Informatik, 46oo Dortmund 5o

0 ÜBERBLICK

In diesem Artikel werden Verfahren für die Implementierung von Datenbanksystemen vorgestellt werden, die die Vorzüge des jeweiligen Rechnersystems bzgl. Hardware, Software und Firmware so weit als möglich ausnutzen.
Ausgangspunkt für den Entwurf des DBMS ist das ANSI/SPARC Schichtenmodell. Für die Implementierung der einzelnen Ebenen sollte möglichst auf bereits existierende Hardware oder Software zugegriffen werden.
Das zugrundeliegende Datenmodell soll im wesentlichen die Züge des Relationenansatzes tragen.
Ein weiterer wichtiger Gesichtspunkt der Implementierung wird die Dialogorientierung des DBMS sein. Die Anwendungsprogramme müssen daher durch eine leicht bedienbare Abfragesprache - wie etwa QUERY BY EXAMPLE (18) - unterstützt werden.
Letztendlich soll bei der Realisierung ein möglichst hoher Grad an Datenunabhängigkeit und Unabhängigkeit von der Größenordung der Anwendung sowie vom Spektrum der Anwender erreicht werden.

In (3) wird das Design und die Implementierung eines DBMS für ein handelsübliches Kleinrechnersystem konsequent durchgeführt.
Im Abschnitt 2 sind die dabei gewonnenen Erfahrungen für die Entwicklung von DB-Systemen auf beliebige Rechner verallgemeinert worden.
Kapitel 3 zeigt insbesondere die Problematik der Implementierung von DB-Systemen auf einem kleinem System anhand eines Rechners mit 16 K Bytes Hauptspeicher und mit Floppy Disk als Sekundärspeichermedium.
Im folgenden Abschnitt 1 werden im top down Verfahren die wesentlichen Konzepte der Datenbankarchitektur festgelegt. Die Implementierung erfolgt wie bei vielen größeren Softwareprojekten bottom up. Allein dadurch kann gewährleistet werden, daß die unteren Ebenen der Hardware und Software optimal ausgenutzt werden.

1 SYSTEMENTWURF

Die wichtigsten Kriterien für den Entwurf eines DB-Systems sind allgemeine Datenunabhängigkeit, Portabilität und Modularität. Der Ansatz, der hier verfolgt werden soll, orientiert sich stark an dem von Härder (9) beschriebenen "Aufbau eines datenunabhängigen Datenbanksystems".
Danach ist das Ziel eines hierarchischen Systementwurfs die Realisierung mehrerer möglichst unabhängiger Ebenen, auf denen Objekte und Operatoren zur Verfügung gestellt werden, mit denen die Implementierung der nächsthöheren Ebene durchgeführt werden kann. Paolini (15) bevorzugt diesen operationalen Ansatz für Kleinrechner, da aufwendige Abbildungsprozeße (transforms, mappings) von einer in die andere Ebene vermieden werden. Die Implementierungsdefinition wird nämlich selber aktiver Teil eines Ebenenüberganges.

Die im folgenden vorgestellte Systemarchiktektur erfüllt daher alle Anforderungen, die an ein modernes DB-System gestellt werden müssen.

MONITOR .Anwendungsauswahl
ANWENDUNGSSYSTEM .ABFRAGE .RELATION-EDITOR .BENUTZERPROGRAMM .SICHERUNG
DATENSYSTEM .MENGEN-OPERATOREN .RELATIONALE-OPERATOREN
ZUGRIFFSSYSTEM .TUPEL .INDEX .Rel-Scan .Ind-Scan
SPEICHERSYSTEM .SEGMENT

Die eigentlichen System- und Benutzeranwendungsprogramme werden mit den Operatoren der DB-Sprache realisiert. Zu Systemanwendungsprogrammen würde man z.B. ein interaktives DB-Sprachmodul ähnlich QUERY BY EXAMPLE oder einen Relation-Editor rechnen.

Benutzeranwendungsprogramme sind z.B. Lagerverwaltung, Lohnabrechnung, Buchhaltung, Fakturierung usw.

Das Datensystem soll dem Benutzer bzw. dem Anwendungsprogramm ausschließlich Aspekte der Problemlösung präsentieren. Im Idealfall würde vom Benutzer keine Kenntnis der Speicherstrukturen der Relationen und Zugriffspfade erwartet. Auf dieser Ebene werden die Relationalen Operatoren für eine deskriptive DB-Sprache bereitgestellt.

Die Prozeduren IND-SCAN und REL-SCAN des Zugriffssystems arbeiten eine Relation Tupel für Tupel ab und zwar in der Ordnung der Relationspeicherstruktur oder in der Reihenfolge der Sortierung eines bestimmten Attributes, zu dem ein Index existiert.

Auf der Ebene des Zugriffssystems sind nur Tupel und Zugriffspfade bekannt. Das Modul TUPEL verwaltet die Relationspeicherstruktur auf den Seiten, die durch das Modul SEGMENT des Speichersystems zur Verfügung gestellt werden. Indexe sind spezielle Zugriffspfade der Relationen, die einen schnellen sequentiellen oder direkten Zugriff in der Sortierreihenfolge eines bestimmten Attributes unterstützen. Um einen hohen Grad an Datenunabhängigkeit zu erreichen, erhalten die Tupel für die interne Verwaltung eindeutige Identifikatoren, so daß in den Indexen z.B. keine physischen Adressen gemerkt werden müssen. Indexe sind also immun gegen physisches Verschieben der Relationspeicherstruktur.

Im Speichersystem werden mit Hilfe der Betriebssystemzugriffsmethoden lineare Adreßräume auf Sekundärspeicher abgebildet. Einzige Voraussetzung dazu ist die Definition geeigneter Speicherzuordnungsstrukturen, die dann die Geräteunabhängigkeit des gesamten Systems garantieren.

2 IMPLEMENTIERUNG

2.1 SPEICHERSYSTEM

Die meisten Datenbanken sind von ihrem Volumen her so groß, daß sie auf sekundären Speichermedien verwaltet werden müssen. Falls keine Systemsoftware zur Verwaltung des Speicherplatzes zur Verfügung steht, muß ein Speichermodul entworfen werden, welches die Funktionen "Speicherplatz.bereitstellen" und "Speicherplatz.freigeben" realisiert. Als Sekundärspeicher kommen nur Medien mit Direktzugriff in Frage wie z.B. Floppy-Disk, Magnetplatte, Trommel, Blasenspeicher. Da ein effizientes Arbeiten nur dann gewährleistet ist, wenn ganze Blöcke von Daten bei einem Zugriff übertragen werden, liegt es nahe, die am Geräteaufbau orientierte physische Sektorierung zu übernehmen. Mehrere benachbarte Sektoren können zu Segmenten (Seiten) zusammengefaßt werden, die dem Speichersystem unter einer eindeutigen Adresse SID bekannt sind.

Es geht nun darum, auf i.a. mehreren Datenträgern einen linearen Adreßraum zu realisieren. Dazu muß eine geeignete Speicherzuordnungsstruktur gefunden werden, die die höheren Ebenen des DBMS von den Gerätecharakteristika isoliert. Wenn mit Datenträgern konstanter Kapazität gearbeitet wird, bietet sich folgende einfache Speicherzuordungsstruktur an (Abb. 1):

Jeder Datenträger erhält einen eindeutigen Identifikator DID. Mit §DISK sei die Anzahl der Speichermedien der Datenbank bezeichnet. Jeder Datenträger kann §DISK-SEGM Seiten aufnehmen, die jeweils aus einer festen Anzahl der kleinsten adressierbaren Speichereinheit (Sektoren) bestehen.

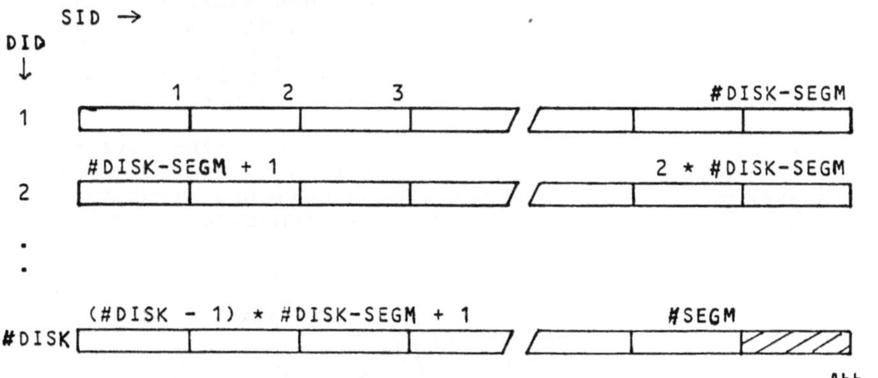

Abb. 1

Zu einem Segment SID müssen also von der Speicherzuordnungsfunktion die Nummer des Datenträgers DID und die Adresse des ersten Sektors (SKT-ID) des Segmentes bzgl. des Datenträgers ermittelt werden. Dazu dienen die beiden folgenden Gleichungen, in denen §SEGM-SKT die Anzahl der Sektoren bezeichnet, aus denen ein Segment besteht.

$$\text{DID} := \lceil (\text{SID} - 1) \,/\, \text{§DISK-SEGM} \rceil$$
$$\text{SKT-ID} := \text{mod}\,(\text{SID} - 1,\ \text{§DISK-SEGM}) * \text{§SEGM-SKT} + 1$$
$$\text{mit } 1 \le \text{SID} \le \text{§SEGM} := \text{§DISK} * \text{§DISK-SEGM}$$

Zur dynamischen Speicherverwaltung wird auf jedem der Datenträger eine linear verkettete Liste der noch verfügbaren Segmente angelegt.

Mit SEGM-BUFF sei ein Hauptspeicherinterner Puffer in der Größe eines Segmentes bezeichnet. Das Speichersystem stellt der nächsthöheren Systemebene folgenden Prozeduren bereit:

```
SPEICHERSYSTEM
            .SEGMENT
                   .Speicherzuordung [SID] -> DID, SKT-ID
                   .laden [SID ] - > SEGM-BUFF
                   .speichern [SID]< -  SEGM-BUFF
                   .anfordern  -> SID
                   .freigeben [SID]
```

alternative Implementierung:
Jedes DOS (disk operating system) oder VS (virtual storage), welches die gerade genannten Funktionen beinhaltet, kann natürlich die Funktion des Speichersystems übernehmen. Es gibt aber auch Sekundärspeicher mit eigenen Prozessoren, die diese Operatoren hardwaremäßig realisieren (4).

Die folgenden Abschnitte zeigen, wie die eigentlichen Datenstrukturen in die Segmente eingebettet werden.

2.2 ZUGRIFFSSYSTEM

2.2.1 SPEICHERUNGSSTRUKTUR FÜR RELATIONEN

Im relationalen Datenmodell ist die Reihenfolge der Tupel in der Tabelle ohne Bedeutung. In konventionellen Rechensystemen ist es allerdings wichtig, auf die einzelnen Sätze (Zeilen) der Relation direkt zugreifen zu können. Zu diesem Zweck wird eine Relationspeicherstruktur definiert, die einen schnellen direkten Zugriff über einen eineindeutigen Tupelidentifikator (TID) auf ein beliebiges Tupel der Relation unterstützt.

Bei der Implementierung wird von einer konstanten Tupellänge (TU-L) ausgegangen, um die Einbettung in die Segmente zu erleichtern. Die Tupel selber können beliebig strukuriert werden. Abb. 2 zeigt das Schema der Relationspeicherstruktur.

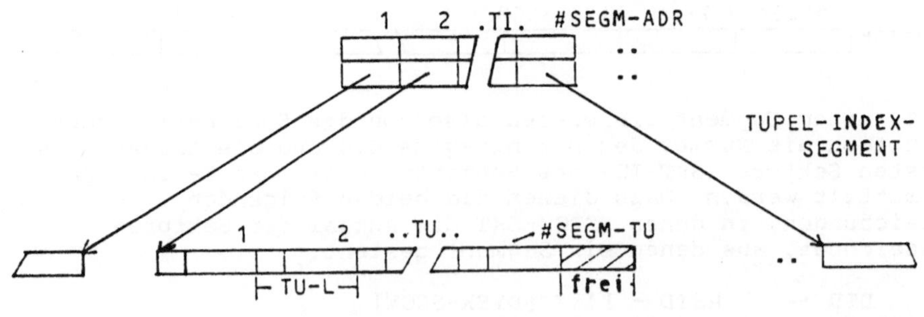

Abb. 2

Die Länge der Segmente sei mit SEGM-L bezeichnet. Insgesamt können daher

```
§SEGM-TU :=  SEGM-L / TU-L
```

Tupel in einem Segment abgespeichert werden. Als Relation-Speicherstruktur werden nun einfach soviel Segmente wie benötigt linear angeordnet und als Adreßraum für den Tupelidentifikator TID betrachtet. Die Anordnung wird durch ein Tupelindex-Segment vorgenommen, das ein Feld von Tupelsegment-Adressen realisiert. So erhält man eine zweistufige Relationspeicherstruktur, in der die Adressierung eines Tupels über die folgenden Beziehungen vorgenommen wird:

```
TU :=   mod (TID - 1, §SEGM-TU) + 1
TI :=   mod (TID - 1, §IND-SEGM-TU) + 1
mit  IND-SEGM-TU := §SEGM-ADR * §SEGM-TU
```

Für kleinere Anwendungen (Größenordung ca. 10**3 bis 10**4) reicht diese Speicherstruktur sicherlich schon aus. Bei größeren Anwendungen kann auf die Speicherstrukur eine weitere Stufe mit Tupelindex-Segmenten aufgesetzt werden.

Der nächsthöheren Ebene des DB-Systems werden für die Relationspeicherstruktur die Operatoren

```
ZUGRIFFSSYSTEM
                .TUPEL
                       .laden [TID]
                       .speichern [TID]
                       .einfügen [TID]
                       .löschen [TID]
                       .Test [FILTERPRÄDIKAT]
```

zur Verfügung gestellt. Die Prozedur "TUPEL.einfügen" stellt den Platz für das Abspeichern eines neuen Tupels bereit und gibt die neue Adresse (TID) an das aufrufende Modul zurück. Umgekehrt kann durch "TUPEL.löschen" der von einem Tupel belegte Platz freigegeben werden. Die Prozedur "TUPEL.Test" wird bei den Scan-Operatoren des Zugriffssystems erklärt.

alternative Implementierung:
Wenn auf dem Rechner eine Zugriffsmethode wie VSAM oder ISAM benutzt werden kann, so erübrigt sich u.U. die Implementierung des Speichersystems und der Relationspeicherstruktur. Ein beliebiges Attribut der Relation wird als Primärattribut ausgezeichnet und dient als Sortierkriterium für die Zugriffsmethode. Wenn das Attribut die Tupel eindeutig identifiziert, kann es gleichzeitig als TID benutzt werden. Auf diese Weise können also auch die Funktionen des Moduls TUPEL - wie sie oben festgelegt wurden - durch vorhandene Betriebssystemsoftware bzw. -Firmware realisiert werden.

Da man als normaler Anwendungsprogrammierer kaum Eingriffe in die interne Struktur dieser Zugriffsmethoden nehmen kann, wird es einem schwer fallen, die Effizienz der Speicherausnutzung zu kontrollieren oder etwa geeignete Konzepte für parallelen Zugriff oder Datenschutz bzw. Datensicherheit bereitzustellen.

2.2.2 ZUGRIFFSPFADE FÜR RELATIONEN

Im Relationenmodell wird grundsätzlich keine Annahme über die Anordnung der Tupel in einer Relation gemacht. Um eine Abfrage an die Datenbank beantworten zu können, müssen die angesprochenen Relationen also ganz - u.U. mehrfach - durchlaufen werden.
Zugriffspfade sollen die Suche erheblich beschleunigen und die Menge der zu untersuchenden Tupel auf eine möglichst kleine Teilmenge reduzieren (1).

Zugriffspfade enthalten keine logischen Informationen, die sich nicht schon aus den Daten selbst ableiten lassen (9). Lediglich die Wirksamkeit des Zugriffs ist durch das Einführen oder Entfernen von Zugriffspfaden betroffen. Diese Redundanz drückt sich in zusätzlichem Speicheraufwand der Programme und Daten aus.

Im folgenden sei eine Liste der wichtigsten Zugriffspfadtypen angegeben (5):
- sequentielle Dateien, Mehrwegbäume, Hash-Verfahren
- Bitlisten, vollständige Indexe, k-d Bäume usw.

Implementierung:
Es müssen die in sich widersprüchlichen Anforderungen eines optimalen Zugriffsverhaltens und einer optimalen Speicherplatzausnutzung berücksichtigt werden. I.a. sollte ein Zugriffspfad sowohl sequentiellen als auch direkten Zugriff auf eine Relation unterstützen.

Für kleinere Anwendungen wurde in (3) ein zweistufiger Index entwickelt, der bzgl. der gestellten Anforderungen einen guten Kompromiß schließt. Es handelt sich dabei um ein kombiniertes Verfahren aus dynamischen Hashing (8) und digitalen Suchbäumen (5). Das Konzept baut auf dem allgemeinen Indexentwurf von (16) auf (Abb. 3).

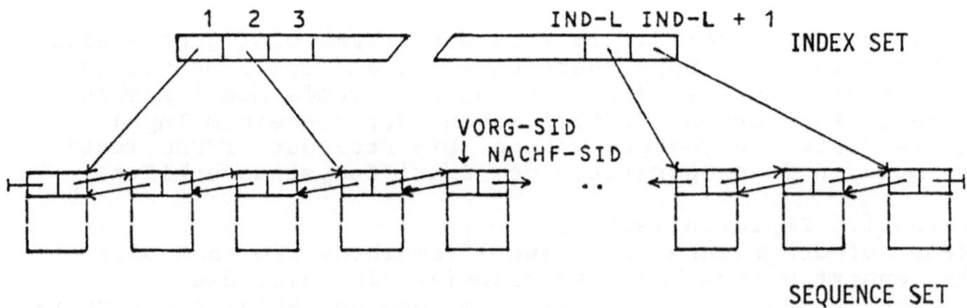

Abb. 3

Auf dem niedrigsten Level, dem SEQUENCE SET, wird eine doppelt verkettete Liste von Segmenten verwaltet, die in aufsteigender Ordnung des indexierten Attributes die Attributwert/TID-Paare enthält. Aus der Bezeichnung geht bereits hervor, daß diese Liste den sequentiellen Durchlauf ermöglicht. Die darüberliegende 2. Ebene besteht zunächst nur aus einem Segmetn (INDEX SET) und ermöglicht aufgrund einer schlüsselsequenzerhaltenden Hashfunktion den direkten Einstieg in den Sequence Set. In (3) werden verschiedene Methoden zur Erweiterung dieses Konzeptes vorgestellt.

Einbettung in die Segmente der Speicherverwaltung:
Ähnlich zur Einbettung der Tupel in die Segmente geht man hier von konstanten Feldlängen für die Attributwert/TID-Paare aus. Bei Überlaufen von Blattseiten werden neue Segmente angefordert und in den Sequence Set eingefügt.

Das Segment des Index Set braucht nur Adressen von Segmenten des Sequence Set zu verwalten, da die Hash-Funktion aus dem Attributwert gleich die richtige Adresse des Index Set auswählt.

Das Modul INDEX stellt neben den Standardmanipulationsfunktionen verschiedene Funktionen für den Zugriff auf den Index bereit:

```
ZUGRIFFSSYSTEM
            .INDEX
                  .Eintrag [KEY, TID]
                  .Austrag [KEY, TID]
                  .Suche [KEY] -> TID, VORHANDEN
                  .erster-Eintrag   -> KEY, TID
                  .letzter-Eintrag  -> KEY, TID
                  .Vorgänger   -> KEY, TID
                  .Nachfolger  -> KEY, TID
```

alternative Implementierung:
Ähnlich zur alternativen Realisierung der Relationspeicherstruktur können auch bei der Implementierung von Zugriffspfaden Betriebssystem-Zugriffsmethoden wie ISAM und VSAM verwendet werden. Wenn man Indexe als binäre Relationen mit den Attributen KEY und TID ansieht, so ergibt sich direkt die Analogie zur Implementierung von Relationen mittels Standardzugriffsmethoden.

2.2.3 OPERATOREN DES ZUGRIFFSSYSTEMS

Aufgabe des Zugriffssystems ist es, wirksame Primitive zur Realisierung einer deskriptiven DB-Sprache auf der nächsthöheren Ebene des Datenbanksystems zur Verfügung zu stellen (9). Dazu können die Module SEGMENT, TUPEL und INDEX herangezogen werden. Die im folgenden angegebenen Operatoren stellen die Tupel einer Relation in der Ordnung eines bestimmten Zugriffspfades zur Verfügung.

Wenn dieser Zugriffspfad die Relationspeicherstruktur selber ist und der Zugriff sequentiell aufgrund des Tupelidentifikators TID erfolgt, so spricht man vom Relationenscan. Wird ein Index über ein Sekundärattribut als Zugriffspfad benutzt, so spricht man von einem Indexscan.

Die Tupel die der aufrufenden Prozedur zur Weiterverarbeitung übergeben werden, können durch ein Filterprädikat weiter eingeschränkt werden. Filterprädikate sind hier konjunktive Verknüpfungen einfacher Prädikate der Form

<attributname> <op> <attributwert>

wobei op ein Vergleichsoperator aus der Menge {=, <>, <, <=, >=, >} ist.

Implementierung:
Die Implementierung der Scan-Operatoren ist einfach, da nur einfache Schleifen programmiert werden müssen. Der formale Parameter "WEITERVERARBEITUNG" bestimmt die Prozedur, die für jedes vom Scan-Operator bereitgestellte Tupel ausgeführt werden soll. Zuvor wird von der Prozedur

```
procedure TUPEL.Check;
  TUPEL.laden [TID];
  TUPEL.Test [FILTERPRÄDIKAT] -> ERFÜLLT;
  if ERFÜLLT then WEITERVERARBEITUNG
end
```

ein bestimmes Tupel geladen und gegen das Filterprädikat getestet. Wenn das Tupel sich gegen das Filterprädikat qualifiziert, gibt die Prozedur "TUPEL.Test" den Wert "true" zurück. Die Scan-Prozeduren können nun folgendermaßen definiert werden:

```
procedure REL-SCAN [RID, START-TID, END-TID,
                    FILTERPRÄDIKAT, WEITERVERARBEITUNG] ;
  for TID := START-TID to END-TID do TUPEL.Check
end
```

Beim Indexscan wird über den Parameter AID das Attribut ausgewählt, dessen Index als Zugriffspfad benutzt werden soll. START-AW und END-AW legen den Bereich des Indexes fest, aus dem Einträge bereitgestellt werden.

```
procedure IND-SCAN [RID, AID, START-AW, END-AW,
                    FILTERPRÄDIKAT, WEITERVERARBEITUNG] ;
  AW := START-AW;
  while AW <= END-AW do
    begin
    INDEX.Suche [AW] -> TID, VORHANDEN;
    while not VORHANDEN and AW <= END-AW
      do INDEX.Nachfolger -> AW, TID, VORHANDEN;
    if VORHANDEN then do TUPEL.Check
    end
end
```

Zur Implementierung der Operatoren der nächsthöheren Ebene stehen also folgende Prozeduren zur Verfügung:

```
ZUGRIFFSSYSTEM
              .REL-SCAN [RID, START-TID, ...    ]
              .IND-SCAN [RID, AID, START-AW, ...]
```

alternative Implementierung:
Dem Autor ist nicht bekannt, ob es Betriebssystemsoftware gibt, die die gerade genannten Funktionen wahrnehmen können. Die Forschung auf dem Gebiet der DB-Systeme hat aber bereits einige Hardwaremäßige Ansätze in Form der relationalen assoziativen Prozessoren (2, 12, 14) hervorgebracht.
Durch Ausnutzung höchstmöglichen parallelen Zugriffs können die Relationen ohne Unterstützung durch Zugriffspfade schnell durchlaufen werden. Durch assoziative Prozessoren können also die unteren Ebenen des DB-Systems einschließlich des Zugriffssystems ersetzt werden.

2.3 DATENSYSTEM

Die Aufgabe des Datensystems ist es, eine deskriptive DB-Sprache bereitzustellen, die in gleicher Weise zur Definition, Manipulation und Kontrolle der Daten herangezogen werden kann. Je nach Größenordnung der Anwendung müssen dabei mehr oder weniger große Einschränkungen in Bezug auf die relationale Vollständigkeit der Sprache gemacht werden. Der im folgenden entwickelte Satz relationaler Operatoren kann auch noch auf kleinsten Systemen sinnvoll implementiert werden (3). Eine Erweiterung des Funktionsumfangs kann aufgrund des sauberen Entwurfs jederzeit vorgesehen werden, wenn die Voraussetzungen von Seiten der Hardware geschaffen wurden.

Die vollständige Relationenalgebra besteht aus zwei Gruppen von Operationen, den Mengenoperationen (Vereinigung, Durchschnitt, Differenz, kartesisches Produkt) und den speziellen relationalen Operatoren (Selektion, Projektion, Verbund, Division (9)). Im folgenden werden die wichtigsten davon vorgestellt und mögliche Implementierungen mit Hilfe der Operatoren der niedrigeren Ebenen des Datenbanksystems gegeben.

2.3.1 MENGENOPERATIONEN

- VEREINIGUNG
  Im Arbeitsspeicher wird ein Tupel aufgebaut. Falls kein anderes Tupel der Relation die gleiche Kombination von Schlüsselattributwerten besitzt, wird das neue Tupel in die Relationspeicherstruktur eingefügt. Gemäß der Datendefinition werden alle Zugriffspfade der Relation aktualisiert.

- DIFFERENZ
  Aus der Relationspeicherstruktur werden alle Tupel entfernt, die dem Filterprädikat genügen. Die Indexe der Relation werden aktualisiert.

Implementierung:
Die Vereinigungsoperation kann direkt mit den Prozeduren der Module TUPEL und INDEX realisiert werden.
Für das Löschen können die Operatoren des Zugriffssystems eingesetzt werden. Die Ordnung (Primär-/Sekundärattribute) des Relationdurchlaufs kann einen starken Einfluß auf die Effektivität der Abarbeitung haben und sollte vom Benutzer bzw. von der aufrufenden Prozedur aufgrund der bekannten Fakten optimiert werden.
Der Aufruf

```
ZUGRIFFSSYSTEM.IND-SCAN [RID, AID, START-AW, END-AW,
                        FILTERPRÄDIKAT, TUPELLÖSCHEN] ;
```

realisiert die Differenz mit der Prozedur

```
procedure TUPELLÖSCHEN;
  TUPEL.löschen [TID];
  for [alle Attribute, zu denen ein Index existiert]
    do INDEX.Austrag [KEY, TID]
end
```

2.3.2 RELATIONALE OPERATOREN

- PROJEKTION
  Für jedes in einer Abfrage beteiligte Attribut einer Relation kann festgelegt werden, ob seine Werte zur Weiterverarbeitung zur Verfügung gestellt werden sollen. Je nachdem enthält die Ergebnisrelation eine bzw. keine Spalte für das Attribut.

- SELEKTION
  Um die Anzahl der zu verarbeitenden Tupel weitgehend einzuschränken, kann mit Hilfe der Filterprädikate eine Selektion vorgenommen werden. Die Definition der Filterprädikate erfolgt implizit in der Abfragedefinition.

- VERBUNDE
  Im ungünstigsten Fall erfordert die Verbundbildung die Konstruktion des kartesischen Produktes aller in der Abfrage angesprochenen Relationen. Das Ziel ist es nun, aufgrund der vorhandenen Zugriffspfade, Selektionen usw. die Ausführung einer Abfrage zu optimieren.

Implementierung:
In praktischen Anwendungen spielt der natürliche Verbund die größte Rolle. Die Implementierung erfolgt mit den Operatoren der nächstniedrigeren Ebene des Datenbanksystems. Die Effizienz der Ausführung hängt dabei im wesentlichen von der Reihenfolge der Abarbeitung ab. Bei mehreren Möglichkeiten sollte aufgrund der Informationen des data dictionarys bzw. mit Hilfe des Benutzers eine Entscheidung herbeigeführt werden. Zur Verfügung gestellt werden sollen daher verschiedene Typen von Verbunden auf zwei Relationen, die die vorhandenen Zugriffsunterstützungen optimal ausnutzen und zu einer allgemeinen Verbundoperation fortgesetzt werden können.

Beispiel:
Natürlicher Verbund der Relationen R und S über die verbundverträglichen Attribute Ar und As. Zu As existiere ein Zugriffspfad in Form eines Indexes.
Die folgende Realisierung spiegelt genau die Vorgehensweise einer ad hoc Lösung dieses Problems wieder. Die Prozedur

```
procedure INDEX-VERBUND;
  ZUGRIFFSSYSTEM.REL-SCAN [R, 1, §R-TU, IND-TID-LADEN]
end
```

ruft für alle Tupel (1..§R-TU) der Relation R die Prozedur IND-TID-LADEN auf. Für den Wert des Attributes Ar des aktuellen Tupels der Relation R werden von IND-TID-LADEN über den Index des Attributes As alle die Tupel der Relation S aufgesucht, deren Wert für Attribut As mit dem von Ar übereinstimmt:

```
procedure IND-TID-LADEN;
  AW := [Wert des Attributes Ar im aktuellen Tupel von
         Relation R];
  ZUGRIFFSSYSTEM.IND-SCAN [ S, As, AW, AW, WEITERVERARBEITUNG]
end
```

An diesem Beispiel kann gesehen werden, daß die Operatoren des Zugriffssystems mächtige Konzepte für die Implementierung relationaler Operatoren bereitstellen. Die Verallgemeinerung von Verbunden kann durch entsprechende Kombination der Operatoren REL-SCAN und IND-SCAN sowie durch geeignete Spezifizierung der Prozedur WEITERVERARBEITUNG erfolgen. Operatoren des Datensystems sind also:

```
DATENSYSTEM
           .MENGEN-OPERATOREN
                             .Vereinigung
                             .Differenz

           .RELATIONALE-OPERATOREN
                                  .Projektion
                                  .Selektion
                                  .Verbund
```

alternative Implementierung:

Das Datensystem ist die oberste Ebene des DBMS. Seine Funktionen werden dem Benutzer oder den Anwendungsprogrammen direkt zur Verfügung gestellt.

Als Alternative zu Systemen, die bereits eine Schnittstelle mit relationalen Operatoren bereitstellen, sind eigentlich nur dedizierte DB-Computer (DB-Maschinen) denkbar (10, 11).

2.4 ANWENDUNGSSYSTEM

Das Anwendungssystem stellt verschiedene Module für System- und Benutzeranwendungen zur Verfügung. Die wichtigsten seien hier aufgeführt:

```
ANWENDUNGSSYSTEM
                .BENUTZERPROGRAMM
                                 ."Prozeduren"

                .ABFRAGE
                        .editieren
                        .ausführen

                .RELATION-EDITOR
----------------------------------------------
MONITOR
       .Anwendungsauswahl
```

Stellvertretend für die eigentlichen Anwendungsprogramme steht hier das Modul BENUTZERPROGRAMM.

Das Modul ABFRAGE gehört wie die anderen aufgeführten Module auch zu den Systemanwendungsprogrammen und gestattet auf dem Bildschirm interaktives Editieren von Abfragen und deren anschließende Ausführung.

Der RELATION-EDITOR betrachtet eine Relation als Tabelle mit den Tupeln als Zeilen. Mit dem TID als Zeilennummer ist ein deskriptives Navigieren und Manipulieren in der Tabelle möglich.

Die gesamte Ablaufkontrolle wird durch das Modul MONITOR vollzogen, welches den Dialog abwickelt, Anwendungen auswählt und deren Ausführung überwacht.

3 ERFAHRUNGEN MIT EINER KLEINRECHNER DB-IMPLEMENTIERUNG

In diesem Kapitel sollen anhand einer konkreten Implementierung (3) die verschiedenen Phasen des Datenbankentwurfs erläutert werden. Besondere Bedeutung wird der Darstellung der Problematik bei der Benutzung von Kleinrechnern beigemessen. Außerdem wird auf geräteabhängige Details eingegangen, wie Programmiersprache, Betriebssystem und Platten-Betriebssystem (DOS).

Entscheidend ist dabei, Mittel zu finden, die den Systementwurf in geeigneter Weise auf die gegebene Kombination von Hardware und Software übertragen.

3.1 HARDWAREKONFIGURATION

Das DB-System wurde auf einem WANG 2200 T Computer implementiert. In der minimalen Ausbaustufe gehören zur Anlage eine CPU mit 16 K Bytes RAM, ein Bildschirmterminal (16 x 64 Zeichen), ein Drucker und eine Floppy Disk Station mit drei Laufwerken a´ 256 K Bytes. Von der Größenordnung her ist die Anlage für Einzelbenutzer ausgelegt, speziell also für kleine Firmen. Für diese Anwender wird mit einem Datenvolumen von ca. 10**3 bis 10**4 Datenobjekten (z.B. Artikel am Lager, Anzahl Kunden, Anzahl Lieferanten, Anzahl Konten in der Buchhaltung usw.) gerechnet. Als Programmiersprache steht ein komfortabler BASIC-Interpreter zur Verfügung, der Aufwärtskompatibilität auf Anlagen des gleichen Herstellers garantiert. Ebenso können die Direktzugriffsmöglichkeiten des Platten Betriebssystems auch auf größere Sekundärspeichermedien übernommen werden. Anlagen, die der Leistungsfähigkeit der gerade beschriebenen Minimalkonfiguraton entsprechen, kosten heute bereits weniger als 10000 DM.

3.2 ANWENDUNG MODERNER SOFTWARETECHNOLOGIEN

Man kann schnell absehen, daß die geringe Hauptspeichergröße einen Engpaß für die Programmentwicklung darstellt. Es wird also nicht genügen, möglichst einfache Prozeduren und Speicherstrukturen zu entwerfen, sondern ein besonderes Augenmerk muß auf eine möglichst effiziente Implementierung des Überganges von einer Ebene des Systems zur anderen gerichtet werden. Durch Anwendung des Modul-Konzeptes (17) konnte ständig der Gesamtentwurf überblickt werden.

Beim hierarchischen Datenbank-Entwurf pflanzen sich gute und schlechte Details gleichermaßen von unten nach oben durch alle Ebenen des DB-Systems fort. Also muß der Entwurf auf den unteren Ebenen besonders sorgfältig durchgeführt werden.

Leider müssen wegen der Kapazitäten häufig Kompromisse gemacht werden, die zu Lasten der Datenunabhängigkeit oder zu Lasten eines einheitlichen Designs gehen. Im folgenden Text werden entsprechende Verbesserungenmöglichkeiten angedeutet.

Erfolgversprechend scheint es zu sein, ähnliche Prozeduren und Datenstrukturen auf die Teilprobleme der verschiedenen Ebenen zu übertragen. Dies Verfahren läßt auch eine geringe Fehleranfälligkeit des Systems erwarten. Je nach der vorhandenen Hardware sollte auch eine Priorität bzgl. der Ausnutzung des Hauptspeichers im Vergleich zum Sekundärspeicher festgelegt werden. Bei der benutzten Anlage besteht kein Zweifel, daß der Vorrang bei der Hauptspeicherausnutzung liegen muß.

3.3 BENUTZER, DATENVERWALTUNG UND DATENWÖRTERBUCH

Bei kleinen DB-Systemen sind die Datenstrukturen für den Benutzer noch recht gut überschaubar, sowohl in Bezug auf die Datendefinition, als auch bzgl. der tatsächlich gespeicherten Daten. Daher liegt es nahe den Anwender als aktiven Teil der Datenbankverwaltung miteinzubeziehen.

Voraussetzung dafür ist natürlich, daß ihm in einem komfortablen Dialog Zugang zum Datenwörterbuch verschafft wird. Auch die eigentlichen Anwendungsprogramme müssen entsprechend unterstützt werden, etwa in Form der "parametric buttons" wie sie in (13) beschrieben sind.

Bei kleineren DB-Systemen werden die Aufgaben des Datenbankverwalters also von zwei Personengruppen mit unterschiedlicher Qualifikation wahrgenommen:

Der Entwurf und die Implementierung des Datenmodells wird aufgrund der Spezifikation des Anwenders vom Anwendungsprogrammierer durchgeführt. Dabei ist die Stabilität des konzeptuellen Schemas von besonderer Wichtigkeit (6).

Im laufenden Betrieb können Änderungen des Datenmodells z.B. aufgrund geänderten Zugriffsverhaltens notwendig werden. Daher müssen Teile der Datendefinition auch vom Anwender ausgeführt werden können. Dazu gehören u.a. das Hinzufügen und Löschen von Zugriffspfaden, Änderungen von Zugriffsberechtigungen, Festlegung von Ausgabeformaten, Hinzufügen und Löschen von Attributen in Relationen usw.

Implementierung des Datenwörterbuchs:

Wegen der Langsamkeit des Interpreters und des Mangels an Hauptspeicherkapazität ist es nicht möglich, die Systemrelationen, die Beschreibungen der Relationen, Attribute, Zugriffspfade, Gerätecharakteristika, Hardwarekonfiguration usw. enthalten, wie normale Anwendungsrelationen mit den entsprechenden Möglichkeiten der Datendefinition und Manipulation zu verwalten. Dadurch, daß die Datendefinition direkter Bestandteil der Prozeduren wird, kann Speicherplatz und Zeit eingespart werden, was allerdings mit einem großen Verlust an Datenunabhängigkeit bezahlt werden muß. Bei größeren Hardwarekapazitäten muß dieser Verlust wieder gut gemacht werden mit dem Ziel, keinen Unterschied zwischen Datendefiniton und Datenmanipulation zu machen (9).

3.4 SPEZIELLE DETAILS DER IMPLEMENTIERUNG

3.4.1 DER BENUTZER ALS DISK JOCKEY

Wegen der geringen Kapazität der Disketten ist es möglich, daß die Anzahl der Datenträger der Datenbank die Anzahl der verfügbaren Laufwerke übersteigt. Die Daten der einzelnen Anwendungen müssen so aufgeteilt werden, daß möglichst wenig Diskettenwechsel nötig werden. Als Ersetzungsstrategie wurde daher ein LRU-Algorithmus implementiert, der unter diesen Voraussetzungen das beste Zugriffsverhalten verspricht.

3.4.2 SPEICHERSTRUKTUREN

Die Verwaltung der Speicherstrukturen für Relationen und Indexe kann durch Verwendung fester Längen für Tupel und Indexeinträge stark vereinfacht werden. Da beide Speicherstrukturen auf der Speicherverwaltung fußen, konnten viele Berechnungsschemata und Prozeduren gemeinsam benutzt werden.

Da effiziente Indexstrukturen im Vergleich zu anderen Komponenten des DB-Systems relativ komplex sind, muß versucht werden, den algorithmischen Aufwand möglichst gering zu halten und dabei trotzdem dem dynamischen Verhalten der Datenbank gerecht zu werden. Ein Ansatz dazu wurde in der Kombination eines dynamischen Hashings und eines digitalen Suchbaums vorgestellt. Diese Struktur kann in ihrer Detailierungstiefe den vorhandenen Hardwarekapazitäten angepaßt werden.

Von besonderem Interesse sind natürlich Zugriffspfade, die keinen zusätzlichen Speicherplatz belegen. Z.B. läßt sich der Tupelidentifikator (TID) der Relationspeicherstruktur zur Adressierung verwenden, insbesondere bei Relationen, die ein dichtes numerisches Schlüsselattribut besitzen wie Rechnungs-Nr., Buchungs-Nr., Angestellten-Nr, usw. Generell kann gesagt werden, daß bei den Speicherstrukturen eine Verbesserung der Speicherausnutzung durch Verkleinern der Segmentgröße erreicht werden kann, während eine Verbesserung des Zugriffsverhaltens umgekehrt durch das generelle Vergrößern der Segmente leicht möglich ist.

3.4.3 DARSTELLUNG VON RELATIONEN AUF DEM BILDSCHIRM UND DEFINITION VON ABFRAGEN

Normale Bildschirme lassen nur eingeschränkte Möglichkeiten zur Darstellung von Relationen und zur Definiton von Abfragen zu. Ein geeigneter Kompromiß wurde in der Verwendung von frei verschiebbaren Relationenmasken gefunden. Sie bilden die Basis für die interaktive Formulierung von Abfragen, da gleichzeitig mehrere verschiedene Relationen sichtbar gemacht werden können. Da die Darstellung zweidimensional ist, kann für jede beteiligte Relation nur das Tupel angezeigt werden, auf das der zugehörige TID zeigt (Abb. 4). Eine wesentliche Verbesserung läßt sich höchstens von der Benutzung graphischer Bildschirme erwarten (7).

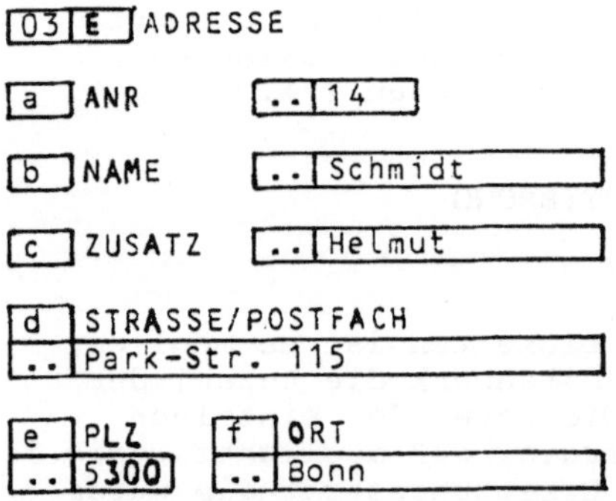

```
[03][E ] ADRESSE

[a ] ANR        [..][14  ]

[b ] NAME       [..][Schmidt        ]

[c ] ZUSATZ     [..][Helmut         ]

[d ] STRASSE/POSTFACH
[..][Park-Str. 115                  ]

[e ] PLZ      [f ] ORT
[..][5300]    [..][Bonn             ]
```

Abb. 4

Das interaktive Abfragemodul ermöglicht einfaches Definieren von Abfragen in den Relationmasken des Bildschirms. Die eingegebenen Daten werden direkt in die Tabellen des sogenannten Verständigungsbereiches eingetragen. Dabei ermöglicht die Einschränkung auf einen noch ausreichenden Satz von relationalen Operatoren, daß eine zeitraubende Übersetzung der Abfrage umgangen wird, da die Operatoren des Datensystems die Informationen des Verständigungsbereiches direkt interpretieren können.

Wenn die Speicherkapazität es zulassen würde, könnte der Funktionsumfang der DB-Sprache durch Verallgemeinerung der Abfragedefinition und Interpretation erweitert werden. Die Minimisierung des Übersetzungsvorganges und die Optimierung der Abfrageausführung setzen zum Teil auch die Mitarbeit des Anwendungsprogrammierers voraus. Bei größeren DB-Anwendungen übernimmt diese Aufgabe natürlich ein Optimierungsprogramm, das den Anwender gänzlich von der Kenntnis der internen Struktur der Datenbank befreit.

3.4.4 AUSFÜHRUNG VON ABFRAGEN

Aus der vorausgegangenen Darstellung wurde deutlich, daß eine deskriptive DB-Sprache nicht in vollem Umfang auf einem Kleinrechner implementiert werden kann. Gesucht wird also eine sinnvolle Teilmenge von Operationen, die gängige Anwendungen befriedigen können. Grenzen allgemeiner Verbundoperationen sind z.B. allein durch die Langsamkeit der Diskettenlaufwerke und des BASIC Interpreters vorgezeichnet. Außerdem darf der Benutzer nicht zu lange auf eine Antwort auf eine Anfrage warten müssen. Daraus resultiert die Idee, keine Zwischenrelation zu generieren, sondern erfolgreich verbundene Tupel gleich zur Ausgabe bereitzustellen. Abfragen, die auf diese Weise nicht befriedigend abgearbeitet werden können, müssen off-line ausgeführt werden. Die bereits angesprochene Beschränkung auf bestimmte Verbundtypen ermöglicht erst den sinnvollen Einsatz von DB-Systemen auf Kleinrechnern. Dabei handelt es sich um den natürlichen Verbund zweier Relationen. Zu jeder Relation kann ein Filterprädikat angegeben werden und die verbundenen Tupel können auf beliebige Spalten projiziert werden.
Um Vorteile existierender Zugriffspfade ausnutzen zu können, wurden insgesamt 3 verschiedene Verbundtypen implementiert. Der Anwender bzw. der Anwendungsprogrammierer kann bei der Definition einer Abfrage bzw. bei der Implementierung einer Anwendung durch Auswahl einer der Verbundtypen die entsprechend optimale Ausführungsmöglichkeit bestimmen.

Ein kritischer Punkt bei der Implementierung kleiner relationaler DB-Systeme ist die Aufrechterhaltung der Integrität der Relationen, die sich i.a. in 3. NF befinden. Beim Neueinfügen eines Tupels in einer Relation kann das Überprüfen des Tupels auf Eindeutigkeit sehr aufwendig werden, wenn der Schlüssel aus einer Kombination von Attributen besteht. Um z.B. bei Fehlen eines Zugriffspfades dann einen vollständigen Relation-Scan zu vermeiden, sollte man dem Benutzer die Verantwortung für die Erhaltung der Integrität geben.
Ein zum Abfrage-Modul alternatives Datenmanipulationsprogramm wurde bereits als Relation-Editor vorgestellt. Dieser erlaubt dem Anwender explizit das deskriptive Navigieren auf der Relation (9).

3.5 STEUERUNG UND ABLAUF DER PROGRAMMAUSFÜHRUNG

Die Prozeduren des DBMS belegen weit mehr Platz als die zur Verfügung stehenden 16 K Byte des Hauptspeichers, von denen außerdem noch 6 K Byte für die Segmentpuffer abgerechnet werden müssen. Von den verschiedenen Anwendungen muß also kontrolliert werden, welche Programmteile für die Ausführung genötigt werden. Alle nicht benötigten Prozeduren werden gelöscht und geben Platz frei für neu einzulagernde Programmteile. Häufig benutzte Prozeduren - z.B. die der Speicherverwaltung, der Bildschirmverwaltung, der Ein/Ausgaberoutinen usw. - werden als Nucleus ständig im Hauptspeicher gehalten. Die Implementierung der Übergabe von Prozeduren als Parameter an Prozeduren wurde ebenfalls durch Overlay-Techniken gelöst.

4 PERSPEKTIVEN DER DB-ENTWICKLUNG

Trotz aller Kompromisse und Unzulänglichkeiten kann man bei der hier diskutierten Implementierung die entscheidenden Kriterien für DB-Systeme als realisiert erkennen. Als wesentliche Engpäße erwiesen sich dabei die geringe Kapazität von Haupt- und Sekundärspeicher, die Langsamkeit des BASIC-Interpreters und der Diskettenlaufwerke, sowie das begrenzte Bildschirmformat.

Der technologische Fortschritt deutet nicht nur an, daß diese physischen Grenzen auf die Dauer mehr und mehr an Bedeutung verlieren werden. Heute werden bereits Mikro-Computersysteme angeboten, die über eigene Mikroprozessoren in den Diskettenlaufwerken verfügen und die Funktionen des Speichersystems hardwaremäßig realisieren (4). Es werden immer mehr Ebenen des DBMS bottom up in der Hardware verschwinden, wie es sich schon bei den relationalen assoziativen Prozessoren andeutet.

Da die Systeme immer komplexer werden, kann es wie hier gezeigt von Zeit zu Zeit nützlich sein, kleinere Datenbanken zu implementieren, um sich die beteiligten globalen Strukturen zu verdeutlichen.

Anerkennung:
Viele hilfreiche Kommentare zu diesem Bericht verdanke ich Herrn Prof. Dr. A. B. Cremers, Universität Dortmund, Lehrstuhl Informatik VI.
Von Prof. Dr. Th. Härder, Technische Hochschule Darmstadt und von Dr. H. Weber, Hahn-Meitner Institut, Berlin wurde ich entscheidend zur Abfassung dieses Berichtes ermutigt.

Literatur:

(1) M.M. Astrahan, D.D. Chamberlin
IMPLEMENTATION OF A STRUCTURED ENGLISH QUERY LANGUAGE
CACM 18, No. 10 (October 1975)

(2) Jayanta Banerjee, David K. Hsiao
PERFORMANCE STUDY OF A DATABASE MACHINE IN SUPPORTING RELATIONAL DATABASES
Proceedings of IV. VLDB 1978, p. 319-329

(3) Hermann Bense
IMPLEMENTIERUNG EINES MODULAREN DATENBANK-SYSTEMS AUF EINEM KLEINRECHNER
Forschungsbericht No. 93, 1979 Universität Dortmund

(4) Commodore Büromaschinen GmbH
PRELIMINARY USER´S MANUAL
COMMODORE 2040 DUAL FLOPPY DISK (320830)
D-6078 Neu Isenburg

(5) Armin B. Cremers
EXTERNE SORTIER- UND SUCHVERFAHREN
Notizen zur Vorlesung, Universität Dortmund, 1978

(6) C.J. Date
AN INTRODUCTION TO DATABASE SYSTEMS
Addison-Wesley Publishing Company., 1977 (Second Edition)

(7) N. Mc Donald, M.R. Stonebraker
CUPID - THE FRIENDLY QUERY LANGUAGE
Proceedings ACM Pacific Conference, San Francisco (5/1975)

(8) R. Fagin, J. Nievergelt, N. Pippenger, H.R. Strong
EXTENDIBLE HASHING- A FAST ACCESS METHOD FOR DYNAMIC FILES
RJ 2305 (31047) Research Report, IBM Research Division, Yorktown Heights, New York

(9) Theo Härder
IMPLEMENTIERUNG VON DATENBANK-SYSTEMEN
Carl Hanser Verlag München Wien 1978

(10) Hewlett-Packard
DATENBANKEN AUF EINEM KLEINCOMPUTER - DEM HP 250
Computer Advances, Nr. 5, 1978

(11) IBM Deutschland GmbH
DAS IBM SYSTEM /38, DER DATENBANK-COMPUTER IN DER FERTIGUNGSINDUSTRIE
Basis Datenverarbeitung, 7000 Stuttgart 80

(12) C.S. Lin, D.C.P. Smith, J.M. Smith
THE DESIGN OF A ROTATING ASSOCIATIVE MEMORY FOR RELATIONAL DATABASE APPLICATIONS
ACM Transactions on Database Systems
Vol. 1, No. 1, March 1976, p. 53-65

(13) D. McLeod, M. Meldman
RISS - A GENERALIZED MINICOMPUTER RELATIONAL DATABASE MANAGEMENT SYSTEM
NCC 1975, Vol. 44, p. 397-402

(14) E.A. Ozkarahan, S.A. Schuster, K.C. Smith
RAP - AN ASSOCIATIVE PROCESSOR FOR DATA BASE MANAGEMENT
Proceedings of IV. VLDB 1978, p. 243-254

(15) P. Paolini
AN ALTERNATIVE STRUCTURE FOR DATA BASE MANAGEMENT
Proceedings of IV. VLDB 1978, p. 243-254

(16) R.E. Wagner
INDEX DESIGN CONSIDERATIONS
IBM Systems Journal, Vol. 12, 1973, p. 351-367

(17) H. Weber
A SOFTWARE ENGINEERING VIEW OF DATA BASE SYSTEMS
Proceedings of IV. VLDB 1978, p. 36-51

(18) M.M. Zloof
QUERY BY EXAMPLE
NCC 1975, Vol. 44, p. 431-437

Abhängigkeiten von Systemkomponenten in Datenbanksystemen

Theo Härder, Andreas Reuter
FB Informatik
TH Darmstadt

1. Einleitung

Die Datenbankliteratur ist reich an Vorschlägen zur optimalen Implementierung einzelner Komponenten eines Datenbanksystems. Bei der Analyse einschlägiger Literaturübersichten, wie z.B. [Sch78] , finden sich zahlreiche Arbeiten, in denen Algorithmen für folgende Aufgaben vorgestellt bzw. auf ihre Leistungsfähigkeit untersucht werden:

- Optimierung von Zugriffspfadstrukturen
- Verwaltungsstrategien für Externspeicher, Clusterungstechniken usw.
- Bestimmung optimaler Sicherungspunkt-Intervalle
  Hier werden meist stark vereinfachte Warteschlangenmodelle auf der Grundlage idealisierter Annahmen betrachtet; Analysen implementierter Systeme sind rar.
- Sperrstrategien, Deadlockbehandlung und Konsistenzsicherungsmaßnahmen
- Verwaltung des Datenbankpuffers

Die meisten dieser Arbeiten behandeln ihr Thema so, als könne es losgelöst von den anderen Bestandteilen eines Datenbanksystems betrachtet werden - wobei diese Voraussetzung niemals explizit genannt wird. Die Entscheidung allerdings, ob ein für sich gesehen vielversprechendes Verfahren sich zur Verwendung in einer wesentlich komplexeren Struktur eignet, setzt die genaue Kenntnis aller seiner Nebenwirkungen und Abhängigkeiten voraus.

Systematische Untersuchungen hierzu sind bis jetzt sehr selten [BS77]; Hinweise auf die Art und Auswirkung solcher wechselseitigen Abhängigkeiten finden sich eher implizit in Darstellungen über Eigenschaften und Leistungsaspekte existierender Systeme [Gr79],[St76].

Diese Arbeit unternimmt den Versuch, einige der wichtigsten Wechselwirkungen zwischen den Funktionsgruppen eines Datenbanksystems (DBS) zu benennen und ihre Konsequenzen kurz aufzuzählen. Wir werden dabei zwei Arten von Beziehungen unterscheiden:

a) die konzeptionellen Abhängigkeiten im zentralen Bereich eines DBS; das sind zwingende Konsequenzen, die sich aus Entwurfsentscheidungen zur Implementierung einer Komponente auf die Implementierung der anderen ergeben,

b) Abhängigkeiten unter Leistungsaspekten zwischen den zentralen Funktionen und den übrigen Komponenten des DBS einerseits und dem Betriebssystem andererseits; damit sind Abstimmungen zwischen Komponenten gemeint , die zum Funktionieren des Systems nicht notwendig, zur Optimierung seiner Leistung aber wünschenswert sind.

All diese Aspekte können in einem so beschränkten Rahmen natürlich eher aufgezählt denn diskutiert werden.

2. Wechselwirkungen zwischen den zentralen DBS-Komponenten

Die in Abb. 1 aufgeführten Komponenten eines DBS werden als zentral in dem Sinne aufgefaßt, daß sie alle Betriebsmittel eines Datenbanksystems auf der untersten Abstraktionsebene, d.h. unmittelbar an der Schnittstelle zum Betriebssystem, verwalten. Alle Datentypen auf höheren Stufen der Abstraktion, von Zugriffspfaden über logische Sperren bis hin zu benutzerdefinierten rücksetzbaren Transaktionen benutzen zu ihrer Realisierung die von diesen vier Komponenten bereitgestellten elementaren Datenobjekte und Operationen.

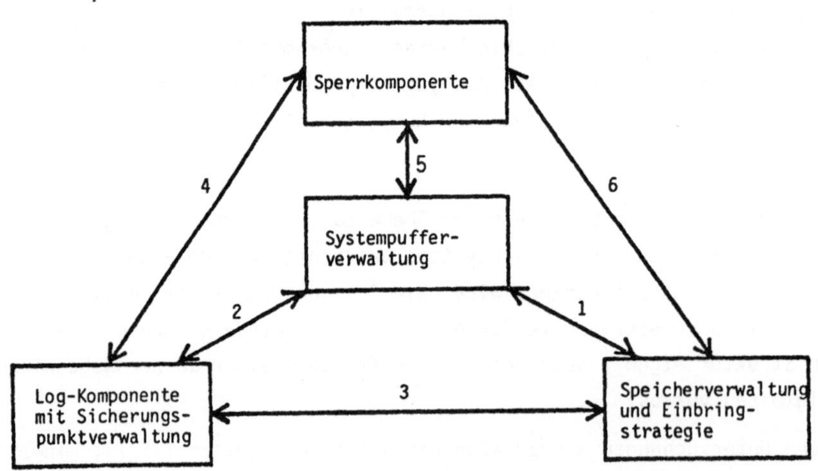

Abb.1: Konzeptionelle Abhängigkeiten zwischen den zentralen Komponenten eines DBMS

Natürlich ist es im Rahmen dieses Papiers nicht möglich, Funktionsweise und -umfang jeder der Komponenten ausführlich zu definieren; wir werden vielmehr eine stichwortartige Kurzbeschreibung verbunden mit Hinweisen auf die einschlägige Literatur geben und uns ansonsten auf ein mehr oder weniger detailliertes Vorverständnis des Lesers stützen.

- *Sperrkomponente:* Die Sperrkomponente hat im Mehrbenutzerbetrieb für alle parallel ablaufenden Transaktionen n.M. den logischen Einbenutzerbetrieb zu gewährleisten, d.h. jede Transaktion soll so arbeiten können, als sei sie alleiniger Benutzer der Datenbank; s.[EGLT76],[GLPT76]. Die wichtigste Bedingung hierfür ist die Einhaltung eines zweiphasigen Sperrprotokolls, das eine Wachstumsphase umfaßt, in der nur Sperren angefordert werden dürfen, und eine Schrumpfungsphase, in der nur erworbene Sperren freigegeben werden dürfen. Die Unterscheidung logischer Sperren, bei denen die Menge der zu sperrenden Datenobjekte durch ein Prädikat beschrieben wird, und physischer Sperren, bei denen jedes einzelne Datenobjekt und mit ihm alle darin enthaltenen (Datei, Satztyp, Satz, Feld) explizit gesperrt werden, ist für unsere Diskussion nicht von Belang, da jede bekannte Implementierung logischer Sperren auf der Benutzerschnittstelle auf einer tieferen Ebene physische Sperren benutzt [Hä78] . Die kleinsten mit einer Sperre zu belegenden Einheiten (Granulate) sind in den existierenden DBS verschieden; üblich sind Sperren in Einheiten von logischen Sätzen (Tupel-Sperren) oder physischen Blöcken (Seitensperren), Vor- und Nachteile beider Methoden werden in [RS79] diskutiert.

- *Systempufferverwaltung:* Im Systempuffer eines DBS werden die zum Lesen oder Ändern benötigten Seiten der Datenbank im Hauptspeicher bereitgestellt. Die in der "Benutzt"-Hierarchie oberhalb der Pufferverwaltung stehenden Komponenten fordern bei dieser eine bestimmte Seite an (logische Referenz, s. [Ef79]). Wenn die Seite nicht schon im Puffer steht, muß die Pufferverwaltung, sofern kein freier Platz mehr vorhanden ist, eine Seite auswählen, die ersetzt werden soll; hierfür werden meist "least recently used"-(LRU) Algorithmen verwendet. Wurde diese Seite geändert, muß bei der Externspeicherverwaltung ihr Rückschreiben in die Datenbank veranlaßt und danach die angeforderte Seite eingelesen werden. Die Probleme der Seitenersetzung werden in [RR76] und [SB76] diskutiert.

- *Log-Komponente und Sicherungspunkt-Verwaltung:* Beide Komponenten haben die Aufgabe, Informationen zu sammeln und an einem sicheren Platz zu speichern, die zum Rücksetzen einer nicht erfolgreichen Transaktion, zur Wiederherstellung eines konsistenten Zustandes nach einem Systemzusammenbruch und zum Nachholen aller vollständigen Transaktionen nach dem Verlust einer Magnetplatte erforderlich sind [Gr78]. Hierfür können die DML-Befehle samt ihrer Argumente benutzt werden (logisches Übergangs-Logging) oder es werden die Inhalte geänderter Datenobjekte vor bzw. nach der Änderung aufgezeichnet (physisches Zustands-Logging). Ein Sicherungspunkt (SP) dient dazu, den Aufwand zur Wiederholung vollständiger Transaktionen nach einem Systemzusammenbruch zu begrenzen. Man unterscheidet, abhängig vom Zeitpunkt ihrer Erzeugung, drei Arten von Sicherungspunkten: speicherkonsistente SP's, wenn quer durch laufende Transaktionen ein SP dann geschrieben wird, wenn kein ändernder DML-Befehl aktiv ist; logisch konsistente SP's, die erzeugt werden, wenn keine Änderungstransaktion aktiv ist; transaktionsbezogene SP's, die am Ende einer Änderungstransaktion deren Modifikationen sicherstellen. Näheres hierzu findet sich in [HR79b].

- *Speicherverwaltung:* Hierüber werden die von der Pufferverwaltung ausgelösten physischen Lese- und Schreiboperationen abgewickelt. Von besonderem Interesse ist in unserem Zusammenhang die zum Zurückschreiben geänderter Seiten angewendete Strategie. Es gibt das direkte Einbringen von Änderungen, meist als "update in place" bezeichnet (IMS, UDS), sowie das verzögerte Einbringen zum Sicherungspunkt mittels sog. "side file"-Konzepte ([SL76],[Lo77])für dateibezogene Sicherung oder aber transaktionsbezogene wie in [HR79a] und [Re79]. Die Konsequenzen verschiedener Einbringstrategien werden in [Gr79] und [HR79b] ausführlich erörtert.

Die Verbindungslinien in Abb. 1 sind nicht als Pfade im Sinne einer "Benutzt"-Hierarchie zu verstehen. Vielmehr bezeichnen sie konzeptionelle Abhängigkeiten zwischen den zur Implementierung der einzelnen Komponenten in Frage kommenden Algorithmen, deren Untersuchung und Bewertung eigentlicher Gegenstand dieser Arbeit ist.

2.1 Wechselwirkungen zwischen Systempuffer- und Externspeicherverwaltung

Betrachtet man die Seitenersetzung als eigentliche Aufgabe der Pufferverwaltung, dann sind vor allem die Einflüsse anderer Komponenten auf die hierfür üblicherweise verwendeten Strategien interessant. Ein vollkommen isolierter Ersetzungsalgorithmus z.B. nach LRU würde jede logische Referenz auf eine (vorhandene) Seite gleich behandeln und die betreffende Seite an die Spitze der LRU-Kette setzen.
Bedenkt man nun aber das isolierte Zurücksetzen einer Transaktion unter Benutzung physischer Before-Images, dann ist leicht einzusehen, daß die daraus sich ergebenden Referenzen vom Pufferverwalter eigentlich anders behandelt werden sollten:
Da jede geänderte Seite (in umgekehrter Änderungsreihenfolge) von der Protokolldatei ersetzt wird, hat jede einzelne eine geringe Wiederbenutzungswahrscheinlichkeit und sollte nicht an die Spitze der LRU-Kette. Einige Pufferersetzungsstrategien unterscheiden geänderte und nur gelesene Seiten, da die Ersetzung einer geänderten Seite wegen des damit verbundenen Schreibens aufwendiger ist als das einer nur von Lesern benutzten. Dafür wird in bestimmten Abständen der ganze Puffer ausgeschrieben (d.h. alle geänderten Pufferseiten). Ein Beispiel hierfür ist das DBS ADABAS [ADAB]. Auch hier muß eine Verbindung zwischen Puffer- und Speicherverwaltung bestehen.

Die stärkste Wechselwirkung erfordern Einbringstrategien, die einen transaktionsbezogenen Sicherungspunkt ermöglichen. Hierbei werden die durch dieselbe Transaktion geänderten Seiten durch Vorwärtszeiger miteinander verkettet, was bedeutet, daß von jeder Änderungstransaktion zu jedem Zeitpunkt (außer der Ende-Behandlung) mindestens eine Seite im Puffer bleiben muß. Diese Notwendigkeit durchbricht jede rein an den logischen Seitenreferenzen orientierte Ersetzungsstrategie. Auch dieser Aspekt wird in der oben zitierten Literatur diskutiert.

2.2 Wechselwirkungen zwischen Systempuffer- sowie Log- und Sicherungspunkt-Verwaltung

Die wohl wichtigste Verknüpfung zwischen beiden Komponenten wird durch das sog. "write ahead log"-(WAL) Prinzip festgelegt (s.[Gr78]). Dieses Prinzip besagt in der in[HR79b] verallgemeinerten Version, daß Log-Informationen, die dem Rücksetzen unvollständiger Transaktionen dienen, geschrieben werden müssen, bevor die entsprechenden Änderungen in die Datenbank eingebracht werden. Bei dem gängigen update in place mit physischem Zustands-Logging bedeutet dies, daß der alte Wert (before image) auf die Protokolldatei geschrieben werden muß, bevor die Seite selbst geschrieben werden kann. Da diese Forderung u.U. zu einer Engpaß-Situation an der Log-Datei führen kann, die durch Pufferung einzelner Log-Einträge gemildert werden könnte, bedeutet eine derartige Optimierung eine "Störung" jeder isolierten Puffer-Ersetzungsstrategie.

Ähnliches gilt bei der Erzeugung segmentorientierter Sicherungspunkte in Verbindung mit indirekten Einbringstrategien. Hier müssen zum Sicherungspunkt alle geänderten Seiten ausgeschrieben werden (was ein Schreiben aller Rücksetzinformationen erzwingt), wodurch ebenfalls - wie dies schon in 2.1 in Zusammenhang mit der Transaktions-Ende-Behandlung erläutert wurde - Einfluß auf die Pufferverwaltung genommen werden kann.

2.3 Wechselwirkungen zwischen Log-Komponente und Externspeicherverwaltung

Die Einbringstrategie der Speicherverwaltung beeinflußt maßgeblich die Anzahl der für die Log-Komponente anwendbaren Verfahren. Grundsätzlich gilt, daß bei allen Methoden des direkten Einbringens von Änderungen logisches Logging zum Zurücksetzen unvollständiger Transaktionen nach einem Systemzusammenbruch nicht möglich ist, da die Ausführung (in diesem Falle inverser) DML-Befehle einen speicherkonsistenten Zustand der Datenbank voraussetzt, der bei update in place nach einem abrupten Anhalten des Systems im allgemeinen nicht gegeben ist. Bei indirekten Einbring-Methoden können alle Log-Verfahren benutzt werden (soweit sie überhaupt erforderlich sind; s.[HR79b]).

Weiterhin hat die Einbringstrategie eine Rückwirkung auf die Log-Komponente, die sich weiter bis auf den Systempuffer erstreckt (s.2.2). Bei direktem Einbringen der Änderungen gilt das strikte WAL-Prinzip, bei indirektem Einbringen können geänderte Seiten beliebig zurückgeschrieben werden, das "write ahead" bezieht sich hier lediglich auf den jeweils nächsten Sicherungspunkt.

Schließlich gibt es noch einen Zusammenhang zwischen der physischen Blockgröße und dem Log-Granulat bei physischem Logging (d.i. die Größe der protokollierten Zustandsinformationen): Wenn bei direktem Einbringen das Log-Granulat kleiner ist als die physische Blockgröße, kann schon ein auf einen Block beschränkter Schreibfehler den Verlust der Datenbank mit Wiederholen aller Transaktionen ausgehend von der letzten Kopie bedeuten.

2.4 Wechselwirkungen zwischen Log- und Sperrkomponente

Das Grundgesetz, das die Beziehungen beider regelt, lautet: Das Sperrgranulat muß mindestens so groß sein wie das Log-Granulat. Im Falle von logischem Logging ist das Log-Granulat die Menge aller durch den DML-Befehl geänderten Datenobjekte. Das wird unmittelbar verständlich, wenn man bedenkt (in diesem Beispiel sei physisches Logging unterstellt), daß beim Rücksetzen einer Transaktion mit Hilfe der before images die alten Werte der Datenobjekte restauriert werden, wobei alle Werte verändert werden, die auf dem Protokoll stehen; somit müssen - und zwar nur wegen der Möglichkeit des Rücksetzens - auch alle diese Werte gesperrt werden. Das bedeutet insbesondere, daß, wenn ganze Seiten auf die Log-Datei geschrieben werden, auch ganze Seiten gesperrt werden müssen.

Wenn das DBS die Möglichkeit transaktions-interner Sicherungspunkte bietet, dann müssen zu diesen Sicherungspunkten alle in diesem Moment gehaltenen Sperren zusätzlich zu den Zustandsinformationen der Datenobjekte protokolliert werden; näheres hierzu siehe z.B. in [Gr78].

Wenn die Sperrkomponente nur ein einfaches 2-Phasen-Protokoll befolgt anstelle des strikten 2-Phasen-Protokolls (Freigabe aller Sperren erst am Ende der Transaktion), müssen alle Interferenzen zwischen Transaktionen (auch solchen, die nur lesen) über gemeinsam genutzte Datenobjekte protokolliert werden, um ein rekursives Zurücksetzen im Fehlerfall zu ermöglichen.

2.5 Wechselwirkungen zwischen Sperrkomponente und Systempuffer-Verwaltung

Neben der zentralen Aufgabe, den logischen Einbenutzerbetrieb für alle Transaktionen sicherzustellen, muß die Sperrkomponente in Zusammenarbeit mit der Pufferverwaltung weiter gewährleisten, daß die nach der Anforderung einer Seite durch irgendein Modul an diese übergebene Pufferadresse der Seite solange gültig bleibt (Fix-Phase), bis der Modul ausdrücklich auf die weitere Benutzung der Seite verzichtet (Unfix). Da eine Seite während der Fix-Phase der Verfügung der Puffer-Verwaltung teilweise entzogen ist, (sie kann zwar ihre Position in einer LRU-Kette ändern, darf aber nicht ersetzt werden), kann es insbesondere bei langen Fix-Phasen zu Betriebsmittel-Mangel im Puffer kommen, wenn ein Modul auf diese Weise alle Seiten im Puffer festhält und eine weitere Seite anfordert, die nicht im Puffer steht, die aber auch nicht bereitgestellt werden kann, da eben wegen dieses Moduls keine der vorhandenen Seiten ersetzt werden darf. Diese Wechselwirkung hat weitreichende Konsequenzen für die Modulstruktur des gesamten DBS. Das Bestreben, solche Situationen zu vermeiden und alle Fix-Phasen möglichst kurz zu halten, kann andererseits zu einer "Übermodularisierung" mit erheblichen Leistungsverlusten führen.

2.6 Wechselwirkungen zwischen Sperrkomponente und Speicherverwaltung

In existierenden Datenbanksystemen sind beide Komponenten im Prinzip unabhängig; die hier zu diskutierende Beziehung ergibt sich aus einigen bislang nur theoretisch untersuchten Implementierungen . In [Ba79] wird ein Sperrkonzept mit dem Ziel erhöhter Parallelität vorgeschlagen, was darauf beruht, daß Datenobjekte, die von Änderungstransaktionen gesperrt sind, gleichzeitig ablaufenden Lesetransaktionen in Gestalt ihres jew. before image zugänglich gemacht werden können. Das setzt voraus, daß die Speicherverwaltung eine Art transaktionsorientiertes Schattenspeicherkonzept unterstützt, wie es etwa in [HR79a] und [Re79] beschrieben wird. Da diese Verfahren auf Ketten von Schattenseiten beruhen, die jeweils allen von einer Transaktion geänderten Seiten entsprechen, müssen, aus dem gleichen Grund, der in 2.3 die Beziehung zwischen Log- und Sperr-Granulaten festgelegte, bei den genannten Algorithmen Seiten als kleinste Einheit gesperrt werden.

3. Abhängigkeiten höherer Systemfunktionen

Die bisher diskutierten Wechselwirkungen zwischen den zentralen Komponenten eines DBS sind Abhängigkeiten zwischen Konzepten und deshalb beim Systementwurf in jedem Fall zu berücksichtigen, um die gewünschten Funktionen gewährleisten zu können.
Es sollen jetzt Abhängigkeiten zwischen Systemkomponenten betrachtet werden, die vor allem die Performance des Systems beeinflussen. Diese Abhängigkeiten sind nicht konzeptbedingt, d.h. die Abstimmung des Zusammenwirkens dieser Komponenten ist nicht prinzipiell erforderlich; aus Gründen der Wirksamkeit kann jedoch darauf im praktischen Einzelfall nicht verzichtet werden. Für die beispielhafte Betrachtung solcher optimierungsbedingter Abhängigkeiten beschränken wir uns auf die in Abb. 2 dargestellten Beziehungen zwischen Systemkomponenten.

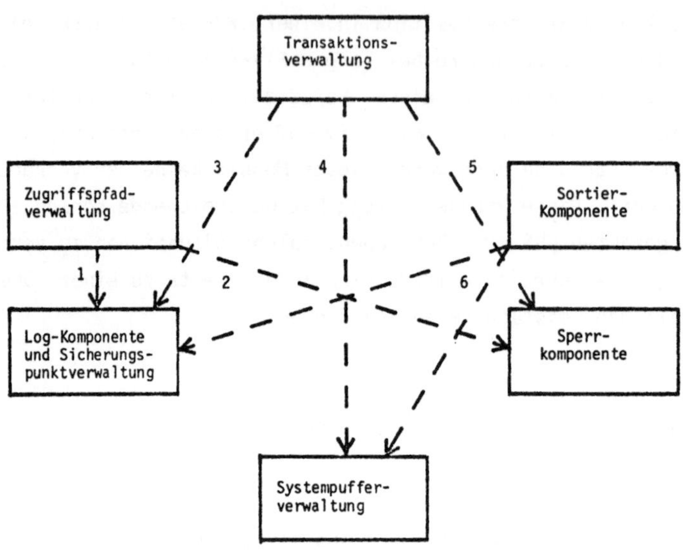

Abb. 2: Optimierungsbedingte Abhängigkeiten höherer Systemkomponenten

- *Zugriffspfadverwaltung:* Die Zugriffspfadverwaltung hat eine Reihe von Strukturen bereitzustellen, die das Aufsuchen von Datensätzen in wirksamer Weise unterstützen. Dazu zählen Zugriffspfade für Primärschlüssel und Sekundärschlüssel, sowie für Beziehungen hierarchischer Art zur Verknüpfung von Datensätzen verschiedenen Typs (Setstrukturen nach CODSAYL). In einer Datenbank sind gewöhnlich eine Vielzahl solcher Zugriffspfade verschiedenen Typs zu warten, die bei Änderungsoperationen auf Datensätzen automatisch durch die Zugriffspfadverwaltung zu aktualisieren sind. Einen Überblick über häufig in DBS eingesetzte Zugriffspfadstrukturen findet man in [WH76] und [Sch78] . Von besonderer Wichtigkeit für DB-Anwendungen sind Indexstrukturen, die den schnellen direkten Zugriff über Schlüssel und den sortiert sequentiellen Zugriff zu allen Datensätzen eines Typs erlauben. Als Implementierungstechniken eignen sich vor allem B^*-Bäume wegen ihrer dynamischen Erweiterbarkeit durch Splittechniken.
- *Transaktionsverwaltung:* Durch das DBS ist pro Benutzer eine Transaktion zu verwalten. Sie dient dem DBS als Einheit der Zuteilung DBS-interner Betriebsmittel, des Scheduling von Anforderungen, der physischen Wiederherstellung von Daten im Fehlerfall und der Erhaltung der logischen Konsistenz der Datenbank. Eine Transaktion, bestehend aus einer beliebig langen Folge von DML-Operationen eines Benutzers, führt bei erfolgreichem Abschluß die Datenbank von einem gültigen in einen neuen gültigen Zustand über, wobei idealerweise das DBS die Zulässigkeit des Zustandsüberganges mit Hilfe von sogenannten Zusicherungen oder Konsistenzbedingungen [EC75] kontrolliert. Änderungen von Transaktionen, die aus Gründen von Konsistenzverletzungen oder durch Eintreten von Fehlerzuständen nicht erfolgreich abgeschlossen werden, müssen so zurückgesetzt werden, als wären die Transaktionen nie ge-

startet worden. Die Transaktionsverwaltung hat den parallelen Ablauf von Transaktionen zu kontrollieren, bei erfolgreichem Abschluß (EOT) die Betriebsmittel freizugeben und im Fehlerfall geeignete Recovery-Aktionen anzustoßen.

- *Sortierkomponente:* Datenbanksysteme, die eine Spezifikation von Benutzeranforderungen in einer deskriptiven Sprache erlauben, müssen durch spezielle Algorithmen den Zugriff auf Mengen von Datensätzen optimieren. Um solche Anforderungen effizient abwickeln zu können, ist es erforderlich, intern Mengen von Datensätzen umzuordnen, beispielsweise zur Unterstützung komplexer Relationsoperationen [Hä78]. Aus Gründen der Benutzerfreundlichkeit sollte außerdem die Spezifikation einer Ausgabefolge der qualifizierten Datensätze angeboten werden. Beide Arten von Benutzeranforderungen setzen eine wirksame Sortierkomponente des DBS voraus.

3.1 Auswirkungen der Log-Funktion auf die Zugriffspfadverwaltung

Die Art der Log-Information, die die Log-Komponente als redundante Information für den Fehlerfall auf einem sicheren Platz sammelt, hat erhebliche Auswirkungen auf das Zeitverhalten von Änderungsoperationen des DBS. Am Beispiel von Änderungen in B^*-Bäumen als redundante Zugriffspfade soll dieser Einfluß kurz diskutiert werden. Für den praktischen Einsatz sind vor allem zwei Log-Techniken relevant [HR79b]: Das logische Übergangs-Logging und das physische Zustands-Logging (s. Kap. 2).

Nehmen wir an, daß ein Datensatz, für den über n Attribute Zugriffspfade vorhanden sind, neu in die DB eingebracht werden soll. Neben dem eigentlichen Einfügen des Datensatzes müssen durch die Zugriffspfadverwaltung n Indexstrukturen - typischerweise B^*-Bäume - aktualisiert werden, damit sie auf den neuen Satz verweisen. Logisches Übergangslogging erfordert für die Wartung der Zugriffspfade keinerlei zusätzlichen Log-Aufwand, da durch die Protokollierung der Einfügeoperation - unter der Annahme einer indirekten Einbringstrategie (s. 2.3) - die Operation im Fehlerfall jederzeit zurückgesetzt oder wiederholt werden kann.

Physisches Zustandslogging dagegen erzwingt bis zu 2n Schreibvorgänge (abhängig von möglichen Blockungstechniken) für zugriffspfadbezogene Log-Informationen.

Ein Musterbeispiel für extrem hohe verborgene Kosten, die oft durch Implementierungsdetails eingeführt werden, soll die Effizienzabhängigkeit der betrachteten Komponenten verdeutlichen. Zur Unterstützung von navigierenden Operationen könnte in B^*-Bäumen für jeden Knoten ein Rückwärts-Pointer zum Vater vorgesehen werden. Beim Splitten eines Vaterknotens bringt diese "unscheinbare Maßnahme" hohe Folgekosten durch die notwendige Aktualisierung der Vater-Pointer in den Söhnen mit sich. Verstärkt wird dieser Wartungsaufwand durch die Log-Kosten vor allem beim physischen Zustandslogging auf Seitenbasis.

Unter der Annahme, daß ein Vaterknoten mit 400 Söhnen gesplittet wird und der neu eingeführte Vaterknoten auf 200 Söhne verweist, lassen sich für die Aktualisierung der Vater-Pointer folgende Zusatzkosten angeben:

- 200 Seiten (Söhne) lesen und geändert zurückschreiben
- 200 Seiten Before-Images in die Log-Datei schreiben
- 200 Seiten After-Images in die Log-Datei schreiben.

Dieses Beispiel soll in drastischer Weise zeigen, daß Optimierungsmaßnahmen für Zugriffspfade in einem DBS die Abstimmung mit der Log-Funktion, der Systempufferverwaltung und der Einbringstrategie der Speicherkomponente erfordern.

3.2 Auswirkungen der Sperr-Funktion auf die Zugriffspfadverwaltung

Im Mehrbenutzerbetrieb müssen im Hinblick auf die Optimierung von Zugriffsvorgängen zusätzliche Auswirkungen weiterer Systemkomponenten berücksichtigt werden. Besonders bei B^*-Bäumen kann ein schlecht angepasstes Sperrkonzept gravierende Folgen für die Parallelität von Transaktionen haben. Exklusive Seitensperren auf der Wurzel von B^*-Bäumen können nicht toleriert werden, da dadurch alle Pfade zu den Blättern blockiert werden. Wegen der typischerweise hohen Frequenz von Suchvorgängen in B^*-Bäumen sollte ein DBS spezielle Algorithmen für das Sperren von solchen Strukturen anbieten. Eine Reihe von verklemmungsfreien Sperralgorithmen werden in [BS77] diskutiert.

3.3 Auswirkungen der Log-Funktion auf die Transaktionsverwaltung

Das Ende einer Transaktion ist der spätest mögliche Zeitpunkt zum Ausschreiben aller REDO-Informationen einer Transaktion, die erforderlich sind, um im Fehlerfall die Änderungen aller abgeschlossenen Transaktionen in ihrer ursprünglichen Reihenfolge wiederholen zu können. Das Ausschreiben der UNDO-Information zum Zurücksetzen einer unvollständigen Transaktion wird in Abhängigkeit von der Einbringstrategie durch das WAL-Prinzip oder durch die SP-Generierung vorgeschrieben (s. 2.2 und 2.3).

Die Transaktionsverwaltung hat folglich bei der EOT-Behandlung jeder Transaktion über die Log-Komponente sicherzustellen, daß die REDO-Information und ein EOT-Quittungsvermerk vor dem Abschluß der Transaktion in der Log-Datei stehen. Werden transaktionsbezogene SP erzeugt, so gilt zusätzlich der Schreibzwang bei EOT für alle geänderten Seiten einer Transaktion, so daß sowohl DB- als auch Log-Ausgabe anfällt. Solche synchronen SP belasten die Kanäle und Speichermedien in erhöhtem Maße, so daß sie potentielle Engpässe darstellen. Abhängig von der Verfügbarkeit von Kanälen wird eine *relative* Serialisierung der Ausgabe erzwungen, die sich auf die Laufzeiten der Transaktionen auswirkt. Um solche graduellen Verstopfungen bei der EOT-Behandlung zu vermeiden, sollten ggf. asynchrone SP-Verfahren gewählt werden.

Bei hohem Verkehrsaufkommen mit kurzen Transaktionen, wie sie typischerweise bei DB/DC-Anwendungen anfallen, wird die reine Log-Ausgabe bei EOT der Systemengpaß. Bei transaktionsbezogener Ausgabe der REDO-Information auf die Log-Datei bestimmt die Geschwindigkeit des externen Speichermediums die maximale Transaktionsrate. Abhilfe in dieser Situation könnte dadurch geschaffen werden, daß die Transaktionsverwaltung die EOT-Behandlung von Transaktionen in bestimmten Zeitintervallen (∿ 50-100 ms) verzögert und die Log-Komponente veranlaßt, die Log-Information aller verzögerten Transaktionen geblockt auszugeben.

3.4 Einflußmöglichkeiten der Transaktionsverwaltung auf die Systempufferverwaltung

Die Transaktionsverwaltung interpretiert die Anforderungen der Benutzer (DML-Anweisungen) und verteilt sie zur Bearbeitung an die entsprechenden Systemkomponenten. Da sich durch die Art der Operatoren und ihres Kontextes Information über eine mögliche Lokalität der Seitenreferenzen ableiten läßt, könnte durch dieses Wissen die Ersetzungsstrategie der Systempufferverwaltung beeinflußt werden. Seitenanforderungen für verschiedenartige DB-Operationen können durch charakteristische Seitenersetzungsstrategien optimiert werden [AIM] , beispielweise

- sequentielle Anforderungen durch FIFO
- zufällige Anforderungen durch LRU
- baumstrukturierte Anforderungen durch GCLOCK ("biased" LRU).

Bei vorgegebener Puffergröße hat die Anzahl paralleler Transaktionen einen erheblichen Einfluß auf die Seitenwechselrate. Dadurch, daß für jede Transaktion bei jeder DML-Operation einige Seiten im Puffer kurzfristig exklusiv gesperrt (Fix-Phase) und dabei neue Seiten zur Fortsetzung der Verarbeitung angefordert werden, kann es vor allem bei kleinen Puffergrößen zu Verklemmungssituationen (Betriebsmitteldeadlock) kommen (s. 2.5). Aber auch das gegenseitige Wegnehmen von Pufferrahmen und Verdrängen von Seiten beeinträchtigt das gesamte Systemverhalten in gravierender Weise. Über ein zeitweiliges Zurückhalten von Anforderungen durch die Transaktionsverwaltung bei drohenden Betriebsmittelengpässen läßt sich ein wirksamer Thrashing-Schutz für den Systempuffer einführen.

3.5 Abstimmung von Transaktionsverwaltung und Sperrverwaltung

Über die Sperrverwaltung wird die Zugriffssynchronisation zu den Objekten der Datenbank in zentraler Weise durchgeführt. Die Transaktionsverwaltung und ggf. andere Komponenten des DBS rufen vor dem aktuellen Zugriff entsprechend der "Benutzt"-

Hierarchie die Sperrverwaltung zum Sperren des betreffenden Objektes. Beim Rücksetzen im Fehlerfall oder bei EOT veranlaßt die Transaktionsverwaltung die Freigabe aller Sperren der betroffenen Transaktion. Wird eine Verklemmungssituation erkannt, ist eine Transaktion als "Opfer" auszuwählen und durch Zurücksetzen die zyklische Wartesituation zu brechen. Zur Minimierung des Verlustes ist eine Abstimmung zwischen Transaktionsverwaltung und Sperrverwaltung sehr hilfreich. Durch zusätzliche Informationen der Transaktionsverwaltung können so Kostenkriterien wie verbrauchte Rechenzeit und Anzahl der durchgeführten Änderungen zusammen mit der Anzahl der gehaltenen Sperren berücksichtigt werden.

3.6 Ausführung spezieller Funktionen

Im allgemeinen besitzen die Primitive der zentralen Systemkomponente nur eine geringe Tauglichkeit für die Ausführung spezieller Funktionen. Ein Musterbeispiel ist die Realisierung der Sortieroperation [Hä77], die in relationalen DBS unerläßlich ist. Es ist davon auszugehen, daß zur Unterstützung komplexer Relationenoperationen (Verbund) häufig große Mengen von Datensätzen (ganze Relationen) mit Hilfe von externen Sortier- und Mischverfahren umzuordnen sind.

Die Abwicklung solcher E/A-intensiver Operationen über die normale Systempuffer- und Log-Schnittstelle hat weitreichende Konsequenzen auf die Performance des DBS. Falls ein m-phasiges Mischen von n Datenseiten über die normale E/A-Schnittstelle durchgeführt wird, sind, explizite Auslagerung der Daten in jeder Mischphase vorausgesetzt, beim physischen Zustandslogging $n \cdot m$ Before-Images und $n \cdot m$ After-Images zu schreiben. Die LRU-Ersetzungsstrategie bei der Pufferverwaltung ist in diesem Fall auch wenig geeignet, da die Mischoperationen vorwiegend sequentieller Natur sind. Bei Einsatz eines Schattenspeicherkonzeptes durch die Speicherkomponente ergeben sich zusätzliche hohe Reibungsverluste, da dieses Konzept für das wiederholte Umspeichern ganzer Segmente, das durch jede Mischphase erzwungen wird, unverhältnismäßig aufwendig ist.

Obwohl grundsätzlich durchführbar, erfordern spezielle höhere Systemfunktionen bei einem brauchbaren Systementwurf eine detaillierte Abstimmung mit den zentralen Komponenten des DBS.

4. Schlußbemerkungen

Beim konkreten Systementwurf sind neben den Abhängigkeiten zwischen den Komponenten des DBS auch die Randbedingungen zu berücksichtigen, die durch die Systemumgebung zur Ablaufzeit vorgegeben sind. Dazu gehören

- die Beziehung zwischen DBS und Anwendungsprogramm
- die Verbindung von DBS und DC-System.

Ähnlich wie *innerhalb* des DBS sind auch *zwischen* den Systemen konzeptbedingte Wechselwirkungen und optimierungsbedingte Abhängigkeiten zu unterscheiden. Eine Reihe von Problemen, die in diesem Zusammenhang auftreten, sind in [Hä79] ausführlich untersucht worden, so daß an dieser Stelle eine Aufzählung der wichtigsten Fragen genügt.Zu den konzeptionellen Problempunkten gehören:

- Ein virtuelles E/A-Konzept des Betriebssystems (BS), bei dem E/A-Aufträge angenommen werden, die aktuelle Ausgabe aber unbestimmt ist, führt auf Unverträglichkeiten mit Log-Konzepten, die Annahmen über definierte Schreibzeitpunkte machen.
- Zugriffskontrolle durch das DBS ist nur möglich, wenn das BS eine hinreichende Isolation von DBS und Anwendungsprogramm (AP) gewährleistet.
- Die Kooperation zwischen AP und DBS setzt die Möglichkeit der Interprozeß-Kommunikation voraus.

Folgende Abhängigkeiten sind aus Performance-Gründen zu berücksichtigen:

- Die Aufteilung der Kontrolle über Betriebsmittel auf verschiedene selbständige Systeme führt hohe Verwaltungskosten ein. Ein Beispiel ist die Verwaltung des virtuellen Speichers durch das BS und des Systempuffers - im virtuellen Speicher realisiert - durch das DBS. Dadurch wird das Problem des Double Paging eingeführt; zusätzlich können sich mit unterschiedlichen Zielsetzungen optimierte Seitenersetzungsstrategien in ihrer Wirkung neutralisieren.
- Unabhängige Recovery-Mechanismen für BS und DBS können die Kosten der Vorsorgemaßnahmen für den Fehlerfall verdoppeln.
- Der vorzeitige Entzug des Rechnerkerns(preemptive scheduling) kann bei der DB-Synchronisation zu Verstopfungen führen (Konvoi-Phänomen).
- Falls DBS und DC-System als unabhängige Prozesse ablaufen, ist ein sehr hoher Aufwand an zusätzlicher Prozeßkommunikation erforderlich. Die Abstimmung bei der Recovery im Fehlerfall ist sehr umständlich.

Diese Übersicht legt nahe, daß weitere Forschungen auf diesem Gebiet unter zwei Gesichtspunkten durchgeführt werden sollten:

- Zur Unterstützung sowohl bei der Implementierung eines DBS als auch beim Entwurf einer DBS-Anwendung sind eine präzise Untersuchung der wechselseitigen Abhängigkeiten von Systemkomponenten, ihre Nachbildung in analytischen Modellen oder durch Simulation und die Voraussage ihres Verhaltens bei isolierten Optimierungsversuchen erforderlich.
- Für Zwecke der Optimierung existierender Systeme oder des Tuning konkreter Anwendungen in einer vorgegebenen Systemumgebung sind bereits beim Entwurf des DBS geeignete Meßschnittstellen vorzusehen, die im laufenden Betrieb die zur

Anwendung der oben genannten Modelle erforderlichen Parameter zu bestimmen erlauben.

Erste Ansätze zur Verknüpfung beider Aspekte werden z.B. in [SB76] und [EHR80] diskutiert.

Literaturverzeichnis:

ADAB ADABAS Benutzer-Handbuch, Broschüre der Software AG, Darmstadt.

AIM AIM, Advanced Information Manager, Reference Manual, Fujitsu, Japan.

Ba79 Bayer, R.;et al.: Parallelism and Recovery in Database Systems, in: Proc. 4th Int. Conf. on Software Engineering, Munich, Sept. 1979.

BS77 Bayer, R., Schkolnick, M.: Concurrency of Operations on B-Trees, in: Acta Informatica, Vol.9, 1977, S. 1-21.

EC75 Eswaran, K.P., Chamberlin, D.D.: Functional Specification of a Subsystem for Database Integrity, in: Proc. 1st Int. Conf. on VLDB 1975, Framingham, Ma., Sept. 22-24, 1975, S. 48-68.

Ef79 Effelsberg, W.: Messung und Auswertung des Seitenreferenzverhaltens von Datenbanksystemen, in: Angewandte Informatik 10/79, S. 434-440.

EGLT76 Eswaran,K.P., Gray, J.N., Lorie R.A., Traiger, I.L.: The Notions of Consistency and Predicate Locks in a Database System, in: Comm. ACM, Vol. 19, No.11, 1976, S. 624-633.

EHR80 Effelsberg, W., Härder, Th., Reuter, A.: Measurment and Evaluation of Techniques for Implementing COSETs - A Case Study, erscheint im Tagungsband der Int. Conference on Database Systems, Aberdeen, Juli 1980.

GLPT76 Gray, J.N., Lorie, R.A., Putzolu, G.R., Traiger, I.L.: Granularity of Locks and Degrees of Consistency in a Large Shared Data Base, in: Modelling in Data Base Management Systems, North Holland Publ. Comp. 1976, S. 365-394.

Gr78 Gray, J.N.: Notes on Data Base Operating Systems, in: Lecture Notes in Computer Science 60, Advanced Course on Operating Systems, Springer-Verlag, Berlin, 1978, S. 393-481.

Gr79 Gray, J.N.; et.al.: The Recovery Manager of a Data Management System, IBM Research Report RJ2623, San Jose, Aug. 1979.

Hä77 Härder,T.: A Scan-Driven Sort Facility for a Relational Database System, in: Proc. 3rd Int. Conf. on VLDB, Tokyo, Japan, Oct. 1977, S. 236-243.

Hä78 Härder, T.: Implementierung von Datenbanksystemen, Carl-Hanser-Verlag, 1978.

Hä79 Härder,T.: Die Einbettung eines Datenbanksystems in eine Betriebssystemumgebung, in: Datenbanktechnologie, J. Niedereichholz (Hrsg.), B.G. Teubner-Verlag, Stuttgart, 1979, S.9-24.

HR79a Härder,T., Reuter, A.: Optimization of Logging and Recovery in a Database System, in: Data Base Architecture, Proc. IFIP TC2-Working Conf., Venice 1979, G. Bracchi and G.M. Nijssen (eds.), North Holland Publ. Comp., Amsterdam 1979, S. 151-168.

HR79b Härder,T., Reuter, A.: A Systematic Framework for the Description of Transaction Oriented Logging and Recovery Schemes, DVI 79-4, Forschungsbericht TH Darmstadt, Dez. 1979.

Lo77 Lorie, R.A.: Physical Integrity in a Large Segmented Database, in: ACM TODS, Vol. 2, No.1, March 1977, S. 91-104.

Re79 Reuter, A.: Minimizing the I/O-Operations for UNDO-Logging in Database Systems, in: Proc. 5th Int. Conf. on VLDB, Rio de Janeiro, Oct. 1979, S. 164-172.

RR76 Ragaz, N., Rodriguez-Rosell, J.: Empirical Studies of Storage Management in a Data Base System, IBM Research Report, RJ1834, San Jose, July 1976.

RS79 Ries, D.R., Stonebraker, M.: Locking Granularities Revisited, in: ACM TODS, Vol. 4,No.2, 1979, S. 210-227.

SB76 Sherman, S.W., Brice, R.S.: Performance of a Database Manager in a Virtual Memory System, in: ACM TODS, Vol. 1, No. 4, 1976, S. 317-343.

Sch78 Schkolnick, M.: A Survey of Physical Database Design Methodology and Techniques, in: Proc. 4th Int. Conf. on VLDB, Berlin, Sept. 1978, S. 474-487.

SL76 Severance, D.G., Lohmann, G.M.: Differential Files: Their Application to the Maintenance of Large Databases, in: ACM TODS, Vol. 1, No.3, 1976, S. 256-267.

St76 Stonebraker, M.; et.al.: The Design and Implementation of INGRES, in: ACM TODS, Vol. 1, No.3, 1976, S. 189-222.

WH76 Wedekind, H., Härder,T.: Datenbanksysteme II, Reihe Informatik/18, Bibliographisches Institut Mannheim, 1976 .

Diese Arbeit wurde teilweise vom Bundesminister für Forschung und Technologie, Förderkennzeichen 081 5186 und von der Siemens AG unterstützt. Wir danken den Gutachtern für wertvolle Hinweise zur deutlicheren Formulierung des zentralen Anliegens dieses Papieres.

AN INTERFACE TO INTERROGATE HETEROGENEOUS DISTRIBUTED DATABASES

Patrick BOSC
IRISA, INRIA
Campus de Beaulieu
35042 RENNES CEDEX - FRANCE

Recent development in communication networks, such as ARPA, CYCLADES, EIN or TRANSPAC, allows the exchange of information between computers and the conception of distributed applications. In this area, distributed database management systems -DDBMS- constitute an example and many works have been undertaken, among which ADD, POREL, POPLYPHEME and SDD-1.

Inside distributed database domain, it seems interesting to conceive a distributed database composed of *existing databases or files* managed by their own system. This approach, called *cooperation of local databases*, tends to define a *global database* managed by a DDBMS using local databases and management systems.

We want here to address the problem of interrogation in such a context. One of major problems to solve lies in the heterogeneousness of both database systems and data which are to cooperate. So, it is convenient to provide users with a homogeneous schema of the distributed database, called *global view* and a query language hiding heterogeneousness. We have choosen the global view to be composed of entities represented by trees refering to each other and a language inspired from SOCRATE.

Any user query is split into parts called *local subqueries* which must be processed on local databases and the question is : how to process them ? One way consists in the translation of each subquery into the data manipulation language of the concerned local DBMS. Such a solution leads to problems for language translation and seems inaccurate for files. So we suggest another way, based on a standard description of any local database, called the *local view*. Each local database may be represented by a subset of the trees contained in the global view. Each of these trees is decomposed into subtrees called *logical files*. A logical file defines a logical record which constitutes the unit of exchange between the DDBMS and the local system managing the local database. Every logical file possesses at least one *access function* (sequential, keyed, ...) delivering the logical record.

Thus, a local subquery is translated into an intermediate procedural language allowing calls to the available access functions. Then a local subquery is executed by an internal evaluator using the access functions. In this approach, the local DBMS is only used to provide data needed by a subquery, but not to process the subquery by itself.

This method has been implemented in a project called FRERES, for which a prototype presently runs upon CYCLADES network.

Rekonstruktion eines global-konsistenten Zustandes in verteilten Datenbank-Systemen

Peter Dadam
Fachbereich Mathematik
Praktische Informatik
FernUniversität Hagen

Das Thema befaßt sich mit dem Problem des "globalen Backup", d.h. dem Zurücksetzen der gesamten verteilten Datenbank (vDB) in einen lokal und global konsistenten Zustand. Da man davon ausgehen kann, daß durch geeignete Vorkehrungen eine solche Maßnahme in einer vDB im allgemeinen äußerst selten erforderlich sein wird, sollte während des normalen Betriebes des Systems hierfür möglichst wenig Aufwand erforderlich sein. Eine direkte Übertragung der von zentralen DBn her bekannten Vorgehensweise wurde in /JOUV77/ vorgeschlagen. Hierbei wird von Zeit zu Zeit an allen Knoten *gleichzeitig* ein sog. *globaler Checkpoint* in das System-Log geschrieben. (Wenn ein Checkpoint geschrieben wird, ist lokal keine Transaktion mehr aktiv, die lokale DB ist daher in einem konsistenten Zustand.) Dieses Verfahren kann während des normalen Betriebes zu einer nicht unerheblichen Leistungs-Einbuße des Systems führen.

Ein anderes Verfahren, das - bei geringem zusätzlichen Aufwand - einen geringeren Performance-Verlust erwarten läßt, wurde in /SCDA79/ vorgeschlagen. Hierbei wird zwar die Notation eines "globalen" Checkpoints beibehalten, dieser aber als Menge von lokalen Checkpoints, die nicht unbedingt "gleichzeitig" erzeugt werden müssen, realisiert. *(lose synchronisierte Lösung)*. Ein weiteres Verfahren, das ganz auf globale Checkpoints verzichtet, wurde in /DASC 79/ vorgestellt. Die lokalen Checkpoints können hierbei völlig unabhängig voneinander - sowohl in Bezug auf den Zeitpunkt als auch in Bezug auf die Häufigkeit - erzeugt werden, auch sonst tritt praktisch kein nennenswerter zusätzlicher laufzeit-relevanter Aufwand auf *(nicht-synchronisierte Lösung)*. Der Preis hierfür ist allerdings eine erhöhte Komplexität und damit verbunden ein höherer Zeit-Aufwand beim Backup selbst.

Literatur

/DASC79/ Recovery in distributed databases based on non-synchronized local checkpoints. Forschungsbericht Nr. 92/1979. Abt. Informatik, Universität Dortmund (Zum Vortrag angenommen für IFIP Congress 80)

/JOUV77/ JOUVE, M.: Reliability Aspects in a distributed data base management system. Proc. AICA'77 DATA BASES, 199-209

/SCDA79/ Reconstruction of consistent global states in distributed databases. Proc. Int. Symp. on Distributed Data Bases, Paris, March 1980, North-Holland Publ. Comp., 191-199

IMPLEMENTATION OF A RELATIONAL DATA BASE SYSTEM ON TOP OF A COMMERCIAL DBMS

M. Böhm, M. Riemer, K.-H. Höhne

Institut für Mathematik und Datenverarbeitung in der Medizin
Universitätskrankenhaus Hamburg-Eppendorf and
Deutsches Elektronen-Synchrotron DESY, Hamburg, F.R.G.

While studying data base structures for medical information systems we have implemented a data base system based on the relational model. To reduce the necessary implementation effort we decided to build our system on top of a suitable commercial system (ADABAS in our case). Having this basis for solving the problems of basic data access methods, recovery, privacy and concurrency we could concentrate on the implementation of a high-level query and manipulation language and a comfortable terminal interface.

The basic concepts of this language stem from SEQUEL, however several features of SEQUEL have been omitted in our current implementation in favour of some extensions required more urgently in our application. It is e.g. often convenient in routine use to generate recurring lengthy transactions with a single and short statement. In order to do this the desired transaction may be defined as a macro.

Data base languages based on the relational model are on the one hand well suited to express set-oriented operations, but on the other hand some very simple and often used operations like updating or deleting a single tuple which is already displayed on the screen require unneccessarily lengthy input. In our system such updates of individual tuples are possible by direct overtyping instead of issuing explicit commands. The system determines automatically the corresponding tuple in the data base and generates the necessary update command. To some extent this gives the user the impression of working with relations as if he were working with tables on paper. These facilities are part of a terminal interface system which handles several larger virtual screens and displays userdefined windows of them on the real terminal screen. These windows can be moved across the virtual screen by simply pressing function keys. This is useful in order to examine result relations of queries which do not fit on the terminal screen or to recall previous commands in order to issue them once more with slight modificatons.

Having several tasks for each user leads to short response times since user and system activities can be performed in parallel. Suppose that a user's query is fulfilled by 50 tuples. The first 10 tuples are read and passed via a FIFO to the users screen. While the user examines these tuples the remaining tuples are read and buffered in the FIFO. When the user requests the next portion of tuples they are in most cases already read and immediately available.

The system has been implemented in PL/1 on a configuration of one IBM 3033 and two IBM 370/168 in the DESY computing center. Tests are performed with real data from 35.000 patients including 500.000 measurement values from the central clinical laboratory of the University Hospital Hamburg-Eppendorf.

Schutz im OSKAR-Betriebssystem

Klaus Dittrich, Karlheinz Hug, Peter Kammerer,
Dieter Lienert, Hans Mau, Klaus Wachsmuth

Institut für Informatik II, Universität Karlsruhe
PF 6380, D 7500 Karlsruhe 1

Kurzfassung

Zu den Zielen des Betriebssystemprojekts OSKAR gehört die Integration umfassender Schutzmaßnahmen in das System. Damit soll einerseits die sichere Austauschbarkeit von Systemkomponenten ermöglicht, andererseits die Voraussetzung zur Realisierung einer Vielzahl von Datenschutzstrategien geschaffen werden. Das Papier nennt die Anforderungen an das Schutzsystem in OSKAR, vermittelt die notwendigen Grundlagen der Architektur des Gesamtsystems und beschreibt die vorgesehenen Schutzmechanismen. Schließlich wird auf einige Implementierungsgesichtspunkte eingegangen.

Das Projekt OSKAR wird von der Deutschen Forschungsgemeinschaft (DFG) unter der Nummer Go 323/1 gefördert.

0. Einleitung

OSKAR (Operating System Karlsruhe) ist ein Betriebssystemprojekt an der Universität Karlsruhe. Hauptziel ist der Entwurf und die Implementierung eines Forschungs- und Experimentierbetriebssystems (Zielmaschine: Siemens 7.700-Serie). Genauer geht es darum,

- in den letzten Jahren separat entstandene Konzepte der Betriebssystemforschung in einem System substantieller Größe zu integrieren und zu erproben (z.B. Kommunikationskonzepte),

- ein für Experimente im Betriebssystembereich selbst zugängliches Produkt zu erhalten, was insbesondere die Austauschbarkeit einzelner Komponenten fordert,

- im System weitgehende Maßnahmen zum Schutz vor Mißbrauch und vor dem Fehlverhalten einzelner Komponenten anzubieten,

- ein Betriebssystem mit übersichtlicher Architektur und Schnittstellengestaltung zu schaffen (z.B. einheitliche Benutzerschnittstelle, Trennung von logischen und physikalischen Aspekten der Datenverwaltung).

Schutzmaßnahmen im Betriebssystem sind die Vorbedingung für Sicherheit und Zuverlässigkeit einerseits sowie für Datenschutz (auch zur Erfüllung der mittlerweile erlassenen gesetzlichen Vorschriften) andererseits. In der Literatur wird zurecht darauf verwiesen, daß Schutzmaßnahmen in einem DV-System so tief wie möglich verankert werden müssen. Sind die von der Hardware gebotenen Möglichkeiten nicht ausreichend (wie heute üblich), so muß dies auf alle Fälle im Betriebssystem erfolgen.

Damit sollte verständlich sein, warum das Thema "Schutz" im OSKAR-Projekt eine wesentliche Rolle spielt. Wir wollen dabei künftig unter Schutzmaßnahmen in einem weiten Sinne alle Vorkehrungen im Betriebssystem verstehen, die zur Festlegung und Durchsetzung wohldefinierter Regelungen zur Verwendung des Gesamtsystems oder Teilen davon durch (menschliche) Benutzer oder andere Systemteile getroffen werden. Die Gesamtheit dieser Vorkehrungen wird oft auch als das "Schutzsystem" als Teil eines umfassenderen Systems bezeichnet. Man muß sich jedoch vor der Vorstellung hüten, dies sei ein Systembestandteil, den man dazutun kann oder nicht. Alle Erfahrungen zeigen, daß Schutzmaßnahmen eng mit dem zu schützenden System verflochten und damit integraler Bestandteil statt hinzugefügte, abgeschlossene Einheit sein müssen. Dies stellt übrigens (neben allgemeinen, anerkannten Konstruktionsprinzipien für gute Software) eine weitere Motivation dar, das System nach möglichst wenigen, einheitlichen Grundsätzen zu entwerfen, um zu einer durchsichtigen Struktur zu kommen.

Im folgenden Papier sollen die wesentlichen Schutzaspekte von OSKAR vorgestellt werden. Wir beginnen mit der Aufzählung der Anforderungen, denen das OSKAR-Schutzsystem genügen soll und stellen soweit notwendig die Architektur des Gesamtsystems dar. Den Hauptteil machen die Beschreibung der Schutzkonzepte sowie Überlegungen zu deren Implementierung aus. Schließlich werden Lösungen einiger aus der Literatur bekannter Schutzprobleme mit OSKAR-Mitteln besprochen.

1. Anforderungen an das OSKAR-Schutzsystem

Bei Schutz ist keine Ja-Nein-Entscheidung zu treffen, sondern es handelt sich um eine graduelle Eigenschaft. Demzufolge muß man sich auch bei einem Betriebssystementwurf entscheiden, in welchem Umfang man Schutzmaßnahmen anbieten will. Wir gehen diesbezüglich in OSKAR von folgenden Annahmen und Anforderungen aus.

1. Jeglicher Systembetrieb besteht in der Ausführung von Operationen, d.h. im Aufruf von Operatoren mit bestimmten Parametern. Schutzmaßnahmen müssen daher an Erlaubnis bzw. Verbot der Ausführung von Operationen (durch sog. Subjekte, vgl. [GD 72]) ansetzen.

2. Wir verlangen ein positives Schutzsystem: alles ist verboten, was nicht explizit erlaubt ist.

3. Die Erlaubnis zur Durchführung einer Operation soll individuell an Subjekte vergebbar sein.

4. Die Erlaubnis zur Durchführung einer Operation soll weitergebbar sein. Dies kann jedoch wiederum von einer speziellen Erlaubnis dazu abhängig sein.

5. Eine einmal erteilte Erlaubnis zur Durchführung einer Operation kann wieder entzogen werden. Auch dies kann wieder von einer speziellen Erlaubnis dazu abhängig sein.

6. Es soll nicht während der gesamten Lebensdauer des Systems ein Subjekt geben <u>müssen</u>, dem alle Operationen erlaubt sind.

7. Das Schutzsystem soll lediglich Mechanismen zur Verfügung stellen. Diese sollen <u>per Programmierung</u> möglichst beliebige

Schutzstrategien zulassen.

Das Schutzsystem sorgt für die Einhaltung der getroffenen Schutzregelungen. Damit ist es außerordentlich kritisch hinsichtlich der korrekten Funktion des Gesamtsystems. Das ordnungsgemäße, unkompromittierbare Arbeiten des Schutzsystems muß also durch besondere Maßnahmen gewährleistet werden (z.B. durch Verifikation oder zumindest Validierung).

2. Grundlagen der OSKAR-Systemarchitektur

Schutzmaßnahmen und Systemarchitektur sind eng miteinander verbunden: Die Wahl der Schutzmechanismen beeinflußt die Art und Weise der Strukturierung und umgekehrt.

Die Strukturierungseinheit von OSKAR muß somit derart gewählt werden, daß Zugriffe von einer solchen Einheit zu einer anderen ausschließlich unter Einschaltung des Schutzsystems möglich sind. Dies ist das bekannte Prinzip der Isolation verbunden mit kontrollierten Zugriffsmöglichkeiten. Nach obiger Forderung 1 könnte man zunächst an einen Operator als Strukturierungseinheit denken. Dies scheitert jedoch daran, daß häufig mehrere Operatoren auf gemeinsamen Daten arbeiten. Wir gehen daher von funktionalen Moduln aus, d.h. von Programmstücken, die eine Menge von Operatoren realisieren und genau diese nach außen zur Verfügung stellen. (Vgl. information hiding, encapsulation; [PAR 72], [SS 75], [LÖH 79]). Das Betriebssystem soll jedoch nicht unnötig für Isolation sorgen, wo bereits durch Sprachübersetzer etc. entsprechende Überprüfungen vorgenommen worden sind. Als Strukturierungseinheit lassen wir daher einen oder eine Gruppe solcher Moduln zu und bezeichnen sie als Subsystem.

Ein Subsystem ist also eine Menge von Operatoren zusammen mit allen Daten, auf denen diese Operatoren arbeiten können. Da der Subsystembegriff auf dem Modulbegriff aufbaut ist klar, daß die Datenmengen verschiedener Subsysteme jeweils paarweise disjunkt sind.

Da man häufig mehrere Subsysteme benötigt, die sich nicht in ihren Operatoren, sondern lediglich in ihren Daten unterscheiden, bezeichnen wir die Programmteile zur Realisierung der Operatoren (samt der Beschreibung der zugehörigen Datenobjekte) als einen Subsystemtyp. Ein Subsystem ist dann stets ein Exemplar genau eines Subsystemtyps.

Benutzerprogramme im herkömmlichen Sinn können als Subsysteme mit einem einzigen Operator ("ausführen") betrachtet werden. Damit gelingt es, sowohl Betriebssystem wie auch Benutzer- und Dienstleistungsprogramme einheitlich mit einem Konzept zu beschreiben.

Zwischen den einzelnen Subsystemen von OSKAR besteht dahingehend eine Relation, daß Operatoren, die in der Schnittstelle eines Subsystems enthalten sind, in der Implementierung von Operatoren anderer Subsysteme verwendet (d.h. prozedural aufgerufen) werden können. Ein solcher Aufruf bedeutet zur Laufzeit einen Wechsel des Subsystems, der wegen Isolation und kontrolliertem Zugriff auf seine Zulässigkeit überprüft werden muß. Da herkömmliche Hardware dazu nicht in der Lage ist, sehen wir zu diesem Zweck eine hardwarenahe Softwarekomponente vor, die selbst natürlich kein Subsystem sein kann. Sie verfügt aber ebenfalls über eine funktionale Schnittstelle und heißt der Kern des Systems. Bei der (quasi auf höherem Abstraktionsniveau) als Aufruf eines Operators eines anderen Subsystems interpretierten Aktion handelt es sich also genauer um den Aufruf einer Kernfunktion, die die Zulässigkeit des Aufrufwunsches überprüft und im Erfolgsfall die Ablaufkontrolle an die entsprechende Stelle im Zielsubsystem übergibt. Entsprechendes gilt für die Rückkehr in das Quellsubsystem. Direkte Aufrufe von Subsystem zu Subsystem unter Umgehung des Kerns sind nicht möglich.

Der Kern wird damit zu einer zentralen Komponente des OSKAR-Schutzsystems, zumal er zur Ausführung seiner Aufgabe über die festgelegten Schutzregelungen informiert sein muß. Wir sehen im Kern jedoch nicht eine Instanz, in der alle schutzrelevanten Daten und Aktivitäten zusammengefaßt sind und deren Korrektheit alleine zu einem "schutzgerechten" Systembetrieb führt. Dies erscheint uns aus vielerlei Gründen nicht sinnvoll (die Systemkomponente zur Dialogverwaltung, die die Benutzeridentifikation akzeptiert, müßte sonst z.B. ebenfalls dem Kern zugeschlagen werden). Auch in der Literatur über Sicherheitskerne ist stets von zusätzlichen "trusted processes" die Rede ([PK 78]). Unser Ansatz zielt dahin, den Kern möglichst klein zu halten und soweit durchführbar Arbeiten in Subsysteme zu verlagern. So wurde etwa für die Hauptspeicherverwaltung, der wesentliche Aufgaben im Rahmen des Schutzes zukommen, ein eigenes Subsystem vorgesehen. Die korrekte Funktion einer Reihe von "trusted subsystems" ist also für die Systemsicherheit ebenso wichtig wie die des Kerns.

Einheit für die Systemabläufe ist in OSKAR wie anderswo der Prozeß, der aus einem entsprechenden Auftrag hervorgeht. Dabei folgen wir der Philosophie eines prozedurorientierten Entwurfs (in-process design). Bei diesem Konzept geht es darum, möglichst viele Betriebssystemaufgaben durch "gewöhnliche" Prozeduraufrufe (genauer: Subsystemoperatoraufrufe) von den Benutzerprozessen selbst durchführen zu lassen und nur dort für Teilaufgaben Systemprozesse einzusetzen, wo dies aus Effizienzgründen geboten ist. Im anderen Fall, dem prozeßorientierten Entwurf (out-of-process design, botschaftenorientierten Entwurf) werden Systemaufgaben grundsätzlich durch eine Anzahl (zyklischer) Systemprozesse übernommen, mit denen Benutzerprozesse via Botschaftenaustausch kommunizieren. Die Entscheidung zwischen beiden Konzepten ist prinzipiell unabhängig von Schutzfragen. Wir wählten für OSKAR das Konzept des prozedurorientierten Entwurfs wegen der in der Literatur erwähnten besseren dynamischen Leistungsfähigkeit (bei Vorliegen bestimmter Hardwareeigenschaften; vgl. [LN 78], [KEE 79]).

Im Sinne der eingeführten Begriffe ist ein Prozeß in OSKAR der Ablauf einer prozedural erzeugten Folge von Subsystemoperatoren auf einem (virtuellen) Prozessor, wobei den Wechsel zwischen zwei Subsystemen jeweils der Kern vermittelt.

Abbildung 1 gibt einen groben Eindruck von der OSKAR-Architektur. Für die nachfolgende Diskussion werden insbesondere die Komponenten Datenverwaltung (FM) und Subsystemverwaltung (SSM) von Interesse sein.

3. Schutzmechanismen

Ausgehend von den oben beschriebenen Strukturierungseinheiten soll nunmehr das Konzept der kontrollierten Ausführung von Operationen erläutert werden. Wir setzen dabei voraus, daß die im System tätigen Benutzer ausreichend identifiziert und authentisiert wurden, wozu eine Fülle von Verfahren (Codekarten, Paßworte, Algorithmen) existiert.

Zur Erfüllung der Forderung nach einem positiven Schutzsystem gehen wir wie folgt vor. Jedem Operator ω des Systems sind k Eingabeparameter mit Wertebereichen $A_1,\ldots,A_k$ und n-k Ausgabeparameter mit Wertebereichen $A_{k+1},\ldots,A_n$ zugeordnet. $A_1,\ldots,A_n$ hängen von ω ab.

Ein Recht ist ein Tupel $r = (\omega, p_1,\ldots,p_n)$ mit $p_i \in A_i$, $i = 1,\ldots,n$, und stellt die Erlaubnis dar, den Operator ω mit den Eingabeparametern $p_1,\ldots,p_k$ auszuführen und die Ausgabeparameter $p_{k+1},\ldots,p_n$ zu erhalten.

Damit können wir das Grundprinzip des OSKAR-Schutzsystems wie folgt formulieren: eine Operation darf nur ausgeführt werden, wenn der Aufrufer über das entsprechende Recht verfügt.

Die Begriffe "ausführen" und "Aufrufer" bedürfen noch einer Erläuterung. Der Kern überprüft die Zulässigkeit jedes Aufrufs. Selbstverständlich kann dabei zunächst nur festgestellt werden, ob bezüglich der Eingabeparameter ein Recht vorliegt. Ist dies nicht der Fall, so wird die gewünschte Operation gar nicht erst ausgeführt.

Die Behandlung von Ausgabeparametern ist problematisch. Eine Prüfung kann hier erst beim Rücksprung (der ebenfalls via Kern läuft) erfolgen. Wird dabei Unzulässigkeit erkannt, so ist die Operation bereits ausgeführt und müßte rückgängig gemacht werden. Wir begnügen uns in diesem Fall jedoch damit, die (unzulässigen) Ergebnisse nicht an den Aufrufer weiterzugeben. Ein Rücksetzen der Operation ist insbesondere bei Mehrbenutzerbetrieb mit beträchtlichen Konsequenzen (z.B. Dominoeffekt) verbunden und gehört daher nicht zu den Mechanismen des Schutzsystems.

Zu beantworten bleibt auch die Frage, was unter einem "Aufrufer" verstanden werden soll, d.h. wem Rechte zugeordnet werden müssen. Da alle Systemaktivitäten letztlich nicht um ihretwegen selbst stattfinden, gehen alle Operationen auf den Wunsch irgendeines (externen, menschlichen) Benutzers bzw. dessen systeminterne Repräsentation zurück. Jedoch ist es nicht ausreichend, jedem zugelassenen Benutzer u eine Menge von Rechten R(u) zuzuweisen. Beispielsweise soll ein Zugriff auf eine Menge von Gehaltsdaten nur erlaubt werden, wenn er aus einem Subsystem heraus erfolgt, in dem der Durchschnitt dieser Daten ermittelt wird. Jedoch ist es ebenso ungenügend, jedem Subsystem s unabhängig vom Benutzer eine Rechtemenge R(s) zuzuordnen. Um beiden Erfordernissen gerecht zu werden, entscheiden wir uns daher, Paare (u,s) als "Aufrufer" zu betrachten und ihnen Rechtemengen R(u,s) zuzuordnen. Die Gesamtheit aller jeweils existierenden Mengen R(u,s) bezeichnen wir als den <u>Schutzzustand</u> des Systems.

Alle Mengen R(u,s) müssen damit dem Kern bekannt sein. Außerdem muß er für alle Prozesse darüber informiert sein, wer der Benutzer u, für den die Aktivität stattfindet, und welches das "aktuelle" Subsystem s ist. Für einige der Systemprozesse (z.B. den zyklischen Seitenrahmenleerer), die nicht für einen speziellen Benutzer arbeiten, kann ein zusätzlicher, fiktiver Benutzer u_s (≙ "System") eingeführt werden.

Wenden wir uns nun der Frage zu, wie die Paare (u,s) zu Rechten kommen:

(a) durch Initialisierung bei Systemstart,
(b) durch Erzeugung neuer Subsysteme,
(c) durch Rechteweitergabe.

In OSKAR gilt der Grundsatz, daß "neue" Rechte grundsätzlich nur aus Anlaß der Schaffung neuer Subsysteme mit den entsprechenden Operatoren entstehen. Rechteerweiterungen (amplifications) wie etwa in HYDRA ([CJ 75]) sind nicht vorgesehen. Natürlich müssen bereits bei Systemstart eine Reihe notwendiger Subsysteme per Urladeprogramm (und nicht durch Aufruf einer Funktion "create_subsystem" der Subsystemverwaltung, die ja noch nicht existiert) erzeugt werden. Auch Rechte für die Operatoren dieser Subsysteme müssen im Zuge der Systeminitialisierung geschaffen und sinnvoll (schutzkritische Entscheidung!) auf die dann vorhandenen R(u,s) verteilt werden (wobei man eingangs von einem einzigen "Urbenutzer" u_0 ausgeht).

Im Anschluß an die Initialisierungsphase ist die Subsystemverwaltung (die selbst ein Subsystem ist) für die Erzeugung und Vernichtung von Subsystemen zuständig. Will Benutzer u aus dem Subsystem s heraus (also im Zustand (u,s)) ein neues Subsystem erzeugen, so muß er ein entsprechendes Recht für die "create_subsystem"-Funktion besitzen. Im Rahmen einer Subsystemerzeugung wird R(u,s) um sämtliche Rechte für die Operatoren des neuen Subsystems (d.h. für alle möglichen Parameterkombinationen) erweitert. Zusätzlich erhält R(u,s) das Recht, eine Funktion "delete_subsystem" der Subsystemverwaltung zur Vernichtung des eben erzeugten Subsystems aufzurufen.

Nach unseren Forderungen 3 und 7 ist jedoch die wichtigste Möglichkeit des Rechteerwerbs die durch explizite Rechteweitergabe. Wir sehen hierzu drei Operatoren vor:

- COPY : der Empfänger erhält eine Kopie des Rechts, d.h. der Sender behält selbst ebenfalls das Recht,
- TRANSFER: der Sender verliert das weitergegebene Recht,
- REVOKE : ein früher weitergegebenes Recht geht unter Verlust beim Empfänger an den Sender zurück.

Selbstverständlich sind unter "Sender" und "Empfänger" wiederum Paare (u,s) bzw. die entsprechenden Mengen R(u,s) zu verstehen.

Offensichtlich handelt es sich bei COPY, TRANSFER und REVOKE um Operatoren, die den Schutzzustand verändern. Diese Funktionen werden daher im Kern realisiert. Außerdem sollen auch sie nicht von jedermann beliebig verwendet werden dürfen, da der Sender eines Rechts oftmals vermeiden möchte, daß es vom Empfänger an Dritte weitergegeben wird. Damit liegt jedoch der Fall vor, daß man für Operationen zur Manipulation des aus Rechten bestehenden Schutzzustandes wiederum Rechte benötigt usw. Zur Vermeidung einer derartigen "Rechteschachtelung" sehen wir vor, daß die Rechte zur Ausführung von COPY, TRANSFER und REVOKE nicht ebenfalls explizit weitergegeben werden können. Vielmehr wird durch zusätzliche Parameter bei COPY und TRANSFER festgelegt, ob der Empfänger mit dem Recht auch COPY- und/oder TRANSFER-Rechte bzw. der Sender das REVOKE-Recht dafür erhalten soll. Die Schutzzustandsänderungsoperationen laufen also im Rahmen der systemweiten Schutzmaßnahmen ab. Zusätzlich kann dabei eine implizite Rechteweitergabe stattfinden.

Schutzzustandsänderungsoperationen realisieren zusammen mit einigen weiteren Kernfunktionen (etwa zum Lesen des Inhalts von R(u,s) im Zustand (u,s)) einen eigenen, neuen Datentyp, mittels dem in den Subsystemen selbst beliebige Vergabealgorithmen für Rechte programmiert werden können. Man beachte, daß dabei durch die Verwendung von Kernfunktionen gewährleistet wird, daß der Schutzzustand nicht unzulässig manipuliert werden kann (z.B. durch Hinzufügen von Rechten durch böswillige Benutzer).

4. Implementierungsgesichtspunkte

Nachdem wir die grundlegenden Konzepte zur Festlegung und Überwachung von Schutzregelungen dargelegt haben, soll in diesem Abschnitt - ohne allzu große Detaillierung - auf einige Aspekte eingegangen werden, die bei der Implementierung dieser Konzepte zu beachten sind.

Für die erforderliche Isolation der einzelnen Schutzeinheiten bietet sich die Verwendung getrennter Adreßräume an. Allerdings reicht es dazu nicht aus, in konventioneller Weise jedem Prozeß einen Adreßraum zuzuordnen. Stattdessen sehen wir in OSKAR für jede Aktivierung eines Subsystems durch einen Prozeß einen eigenen Adreßraum vor, der folgende Bestandteile umfaßt:

(a) einen Kernanteil (Code + Daten),

(b) einen Subsystemanteil (Code + subsystemspezifische Daten),

(c) für den jeweiligen Prozeß und das "aktuelle" Subsystem spezifische Daten (z.B. aktuelle Parameter etc.).

Vom Kern müssen Adreßraumwechsel vorgenommen werden; sein Code muß daher allen Adreßräumen gemeinsam sein. Eine Aufteilung in (b) und (c) ist erforderlich, da sich durchaus mehrere Prozesse im gleichen Subsystem "aufhalten" können. Die Festlegung, was zu den subsystemspezifischen und was zu den prozeßspezifischen Daten gehört, ist bei der Programmierung der Subsysteme zu treffen. Ebenso muß dort, falls erforderlich, für Synchronisation auf den Daten von (b) gesorgt werden.

Aus der Adreßraumgestaltung geht bereits hervor, daß ein Prozeß bei jedem Subsystemwechsel auch den Adreßraum wechseln muß. Somit ist eine strenge Isolation der einzelnen Subsysteme untereinander gewährleistet. Für die Trennung der Subsysteme vom Kern wird der hardwareseitig vorhandene Ringschutz verwendet. Dabei genießt der Kern freien Zugang zu den Adreßraumteilen (b) und (c). Dies stellt keine Schutzverletzung dar, da ohne korrekte Funktionsweise des Kerns ohnehin kein sinnvoller Systembetrieb möglich ist. Umgekehrt darf aus dem jeweiligen Subsystemcode heraus nur durch Aufruf der wohldefinierten Kernfunktionen auf Teil (a) zugegriffen werden. Dies läßt sich durch Verwendung spezieller Hardwareeigenschaften der zugrunde liegenden Rechenanlage (Steuer- und Datenkeller, Zugriff über CALN-Befehl; vgl. [SIE 75]) in sicherer Weise realisieren.

Als zweiter wesentlicher Implementierungsgesichtspunkt ist die Realisierung der Rechte zu betrachten. Zwar ist es ganz selbstverständlich, daß die Anwendung von Schutzmaßnahmen ihren Preis in Form von Laufzeit- und Speicheraufwand fordert. Jedoch müssen diese Aufwendungen in solchen Grenzen bleiben, daß noch ein akzeptabler Systembetrieb möglich ist.

Aus diesem Grund sind die oben eingeführten Rechte zwar zur Erläuterung des Konzepts gut geeignet, nicht jedoch für den Umgang und die Implementierung. Wir fassen daher in einem ersten Schritt jeweils all die Rechte in einem R(u,s) zusammen, die sich auf die Operatoren eines einzigen Subsystems beziehen, und erhalten dadurch eine Befähigung (capability) für dieses Subsystem. Befähigungen stellen dann die Einheit für die Rechteverwaltung und -weitergabe dar. Entsprechend müssen die Operatoren zur Änderung des Schutzzustandes auf Befähigungen erweitert werden. Bei der Weitergabe muß dabei zusätzlich die Möglichkeit zur Einschränkung der durch eine Befähigung dargestellten Rechtemenge geschaffen werden.

Bei den Überprüfungen durch den Kern muß nunmehr festgestellt werden, ob der Aufrufer über eine Befähigung verfügt, die das für die gewünschte Operation benötigte Recht enthält. Die Suche nach Rechten läßt sich mit vertretbarem Aufwand implementieren, da Rechte durch die Befähigungen nach Subsystemen geordnet sind.

Weiterhin sollte die Implementierung eines Schutzsystems gewährleisten, daß an den Stellen, wo auf einzelne Schutzmechanismen verzichtet wird, möglichst auch kein Aufwand entsteht. Ein solcher Verzicht bedeutet bei einem positiven Schutzmechanismus beispielsweise, daß Operatoren mit allen von der Schnittstelle her möglichen Parametern aufgerufen werden dürfen (oder daß dies sogar für alle Operatoren eines Subsystems gilt). Für diesen (in der Praxis sicher nicht seltenen) Fall sehen wir eine spezielle Befähigungsdarstellung derart vor, daß er vom Kern sofort erkannt werden und die sonst erforderliche Parameterprüfung unterbleiben kann. Zudem wird für diese Situation für eine sehr platzsparende Unterbringung der Befähigungen gesorgt.

Trotzdem muß man sich weitere Gedanken über die Speicherung der Befähigungen machen. Dies umso mehr, als Dateien im traditionellen Sinne in OSKAR ebenfalls Subsysteme sind (worauf hier nicht näher eingegangen werden kann; siehe jedoch die Beispiele im nächsten Abschnitt). Dadurch hat man eine große Anzahl von Subsystemen und entsprechend viele Befähigungen zu verwalten.

Grundsätzlich enthalten Befähigungen Schutzinformation, die nur für den Kern bestimmt ist und am sichersten von ihm verwaltet wird. Ein dazu erforderlicher "eigener" Hintergrundspeicher (anteil) für den Kern ist jedoch aus Hardwaregründen nicht mit vertretbarem Aufwand realisierbar. Somit verbleibt nur die Möglichkeit, Befähigungen zeitweise aus dem Kern herauszunehmen und der Datenverwaltung anzuvertrauen. Teile davon werden dadurch ebenfalls zu sicherheitskritischen Systemkomponenten. Durch den Einsatz kryptographischer Methoden kann dem Mißbrauch von Befähigungen auf Magnetplatten etc. (durch Herausnehmen des Stapels) entgegengetreten werden.

Da der Kern Befähigungen für seine Prüfaufgaben benötigt, muß man genau überlegen, welche davon man in die Datenverwaltung auslagert. Wir sehen vor, zunächst die Befähigungen solcher Mengen R(u,s) als Auslagerungskandidaten zu betrachten, für die entweder u im Augenblick nicht angemeldet oder s ein "geschlossenes" Subsystem (vergleichbar mit einer geschlossenen Datei) ist. Auf diese einfache Weise wird die Anzahl der im Kern zu haltenden Befähigungen bereits drastisch reduziert.

Abschließend zu diesem Abschnitt sei nochmals deutlich darauf hingewiesen, daß hier nicht alle Implementierungsprobleme angesprochen werden konnten. Weitere kritische Punkte wären etwa das dynamische Hinzufügen neuer Subsystemtypen, die

Auswahl geeigneter Datenstrukturen für die Schutzinformation oder die schutzgerechte Speicherbeschaffung und -rückgabe.

5. Lösung einiger Schutzprobleme in OSKAR

Hier sollen in aller Kürze einige Beispiele für bekannte Schutzprobleme sowie deren Lösungen in OSKAR skizziert werden.

Programmschutz

Ein Programm kann in OSKAR als ein Subsystem mit einer einzigen Operation ("ausführen") eingebracht werden. Durch entsprechende Rechtevergabe kann dafür gesorgt werden, daß nur bestimmte Benutzer und diese nur an bestimmten Stellen ihrer Arbeit (d.h. von bestimmten Subsystemen aus) das Programm verwenden können.

Dateischutz

Auch Dateien werden in OSKAR als Subsysteme behandelt. Dabei werden die Daten in einen Modul eingeschlossen, dessen Operatoren gerade die Zugriffsmethode ausmachen. Subsystemtypen für die üblichen Zugriffsarten können standardmäßig angeboten werden. Datenübertragungen von und zu den Hintergrundspeichern sowie Pufferung verbergen sich in den jeweiligen Subsystemen.

Damit kann Dateischutz genau wie der Schutz anderer Systemteile erfolgen. Der Ersteller einer Datei erhält die Rechte für alle im Rahmen der jeweiligen Zugriffsmethode möglichen Operatoren. Er kann diese selektiv an andere Paare (u,s) weitergeben und dabei auch zwischen Lese- und Schreibzugriffsrechten differenzieren. Außerdem wird dadurch das Problem gelöst, daß manchen Benutzern nur aus bestimmten Subsystemen heraus der Dateizugriff gestattet werden darf (z.B. Lesen einer Datei nur zu Zwecken der Durchschnittsberechnung, aber nicht zur Kenntnisnahme der Einzeldaten). Es wird also die enge Verknüpfung von Daten und sie bearbeitenden Operatoren erzwungen.

Weitergabe von Rechten

Der Inhaber eines Rechts (bzw. einer Befähigung) möchte dieses oft gezielt weitergeben, eine weitere Vergabe an Dritte jedoch verhindern. Dieses Problem wird dadurch gelöst, daß die entsprechende COPY- bzw. TRANSFER-Operation mit der Option "kein Recht für COPY/TRANSFER dieses Rechts beim Empfänger erzeugen" ausgeführt wird.

Modifikation

Das in der Literatur ([CJ 75]) genannte Problem der mißbräuchlichen Änderung von Parameterobjekten durch aufgerufene Operatoren tritt in dieser Form nicht auf, da aus Gründen der strengen Isolation alle Parameter (via Kern) per Wert übergeben werden.

Sonstiges

Genaue Untersuchungen haben gezeigt, daß auch andere Probleme, wie etwa Informationsflußkontrolle, gegenseitiges Mißtrauen (mutual suspicion) usw. mit OSKAR-Mitteln lösbar sind (soweit dies überhaupt durch programmierte Prüfmaßnahmen allein möglich ist; vgl. etwa das Confinement-Problem, [LAM 73], [CJ 75]).

6. Zusammenfassung

Wir versuchen, in OSKAR extensive Schutzmaßnahmen in einem Mehrzweckbetriebssystem substantieller Größe für konventionelle Hardware zu realisieren. Wir haben dazu in diesem Papier eine Reihe von Anforderungen genannt und ein relativ einfaches Schutzkonzept auf der Basis sogenannter Rechte vorgestellt, das unsere Forderungen - obwohl dies hier nicht in allen Einzelheiten nachgewiesen wurde - erfüllt. Die Einfachheit des Konzepts zeigt sich zum Beispiel darin, daß weder für Dateien eine Sonderbehandlung erforderlich ist, noch komplizierte, schwer handhabbare (und hinsichtlich Schutz fragwürdige!) Möglichkeiten wie die der Rechteerweiterung notwendig sind. Einen weiteren, wesentlichen Fortschritt sehen wir darin, die Rechtevergabe programmierbar zu machen. Damit kann auf der Grundlage einfacher Mechanismen eine Vielzahl flexibler Datenschutzstrategien bereitgestellt werden.

Für die Implementierung dieses Schutzkonzepts wurden einige kritische Punkte angesprochen. Insbesondere kommen wir nicht umhin, einen Teil der Rechte außerhalb des Kerns zu halten und damit zusätzliche Systemkomponenten schutzkritisch zu machen. Wir sehen darin jedoch den Preis dafür, mit einer nicht auf unsere Schutzforderungen zugeschnittenen Hardware arbeiten zu müssen.

Unsere Implementierungsarbeiten sind bis jetzt soweit fortgeschritten, daß eine zunächst vereinfachte Kernversion (noch keine Parameterprüfung) kurz vor der Vollendung steht. Aufbauend darauf soll eine erste OSKAR-Version erstellt werden. Der Vollausbau des Schutzsystems ist für das nächste Jahr vorgesehen. Zur Implementierung wird die Systemimplementierungssprache LIS ([SIE 78]) verwendet.

7. Literatur

[CJ 75] Cohen, E.; Jefferson, D.: Protection in the HYDRA Operating System. Operating Systems Reviews 9(1975)5, 141 - 160

[GD 72] Graham,G.S.; Denning, P.J.: Protection - principles and practice. Proceedings Spring Joint Computer Conference 1972, 417 - 429

[KEE 79] Keedy, J.L.: A comparison of two process structuring models. Monads Report No. 4, Department of Computer Science, Monash University, Clayton, Victoria, Australien, 1979

[LAM 73] Lampson, B.W.: A note on the confinement problem. CACM 16(1973)10, 613 - 615

[LN 78] Lauer, H.C.; Needham, R.M.: On the duality of operating system structures. Second Int. Symp. on Operating Systems, IRIA, Rocquencourt, Frankreich, 1978 (nachgedruckt in Operating Systems Reviews 13(1979)2, 3 - 19)

[LÖH 79] Löhr, K.-P.: Architektur von Betriebssystemen. Interner Bericht, Universität Bremen, 1979

[PAR 72] Parnas, D.L.: On the criteria to be used in decomposing systems into modules. CACM 15(1972)12, 1053 - 1058

[PK 78] Popek, G.J.; Kline, C.S.: Issues in Kernel design. Proc. NCC 1978, 1079 - 1086

[SIE 75] Siemens AG: Serie 7.000 Beschreibung und Befehlsliste. 1979

[SIE 78] Siemens AG: LIS Reference Manual. 1979

[SS 75] Saltzer, J.H.; Schroeder, M.D.: The protection of information in computer systems. Proc. IEEE 63(1975)9, 1278 - 1308

Abb. 1: OSKAR-Grobarchitektur

Die Abbildung zeigt in groben Zügen die Komponenten von OSKAR (durchgezogene Kästchen):

PD Verwaltung der physikalischen Geräte

LD Logische Geräte

VMM Virtuelle Speicherverwaltung

RC Betriebsmittelsteuerung

SSM Subsystemverwaltung

PM Prozeßverwaltung

FM Datenverwaltung

DS Dialogsystem

JM Auftragsverwaltung

SC Systemsteuerung

Die Komponenten FM, LD und PD umfassen jeweils eine Menge von Subsystemen (FM insbesondere alle Dateien), die übrigen genau ein Subsystem.

Einfache Pfeile repräsentieren die Aufrufstruktur zwischen den einzelnen Komponeten. Prozesse sind durch [dargestellt und mittels Doppelpfeilen ihren Ausgangssubsystemen zugeordnet.

Gestrichelt eingezeichnet sind eine Reihe möglicher Anwender- bzw. Dienstleistungssubsysteme samt ihrer Aufrufbeziehungen untereinander und mit dem Betriebssystem selbst.

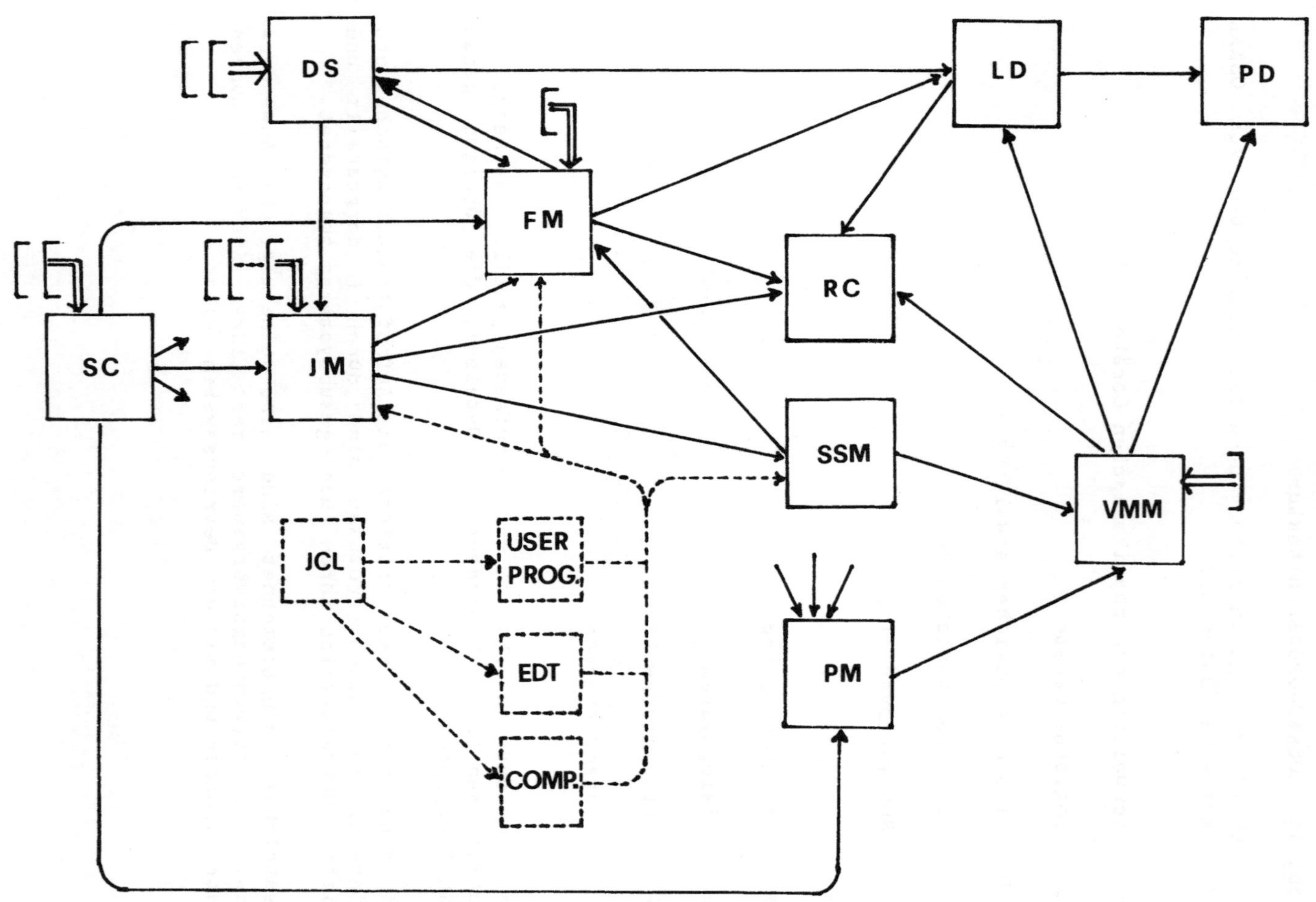
DS
LD
PD
FM
RC
SC
J M
SSM
VMM
JCL
USER PROG.
EDT
COMP.
PM

SYNCHRONIZATION AND PROTECTION FEATURES FOR DATA ABSTRACTION

D. HERMAN*, M. RAYNAL**

* IRISA, Université de Rennes
** IRISA, INRIA
35042 RENNES CEDEX, France

Abstract :

Program structuring relies on data abstraction concept. It is shown this concept can be used to write operating systems ; to this end two system aspects are tackled : protection and synchronization. On protection hand some visibility and access control problems, usually solved by dynamic mechanisms, are statically solved by using modules or abstract data type constructs. On synchronization hand some expressions well-suited to module exist but they need extensions to cope with data abstraction mechanism : so an appropriate proposal is made. Finally a common base for synchronization and protection expression is sketched.

Key-words :

Abstract Data Type, Access Control, Binding-time, Capability, Cluster, Module, Protection, Type Checking, Scope, Synchronization.

1 - INTRODUCTION

Modules [1] and Clusters [2] are abstraction implementation mechanisms which increase software reliability. They allow the division of programs into units making the maximum set of assumptions on their mutual behaviour. Relations between these units must be strongly controlled. Thus, when separately compiled units are linked together, type and scope checking are performed. These controls can be considered as the enforcement of protection policies ; that enforcement is statically ensured (i.e., the enforcement is done only once and before execution).
We display, in section 2, some static protection mechanisms with regard to dynamic ones. Postponing protection checks till run-time will always allow more flexible protection regimes but using abstraction mechanisms could be sufficient in many cases. System writing languages are more and more provided with abstraction mechanisms [4, 5]. When such mechanisms are used in a parallel environment they must be supplied with synchronization mechanisms which ensure object coherence. Several proposals of synchronization mechanisms have been made for modules [6, 7]. We display, in section 3, their inconvenience in the case of CLU-like abstract data types and we make an appropriate proposal.
In section 4, we sketch a common base for expressing synchronization policies together with protection ones. The start point of this common base is the "right" notion developped in [8].

2 - PROTECTION AND DATA ABSTRACTION

An operating system which carries program executions must avoid malversations and must limit the effects of errors. To do that, techniques based on keys and locks have been initially used ; they are implemented at the hardware level : a current key is associated to processes and locks are associated to memory cells. Each time an access is performed, a check for the concordance between key and lock is done. Keys are only made up by the system and the key of a given process may vary according to its execution locus (e.g., user program or system function). The domain concept has been developped to model the notion of process execution locus [9, 10] ; at a given time, a process is running in a domain which :

- defines the set of accessible objects and
- limits accesses to these objects to a given subset of all the potential ones.

Some entry points are associated to each domain. A mechanism must check if the accesses made by a process, into a domain, belong to the authorized subset. So domain implementation requires an access validation mechanism which may be either static (each access is validated by the compiler) or dynamic (each access is controlled and interpreted via a capability). An access control mechanism classification is allowed by

the static/dynamic criterion. Independently of this criterion, another one can be found : the binding-time of an object to the domain ; the binding can occur once at the domain creation, or each time a domain entry point is invoked (we call mechanisms endowed with such binding mode respectively encapsulation and renaming mechanisms). Consequently, with these two criteria four classes of access control mechanisms may be defined. We illustrate differences and similarities between these clàsses ; for each one we discuss briefly its noteworthy properties. For didactic purposes the same (and very simple) following example will be treated each time :
A domain BASE contains objects of type FILE which can only be accessed by the procedures READ and WRITE. For users, these objects must appear as objects of type BASE ; this type is supplied with two access procedures CONSULT and UPDATE. Hence direct use of READ, WRITE and FILE is forbidden to users ; indirect use is, nevertheless, provided via CONSULT and UPDATE. When it is possible an access procedure, namely MERGE, will be added to the type BASE. MERGE is a diadic procedure : it has two parameters of type BASE and it can use READ and WRITE on each one.

2.1. Static mechanisms

We present successively two abstraction mechanisms which are of interest from the static protection point of view : abstract types and modules.

2.1.1. Abstract types

Languages such as CLU [2] or ALPHARD [11] provide the user with abstract data type constructs (ADT) such as *Cluster* or *Form*. An ADT is characterized by a name and a set of access procedures names together with their types ; access procedures can be polyadic (i.e., take as parameters several objects of the type) and at least one of them can create objects of the type. Domains can be expressed with ADT constructs, and our example can be treated in the following way. (We use self-explanatory constructs for ADT and module).

```
(1) ADTREALIZATION BASE
      BEGIN
(2)      ADT BASE = REPRESENTATION TYPE (F : FILE) ;
         PROC CREATE = BASE : ... ;
         PROC CONSULT = (BASE B) ITEM : % this procedure returns a value of type ITEM
             from an object of type BASE ; it can use READ(B.F) to perform this action%
         PROC UPDATE = (BASE B, ITEM I) : % it can use WRITE(I, B.F) %
         PROC MERGE = (BASE B1, B2) : % it can use READ and WRITE on B1.F and B2.F %
(3)      DELIVERS ACCESS PROCEDURES CREATE, CONSULT, UPDATE, MERGE
             % these procedure names, together with their types, are the ones of the
             access procedures of the type BASE. Each realization of the ADT BASE must
             provide such a DELIVERS statement %
      END
```

(These constructs, except for the CLU cvt and the BASE declaration, are similar to the

CLU ones : ADTREALIZATION, REPRESENTATION TYPE and DELIVERS stand for cluster, rep and is).

In the domaine BASE defined by this ADT realization (line 1) FILE is a representation type for the abstract type BASE (line 2), this representation type is of course hidden (scope rule of the BEGIN ... END construct) ; thereby CONSULT, UPDATE, MERGE and CREATE (left to the users by the key-word DELIVERS at line 3 which breack scope rule) can manipulate objects of type BASE as being of type FILE (consequently then can apply READ and WRITE on their parameters of type BASE). All those type and scope checking are statically done by the compiler ; if X is a BASE it will reject expressions like : READ(X), X.F (standing outside the BEGIN ... END scope) and CONSULT(F) where F is of type FILE. Within a program, the declaration X : BASE authorizes only manipulating X as a BASE (assignation, passing as parameter). Thus links between domain entry points (access procedures) and objets are fugitive (they are established by the access procedure call and destroyed at the corresponding return) and access procedures can be polyadic (that is the case of MERGE) (Figure 1).

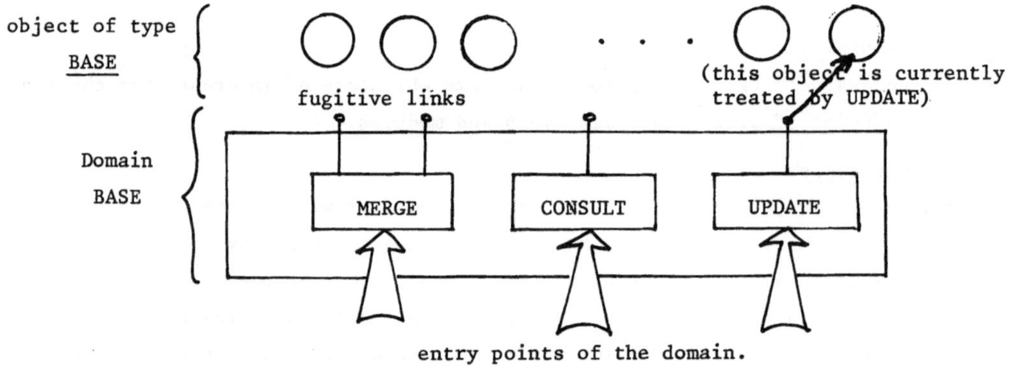

Fig. 1 : Static renaming tool.

We call such a programming tool a static renaming tool : when an entry point is invoked, a BASE is renamed and becomes a FILE ; obviously FILE and BASE have, each one, their own access procedures. Let us point out the fact that since objects are passed as parameters CONSULT, UPDATE and MERGE are never duplicated and are able to manipulate any object of the type BASE.

Let us finally notice that many realizations of the same ADT can exit simultaneously, with different representation types ; they must define the same set of access procedures. Moreover the components of a representation type used to implement an ADT can be primitive or abstract types.

2.1.2. Modules

The module concept provides abstraction features [1]. It gathers procedures which share private data ; these data are hidden and consequently protected. Only some procedure names, together with their types, are available to users ; they constitute the interface module. The module construct can be used in the following way to express the domain BASE.

```
MODULE BASE
BEGIN
     F : FILE ;
     PROC CONSULT = ITEM : % returns an item from F using READ(F) %
     PROC UPDATE = (ITEM I) : % update F with the item I using WRITE %
       % initialization of the module components %
     DELIVERS CONSULT, UPDATE
END
```

From the user point of view datum F, created and initialized at the module creation, can only be referred to by the access procedures CONSULT and UPDATE (left to users by the DELIVERS statement). Links between F and these access procedures are established at compile-time : that is a permanent binding. Thus module and created object can be assimilated : the module is an abstract object which can be seen as a t-uple of access procedures encapsulating the created object. As we can see in the example there is no access procedure which can create object of type BASE within the module. The module BASE is the only object of type BASE, consequently module name and type name can be confounded and access procedures have no parameters of type BASE ; furthermore, polyadicity, as in the MERGE procedure, and expression of CLU-like ADT is impossible. We call such a programming tool a static encapsulation tool. As in ADT case, protection is ensured by the compiler thanks to the scope rule (F is not accessible outside of the module).
Some languages provide module patterns such as SIMULA classes [12]. The same pattern may dynamically provide instances of the same "abstraction" (Figure 2).

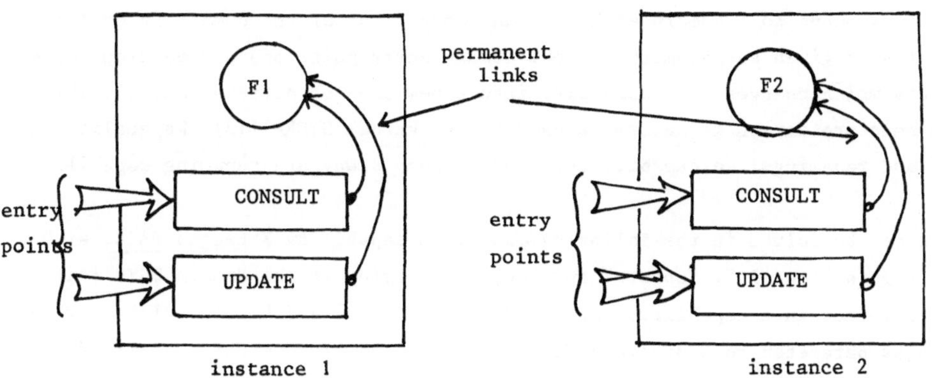

Fig. 2 : Static encapsulation tool.

For a particular instance, links between access procedures and data are permanent (they are established at the instance creation). New copies of CONSULT and UPDATE are created for each new instance which can be seen as a couple of access procedures.

2.2. Dynamic mechanisms

Most dynamic protection mechanisms are based on the capability concept. We limit our study to a part of these ones. A *capability* acts like a ticket allowing the use of some object [3]. It is composed of three parts :

- a tag specifying the class to which the object belongs. (This part is sometimes omitted).
- some information to reach the object.
- some access rights to the object.

An object can only be accessed through a capability. An access control is performed each time a capability is used.

We do not present anymore the capability concept and we only study how a domain can be implemented with capabilities.

The capability concept allows to implement the domain notion in defining a domain as a set of capabilities. Let us note a domain is considered as an object : so it is referred to by a capability ; its tag is DOMAIN and the associated right is "call". A CALL operation on domain must indicate an entry point. In this study we are not concerned by the call mechanism ; it is more detailled in [9, 10]. Two classes of mechanisms can be distinguished according to the way (fugitive or permanent) a capability is included into a domain. We call these classes respectively *renaming* and *encapsulation* mechanisms.

2.2.1. HYDRA-like capabilities

Two or several capabilities may refer to the same object. These one are said to be of different kind if their tag and right parts are different. Thus when an object may be referred to by several capabilities of different kind, accesses to that object may vary.

If an object is bound to a domain each time an entry point of the domain is called, its capability is given as parameter to the domain entry point and a "coercion" operation occurs which changes the capability into a new one (of different kind). This sort of dynamic protection mechanism is used by the kernel HYDRA [13]. We qualify it as dynamic and renaming ; so capabilities used in such a way are renaming capabilities.

Our example can be solved in the following manner. A capability X tagged BASE, with the access rights "consult", "update" and "merge" is lying in the domain USER ; it will be transformed in a capability tagged FILE with "read" and "write" rights, when it is given as parameter to a domain BASE entry point, namely CONSULT, UPDATE or MERGE (Figure 3).

Relations between renaming capabilities and CLU-like abstract data type are apparent. Both act in the same manner : one at run-time, the other at compile-time. Domain entry points can be polyadic and a creation operation must exist in both cases.

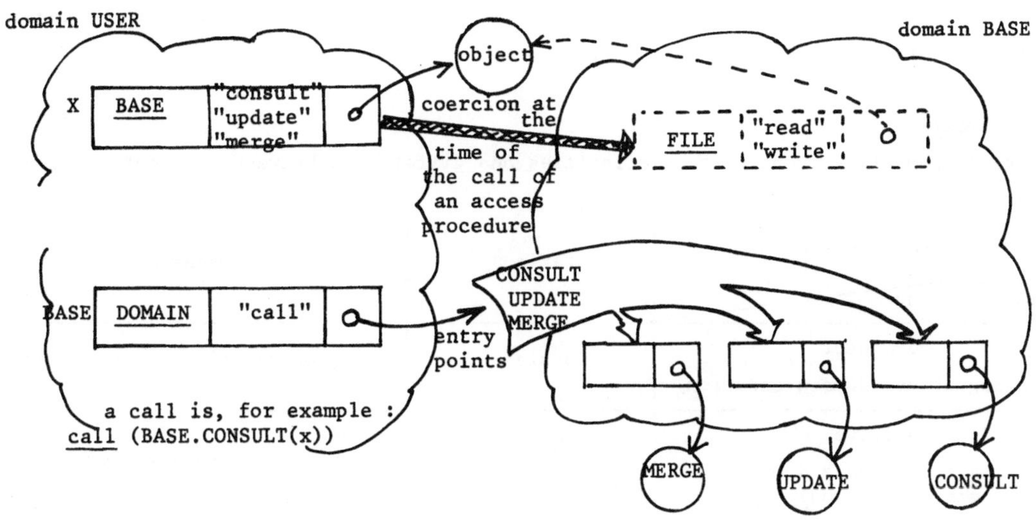

Fig. 3 : Dynamic renaming mechanism.

2.2.2. PLESSEY 250-like capabilities

Another dynamic protection mechanism using capabilities works by encapsulation. In this case, with regard to the protected object, the domain USER of our example contains only a capability referring to the domain BASE. A single capability for the protected object F, (tagged FILE), is located in the domain BASE. This capability can only be accessed by CONSULT and UPDATE (Figure 4).

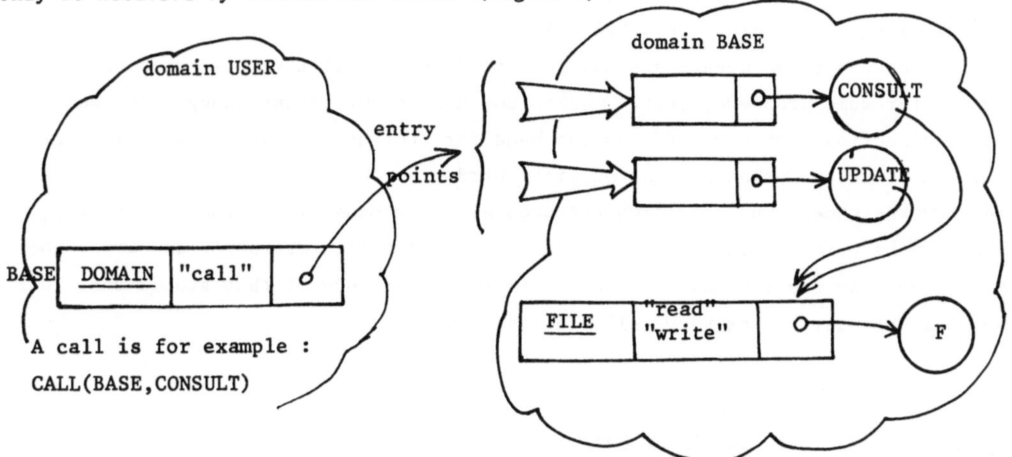

Fig. 4 : Dynamic encapsulation tool.

Such a mechenism is used in the PLESSEY 250 Machine [14]. Similarities with modules are obvious. The object F is encapsulated in the domain BASE ; it is bound to the procedures CONSULT and UPDATE at the domain creation.

Capabilities used in such a way are called encapsulation capabilities. They mainly differ from renaming capabilities by the fact an object cannot be referred to by capabilities of different kind.

2.3. Summary

Figure 5 summarizes properties, similarities and differences between the four protection mechanisms presented.

Criteria: Access control / Object binding	Static	Dynamic
Permanent (binding at the domain creation)	modules	encapsulation capabilities
Fugitive (binding each time a domain entry point is called)	CLU-like abstract types	renaming capabilities

Fig. 5 : Protection mechanism classification.

As dynamic ones, static protection mechanisms seem to be useful for writing system kernels. Their use requires less sophisticated hardware and saves expensive access control (this technique needs, of course, the compiler reliability). In [8] Jones and Liskov present an other static protection mechanism well-suited to CLU-like abstract data types ; it allows further checking about the access procedures use.

Our aim was not to prove the "equivalence" between static and dynamic mechanisms ; moreover such a proof is impossible : dynamic mechanisms allow more flexible programs to be written and are more powerful (in many senses) that the static ones (for example for revoking or granting a capability).

The facing between these mechanisms has permitted to exhibit their features and to show that, for some problems, static mechanisms can be sufficient enough. So two application directions can come off. On one hand for protection-poor hardware the use of static protection mechanisms can palliate hardware checking for some problem classes. On the other hand, for architectures allowing many protection facilities, programs can be written (when possible) in term of a static mechanism and implemented by the dynamic one ; dynamic mechanism is the understudy of that static one. This method could be usefull for very reliable systems.

3 - SYNCHRONIZATION AND DATA ABSTRACTION

Abstraction implementation mechanisms like module or abstract data type since they allow construction of domains, would be helpful for operating systems designers, provided they offer means of synchronizing concurrent accesses to the same domain. Using modules or abstract data types in a parallel environment may indeed lead to conflicting accesses : in the previous example, when two simultaneous WRITE accesses on the same object FILE occur, one of them must be delayed. We present in this section a synchronization expression well-suited to modules and make a proposal for abstract data types.

3.1. Synchronization expression for modules

As we have noticed in section 2, a module may be considered by users as a t-uple of access procedures. Hence accesses to a module may be managed using a language based on procedure names. Examples of such languages are path expressions [6] and control modules [7]. Introduced by Robert and Verjus the control module concept (presented here), like path expressions, differs from the monitor concept [15, 16] by physically separating the synchronization expression from the processing statement. However, control modules, like monitors and path expressions, are strongly related to the "monadic" character of modules and need extensions to cope with the polyadic aspect of abstract data types.

To express synchronization policies, a control module associates implicitly status counters to each access procedure of a given module. These counters are set to zero at the initialization of the control-module and are updated when procedures are invoked, activated, or terminated. They are :

- REQ(P) : total number of invocations of P.
- AUT(P) : total number of execution beginings of P.
- TERM(P) : total number of terminations of P.

In addition two others counters are defined in terms of the previous ones :

- ACT(P) = AUT(P) - TERM(P) : number of instances of P currently executing.
- WAIT(P) = REQ(P) - AUT(P) : number of invocations which have not yet led to execution.

The history of accesses to a particular module is recorded by its status counters. Synchronization problems may be solved by giving constraints expressed with them ; such constraint expressions (built with logical operators and tests on counter values) are called conditions. Each access procedure is controlled by such a condition which delays the execution until its value is true. Counter updating is done by the control module and the values of conditions change consequently. As an example, the module implementing the domain BASE may be controlled according to the readers and writers discipline [17]. The associated control module is :

```
CONTROL-MODULE RW
BEGIN
    COND (CONSULT) : ACT(UPDATE) = 0 ;
    COND (UPDATE)  : ACT(UPDATE) = 0 AND ACT(CONSULT) = 0 ;
END
```

These two conditions ensure that at most one UPDATE execution is activate at any time and, if no UPDATE is active, the number of CONSULT which are running may be any. We do not present any more this synchronization expression [7].

3.2. Synchronization expression for abstract data types

Consider again the abstract data type BASE which besides monadic procedures (CONSULT, UPDATE), includes a diadic one (MERGE). MERGE merges two objects BASE B1 and B2, and puts its results in B1. The usual execution condition for MERGE is twofold :

- B1 should be neither currently modified, nor consulted.
- B2 should not be currently modified.

Since the name MERGE is not sufficient to express the different kinds of access on its two parameters, the execution condition cannot be expressed with a language using only procedure names.

Several kinds of accesses (for a given cluster) may be defined with respect to synchronization needs. In our example they are of course "reading" and "writing". In the authors proposal, a name (called attribute), is associated to each kind of accesses (hence R stands for "reading", W for "writing"). Attributes are associated to formal parameters in the abstract data type definition according to the way the procedure deals with them. Thus the definition of the abstract data type BASE becomes :

```
ADTREALIZATION BASE
     BEGIN
       ATTRIBUTE R, W ;
       ...
       PROC CONSULT = (BASE {R} B) ITEM : ... ;
       PROC UPDATE  = (BASE {W} B, ITEM I) : ... ;
       PROC MERGE   = (BASE {W} B1, BASE {R} B2) : ... ;
     END
```

The definition of attributes makes possible the expression of synchronization rules without using procedure names. So the control module notion is slightly modified : status counters are henceforth associated to attributes instead of procedures. Thus the control module, for the abstract date type BASE, expressing the readers-writers discipline without priority is the following :

```
CONTROL-MODULE RW
BEGIN
     COND(R) : ACT(W) = 0 ;
     COND(W) : ACT(W) = 0 AND ACT(R) = 0 ;
END
```

At a declaration like :

```
BASE(RW) B ;
```

The control module RW associates two sets of status counters to the object B (one set for each attribute). Control on each procedure execution must ensure the respect on the conditions COND(R) and/or COND(W) for each parameter. For example an access procedure accessing a parameter with a W attribute can start its execution if, and only if, the condition associated to W is true, i.e., if the counters ACT(W) and ACT(R) associated to that parameter are equal to zero.

The enforcement of the constraints on which procedure executions depend is an implementation problem for which the frame of pre- and post-operations (performed in mutual exclusion) provides a solution. Each access procedure is implicitly bracketed by two such control operations. (When the counter REQ is used, two distinct pre-operations are necessary : the first one to record the request, the second one to allow the execution). Thus from the heading of the procedure MERGE for example,

```
PROC MERGE = (BASE {W} B1, BASE {R} B2)
```

the compiler can derive these pre- and post-operations (the dot notation of SIMULA is used).

```
pre-MERGE =
   BEGIN
     WAIT B1.(ACT(W) = 0 AND ACT(R) = 0) AND B2.(ACT(W) = 0) ;
     B1.AUT(W) := B1.AUT(W) + 1 ;
     B2.AUT(R) := B2.AUT(R) + 1 ;
   END
post-MERGE =
   BEGIN
     B1.TERM(W) := B1.TERM(W) + 1 ;
     B2.TERM(R) := B2.TERM(R) + 1 ;
   END
```

These control operations can be easily implemented without busy waiting with generalized semaphores [18], Kessels' monitor conditions [19] (the expression of which is very close to the present one) or eventcounts and sequencers [20].

4 - TOWARDS A COMMON BASE FOR SYNCHRONIZATION AND PROTECTION EXPRESSIONS

Our synchronization proposal can be related to a compile-time protection expression defined by Jones and Liskov [8]. That expression was given for CLU-like abstract data types (Clusters) : particular access rights are specified in any object reference. The set of all the relevant rights for a given-type is declared within the cluster ; each right has a particular semantics with regard to protection policy. In the formal parameters list of each access procedure a subset of rights is associated to each parameter. When an access procedure is called, the actual parameters must have (at least) the required rights. This requirement is statically enforced by the compiler. Let us consider the abstract type <u>BASE</u>. Four meaningful rights are needed to express usual protection policy : C, U, MT and M which are associated to consulting, updating and merging manipulations. The definition becomes :

```
ADTREALIZATION BASE
   BEGIN
     RIGHT C, U, MT, M ;
     ...
     PROC CONSULT = (BASE {C} B) ITEM : ... ;
     PROC UPDATE  = (BASE {U} B, ITEM I) : ... ;
     PROC MERGE   = (BASE {MT} B1, BASE {M} B2) : ... ;
   END
```

With the declarations :

```
B1 : BASE {C,U} ;
B2 : BASE {M} ;
B3 : BASE {C, U, M, MT} ;
```

The compiler forbids expressions like MERGE (B1, B2), UPDATE (B2, I), B1 := B2, and authorizes MERGE (B3, B2), UPDATE (B1, I) and B2 := B3. (Let us note that access rights are associated with identifiers ; hence, when several identifiers are referencing the same object, access rights variation is allowed : rights are, in fact, associated to access paths).

This protection mechanism can be combined with our synchronization mechanism. From user point of view, a right is associated to a particular and semantically "indivisible" manipulation. In a concurrent environment, as we have noticed, keeping object coherence needs synchronization constraints to be associated to each manipulation. In the most general case, the same synchronization attribute should correspond to several rights. This correspondance may be declared in the abstract data type and the set of rights associated to formal parameter is then sufficient to characterize the synchronization conditions.

With this common base for synchronization and protection the abstract data type BASE is now defined by :

```
ADTREALIZATION BASE
   BEGIN
     RIGHTS C, U, MT, M ;
     ATTRIBUTE R = {C,M}, W = {U,MT}
     ...
     PROC CONSULT = (BASE {C} B) ITEM : ... ;
       % The parameter is accessed in a "reading" mode, because C is in the list of
        the "reading" attribute R %
     PROC UPDATE (BASE {U} B, ITEM I) : ... ;
     PROC MERGE = (BASE {MT} B1, BASE {M} B2) : ... ;
     ...
   END
```

5 - CONCLUSION

It has been shown that, thanks to separation between definition and implementation of objects and use of type and scope notions, data abstraction concept constitutes a static protection mechanism. In some cases this mechanism is powerful enough to solve visibility and access control problems involved by domain construction. That approach was experimented by the authors in implementing a CLU-like abstraction which allow long term storage of typed objects [21].

It has also been seen that protection mechanisms must be supplied with synchronization mechanisms because they can be used in a concurrent environment. If several synchronization expressions suited to modules exist they are not suited to abstract data types ; to cope with these ones they need extensions : the linguistic notion of attribute has been introduced to this end [22]. Thus supplied with synchronization expressions, data abstraction facilities seem well-suited to solve some problems generally encountered at the operating system level. The suggestion of a common base for synchronisation and protection expressions can be a first step towards a better understanding of these mechanisms. Such an approach can narrow the gap between languages and operating systems [23]. Other studies have also made attempts to narrow this gap in the protection area [24, 25].

REFERENCES

[1] D.L. Parnas, "On the Criteria to be Used in Decomposing Systems into Modules", *Commun. Ass. Comput. Mach.*, vol. 15, pp. 1053-1058, December 1972.

[2] B. Liskov, A. Snydern, R. Atkinson, C. Schaffert, "Abstraction Mechanisms in CLU", *Commun. Ass. Comput. Mach.*, vol. 20, pp. 564-576, August 1977.

[3] J.B. Dennis and E.C. Van Horn, "Programming Semantics for Multiprogrammed Computations", *Commun. Ass. Comput. Mach.*, vol. 9, pp. 143-155, March 1966.

[4] M. Geschke, J.H. Morris and E.H. Satterwaite, "Early Experience with MESA", *Commun. Ass. Comput. Mach.*, vol. 20, pp. 540-552, March 1977.

[5] N. Wirth, "Towards a Discipline of Real-Time Programming", *Commun. Ass. Comput. Mach.*, vol. 20, pp. 577-584, August 1977.

[6] R.H. Campbell, "The Specification of Process synchronization by Path Expressions", in *Proc. on aspects theoriques et pratiques des systèmes*, Rocquencourt, Ed. by IRIA, pp. 93-106, April 1974.

[7] P. Robert and J.P. Verjus, "Towards Autonomous Descriptions of Synchronization Modules", in *1977 IFIP Congress Proc.*, B. Gilchrist Ed., North-Holland, pp. 981-986, August 1977.

[8] A.K. Jones and B. Liskov, "A Language Extension for controlling Access to shared Data", *IEEE Trans. Soft. Eng.*, vol. SE2, pp. 277-285, December 1976.

[9] B.W. Lampson, "Dynamic Protection Structures", in *1969 Fall Joint Comput. Conf., AFIPS Conf. Proc.*, vol. 35, Montvale, NJ.: AFIPS Press, 1969, pp. 27-38.

[10] R.M. Needham, "Protection Systems and Protection Implementations", in *1972 Fall Joint Comput. Conf., AFIPS Conf. Proc.*, vol. 41, Montvale, NJ : AFIPS Press, 1972, pp. 571-578.

[11] W.A. Wulf, R.L. London and M. Shaw, "An Introduction to the Construction and Verification of ALPHARD Program", *IEEE Trans. Soft. Eng.*, vol. SE2, pp. 253-265, December 1976.

[12] O.J. Dahl, B. Myrhaug and K. Nyggard, "SIMULA 67 a Common Base Language", *Tech. Rep. 22*, Norvegian Computing Center, 1969.

[13] W. Wulf, E. Cohen, A. Corwin, A. Jones, R. Levin, C. Pierson and F. Pollack, "HYDRA : The Kernel of a Multiprocessor Operating System", *Commun. Ass. Comput. Mach.*, vol. 17, pp. 337-345, June 1974.

[14] D.M. England, "Capability Concept Mechanisms and Structure in System 250", in *Proc. int. workshop on protection in operating systems*, Rocquencourt : France, Ed. by IRIA, pp. 63-82, August 1974.

[15] P. Brinch Hansen, *Operating System Principles*. Englewood Cliffs, NJ : Prentice Hall, July 1973.

[16] C.A.R. Hoare, "Monitors : An Operating System Structuring Concept", *Commun. Ass. Comput. Mach.*, vol. 17, pp. 549-557, October 1974.

[17] P.J. Courtois, F. Heymans and D.L. Parnas, "Concurrent Control with Readers and Writers", *Commun. Ass. Comput. Mach.*, vol. 14, pp. 667-668, October 1971.

[18] L. Presser, "Multiprogramming Coordination", *Comput. Surveys*, vol. 7, pp. 21-44, 1975.

[19] J.L.W. Kessels, "An Alternative to Event Queues for Synchronization in Monitors", *Commun. Ass. Comput. Mach.*, vol. 20, pp. 500-503, July 1977.

[20] D.P. Reed and R.K. Kanodia, "Synchronization with Eventcounts and Sequencers", *Proc. 6th int. ACM Conf. on O.S. Principles*, Purdue University, November 1977.

[21] M. Banâtre, A. Couvert, D. Herman and M. Raynal, "Présentation et évaluation du projet Systèmes d'Objets Conservés", *Proc. AFCET Congress*, Paris, November 1978.

[22] M. Raynal, "Une Expression de la Synchronisation pour les Types Abstraits", *RAIRO Informatique/Computer Sciences*, vol. 12, December 1978.

[23] A.K. Jones, "The Narrowing Gap between Language Systems and Operating", in *1977 Congress Proc.*, B. Gilchrist Ed., North-Holland, pp. 869-873, August 1977.

[24] R.B. Kieburtz and A. Silberschatz, "Capability Managers", *IEEE Trans. Soft. Eng.*, vol. SE4, pp. 467-477, November 1978.

[25] J.R. McGraw and G.R. Andrews, "Access Control in Parallel Programs", *IEEE Trans. Soft. Eng.*, vol. SE5, pp. 1-9, January 1979.

Probleme beim Entwurf sicherer Datenbanksysteme

Th. von Bomhard, H. vor der Brück, N. Ramsperger
IABG Ottobrunn

1 Einführung und Übersicht

Ein Datenbanksystem ist immer ein Teil eines umfassenden Systems, eines Informations- und Kontrollsystems, das in Beziehung zu einem Ausschnitt aus der Realität, dem Objektsystem, steht. Die in dem Objektsystem vorhandenen Bedürfnisse bezüglich des Schutzes vor unberechtigter Informationsgewinnung erfordern innerhalb des Datenbankverwaltungssystems (DBVS) geeignete Vorkehrungen. Unterschiedliche Bedürfnisse aus Objektsystemen werden in Kapitel 2 betrachtet. Die innerhalb des DBVS möglichen Vorkehrungen zur Erfüllung dieser Bedürfnisse werden in Kapitel 3.2 in die Schema-Architektur eingeordnet. DBVS setzen üblicherweise auf Betriebssystemen (BS) auf. Zur Realisierung ihrer Sicherheitsvorkehrungen haben sichere DBVS Anforderungen an das BS. Die zu erfüllenden Anforderungen werden in Kapitel 3.1 beschrieben. Sichere BS werden in der Literatur seit geraumer Zeit betrachtet. Die Sicherheitskernarchitektur ist ein Ansatz, BS sicher zu machen. Dieser Ansatz wurde auch auf DBVS ausgedehnt. Ein solcher unternommener Versuch wird mit seinen Möglichkeiten und Grenzen in Kapitel 3.3 kritisch gewürdigt. Der Ausblick in Kapitel 4 weist auf offene Probleme beim Entwurf sicherer DBVS hin. Ein Ergebnis ist, daß sichere DBVS noch nicht in Reichweite sind.

2 Sicherheit aus Sicht der Benutzer

2.1 Berechtigungen

Die mit einer Datenbank arbeitenden Benutzer haben im allgemeinen fest umrissene Aufgaben durchzuführen. Ein sicheres DBVS muß es erlauben, für jeden Benutzer genau festzulegen, auf welche Daten, mit welchen Operationen und in welchem Kontext er zugreifen darf. Außerhalb dieser explizit mit dem DBVS festgelegten Berechtigungen soll ein Zugriff auf die Daten unmöglich sein. Die in dieser Arbeit interessierenden grundsätzlichen Möglichkeiten, Sicherheitsbedürfnisse durch Berechtigungen festzulegen, sollen nachstehend kurz erläutert werden /MCLE, FERN/. Das geschieht teilweise am Beispiel der Relation PERSONAL (PNR, NAME, ABT, GEHALT):

Es werden die Daten festgelegt, auf die ein Benutzer zugreifen darf:

(1) Relationen oder Felder von Relationen, etwa PERSONAL oder PNR, NAME, ABT aus PERSONAL,

(2) Tupel einer Relation, deren Werte einer gegebenen Bedingung genügen, etwa alle Tupel von PERSONAL, für die ABT den WERT "SZD" hat,

(3) abgeleitete Daten, etwa eine aus PERSONAL abgeleitete Tabelle der Durchschnittsgehälter der jeweiligen Abteilungen.

Es werden zusätzlich die Operationen festgelegt, mit denen ein Benutzer zugreifen darf:

(4) Operationen des DBVS, etwa Lesen, Schreiben, Ändern, Einfügen und, wenn es das DBVS anbietet, komplexere Operationen wie Durchschnitt, Summe, Maximum,

(5) außerhalb des DBVS definierte Operationen, etwa statistische Auswerteprogramme, Programme zur tariflichen Gehaltserhöhung.

2.2 Übergeordnete Sicherheitsstrategien

Es wird der Kontext festgelegt, in dem der Benutzer zugreifen darf:

(6) Es müssen äußere Randbedingungen gelten, etwa Barauszahlungen nur zu den Kassenstunden.

(7) Ein unerwünschter Informationsfluß über Dritte darf nicht möglich sein. Dazu ein Beispiel:

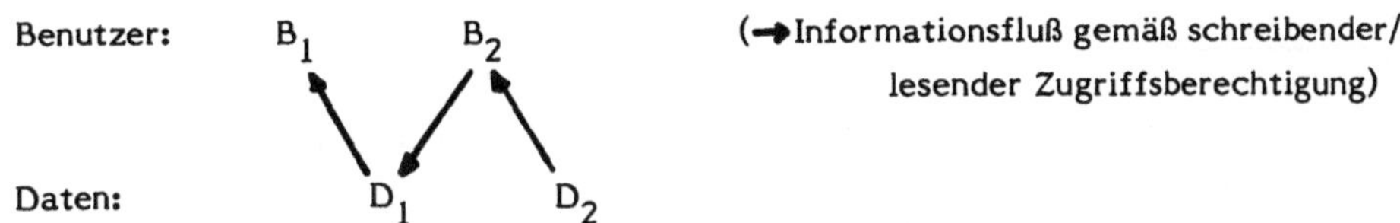

Obwohl B_1 nicht D_2 lesen darf, ist ein Informationsfluß von D_2 nach B_1 über Dritte möglich. Mitunter wird die Forderung gestellt, daß derartige Informationsflüsse nicht möglich sein sollen, daß also alle möglichen Informationsflüsse mit den explizit erlaubten Zugriffen zusammenfallen (*-property /BELL,VDBR/). In manchen Fällen reicht es aus, wenn das DBVS garantiert, daß z. B. nach einem lesenden Zugriff auf D_2 der Benutzer B_2 nicht mehr auf D_1 schreiben darf. Diese kontextabhängige Einschränkung der Berechtigung kann mit jedem "Log-off" aufgehoben werden. Ist das umgebende System des DBVS entsprechend organisiert, so ist der unerwünschte Informationsfluß nur noch manuell möglich, auf jeden Fall nicht mehr innerhalb des DBVS.

(8) Das Herleiten von zu schützenden Informationen aus einer Folge von Abfrageergebnissen darf nicht möglich sein, etwa bei statistischen Abfragen auf Datenbanken, die personenbezogene Daten enthalten /KAMU/. Die dabei auftretenden Probleme sollen in dieser Arbeit nicht weiter erörtert werden.

Es werden Benutzerklassen (alle Benutzer einer Klasse haben die gleichen Berechtigungen) und Datenklassen (auf alle Daten einer Klasse dürfen dieselben Benutzer in gleicher Weise zugreifen) gebildet:

(9) Geheimhaltungsmodell: Die Benutzer dürfen gemäß ihrer Klassenzugehörigkeit zugreifen und gegebenenfalls soll auch hier wieder die *-property (7) gelten, etwa: Die Personaldaten dürfen nur von den Mitarbeitern der Personalabteilung bearbeitet werden. Die militärische Geheimhaltung mit ihren unterschiedlichen Geheimhaltungsstufen (NfD, vertraulich, geheim, streng geheim) ist ein weiteres Beispiel für entsprechende Klassenbil

dungen /BELL/. Hier bedeutet die Einhaltung der *-property, daß ein Benutzer, auf Daten nicht mehr schreiben darf, die niedriger als die bislang gelesenen eingestuft sind (kontextabhängige Berechtigung).

2.3 Vergabe und Rücknahme von Berechtigungen

Berechtigungen können von zentraler Stelle (etwa in der militärischen Geheimhaltung, zur Einhaltung der *-property (7)) oder von den einzelnen Benutzern selbst vergeben werden. Probleme bereitet die Rücknahme weitergegebener Berechtigungen /GRIF/. Je nach Anwendungsfall können unterschiedliche Forderungen vorliegen, etwa:

- Rücknahme aller Rechte, wenn sie von Befugten an Personen aber mißbräuchlich weitergegeben wurden, die diese Berechtigung nicht erhalten sollten,
- keine Rücknahme der Rechte, wenn der Benutzer, der sie vergeben hat, in seiner Funktion durch einen anderen abgelöst wird.

2.4 Protokollierung sicherheitsrelevanter Aktivitäten

In vielen Anwendungen müssen sicherheitsrelevante Aktivitäten zumindest protokolliert werden, etwa:

- Änderung von Berechtigungen,
- berechtigte Zugriffe auf besonders schützenswerte Daten, wie Entwicklungsdaten eines Unternehmens,
- Zugriffe, die die Anwendung verlangt, die aber nur unter Verletzung der *-property (7) möglich sind,
- Schreiben personenbezogener Daten gemäß Datenschutzgesetz.

2.5 Gesonderte Speicherung von Daten

Besonders schützenswerte Daten müssen mitunter auf eigenen Datenträgern abgelegt werden, damit sie isoliert von den anderen Daten eine eigene organisatorische Behandlung erfahren können (streng geheime Daten oder Entwicklungsdaten werden in eigenen Tresoren gelagert).

2.6 Randbedingungen für die Sicherheitsmechanismen

Die Sicherheitsmechanismen eines DBVS müssen nachstehende Eigenschaften aufweisen /MCLE/:

- Flexibilität: Ein breites Spektrum unterschiedlicher Anwendungen muß abgedeckt werden.
- Zuverlässigkeit: Man muß sich auf die Sicherheitsmechanismen verlassen können. Ihre Umgehung über andere Systemteile wie BS oder Wiederanlaufmechanismen darf nicht möglich sein. In manchen Fällen soll bewiesen werden, daß das DBVS die geforderte Sicherheit garantiert. Voraussetzung dafür ist die Beschreibung der geforderten Sicherheit in formalen Sicherheitsmodellen /BELL, VDBR/.

- Effizienz: Die Sicherheitsmechanismen dürfen nicht mehr kosten als durch ihren Schutz gewonnen wird.
- Datenunabhängigkeit: Die Berechtigungen müssen unabhängig von Zugriffs- und Speicherstrukturen formuliert werden, d. h. mindestens auf der gleichen Ebene wie die Schnittstelle zum DBVS.

3 Sicherheit und funktionale Aufteilung

Bei Systemen der Größe und Komplexität von DBVS ist eine unter Sicherheitsaspekten geeignete funktionale Gliederung notwendig, um die Sicherheit abzuschätzen, die das System gegen unbefugte Zugriffe bietet. So muß neben der Korrektheit der Sicherheitsfunktionen auch sichergestellt werden können, daß diese Funktionen nicht umgangen oder durch andere Funktionen getäuscht werden können, auf denen sie aufbauen. Darüberhinaus können kritische Überprüfungen oder gar formale Verifikation des Designs oder von Teilen der Implementierung nur bei geeignet strukturierten Systemen durchgeführt werden.

Da heutige DBVS im allgemeinen unter der Kontrolle und Steuerung eines BS ablaufen, sollen zunächst kurz die Forderungen erläutert werden, die sinnvollerweise an das unterliegende BS gestellt werden.

3.1 Anforderungen an das Betriebssystem

Unter Berücksichtigung der üblichen Funktionsaufteilung müssen zur Gewährleistung der Sicherheit im DBVS vom BS die folgenden Leistungen zur Verfügung gestellt werden:

(1) Isolation: Ein Isolationsmechanismus muß den Schutz von Objekten (hier DBVS mit seinen Dateien) gegen unbefugte Zugriffe von außen garantieren. Hierdurch wird sichergestellt, daß nur über das DBVS auf die entsprechenden Dateien zugegriffen werden kann, so daß bei Korrektheit des DBVS dessen Zugriffsüberprüfungen nicht umgangen werden können. Außerdem werden dadurch auch der Code des DBVS oder dessen Statusdaten gegen unbefugte Zugriffe von außen geschützt.

(2) Identifikation und Authentifizierung: Damit wird sichergestellt, daß das DBVS nicht über die Identität eines Benutzers getäuscht werden kann. Da die Zugriffsüberprüfung im allgemeinen auf der Identität des Zugreifers aufbaut,ist sichere Identifikation von größter Bedeutung.

(3) Korrekte Ein-/Ausgabe: Da das DBVS im allgemeinen auf der E/A des BS aufsetzt, muß für die Sicherheit im DBVS vorausgesetzt werden, daß dieser Teil des BS korrekt arbeitet.

(4) Sichere Kommunikation: Das BS muß sicherstellen, daß beim Austausch von Daten zwischen Anwender und DBVS diese Daten von Dritten nicht unbefugt gelesen oder

verändert werden können, und daß keiner der Kommunikationspartner über die Identität des anderen getäuscht werden kann.

Die Forderungen (1), (3) und (4) müssen auf jeden Fall vom BS garantiert werden, während die Forderung (2) auch vom DBVS übernommen werden kann.

Neben den obigen Forderungen muß eventuell noch die Korrektheit weiterer BS-Funktionen vorausgesetzt werden, falls die Auswertung einer Zugriffsanforderung von Bedingungen abhängig ist, zu deren Überprüfung vom BS aktuelle Werte geliefert werden müssen (z. B. Datum oder Uhrzeit).

3.2 Sicherheitsfunktionen innerhalb der Schema-Architektur

Aus Sicherheitsgründen ist eine möglichst nahe Anordnung der Überprüfungsmechanismen am physikalischen Zugriff wünschenswert. Dadurch wird die Möglichkeit drastisch eingeschränkt, diese Mechanismen aufgrund von Systemschwächen zu umgehen. Außerdem kann der Teil der Bearbeitung eines Auftrags, der vor der Berechtigungsprüfung ausgeführt wird, bei einer geeigneten Strukturierung des Gesamtsystems, wie sie in Abbildung 1 angegeben ist, nicht zu sicherheitsrelevantem Fehlverhalten führen.

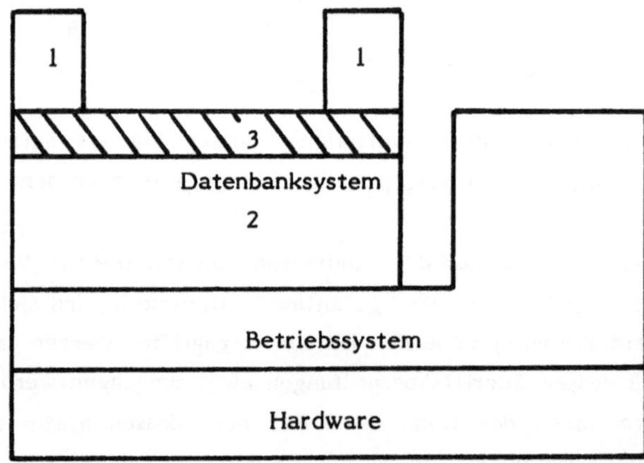

(1) anwenderspezifische DBVS-Teile, durch Isolationsmechanismen des BS gegeneinander isoliert,
(2) Teil des DBVS, der für alle Anwender gemeinsam ist,
(3) Schicht des DBVS, in der die Überprüfung stattfindet.

Abbildung 1: Aufteilung des DBVS in anwenderspezifische und globale Systemteile

Die Bereiche (1) in Abbildung 1 sind durch das Betriebssystem isoliert und anwenderspezifisch. Dadurch kann ein Fehlverhalten in diesen Teilen weder einen anderen Anwender stören, noch kann das DBVS über die Identität des zugehörigen Anwenders durch einen solchen Fehler getäuscht werden. Fehler im Bereich (2) des DBVS, d. h. nach Überprüfung der Rechtmäßigkeit einer Zugriffsanforderung, können dagegen zu sicherheitsrelevantem Fehlverhalten führen.

Neben dem Aspekt der Isolation muß auch untersucht werden, wie der mögliche sicherheitsrelevante Funktionsumfang der Anwenderschnittstelle des DBVS von der Anordnung der Sicherheitsfunktionen im DBVS abhängt. Bei der folgenden Untersuchung wird von der Schema-Architektur des "Koexistenzmodells" (externes, konzeptionelles und internes Schema /NIJS/) ausgegangen. Hierbei sollen zunächst nur die Fälle diskutiert werden, bei denen die Überprüfungen eindeutig einer Ebene zugeordnet werden können.

3.2.1 Überprüfung auf der Ebene des externen Schemas

In diesem Fall muß das externe Schema die gesamte Information enthalten, die zur Berechtigungsprüfung einer Zugriffsanforderung notwendig ist. Der Anwender sieht im allgemeinen nur den Teil der Daten, auf die er zugreifen darf (z. B. Subschema in DBTG-DB's /DATE/, View in System R /CHAM/), wobei der Zugriff noch auf bestimmte Arten eingeschränkt sein kann. Mittels speziell definierter Views können komplexe Schutzanforderungen realisiert werden, wie z. B. Zugriff auf abgeleitete Daten, auf deren Basisdaten der Anwender nicht zugreifen darf (Forderung (3) aus 2.1). Die Anwenderschnittstelle, die durch ein Subschema gebildet wird, stellt dagegen bereits eine Einschränkung dar, da ein Subschema nicht erlaubt, abgeleitete Daten zu definieren. Somit muß ein Anwender in diesem Fall zum Zugriff auf die Basisdaten berechtigt sein, wenn er eine solche Ableitung bilden will.

Da der gesamte Schutz des Systems auf der korrekten Definition der externen Schemata aufbaut, muß deren Definition den für die Vergabe von Befugnissen Berechtigten vorbehalten bleiben. Dem Vorteil der großen Flexibilität in der Definition der Schutzanforderungen, die durch die Überprüfung auf der Ebene des externen Schemas gegeben ist (die Forderungen (1) bis (4) aus 2.1 können prinzipiell erfüllt werden), steht gegenüber, daß die Sicherheit gegen unbefugte Zugriffe nur gegeben ist, wenn das gesamte System korrekt arbeitet. Ein Fehler unterhalb der Schnittstelle des DBVS zur Umwelt kann potentiell zur unbefugten Kenntnisnahme oder Manipulation von Daten führen.

3.2.2 Überprüfung auf der Ebene des konzeptionellen Schemas

Wird die Überprüfung der Berechtigungen auf der Ebene des konzeptionellen Schemas durchgeführt, so können einerseits Fehler in der Transformation vom externen zum konzeptionellen Schema bei geeigneter Strukturierung (Abb. 1) keine Sicherheitsverletzungen bewirken und zum anderen ist das Recht zur Definition von Subschema oder View nicht sicherheitskritisch und kann den Anwendern ohne Einschränkung gegeben werden.

Ohne Erweiterung der elementaren Zugriffsrechte (z. B. lesen, schreiben, einfügen) tritt jedoch eine wesentliche Einschränkung der sicherheitsrelevanten DBVS-Schnittstelle ein. So ist es im allgemeinen nicht mehr möglich, einem Anwender das Recht zu geben, auf ein abgeleitetes Datum zuzugreifen, falls der Anwender nicht das Recht hat, auf die Basisdaten zuzugreifen (z. B. INGRES /STON1,MCLE/). Dies wird erst möglich, wenn es das System erlaubt, komplexe Operationen zu definieren, die solche Ableitungen durchführen, und dem Anwender die Befugnis zu geben, über solche Operationen mittelbar auf solche Daten zuzugreifen, auf die er keinen direkten Zugriff hat. Diese Operationen stellen jedoch bereits wieder eine Abbildung eines Teils des konzeptionellen Schemas auf eine weiter außen liegende Ebene dar, so daß hierbei der Übergang zum externen Schema fließend wird.

Eine elegante Möglichkeit der Zugriffsüberwachung auf der konzeptionellen Ebene stellt die sogenante Query-Modifikation dar /STON2,MCLE/. Hierbei wird die Schutzanforderung einfach durch eine Konjunktion an die Suchanfrage angehängt. Da hier die Berechtigungsüberprüfung durch denselben Mechanismus durchgeführt wird, der auch den eigentlichen Zugriff ausführt, wird ein hohes Maß an struktureller Einfachheit und damit ein gesteigertes Vertrauen in die Zuverlässigkeit erreicht.

3.2.3 Überprüfung auf der Ebene des internen Schemas

Bei der Überprüfung der Zugriffsbefugnisse auf der Ebene des internen Schemas kann bei geeigneter Strukturierung (Abb. 1) ein Großteil des Codes des DBVS als nicht sicherheitsrelevant angesehen werden. Alle Fehler, die im DBVS oberhalb des internen Schemas auftreten, sind in diesem Fall nicht sicherheitsrelevant, da sie vor der Berechtigungsüberprüfung auftreten.

Da auf der Ebene des internen Schemas keine Kenntnisse über logische Datenstrukturen vorhanden sind, wird das Spektrum der definierbaren Befugnisse an der Anwenderschnittstelle stark eingeschränkt (etwa auf die Forderungen (1), (4) und (9)). Inhaltsabhängiger Schutz oder der Zugriff auf abgeleitete Daten lassen sich auf dieser Ebene nicht mehr darstellen. Realisierbar ist lediglich ein Schutz auf Behälterebene. Damit erscheint eine Überprüfung der Zugriffsbefugnisse ausschließlich auf der Ebene des internen Schemas nur für ein sehr begrenztes Spektrum von Datenbankanwendungen geeignet.

3.3 Diskussion einer Sicherheitskernarchitektur

3.3.1 Sicherheitskerne

Ein Sicherheitskern ist ein isolierter Teil von geringem Umfang in der untersten Schicht eines BS, der alle Funktionen enthält, die für die Erfüllung der Sicherheitsbedürfnisse des BS von Bedeutung sind /POPE/. Die Ansiedlung in der untersten Schicht des BS macht den Kern unabhängig von anderen Teilen des Systems. Das sowie sein geringer Umfang erhöht in erheblichem Ausmaß die Chance, formale Verifikationstechniken in kosteneffektiver Weise auf einen Sicherheitskern anzuwenden. Die für eine Verifikation notwendige Kleinheit eines Kerns kann jedoch dazu führen, daß nicht alle Sicherheitsfunktionen in den Kern aufgenommen werden können. Das führt auf das schwierige Problem, die innerhalb eines Systems erbrachten Funktionen so zu entwerfen und aufzuteilen, daß die für die Sicherheit grundlegenden Funktionen in den Kern zusammengefaßt werden. Dies Problem wird in /FEIE/ als ein Nachteil der Sicherheitskernarchitektur empfunden. Es ist jedoch wohl eher ein inhärentes Entwurfsproblem der funktionalen Aufteilung, das sich hier vor dem Entwurfsziel Sicherheit wieder stellt.

Sicherheitsbedürfnisse können auf vielen Schichten eines Systems existieren. Es mag unpraktisch oder auch unnatürlich sein, die Funktionen zur Erfüllung aller Sicherheitsbedürfnisse des gesamten Systems in den Sicherheitskern hineinzuzwängen. In diesen sollen vielmehr nur die kritischen und elementaren Funktionen aufgenommen werden, die ihrerseits der Realisierung der übrigen Sicherheitsfunktionen dienen können. Diese übrigen Funktionen sind in "trusted processes" /FEIE,MCCA/ oder Sicherheitskernen auf höheren Ebenen ("levels of kernels" /POPE/) zusammenzufassen. Die Unabhängigkeit dieser weiteren Sicherheitskerne von den anderen nicht sicherheitsrelevanten Teilen des Systems bleibt gewährleistet, wenn sie nur Funktionen tieferer Sicherheitskerne oder der Hardware benutzen. Durch "levels of kernels" kann der sicherheitsrelevante Code eines Systems neben der Abtrennung von dem übrigen System selbst eine Modularisierung erfahren, die mit einer vorteilhaften Aufteilung der Verifikation einhergeht /POPE/.

In /DOWN 1,2/ wird eine Ausdehnung der bei BS verschiedentlich angewendeten Sicherheitskernarchitektur auf DBVS beschrieben.

3.3.2 Ein DBVS mit Sicherheitskern

Zwei "levels of kernels" finden sich in der Beschreibung einer Sicherheitskernarchitektur für ein DBVS in /DOWN1,2/. Einer der Kerne ist für die Sicherheit des BS verantwortlich. Dieses bietet eine sichere Identifikation der Benutzer, eine sichere Isolierung der Prozesse zusammen mit einer sicheren Überwachung ihrer Kommunikationen und schließlich eine sichere Kontrollierung der Zugriffe der Prozesse auf Dateien. Auf diesem BS ist das sichere DBVS mit Hilfe eines zweiten Kernes realisiert.

Eine in Anlehnung an /DOWN2/ erstellte Übersicht über das DBVS findet sich in Abb. 2. Berechtigungsdaten enthalten alle Aussagen darüber, welche Benutzer auf welchen Daten welche Operationen durchführen dürfen. Die Planung physikalischer Zugriffe (PPZ) faßt alle Aktivitäten des DBVS zusammen, die sich auf die Vorbereitung der Zugriffe auf die Daten beziehen, und die nicht die vom DBVS zu garantierende Sicherheit unterwandern können. Dazu gehören Bestimmung von Zugriffspfaden und Zugriffsstrategien, Verwalten von Indexdaten, Zugriffssynchronisation usw. Die Kontrolle logischer Zugriffe (KLZ) und die Kontrolle physikalischer Zugriffe (KPZ) bilden zusammen den zu verifizierenden Sicherheitskern des DBVS.Die KLZ stellt mit Hilfe der Berechtigungsdaten fest, ob der Benutzer auf die in dem DB-Befehl angesprochenen Daten den angegebenen Zugriff durchführen darf. Dazu setzt sie zuvor den benutzerspezifischen in den systemweiten logischen Datennamen um. Im Fall der Berechtigung wird der DB-Befehl sowohl an die PPZ als auch mit dem systemweiten logischen Datennamen an die KPZ weitergereicht.

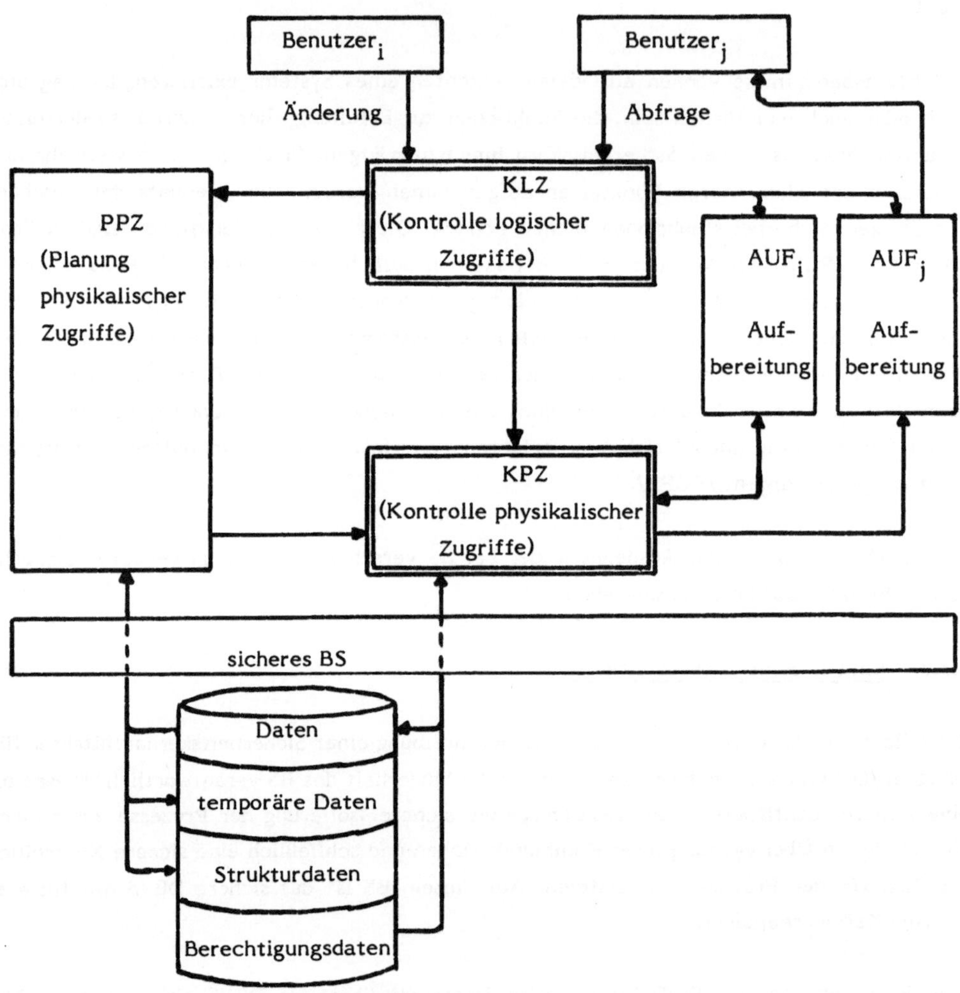

Abbildung 2

Die KPZ erhält von der PPZ die Adressen der Speicherbereiche mit den Daten, auf die der Zugriff des Benutzers geschehen soll. Die KPZ stellt fest, ob die in diesen Speicherbereichen gefundenen Daten tatsächlich zu dem systemweiten logischen Namen gehören. Das geschieht mit Hilfe der Berechtigungsdaten, die eine Zuordnung zwischen den "tags" der gefundenen Daten und den logischen Namen enthalten (die tags sind auffaßbar als eine Codierung der logischen Namen). Bei Übereinstimmung werden im Fall eines lesenden Zugriffs die Daten dem zugreifenden Benutzer über die Aufbereitung (AUF) zugestellt, die die Daten für den Benutzer in der Form aufbereitet, die von der KLZ vorgeschrieben wurde. Im Fall eines ändernden Zugriffs werden die zu ändernden Daten der AUF zugestellt, von dieser gemäß der Vorschrift der KLZ geändert und dann von der KPZ wieder zurückgeschrieben.

Diese Vorgehensweise läßt zu, daß die von der PPZ vorgesehenen Zugriffe nicht die Daten treffen, die den Absichten des Benutzers entsprechen, und sie läßt auch zu, daß die Daten von der AUF unkorrekt aufbereitet werden. PPZ und AUF führen Tätigkeiten durch, die nicht eigentlich sicherheitsrelevant sind. Sind PPZ und AUF durch das BS isoliert, so sind keine unerlaubten Informationsflüsse in Richtung Benutzer möglich. Es ist garantiert, daß Zugriffe eines Benutzers nur dann durchgeführt werden, wenn er prinzipiell auf die Daten zugreifen darf.

Die vorgenommenen Sicherheitsüberprüfungen lassen sich in die Schema-Architektur einordnen: die KLZ prüft auf der Ebene des konzeptionellen Schemas die Berechtigung des Benutzers zum Zugriff auf das Datenobjekt mit dem umgesetzten systemweiten logischen Namen. Die KPZ überprüft beim physikalischen Zugriff die von der PPZ vorgenommene Abbildung vom konzeptionellen auf das interne Schema. Dazu überprüft die KPZ, ob die Speicherbereiche, auf die zugegriffen wird, in einer erlaubten Beziehung zum systemweiten Namen des konzeptionellen Datenobjekts stehen. Die Umsetzung des benutzerspezifischen Namens in den systemweiten ist nicht sicherheitsrelevant und könnte daher wie die andere Abbildung außerhalb von KLZ und KPZ geschehen. Der Umfang des Sicherheitskerns könnte hier noch reduziert werden.

3.3.3 Grenzen der Sicherheitskernarchitektur

Die beschriebene Architektur führt Schutzbedürfnisse auf mit "tags" versehene Speichereinheiten zurück. Alle externen Datenobjekte, die sich unmittelbar und eineindeutig auf solche Speichereinheiten abbilden lassen, sind daher in einfacher Weise geschützt. Noch schützbare Objekte können Felder von Relationen sein. Damit können Subschemas (Forderung (1) aus 2.1) geschützt werden. Werteabhängiger Schutz (Forderung (2)) wird nach /DOWN1,2/ durch das tagging-Verfahren nicht unterstützt. Schutz von abgeleiteten Daten (Forderung (4)), wie etwa Summe, Maximum, arithmetisches Mittel, ist wohl noch schwieriger zu erreichen.

Manche Sicherheitsstrategien (Forderung (9) aus 2.1) verlangen, daß Benutzer und Daten, auf die der Benutzer zugreift, zu derselben Kategorie gehören. Diese Strategie läßt sich offensichtlich mit Hilfe des tagging-Mechanismus realisieren. In ähnlicher Weise könnte sichergestellt werden, daß eingestufte Benutzer nur auf nicht höher eingestufte Daten zugreifen können. Zusätzlich wäre eine Erweiterung des Sicherheitskerns denkbar, die die Überprüfung der kontextabhängigen Strategie gewährleistet (Forderungen (7),(8)), daß ein Benutzer nach dem Lesen eingestufter Daten innerhalb derselben Terminalsitzung nicht mehr in niedriger eingestufte Daten schreiben kann. Dazu muß der Kern sich innerhalb einer Terminalsitzung des Benutzers das Maximum der Einstufung der gelesenen Daten merken und schreibende Zugriffe nur noch auf solche Daten erlauben, deren Einstufung nicht niedriger als dieses Maximum ist.

4 Ausblick

Die obigen Untersuchungen haben insbesondere die folgenden Problemkreise beim Entwurf sicherer DBVS aufgezeigt:

- Übergeordnete Strategien zur Kontrolle des Informationsflusses (wie die *-property) werden durch gegenwärtige DBVS nicht realisiert. Es bleibt zu untersuchen, wie für solche Aufgaben, die systemweit erbracht werden müssen, DBVS und BS zusammenarbeiten können.
- Je tiefer die Überprüfungen innerhalb des DBVS angeordnet sind, um so kleiner ist bei geeigneter Strukturierung der Anteil des Codes, der zu sicherheitsrelevanten Fehlern führen kann. Dabei wird gleichzeitig die Anwenderschnittstelle in ihrem sicherheitsrelevanten Teil zunehmend eingeschränkt. Es bleibt hier zu untersuchen, wie durch geeignete Kombination von Überprüfungen auf verschiedenen Ebenen und Separierung des sicherheitsrelevanten Codes vom Restsystem einerseits der Teil des sicherheitsrelevanten Codes relativ klein bleibt und andererseits das volle Spektrum der Sicherheitsforderungen der Anwender abgedeckt werden kann. Der Ansatz von /DOWN1,2/ kann hierzu ein erster Schritt sein, falls es gelingt, ihn so zu erweitern, daß die bisher noch starken Einschränkungen bezüglich der potentiellen Anwenderschnittstelle ganz oder teilweise aufgehoben werden können.

Zwei weitere Problemkreise, die Protokollierung und der Wiederanlauf, wurden bisher bei den Diskussionen der Sicherheitsproblematik von DBVS praktisch völlig ausgeklammert. Je nach der Anforderung an den Umfang der Protokollierung (z. B. BDSG: jeder Schreibzugriff mit Angabe des Zugreifenden, militärische Anforderung: jeder Schreib- und jeder Lesezugriff mit Angabe des Zugreifenden) ergeben sich hier bereits rein mengenmäßig erhebliche Probleme. Daneben muß sichergestellt sein, daß auch nicht über den Umweg der Protokollierung unbefugte Zugriffe realisiert werden können. Hier erhebt sich die Frage, ob und inwieweit für Daten mit unterschiedlichen Schutzanforderungen (etwa Klassen) eventuell verschiedene Protokolldateien verwendet werden müssen. Ähnlich problematisch sind die Sicherheitsprobleme beim Wiederanlauf. Beim Wiederanlauf muß mit Berechtigungen, die im allgemeinen umfassender sind als die Berechtugungen einzelner Benutzer, auf Daten unterschiedlicher Schutzanforderungen zugegriffen werden. Wie wird sichergestellt, daß dabei keine Sicherheitsverletzungen auftreten? Wie können Wiederanlauffunktionen in das Gesamtsystem des DBVS so eingeordnet werden, daß weiterhin eine Separierung der sicherheitsrelevanten Systemteile möglich ist?

Zusammenfassend muß festgestellt werden, daß im Gegensatz zu dem Bereich der Betriebssysteme bei den Datenbanken die Untersuchungen über die Sicherheitsproblematik noch ganz am Anfang stehen.

Literaturverzeichnis

/BELL/ D. Bell, L. La Padula: Secure Computer System: Unified Exposition and Multics Interpretation, EDS-TR-306, 76

/CHAM/ D. Chamberlin, J. Gray, I. Traiger: Views, Authorisation, and Locking in a Relational Data Base System, IBM RJ 1466, 74

/DATE/ C. Date: An Introduction to Database Systems, Second Edition, Addison-Wesley Publishing Company, 77

/DOWN1/ D. Downs, G.J. Popek: A Kernel Design for a Secure Data Base Management System, Proc. of the 3th Very Large Data Base Conf., 77

/DOWN2/ D. Downs, G.J. Popek: Data Base Management Systems Security and INGRES, Proc. of the 5th Very Large Data Base Conf., 79

/FEIE/ R.J. Feiertag, P.G. Neumann: The Foundations of a Provably Secure OS (PSOS), Proc. of the National Computer Conf., 79

/FERN/ E.B. Fernandez, C. Wood: The Relationship between Operating System and Database System Security: A Survey, Proc. of the First Intern. Software and Application Conf., Nov. 77

/GRIF/ P. Griffiths, B. Wade: An Authorisation Mechanism for a Relationel Database System, TODS v1n3, 76

/HÄRD/ Th. Härder: Implementierung von Datenbanksystemen, Hanser Verlag, 78

/KAMU/ J. Kam, J. Ullmann: A Model of Statistical Database and Their Security, TODS v2n1, 77

/MCCA/ F.J. McCauley, P.J. Drongowski: KSOS - The Design of a Secure Operating System, Proc. of the National Computer Conf., 79

/MCLE/ D. McLeod: A Framework for Data Base Protection and its Application to the INGRES and System R Data Base Management Systems, Proc. of the First Intern. Software and Application Conf., Nov. 77

/NIJS/ G.M. Nijssen: On the Gross Architecture for the Next Generation Data Base Management Systems, in Information Processing 77, B. Gilchrist (Ed.), North Holland Publ. Comp., Amsterdam, 77

/POPE/ G.J. Popek, C.S. Kline: A Verifiable Protection System, Proc. of the Intern. Conf. of Reliable Software, Los Angeles, 75

/STON1/ M. Stonebraker, P. Rubinstein: The INGRES Protection System, Proc. of the ACM National Conf., 76

/STON2/ M. Stonebraker, E. Wong, P. Krebs, G. Held: The Design and Implementation of INGRES, TODS v1n3, 76

/VDBR/ H. vor der Brück: Abstrakte Modelle zur Untersuchung sicherer Systeme, Computing 19, 77

Subjektorientierte Zugriffsautorisierung

W. Ballin
Universität Karlsruhe
Institut für Informatik III
- Betriebssysteme -
Postfach 6380, 7500 Karlsruhe 1

In einem abstrakten Schutzmodell wird der Begriff Zugriffsauthorisierung im Sinne der Veränderung der Zugriffsrelation $ZR \subseteq S \times R \times O$ mit S = Menge der Subjekte, R = Menge der Zugriffsrechte, O = Menge der Objekte, verwendet. ZR beschreibt, welche Subjekte welche Zugriffsrechte an welchen Objekten besitzen, d.h. $s \in S$ besitzt $r \in R$ an $o \in O \Longleftrightarrow (s,r,o) \in ZR$. Die Zugriffsauthorisierung wird üblicherweise von Objekteigentümern bzw. -verwaltern durchgeführt, die ihre Objekte vor Mißbrauch schützen wollen (objektorientierte Zugriffsauthorisierung). Analog dazu können wir uns auch Eigentümer bzw. Verwalter von Subjekten vorstellen, die ihre Subjekte an bestimmten Zugriffen hindern wollen (subjektorientierte Zugriffsauthorisierung). Wir stellen uns daher vor, daß: $(s,r,o) \in ZR \Leftrightarrow$ sowohl der Eigentümer von o als auch der Eigentümer von s haben eine entspr. Rechtevergabe durchgeführt. Die zusätzliche Kontrollmöglichkeit durch den Subjekteigentümer kann durch folgendes Beispiel motiviert werden:

Ein Projektleiter (Subjektverwalter der Subjekte des Projekts) möchte bei der Durchführung des Projekts die Verwendung bestimmter Programme auf bestimmte Mitarbeiter beschränken oder ganz verbieten, weil
1) die Programme für das Projekt ungeeignet sind und
2) fremde Programme ein Sicherheitsrisiko darstellen (beachte das sog. "Confinement problem")

Eine derartige Zugriffsbeschränkung liegt allein im Interesse des Projektleiters (Subjektverwalter) und nicht im Interesse der Programmersteller (Objekteigentümer), die im Gegenteil an einer häufigen Benutzung ihrer Programme interessiert sind. Eine differenzierte Kontrolle der Benutzung von Programmen (und anderen Hilfsmitteln) innerhalb des Projektes kann deswegen nur durch eine subjektorientierte Zugriffsauthorisierung durchgeführt werden.

SCHUTZMECHANISMEN IN EINEM BETRIEBSSYSTEM FÜR EINE MULTIMIKROCOMPUTERKONFIGURATION

S. Keramidis
M. Reitenspieß

Universität Erlangen, IMMD IV, Martensstraße 3
D-8520 Erlangen

Zur Zeit wird am IMMD IV (Betriebssysteme) der Universität Erlangen-Nürnberg ein Multimicrocomputersystem entwickelt. Die Hardware-(HW) Konfiguration basiert auf Single-Chip-Computern der Serie Intel 8086. Die Benutzerschnittstelle des zugehörigen Betriebssystems orientiert sich am System UNIX. Schutzmechanismen werden zum Teil bei der Konfiguration der HW, zum Teil bei Software (SW)-Erstellung verwirklicht. Grundlegend für das Betriebssystem ist die Existenz von Capabilities in Zusammenhang mit Segmentierung. Mit Capabilities wird die eindeutige Identifizierung aller Objekte ermöglicht, während Segmentierung die Darstellung sehr kleiner Objekte zuläßt. Damit wird die Realisierung kleiner Schutzdomänen unterstützt. Directories dienen dem Schutz von Capabilities und der Definition von Objektumgebungen. Der ebenfalls in Directories definierte Schlösser-Schloß-Mechanismus erlaubt eine feine Unterscheidung bezgl. des Zuganges zu einem Directoryeintrag, d.h., zu einer Capability. Die Verwendung abstrakter Datentypen bei SW-Entwicklung hat einen wesentlichen Anteil an der Realisierung der genannten Schutzmechanismen.

Das HW-Konzept unterstützt die Realisierung der vorgestellten Schutzmechanismen. Einerseits wird ein spezieller Baustein (ZILOG MMU Z 8010) zur Adressierung mit Hilfe von Capabilities und zur Implementierung kleiner Schutzdomänen eingesetzt. Andererseits wird durch die Anordnung der Prozessoren und der Busse die Zuverlässigkeit erhöht.

POLYNOMIALS -
THE SPECIFICATION, ANALYSIS AND DEVELOPMENT OF AN ABSTRACT DATA TYPE +)

W. Dosch, M. Wirsing

Institut für Informatik
Technische Universität München
Postfach 202420
D-8000 München 2

G. Ausiello, G.F. Mascari

Istituto di Automatica
Via Eudossiana 18
I-00100 Roma

ABSTRACT

Abstract data types provide a powerful tool for the representation independent specification of data structures. This paper applies theoretical results to a simple example and demonstrates how to work with this algebraic specification technique: Polynomials are defined by a hierarchical type. For this specification the class of all models is analyzed and properties of initial and terminal models are discussed.

A normal form serves as the basis for data type developments leading to a specification of polynomials with efficient sequential or parallel evaluation. Then relations between the derived types are studied and their implementation is discussed. Finally additional operations are added by a data type extension.

Throughout the paper program transformation methods like embedding, recursion introduction and recursion elimination are used.

1. INTRODUCTION

In the recent years (abstract data) types were included into several programming languages (as e.g. into SIMULA, EUCLID, ADA, CIPL or CLEAR) since they were considered as a basis for the specification of data structures. By their signature and axioms types describe the "world" of a program. From an intuitive point of view it seems simple to write down the axioms and to understand them. But in fact types pose severe problems, like consistency, they may be not computable and in general the laws do not uniquely characterize one (isomorphism class of) data structure(s) but a rich lattice of isomorphism classes. On the other hand it is desirable to have a large variety of models: An abstract algorithm developed for such a type describes in fact a class of algorithms, i.e. a program family. The understandability of the properties of a type is increased by omitting unnecessary details. This provides also more freedom for the choice of implementations, which can be seen as a type, too. Based on a theoretical analysis of a type one can apply program transformation methods (like embedding, recursion elimination) and algebraic methods (like the definition of normal forms) to the axioms. In this way efficient implementations can be obtained by "data type developments".

+) This research was supported in part by the Sonderforschungsbereich 49 - Programmiertechnik, Munich.

In this paper we specify polynomials by a hierachical type. Polynomials as abstract data types have already been defined in /GUTTAG,HOROWITZ,MUSSER 76/. In /AUSIELLO, MASCARI 79/ the axioms for about ten operations are transformed in order to obtain an implementable rewrite system. Here we use a different axiomatization: we are not only interested in polynomials as symbolic objects but also in their evaluation. Furthermore we start from a very simple specification (with only three functions) which is developed by transformations. The specification is as liberal as possible: the models form a complete lattice with a terminal model determined by the mathematical equality and an initial model determined by the syntactic equality. This variety of models is reduced when developing the type towards an efficient implementation.

By this simple type we intend to show how one can analyze and transform a specification. First we study syntactic and semantic properties like sufficient completeness, hierarchy preservation, existence of initial and terminal models; then we analyze specific models themselves by asking for their computability, their equality relation and possible normal forms. Based on these informations we transform the type leading to a specification of polynomials with efficient sequential or parallel evaluation. Using the criteria above, the derived types and their interrelationship to the original one are investigated. Finally, additional operations are introduced by specifying their required input/output behaviour; using data type induction direct recursive definitions for these operations are developed from the specification.

For the theoretical background and the basic definitions we refer to the appendix.

2. THE TYPE POLY : SPECIFICATION AND ANALYSIS

In mathematics a polynomial p(X) with integral coefficients is defined as the formal expression

$$a_n X^n + a_{n-1} X^{n-1} + \dots + a_1 X + a_o \qquad (n \geq 0 \text{ and } a_i \in \mathbb{Z})$$

In computer science one often is interested to calculate the value of a polynomial when the symbol X is replaced by an integral number.

2.1. SPECIFICATION OF THE TYPE POLY

Consequently an algebraic specification should reflect the input/output behaviour of polynomials, i.e. the polynomial functions, independent from their internal structure and/or representation in order to have freedom for choosing adequate implementations. So the following type POLY contains a single output function eval associating the value p(b) with a polynomial p and an integer b .

The mathematical definition also suggests the proper hierarchical structure for the specification: POLY is based on two primitive types, the type NAT of natural numbers for the exponents and the type INT of integral numbers for the coefficients. Both primitive types NAT and INT are assumed to be monomorphic. This can be reached by including the inequation $n \neq succ(n)$ into their axioms.

```
type POLY ≡ NAT, INT, poly, zero, attach, eval :
    primitives  NAT, INT ;
    sort        poly ;
    functions   poly zero ,
                (poly, int, nat) poly attach ,
                (poly, int) int eval ;
    laws        ∀ poly p, int a, b, nat n :
                eval(zero, b)                = 0 ,
                eval(attach(p, a, n), b)     = eval(p, b) + a × b^n
endoftype
```

Of course, arbitrary polynomials can be specified analogously by a type scheme (parameterized type, cf. /ADJ 78a/) allowing any commutative finitely generated ring for the coefficients.

This specification actually meets the idea of polynomials as the following family of provable equations shows :

Lemma

$$\text{POLY} \vdash \text{eval}(\text{attach}(\ldots(\text{attach}(\text{zero},a_1,n_1),\ldots),a_k,n_k),b) = \sum_{1\le j\le k} a_j \times b^{n_j}$$

2.2 ANALYSIS OF THE TYPE POLY

The algebraic specification of abstract data types has to meet some important properties to be of practical use:

Sufficient completeness (cf. /GUTTAG 75/), a deduction oriented condition, ensures that the result of an output operation is independent from a particular model. Thus the validity of the structural induction in the primitive types is preserved.

Hierarchy preservation (cf. /WIRSING et al. 80/) and persistency (cf. /ADJ 78a/), both model-theoretic conditions, describe the reduction resp. extension of primitive models to models of the overall type. Thus they guarantee the independent implementation of the primitive and non-primitive parts of a type.

Furthermore the existence of initial and terminal models and their recursiveness provides an information about the quality of a specification.

THE CLASS GEN_{POLY} OF MODELS

We summarize the semantic properties of the specification:

Theorem POLY is a sufficiently complete, hierarchy preserving and persistent polymorphic type forming a complete lattice. Thus for POLY initial and terminal models exist.

Sketch of the Proof

Since POLY is an equational type with monomorphic primitive types it is persistent and forms a complete lattice (cf. /WIRSING, BROY 80/ or /GIARRATANA, GIMONA, MONTANARI 76/). Sufficient completeness and hierarchy preservation can easily be proved by structural induction using the axioms.

□

INITIAL MODELS

In order to understand the properties of initial models we characterize the equality in an initial model I :
Two terms p, q of sort poly are equal in I , iff they are equal in any model of POLY (cf. /ADJ 78/, /WIRSING et al. 80/). Thus the model-theoretic equality of I coincides with the syntactic equality of the term algebra W(POLY) . So we get e.g. the following models:

I1 the term algebra W(POLY)

I2 finite sequences of pairs of an integral and a natural number

I3 a pair of a sequence of natural numbers and a sequence of integral numbers having the same length

I4 polynomials with unordered (eventually multiply occurring) exponents

Here I2 and I3 suggest a lot of concrete implementations by linked lists or flexible arrays (cf. /KNUTH 75/).

Note that in each initial model of POLY there exist infinitely many different objects of sort poly defining the same mapping. For example in I2 X + 2 may equivalently be represented by << 1,1>, < 2,0 >> or << 2,0 > , < 1,1 >> .
In each initial model the operation attach can simply be implemented by the concatenation whereas eval is rather inefficient since even powers with the same exponent are computed separately. So if one is not interested in the internal structure of polynomials but only in their I/O behaviour an initial model is redundant since it reflects the complete generation process by the constructor functions.

TERMINAL MODELS

In a dual way terminal models Z can be characterized: Two terms p, q of sort poly are different in Z , iff there exist integers b, c, d with

$$\text{POLY} \vdash \text{eval}(p,b) = c \ \text{ and } \ \text{eval}(q,b) = d \ \text{ and } \ c \neq d \ .$$

Equivalently p and q are equal in Z , iff

$$\text{POLY} \vdash \forall \ \underline{\text{int}} \ b : \ \text{eval}(p,b) = \text{eval}(q,b) \ ,$$

i.e. they describe the same mapping ("mathematical equality", cf. /BROY, WIRSING 80/). Furthermore transformed into a normal form they must have the same coefficients. This property is decidable and therefore the class of all terminal models is computable.

From each initial model I we get a corresponding terminal model Z by regarding only terms with non-zero coefficients and, for example, strictly monotonically decreasing exponents. Thus $3\ X^2 + 2$ uniquely corresponds to << 2,0 >, < 3,2 >> . Another terminal model is based on simple sequences of integral numbers beginning with a non-zero element. Here $3\ X^2 + 2$ is represented by < 2,0,3 >.

In terminal models eval is more efficient than in initial ones since terms with the same exponent are computed only once. Conversely in terminal models attach does not simply correspond to the concatenation.

Of course, in Gen_{POLY} there exist infinitely many different non-isomorphic models - computable and non-computable ones - , for examples sequences of pairs of an integral and a natural number containing a limited number of equal exponents.

3. DATA TYPE DEVELOPMENT

The axioms of a type characterize the class of all models, thus they are not related to efficiency in any way. But if the axioms are equations they can additionally be considered as a (left-to-right) term rewrite system (cf. /AUSIELLO, MASCARI 79/, /KNUTH, BENDIX 70/, /LESCANNE 79/). Thus we can introduce a simple efficiency measure by counting the (minimal) number of primitive operations which must be executed in a deduction in order to obtain an equivalent primitive term.

We now investigate different data type developments in order to get related types with more "efficient" equations allowing a better implementation of eval .

The general method is to select a normal form in such a way that the class of models, i.e. the breadth of the specification, is restricted to those models allowing efficient implementations.

NORMAL FORM

As normal form we select terms of W(POLY) with a complete strictly descending sequence of exponents, i.e. each poly p is represented by a term

(NF) $\text{attach}(\text{attach}(\ldots(\text{attach}(\text{zero}, a_k, k), \ldots), a_1, 1), a_0, 0)$

for some $k \in \mathbb{N}$.

Note that this normal form (NF) neither is initial (cf. /ADJ 78/) nor terminal. E.g. the terms attach(attach(zero,1,0)2,1) and attach(attach(zero,2,1),1,0) are different in an initial model I , although they can be identically represented by (NF). On the other hand attach(attach(zero,0,1),2,0) and attach(zero,2,0) are different terms in (NF) although they are identically interpreted in each terminal model Z .

EMBEDDING OF EVAL

In the computation of eval(p,b) with p in (NF) the powers b^i are separately computed for each exponent $i \in \{0,\ldots,k\}$. According to the "embedding technique" of program transformations (cf. /BAUER,WÖSSNER 80/, /BROY,GNATZ,WIRSING 79/) we add a further parameter pow on which the powers b^i are subsequently computed using b^{i-1} . Thus we introduce an embedding function

funct (poly, int, int) int embeval

with the axioms

```
embeval(zero, b, pow)             = 0 ,
embeval(attach(p, a, n), b, pow) = embeval(p, b, pow × b) + a × pow
```

and conclude:

Lemma ∀ int b, poly p in (NF) : eval(p,b) = embeval(p, b, 1) .

Proof By structural induction using the axioms of POLY .

THE TYPE NORMPOLY

Thus we get a new type NORMPOLY by replacing the axioms for eval by those for embeval :

```
type NORMPOLY ≡ INT, npoly, nzero, nattach, neval :
     primitive    INT ;
     sort         npoly ;
     functions    npoly nzero ,
                  (npoly, int) npoly nattach ,
                  (npoly, int) int neval ,
                  (npoly, int, int) int embeval ;
     laws         ∀ npoly p, int a,b,pow :
                  neval(p,b)                        = embeval(p, b, 1) ,
                  embeval(nzero, b, pow)            = 0 ,
                  embeval(nattach(p, a), b, pow) = embeval(p, b, pow × b) + a × pow
endoftype
```

In NORMPOLY polynomials are constructed according to the normal form (NF) for which the exponent does not play any role. Thus the constructor function nattach has only two arguments and the primitive type NAT can be dropped.

Here embeval is regarded as a hidden function (cf. /MAJSTER 79/, /ADJ 78a/) and thus not provided among the exported items in the first line of the type.

In the sequel NORMPOLY serves as the basis for two different developments: Aiming at an efficient sequential evaluation we arrive at a specification of polynomials in HORNER's form. But looking for an efficient parallel computation one can also derive a specification for parallel evaluation.

3.1 SEQUENTIAL EVALUATION OF POLYNOMIALS: THE TYPE HORNER

In the recursion equation of the embedding function the multiplication by pow is compatible with embeval (cf. /KNUTH 71/):

Lemma ∀ int a, b, x, npoly p :

neval(nattach(p, a), b) = neval(p,b) × b + a

Proof By structural induction using the axioms of NORMPOLY .

Using this equation we define a new abstract data type HORNER :

```
type HORNER  =  INT, hpoly, hzero, hattach, heval :
     primitive  INT ;
     sort       hpoly ;
     functions  hpoly hzero ,
                (hpoly, int) hpoly hattach ,
                (hpoly, int) int heval ;
     laws       ∀ hpoly p, int a,b :
                heval(hzero, b)          = 0 ,
                heval(hattach(p, a), b) = heval(p, b) × b + a
endoftype
```

3.2 PARALLEL EVALUATION OF POLYNOMIALS : THE TYPE PARPOLY

The recursion equation for embeval in NORMPOLY is of linear, but not of tail-recursion type. Using the associativity of the addition in INT we can remove this recursion by an iterative embedding function (cf. /BAUER,WÖSSNER 80/)

funct (npoly, int, int, int) int pembeval1

with the axioms

```
pembeval1(nzero, b, pow, res)          = res ,
pembeval1(nattach(p, a), b, pow, res) = pembeval1(p, b, pow × b, res + a × pow)
```

To execute on each parameter of pembeval1 at most one arithmetic operation we compute a × pow using a further parameter h . In analogy to the development of HORNER we finally get (cf. /BAUER 80/) :

```
type PARPOLY ≡ INT, ppoly, pzero, pattach, peval :
     primitive   INT ;
     sort        ppoly ;
     functions   ppoly pzero ,
                 (ppoly, int) ppoly  pattach ,
                 (ppoly, int) int  peval ,
                 (ppoly, int, int, int, int) int pembeval ;
     laws        ∀ ppoly p, int a, b, pow, res, h :
     peval(p, b)                            = pembeval(p, b, 1, 0, 0) ,
     pembeval(pzero, b, pow, res, h)        = res + h ,
     pembeval(pattach(p, a), b, pow, res, h) =
                       pembeval(p, b, pow × b, res + h, a × pow)
endoftype
```

3.3 COMPARISON OF THE TYPES HORNER AND PARPOLY

For a polynomial of degree k without leading zeros HORNER's evaluation heval is optimal with respect to the number of primitive operations: heval needs only $k + 1$ additions and $k + 1$ multiplications but unfortunately these operations can be executed only sequentially in $2 \times (k + 1)$ computation steps.

Conversely the evaluation peval needs $k + 2$ additions and even $2 \times (k + 1)$ multiplications. But three operations may be executed in parallel exploiting the "Call-in-Parallel" computation rule of /BROY 80/. Thus only $k + 2$ computation steps are necessary.

4. RELATIONS BETWEEN THE TYPES POLY AND HORNER

4.1 ANALYSIS OF NORMPOLY AND HORNER

Following the arguments of section 2.2 we see that the properties of theorem 2.2 also apply to the derived types NORMPOLY and HORNER . As an initial model of HORNER we get for example:

- the term algebra W(HORNER)
- finite sequences of integral numbers
- polynomials in HORNER's form

From each initial model we get a terminal model by deleting leading zeros. So e.g. sequences with a first non-zero element form a terminal model of HORNER .

For NORMPOLY we get a quite a similar analysis. Thus we can prove:

<u>Theorem</u> HORNER and NORMPOLY are definitionally equivalent. They are persistent, hierarchy preserving polymorphic types forming complete lattices.

4.2 RELATIONSHIP BETWEEN POLY AND NORMPOLY

Every model of NORMPOLY can be extended to a model of POLY by associating zero resp. eval with nzero resp. neval and by defining the operation attach of POLY for terms of NORMPOLY by structural recursion:

```
attach(nzero, a, n) =def
     if n = 0 then nattach(nzero, a)
               else nattach(attach(nzero, a, n - 1), 0) fi ,

attach(nattach(p, b), a, n) =def
     if n = 0 then nattach(p, b + a)
               else nattach(attach(p, a, n - 1), b) fi
```

Therefore we obtain:

Theorem NORMPOLY is a descendant of POLY .

Since the descendant relation is transitive we finally get:

Theorem HORNER is a descendant of POLY .

5. TRANSITION TO PROCEDURAL TYPES

So far abstract data types specify operations in a purely functional style using case analysis and recursion. In order to implement a type efficiently using machine-oriented language constructs we pass from an algebraic specification to a procedural type, i.e. a type with program variables and while-statements. For the type HORNER we exemplarily show this transition. Using the program transformation technique of "function inversion" (cf. /BAUER,WÖSSNER 80/) the recursive definition of heval can be changed into an iterative one by inverting the argument of the recursive call. Thus we introduce a function

```
funct (hpoly) hpoly reverse
```

with the axioms

```
reverse(hzero)          = hzero ,
reverse(hattach(p, a)) = insert(reverse(p), a)
```

where the auxiliary function

```
funct (hpoly) hpoly insert
```

may be specified by

```
insert(hzero, a)          = hattach(hzero, a) ,
insert(hattach(p, b), a) = hattach(insert(p, a), b)  .
```

Then we use an iterative embedding function heval :

```
heval(p, b) = iteval(reverse(p), b, 0)
```

where

```
funct (hpoly, int, int) int iteval
```

is defined by

```
iteval(hzero, b, res)           = res
iteval(hattach(p, a), b, res) = iteval(p, b, res × b + a)   .
```

Transforming the iterative recursion of iteval into a while-statement we get a procedural type ITHORNER based on complete ascending normal forms. By the introduction of destructor functions irest and itop the operation reverse is no longer needed. Note that the recursive definition of iteval provides the invariant of the while-statement.

```
type ITHORNER ≡ INT, ipoly, izero, iattach, ieval :
    primitive   INT ;
    sort        ipoly ;
    functions   ipoly izero ,
                (ipoly, int) ipoly iattach ,
                (ipoly, int) int ieval ,
                (ipoly p : p ≠ izero ) ipoly irest ,
                (ipoly p : p ≠ izero) int itop ;
    laws        ∀ ipoly p, int a,b :
                itop(iattach(p, a)) = a ,
                irest(iattach(p, a)) = p ,
                ieval(p, b) =
                   ⌈(var ipoly P, var int RES) := (p, 0) ;
                    while P ≠ izero
                     do (P, RES) := (irest(P), RES × b + itop(P)) od ;
                    RES                                              ⌋
endoftype
```

For a formal treatment of partial functions in abstract data types see e.g. /WIRSING et al. 80/.

This type ITHORNER is again polymorphic forming a complete lattice with initial and terminal elements. Note that the procedures work uniformly in every model independently whether leading zeros are admitted or not.

Furthermore HORNER and ITHORNER are descendants of each other; thus ITHORNER also is a descendant and therefore an implementation of POLY .

6. DATA TYPE EXTENSIONS: INTRODUCTION OF ADDITION AND MULTIPLICATION

After the analysis of POLY we can introduce further operations. As an example we choose the addition and multiplication :

```
funct (poly, poly) poly add
funct (poly, poly) poly mult
```

Using the output operation eval we can simply define these operations.

SPECIFICATION OF ADDITION AND MULTIPLICATION

∀ poly p,q, int b :

eval(add(p, q), b) = eval(p, b) + eval(q, b)

eval(mult(p, q), b) = eval(p, b) × eval(q, b)

If we enlarge POLY by these functions and axioms, then add and mult are further constructor functions in the extended type POLY' . In the initial models of POLY' they introduce new polynomials different from all terms of POLY . Thus POLY' is not a descendant of POLY and therefore POLY and POLY' are not definitionally equivalent.

RECURSIVE DEFINITION OF ADDITION AND MULTIPLICATION

In oder to obtain a definitionally equivalent extension (i.e. an enrichment, cf. /ADJ 78/) of POLY , we use structural induction on POLY and calculate for example

eval(add(zero, q), b) = eval(zero, b) + eval(q, b) = 0 + eval(q, b)
= eval(q, b) .

Then the law

(L1) add(zero,q) = q

implies the equation

eval(add(zero, q), b) = eval(q, b)

too, but not vice versa. Analogously we get the following recursive equations:

(L2) add(attach(p, b, n), q) = add(p, attach(q, b, n))

(L3) mult(zero, q) = zero

(L4) mult(attach(p, b, n), q) = add(mult(p, q), mult(attach(zero, b, n), q))

(L1) - (L4) do not hold in initial models of the extended type POLY' but in terminal ones. They extend POLY in a definitionally equivalent way.

7. CONCLUDING REMARKS

In the construction of an abstract type one often starts with a well-structured hierarchical type (cf. /BURSTALL, GOGUEN 77/) having a "natural" terminal semantics (cf. /WAND 77/, /BROY et al. 79/). Then data type development leads to a type in which the equations can be regarded as a reasonably efficient term rewriting system. The correctness proof for this transition can be restricted to a small set of constructor functions if the remaining operations are defined in terms of these constructors (cf. /GAUDEL 78/).

The resulting type may be monomorphic. But there exist examples of polymorphic types (cf. the types of primitive recursive functions in /BERGSTRA,TUCKER 80/ and /WIRSING, BROY 80/) where the equality in a terminal model, i.e. the mathematical equality, is not recursively enumerable. On the other hand, for equational types the equality in initial models is always recursively enumerable. Therefore, when specifying e.g. a programming language by an abstract data type (cf. /BROY,WIRSING 80/), a type development can never lead to an equational type the initial models of which describe exactly the mathematical semantics.

Often the initial models I of the final type are somewhere between the original initial and terminal models. These initial models I are determined during the data type development by successive (program) transformations: An algorithm working over I-normal forms works uniformly over every quotient structure of I (provided a hierarchical, sufficiently complete equational specification).

So program transformation methods for the transition from a type to a descendant joined with a careful analysis of every derived type seem to be a promising tool for developing reliable data structure specifications.

Acknowledgement

We gratefully acknowledge valuable discussions with Prof. F. L. Bauer and Prof. K. Samelson. We are indebted to our colleages M. Broy, Th. Matzner and B. Möller from the project CIP in Munich for critically reading drafts of this paper.

References

/ADJ 78/
J.A. Goguen, J.W. Thatcher, E.G. Wagner: An initial algebra approach to the specification, correctness and implementation of abstract data types. In: R.T. Yeh (ed.): Current Trends in Programming Methodology, Vol. 3, Data Structuring, N.J. : Prentice Hall, 1978

/ADJ 78a/
J.W. Thatcher, E.G. Wagner, J.B. Wright: Data type specification: Parameterization and the power of specification techniques. Proc. SIGACT 10th Annual Symposium on the Theory of Computing, 1978

/AUSIELLO,MASCARI 79/
G. Ausiello, G.F. Mascari: On the design of algebraic data structures with the approach of abstract data types. In: E.W. Ng (ed.): Symbolic and Algebraic Computation, LNCS 72, 515 - 530 (1979)

/BAUER 80/
F.L. Bauer: Einführung in die Informatik I . Vorlesungsskriptum, Technische Universität München (1980)

/BAUER,WÖSSNER 80/
F.L. Bauer, H. Wössner: Algorithmic language and program development. Berlin-Heidelberg-New York: Springer-Verlag. To appear

/BERGSTRA,TUCKER 79/
J.A. Bergstra, J.V. Tucker: Algebraic specifications of computable and semicomputable data structures. Afdeling Informatice Amsterdam, IW 115/79

/BERGSTRA,TUCKER 80/
J.A. Bergstra, J.V. Tucker: A natural data type with a finite equational final semantics specification but no effective equational initial semantics specification. To appear

/BERTONI et al. 79/
A. Bertoni, G. Mauri, P.A. Miglioli, M. Wirsing: On different approaches to abstract data types and the existence of recursive models. Bulletin of EATCS 9, 47-57 (1979)

/BROY 80/
M. Broy: Transformation parallel ablaufender Programme. Dissertation, Technische Universität München, Fakultät für Mathematik (1980)

/BROY et al. 79/
M. Broy, W. Dosch, H. Partsch, P. Pepper, M. Wirsing: Existential quantifiers in abstract data types. In: H.A. Maurer (ed.): Proc. 6th ICALP, Graz, LNCS 71, 73-87 (1979)

/BROY,GNATZ,WIRSING 79/
M. Broy, R. Gnatz, M. Wirsing: Problemspezifikation - eine Grundlage für Programmentwicklung. Workshop on Reliable Software, Bonn University, Sept. 22-23, 1978. Hanser Verlag (1979)

/BROY,WIRSING 80/
M. Broy, M. Wirsing: Programming languages as abstract data types. Proc. 5th Colloquium on "Arbres en Algèbre et en Programmation", Lille 1980

/BURSTALL,GOGUEN 77/
R.M. Burstall, J.A. Goguen: Putting theories together to make specifications. Proc. of the Fifth Int. Joint Conf. on Artificial Intelligence, MIT, Cambridge, Mass., 1045-1058 (1977)

/EHRICH 79/
H.D. Ehrich: On the theory of specification, implementation and parameterization of abstract data types. To appear

/EHRIG et al. 78/
H. Ehrig, H.J. Kreowski, P. Padawitz: Stepwise specification and implementation of abstract data types. Proc. 5th ICALP, Udine, LNCS 62, 205-226 (1978)

/GAUDEL 78/
M.C. Gaudel: Spècifications incomplètes mais suffisantes de la représentation des types abstraits. IRIA Rapport de Recherche No. 320 (1978)

/GIARRATANA,GIMONA,MONTANARI 76/
V. Giarratana, F. Gimona, U. Montanari: Observability concepts in abstract data type specification. Proc. of the 5th MFCS Symposium. LNCS 45, 576-587 (1976)

/GUTTAG 75/
J.V. Guttag: The specification and application to programming of abstract data types. Ph. D. Thesis, Univ. of Toronto, Dept. of Comp. Science, Rep. CSRG-59 (1975)

/GUTTAG,HOROWITZ,MUSSER 76/
J.V. Guttag, E. Horowitz, D.R. Musser: The design of data specifications. USC/Information Sciences Institute, RR-76-49 (1976)

/KNUTH 75,71/
D.E. Knuth: The art of computer programming., Vol. 1,2. Reading Mass.: Addison-Wesley (1971,1975)

/KNUTH,BENDIX 70/
D. Knuth, P. Bendix: Simple word problems in universal algebras. In: J. Leech (ed.): Computational Problems in Abstract Algebra. Pergamon Press 1970

/LESCANNE 79/
Etude algébrique et relationnelle des types abstraits et de leurs représentations. Thèse de Doctorat, Université de Nancy 1979

/MAJSTER 79/
M. Majster: Data types, abstract data types and their specification problem. TCS 8, 89-127 (1979)

/WAND 77/
M. Wand: Final algebra semantics and data type extensions. Indiana University, Comp. Science Department, Technical Report No. 65 (1978)

/WIRSING,BROY 80/
M. Wirsing, M. Broy: Abstract data types as lattices of finitely generated models. To appear in the Proc. 9th MFCS, Rydzyna, Poland (1980)

/WIRSING et. al 80/
M. Wirsing, P. Pepper, H. Partsch, W. Dosch, M. Broy: On hierarchies of abstract data types. Technische Universität München, Institut für Informatik, TUM I8007 (1980)

APPENDIX DEFINITIONS AND BASIC RESULTS

The formal treatment of abstract data types employs tools from algebra, logic and category theory. Since a uniform terminology has not yet prevailed we briefly summarize the basic notions to make the above applications precise.

A *heterogeneous algebra* $A = \langle (s^A)_{s \in S}, (f^A)_{f \in F} \rangle$ consists of a family of *carrier sets* s^A and of a family of total *operations (functions)* f^A on these carrier sets. Each function $f^A : s_1{}^A \times \ldots \times s_n{}^A \to s_{n+1}{}^A$ has a *functionality* $s_1 \times \ldots \times s_n \to s_{n+1}$ where $s_1{}^A \times \ldots \times s_n{}^A$ is the *domain* and $s_{n+1}{}^A$ the *range* of $f^A (s_i \in S, \ n \geq 0)$. For $n = 0$ f^A is a *nullary function* or *constant*. The countable index sets S of *sorts* s and F of *function symbols* f define the *signature* $\Sigma = \langle S, F \rangle$. So $A = \langle S^A, F^A \rangle$ becomes a Σ-*algebra*, where S^A (resp. F^A) abbreviates $(s^A)_{s \in S}$ (resp. $(f^A)_{f \in F}$).

A Σ-algebra $A = \langle S^A, F^A \rangle$ is called a *(primitive) reduct* of an algebra $A' = \langle S^{A'}, F^{A'} \rangle$ iff $S^A \subseteq S^{A'}$ and $F^A \subseteq F^{A'}$. Conversely A' is called an *extension* of A.

A Σ-algebra A' is called Σ-*subalgebra* of a Σ-algebra A, if for all $s \in S$ $s^{A'} \subseteq s^A$, for all $f \in F$ $f^{A'}$ is the restriction of f^A to A' and A' is closed under all the operations of A. For every Σ-algebra A there exists a smallest Σ-subalgebra Sub(A) of A (with respect to set inclusion). A is called *finitely generated*, iff Sub(A) = A .

From the function symbols themselves we obtain particular Σ-algebras: Let $x_1, \ldots, x_k$ be (free) variables of sort $s_1, \ldots, s_k \in S$. Then $W(\Sigma; x_1, \ldots, x_k)$ is the Σ-algebra consisting of all wellformed expressions which can be finitely generated from $x_1, \ldots, x_k$ and the constants $f \in F$. If $k = 0$ we write $W(\Sigma)$ and call it the *term algebra* of Σ. Clearly, $W(\Sigma)$ is finitely generated and Σ-subalgebra of all $W(\Sigma; x_1, \ldots, x_k)$. The elements of $W(\Sigma)$ are called *terms*.

For two Σ-algebras A and B a family $\varphi = (\varphi_s)_{s \in S}$ of total mappings $\varphi_s : s^A \to s^B$ is called Σ-*homomorphism* if for all $f : s_1 \times \ldots \times s_n \to s_{n+1} \in F$ and elements $a_1 \in s_1{}^A, \ldots, a_n \in s_n{}^A$:

$$\varphi_{s_{n+1}}(f^A(a_1, \ldots, a_n)) = f^B(\varphi_{s_1}(a_1), \ldots, \varphi_s(a_n)).$$

Then every finitely generated Σ-algebra is a homomorphic image of $W(\Sigma)$; there exists at most one homomorphism between two finitely generated Σ-algebras and this homomorphism, if it exists, is surjective.

Properties of Σ-algebras are expressed by *equations* $t_1 = t_2$ and *inequations* $t_1 \neq t_2$ where $t_1, t_2 \in W(\Sigma; x_1, \ldots, x_k)$. The *interpretation* is defined as usual in the classical two-valued first order logic: $t_1 = t_2$ holds in A, i.e.

$A \models t_1 = t_2$, iff for all $a_1, \ldots, a_k \in A$ of appropriate sort

$$t_1[a_1/x_1, \ldots, a_k/x_k]^A = t_2 [a_1/x_1, \ldots, a_k/x_k]^A$$

Now an *(abstract data) type* $T = < \Sigma, E >$ consists of a signature Σ and a (countable) set E of equations, called *axioms*. A Σ-algebra A is called *model* of type T, if A is finitely generated and $A \models t_1 = t_2$ for all equations $t_1 = t_2 \in E$. The *class of all models* of a type T is denoted by Gen_T. If $E = \emptyset$ we write Gen_Σ for $Gen_{< \Sigma, \emptyset >}$. We say that an equation $t_1 = t_2$ is *valid* in T iff for all $A \in Gen_T$ $A \models t_1 = t_2$. T is *satisfiable* if $Gen_T \neq \emptyset$ and T is called *monomorphic* if all elements of Gen_T are isomorphic; otherwise T is *polymorphic* (cf./ BAUER, WÖSSNER 80/).

The usual equational axioms (see e.g. /WAND 77/) and logical rules of interference as well as a structural induction (cf. /GUTTAG 75/) hold for types. An equation $t_1 = t_2$ is called *provable* in T, i.e. $T \vdash t_1 = t_2$, if $t_1 = t_2$ can be deduced from the laws of T using the above axioms and rules. The *completeness theorem* of first order logic holds for equations, i.e.

$$T \vdash t_1 = t_2 \quad \Leftrightarrow \quad t_1 = t_2 \quad \text{is valid in } T .$$

For Σ-algebras $A, B \in Gen_T$ we define

$$A \leq B \text{ iff there exists a } \Sigma\text{-homomorphism } \varphi : B \to A$$

$$A \cong B \text{ iff } A \leq B \text{ and } B \leq A ,$$

$$|Gen_T| =_{def} Gen_T/\cong$$

$|Gen_T|$ can be viewed as the set of quotient structures of $W(\Sigma)$ which are models of T. The relation $\leq$ is reflexive and transitive on Gen_T and antisymmetric on $|Gen_T|$. Thus $\leq$ is a partial ordering on $|Gen_T|$. Using this ordering we define for $\emptyset \neq H \subseteq |Gen_T|$ and $A, B \in |Gen_T|$ upper and lower bounds, least upper bound $lub_T(H)$ and greatest lower bound $glb_T(H)$ as usual. A is called initial in T, if $A = lub_T(|Gen_T|)$ and terminal in T, if $A = glb_T(|Gen_T|)$. Furthermore T is called a lattice, if $Gen_T \neq \emptyset$ and $A \sqcup B =_{def} lub_T(\{A, B\})$ and $A \sqcap B =_{def} glb_T(\{A, B\})$ exist for all $A, B \in |Gen_T|$. A lattice A is called *complete*, if $lub_T(H)$ and $glb_T(H)$ exist for all $\emptyset \neq H \subseteq |Gen_T|$.

If T is a complete lattice it always has a terminal element and an initial element. Obviously every monomorphic type forms a complete lattice. Due to the equational form of the axioms the notions of initial and terminal coincide with the respective notions defined in /ADJ 78/, /WAND 77/ or /BROY et al. 79/ (cf. /BERTONI et al. 79/ and /WIRSING,BROY 80/).

We want to define types in hierarchies (cf. /WIRSING et al. 80/). A type $T = <\Sigma, E>$, with $\Sigma = < S, F >$ is called *hierarchical,* if a type $T' = <\Sigma', E'>$ is signed as primitive in T, where $\Sigma' = <S', F'>$ and $S' \subseteq S$, $F' \subseteq F$ and $E' \subseteq E$ hold. T' is called the *primitive type* of T. Furthermore we call a term $p \in W(\Sigma)$ a *primitive term* if p is built from primitive function symbols only, i.e. $p \in W(\Sigma')$. A term $t \in W(\Sigma)$ is called to be of *primitive sort,* if t is of sort s' and s' is primitive, i.e. $s' \in S'$. Consequently every primitive term is of primitive sort but not vice versa.

Then a model A of a type T is called *hierarchy-preserving* if for the primitive type T' of T the Σ'-reduct of A is a model of T'. A type is called *hierarchy preserving,* if all its models are hierarchy preserving. The corresponding notion of provability is GUTTAG's condition: A type T is called *sufficiently complete* if for every term t of primitive sort there exists a primitive term p with $T \vdash t = p$. Due to the completeness theorem an equationally specified type is sufficiently complete iff it is hierarchy preserving (cf. /WIRSING et al. 80/). We call a type *persistent* (cf. /ADJ 78a/) if it is hierarchy preserving and every model of the primitive type of T is a reduct of some model of T. Clearly every hierarchy preserving type with monomorphic primitive types is persistent.

Finally we define computability, normal forms and implementation of types: An isomorphism class C of finitely generated Σ-algebras, e.g. the class of all initial models of some type, is called *computable* if the equality is recursive, i.e.

$$\{(t_1, t_2) \in W(\Sigma) \times W(\Sigma) : A \models t_1 = t_2 \text{ for all } A \in C\}$$

is recursive. For related notions see /BERTONI et al. 79/ or /BERGSTRA,TUCKER 79/

A *C-normal form (system)* is a set $M \subseteq W(\Sigma)$ such that

(1) $C \models c \neq c'$ for distinct $c, c' \in M$ and

(2) for every term $t \in W(\Sigma)$ there exists $c \in M$ with $C \models t = c$.

(cf. "traversal" in /BERGSTRA,TUCKER 79/).

For two types $T = \langle\langle S, F\rangle, E\rangle$ and $T' = \langle\langle S, F'\rangle, E'\rangle$ with common sorts S let the type $T'' = \langle\langle S, F \cup F' \cup F''\rangle, E' \cup E''\rangle$ be the enrichment of T' by the operations F, by some further operations F'' and by some equations E'' for $F \cup F''$. T' is called a *descendant* of T if for every model A'' of T'' the $<S, F>$-reduct of T'' is a model of T. Two mutually descendant types are called *definitionally equivalent.* The notion of descendant is stronger than the notion of *implementation* which requires only the existence of a $<S, F>$-epimorphism from the finitely generated $<S, F>$-subalgebra of A'' onto some model of T (cf. the notion of implementation in /ADJ 78/, /EHRICH 79/ and /EHRIG et al. 78/, but note that a descendant as well as an implementation in our sense implements (in the terminology of /ADJ 78/) always the terminal algebra, but may not implement the terminal one).

A LR-Like Analyzer Algorithm for Graphs

Helmut J. Ludwigs
Universitaet Dortmund

The lack of linear orderings in graphs is a major obstacle in the extension of powerful syntactic analysis methods to graphs. One method to describe an ordering on a graph is the specification of a spanning ordered tree, a so-called visitation-tree. If such trees are given for all graphs occuring in a graph-grammar, for all generated graphs visitation-trees may be generated as well by the same derivation mechanism. Thus, the graphs generated by ordered graph grammars carry an implicit ordering with them, which may be reconstructed on need. We will show that such visitation-trees form a solid basis for the extension of LR-Parsing to graphs.

1. Introduction

Sets of graphs can be described by graph-grammars like string languages can be specified by Chomsky-type grammars. Graph-grammars have been studied by a number of authors, an extensive survey can be found in /Nag-78/. Although these concepts differ somewhat from each other, they can be viewed as special cases of the graph-grammars described by Nagl /Nag-76/ or Ehrich /Ehr-75/.

There exist a number of algorithms for constructing analyzers for string languages from a contextfree grammar, e.g. the precedence-method, LL- and LR-methods. Until yet, only the comparatively weak precedence-method has been extended to graph-grammars and is used in the PLAN-2D compiler system /Fra-77/.

Unfortunately, the class of precedence graph grammars is too small for many important applications as the analysis of program-graphs.

Therefore it has been suggested /Nag-79/ to apply more advanced parsing methods (e.g. the LR-method) to graphs. These methods rely very heavily on the unique right-to-left order in strings, and cannot be adapted to graph-grammars as easy as precedence-parsing. In this paper we will present a modification to the usual definition of graph-grammars which assigns each generated graph a definite ordering, which can be used to apply the ideas of LR-parsing to graph-grammars.

For the sake of simplicity and understandability we will limit ourselves to context-free graph-grammars with constant embedding functions which do not allow relabelling or reversion of embedding edges, deletion or generation of new ones. This restriction is not necessesary, the same ideas may be applied to grammars which generate new edges and/or relabel and/or revert edges.

2. Graphs

We will draw graphs like the following example:

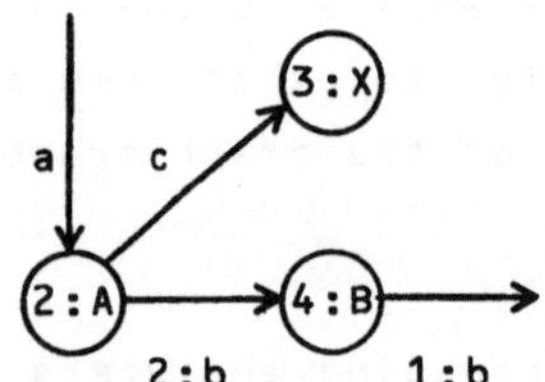

Nodes and edges are labelled by alphameric symbols, uppercase is used for nonterminal labels, lowercase for terminals. Because labels must not be unique in a graph, we add an indentification-number for edges and nodes, which may be skipped if the label alone provides a basis for unique identification. The notation "2:A" means the node number 2 with label "A", and "a" means the edge with label "a" in the graph above. We will interprete these edges as a rule how the graph-body shall be "embedded" into a host-graph. They will be used to specify embedding mappings in graph-productions. For simplicity, we will mainly use examples without edgelabels in the following.

3. Graph-Grammars

The productions of (ordinary) graph-grammars are usually written as triples

p = (g, h, f) where

- g is the leftside graph, which will consist of only one node and some embedding edges,
- h is the rightside graph, which will replace g, and
- f is the embedding function which describes an embedding of h in place of g. It must be bijective in our case.

We will extend this type of production to a quadruple

p = (g, h, b, f) where

b is a ordered spanning tree of the undirected equivalent of h, the so-called visitation-tree. The root of b must have an ingoing edge in the embedding of h.

This (ordered) tree will be used to establish orderings for all graphs generated by the grammar, orderings which can be used to drive a LR-like Analyzer.

Productions will be written as follows: Three boxes in a row, the leftmost contains the leftside graph together with its embedding edges. The middle box contains the rightside graph with its embedding, and the right one the (ordered) visitation tree. Corresponding embedding edges in the left- and rightside graphs are connected by dotted arrows:

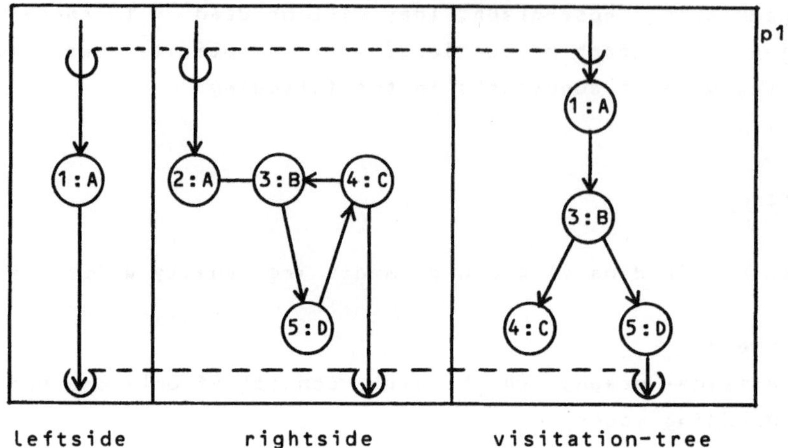

An extended graph grammar has a unique startproduction of the form:

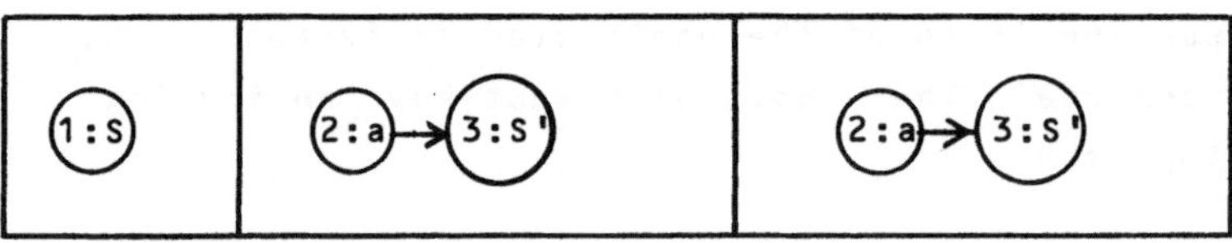

where "a" is a unique labelling, the anchor-label, which may not be used in other places in the grammar. In most practical applications it is easily possible to find such an anchor-label. Extended graph-grammars are written as 5-tuples

G = (T, N, E, S, a) with

T is a set of terminal node-labels,

N is a set of nonterminal node-labels,

E is a set of edge-labels,

S ε N is the startlabel,

a ε T is the anchor-label.

We will require all left- and rightside graphs in productions to use embeddings consistently, that means the embedding for a given nonterminal label must be the same at all occurences in the grammar. Otherwise we would try to analyze context-sensitive languages, which is known to be a np-complete problem.

4. Construction of Graphs and Visitation-Trees

Let us consider the graph-grammar in the appendix, which describes simple program-graphs, and the following host graph:

[g1]

By applying production 4 to the node "3:P" we get

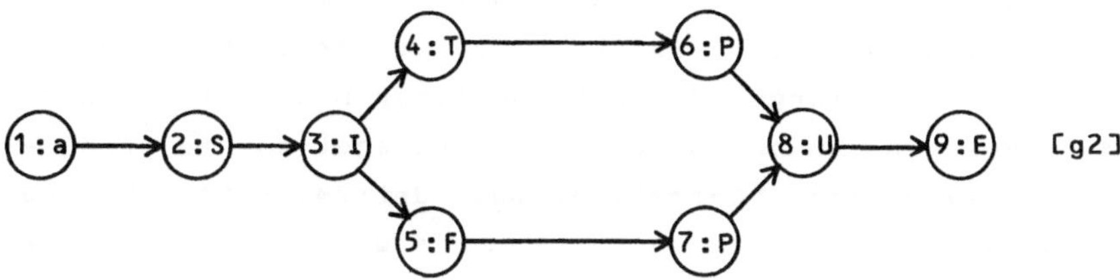

[g2]

This transformation is accomplished by removing the node except for its embedding edges and "catenating" the embedding edges of the rightside as described by the embedding function.

Putting the visitation trees together with the same mechanism, we may create a visitation tree for each produced graph. For example, the host-graph [g1] has a visitation-tree which is equal to itself. By applying production 4 we get the visitation-tree (laid on its left side)

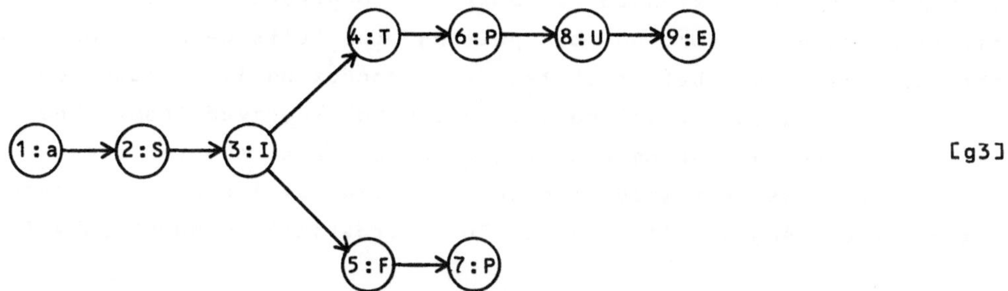

[g3]

If all visitation-trees in the grammar match each other, the result will always be an ordered tree. This property can be checked for statically. Note, that this does not really restrict the class of languages accepted, the visitation-tree is simply a kind of "guide" for the analyzer, and for nearly every grammar a suitable combination of visitation-trees can be found. As a matter of fact, they could be chosen by a backtracking algorithm which would try all possible combinations of visitation trees and generate PRE-Analyzers for them. But this would be a very time-consuming process and unpractical; and because the algorithm is intended to be used in a compiler-like way, the user must have complete knowlege of the sequence the analyzer choses beforehand.
Each graph produced by an extended graph-grammar carries its own (invisible) visitation-tree which may be reconstructed during analysis. For string languages, a LR-analyzer must only figure out, which productions in which sequence were applied to produce the sentential form given. The PRE-analyzer must determine too, by looking at the graph and its labels, which sequence was used to produce the input-graph.

Since each graph is assinged an order on its nodes, we may choose special derivation-sequences as "canonical" or "anticanonical". We will christen the preorder "canonical".

5. Derivation Graphs

An analog to the derivation-trees for string-grammars are the derivation-graphs which are defined as follows: For each production p=(g,h,b,f) of an extended grammar we construct the corresponding derivation-graph production by putting the leftside node above the rightside, with its label bracketed, and connecting it to each node in the rightside graph with edges labelled "d" (derived from). The new node gets a new embedding edge labelled "d", also the leftside node. The order which is impressed upon the rightside by its visitation-tree is marked by edges with label "o" (ordering). Production 5 from grammar A1 will yield the following:

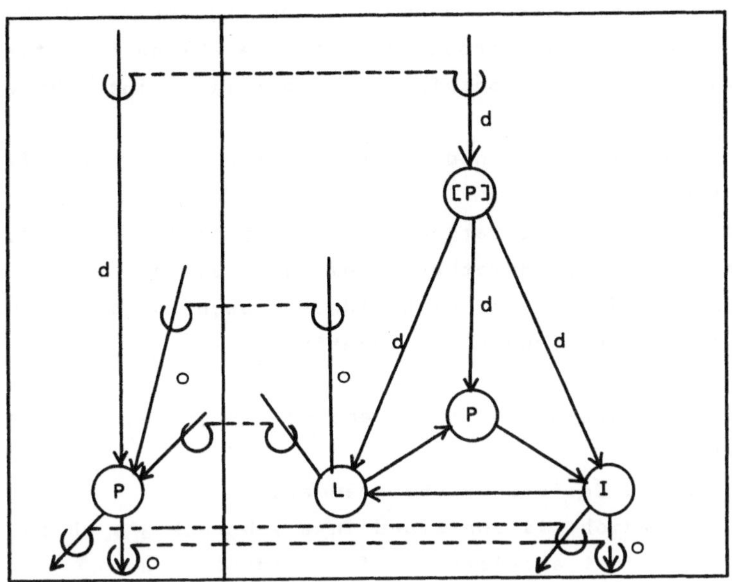

The derivation-graph productions form the derivation-graph-grammar which generates derivation graphs for all graphs produced by the original grammar. We simply apply the corresponding derivation-grammar production to the corresponding node in the derivation-graph at each step in the derivation. There is no need for a visitation tree in this production, since we use it only as a description tool.

A graph is called ambigous, if more than one different corresponding derivation-graph exists. Ambiguity may arise from two different causes:

- "real" ambiguity known from string-languages, which means that there are two or more sequences of productions for a given graph, and
- "visitation-tree"-ambiguity which arises if there exists more than one visitation-tree for a given graph.

Naturally, the algorithm will work only for unambigous grammars.

6. PRE - Classes

Our projected analyzer will walk through the input-graph along the visitation-tree, shifting and reducing like a LR-parser for string-grammars. We will divide the possible configurations into three groups:

- "shift": Shift the current input node, the "position" and identify it in the grammar.
- "backup": A leaf of the visitation-tree has been encountered, go to the father (grandfather..) of the position.
- "reduce": The last leaf of an rightside has been found. Apply the inverse of the production identified.

The parsing-decisions are based upon the scene of the graph: A scene is a triple sc=(g,v,i) where

- g is a graph which can be derived by the grammar,
- v is a node in g, which is contained in a subgraph g', which was generated by the final application of a production p.
- i is a natural number, which gives the number of times node v has already been visited during analysis. Another interpretation of i is that i gives the number of the son which will be the node-component in the successor-scene of sc.

Each possible scene belongs to at least one of the classes

- i shift(p,v) for all pairs of productions p and nodes v in p.
- ii backup(n) for all integers 1<=n<=m with m is the maximum depth of all visitation-trees.
- iii reduce(p) for all productions p.

Because the analyzer-algorithm is based upon the prefix-ordering of the visitation-tree, we will call these classes PRE-classes. They are an analog to the reduction-classes known from LR-theory.

The shift-type of classes has only one homologue in LR-analysis, because in strings one must not tell which way to go next in the string; there is only one way: left-to-right. In PRE-analysis, this single LR-shift-class has to be split into several new classes, because there may be more than one way to continue analysis.

There is no equivalent to the backup-classes in LR-analysis because the "visitation-tree" for string-languages would have only one branch and backing up in this tree is not required.

The classes for a given Grammar G will now be discussed in more detail.

The class shift(p,v) contains (g,v',i) iff:
- g is produced by the grammar G and
- there is a subgraph g' of g which was generated by final application of production p. v' is the father of the equivalent of v in g'; and v is the ith son and
- node v' has been visited i times during analysis so far.

With other words: let v' denote a position in g. Looking at the graph g around v', we see a subgraph which was constructed by application of production p. Sons 1..i-1 are already processed and the node v is equivalent to son number i. This son will be identified as v and shifted next.

The class backup(n) contains (g,v,1) iff
- g is generated by grammar G and there exists a subgraph g' of g which was generated by final application of a production p. v is a leaf of g', but not the last leaf.
- the differences in the levels (with respect to the visitation tree) of v and its successor is n-1.

"Backup" means that a leaf of a production was encountered, but other nodes must still be processed. Go back to the positions father (grandfather,...) and try again. Note that the visitation-counter for this type of class is always 1, since leafs are visited only once in a preorder walk on the tree.

The class reduce(p) contains (g,v,1) iff
- g can be derived by grammar G and there exists a subgraph g' of g which was generated by a final application of production p and
- v is the last (rightmost) leaf of g'.

The current position, e.g. the last node shifted, is the last node in the visitation-tree for production p. Apply the inverse of p to g'. If the rightside graph of production p contains n nodes, the last n nodes shifted (on the parsestack) are equivalent to p's rigthside nodes.

We will now give an example on how the parser walks along the graph given in [g2]. Analysis will start with the scene
(g2, #1:a, 1):
There is only one way to continue: shift node #2:S and identify it as being node #2:S in production 3. Next scene will be (g2, #2:S, 1):
The rightside of production 3 has entirely been shifted, now we may apply the inverse to the last shifted node, and get a new sentential form as input-graph:

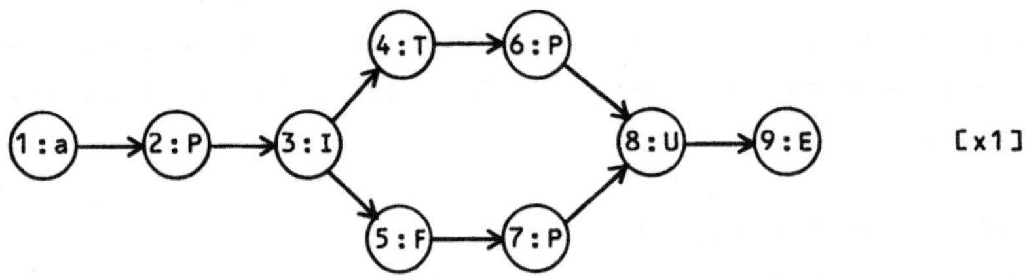

[x1]

The position after this manipulation is set back to the previous scene
(x1 , #1:a, 1):
Now we will shift again the next node in sequence:
(x1 , #2:P, 1):
According to our grammar, we can not reduce further, first (see production 2) all nodes past #2:P must be reduced to a single node with nonterminal label 'P'. What is to be done, is shift the next node, which appears to be element of PRE-class shift(5,#2), yielding scene
(x1, #3:I, 1):
The shifting will continue with shift(5,#3)
(x1, #5:T, 1):
and next action is shift(5,#5)
(x1, #7:P, 1):

Now we can't continue shifting, we have reached a leaf node of the visitation tree. We must backup two levels to node #3 and get
(x1, #3:I, 2):
We have already been in a scene with position on node #3 and decided then to go along the branch starting at node #5:T. But this was only at the first time. The vivisation-counter of node #3 beeing 2, we decide to shift node #4:F; the scene belongs to shift(5,#4).
(x1, #4:F, 1):
Now the parser continues to shift in the following steps

shift (5,#6)

(x1, #6:P, 1): shift (5,#7)

and we reach the scene
(x1, #8:U, 1):
This is the rightmost (last) leaf of the visitation tree in the production 4. If we apply the inverse of production 4 to the nodes shifted last, we will get the graph

[x2]

as new input to our analyzer. The position is reset to its last node before we entered the subgraph just removed (node 2:P). The parser will continue shifting, backing up and reducing until a scene in the class reduce(startproduction) is reached.

The PRE-classes in this form cannot be used for practical purposes. They are nonregular and of infinite size. But if the graph g in the scenes of form (g,v,i) are cut down to a fixed "look-around-depth" k around v and to the predecessor nodes of v, then we will get PRE(k)-classes which are regular sets.

7. PRE(k)-Classes

We will denote the subgraph spanned by a set of nodes M in a graph g by

SPAN(g,M)

and the set of nodes which can be reached from a node v in g on paths not longer than k edges by

CIRC(g,k,v).

The visitation-tree of a graph g with respect to Grammar G is written as

VT(G,g)

and the set of nodes with lower prefix-order than node v in an ordered tree b as

HEAD(b,v).

Then

CUT(g,k,v):= SPAN(g,HEAD(VT(G,g),v)∪CIRC(g,k,v))

is the subgraph of of g which contains only nodes with lower order than v or within a "radius" of k edges around v. This enables us to define the set of PRE(k)-classes for a given extended Grammar G:

Let Q be a PRE-class of G. The PRE(k)-class Q' for Q is

Q':= { (g',v,n) | (g,v,n) Q and g'=CUT(g,k,v) }.

If all PRE(k)-classes for G are disjoint, the grammar is unambiguos and we may apply the following algorithm to reconstruct the leftmost derivation for a given graph.

8. The Analyzer Algorithm

The following algorithm performs a syntactical analysis of an input graph, given a set of PRE-classes. It assumes the existence of functions SPAN(h,v) and CUT(g,k,v), which are defined as in section 7. Two different stacks are used, the parsestack, which is equivalent to the stack used in LR-parsers, and the visitstack, which is used to perform the prefix-walk on the visitation-tree of input-graph q. The function COUNT denotes the visitation-counter of q's nodes. q is destroyed during analysis; it is changed on each reduction.

```
Algorithm:    Syntaxanalyzer

q :           input-graph;
k :           integer;         (lookaround-depth)
i :           integer;
v :           node;
g :           graph;
parsestack : stack of nodes;  (for real parsing)
visitstack : stack of nodes;  (for walking the visitation tree)
begin
   v:= anchor-node;
   g:= CIRC(q,k,v);
   i:= COUNT(v):=COUNT(v)+1;
   while (g,v,i) reduce(startproduction) do
   begin
      if (g,v,i) shift(p,v') then
         push v onto parsestack;
         push v onto visitstack;
         v:=  equivalent of v' in g;
      else
      if (g,v,h) backup(n) then
         pop n entries from visitstack;
         v := top of visitstack;
      else
      if (g,v,h) reduce(p) then
         Apply the inverse of p to the last nodes
               pushed onto parsestack, modifying q;
         pop rightside of p off parsestack;
         pop last branch off visitstack;
         v:= position before entereing reduced subgraph;
      else
         syntax-error;
      fi;  fi;  fi;
      i := count(v) := count(v) + 1;
      g := CUT(g,k,v);
   end;    (analysis successful)
end;
```

9. Future Activities

A parser-generator for k=1 is currently under implementation at Dortmund. One of the next things to be done is to extend theory and the generator itself to grammars with non-constant embedding functions, which may allow generatioen, reversion and relabelling of edges in a production's embedding. There arise some new problems, like that canonical and anticanonical derivations may generate different languages (Due to the fact that embeddings cannot be consistent throughout the whole grammar in both types of derivations). Not all these problems are really solved yet, and much work remains to be done.

Another field for future research is the implementation of practical applications of graph-parsers.

10. Literatur

Ehr-75 H. Ehrig: Graph-Grammars. Problems and Results in View of Computer Science Applications. Techn. Rep. 75-21, FB Kybernetik, TU Berlin 1975

Fra-77 R. Franck: Precedence Graph Grammars. Theoretical Results and Documentation of an Implementation. Techn. Rep. 77-10, FB 20, TU Berlin 1977

Nag-76 M. Nagl: Formal Languages of Labelled Graphs. Computing 16, (1976), pp 113-137

Nag-78 M. Nagl: A Tutorial and Bibliographcal Survey on Graph Grammars. Universitaet Dortmund, Abteilung Informatik, Bericht Nr. 69, 1978

Nag-79 M. Nagl: Graph-Grammatiken. Theorie Implementierung Anwendungen. Vieweg & Sohn, Braunschweig 1979

Appendix: Example Grammar A1

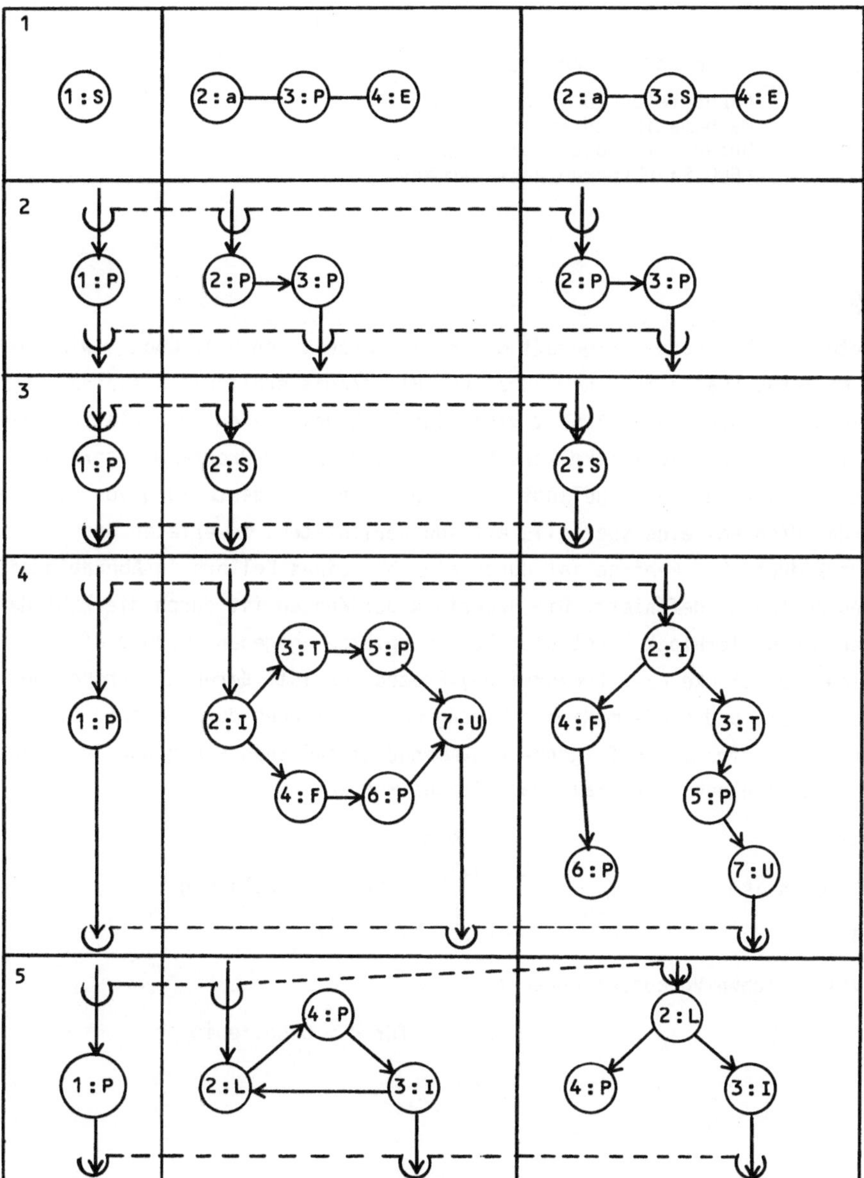

PLATZ- UND ZEITEFFIZIENTE REALISIERUNG DES LAUFZEITKELLERS BEI BLOCK-STRUKTURIERTEN PROGRAMMIERSPRACHEN

Bernd H. Schmidt

Fachbereich 10 - Angewandte
Mathematik und Informatik
Universität des Saarlandes
6600 Saarbrücken/West Germany

ZUSAMMENFASSUNG

Vor kurzem zeigte Kurt Mehlhorn - angeregt durch eine Arbeit von S.A. Cook - wie deterministische Kellerautomaten in einem günstigen Platz/Zeitverhältnis auf einer RAM implementiert werden können. Seine Arbeit gibt eine Methode, die auf die platz/zeiteffiziente Realisierung des Laufzeitkellers blockstrukturierter Programmiersprachen verallgemeinert werden kann. Damit gelingt die Lösung einer Fragestellung von G. Hotz. Wir betrachten das Problem, eine spezielle Art von gerichteten, bewerteten Graphen (Gebirgen) zu markieren. Ein Gebirge ist durch die Höhe eines Kellers in Abhängigkeit vom betrachteten Zeitpunkt definiert. Die Bewertung der Knoten ist durch die Zahl der von dem zugeordneten Kellerblock benötigten Speicherplätze gegeben. Wenn m die Anzahl der durchlaufenen Blöcke bzw. (rekursiven) Prozeduren ist, deren Kellerspeicherbedarf insgesamt n ist, und k die maximale Blockgröße, so können durch Angabe einer Familie von Markierungsstrategien folgende Zusammenhänge zwischen Platz und Zeit einer Realisierung für den schlechtesten Fall hergeleitet werden :

Platz	Zeit
$O((1/c)6^c \log n \cdot k)$	$n^{1+1/c}$ für $c > 0$ beliebig
$O(\sqrt{n} \cdot k)$	$n \cdot 2^{O(\log \log n)}$

und mit zusätzlichen Voraussetzungen :

$O((c+c \cdot n^{1/c}) \cdot k)$	$6^{c-1} \cdot n$ für $c > 0$ beliebig

I. EINFÜHRUNG

K. Mehlhorn zeigte kürzlich, wie deterministische Kellerautomaten mittels einer Strategie für das Markenspiel auf Graphen effizient implementiert werden können. Das Markenspiel wird auf gerichteten Graphen gespielt. Das Ziel des Spiels ist, ausgehend von einem (oder mehreren) ausgezeichneten Anfangsknoten durch sukkzessives Belegen der Knoten mit Spielsteinen (Marken), einen (oder mehrere) ausgezeichnete Endknoten zu markieren. Dabei darf ein Knoten nur dann markiert werden, wenn alle seine "Vorgänger" bereits mit Marken belegt sind.

Wir betrachten nun eine beliebige blockstrukturierte Programmiersprache (für die formale Definition siehe z.B. Hotz bzw. Kopp). Zur Implementierung von Blockstrukturen bzw. (rekursiven) Prozeduren zur Laufzeit werden i. allg. Keller benutzt. Außer einigen technischen Daten wie Rücksprungadresse usw. werden die lokalen Variablen jedes Blocks auf dem Keller abgelegt. Dies kann jedoch gerade bei rekursiven Prozeduren platzaufwendig sein. Da man jeden Block eines Programms als Prozedur auffassen kann (Prozedurdefinition gefolgt von "call"), wollen wir uns im folgenden der Einfachheit halber auf Prozeduren beschränken. Genau wie Gurari/Ibarra lassen wir rekursive Unterprogrammtechniken zu mit gewissen Einschränkungen an die Parameter und globalen Variablen. Wir können allerdings bei gleicher Schranke für den Platzbedarf einer Kellerrealisierung eine kleinere, $n^{1+1/k}$-Schranke für die Zeit nachweisen, wo Gurari/Ibarra eine exponentielle Zeitschranke angeben. Swami/Savage betrachten ausschließlich linearrekursive Prozeduren (d.h. ein Aufruf kann höchstens einen weiteren Aufruf hervorrufen). Sie zeigen z.B. für ein Programm, das m-fach rekursiv aufgerufen wird, daß der Speicherplatz auf $\sqrt{m}$ beschränkt werden kann bei nur einem konstanten Zuwachs in der Rechenzeit; uns gelingt es, das gleiche Ergebnis für generelle blockstrukturierte Programme zu zeigen. Außerdem können sie für ihre Methode (ebenfalls ein Markenspiel auf speziellen Graphen) eine untere Schranke zeigen.

Im zweiten Teil wollen wir die Verbindung von blockstrukturierten Programmen bzw. deren Laufzeitkeller-Realisierung zu einem dadurch definierten speziellen Graphen (Gebirge) aufzeigen. Im dritten Teil geben wir eine Familie von Algorithmen an, die unter Benutzung des Gebirge-Modells eine Zeit/Platz-Hierarchie für die Realisierung des Laufzeitkellers definiert. Platz- und Zeitbedarf unserer Algorithmen schätzen wir im vierten Teil ab und gehen zuletzt auf praktische Aspekte wie Realisierbarkeit und Anpassungsfähigkeit ein. Kurt Mehlhorn gilt der Dank für viele fruchtbare Diskussionen.

II. BLOCK-STRUKTURIERTE PROGRAMME UND GEBIRGE

Wir wollen zunächst eine Zuordnung zwischen dem Laufzeitkeller spezieller blockstrukturierter Programme und dadurch definierten gerichteten Graphen, die wir Gebirge nennen, herstellen.

Da man jeden Block als Prozedurdefinition gefolgt vom zugehörigen Prozeduraufruf auffassen kann, wollen wir uns aus Gründen der Benennung ausschließlich auf (ineinander verschachtelte) Prozeduren beschränken. Die Prozeduren können, wie bei Gurari/Ibarra, folgende Parameter und Variablen benutzen :

(1) Eingabe-Parameter
(2) Ausgabe-Parameter

(3) lokale Variablen

(4) globale nur-lese Variablen

(5) globale nur-schreibe Variablen

Wir wollen alle Parameter als "value"-Parameter (oder äquivalent dazu) vereinbaren .

Eine Prozedur p habe etwa folgendes syntaktische Aussehen :

<u>procedure</u> $p(v_1,\ldots,v_s)$

<u>var</u> $v_{s+1},\ldots,v_{n_p}$

<Anweisungsteil>

<u>return</u> p

Unsere Einschränkungen an die Programme sind rein syntaktisch bereits zur Compile-Zeit überprüfbar.

<u>Definition:</u> Die Anzahl der lokalen Variablen und Übergabeparameter n_p einer Prozedur p bezeichnen wir als <u>Gewicht</u> von p.

Da die globalen Variablen nicht auf dem Keller abgelegt werden müssen, lassen wir sie bei allen Komplexitätsbetrachtungen unbeachtet.

Sei jetzt $(p_1,\ldots,p_m)$ die Liste von nicht notwendig verschiedenen Prozedurnamen in der Reihenfolge ihres Aufrufs zur Laufzeit.

Wir bezeichnen mit c_i den Aufruf von p_i und mit r_i die Rückkehr aus p_i für $1 \leq i \leq m$. n_i ist das Gewicht von p_i.

Bei jedem call p_i wird zur Laufzeit ein weiterer Block zur Aufnahme der technischen Daten von p_i sowie der Variablen $v_1,\ldots,v_{n_i}$ gekellert.

Dieser Block wird beim entsprechenden return p_i wieder freigegeben.

Die Höhe des Kellers zum Zeitpunkt t entspricht der Anzahl der zu diesem Zeitpunkt benutzten Blöcke.

Um die Höhe des so benutzten Kellers in Abhängigkeit von der Zeit genauer beschreiben zu können, wollen wir jetzt eine Graphenklasse definieren, die uns als Abbild der Kellerbewegungen zu verschiedenen Zeiten und damit als Werkzeug zur effizienten Implementierung einer Folge $(p_1,\ldots,p_m)$ von Prozeduraufrufen dienen wird.

Wir können uns die Prozeduren entsprechend ihrer Aufruffolge syntaktisch ineinander geschachtelt vorstellen. Dann ist der Folge $(p_1,\ldots,p_m)$ eine Folge $S = (s_1,\ldots,s_{2m})$ eindeutig zugeordnet mit

$s_i \in \{c_1,\ldots,c_m\} \cup \{r_1,\ldots,r_m\}$ für $1 \leq i \leq 2m$

Wir geben für die geplante Konstruktion ein Beispiel :

Wir nehmen an, die Prozeduren $f(x_1,x_2,x_3)$ mit var x_4

$g(y_1,y_2)$ (ohne lokale Variablen)

und $h(z_1,z_2,z_3,z_4)$ mit var z_5,z_6,z_7

seien gegeben (n_f=4, n_g=2, n_h=7). In Abhängigkeit von Bedingungen und Werten, auf die wir nicht näher eingehen, soll der Aufruf jeder Prozedur (inklusive sich selbst) in jeder Prozedur möglich sein.

Wir stellen uns vor, die Prozeduren wären gemäß der Semantik zur Laufzeit syntaktisch geschachtelt, z.B.

```
call f(x1,x2,x3)
 :
    call f(x1',x2',x3')
     :
        call g(y1,y2)
         :
        return g
         :
        call h(z1,z2,z3,z4)
         :
            call f(x1",x2",x3")
             :
            return f
             :
        return h
         :
    return f
     :
    call g(y1',y2')
     :
    return g
     :
return f
```

Wir haben damit $(p_1,\ldots,p_6)$ = (f,f,g,h,f,g) und $(s_1,\ldots,s_{12})$ =

$(c_f,c_f,c_g,r_g,c_h,c_f,r_f,r_h,r_f,c_g,r_g,r_f)$.

Es ergibt sich das folgende Gebirge :

Abbildung 1: Ein Gebirge mit 2m+1 = 13 Knoten für 6 Prozeduraufrufe und dem Speicherbedarf n = 29

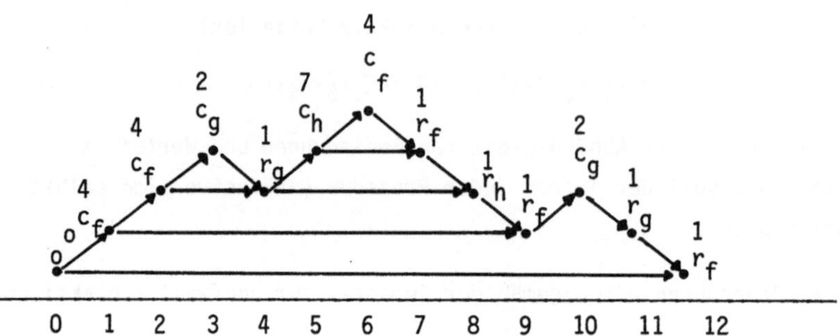

Wir wollen jetzt ein zu einer Folge S gehöriges Gebirge G(S) genauer definieren :

Definition:

Ein Gebirge der Länge 2m+1 zu einer Folge S ist ein gewichteter Graph G(S)=G=(V,E) mit bewerteter Knotenmenge V (der Einfachheit halber verzichten wir auf den Bezug zu S), wobei

1) $V = V' \cup \{0\}$

$$V' = \{c_1,\dots,c_m\} \cup \{r_1,\dots,r_m\} = \{s_1,\dots,s_{2m}\}$$

2) Es existiert eine Funktion

Höhe : $V \to \mathbb{N} \cup \{0\}$ mit

Höhe(0) = 0; Höhe(c_1) = 1

und für $2 \leq i \leq m$ ist

$$\text{Höhe}(s_i) = \begin{cases} \text{Höhe}(s_{i-1})-1 & \text{falls } s_i \in \{r_1,\dots,r_m\} \\ \text{Höhe}(s_{i-1})+1 & \text{falls } s_i \in \{c_1,\dots,c_m\} \end{cases}$$

3) Es existiert eine Bewertungsfunktion

$n^*: V \to \mathbb{N} \cup \{0\}$ mit

$n^*(0) = 0$

$$n^*(s_i) = \begin{cases} 1 & \text{falls } s_i \in \{r_1,\dots,r_m\} \\ n_i & \text{falls } s_i \in \{c_1,\dots,c_m\} \end{cases}$$

4) $E = \{(s_i,s_{i+1});\ 1 \leq i \leq 2m-1\} \cup \{(0,s_1)\} \cup$

$$\{(s_i,s_j);\ i < j \text{ und Höhe}(s_i) = \text{Höhe}(s_j) < \text{Höhe}(s_r) \quad \text{für alle } i < r \leq j\}$$

Bemerkung:

(1) Wegen einer übersichtlicheren Darstellung definieren wir eine Funktion

$\bar{n} : [0:2m] \to \mathbb{N} \cup \{0\}$ durch

$\bar{n}(0) = 0$

$\bar{n}(i) = \sum_{k=1}^{i} n^*(s_k)$; wir setzen $n := \bar{n}(2m)$

$\bar{n}$ läßt sich bei gegebenem n^* leicht berechnen (und umgekehrt).

(2) Da genau zum Zeitpunkt des Aufrufs einer Prozedur ein weiterer Block gekellert wird, bewerten wir die c_i (d.h. call p_i) mit der von p_i benötigten Blockgröße.

Definition:

a) Der linke Nachbar von s_i ist

s_{i-1} falls Höhe(s_{i-1}) < Höhe(s_i)

oder

s_j falls $(s_j,s_i) \in E$ mit $j < i$ und Höhe(s_j) = Höhe(s_i)

b) s_j heißt sichtbar von s_i, falls $j \leq i$ und für alle r; $j < r \leq i$ ist Höhe(s_j) < Höhe(s_r)

Die hier gegebenen Definitionen unterscheiden sich von den Mehlhorn'schen nur insofern, als daß die Knoten bewertet und gleich entsprechend der Anwendung bezeichnet sind.

III. DER ALGORITHMUS

Wenn wir den benötigten Laufzeitkeller möglichst klein halten wollen, so können wir das nur, indem wir gewisse Teile des Kellers nicht aufheben, sondern uns darauf verlassen, sie wieder erzeugen zu können. Das Markieren eines Knoten c_j entspricht dem Abspeichern des zur Prozedur p_j gehörenden Verwaltungsblocks. Das Wegnehmen einer Marke von c_j entspricht dem Freigeben des Blockes von p_j. Es ist klar, daß bei gewöhnlicher Kellerverarbeitung alle von einer Stelle t des Gebirges aus sichtbaren Punkte gerade den Inhalt des gesamten Kellers zum Zeitpunkt t beschreiben. Um den benötigten Speicherplatz zu verringern, müssen von diesen sichtbaren Punkten diejenigen markiert werden, die zur Auswertung der Prozedur an der Stelle t benötigt werden und die bei der Wiederberechnung der bereits gelöschten Kellerblöcke von Nutzen sind. Unsere Markierungsstrategie wird von drei Prinzipien dominiert :

1. Je mehr Zeit zwischen dem aktuellen und einem früheren Prozeduraufruf vergangen ist, desto wichtiger wird der diesem früheren Prozeduraufruf zugeordnete Punkt des Gebirges. (Dies wird sich in der Definition des Typs einer Marke widerspiegeln).
2. Da unsere Prozeduren sich wegen obiger Einschränkung nur auf eine lokale Umgebung

beziehen, wollen wir möglichst viel dieser Umgebung in unserem Keller lassen. (Dies spiegelt sich in der Definition unserer Funktion f wider).

3. Täler sind wichtiger als Berge.

Da die eben aufgezeigten Prinzipien jeden Zeitpunkt t gleichermaßen betreffen, liegt eine "teile und beherrsche"-Strategie nahe.
Das Teilen wird mittels einer Funktion f realisiert, die wie folgt definiert wird :

Sei $f : \mathbb{N} \cup \{0\} \to \mathbb{N}$ eine Funktion mit

(1) $f(0) = 1$

(2) $f(d+1) \geq 2f(d)$; also $f(d) \geq 2^d$

(3) Die Binärdarstellung von f(d) kann bei gegebener Binärdarstellung von d in log f(d) Platz berechnet werden.

Die Anzahl der Stufen der "teile und beherrsche"-Strategie wird durch d gegeben. Der Einfachheit halber schreiben wir dort, wo kein Mißverständnis möglich ist, statt s_i einfach i. Eine Strategie der Ordnung d kann auf ein Gebirge M der Länge 2m+1 angewendet werden, falls $\bar{n}(2m) = n \leq f(d+1)$. Seien v,v+1,...,v+2m die Knoten von M. Ziel der Strategie ist das Markieren des Knoten v+2m.

Definition: Eine Menge von Marken, die sich auf eine Marke (g,r), die auf u liegt, stützt, besteht aus (g,r) selbst und aus allen Marken mit Typ < g auf Knoten z, wo $u \leq z$, und kein Knoten zwischen u und z trägt eine Marke vom Typ $\geq$ g.

Es werden zwei Arten von Marken benötigt :
Rekursionsmarken und gewöhnlich Marken. Eine Strategie der Ordnung d benötigt d Rekursionsmarken für jedes e, $1 \leq e \leq d$, und für jedes g, $0 \leq g \leq d$ werden $\lceil f(g+1)/f(g) \rceil$ normale Marken vom Typ g benötigt. Diese werden mit (g,0),(g,1),... bezeichnet. Die zweite Komponente einer Marke wollen wir als ihren Index, die erste als ihren Typ bezeichnen.

Wir speichern in jeder Marke den Block von p_i, falls sie auf c_i liegt.
Wir wollen annehmen, daß auf v zu Beginn eine Marke vom Typ > d liegt.
Diese Marke wird während des ganzen Spiels auf M auf v verbleiben.
Eine Strategie der Ordnung d wird folgendermaßen gespielt:

Falls $n \leq f(d)$ wird auf M eine Strategie der Ordnung d-1 gespielt.

Falls d = o (d.h. $n \leq f(1)$), markieren wir nacheinander die Knoten v+i mit den Marken (0,i), und entfernen dann die Marken von allen Knoten, die nicht von v+2m aus sichtbar sind. Sei jetzt $d \geq 1$ und $n > f(d)$, dann wird M in n/f(d) Teilgebirge geteilt. Genauer enthält für $0 \leq j \leq \lceil n/f(d) \rceil - 1 \leq \lceil f(d+1)/f(d) \rceil - 1$ das j-te Teilgebirge diejenigen Punkte s mit

$\bar{n}(s) \in [\bar{n}(v) + j \cdot f(d), \min(\bar{n}(v+2m), \bar{n}(v) + (j+1)f(d) - 1)]$

Das Spielen von M beginnt damit, eine Marke (d,0) auf v zu legen. (Index-0 Marken werden immer auf bereits markierte Knoten gelegt). Dazu ist u.U. vorher das Aufnehmen der Marke (d,0) und aller sich darauf stützenden Marken notwendig.
Wir nehmen jetzt an, daß wir gerade die Marke (d,j) auf den ersten Knoten des j-ten Teilgebirges gelegt haben.
Sei i dieser Knoten. Dann gilt die folgende Invariante :

a) Sei $j' \leq j$. Falls das j'-te Teilgebirge einen von i sichtbaren Punkt enthält, dann trägt der meistlinke sichtbare Punkt dieses Teilgebirges die Marke (d,j').

b) Falls $u \leq i$ markiert ist, dann ist u von i aus sichtbar. Sei weiterhin w irgendein von i aus sichtbarer Punkt und sei d' $0 \leq d' \leq d$ beliebig. Sei $u \leq w$ der meist rechte Knoten, der eine Marke vom Typ d' hält (falls existiert). Dann ist $\bar{n}(w) < \bar{n}(u) + f(d')$.

Bemerkung: Folgende Idee liegt unserer Invarianten zugrunde :
Eine Marke vom Typ d' dient der Bewältigung eines Teilgebirges mit einer Länge von höchstens f(d') (falls alle Gewichte 1 sind). Falls w sichtbar ist, und u der meist rechte Punkt $\leq w$, der eine Marke trägt, dann dient die Marke auf u zum Spielen von w.

Man betrachte das j-te Teilgebirge genauer :
Sei die Folge $v_0, v_1, \ldots, v_k$ von Punkten im j-ten Teilgebirge definiert durch

a) v_0 ist der erste Punkt im j-ten Teilgebirge

b) $v_{\ell+1} = \min\{r;\ v_\ell < r \text{ und Höhe}(v_\ell) \geq \text{Höhe}(r)\}$.

Weiterhin ist v_{k+1} der erste Punkt im (j+1)-ten Teilgebirge. Dann ist entweder

$$\text{Höhe}(v_\ell) \leq \text{Höhe}(v_{\ell+1}) \qquad (= \text{ für } \ell < k)$$

oder

$$\text{Höhe}(v_\ell) - 1 = \text{Höhe}(v_{\ell+1}) \text{ und } v_{\ell+1} = v_\ell + 1$$

Das j-te Teilgebirge wird nun folgendermaßen gespielt :

<u>for</u> $\ell = 0$ <u>to</u> k <u>do</u>

<u>begin</u> <u>*co*</u> *Die Marke (d,j) ist auf Knoten* v_ℓ *und die Invariante gilt mit* $i = v_\ell$

    <u>if</u> $\text{Höhe}(v_\ell) \leq \text{Höhe}(v_{\ell+1})$

    <u>then</u> Sei d' minimal mit $\bar{n}(v_\ell) + f(d') \geq \bar{n}(v_{\ell+1})$

        <u>*Co*</u> *d' ist sicher* $\leq$ *d;*

(A)   Spiele Strategie der Ordnung (d'-1) auf dem Gebirge $v_\ell, v_{\ell+1}, \ldots, v_{\ell+1}-1$;
        <u>*Co*</u> *An dieser Stelle liegt die Marke (d,j) immer noch auf* v_ℓ *und auch* $v_{\ell+1}-1$ *ist markiert;*

    <u>fi</u>

        ersetze die Marke auf $v_{\ell+1}-1$ durch die Rekursions-Marke vom Typ d;
        Sei t der linke Nachbar von $v_{\ell+1}$,

sei $u \leq t$ der meist rechte Knoten, der eine Marke trägt,und sei d' der Typ der Marke auf u

co *Wegen Teil b) der Invariante ist $\bar{n}(u) + f(d') \geq \bar{n}(t)$;*

Sei d" minimal mit $\bar{n}(u) + f(d'') \geq \bar{n}(t)$;

(B) Spiele eine Strategie der Ordnung (d"-1) auf u,...,t

Entferne Marke (d,j) (bzw. (d,j+1)) und alle Marken, die sich auf sie stützen, vom Gebirge

(C) Lege Marke (d,j) (bzw. (d,j+1)) auf den Knoten $v_{\ell+1}$, falls $\ell < k$ (bzw. $\ell = k$);

entferne von allen Punkten, die von $v_{\ell+1}$ nicht sichtbar sind, die Marken

co *hier gilt die Invariante für $i = v_{\ell+1}$;*

end

Damit ist die Beschreibung einer Strategie der Ordnung d in Abhängigkeit einer gegebenen Funktion f abgeschlossen.

Auf einem beliebigen Gebirge M der Länge 2m+1 mit $n = \bar{n}$ (2m) spielen wir immer eine Strategie der Ordnung d mit dem kleinstmöglichen d, d.h. $f(d) < n \leq f(d+1)$.

Die Einschränkung unserer Prozeduren bzgl. der globalen Variablen stellt sicher, daß beim Wiederberechnen eines linken Nachbarn immer das gleiche Resultat erzielt wird.

IV. PLATZ- UND ZEITBEDARF

Zunächst wollen wir den Platzbedarf unserer Markierungsstrategie und somit einer Realisierung des Laufzeitkellers einer blockstrukturierten Programmiersprache mittels unserer Algorithmen abschätzen. Im schlechtesten Fall kann eine Prozedur allein den Hauptanteil der insgesamt benötigten Speicherplätze (nämlich n-2(m-1)) benötigen. In einem realen Programm werden jedoch sinnvollerweise mehr Prozeduren aufgerufen als definiert. Die maximal benötigte Kellerblockgröße kann zur Compile-Zeit bereits bestimmt werden. Wir wollen deshalb $k = \max\{n_i | 1 \leq i \leq m\}$ setzen. Wir legen eine RAM mit Einheitskostenmaß als Berechnungsmodell zugrunde. (Speicherkosten einer (beliebig langen) Zahl sind 1).

Da nur sichtbare Marken auf dem Gebirge liegen können, ist sichergestellt, daß die sowieso benötigte, maximale Kellerhöhe niemals überschritten werden kann.

Beim Markieren eines return-Knotens r_i wird ein call-Knoten weniger sichtbar, was dem Freigeben eines Blockes auf dem Keller entspricht.

Definition: Sei f wie oben beschrieben, $n \in \mathbb{N}$

$$d_0(n,f) = \min\{d;\ n \leq f(d+1)\}$$

$$N(n,f) = \sum_{d=0}^{d_o(n,f)} (2 + \lceil f(d+1)/f(d) \rceil)$$

$N(n,f) = \Omega(\log n)$ für alle Funktionen f, die der angegebenen Definition genügen.

Aus der Beschreibung unserer Strategie folgt, daß nie mehr als N(n,f) Marken benutzt werden.

Daraus folgt das

Lemma 1: Sei f wie oben beschrieben und sei M ein Gebirge mit 2m+1 Knoten und $\bar{n}(2m) = n$. Dann benutzt unsere Strategie höchstens N(n,f) Marken auf M.

Wir wollen uns nun der Zeitanalyse unserer Strategie zuwenden.

Wir gehen davon aus, daß der Zeitbedarf einer Prozedur im wesentlichen von der Zahl der von ihr benutzten Parameter bestimmt wird.

Durch geeignete Verallgemeinerung und mit der Beobachtung, daß die Definitionen von "sichtbar", "Höhe" und "Nachbarschaft" von der Bewertung der Knoten unabhängig sind, folgt analog zu Mehlhorn das

Lemma 2: Sei f beliebig wie oben beschrieben. Sei T(n,d) die maximale Anzahl von Zügen einer Strategie der Ordnung d auf einem Gebirge M der Länge 2m+1 mit $\bar{n}(2m) = n$. Dann ist

$$T(2,d) = 3 \qquad T(n,0) \leq 2m+1$$

$$T(n,d) \leq T_A + T_B + T_C + (\lceil n/f(d) \rceil - 1)\, T(f(d-1),d-2) + (\lceil n/f(d) \rceil - 2)\, T(f(d),d-1)$$

wobei

$$T_A = \max \left\{ \sum_{i=o}^{k} (1+T(y_i,e_i)); \quad \begin{array}{l} 0 \leq e_i \leq d-1 \\ f(e_i) < y_i \leq f(e_i+1) \\ y_o+\ldots+y_k \leq n \end{array} \right\}$$

$$T_B = \max \left\{ \sum_{i=o}^{k'} T(\min(f(h_i+1),2z_i),h_i) \quad \begin{array}{l} 0 \leq h_i \leq d-1 \\ f(h_i) < z_i \leq f(h_i+1) \\ z_o+\ldots+z_{k'} \leq n \end{array} \right\}$$

$$T_C = \sum_{g=1}^{d-1} \left(\left\lceil \frac{n}{f(d)} \right\rceil - 1\right) \left\lceil \frac{f(d)}{f(d-1)} \right\rceil \cdots \left\lceil \frac{f(g+1)}{f(g)} - 1 \right\rceil \cdot T(f(g),g-1)$$

Durch Induktion über d läßt sich eine einfache Schranke für T(n,d) zeigen, so daß die Maximalzahl der Züge abgeschätzt wird durch das

Lemma 3: $T(n,d) \leq n \cdot 6^{d-1}$

Die Folge $S = (s_1,\ldots,s_{2m})$ definiert in natürlicher Weise ein Gebirge.
Man hat in jeder Marke ihre Position (d.h. den Zeitpunkt des Markierens), Typ und Index, die Position des größten sichtbaren Knotens, die Adresse der gerade aufzurufenden bzw. zu verlassenden und, falls der Knoten, auf dem sie liegt, ein c-Knoten

ist, den zu diesem gehörenden Block zu speichern. Dies benötigt im Einheitskostenmaß k+3 Speicherzellen, wobei $k = \max\{n_i | 1 \leq i \leq m\}$ wie oben definiert.

Man kann $s_1,\ldots,s_{2m}$ als Wort einer speziellen Klammersprache auffassen, indem man für jede syntaktisch definierte Prozedur (endlich viele!) einen neuen Klammertyp definiert, bei dem ein c eine öffnende und ein r eine schließende Klammer bedeutet. Mit jedem Eingabezeichen ändert sich die Höhe des Kellers. Wir haben also eine spezielle Sprache eines eingabebetriebenen deterministischen Kellerautomaten vor uns (Mehlhorn). Die Höhe des Kellers als Funktion der Zeit definiert ein Gebirge. Allerdings müssen wir uns im Unterschied zu Mehlhorn in jeder Marke anstatt eines Kellersymbols den Block und die Adresse der entsprechenden Prozedur speichern. Dadurch benötigt eine Marke höchstens Platz O(k). (Die Zahl k kann bereits vom Compiler ermittelt und zusammen mit dem Wort $s_1,\ldots,s_{2m}$ an den Kellerautomaten übergeben werden).

Satz: Der Laufzeitkeller eines blockstrukturierten Programms mit m Block-(Prozedur-) Aufrufen, deren Speicherbedarf insgesamt n ist und dessen Anzahl im wesentlichen der Anzahl der benutzten Speicherplätze entspricht, kann in Platz/Zeit

a) $O((1/c)\ 6^c \log n \cdot k)$ $\quad n^{1+1/c}$ für $c > o$ beliebig

b) $O(\sqrt{n} \cdot k)$ $\quad n2^{O(\log \log n)}$

und bei Kenntnis von n

c) $O((c+cn^{1/c}) \cdot k)$ $\quad O(6^{c-1}n)$ für $c > o$ beliebig

realisiert werden.

Beweis: Teil a) Benutze $f(g) = s^g$ wobei s so gewählt ist, daß $\log 6/\log s = 1/c$. Dann ist $d+1 = \log n/\log s$, wodurch die Anzahl der Marken durch $(d+1)(2+s) = \log n \cdot (2+s)/\log s = \log n(2+6^c)/(c \log 6)$. Die Zeitschranke ist $n^{1+1/c}$. Benutze für Teil b) $f(g) = 2^{2g}$ und für Teil c) $f(g) = (n^{1/c})^g$. Dann ist $d+1 = c$ und somit die Platzschranke $2c+c \cdot n^{1/c}$ und die Zeitschranke $6^{c-1} \cdot n$. Die Zahl n kann durch Iteration mit konstantem Platz in linearer Zeit im voraus berechnet werden.

Teil a) unseres Satzes reduziert die bei Gurari/Ibarra benötigte Zeit vom Exponentiellen zum nahezu Linearen. Teil c) verallgemeinert das erstaunliche Ergebnis von Swami/Savage, daß konstante Vervielfältigung der Rechenzeit einen Gewinn der Größenordnung der Wurzel im Platz erbringt, auf allgemein blockstrukturierte Programme bei gleichen Voraussetzungen.

V. REALISIERBARKEIT UND ANPASSUNGSFÄHIGKEIT

Unsere Strategie kann als Betriebssystemkomponente im Laufzeitsystem implementiert werden. Die Markierungsstrategie, versorgt mit dem aktuellen Laufzeitkeller und der aktuellen Teile-Funktion f, kann als Unterprogramm eines Programms zur Kellerverwal-

tung realisiert werden. Die Markengröße läßt sich mittels Zeigerverwaltung bzw. Adressrechnung jeweils der aktuell benötigten Blockgröße anpassen, so daß man u.U. wesentlich unter dem in der Schranke unseres Satzes angegebenen Speicherplatzaufwand bleibt.
Durch geschickte Wahl der jeweils entsprechenden Funktion f ist eine dynamische Anpassung an reale Speicherplatzgegebenheiten leicht möglich.

Zunächst folgende Beobachtungen :
Wir betrachten Funktionen der Form $f(d) = (2^i)^d$, $i \in \mathbb{N}$.
Es gelten folgende Zusammenhänge:

(1) Je größer i gewählt werden kann, desto mehr Marken werden von unserer Strategie benutzt.

(2) Aus gegebener maximaler Kellergröße r läßt sich leicht ein maximales $i_0 = i(r)$ berechnen.

Man geht nun folgendermaßen vor : Zunächst benutzt man den üblichen Kellermechanismus. Wird mehr als r Platz benutzt, beginnt man mit einer Strategie der Ordnung d, wobei $f(d) = (2^{i_0})^d$ benutzt wird. Reicht dann im Verlauf der Rechnung wiederum der Platz nicht, so geht man zu $f_{i_0-1}(d) = (2^{i_0-1})^d$ über, u.s.w.

Diese Art der Realisierung hat den Vorteil, bei normalem Kellerbetrieb höchstens den Programmspeicherplatz der Markierungsstrategie als "overhead" zu haben, da zunächst das Hauptprogramm die Aufträge an den Kellermechanismus sofort durchreicht.

Betriebssysteme, die mit einer solchen Markierungsstrategie ausgerüstet sind, erlauben jetzt das Implementieren stark rekursiv und prozedural orientierter, höherer Programmiersprachen (LISP, PASCAL, PL/1,...) auf kleinen und kleinsten Rechnern. Dies ist im Moment in der Praxis ein besonders relevantes Problem. Gerade wo intelligente, wirkungsvolle Programme mit relativ geringem eigenen Speicherbedarf zum Aufbau komplizierter Datenstrukturen eingesetzt werden (Datenbanken), ist die Verwendung rekursiver Unterprogrammtechniken unumgänglich. Besonders dann aber (Rekursionstiefe hängt von Daten ab), ermöglicht unsere Strategie noch die Programmausführung, wo bei gewöhnlichen Kellermechanismen der Speicherplatz nicht gereicht hätte. Dafür wird ein vertretbarer Preis an Berechnungszeit gezahlt.

Eine Markierungsstrategie der angegebenen Art läßt sich leicht in ein Betriebssystem einfügen und kann unabhängig von Art und Umfang der gegebenen Programmiersprachen bzw. deren Compiler arbeiten, da sie eine einfache und eindeutige Schnittstelle besitzt $((s_1,n^*(1)), (s_2, n^*(2)),\ldots,)$. Der Umfang der Implementierungsarbeit läßt sich leicht aus dem angegebenen Algorithmus ablesen und dürfte begrenzt sein. (Das Hauptprogramm ist sehr einfach). Auch der Speicherbedarf des Programms liegt in realistischen Grenzen.

LITERATUR

S.A. Cook : Deterministic CFL's are accepted simultaneously in polynomial time and log squared tape, 11th ACM-STOC, 1979, 338-345

E.M. Gurari, O.H. Ibarra : On the Space Complexity of Recursive Algorithms, Inf. Proc. Letters, Vol. 8, No. 5, 1979, 267-272

G. Hotz : Grundlagen einer Theorie der Programmiersprachen II : Rekursive und nichtrekursive Unterprogramme, FB 10, Universität des Saarlandes, Bericht Nr. A 01/72, 1972

H. Kopp : Beiträge zur Theorie der Programmiersprachen, BMFT-GMD 97, 1975

K. Mehlhorn : Pebbling Mountain Ranges and its Application to DCFL-Recognition, Bericht Nr. A 79/13, FB 10 der Universität des Saarlandes, erscheint bei 7. ICALP, Nordwijkerhout 1980

B.H. Schmidt : Über den Zusammenhang von Platz und Zeit bei der Implementierung von Blockstrukturen, Dissertation, FB 10, Universität des Saarlandes, in Vorbereitung

S. Swami, J. Savage : Space-Time Tradeoffs for linear Recursion, 6th ACM Symposium on Principles of Programming Languages, 1979, 135-142

Ein Sortierverfahren für Registermaschinen+

(Zusammenfassung)

Stefan Reisch
Fakultät für Mathematik
Universität Bielefeld
D-4800 Bielefeld 1

Wir geben einen Sortieralgorithmus für Registermaschinen an, wie sie in [1] definiert sind und die Additionen, modifizierte Subtraktionen, Multiplikationen und ganzzahlige Divisionen in einem Schritt durchführen können. Dieser Sortieralgorithmus sortiert n natürliche Zahlen $x_1,\dots,x_n$, die die Bedingung (*) erfüllen, in uniformer Zeitkomplexität von $O(n)+O(c)$.

(*) $$\forall_{i,j}(1\le i,j\le n):(x_1>x_j)\Rightarrow x_i\ge(1+1/2^c)x_j.$$

Grundlegend hierfür ist ein linearer Sortieralgorithmus, der unter der schwächeren Bedingung (**) korrekt arbeitet.

(**) $$\forall_{i,j}(1\le i,j\le n):x_i|x_j\notin\{1/n-1,n-1\}.$$

(Hieraus folgt die Existenz eines stets korrekt arbeitenten linearen Sortieralgorithmus für Registermaschinen, die zusätzlich Zweierpotenzen in einem Schritt berechnen können).

Das gewünschte Verfahren gewinnt man, wenn der unter Bedingung (**) arbeitende Sortieralgorithmus mit einem Algorithmus zur Berechnung der Funktion $h:\mathbb{N}^{n+1}\to\mathbb{N}^n$, mit $h(x_1,\dots,x_n)c)=x_1^{2c},\dots,x_n^{2c}$, kombiniert wird, die in Zeit $O(n)+O(c)$ berechnet werden kann.

Zahlen $x_1,\dots,x_n\le 2^{cn}$ lassen sich damit in Zeit $O(cn)$ sortieren. Durch zusätzliches Anwenden der "Bucket-sort"-Technik verbessert sich die Zeitschranke auf $O(c^{1/2}n)$.

Literatur

[1] A.V. Aho, J.E. Hopcroft, J.D. Ullmann, *The Design and Analysis of Computer Algorithmus*", Addison Wesley 1974.

[2] W. Paul, J. Simon, *Decision Trees and Random Access Machines*, Symposium über Logik und Algorithmik, Zürich 1980.

[3] S. Reisch, *Efficient Sorting by Random Access Machines*, preprint 1980.

+Der Autor hat davon erfahren, daß Kirckpatrick zu ähnlichen Resultaten gelangt ist.

Sortieren in Magnetblasenspeichern

Michael Breder
Volkswagenwerk AG, 3180 Wolfsburg;
vorm. Universität des Saarlandes, 6600 Saarbrücken

Eine der interessantesten Entwicklungen der letzten Jahre auf dem Gebiet der Speichertechnologie sind die Magnetblasenspeicher. Gegenüber Speichermedien wie Magnetplatte und -trommel bieten sie durch fehlende mechanische Teile wesentliche Vorteile wie geringere Zugriffszeiten, geringeren Platzbedarf, geringeren Stromverbrauch und niedrigere Fehlerraten, so daß in den nächsten Jahren mit einem weiteren Vordringen von Magnetblasenspeichern zu rechnen ist.

Ein Magnetblasenspeicher arbeitet wie ein Schieberegister, so daß kein Direktzugriff zu den Daten besteht. Um eine Leseoperation durchführen zu können, müssen deshalb die gespeicherten Daten solange durch den Speicher geschiftet werden, bis die gewünschte Information an der Lesestation bereitsteht.

Die Magnetblasentechnologie kann jedoch nicht nur zur Konstruktion von Speichern, sondern auch zur Implementierung logischer Funktionen verwendet werden. Dadurch ist es möglich, auf einem Chip Speicher und Logik in derselben Technologie zu realisieren.

Diese Eigenschaft wird nun benutzt, um einen "schnellen" Sortieralgorithmus in einem Magnetblasenspeicher zu implementieren. Die Idee dazu ist folgende: Der Speicher wird so organisiert, daß eingelesene Schlüssel während eines Schifts durch den Speicher automatisch sortiert werden. Es läßt sich zeigen, daß die zum Sortieren erforderliche Zeit in der Größenordnung des Einlesens der Daten liegt.

Da bei Konstruktion eines solchen Speichers im wesentlichen die Struktur des Blasenspeichers beibehalten wird und Logik, die an bestimmten Positionen des Speichers benötigt wird, in derselben Technologie realisiert werden kann, dürften die Fertigungskosten eines solchen Sortierchips nicht wesentlich über denen eines Speicherchips liegen. Ein weiterer Vorteil besteht darin, daß durch Hintereinanderschalten einer entsprechenden Anzahl dieser Sortierchips sogar beliebig große Datenmengen sortiert werden können.

Das P = NP-Problem in der Kategorie der partiellen Ordnungen mit 2-stelligen Suprema

H. Huwig
Abteilung Informatik
Universität Dortmund

Einleitung:

Unter dem P = NP-Problem verstehen wir die Formalisierung des entsprechenden Problems in der Zermelo-Fraenkel'schen Mengenlehre. Die Lösung dieses Problems gilt als schwierig. Allgemein wird erwartet, daß P = NP gilt.

In dieser Arbeit stellen wir uns die Frage: Wie schwer ist das P = NP-Problem. Wir erachten dabei eine Aussage A für umso schwieriger (in der Zermelo-Fraenkel'schen Mengenlehre) beweisbar, je stärker strukturierte Kategorien wir angeben können, in denen $\neg$A gilt. Dies ist vor dem Hintergrund der Lawvere'schen Mengenlehre zu sehen, bei der ausgehend von der elementaren (= first order) Theorie einer Kategorie, ETAK, durch Axiome, die sich in dieser Theorie formulieren lassen, die Kategorie der Mengen und Funktionen, die von der Zermelo Fraenkel'schen Mengenlehre herrührt, herausgefiltert wird.

Wir analysieren dazu die Sprachmittel, die benötigt werden, das P = NP-Problem in Set zu formulieren. Es stellt sich heraus, daß jede symmetrisch monoidale und monoidal abgeschlossene Kategorie mit einem Objekt natürlicher Zahlen, NNO, Pullbacks und Bildzerlegungen über ihr eigenes P = NP-Problem verfügt. Die Kategorie SPord, deren Objekte Ordnungen mit zweistelligen Suprema und deren Morphismen monotone, Suprema respektierende Abbildungen sind, verfügt über genügend Struktur, eine Formulierung des P = NP-Problems zu gestatten. Für dieses P = NP-Problem gilt: P = NP.

Das NNO in SPord läßt diese Untersuchungen als eine interessante Alternative zu Lipton's modelltheoretischen Untersuchungen dieser Fragestellung erscheinen. Erfüllt es doch alle Peano Axiome einschließlich dem der Nichttrivialität. Darüberhinaus besitzt jedes primitive und jedes syntaktische Iterationsproblem genau eine Lösung. Dies kann man von den Lipton'schen Modellen natürlicher Zahlen nicht erwarten. Der Vorteil von Liptons Vorgehen liegt hingegen darin, daß er eine Liste von Axiomen aufstellen kann, von denen die (erwartete) Lösung des P = NP-Problems unabhängig ist. Leider verfügt SPord über kein "Potenzmengenaxiom", daher müssen wir zur Bildung neuer Kategorien externe (= second order) Statements benutzen. Dies macht es schwierig, die benutzte Sprache exakt einzugrenzen. Andererseits benutzen wir keineswegs mehr als die alltägliche Sprache eines Mathematikers. Hiermit lassen sich relativ zu Kategorien mit oben erwähnten Axiomen große Teile der abstrakten Algebra mit den erwarteten Resultaten - i.e. denselben Ergebnissen wie in Set nachspielen. Daher besteht eine gewisse Berechtigung unser Resultat dahingehend zu interpretieren, daß die Lösung des P = NP-Problems schwieriger als die Standardkonstruktionen der abstrakten Algebra ist. Die Lawvere'sche Mengenlehre liefert die Richtschnur, entlang derer man die hier entwickelte Theorie im Hinblick auf die Abgrenzung der benutzten Sprachmittel einerseits und auf die von Hartmanis und Hopcroft aufgestellte These, daß die Lösung von P = NP möglicherweise unabhängig von der Zermelo-Fraenkel'schen Mengenlehre ist, andererseits, weiter verfolgen sollte: Zunächst gilt es stärker strukturierte Kategorien als SPord zu finden in denen auch P = NP zumindest unter Verwendung externer Argumente gilt. Gilt dies sogar für ein Topos - dazu bedarf es der Ersetzung des monoidalen durch kartesischen Abschluß und der Hinzufügung des Potenzmengenaxioms - sollte die Internalisierung dieses Resultats, i.e. sein Beweis mit ausschließlich first order Statements keine unüberwindlichen Schwierigkeiten bereiten. Die Axiome, die danach zum Nachweis von P ≠ NP in Set benötigt werden, sind dann schon von sehr spezieller Natur.

1. Pfeilorientierte Formalisierung von P = NP in Set.

Wir geben zunächst eine Formulierung des P = NP-Problems an, die sich auf hinreichend strukturierte Kategorien übertragen läßt. Wir definieren dazu zunächst Polynomialzeit berechenbare Funktionen und danach Polynomialzeitsprache als diejenigen $L \subset \mathbb{N}$, die sich vermöge einer Polynomialzeit berechenbaren Funktion $f:\mathbb{N} \to \mathbb{N}$ schreiben lassen als: $L = \{x | x \in \mathbb{N} \wedge xf = o\}$. Zur Definition von nichtdeterminierter Sprache benutzen wir eine Formulierung,die auf D.Scott zurückgeht: L heißt in nichtdeterminierter Polynomialzeit berechenbar genau dann, wenn es eine Polynomialzeit berechenbare Funktion $f:\mathbb{N} \times \mathbb{N} \to \mathbb{N}$ und ein Polynom $p:\mathbb{N} \to \mathbb{N}$ gibt, so daß

$$L = \{x | x \in \mathbb{N} \wedge \exists y \in \mathbb{N}: y \lg_2 \leq x \lg_2 p \wedge (x,y)f = o\}$$

gilt. Dieses Vorgehen wird häufig als "hidden nondeterminism" bezeichnet. Ein operationales Vorgehen bei der Definition hätte aber die Übertragung von mehr Begriffen erfordert.

Der Schlüssel zu einer Vorstellung von (primitiv rekursiver) Berechenbarkeit in Kategorien liegt in der Definition

(1.1) Def: (Lawvere) Sei K eine monoidal abgeschlossene Kategorie, 1 das neutrale Element bzgl. dem Tensorprodukt. Ein Objekt N heißt Objekt natürlicher Zahlen, NNO, <=> Es gibt Pfeile $1 \overset{o}{\rightarrow} N \overset{s}{\rightarrow} N$, so daß für jedes weitere Paar $1 \overset{x}{\rightarrow} X \overset{f}{\rightarrow} X$ genau ein $x^{\#}: N \rightarrow X$ existiert, der das Diagramm

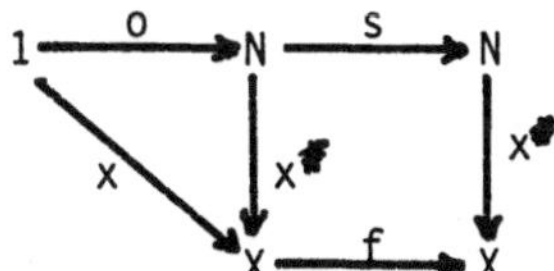

kommutativ ergänzt.

Dies ist die kategorielle Formulierung, der Beobachtung, daß in Set das Axiom der Unendlichkeit äquivalent ist zu der Forderung: "Es gibt eine initiale 0-1-Algebra".

(1.2) Bsp: Kartesischer Abschluß genügt nicht, die Trivialität ($1 \cong N$) eines NNO zu verhindern. Man betrachte hierzu die freie Kategorie über dem Graphen $\underset{A}{.} \longrightarrow \underset{B}{.}$. Diese ist kartesisch abgeschlossen und es gilt $B \xrightarrow{B} B \xrightarrow{B} B$ ist ein NNO. Für Topoi gilt allerdings: $1 \cong N$ <=> Das Topos selbst ist trivial (d.h. isomorph zu freien Kategorie über dem Graphen $\underset{A}{.}$).

(1.3) Satz: (Freyd) In einer monoidal abgeschlossenen Kategorie besitzt jedes primitive Iterationsproblem genau eine Lösung. Das heißt: Zu $X \xrightarrow{g} Y \xrightarrow{f} Y$ existiert genau ein Morphismus $g^{\#}: X \otimes N \rightarrow Y$, der das Diagramm

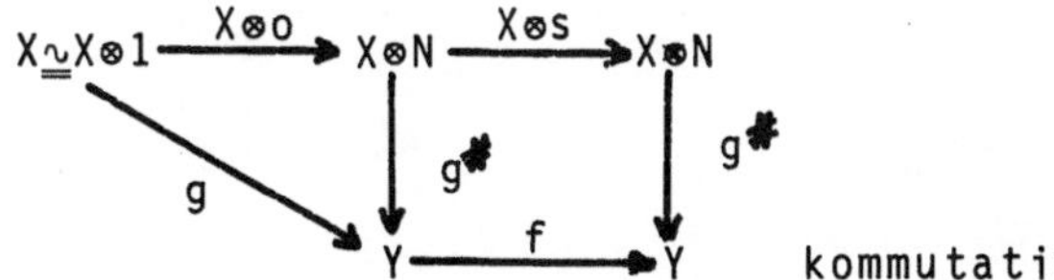

kommutativ ergänzt.

<u>Bew</u>: Die "λ-Transpositionen" von g und f $1 \xrightarrow{\ulcorner g \urcorner} Y^X \xrightarrow{f^X} Y^X$ definieren eine 0-1-Algebra. Es gibt daher genau einen Morphismus von 0-1-Algebren $\tilde{g}: N \to Y^X$, dessen "exponentielle" Übersetzung

$$g^{\#}: X \otimes N \to Y$$

ist die gesuchte, eindeutig bestimmte Lösung.

Eine Konsequenz dieses Satzes ist es, daß man einer monoidalen Kategorie mit NNO alle primitiv rekursiven Funktionen durch geeignete Iterationsschema wiederfindet.

Das einfachste Beispiel ist das Diagramm für die Addition in einer solchen Kategore. Es lautet:

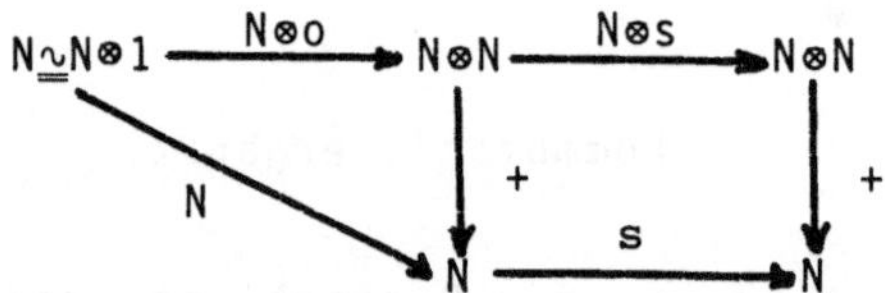

Insbesondere kann man die Morphismen $s_o := \lambda x.2x+1$ bzw. $s_1 := \lambda x.2x+2$ definieren, durch die Schemata:

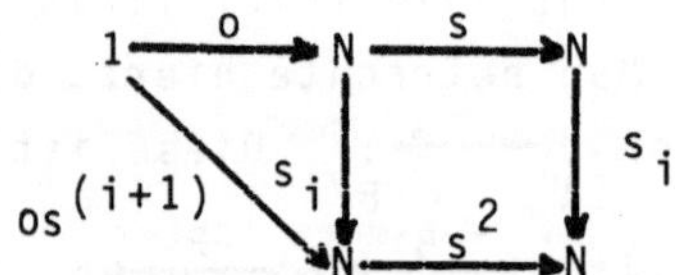

für $i \in \underline{2} = \{o, 1\}$.

(1.4) <u>Korollar</u>: In einer monoidal abgeschlossenen Kategorie mit NNO ist $1 \xrightarrow{o} N \underset{s_1}{\overset{s_o}{\rightrightarrows}} N$ initiale 0-2-Algebra und jedes syntaktische Iterationsproblem besitzt genau eine Lösung. Das heißt zu jedem Diagramm

$X \xrightarrow{g} Y \underset{f_1}{\overset{f_o}{\rightrightarrows}} Y$ gibt es genau ein $g^{\#}: X \otimes N \to Y$, sodaß das

Diagramm

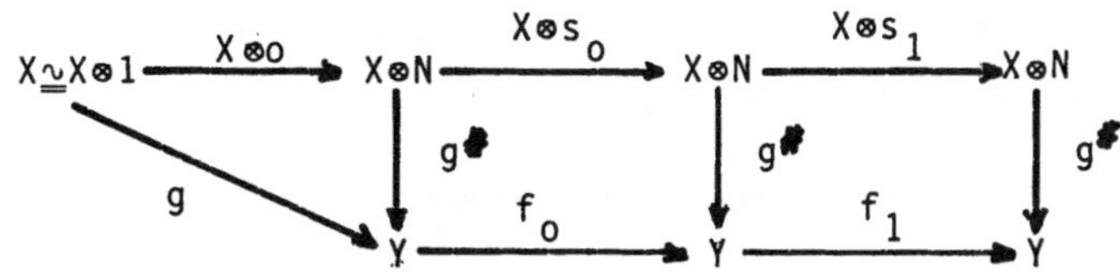

kommutiert.

<u>Bew</u>: Es genügt die Initialität von $1 \xrightarrow{o} N \overset{s_o}{\underset{s_1}{\rightrightarrows}} N$ zu beweisen und dann wie in (1.3) vorzugehen. Die Initialität von $1 \xrightarrow{o} \mathbb{N} \overset{s_o}{\underset{s_1}{\rightrightarrows}} \mathbb{N}$ in <u>Set</u> läßt sich aber mit primitiv rekursiven Argumenten aus derjenigen von $1 \xrightarrow{o} \mathbb{N} \xrightarrow{s} \mathbb{N}$ folgern. Daher kann man diesen Beweis übertragen.

(1.5) <u>Def</u>: Seien X und Y endliche Produkte von Mengen in <u>Set</u>, deren sämtliche Faktoren gleich $\underline{1}$ oder $\mathbb{N}$ sind. Wir sagen g geht aus $X \xrightarrow{g} Y \overset{f_o}{\underset{f_1}{\rightrightarrows}} Y$ durch Polynomialzeit beschränkte Iteration hervor, falls g das durch $X \xrightarrow{g} Y \overset{f_o}{\underset{f_1}{\rightrightarrows}} Y$ aufgeworfene syntaktische Iterationsproblem löst und außerdem gilt:
Es gibt ein Polynom $p\colon \mathbb{N} \to \mathbb{N}$ mit

$$lg_2 \cdot max_{X \times \mathbb{N}} \circ p \geq f \circ lg_2 \circ max_Y .$$

Den Morphismus lg_2, Logarithmus zur Basis zwei, definieren wir dabei als die Lösung des syntaktischen Rekursionsproblems:

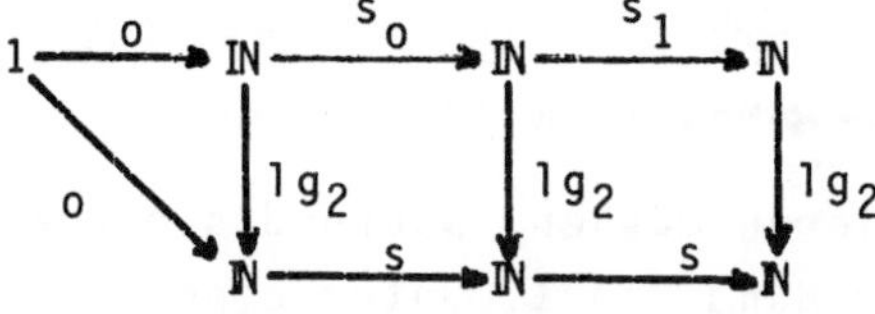

Ausgehend von (irgend) einer primitiven rekursiven Definition von $max\colon \mathbb{N} \times \mathbb{N} \to \mathbb{N}$ definiert man rekursiv die Funktionen $max_r\colon \mathbb{N}^r \to \mathbb{N}$ für $r \in \mathbb{N}$ in der naheliegenden Weise. So dann $max_X\colon X \to \mathbb{N}$

für irgendeine Menge X, die als endliches Produkt aus $\underline{1}$ und $\mathbb{N}$ mit genau r Faktoren $\mathbb{N}$ gegeben ist, durch

$$X \xrightarrow{\alpha} \mathbb{N}^r \xrightarrow{max_r} \mathbb{N}.$$

Dabei bezeichnet $\alpha: X \to \mathbb{N}^r$, den Isomorphismus der auf Grund der Kohärenzeigenschaften von -×- existieren muß.

(1.6) Def: Poltime ist die kleinste Unterkategorie von Set, welche als Objekte genau alle endlichen Produkte von $\underline{1}$ und $\mathbb{N}$ enthält, in der alle "Zahlen" $\underline{1} \xrightarrow{p} \mathbb{N}$ sowie die Morphismen $\mathbb{N} \underset{s_1}{\overset{s_0}{\rightrightarrows}} \mathbb{N}$ liegen, und die schließlich abgeschlossen ist gegen Parallelausführung und Polynomialzeit beschränkte Iteration.

(1.7) Satz: Sei P die Kategorie der Funktionen $f: \mathbb{N}^r \to \mathbb{N}^s$, deren "Dualdarstellung" auf einer Turingmaschine in Polynomialzeit berechenbar ist, dann gilt:
P ist äquivalent zu Poltime.

Bew: Beweise dieser Aussage finden sich in der Literatur sehr häufig, allerdings implizit. [HWI,HUa,To].

Da wir im Folgenden nur an "internen" Eigenschaften von Poltime interessiert sind, ist es erlaubt P durch Poltime zu ersetzen, was größere Freiheit bei der Definition von Morphismen verschafft.

Über welche zusätzlichen Eigenschaften muß nun eine symmetrisch monoidal abgeschlossene Kategorie B verfügen, um die Definition der Kategorie Poltime-B der in ihr in Polynomialzeit berechenbaren Morphismen zu erlauben? Eine Analyse von (1.5) und (1.6) zeigt, daß wir "die" Kleiner-gleich-Relation

$$\leq \rightarrowtail N \otimes N \text{ in } B$$

und Polynome in B definieren müssen, während die Übertragung von lg_2 und max_X bereits auf der Hand liegt. Unter einer Zahl in B verstehen wir einen Pfeil $1 \xrightarrow{p} N$. Die Definition der Addition $+: N \otimes N \to N$ und der Multiplikation $-\cdot-: N \otimes N \to N$ ist klar. Ebenso stehen für alle Substitutionsmorphismen, z.B.

$$D: \mathbb{N} \to \mathbb{N}\times\mathbb{N}$$
$$x \mapsto (x,x) \qquad \text{oder}$$
$$V: \mathbb{N} \times \mathbb{N} \to \mathbb{N} \times \mathbb{N}$$
$$(x,y) \mapsto (y,x)$$

via Iterationsschemata entsprechende Morphismen zur Verfügung. Daher definieren wir die Kategorie der Polynome in B,N[x] -B, als die kleinste Unterkategorie von B, die alle endlichen Produkte von 1 und N als Objekte enthält, an Morphismen alle Zahlen, alle Substitutionsmorphismen sowie $-+-:N\otimes N \to N$ und $-\cdot-:N\otimes N \to N$. Schließlich ist N[x]-B abgeschlossen gegen Parallelausführung, das heißt: mit f und g ist auch $f\otimes g$ aus N[x]-B.

Damit die natürlichen Zahlen in einer monoidal abgeschlossenen Kategorie B über eine Ordnung verfügen, muß diese Eigenschaft formulierbar sein. Es genügt das B zusätzlich über Pullbacks und existentielle Quantifikation verfügt. Letzteres ist z.B. immer dann der Fall, wenn sich jeder Pfeil $f:X \to Y$ eindeutig in den Coequalizer seines Kernpaares und einen Mono zerlegen läßt. Der Pullbackfunktor von der Kategorie der Unterobjekte von Y in diejenige der Unterobjekte von X:

$$f^{-1}:\mathbb{P}Y \to \mathbb{P}X$$

hat dann stets einen Linksadjungierten $\exists f:\mathbb{P}X \to \mathbb{P}X$. Dabei ist für $A \overset{i}{\rightarrowtail} Y$, $(A \overset{i}{\rightarrowtail} Y)\exists f = B \overset{j}{\rightarrowtail} X$, wo $j:B \to X$ der Monomorphismus ist, der von der Zerlegung von $i\cdot f$ geliefert wird. Die Heuristik hinter dieser Definition wird anhand einer Relation $R \overset{i}{\longrightarrow} X\times X$ in Set deutlich:

$$R\,\exists\pi_0 = \{x \mid x\varepsilon X \wedge \exists z\varepsilon R: z\pi_0 = x\}$$
$$= \{x \mid x\varepsilon X \wedge \exists y\varepsilon X:(x,y)\varepsilon R\}.$$

Unter diesen zusätzlichen Voraussetzungen - Pullbacks und Bildzerlegungen - kann man zeigen, daß der Pfeil

$$N\otimes N \overset{\delta}{\to} (N\otimes N)\otimes N \overset{\alpha}{\to} N\otimes(N\otimes N) \xrightarrow{N\otimes +} N\otimes N$$

eine Ordnungsrelation in B definiert. Dies "ist" die übliche Ordnungsrelation in Set. Wir schreiben abkürzend $\leq \overset{r}{\rightarrowtail} N\otimes N$ für diese Relation.

(1.8) Def: Sei B eine symmetrisch monoidale, monoidal abgeschlossene Kategorie mit NNO, Pullbacks und Bildzerlegungen. Dann ist Poltime-B die kleinste monoidale Unterkategorie von B, welche die Objekte 1 und N enthält, alle "Zahlen"-Morphismen-

$1 \xrightarrow{p} N$ sowie die Morphismen $N \overset{s_o}{\underset{s_1}{\rightrightarrows}} N$ und schließlich abgeschlossen ist gegen Polynomialzeit beschränkte Rekursion. Das heißt mit Morphismen $X \xrightarrow{g} Y \overset{f_o}{\underset{f_1}{\rightrightarrows}} Y$ enthält Poltime-B auch die Lösung des zugehörigen syntaktischen Rekursionsproblems $g : X \otimes N \to Y$ falls die Diagonale $\delta : X \otimes N \to (X \otimes N) \otimes (X \otimes N)$ - die mittels syntaktischer Rekursion definiert werden kann - über das Pullback

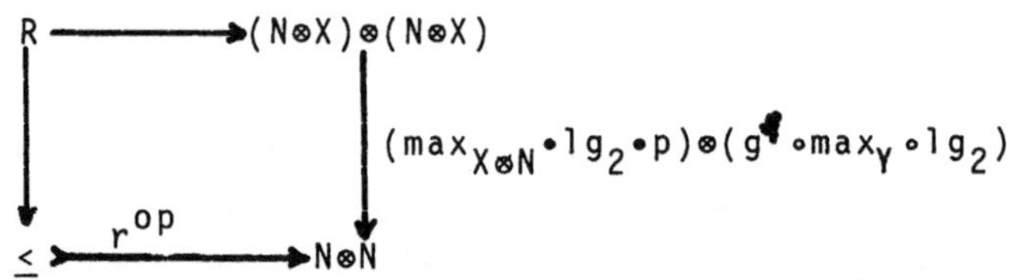

für ein $p \in N[x]$-B faktorisiert.

D-Poltime-B ist die diskrete Kategorie aller $L \xrightarrow{i} N$, die sich für ein $f : N \to N$ als das Pullback

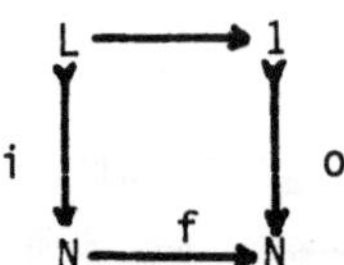

darstellen lassen.

ND-Poltime-B ist die diskrete Kategorie aller $L \xrightarrow{i} N$, zu denen es ein $f : N \otimes N \to N$ aus Poltime-B und ein $p \in N[x]$-B gibt, so daß sich $L \xrightarrow{i} N$ schreiben läßt als $(M \cap R \xrightarrow{j} N \otimes N) \exists \pi_o$. Dabei ist M das Pullback:

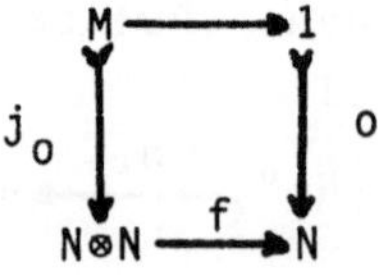

und R das Pullback

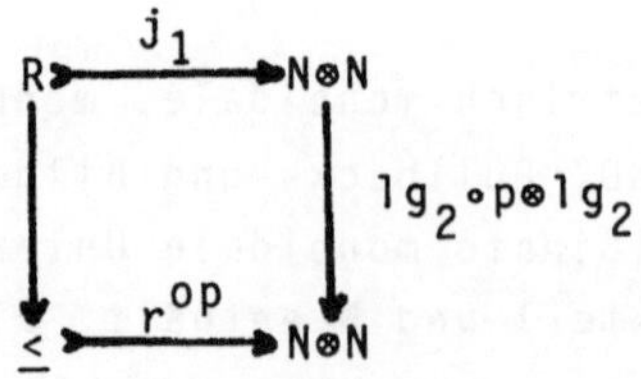

Schließlich $M \cap R \xrightarrow{j} N \otimes N$ das Pullback von j_0 und j_1
Unter $\leq \xrightarrow{r^{op}} N \otimes N$ verstehen wir die Relation
$\leq \xrightarrow{r} N \otimes N \xrightarrow{v} N \otimes N$. Wo v die rekursiv definierte Vertauschung meint. Die Morphismen max_X und lg_2 lassen sich in Analogie zum Set-Fall definieren.

Es ist empfehlenswert sich klar zu machen , daß es sich hierbei um die übliche Definition der entsprechenden Begriffe handelt, wenn wir B = Set setzen. Der Pfeil $1 \xrightarrow{o} \mathbb{N}$ in Set läßt die Interpretation $1 \xrightarrow{o} \mathbb{N}$ ist Komplement von $\mathbb{N} \xrightarrow{s} \mathbb{N}$ zu. In Set oder allgemeiner in Topoi führt dies stets auf dieselben Sprachklassen. In den allgemeinen Kategorien B wie wir sie hier betrachten ist dies nicht der Fall. Dennoch sind beide Definitionen von Sprachklassen für die eingangs diskutierten Fragestellungen gleich relevant. Wir ersetzen daher in obiger Definition $\perp \xrightarrow{o} N$ jeweils durch $C \xrightarrow{j} N$, dabei ist C das Heytingkomplement von $N \xrightarrow{s} N$, das heißt der Durchschnitt beider Unterobjekte ist leer (= dem initialen Objekt der Kategorie B) und $C \xrightarrow{j} N$ ist das größte Unterobjekt mit dieser Eigenschaft.

2. Das P = NP-Problem in SPord.

Es geht jetzt darum sicherzustellen, daß die Kategorie SPord, der partiellen Ordnungen mit zweistelligen Suprema, über genügend Struktur verfügt, die Formulierung eines P = NP-Problems zu erlauben. Dies folgt unmittelbar aus dem Satz:

(2.1) Satz: a) $U: \mathrm{SPord} \to \mathrm{Set}$
$(X, \leq) \longmapsto X$ ist algebraisch.

Dies bedeutet U ist ein Rechtsadjungierter, erzeugt Limiten und Coequalizer von Kernpaaren.

b) SPord ist eine symmetrisch monoidale, monoidal abgeschlossene Kategorie.

Bew: SPord ist äquivalent zur vollen Unterkategorie der kommutativen Halbgruppen, deren Objekte gerade die kommutativen idempotenten Halbgruppen sind. Das Tensorprodukt kann daher wie üblich konstruiert werden. Der Rechtsadjungierte zu $X \otimes \_$ ist an der Stelle Y durch $Y^X = \{f \mid f$ respektiert zweistellige Suprema$\}$ gegeben. Der Linksadjungierte zu U kann als F: Set → S-Pord
$X \longmapsto \{A \mid A \subset X,\ A$ endlich und $A \neq \emptyset\}$
formuliert werden.

(2.2) Korollar: a) $\underline{1}F \xrightarrow{oF} \mathbb{N}F \xrightarrow{sF} \mathbb{N}F$ ist NNO bezüglich des Tensorprodukts in SPord.

b) Dieses NNO erfüllt alle Peano-Axiome

c) Jedes primitive und jedes syntaktische Iterationsproblem besitzt genau eine Lösung in SPord.

Das $\underline{1}F \xrightarrow{oF} \mathbb{N}F \xrightarrow{sF} \mathbb{N}F$ alle Peano Axiome erfüllt, bedeutet, daß durch $1F \xrightarrow{x} X \xrightarrow{f} X$ eindeutig eine "Folge" $X:\mathbb{N}F \to X$ festgelegt ist, daß jedes oF-sF abgeschlossene Unterobjekt von $\mathbb{N}F$ bereits ganz $\mathbb{N}F$ ist, daß sF ein Monomorphismus ist und schließlich, daß $\underline{1}F$ nicht isomorph zu $\mathbb{N}F$ ist. Ein explizites Bild des Tensorproduktes in SPord liefert die Beobachtung, daß auf freien Objekten XF und YF die universelle bilineare Abbildung durch

$$XF \times YF \xrightarrow{h} (X \times Y)F = XF \otimes YF$$
$$(S,T) \longmapsto \{(s,t) | s \in S \wedge t \in T\}$$ gegeben wird.

Eine Konsequenz hiervon ist:

(2.3) Satz: $f \varepsilon$Poltime => $fF \varepsilon$ Poltime-SPord

Bew: Da F das Produkt in Set in das Tensorprodukt in SPord übersetzt, respektiert F syntaktische Iterationsschemata. Darüberhinaus folgt aus $f \leq g$ in Set $fF \leq gF$ in SPord.

Ähnlich wie in Set beweist man:

(2.4) Bem: $f \varepsilon$Poltime-SPord, $f:X \to Y$, => $\exists p \varepsilon N[x]$-Spord mit $f \circ max_Y \circ lg_2 \leq max_X \bullet lg_2 \bullet p$ in SPord.

(2.5) Bem: Zu jedem Polynom $p:\mathbb{N}F \to NF$ aus N[x]-SPord gibt es eine endliche Teilmenge $P \subset \mathbb{N}[x]$ so daß sich p an der Stelle $S \varepsilon \mathbb{N}F$ schreiben läßt als:

$$Sp = \bigcup_{s \varepsilon S} \bigcup_{f \varepsilon P} \{sf\}.$$

In SPord verfügen wir über Nichtstandardzahlen, d.h. solche die sich nicht durch iterierte Anwendung von sF auf oF gewinnen lassen. Ein Beispiel für eine solche Zahl ist:

Satz : ND-Poltime-SPord = D-Poltime-SPord .

Bew: Zunächst überzeugt man sich davon, daß für jedes Polynom $p \in \mathbb{N}[x]$ -SPord der analog zum Set-Fall konstruierte Morphismus $\bar{p} := \lambda x.2^{x \lg_2 p}$ in Poltime-SPord liegt. Zu vorgelegtem $f: \mathbb{N}F \otimes \mathbb{N}F \to \mathbb{N}F$ und $p: \mathbb{N}F \to \mathbb{N}F$ konstruiert man jetzt die Morphismen

$$\phi: \mathbb{N}F \otimes \mathbb{N}F \to (\mathbb{N}F)^4$$
$$\phi = (\delta \otimes \mathbb{N}F) \bullet (\mathbb{N}F \otimes \nu) \circ \alpha \circ (\mathbb{N}F \otimes 0F \otimes \mathbb{N}F \otimes 0F) \circ ((\mathbb{N}F)^3 \otimes f)$$

dabei bedeutet δ die Diagonalisierung $\nu: \mathbb{N}F \otimes \mathbb{N}F \to \mathbb{N}F \otimes \mathbb{N}F$ die Vertauschung und $\alpha: (\mathbb{N}F)^3 \to (\mathbb{N}F)^2 \otimes 1F \otimes \mathbb{N}F \otimes 1F$ den Kohärenzisomorphismus Alle Morphismen sind offensichtlich in Poltime-SPord. Den Morphismus $\tilde{g}: (\mathbb{N}F)^4 \to (\mathbb{N}F)^4$ konstruieren wir als das Kompositum $\tilde{g}_0 \tilde{g}_1 \tilde{g}_2$. Dabei ist

$$\tilde{g}_0 : (\mathbb{N}F)^4 \to (\mathbb{N}F)^4 \quad \text{gegeben durch}$$
$$\tilde{g}_0 := (\mathbb{N}F \otimes \delta \otimes q \otimes \mathbb{N}F) \circ (\nu \otimes Min \otimes \mathbb{N}F),$$

dabei bedeutet q den oben diskutierten Morphismus und Min die Minimumsbildung in SPord.

$$\tilde{g}_1 := (\mathbb{N}F \otimes \delta \otimes \delta \otimes \mathbb{N}F) \circ (\nu \otimes \nu \otimes (\mathbb{N}F)^2).$$

Schließlich ist $\tilde{g}_2 : (\mathbb{N}F)^6 \to (\mathbb{N}F)^4$ durch

$$\tilde{g}_2 := ((\mathbb{N}F)^3 \otimes f \otimes \mathbb{N}F) \circ ((\mathbb{N}F)^3 \otimes Min \otimes \mathbb{N}F) \quad \text{gegeben.}$$

Die Lösung, $\phi^{\#}$, des Iterationsproblems

$$(\mathbb{N}F)^2 \xrightarrow{\phi} (\mathbb{N}F)^4 \overset{\tilde{g}}{\underset{\tilde{g}}{\rightrightarrows}} (\mathbb{N}F)^4$$ liegt in Poltime-SPord,

da man aus der Abschätzung des Wachstums von f eine geeignete Abschätzung für $\phi^{\#}$ konstruieren kann. Zu dem Polynom p konstruieren wir gemäß (2.5) Polynome $p_0, \ldots, p_{r-1}$ in Set mit ihrem Entsprechungen in SPord den Morphismus

$$\mathbb{N}F \xrightarrow{\delta_r} (\mathbb{N}F)^r \xrightarrow{\prod_{i \in \underline{r}} \bar{p}_i} (\mathbb{N}F)^r \xrightarrow{Min_r} \mathbb{N}F.$$

Dabei bezeichnet δ_r die r-fache Diagonale, $\prod_{i \in r} \bar{p}_i$ die Parallelausführung der $\bar{p}_i$ und Min_r die Verallgemeinerung von Min auf r Komponenten.

$$\underline{1} \cong \underline{1}F \xrightarrow{\{1,2\}} \mathbb{N}F$$
$$0 \longmapsto \{1,2\}.$$

{1,2} ist als Zahl in Polynomialzeit berechenbar. Damit auch der Morphismus q den man suggestiv $\lambda x.2x + \{1,2\}$ schreiben möchte: $q = \delta \circ \rho \bullet (\mathbb{N}F \otimes \mathbb{N}F \otimes \{1,2\}) \bullet (+F \otimes \mathbb{N}F) \circ + F$. Dabei bedeutet δ die Diagonalisierung und ρ den natürlichen Isomorphismus $\rho: (\mathbb{N}F \otimes \mathbb{N}F) \to (\mathbb{N}F \otimes \mathbb{N}F) \otimes 1$. Die Lösung, $q^{\#}$, des syntaktischen Iterationsproblems

$$\underline{1}F \xrightarrow{oF} \mathbb{N}F \underset{q}{\overset{q}{\rightrightarrows}} \mathbb{N}F$$ kann durch Polynomialzeit beschränkte Rekursion in SPord gewonnen werden. Sie erfüllt: $\forall S \varepsilon \mathbb{N}F: Sq^{\#} = \{s' | s' \varepsilon \mathbb{N} \wedge s' lg_2 = s lg_2\}$. Das Heyting Komplement von $\mathbb{N}F \xrightarrow{sF} \mathbb{N}F$ ist die Unterhalbgruppe von $\mathbb{N}F$ mit:

$$\forall S \varepsilon \mathbb{N}F: S \varepsilon C \Leftrightarrow 0 \varepsilon S.$$

Die Tatsache, daß $q^{\#}$ in Polynomialzeit berechenbar ist, führt zusammen mit der Struktur des Komplements zur folgenden prinzipiellen Idee eines Polynomialzeitalgorithmus' für eine nichtdeterminierte Polynomialzeitsprache: Sei $f: \mathbb{N}F \otimes \mathbb{N}F \to \mathbb{N}F$ aus Poltime-SPord und $p: \mathbb{N} \to \mathbb{N}$ aus N[x] -SPord vorgelegt. Eine Analyse der Formel (1.8) für das zugehörige Objekt zeigt: Es handelt sich um das Unterobjekt $L \xrightarrow{i} \mathbb{N}F$ für das gilt:

$$S \varepsilon L \Leftrightarrow \exists S' \varepsilon N \otimes N: (o \varepsilon S' f \wedge (\forall (s,t) \varepsilon S': \forall z \varepsilon s lg_2 p: z \geq t lg_2)) \wedge (\forall s \varepsilon \mathbb{N}: s \varepsilon S \Leftrightarrow \exists t \varepsilon \mathbb{N}: (s,t) \varepsilon S')).$$

Es sei $M_i := \{i\}\, q^{\#}$. Testet man nun sukzessive $S \otimes M_0, S \otimes M_1, S \otimes M_2, \ldots$ vermöge f in Polynomialzeit daruf, ob $o \varepsilon (S \otimes M_i) f$ gilt, so kann man sich durch geeignete Minimusbildung an der Stelle i gleichzeitig merken, ob für $j \leq i$ der Test einmal positiv ausgefallen ist. Daher kann man schließlich an einer einzigen Stelle die durch S und p bestimmt ist, feststellen, ob jemals eine o aufgetreten ist. Um den Teil,

$$\forall z \varepsilon s lg_2 p: z \geq t lg_2,$$ der Formel

sicherzustellen muß man eine zusätzliche Schranke bei der Iteration einbauen. Wir können hier nur die benötigten Funktionen angeben. Der Nachweis, daß sie das Gewünschte leisten, findet sich in [Hub].

Diesen Morphismus bezeichnen wir mit U_p. Das Kompositum

$\psi = \delta_2 \circ (\mathbb{N}F \otimes U_p \otimes \bar{p}) \circ \phi^{\#} \circ \pi_3$ ist der gesuchte einstellige Morphismus in Poltime-SPord, der die selbe Sprache wie f und p definiert. $\pi_3 : (\mathbb{N}F)^4 \to \mathbb{N}F$ bedeutet dabei die Projektion. Die Umkehrung ist trivial, es genügt den Morphismus

$$\mathbb{N}F \otimes \mathbb{N}F \xrightarrow{\mathbb{N}F \otimes t} \mathbb{N}F \otimes \underline{1} \xrightarrow{\sim} \mathbb{N}F \xrightarrow{f} \mathbb{N}F$$

und das Nullpolynom zu betrachten.

Die große Anzahl von Kategorien, die über ein NNO mit Nichtstandardzahlen verfügen, läßt die Hoffnung berechtigt erscheinen, daß das Studium ihrer jeweiligen P = NP-Probleme einiges an Erkenntnisse über das P = NP-Problem beizusteuern vermag.

Literaturverzeichnis

[BGS] Baker, T. & Gill,J. & solovay,R. "Relativizations of the P=NP question". SIAM Journal of Computing 4, 1975

[Co] Cook,S. "The Complexity of Theorem Proving Procedures", 3rd ACM Symposium on Theory of Computing, 1971, Seite 151-158

[G] Grzegorczyk, A. "Some classes of recursive functions", Rozprawy Matematyczne, Warszawa 1953

[F] Fachini, E. and Maggiolo-Schettini, "A Hirarchy of Primitive Recursive Sequence Functions", Informatique theorique, Nr. 13, 1979

[Ha,Ho] Hartmanis, J. & Hopcroft,J. "Independee results in Computer Science" SIGACT Newsletter 8, 1976.

[Hu] Huwig, H., "Beziehungen zwischen beschränkter syntaktischer und beschränkter primitiver Rekursion", Dissertation, Berichtsreihe der Abteilung Informatik an der Universität Dortmund 25/76

[Hub] Huwig,H. "Das P = NP-Problem in der Kategorie der kommutativen idempotenten Halbgruppen", Habilitationsschrift, eingereicht bei der Universität Dortmund, 1980

HWI von Henke,F., & Indermark,K. & Weihrauch K. "Hierarchies of primitive recursive wordfunctions and transductions defined by automata", Automata, Languages and Programming, 1972, North-Holland Publishing Company, Amsterdam-London

[Li] Lipton,R.: "On the consistency of P=NP and fragments of arithmetic" FCT'79, Akademie Verlag Berlin

[Ma] Makkai,M. & Reyes,G., "First order categorical logic" Springer Verlag, 1977

[Ra] Radziszowski, S. "Programmability and P=NP Conjecture" Proceedings of FCT'77, Springer Verlag

[Sco a] Scott, D. "Some Definitional Suggestions for Automata Theory", JCSS 1, 1967

[To] Thompson, D. "Subrecursiveness: Machine-Independent Notions of Computability in Restricted Time and Storage", Mathematical Systems Theory, Vol. 6, No. 1, 1972.

UNTERE ZEITSCHRANKEN FÜR DAS RUCKSACK-PROBLEM

P. Klein und F. Meyer auf der Heide
Universität Bielefeld

Abstract:

In dieser Arbeit wird eine Methode zur Anwendung von Entscheidungsbaumargumenten auf Registermaschinen (RAM's) vorgestellt. Wir untersuchen Maschinen, die den Input nicht bitweise,sondern Zahl für Zahl einlesen und zeigen:

- eine exponentielle untere Zeitschranke (im Verhältnis zur Summe der binären Längen der ganzen Zahlen des Inputs) für das Rucksack-Problem auf einer RAM mit Gleichheitsabfragen ("if acc = 0 then goto α");
- eine exponentielle untere Zeitschranke (im Verhältnis zur Anzahl der ganzen Zahlen im Input) für das Komplement des Rucksack-Problems auf der nicht deterministischen Version der obigen Maschine;
- eine quadratische untere Zeitschranke (im Verhältnis zur Anzahl der Zahlen im Input) für das Rucksack-Problem auf einer RAM mit der üblichen Abfrage "if acc > 0 then goto α".

I. Einleitung und Resultate

Paul-Simon [6] und Rackoff zeigten eine untere Schranke von $\Omega(n \log n)$ für die Sortierkomplexität von n natürlichen Zahlen auf einer Registermaschine mit indirekter Adressierung, die neben den üblichen Anweisungen über die Operationen $+, *, \dot{-}$, verfügt. Die dabei angewandte Technik - man ordnet dem Programm einen linearen Baum zu, dessen Tiefe der Laufzeit des Programms entspricht und schätzt anschließend die Tiefe dieses Baumes ab - wird auch hier benutzt und in Kap. II erläutert. Kap. III enthält geometrische Vorbereitungen und die Beweise der Sätze.

Wir beschreiben zunächst kurz die hier untersuchten Typen von Registermaschinen, vgl. auch [5].

Eine deterministische $\mathbb{N}$-RAM ($\mathbb{Z}$-RAM) ist gegeben durch

(a) eine Registermenge mit Adressen aus $\mathbb{N} = \{0,1,\ldots\}$ ($\mathbb{Z} = \{\ldots -1,0,1,\ldots\}$). Das nullte Register heißt Akkumulator. Jedes Register enthält eine natürliche Zahl (ganze Zahl). Der Inhalt des i-ten Registers wird mit $\langle i \rangle$ bezeichnet.

(b) einen Befehlszähler b;

(c) ein Programm, d.h. eine endliche Folge von Anweisungen.

Als Anweisungen sind dabei zugelassen die üblichen Befehle für RAM's (einschließlich indirekter Adressierung); zusätzlich verfügt die $\mathbb{N}$-RAM über die arithmetischen Operationen "+" (add (k)), "$\dot{-}$" (sub* (k)), wobei $a \dot{-} b := \max\{a-b,0\}$, die $\mathbb{Z}$-RAM über "+" und "−" (sub (k)). Abweichend von den in [5] definierten Maschinen lesen unsere Modelle den Input als Folge von ganzen Zahlen (nicht von Bits!) ein.

Wir sagen, <u>eine $\mathbb{N}$-RAM ($\mathbb{Z}$-RAM) M akzeptiert eine Sprache</u> A, $A \subset \mathbb{N}^* = \bigcup_{n \geq 1} \mathbb{N}^n$ $(A \subset \mathbb{Z}^*)$, wenn für alle $\bar{x} \in \mathbb{N}^*(\mathbb{Z}^*)$ gilt:
M gestartet mit $\bar{x} \in A$ berechnet 1 (d.h. M angesetzt auf $\bar{x}$ hält mit dem Akkumulatorinhalt 1), M gestartet mit $\bar{x} \notin A$ berechnet 0. Die Gesamtzahl der Anweisungen, die M gestartet mit $\bar{x}$ ausführt, heißt $t_M(\bar{x})$.

Wir können nun unsere Komplexitätsmaße definieren.

Für eine $\mathbb{N}$-RAM M : $D_M(n) = \max\{t_M(\bar{x}) \mid \bar{x} \in \mathbb{N}^n\}$ falls es existiert, ∞ sonst}.

Für eine $\mathbb{Z}$-RAM M:

$T_M(n) := \max\{t_M(x_1,\ldots,x_m) \mid x_i \in \mathbb{Z}, m \in \mathbb{N}, \sum_{i=1}^{m} \ell(x_i) \leq n\}$; dabei ist $\ell(x_i)$ die Länge der Binärdarstellung von $|x_i|$.

Eine nichtdeterministische $\mathbb{Z}$-RAM (<u>ND-RAM</u>) M ist gegeben durch (a), (b) wie für $\mathbb{Z}$-RAMs und

(c)' ein nichtdeterministisches Programm, d.h. eine endliche Folge von Befehlsvektoren.

Eine Berechnung von M ist dann in der üblichen nicht deterministischen Weise definiert. M akzeptiert eine Sprache $A \subset \mathbb{Z}^*$, wenn es für jedes $\bar{x} \in A$ eine akzeptierende Berechnung gibt, die 1 berechnet und für jedes $\bar{x} \notin A$ keine solche Berechnung. $t_M(\bar{x})$ ist jetzt die Anzahl der ausgeführten Anweisungen in einer kürzesten akzeptierenden Berechnung von M gestartet mit $\bar{x}$, falls eine solche existiert; sonst ist $t_M(\bar{x}) = 0$. Das Komplexitätsmaß ist:
$ND_M(n) := \max\{t_M(x) \mid \bar{x} \in \mathbb{Z}^n\}$, falls es existiert, ∞ sonst.

Das Thema dieser Arbeit ist das <u>Rucksack-Problem</u>, d.h. das Problem, für ein gegebenes $(x_1,\ldots,x_{n+1}) \in \mathbb{N}^{n+1}$ $(\mathbb{Z}^{n+1})$ zu entscheiden, ob eine Teilmenge $I \subset \{1,\ldots,n\}$ existiert mit $\sum_{i \in I} x_i = x_{n+1}$. Die Menge aller Tupel in $\mathbb{N}^*(\mathbb{Z}^*)$, für die eine solche Teilmenge existiert, heißt $K_{\mathbb{N}} \subset \mathbb{N}^* (K_{\mathbb{Z}} \subset \mathbb{Z}^*)$. Wir zeigen:

<u>Satz 1</u>: $T_M(n) \geq 2^{n^{1/3}}$ für jede $\mathbb{Z}$-RAM M, die $K_{\mathbb{Z}}$ akzeptiert.

Aus Satz 1 folgt nicht NP $\neq$ P, weil nicht gezeigt ist, daß die von T_M induzierte polynomielle Klasse gleich P ist.

<u>Satz 2</u>: $ND_M(n) \geq 2^{(n-1)/2}$ für jede ND-RAM M, die $CK_{\mathbb{Z}}$ akzeptiert, das Komplement von $K_{\mathbb{Z}}$ in $\mathbb{Z}^*$.

<u>Satz 3</u>: $D_M(n+1) \geq n^2/2 - 4n \log n$ für jede $\mathbb{N}$-RAM M, die $K_{\mathbb{N}}$ akzeptiert.

II. Das "Aufrollen" eines Programms

In diesem Abschnitt ist die Dimension n+1 des Inputs beliebig aber fest gewählt. Das Aufrollen eines (mit der Maschine identifizierten) Programms M besteht darin, M einem binären Baum T zuzuordnen, der das Verhalten von M gestartet mit $\bar{x} \in \mathbb{N}^{n+1}$ $(\mathbb{Z}^{n+1})$ modelliert. Die Tiefe von T soll dabei der Laufzeit von M entsprechen. In den deterministischen Fällen ändern wir zunächst M aus technischen Gründen um. Sei b* die Nummer des "Halt"-Befehls (o.B.d.A. die größte Nummer der Befehlsfolge). Dann lautet die Modifikation:

```
b* :  if  <0>  > 0 (≠ 0)  then  goto  b* +2
b* +1:  halt
b* +2: c-load(1)
b* +3: goto  b*+1
```

Im Fall einer $\mathbb{N}$-RAM ersetzen wir einen Befehl "b : sub*(k)" durch

```
b : sub*(k)
b': if <0> > 0  then goto  b'''
b": c-load(0)
b''': ....
```

Dabei sind b' und b" neue Befehlsnummern, b''' ist der ursprünglich auf b folgende Befehl. Offensichtlich akzeptiert das so modifizierte Programm M' die gleiche Sprache wie M.

Wir konstruieren jetzt T induktiv:

(i) Die Wurzel v_o von T entspricht dem Zustand von M vor Beginn der Berechnung. v_o hat einen Sohn, der dem ersten Schritt von M entspricht.

(ii) Der Knoten v von T enstspreche einem Befehl "if <0> > 0 (= 0) then goto α" Dann bekommt v zwei Söhne v_1, v_2, die dem α'ten bzw. dem nächsten Befehl entsprechen. Wenn z.B. der "if" Befehl durch die obige Modifikation entstanden ist, gehört zu v_1 "b''' :...", zu v_2 "c-load(0)".

(iii) Jedes Blatt von T entspricht dem "halt"-Befehl.

(iv) Jedem anderen Befehl entspricht ein Knoten mit einem Sohn.

Auf diese Weise entspricht einer Berechnung von M' gestartet mit $\bar{x}$ gerade ein Weg in T von v_o zu einem Blatt ℓ. Im Fall (ii) etwa folgt dieser Weg dem linken Zweig, falls bei Input $\bar{x}$ an der entsprechenden Stelle von M' <0> > 0 (= 0) ist, anderenfalls dem rechten Zweig.

Der nichtdeterministische Fall wird genauso gehandhabt, außer daß ein Knoten für jeden Befehl des nächsten Befehlsvektors einen Sohn hat.

Seien $i_1,\dots,i_m$, $i_1 < \dots < i_m$ die Adressen aller Register, die in den Befehlen von M' explizit vorkommen, wie etwa k in "i-load(k)" und außerdem die Register 0,...,n+1 . Als nächstes soll jedem Knoten v von T ein m-Tupel von linearen Funktionen $L^v = (L^v_{i_1},\dots,L^v_{i_m})$ zugeordnet werden: $L^v_{i_j}(x_1,\dots,x_{n+1})$ ist für gewisse Inputs gerade der Inhalt des i_j-ten Registers, wenn eine Berechnung mit $(x_1,\dots,x_{n+1})$ gestartet wurde und an dem zu v gehörigen Befehl angekommen ist. Wir definieren L^v induktiv:

$$L_k^{v_o} \equiv \begin{cases} x_k, & \text{falls } k \in \{1,\dots,n+1\} \\ 0 & \text{sonst} \end{cases}$$

Sei nun L^v gegeben und der Sohn v' von v entspreche einem der folgenden Befehle: "halt", "if <0> > 0 (= 0) then goto α", "goto α". In diesem Fall definiere $L^{v'} = L^v$. Definiere $L_o^{v'} = L_o^v + L_k^v$, falls v' "add(k)" entspricht, $L_o^{v'} = L_o^v - L_k^v$ falls v' "sub(k)" oder "sub*(k)" entspricht, $L^{v'}_{i_j} = L^v_{i_j}$ für $i_j \neq 0$.

v' entspreche einem Befehl "i-store(k)". Falls $L_k^v \equiv c \in \{i_1,\dots,i_m\}$, definiere $L_c^{v'} = L_o^v$, $L^{v'}_{i_j} = L^v_{i_j}$ für $i_j \neq c$. Andernfalls definiere $L^{v'} = L^v$. Es bleibt der Fall, daß v "i-load(k)" entspricht: Falls $L_k^v \equiv c \in \{i_1,\dots,i_m\}$, definiere $L_o^{v'} = L_c^v$, $L^{v'}_{i_j} = L^v_{i_j}$ für $i_j \neq 0$. Andernfalls werden zwei Fälle unterschieden:

1. Fall: Auf dem Weg in T von v_o zu v gibt es einen Knoten v*, der einem Befehl "i-store(k)" entspricht mit $L_k^{v*} = L_k^v$. Dann nehme man das letzte solche v* und definiere $L_o^{v'} = L_o^{v*}$, $L^{v'}_{i_j} = L^v_{i_j}$ für $i_j \neq 0$.

2. Fall: Einen solchen Knoten v* gibt es nicht. Dann definiere $L_o^{v'} \equiv 0$ und $L^{v'}_{i_j} = L^v_{i_j}$ für $i_j \neq 0$.

Definition 1: $\langle i\rangle_v(\bar{x})$ ist der Inhalt des i-ten Registers nach Ausführung des zu v gehörigen Befehls, vorausgesetzt, daß v erreicht wird, falls M mit $\bar{x}$ gestartet wurde, nicht definiert sonst.

Wir wollen T noch vereinfachen für den Fall von "irrelevanten" Abfragen. Sei v ein Knoten von T, der "if <0> >0 (= 0) then goto α" repräsentiert. Es kann sein, daß für alle $\bar{x}$, für die $\langle 0\rangle_v(\bar{x})$ definiert ist, gilt $\langle 0\rangle_v(x) > 0$ (= 0). In diesem Fall führt für kein $\bar{x}$ der Weg über den rechten Subbaum von v, und wir streichen diesen Subbaum. Entsprechend wird verfahren, falls für alle $\bar{x}$ gilt $\langle 0\rangle_v(\bar{x}) = 0$ ($\neq 0$).

Aus der Definition von $L^v_{i_j}$ folgt nicht, daß tatsächlich in jedem Fall $L^v_{i_j}(\bar{x}) = \langle i\rangle_v(\bar{x})$ ist. Wegen der Definition von $L_o^{v'}$ bei einem "i-load(k)"-Befehl ist es beispielsweise möglich, daß zwischen v* und v der Inhalt des Registers mit der Nummer $L^{v^*}_{k_*}(\bar{x})$ geändert wurde durch einen "i-store(s)" - Befehl am Knoten v" wobei $L^{v''}_{s}(\bar{x}) = L^{v^*}_{k}(\bar{x})$ war. In diesem Fall ist $L^{v'}_{o}(\bar{x}) \neq \langle 0\rangle_{v'}(\bar{x})$. Inputs, bei denen diese Situation auftritt, sollen in Zukunft ausgeklammert werden.

Definition 2: Für $j = 1,\dots,m$ sei f_j die konstante Funktion $f_j \equiv i_j$. Sei ℓ ein Blatt von T und A'_ℓ die Menge (paarweise verschiedener) linearer Funktionen, die während einer zu ℓ führenden Berechnung erzeugt werden, A_ℓ die Menge der paarweise verschiedenen Funktionen aus $A'_\ell \cup \{f_1,\dots,f_m\}$. Für je zwei Funktionen L,L' aus A_ℓ ist $\{\bar{x} \in \mathbb{R}^{n+1} \mid L(\bar{x}) - L'(\bar{x}) = 0\}$ eine Hyperebene, die verbotene Hyperebene für ℓ heißt. Die verbotenen Hyperebenen für ℓ werden mit $F^\ell_1,\dots,F^\ell_{k_\ell}$ bezeichnet. $\bar{x} \in \mathbb{N}^{n+1}(\mathbb{Z}^{n+1})$ heißt ℓ-zulässig, wenn M gestartet mit $\bar{x}$ zu Blatt ℓ führt und $\bar{x}$ nicht auf einer für ℓ verbotenen Hyperebene liegt.
$c(\ell) := \{\bar{x} \in \mathbb{N}^{n+1}(\mathbb{Z}^{n+1}) \mid \bar{x}$ ist ℓ-zulässig$\}$.
Das folgende wichtige Lemma ergibt sich nun sofort aus den Definitionen:

Lemma 1: Sei $\bar{x} \in \mathbb{N}^{n+1}(\mathbb{Z}^{n+1})$ ℓ-zulässig, und sei p der Weg von v_o zu ℓ. Dann gilt:

(i) $\langle i_j\rangle_v(\bar{x}) = L^v_{i_j}(\bar{x})$ für alle Knoten v auf p.

(ii) $c(\ell) = \{\bar{x} \in \mathbb{N}^{n+1}(\mathbb{Z}^{n+1}) \mid \bar{x} \notin \bigcup_{i=1}^{k_\ell} F^\ell_i$ und für alle Verzweigungspunkte v auf p : $L^v_o(\bar{x}) > 0\ (= 0)$ falls p in dem linken Zweig folgt und $L^v_o(\bar{x}) \leq 0$ sonst$\}$

Nach Konstruktion von T und nach der Modifikation von M zu M' gilt für deterministische Maschinen: für jedes Blatt ℓ ist entweder $L^\ell_o \equiv 1$ oder $L^\ell_o \equiv 0$. Im ersten Fall heißt ℓ akzeptierendes Blatt, im zweiten verwerfendes Blatt.

Definition 3: Die Länge eines Weges in T ist die Anzahl der Verzweigungspunkte auf ihm. Im Fall einer $\mathbb{N}$-RAM ($\mathbb{Z}$-RAM) ist die Tiefe D(T) von T die Länge eines längsten Weges von v_o zu einem Blatt ℓ mit $c(\ell) \neq \emptyset$. Im Fall einer ND-RAM ist D(T) die Länge eines längsten Weges p von v_o zu einem Blatt ℓ, so daß $c(\ell)$ ein $\bar{x}$ enthält, für das p einer kürzesten Berechnung von $\bar{x}$ entspricht.

Aus dieser Definition folgt, daß die Länge eines Weges in T genau die Anzahl der "if"-Abfragen in der p entsprechenden Berechnung in M' ist. Diese ist ihrerseits nicht größer als die Schrittzahl der Original-Berechnung von M. Daher gilt:

Fakt: Für eine $\mathbb{N}$-RAM (ND-RAM) M gilt: $D(T) \leq D_M(n+1)$, $(D(T) \leq ND_M(n+1))$, und für jedes Blatt ℓ ist die Anzahl der verbotenen Hyperebenen $k_\ell \leq D(T)(D(T)-1)/2$.

III. Geometrische Vorbereitungen und Beweise

Im folgenden werden einige geometrische Definitionen unf Fakten ohne Beweise aufgelistet. Für vollständige Beweise verwende man etwa Hilfsmittel aus [1].

Definition 4:

(i) G_n^b ist der n-dimensionale Würfel in $\mathbb{R}^n$ der Kantenlänge b und $0 \le x_i \le b-1$ für alle $\bar{x} \in G_n^b$, $\mathbb{R}_+^n = \{\bar{x} \in \mathbb{R}^n \mid x_i \ge 0$ für alle $i\}$.

(ii) Für jede Teilmenge $M \subset \mathbb{R}^n$ ist $i(M) := |M \cap \mathbb{Z}^n|$.

(iii) Für $\bar{\alpha} \in A_n := \{0,1\}^n - \{(0,\ldots,0)\}$ und $b \in \mathbb{N}$ ist $H_{\bar{\alpha}}^b := \{\bar{x} \in \mathbb{R}^n \mid \bar{x}\cdot\bar{\alpha}-b = 0\}$.

(iv) Ein Halbraum in $\mathbb{R}^n$ ist eine Menge $\{\bar{x} \in \mathbb{R}^n \mid \bar{x}\cdot\bar{\beta} \ge a\ (>a)\}$, $\bar{\beta} \in \mathbb{R}^n$, $a \in \mathbb{R}$. Der Durchschnitt einer endlichen Menge von Halbräumen ist konvex und heißt konvexes Polyeder. P heißt n-dimensional, wenn es einen n-dimensionalen Ball vom Radius $r > 0$ enthält. Die Dicke $t_n(P)$ eines n-dimensionalen konvexen Polyeders P ist der kleinste Abstand von zwei parallelen Hyperebenen, zwischen denen P liegt.

Bei den folgenden Abschätzungen wird n als Konstante betrachtet.

Fakt 1: Für alle Hyperebenen $H \subset \mathbb{R}^n$ gilt: $i(H \cap G_n^{2b}) \le O(b^{n-1})$

Fakt 2: (Blaschkes Theorem [2]): Jedes n-dimensional konvexe Polyeder P enthält einen n-dimensionalen Ball vom Radius $r \ge \frac{t_n(P)}{n+1}$.

Fakt 3: Sei $A \subset \mathbb{R}^n$ eine Menge, so daß jeder n-dimensionale Ball vom Radius r_o einen Punkt aus A enthält, sei $k \in \mathbb{N}$. Denn gilt für jede Menge $\{H_1,\ldots,H_k\}$ von k Hyperebenen und jeden Ball $B_n \subset \mathbb{R}^n$ vom Radius $r \ge 4n\,k\,r_o$

$$(B_n - \bigcup_{i=1}^{k} H_i) \cap A \neq \emptyset.$$

Wir können nun unsere Sätze beweisen. Dabei konzentrieren wir uns auf Satz 3. Exakte Beweise der ersten beiden Sätze finden sich in [4].

Beweisidee von Satz 1: Wir untersuchen nur Inputs mit $m+1 = 2^{n^{1/3}}+1$ Komponenten, von denen jede die binäre Länge von höchstens $n/(m+1)$ hat. Wir betrachten dann den Weg p zum Blatt ℓ in T, der in jeder Verzweigung dem "$\neq$"-Zweig folgt. ℓ ist das einzige Blatt, für das sich $c(\ell)$ nicht in eine Hyperebene einbetten läßt; deshalb enthält es, da nur endlich viele Blätter vorhanden sind, fast ganz $CK_{\mathbb{Z}}$. Daher darf $c(\ell)$ keinen ganzzahligen Punkt aus einem $H_{\bar{\alpha}}^b$ enthalten. Da die $H_{\bar{\alpha}}^b$ alle durch verbotene Hyperebenen und Abfragen auf p ausgeschlossen werden müssen, folgt (mit einigen geometrischen Überlegungen), daß auf p mindestens $2^{n^{1/3}}$ Abfragen liegen müssen.

Beweisidee zu Satz 2: Man betrachtet den zum Programm für $CK_{\mathbb{Z}}$ gehörigen Baum für $\bar{x} \in \mathbb{Z}^{n+1}$ und zeigt die Existenz eines "$\neq$"-Weges p, der einer kürzesten akzeptierenden Berechnung entspricht. Argumente analog zum obigen Beweis liefern dann die Länge von p und damit die untere Zeitschranke.

Zum Beweis von Satz 3 benutzen wir - wie in den Beweisen zu den Sätzen 1 und 2 – folgende geometrische Interpretation des Rucksack-Problems: gegeben $(x_1,\dots,x_n,b)$, x_i, $b \in \mathbb{N}$ dann ist $(\bar{x},b) \in K_{\mathbb{N}} \Longleftrightarrow$ es gibt $\bar{\alpha} \in A_n$ mit $\bar{x} \in H^b_{\bar{\alpha}}$.

Definition 5: Sei $H = \{\bar{x} \in \mathbb{R}^n \mid \bar{x}\cdot\bar{\beta}-a = 0\}$ eine Hyperebene in $\mathbb{R}^n$. Wir sagen $\bar{x} \in \mathbb{R}^n$ liegt über (unter) H falls $\bar{x}\cdot\bar{\beta} > a(\bar{x}\cdot\bar{\beta} < a)$. Für $I \subset A_n$ ist $\bar{R}^b_I := \{\bar{x} \in \mathbb{R}^n \mid \bar{x}$ liegt über $H^b_{\bar{\alpha}}$ für $\bar{\alpha} \in I$ unter $H^b_{\bar{\alpha}}$ für $\bar{\alpha} \notin I\}$ und $R^b_I = \bar{R}^b_I \cap \text{int } G^{2b}_n$, wobei int G^{2b}_n die Menge der (topologisch) inneren Punkte von G^{2b}_n ist.

Die R^b_I sind gerade die konvexen Mengen, in die int G^{2b}_n durch die Hyperebene $H^b_{\bar{\alpha}}$, $\bar{\alpha} \in A_n$ zerfällt. Wir schätzen zuerst die Anzahl der nicht leeren R^b_I nach unten ab.

Definition 6: Sei $f_I : \{0,1\}^n \to \{0,1\}$ die charakteristische Funktion für $I \subset \{0,1\}^n$. f_I heißt positive n-Schwellenfunktion mit Schwelle s, falls $s \geq 0$ und $\bar{w} \in \mathbb{R}^n_+$ existieren mit $\bar{w}\cdot\alpha \leq s \Longleftrightarrow \bar{\alpha} \in I$. $N(n)$ ist die Gesamtzahl der positiven n-Schwellenfunktionen.

Lemma 2: Es gibt $b \in \mathbb{N}$, so daß $N(n) \leq |\{I \subset A_n \mid R^b_I \neq \emptyset\}|$.

Lemma 3: $N(n) \geq 2^{(n-1)(n-2)/2}$.

Wir verzichten an dieser Stelle auf die Beweise; vereinfachte Versionen dieser Resultate wurden in [3] bzw. [8] hergeleitet.

Mit Lemma 2 und 3 folgt, daß G^{2b}_n durch die 2^n-1 Hyperebenen $H^b_{\bar{\alpha}}$ in mindestens $2^{(n-1)(n-2)/2}$ paarweise disjunkte offene Mengen zerschnitten wird. Demgegenüber liefert Lemma 4 eine obere Schranke für die maximale Anzahl $C_{m,n}$ von paarweise disjunkten, konvexen Mengen, in die der $\mathbb{R}^n$ durch irgendeine Menge $\{H_1,\dots,H_m\}$ von m Hyperebenen zerschnitten werden kann. Der Beweis folgt schnell aus einem in [7], Kap.2 angegebenen verwandten Resultat.

Lemma 4: $C_{m,n} \leq m^n$ für $n \geq 2$.

Wir wollen im folgenden zeigen, daß für jedes Blatt ℓ von T die Menge $c(\ell)$ der ℓ-zulässigen Punkte von höchstens $\left(\frac{D(T)^2}{2}\right)^n$ verschiedenen konvexen Mengen R^b_I "einen großen Teil" enthalten kann. $c(\ell)$ ist wegen Lemma 1 mit Hilfe folgender Hyperebenen definiert:

(a) der Menge $\{F^\ell_1,\dots,F^\ell_{k_\ell}\}$ der für ℓ verbotenen Hyperebene;

(b) der Menge $\{B^\ell_1,\dots,B^\ell_{r_\ell}\}$ der Hyperebenen, über denen $c(\ell)$ liegt;

(c) der Menge $\{A^\ell_1,\dots,A^\ell_{s_\ell}\}$ der Hyperebenen, unter denen $c(\ell)$ liegt.

Definiere $\underline{g(\ell)} := \{\bar{x} \in \mathbb{R}^n \mid \bar{x}$ liegt über $B_1^\ell,\ldots,B_{r_\ell}^\ell$, unter $A_1^\ell,\ldots,A_{s_\ell}^\ell\}$,

$\bar{g}(\ell) = g(\ell) - \bigcup_{i=1}^{k_\ell} F_i$, d.h. $c(\ell) = \bar{g}(\ell) \cap \mathbb{N}^n$ und $\bigcup_{\ell \text{ Blatt}} g(\ell) = \mathbb{R}^n$.

Lemma 5: Für jedes $R_I^b \neq \emptyset$ gilt:

(i) $i(R_I^b) \geq \Omega(b^n)$

(ii) Es gibt ℓ mit $i(c(\ell) \cap R_I^b) \geq c \cdot b^n$, $c > 0$ unabhängig von b.

Beweis: (i) Für $b > b'$, geht R_I^b aus $R_I^{b'}$ hervor durch Zentralprojektion vom Nullpunkt aus um den Faktor $\frac{b}{b'}$. Aus einem Ball $B' \subset R_I^{b'}$ vom Radius $r > 0$ geht daher ein Ball $B \subset R_I^b$ vom Radius $\frac{b}{b'} \cdot r$ hervor. Deshalb ist das Volumen von B proportional zu b^n und damit auch die Anzahl der ganzzahligen Punkte in B.

(ii) Wegen Fakt 1 ist $i(\bigcup_{i=1}^{k_\ell} F_i^\ell \cap G_n^{2b}) = O(b^{n-1})$. Die Behauptung folgt dann sofort aus (i) und aus $\bigcup_\ell g(\ell) = \mathbb{R}^n$.

Das nächste Lemma besagt, daß eine Menge $g(\ell)$ eine für ℓ nicht verbotene Hyperebene H_α^b nur in "sehr wenigen" Punkten schneiden kann.

Lemma 6: Sei ℓ ein verwerfendes Blatt und H_α^b nicht verboten für ℓ. Dann gilt für die Dicke von $g(\ell) \cap H_\alpha^b$: $t_{n-1}(g(\ell) \cap H_\alpha^b) \leq 4 \cdot D(T)^2 \cdot n^{2.5}$.

Beweis: Nach Definition der H_α^b enthät jeder $(n-1)$-dimensionale Ball vom Radius $\sqrt{n}$ in H_α^b einen Punkt $\bar{x} \in \mathbb{N}$. Wir wenden Fakt 3 auf H_α^b und $H_\alpha^b \cap F_i^\ell$, $i = 1,\ldots,k_\ell$ an. Wegen $k_\ell \leq D(T)^2/_2$ folgt: Jeder Ball vom Radius $r > 4 \cdot D(T)^2/_2 \cdot 4\sqrt{n}$ in $H_\alpha^b \cap g(\ell)$ enthält einen Punkt $\bar{x} \in \mathbb{N}^n$ der auf keiner Hyperebene F_i^ℓ liegt und deshalb ℓ-zulässig ist. Weil ℓ verwerfend ist, folgt andererseits $x \notin g(\ell)$. $g(\ell) \cap H_\alpha^b$ enthält also nur Bälle vom Radius $r \leq 2D(T)^2 \cdot n^{1.5}$. Aus Blaschkes Theorem (Fakt 2) folgt dann $t_{n-1}(g(\ell) \cap H_\alpha^\ell) \leq 4 \cdot D(T)^2 \cdot n^{2.5}$.

Lemma 7: Sei $P \subset \mathbb{R}^n$ ein konvexes Polyeder der Dimension n und F eine Hyperebene mit $F \cap \text{int } P \neq \emptyset$. P^+, P^- seien die Schnitte von P mit den beiden Halbräumen F^+, F^-, die durch F gegeben sind. Dann ist entweder $t_n(P^+) \leq t_{n-1}(P \cap F)$ oder $t_n(P^-) \leq t_{n-1}(P \cap F)$.

Beweisidee: Man gibt parallele Hyperebenen H_1, H_2 an mit:
(a) P liegt über H_1; (b) $P \cap F$ liegt zwischen H_1 und H_2; (c) der Abstand von $H_1 \cap F$ und $H_2 \cap F$ ist t_{n-1} $(P \cap F)$. Dann folgt:
P^+ oder P^- liegt zwischen H_1 und H_2. Ein vollständiger Beweis findet sich in [4].

Lemma 8: Sei ℓ ein Blatt von T, R_I^b, $R_{I'}^b$ verschieden und nicht leer. H_α^b liege zwischen R_I^b und $R_{I'}^b$ und sei nicht verboten für ℓ. Dann ist $i(g(\ell) \cap R_I^b) \leq c' \cdot b^{n-1}$ oder $i(g(\ell) \cap R_{I'}^h) \leq c' \cdot b^{n-1}$, für eine Konstante $c' > 0$ unabhängig von b.

Beweis: Wegen $H_\alpha^b \neq F_i^\ell$ $i = 1,\ldots,h_\ell$ folgt aus Lemma 6 $t_{n-1}(g(\ell) \cap H_\alpha^b) \leq 4n^{2.5} \cdot D(T)^2$. Nach Lemma 7 liegt daher o.B.d.A. $g(\ell) \cap R_I^b$ zwischen zwei parallelen Hyperebenen vom Abstand $4n^{2.5} \cdot D(T)^2$. Aus Fakt 1 folgt $i(g(\ell) \cap R_I^b) \leq 4n^{2.5} \cdot D(T)^2 \cdot O(b^{n-1}) = O(b^{n-1})$.

Wegen der Voraussetzung von Lemma 8 kann der Fall auftreten, daß eine Menge $g(\ell)$ viele Gebiete R_I^b enthält: nämlich dann, wenn die dazwischenliegenden Hyperebenen H_α^b für ℓ verboten sind. Im letzten Lemma wird die maximale Anzahl dieser R_I^b nach oben abgeschätzt.

Definition 7: Für eine konvexe Menge $A \subset \mathbb{R}^n$ sei $Q(A) := |\{R_I^b \mid i(A \cap R_I^b) \geq c \cdot b^n\}|$, wobei c die Konstante von Lemma 5 (ii) ist.

Lemma 9: Für jedes Blatt ℓ von T gilt $Q(g(\ell)) \leq D(T)^2/_{2^n}$.

Beweis: Wähle b so, daß $c' \cdot b^{n-1} < c \cdot b^n$, wobei c' die Konstante von Lemma 8 ist. H_α^b sei nicht verboten für ℓ und $H_\alpha^b \cap g(\ell) \neq \emptyset$. Aus den Lemmas 7 und 8 folgt $i(g(\ell) \cap R_I^b) \leq c' \cdot b^{n-1} < c \cdot b^n$ für alle R_I^b, die in einem der von H_α^b definierten Halbräume liegen. Dieser Halbraum heißt $H_\alpha^{b^-}$, der andere $H_\alpha^{b^+}$. Daher ist $Q(g(\ell)) = Q(g(\ell) \cap H_\alpha^{b^+})$. Wiederholung dieses Verfahrens für alle nicht verbotenen Hyperebenen H_ℓ^b liefert $Q(g(\ell)) = Q(g^*(\ell))$, wobei

$$g^*(\ell) = g(\ell) \cap \bigcap_{H_\alpha^b \text{ nicht verboten}} H_\alpha^{b^+}.$$

$g^*(\ell)$ wird jetzt nur noch von H_α^b geschnitten, die für ℓ verboten sind. Deren Anzahl ist $k_\ell \leq D(T)^2/_2$. Nach Lemma 4 können sie daher höchstens $D(T)^{2n}/_{2^n}$ Gebiete R_I^b definieren. Es folgt:

$$Q(g(\ell) = Q(g^*(\ell)) \leq D(T)^{2n}/_{2^n}.$$

Beweis von Satz 3: Nach Lemma 5 gibt es zu jedem $R_I^b \neq \emptyset$ ein Blatt ℓ_I, mit $i(c(\ell_I) \cap R_I^b) \geq c_4 \cdot b^n$. Andererseits ist wegen Lemma 9

$Q(g(\ell_I) \leq D(T)^{2n}/_{2^n}$. Da die Gesamtzahl der R_I^b mindestens $2^{(n-1)(n-2)/2}$ ist, folgt für die Anzahl L(n) der Blätter von T: $L(n) \geq 2^{(n-1)(n-2)/2} \cdot 2^n / D(T)^{2n}$. Aber wir können annehmen $D(T) \leq n^2/_2$ (sonst ist der Satz bewiesen). Daher gilt

$$L(n) \geq 2^{n^2/_2 - 4n \log n + n} \Rightarrow D(T) \geq n^2/_2 - 4n \log n + n \Rightarrow D_M(n+1) \geq n^2/_2 - 4n \log n + n$$

Literaturverzeichnis

[1] R.V. Benson, Euclidean geometry and convexity . Mc Graw-Hill 1916

[2] W. Blaschke, Über dem größten Kreis in einer konvexen Punktmenge. Jahresbericht der Deutschen Mathematiker-Vereinigung 23, 1914, pp 369-374

[3] D. Dobkin; R. Lipton, A lower bound of $\frac{1}{2} n^2$ on linear search programs for the Knapsack Problem. Journal of Computer and Systems Science 16, 1978, pp. 413-417

[4] P. Klein; F. Meyer auf der Heide, Lower time bounds for the Knapsack-Problem on several Random Access Machines, Preprint

[5] W. Paul, Komplexitätstheorie, B.G. Teubner, 1979

[6] W.J. Paul; J. Simon, Decision trees and Random Access Machines. Symposium über Logik und Algorithmik, Zürich 1980

[7] C.L. Sheny, Threshold Logic. Academic Press, London, New York 1969

[8] S. Yajima; T. Ibanaki, A lower bound on the number of threshhold functions, IEEE - EC 14, 1965, pp. 926- 929

Multidimensional B-tree:An efficient dynamic file structure for exact match queries

H. Güting and H.P. Kriegel
Informatik VI, Universität
D-46oo Dortmund 5o, W.Germany

Abstract: A file structure, called k-dimensional B-tree of order d, $d \geq 1$, is presented which allows each of the operations k-dimensional exact match query ("k-dimensional search"), insertion and deletion to be performed in time $O(\log_{(d+1)} N+k)$ in the worst case, where N is the number of k-dimensional records in the file.

A file F is a collection of N records. Every record is an ordered k-tupel $(x_1,\ldots,x_k)$ of values. Every component of the k-tuple is called a key or an attribute. A partial match query specifies values for s of k keys, $s \leq k$, and asks for all records which have those s values, independant of the other k-s values.

In case s = k the query is called an exact match query. The known dynamic file structures for partial match queries are the k-d trees by Bentley (1975, 1978) and the quintary trees by Lee and Wong (1978). If s < k keys are specified and A is the number of records satisfying the query, then the running times for a partial match query in a file of N records in a k-d tree structure and in a quintary tree structure are upper bounded respectively, by $O(s\ N^{1-s/k} + A)$ and $O(3^{k-s}(s + \log N) + A)$. To be fair, it should be mentioned, that these two file structures can additionally answer other types of queries, i.e. region queries and partial region queries, rather efficiently.

In order to develop a more efficient dynamic file structure for answering partial match queries or/and partial region queries, we should have an efficient dynamic file structure for answering exact match queries. The most efficient dynamic file structure that is known for answering exact match queries are the D-trees by Mehlhorn (1979). If a trie is used to represent the file of N records and each node of the trie is implemented as a D-tree, then exact match query, insertion of a new record and deletion of a record can be performed in time $O(\log_2 N+k)$ in the worst case.

We will give a dynamic file structure which allows each of the operations exact match query, insertion and deletion to be performed in time $O(\log_{(d+1)} N+k)$, $d \geq 1$, in the worst case. The structure called k-dimensional B-tree, kB-tree for short, is a generalization of the usual B-tree storing one dimensional keys to the case of "k-dimensional keys". As expected from this generalization kB-trees are suitable for external stores.

1. Structure of kB-trees

We start from a B-tree of order d. Every node, except for the root, contains l keys, $d \le l \le 2d$. Very few of the nodes of a kB-tree may have less than d keys. These nodes are called underfilled. To every key s in a B-tree there are two pointers associated. The left pointer points to a subtree for keys smaller than s and is called LOSON, the right one points to a subtree for keys larger than s and is called HISON. Thus each key in a B-tree has the function of a separator of two subtrees containing no underfilled nodes. In kB-trees there is an additional pointer called EQSON associated to each key s. In order to explain its function we have to give more information. A kB-tree of order d stores records $x = (x_1,\dots,x_k)$. A kex x_i, $1 \le i \le k$, is called a key of dimension i. Every node in a kB-tree contains keys of the same dimension i, $1 \le i \le k$. Then the node belongs to dimension level i or level i for short. Now let s be a key of dimension 1. For all records with first component equal to s, consider the (k-1) dimensional projection records obtained by omitting their identical first component. Then EQSON of s points to a (k-1)B-tree of order d for these projection records. Thus in a kB-tree, $k > 1$, a key may function as a representative for all the projection records stored in its EQSON subtree. Which of the two functions a key has, determines its height in the kB-tree (key-height-condition).

Example 1:

To give an idea of the kB-tree, we construct a 2B-tree of order 1 from the empty tree for the records

(a, 1), (a, 3), (a, 7), (a, 9),

(b, 2), (b, 4), (b, 5),

(c, 1), (c, 2),

(d, 1), (d, 3), d, 4)

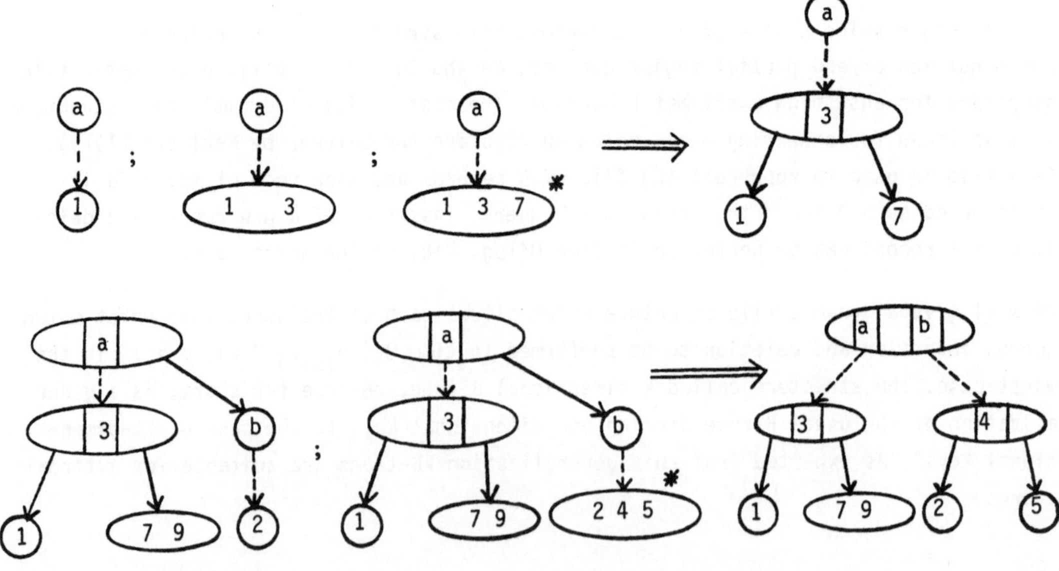

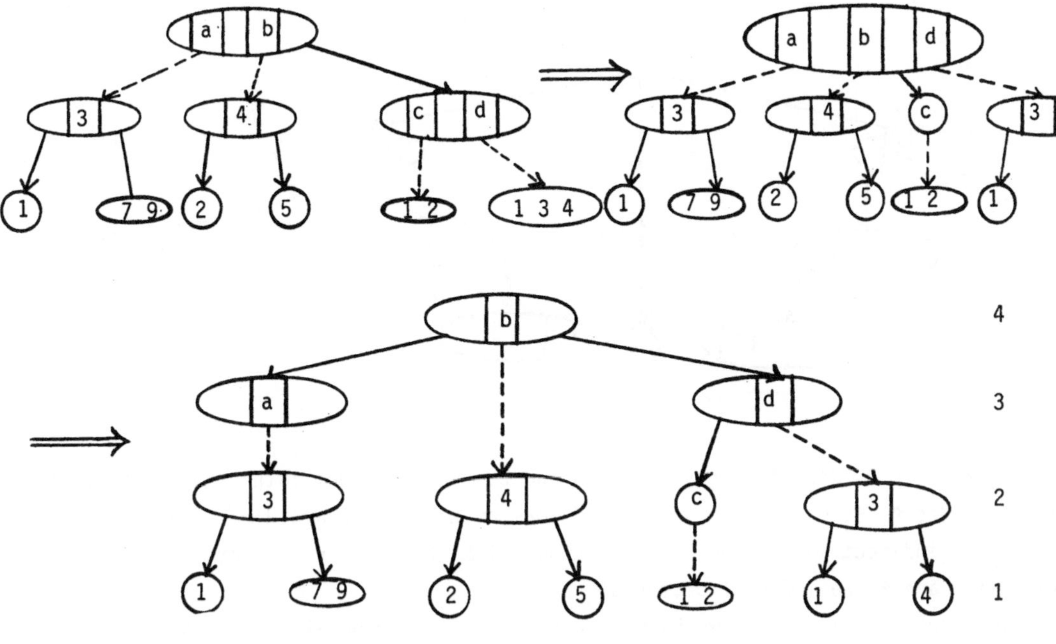

Figure 1

Both B-tree and kB-tree grow bottomup. Instead of the usual notion of level of a node we introduce the height of a node as its distance to the leaves. All leaves have height 1. The height of a node is equal to the height of its highest son increased by 1. The height of a kB-tree is equal to the height of its root.

In the following, the levels are counted from bottom to top, i.e. each leaf belongs to level 1, the root of the tree belongs to level k. This is in contrast to the introductary Example 1. When it is convenient, the records are given in the corresponding sequence, i.e. $x = (x_k,\ldots,x_1)$.

A node of height h and level i is called an (h,i)-node for short, h, i ≥ 1. We use the terms root and leaf as well with respect to a certain level. An (h,i)-node P is called root of level i, if it has no father on the same level.P is called leaf of level i, if h = i (this implies that P has no sons of level i).

Now we introduce relations between keys and nodes. If node P is LOSON or HISON of key k, then k is called direct right or direct left father key of node P, respectively. IfP is EQSON of k, then k is called father key of node P. Given key k, LOSON- and HISON-nodes are called direct sons of k.

If key k is the first or last key in the node, then its left or right son has only one direct father key, respectively. The other father key is in a higher node and is called indirect father key. If key l is indirect left or right father key of node P, then P is indirect right or left son of l, respectively. In an analogous way we distinguish direct and indirect brothers.

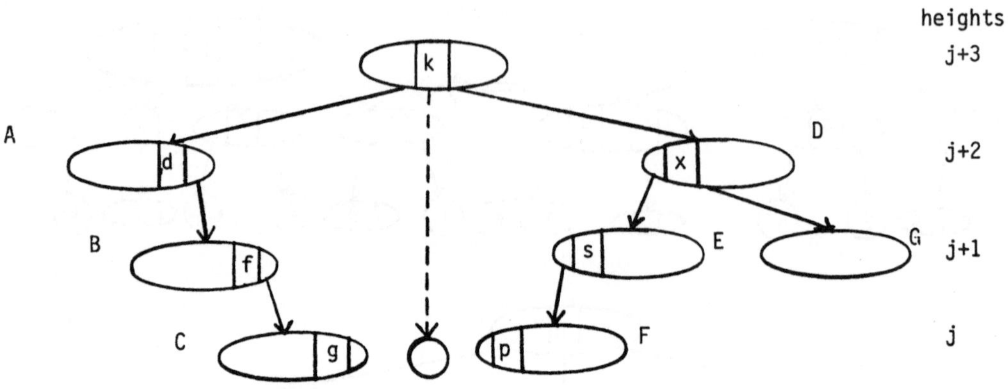

Figure 2

In figure 2, k is direct father key of A and D, k is indirect father key of B, C, E and F. Nodes A, B, C, D, E, F are called sons of k, A and D are direct sons, B, C, E and F are indirect sons. Node G is not a son of k. A and D are direct, B and E as well as C and F are indirect brothers.

For each key k in a kB-tree we have: the height of the node storing k is larger than the height of the EQSON-subtree. Let k be a key in a (h,i)-node, whose EQSON-subtree has height j. k is called <u>sinkable</u> if $h > j + 1$. k is called <u>sinkable to height l</u>, if $j < l < h$. (In case $i = 1$, let $j = 0$.)

k is called a <u>separator on height l</u>, if its (direct or indirect) sons of height l have at least d keys. k is called a <u>separator</u> if k is sinkable and if k is a seperator on all heights to which k is sinkable. k is called a <u>representative</u>, if k is not sinkable.

In figure 2, k is sinkable to heights j+2 and j+1. k is separator on height j+1 if nodes B and E contain at least d keys. k is separator if each of the nodes A, B, D, E contains at least d keys.

A kB-tree of order d satisfies the following structure properties:

(i) Every node contains at least one, at most 2d keys of the same dimension (key-number-condition).

(ii) Every key is either separator or representative (key-height-condition).

(iii) For every key k the following holds: the height of the node storing k is equal to the height of the highest of its three sons increased by 1.

(iv) All leaves (have no sons at all) have height 1.

Condition (iii) positions every key in a kB-tree as high as necessary dependent on the number of records which the key represents or separates. Condition (ii), the key-height-condition, guarantees that every key is as low as possible, i.e. a key has to be separator on each height to which the key is sinkable in order to justify its height. In case k = 1, conditions (i) - (iv) reduce to the usual B-tree conditions. In this case exactly all keys in leaves are not sinkable and are therefore representatives.

According to the key-height-condition all other keys must be separators. Since every key is sinkable to height 1, the definition of separator implies that every node, except for the root, contains at least d keys, and the root contains at least one key. Together with the maximum number 2d of keys per node from condition (i) and condition (iv) we obtain the usual B-tree conditions. Thus B-trees are a special case of kB-trees.

2. Height of kB-trees

Obviously, we are interested in a good upper bound for the height of a kB-tree of order d. Therefore we compute a lower bound for the number of records stored in a kB-tree of order d with a given height h. The root of such a tree is an (h,k)-node. Thus we will compute a lower bound for the number of records represented by an (h,i)-node being the root of a subtree. For this purpose, we will apply the following rule: From a lower bound for nodes of height $\le$ h-1 we derive a lower bound for nodes of height h by adding the lower bounds for those sons which exist for sure.

We only consider two types of nodes.

(i) nodes which are LOSON or HISON of a separator key and therefore have at least d keys. They are of <u>type I</u> (interior node).

(ii) nodes which are the root of some level i, $i \le k$. In case $i = k$, we have the root of the kB-tree, in case $i < k$ we have an EQSON of a representative key. Such nodes are said to be of <u>type R</u> (root).

Let I(h,i) and R(h,i) be a lower bound for the number of records represented by an (h,i)-node of type I and R, respectively. In order to compute R(h,k), we need not consider nodes which are neither of type I nor of type R.

For the lowest level we have:

$$\left.\begin{array}{l} I(1,1) = d,\ I(h,1) \ge (d+1)\cdot I(h-1,1),\ h > 1 \\ R(1,1) = 1,\ R(h,1) \ge 2\cdot I(h-1,1),\ h > 1 \end{array}\right\}(1)$$

If h = i, we have

$$\left.\begin{array}{l} I(i,i) = d \\ R(i,i) = 1 \end{array}\right\}(2)$$

Let P be an (h,i)-node, h, i > 1.

(i) If P is of type R, P contains at least one key which is either representative or separator. Thus we have:

(3) $R(h,i) \ge \min\{R(h-1, i-1),\ 2\cdot I(h-1, i)\}$

(ii) If P is of type I, P contains at least d keys. Either these keys are all representatives or at least one of them is separator.

(4) $I(h,i) \ge \min\{d\cdot R(h-1, i-1),\ (d+1)\cdot \min\{R(h-1, i-1), I(h-1, i)\}$

Recurrence relations (3) and (4) together with initial conditions (1) and (2) yield the following solution (for a more detailed description see [3]):

$$I(h,i) \ge d(d+1)^{h-i}$$

$$R(h,i) \ge \begin{cases} 1 & \text{, if } h = i \\ 2d\,(d+1)^{h-i-1} & \text{, if } h > i \end{cases}$$

Let N be the number of records stored in a kB-tree of order d with a given height h.

We assume $h > k$. Then we have

$$N \geq 2\ d\ (d+1)^{h-k-1} = \frac{2d}{d+1}\ (d+1)^{h-k}$$

Since $\frac{2d}{d+1} \geq 1$, we obtain

$$N \geq (d+1)^{h-k}$$

This yields an upper bound for the height h of a kB-tree of order d storing N keys:

$$h \leq \log_{(d+1)} N + k$$

Obviously an exact match query can be performed in time O(h) and therefore $O(\log_{(d+1)} N + k)$ in the worst case.

We will give insertion and deletion algorithms for kB-trees of order d that operate in O(h) and therefore $O(\log_{(d+1)} N + k)$ time in the worst case.

3. Insertion Algorithm

Let $x = (x_k, x_{k-1}, \ldots, x_1)$ be the record which should be inserted. We assume that x is not stored in the tree.

Case 1: The tree is empty.

Then we create a node of height h = k containing key x_k, pointing with its EQSON pointer to a node of height k-1 containing key x_{k-1}, etc. The leaf contains key x_1. As a result we have the following chain of nodes.

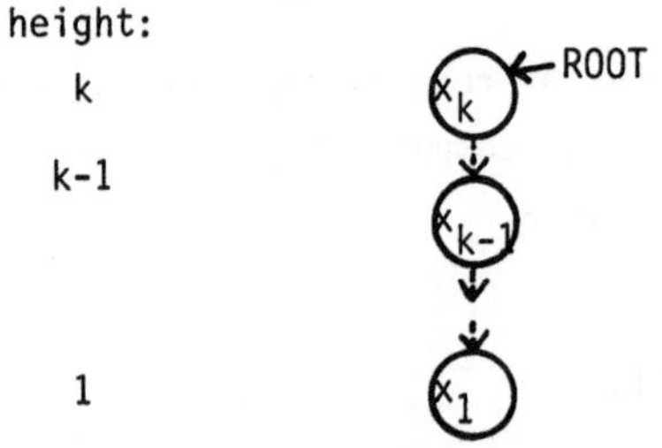

height:

k — (x_k) ← ROOT

k-1 — (x_{k-1})

1 — (x_1)

This structure is a correct kB-tree since all keys are representatives.

Case 2: The tree is not empty.

Searching for the keys $x_k, x_{k-1}, \ldots$ we traverse the levels k, k-1,.... Since record x is not stored in the tree, we will reach some level i which does not contain key x_i. Thus the search ends in an (h,i)-node P in which x_i falls between two keys.

2.1: P is a leaf of level i, i.e. h = i.

We insert key x_i in node P and create a chain of EQSON-nodes below key x_i storing the keys $x_{i-1}, \ldots, x_1$.

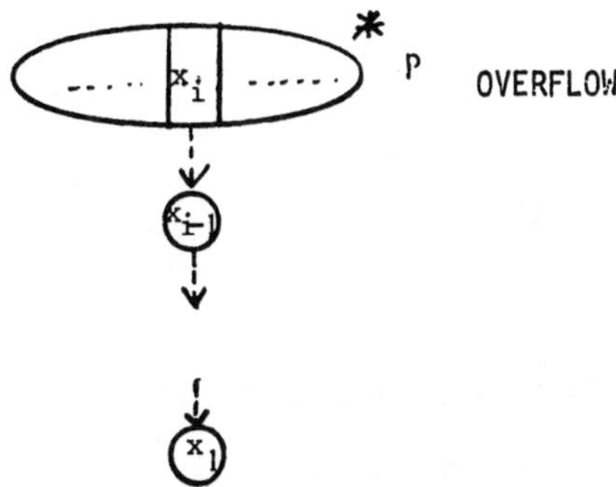

key x_i is a representative. The insertion of key x_i may have created an OVERFLOW in node P, denoted by the star. The restructuring will be described in the next section.

2.2: P is not a leaf of level i, i.e. $h > i$, and the value of the pointer q which we follow from node P, is <u>nil</u>.

We create a chain of nodes storing $x_i,\ldots,x_1$ and let q point to the root of this chain.

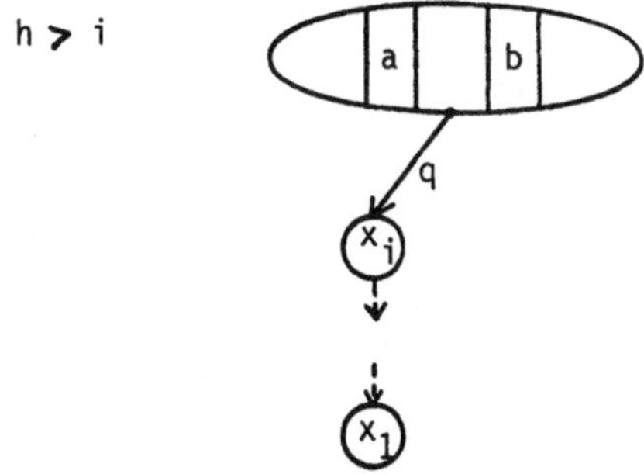

Since pointer q pointed to an empty and thus underfilled node, keys a and b are representatives. Thus the modified structure is correct. Since no OVERFLOW can occur, the insertion is finished.

<u>Restructuring Operations.</u>

We will generalize the three restructuring operations which we know from B-trees: splitting a node, balancing of two brother nodes and collapsing two brother nodes. Additionally, we need two new operations: lift a key in a certain node up to its father and eliminate the root of a level.

1. SPLIT (P)

This operation is performed if an OVERFLOW occurs in node P. The middle key of the 2d+1 keys in node P is pushed up into the father node and splits the overfilled node into two fragments of each d keys. Let P be an (h,i)-node.

<u>Case 1:</u> The father of P has height h+1.

1.1 The father Q of P belongs to level i

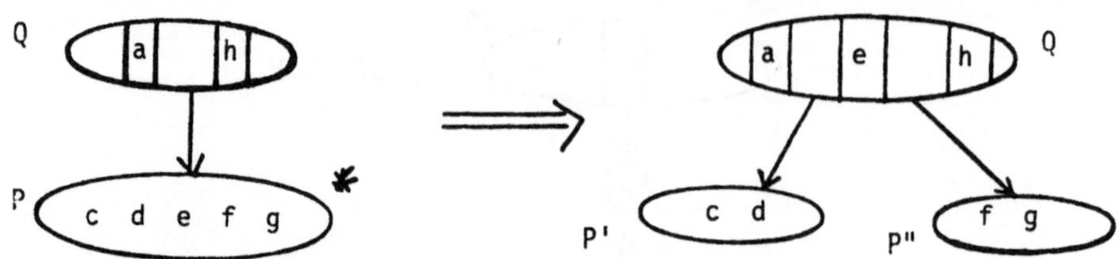

If Q now contains 2d+1 keys, then SPLIT (Q).

1.2 The father Q of P belongs to level i+1.

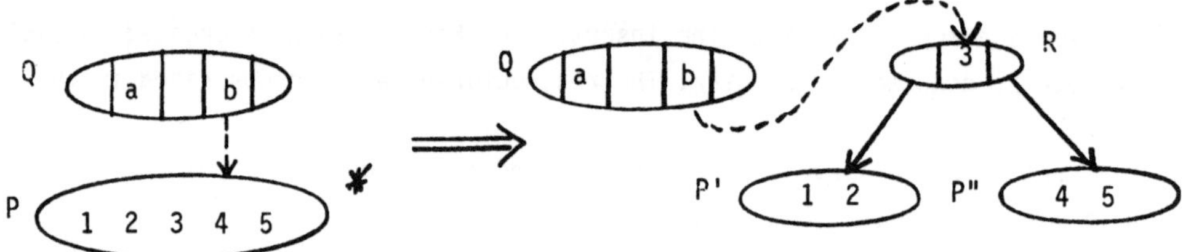

and lift key b in Q:
LIFTKEY (b, Q).

Case 2: The father of P has height > h+1 or does not exist.

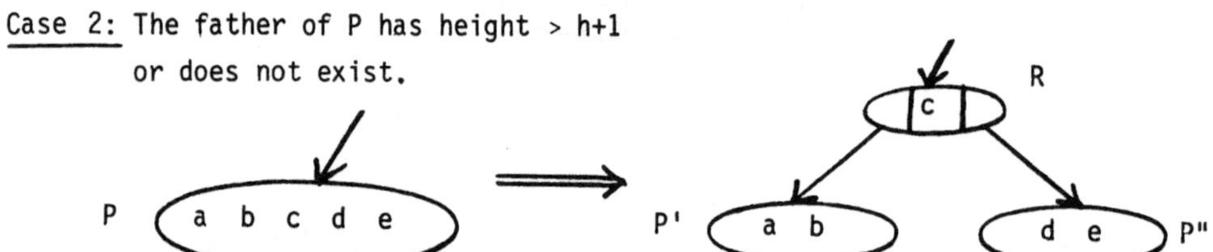

An operation is called correct if the result of the operation violates the structure properties (i) - (iv) of a kB-tree only where further operations are performed. For a verification that SPLIT is correct see [3].

2. LIFTKEY (k,P)

This operation is initiated by case 1.2 in SPLIT. In node P some key k has to be lifted to the father of P. Thus node P is split into two parts of arbitrary size. Let P be an (h,i)-node.

Case 1: The father of P has height > h+1 or does not exist.

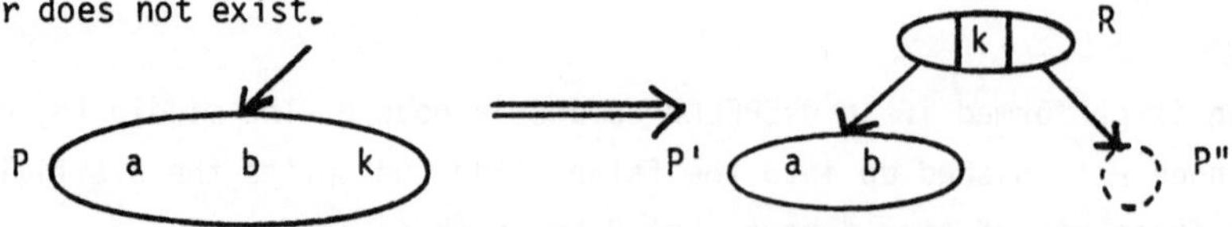

Correctness:

The father key of key k does not exist or is not sinkable. key k is not sinkable. Thus nodes P', P" and R may be underfilled.

Case 2: The father of P has height h+1.

2.1 The father Q of P belongs to level i+1.

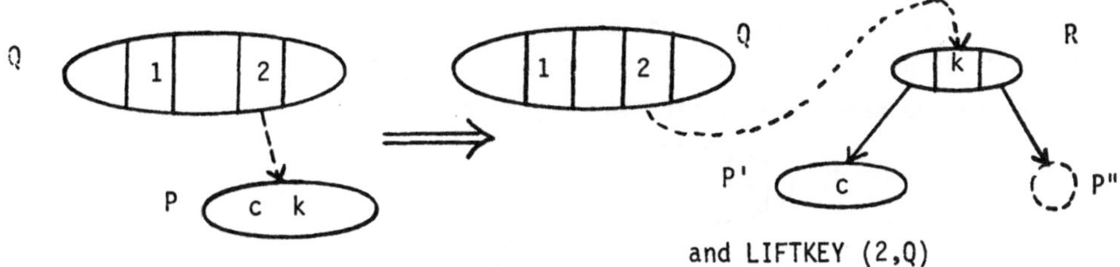

Correctness:

Since for key k there is no sinkable father key of the same level and key k is not sinkable, nodes P', P" and R may be underfilled.

2.2 The father Q of P belongs to level i.

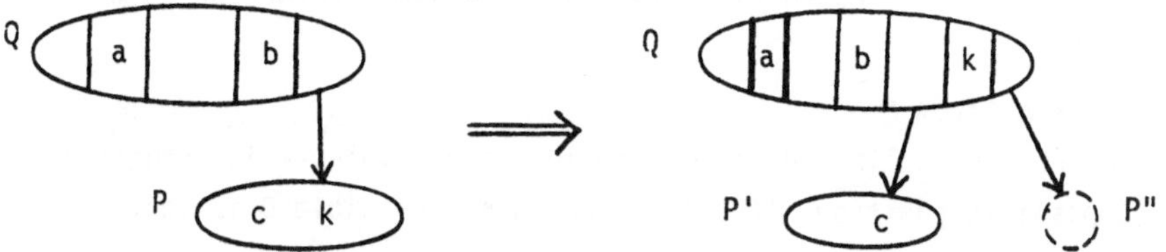

The following violations of the kB-tree structure may have been created by these transformations:

1.) Q has too many keys, OVERFLOW.
2.) P' is underfilled, the left father key of P' may have lost its separator property.
3.) P" is underfilled, the right father key of P" may have lost its separator property.

These violations are eliminated in the following way:

1.) SPLIT (Q).
2.) Balancing or collapsing P' with its left brother.
3.) Balancing or collapsing P" with its right brother.

In each case the situation can be corrected such that only one OVERFLOW or UNDERFLOW remains.

Case a: All father keys of P' and P" are in Q.

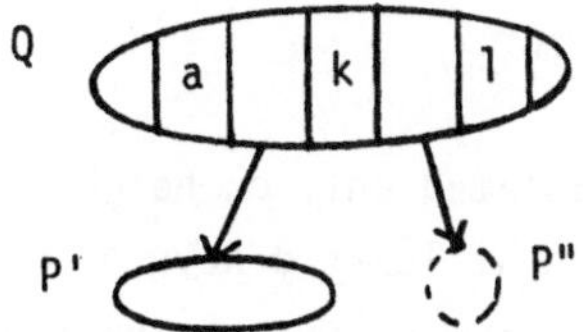

The UNVERFLOWS of P' and P" are treated by sinking keys a and/or l from node Q depending on whether balancing or collapsing is possible. We are left with

- an UNDERFLOW, if a and l were sunk.
- a finish, if one of the two keys was sunk.
- an OVERFLOW, if no key was sunk.

Case b: Exactly one father key except for key k is in Q.

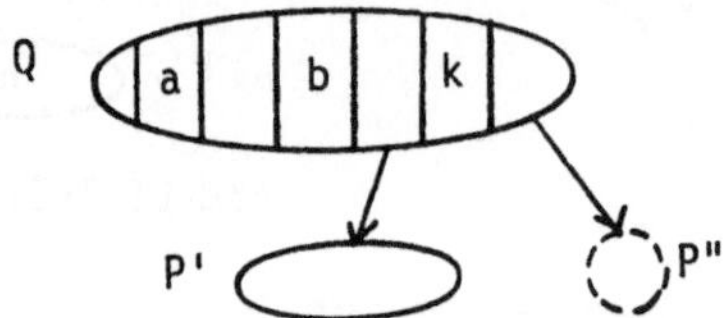

P' is balanced or collapsed with its left brother if b is sinkable.

b.1: The father key b is sunk and P' is balanced or collapsed with its left brother. Then the number of keys in Q is the same as before performing LIFTKEY(k,P). P" is balanced or collapsed with its indirect right brother which may cause an UNDERFLOW.

b.2: No key is sunk from Q. P" is balanced or collapsed. If collapsing is possible, k is brought in the highest possible position. If collapsing is not possible Q is left with an OVERFLOW.

Balancing with a brother

Node p is balanced with its brother Q if P and Q together contain at least 2d keys. Otherwise P and Q are collapsed.

a. Balancing with a direct brother

Let P be the underfilled node which causes balancing.

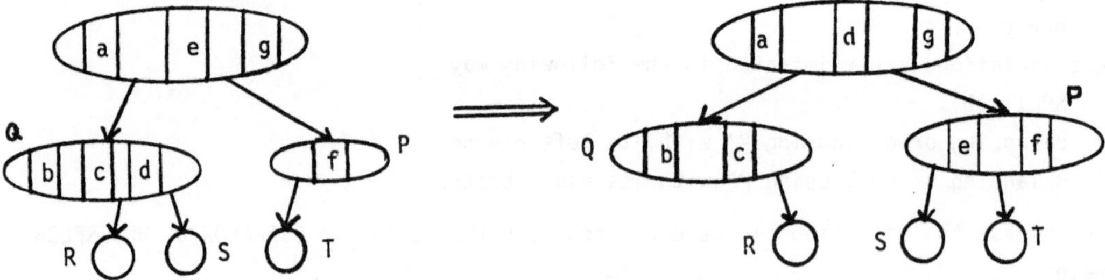

Balancing with a direct brother can be performed if the common father key of the two brothers, in our case key e, is sinkable. If none of the two father keys of P is sinkable the situation is already correct.

Correctness:

The separator property of key e was violated only on height j. Thus nodes S and T and further indirect sons of key e have at least d keys or e is not sinkable to their height. Therefore e is separator in its new position. The separator property of key g was violated but is now repaired by filling up node P. Key d was separator in its old position. Thus nodes R and S contain at least d keys. On height j, key d is separator, since Q and P are not underfilled. Thus d is separator.

b. Balancing with an indirect brother

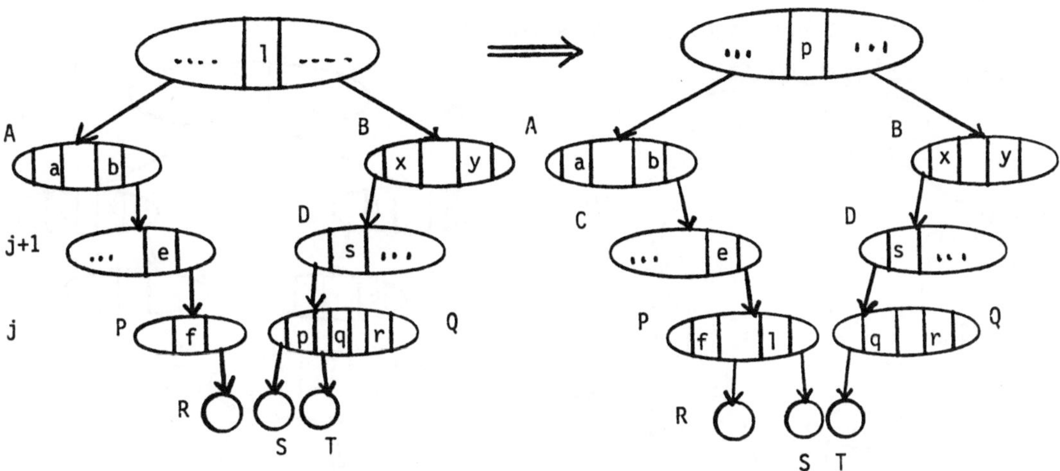

Balancing with an indirect brother is applicable only if the indirect father key of node P, in our case key l, is sinkable to height j. If the direct father key of P, in our case key e, would be sinkable to height j, it would be better to balance with the direct left brother.

Correctness:

Nodes A-D are not underfilled, since key l was sinkable to their height. Thus key p is separator on heights >j. Nodes P and Q on height j are not underfilled any more and below height j, key p has the same sons as before. Therefore key p is separator. Key l is as well separator since the tree fulfilled the kB-tree properties below level j.

Collapsing with a brother

The underfilled node P is collapsed with its brother Q if P and Q together contain less than 2d keys.

a. Collapsing with a direct brother

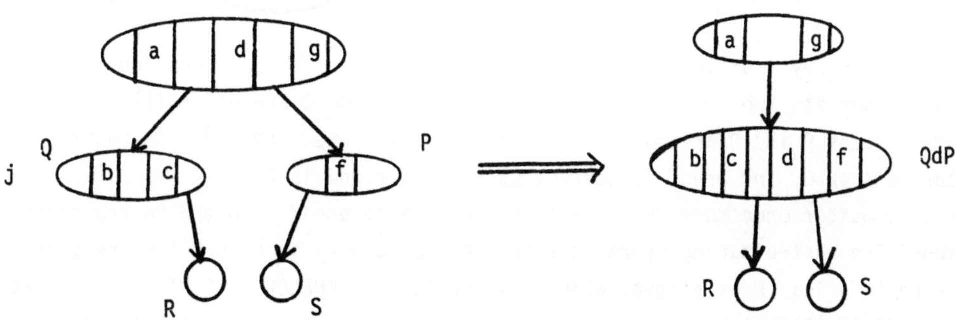

Collapsing with a direct brother is applicable if the common father key d of the nodes Q and P is sinkable to height j. If none of the two father keys of P is sinkable, the situation is already correct.

Correctness:

Key d is separator below height j if it is sinkable.

b. Collapsing with an indirect brother

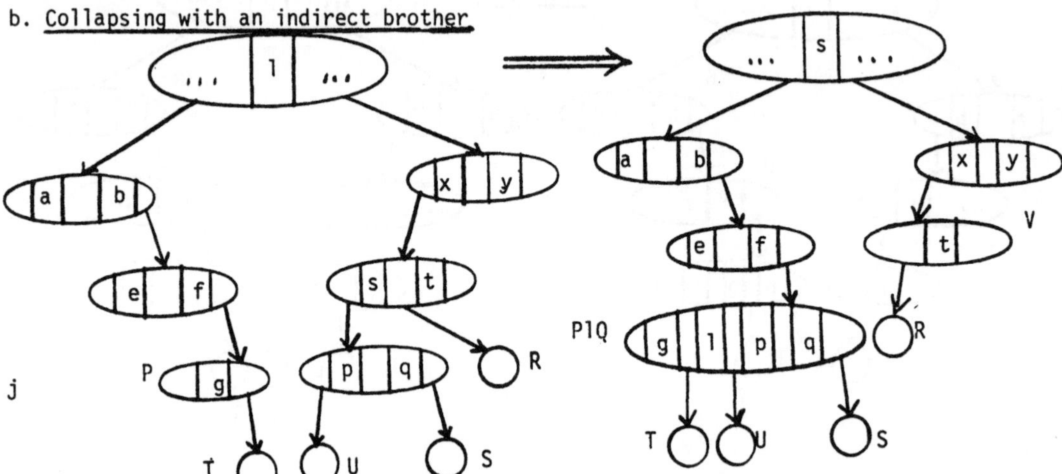

Collapsing with an indirect brother is possible if the indirect father key of node P, in our case key l, is sinkable to height j. An UNDERFLOW may occur in node V which will be treated. The proof of correctness is similar to that for balancing with an indirect brother and can be found in detail in [3].

Eliminating the root of a level

The root of a level can be underfilled. If by collapsing its two sons, the last key is deleted from the root, the root is eliminated.

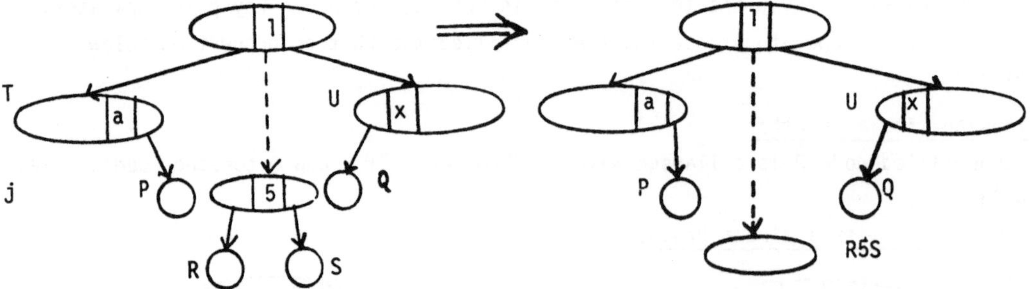

Thus, the father key l of this level is now sinkable to height j. Therefore, we have to check whether its two sons on height j, the nodes P and Q are underfilled. If this is the case nodes P and Q are balanced or collapsed to a new node PlQ. An UNDERFLOW may occur in T or U. The proof of correctness can be found in [3].

Now let us consider once more the insertion algorithm together with the restructuring operations. The restructuring operations are initiated only in case 2.1 where a key is inserted in a leaf P of a level which may create an OVERFLOW in P. This is treated by calling SPLIT (P) which may create again an OVERFLOW (case 1.1 of SPLIT (P)). Thus

SPLIT (P) may be called for the root of a level. If the result violates condition (iii) of a kB-tree LIFTKEY has to be performed. As a result, OVERFLOW, UNDERFLOW or FINISH can occur. OVERFLOW is treated as already mentioned. In case of UNDERFLOW, we try to balance or collapse with direct or indirect brothers. If balancing is possible, the restructuring is finished. Collapsing may result in a further UNDERFLOW. If collapsing eliminates the root of a level, UNDERFLOW may occur in the next higher level. OVERFLOW and UNDERFLOW can walk up a path in the tree until finally reaching the root of the tree which may be split or eliminated.

For the operations balancing with an indirect brother and collapsing with an indirect brother stacking the nodes of the search path guarantees that each node of the search path is visited at most once in the restructuring phase. Thus insertion time is $O(\log_{(d+1)} N + k)$ in the worst case.

4. Deletion Algorithm

Let $x = (x_k, x_{k-1},\dots,x_1)$ be the record which should be deleted. We assume that x is stored in the tree.

We perform an exact match query for record x until key x_1 on level 1 is found. x_1 will be deleted from level 1. If x_1 is the only key on level 1, i.e. the EQSON-subtree of x_2 consists only of one node containing x_1, we have to delete as well key x_2 from level 2. If the EQSON-subtree of x_3 consists only of one node containing x_2, we have to delete x_3 from level 3, etc. This will stop at some level i which contains more keys than just x_i. Otherwise the tree was storing only record x and we finish deletion by changing the tree to the empty tree.

Case 1: x_i is in a leaf of level i.

x_i is deleted from this leaf which may create an UNDERFLOW.

Case 2: x_i is in an (h,i)-node of level i which is not a leaf of level i, i.e. h>i.

The EQSON-subtree of key x_i is a chain $x_{i-1},\dots,x_1$ which we delete.

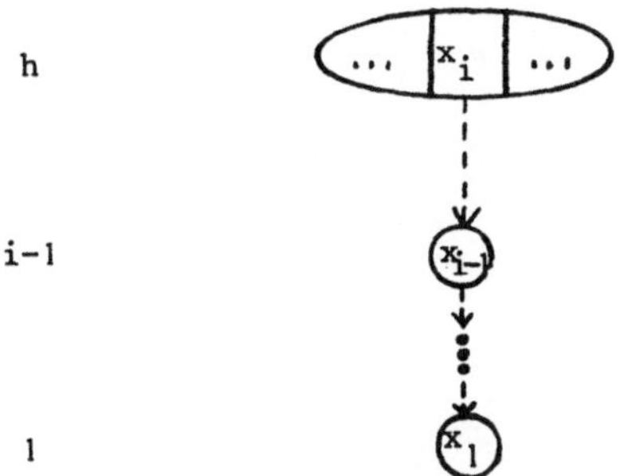

Since the height of the EQSON-subtree of key x_i is i-1 and h > i, key x_i is sinkable (to height i). Thus x_i is a separator and therefore a separator on heights h-1 to i. Now we search in the HISON-subtree of x_i for the successor y of x_i with respect to level i and replace x_i by y. y is in a leaf of level i. The deletion of y from this leaf is performed according to case 1. Key y is a separator in its new position since the key x_i which it is replacing is a separator and both y and x_i are sinkable to height i.

In both cases an UNDERFLOW may occur. UNDERFLOW is treated by balancing or collapsing as already described.

What concerns the time complexity of the deletion algorithm, let us remark that the jump in case 2 from a nonleaf node of level i to a leaf of level i does not extend the restructuring path to more than the height of the kB-tree. Together with the remarks concerning visiting each node of the search path at most once this guarantees $O(\log_{(d+1)} N + K)$ deletion time in the worst case.

We have shown that kB-trees are a very efficient dynamic file structure for answering k-dimensional exact match queries. In [3] it is shown that kB-trees can be used for answering partial match queries in $O(\log_{(d+1)} N + s + A)$ time in the worst case where s is the number of components specified in the query and A is the number of answers to the query.

References:

[1] Bentley, J.L. (1975), Multidimensional search trees used for associative searching, CACM 18, 9 (September 1975), 5o9-517.

[2] Bentley, J.L. (1978), Multidimensional binary search trees in database applications, Carnegie-Mellon Report CMU-CS-78.

[3] Güting, H. and Kriegel, H.P. (198o), Multidimensional B-trees, Computer Science Technical Report, Universität Dortmund, will appear.

[4] Lee, D.T. and Wong, C.K. (1978), Quintary Tree: A File Structure for Multidimensional Database Systems, IBM Research Report, R.C. 7285.

[5] Mehlhorn, K. (1979), Dynamic binary search, SIAM J. COMPUT. 8,2 (May 1979), 175-198.

TOWARDS SINGLE PROBE RETRIEVAL

G. Jaeschke
IBM Scientific Center
Heidelberg

Abstract
A short survey on minimization techniques for reducing the numbers of probes in open addressing schemes is given. Further, universal classes of hash functions (in the sense of Carter-Wegman) are discussed briefly. Finally, methods for constructing single probe retrieval functions are presented such as Sprugnoli's, Cichelli's and the author's approach (Reciprocal Hashing).

Investigations belong to the Information Management Research Project (AIM) at the IBM Scientific Center, Heidelberg

Hash coding generally requires to resolve collisions which can be performed by using

chaining methods or
open addressing methods.

Both kinds of collision resolution aim at minimizing the number of probes for retrieving a key from the table, and at working with compact hash tables.

In order to reduce the number of probes in the open addressing case one tries to arrange the keys to be inserted in an 'optimal' ordering. Several approaches exist for these purposes.

Motivated by the idea that most entries in hash tables are looked up several times Brent /1/ developed in 1973 a method for minimizing the number of probes to look up keys which are already in the table (successful search). Especially, the average successful search time remains bounded as the table gets full. The main ideas of Brent's variation shall be sketched briefly.

Let us assume that a table Tab with the locations Tab(o), Tab(1),.....Tab(M-1) is given, and that some positions i are already occupied: Tab(i) $\neq$ o. The key k is to be inserted into Tab. When open addressing is used a 'probe sequence' $p_o, p_1, \ldots p_s$ is associated to the key k such that

$$\mathrm{Tab}(p_o) \neq o, \ldots . \mathrm{Tab}(p_{s-1}) \neq o,\ \mathrm{Tab}(p_s) = o.$$

In this case k is inserted in position p_s. To this probing Brent introduced what will be called a 'first-order displacement'. For any position p_j, j = o,...,s-1, it will be examined whether the number of probes can be diminished by displacing Tab(p_j) to an open slot and simultaneously by inserting k at location Tab(p_j). The position p_{j_o} of the greatest savings of retrieval probes is chosen for such a displacement. If no probe number reduction can be achieved in this way no item is displaced and k is inserted at location Tab(p_s).

Though Brent's method improves expected retrieval times it can happen that the insertion of new keys negates the value of earlier displacements as for example in the following table where A,B,C,D,E are inserted in this ordering:

Ordering	Item	Hash codes	Normal	Brent
1	A	a d -	1	2
2	B	b - -	1	1
3	C	a b c	3	1
4	D	d e -	1	2
5	E	e f -	1	2

Normal probe number is 7 while Brent needs 8 probes because of the displacements $A \rightarrow d$, $D \rightarrow e$, $E \rightarrow f$.

By introducing recursive insertions (or higher order displacements) which allow displaced items to dislocate other entries when searching for an open slot the above demonstrated negative effect can be avoided and the expected costs for retrieving stored items can be lower (Lyon /2/). Generally, it suffices to apply second-order displacements, since third- and higher-order displacements yield only smaller improvements. For the case of unsuccessful search Lyon introduces so-called KICKOUT-values which indicate the length of longest searches of stored keys. If the number of probes for a key k has reached the KICKOUT-value k can be rejected without having discovered an open slot.

Further, some results in arranging keys optimally in a hash-table are stated in a paper of Rivest /3/. Here it is shown that arrangements minimizing either the average or the worst-case number of probes required to retrieve any key in the table can be found by using efficient algorithms for the assignment problem. Also, in the same way optimality can be maintained when new keys are inserted to the table which is not true with respect to Brent's algorithm.

Finally, a confrontation of these open addressing methods which are efficient in the case of successful search, with chaining in combination with abbreviated keys results in the fact (see a corresponding paper of Schek, to appear in CACM) that the latter can be made optimal with respect to the expected number of probes for a stored key, and more efficient for searches with a lot of rejections.

All mentioned approaches for reducing the number of probes use for determining the table locations (probe sequences etc.) fixed hash functions which do not depend upon the inserted keys.

In contrast to these approaches the following ones work with a suitable set of hash functions and select one of these to perform the retrieval of keys. So, Carter and Wegman /8/ have introduced 'universal' classes K of hash functions which have the defining property that no pair of distinct keys collide under more than 1/b of the functions of K (where each $h \in K$ maps a set A of keys into a set B with b elements). Here, a hash function is chosen

<u>at random</u> and <u>input independent</u> from K (input $S \subseteq A$).

Intuitively speaking, such a universal class K of hash functions contains enough good functions that a random choice is very likely to be a good choice.

Another possibility is to define classes of parametrized functions $f(k,a_1,\ldots a_r)$ with parameters $a_1,a_2,\ldots a_r$, key = k, and to determine suitable parameters dependent upon a given input. If the aim here is to permit no collisions at all we are concerned with so-called 'perfect hashing functions'. These are bijective mappings from a set W of given keys onto a set $\{z_1,\ldots z_n\}$ of integers where n = card W. They enable retrieval and rejection with a single probe per key. If the size of the hash table doesn't play any role then it is easy to find perfect hashing functions : For any set W of n given numerical keys $w_1,\ldots,w_n$ determine the smallest integer M such that all w_i mod M are different from each other. But it turns out that such M-values are generally relatively large and cannot be of practical interest. Therefore, Sprugnoli /4/ has developed some methods for the determination of perfect hashing functions with tables as small as possible (but not necessarily minimal). Especially, his 'quotient reduction with a cut' is to be mentioned which is applicable to smaller identifier sets. Though this method is relatively efficient in the case of uniformly distributed keys, this is not the case if the keys are great integers which are not uniformly distributed. Here hash functions are obtained which in addition to their inefficient discovering yield very sparse tables.

These hash functions are of the following type:

$$h(x) = [(x + a)/b] \quad \text{for} \quad x \leq c$$

$$h(x) = [(x + a')/b] \quad \text{for} \quad x > c$$

with parameters a,a',b,c.

As an example take the following set W of keys

W = {438,977,1233,1844,2769,3145,4722,6300,7942,
7968,8413,9244} with 12 elements.

Here we obtain

$$h(x) = [(x + 188)/627] \quad \text{for} \quad x \leq 7968$$

$$h(x) = [(x + 370)/627] \quad \text{for} \quad x > 7968$$

and a table size of 16.
Other examples (for instance with 20 numerical keys between 10000 and 100000000000) yield tables with a load factor less than 1/300.
Hash functions which yield no collisions and minimal table size (load factor = 1) are called 'minimal perfect hashing functions'. A simple method for generating minimal perfect hashing functions (which, however, does not work in several cases) was given recently by Cichelli /5/. If all keys k $\in$ W are words of Σ * then to every letter ζ of the alphabet Σ an appropriate integer $\alpha(\zeta)$ will be associated and the hash code of k is determined by
(length of k) + α(first letter of k) + α(last letter of k).
Here, it is easy to find nontrivial examples of key sets of arbitrary magnitude for which no mappings α of the above kind exist (cf. Jaeschke-Osterburg, intended to appear as letter to the editor in CACM).

In order to find in any case (i.e. for arbitrary sets of numerical identifiers) minimal perfect hashing functions I have developed the approach of 'Reciprocal Hashing' for static tables which shall be discussed in the following /6/.

It can be proved that to any given finite set W of positive integers there exist three integer constants C,D,E such that the function h with

$$h(w) = [C/(Dw + E)] \bmod n, \quad \text{card}(W) = n$$

is a minimal perfect hashing function. h is then a bijective mapping from W onto the set {0,1,...n-1}. In order to determine the constants C,D,E one needs special algorithms.

The algorithm C determines for a given set W = $\{w_1,...w_n\}$ of integers an integer C such that the residues

$[C/w_1]$, $[C/w_2]$,.....$[C/w_n]$ are different mod n. Such a number C exists if the $w_1, w_2, \ldots w_n$ are pairwise relatively prime. In the general case (where the w_i are not necessarily pairwise relatively prime) it may happen that no such C exists (this actually happened until now in only two linearly independent cases cf./6/).

For such a case the algorithm DE determines for a given set $W = \{w_1, \ldots w_n\}$ of integers two integers D,E such that

$$Dw_1 + E, Dw_2 + E, \ldots\ldots Dw_n + E \in W'$$

are pairwise relatively prime. -

The most critical part of the determination of a minimal perfect hashing function is the algorithm for the C-values related to the set W or W'. Here it is possible that an appropriate integer C exists but its computation requires too much time. In this case one can also apply another algorithm which is described in /6/. This algorithm (called congruence method) corresponds to the constructive proof of the existence theorem of reciprocal hashing. The only disadvantage of the congruence method is that it generally returns very large C-values.

Other possibilities in the case of too large C-values are the application of 'reciprocal hashing with a cut' or of 'reciprocal hashing with grouping'.

Before discussing the algorithms C and DE we present some examples of our approach. Let's take at first the twelve element set W from above. Here we find for D = 1, E = o

$$h(x) = [441558o/x] \bmod (12,$$

and by applying algorithm DE

$$h(x) = [74o19o5/(6x + 49)] \bmod 12$$

as minimal perfect hashing functions.

Up to n = 2o experiments show that there are no great difficulties in finding the appropriate parameters C,D,E for a given set W of cardinality n. For larger cardinalities n $(21 \le n \le 4o)$ one can apply 'reciprocal hashing with a cut'. Let us take as example the set of the 31 most frequently used English words given in /7/. These are

A, AND, ARE, AS, AT, BE, BUT, BY, FOR, FROM, HAD, HAVE, HE, HER, HIS, I, IN, IS, IT, NOT, OF, ON, OR, THAT, THE, THIS, TO, WAS, WHICH, WITH, YOU.

If these words are encoded to a basis 27 we obtain the following set W (increasing ordering)

$$W = \{1,9,46,47,59,79,221,257,262,263,411,419,423,555,1111, 122o,2o45,4797,5863,5985,6o94,1o631,148o1,16813,18651, 131638,158792,399539,399754,459818,12387257\}$$

We determine D,E by algorithm DE and find

$$D = 3oo3o, \quad E = 277.$$

Now we transform W into W' by $w_i' = Dw_i + E$ and obtain

$$W' = \{3o3o7,27o547,1381657,1411687,1772o47,2372647, 66369o7,7717987,7868137,7898167,123426o7,12582847, 127o2967,16666927,333636o7,36636877,61411627, 144o54187,176o66167,179729827,183oo3o97,3192492o7, 4444743o7,5o4894667,56oo898o7,3953o89417,4768524o37, 11998156447,12oo4612897,138o8334817,371989327987\}.$$

Let Y_1 be the set of the 18 smallest numbers of W' and $Y_2 = W'-Y_1$. By determining C-values for Y_1 and Y_2 we obtain

$$C_1 = 17858277 \quad \text{and} \quad C_2 = 184245996.$$

Therefore, the function h defined by

$$h(w) = [17858277/(3oo3ow+277)] \bmod 18 \text{ for } w \leq 4797$$

$$h(w) = 18 + [184245996/(3oo3ow+277)] \bmod 13 \text{ for } w > 4797$$

is a minimal perfect hashing function for the original set W.

For n > 4o we use grouping functions as follows.

A 'grouping function' g maps the set W of identifiers onto a set {1,...m} with $2 \leq m < n$. If $g(w_i) = k$ then we say that w_i belongs to the k.th group G_k with respect to g and W. Let g_k be the number of elements of W belonging to the k.th group G_k: $g_k = |G_k|$. For each group G_k we determine the number C_k by the search algorithm C and put

$$h_k(w) = [C_k/w] \bmod g_k \quad \text{for } w \in G_k.$$

Finally, if

$$h(w) = h_k(w) + \sum_{j=1}^{k-1} g_j \quad \text{with } k = g(w)$$

then h is a minimal perfect hashing function for the set W.

The number of groups should be the smallest integer m such that each group doesn't contain more than 2o elements. A grouping function g may then be defined for example by

$$g(x) = 1 + x \bmod m.$$

Let $\pi(j)$ denote the hash code $h(w_j)$. Then retrieval of an item x is obviously performed as follows

$$i = 1 + x \bmod m$$

$$h(x) = [C_i/x] \bmod g_i + \sum_{j=1}^{i-1} g_i$$

and compare x to w_j with j such that $\pi(j) = h(x)$. If $x = w_j$ then clearly $x \in W$, but if $x \neq w_j$ then $x \notin W$ (single probe).

With respect to practical applications one should work with groups having for instance 12 elements only. If then a new key is to be inserted one has only to recompute a C-value for the group into which this key shall be entered, otherwise we have to form new groups and all C-values have to be recomputed.

Finally, we discuss the algorithms C and DE for finding the parameters C,D,E of a minimal perfect hashing function for the set W:

$$h(x) = [C/(Dx + E)] \bmod n, \quad n = \text{card } W.$$

The Algorithm C.

Let $W = \{w_1, w_2, \ldots, w_n\}$ consist of positive integers with $w_1 < \ldots < w_n$. Then the algorithm C tries to find an integer C such that

$$[C/w_1] \bmod n, \ldots\ldots [C/w_n] \bmod n$$

are different from each other.

The algorithm starts with an arbitrary positive integer $C = C_o$. Then the residues of $[C/w_i] \bmod n$ are calculated. If they are all different from each other the algorithm terminates successfully. Otherwise the actual C is increased conveniently (see below) by a certain amount $\alpha(C,W)$ and the new C will be examined in the same way. The algorithm C terminates unsuccessfully if C exceeds a prescribed limit L.

Now let us discuss which increment $\alpha(C,W)$ is convenient for our algorithm. We need examine only such integers C which are multiples of at least one element w_i of W. This is clear because a C-value that is not a multiple of any element of W gives a remainder

$$r_i \equiv C \bmod w_i \qquad (o < r_i < w_i),$$

and by taking the minimum of these r_i, say r_{i_o}, the quotients $[C/w_i]$ equal the quotients $[C'/w_i]$ where $C' = C - r_{i_o}$; C' is a multiple of w_{i_o}. This means that $\alpha(C,W)$ should be one of the numbers

$$w_1 - r_1,\ w_2 - r_2, \ldots\ldots w_n - r_n \quad \text{with } r_i = C - [C/w_i].w_i.$$

Our aim is to examine as few as possible C-values and to find the smallest one being greater than C_o. If now for example

$$[C/w_i] \equiv [C/w_j] \bmod n$$

for some i,j then no integer C' exists with

$$C < C' < C + \min\{w_i - r_i,\ w_j - r_j\}$$

such that $[C'/w_i] \not\equiv [C'/w_j] \bmod n$ as is easy to be seen. If we therefore define

$$\delta_{ij} = \min\{w_i - r_i,\ w_j - r_j\}$$

$$K(C,W) = \{(i,j) \mid 1 \le i < j \le n \wedge [C/w_i] \equiv [C/w_j] \bmod n\}$$

$$\alpha'(C,W) = \max_{(i,j) \in K(C,W)} \delta_{ij}$$

then $\alpha'(C,W)$ would be an appropriate increment of C. But experimental results show that it is more efficient to work with

$$\alpha(C,W) = \delta_{i_o j_o}$$

as increment of C instead of $\alpha'(C,W)$, where j_o is the greatest index j for which there exists an i with $(i,j) \in K(C,W)$, and i_o is the greatest index i with $(i,j_o) \in K(C,W)$. -

Given $W = \{w_1, \dots, w_n\}$ with $w_1 < \dots < w_n$ and integers C_o, L we perform the following steps.

Step 1.

Put $C = C_o$.

Step 2.

Determine the residues

$[C/w_1] \bmod n, \dots\dots [C/w_n] \bmod n$.

If they are all different from each other the algorithm terminates successfully. Otherwise go to step 3.

Step 3.

If C > L then the algorithm terminates unsuccessfully. Otherwise go to step 4.

Step 4.

Determine

$$j_o = \max\{j \mid \forall_i [C/w_i] \equiv [C/w_j] \bmod n\}$$

$$i_o = \max\{i \mid [C/w_i] \equiv [C/w_{j_o}] \bmod n\}$$

$$\alpha(C,W) = \min\{w_{i_o} - C \bmod w_{i_o},\ w_{j_o} - C \bmod w_{j_o}\}$$

$C = C + \alpha(C,W)$ and return to step 2.-

The Algorithm DE.

Given a set W of positive integers $w_1, w_2, \dots w_n$ the algorithm DE determines integers D and E such that the values

$$Dw_1+E,\ Dw_2+E, \dots\dots\dots,\ Dw_n+E$$

are pairwise relatively prime.

Let P be the set of all primes.

Step 1.

Determine the set

$$I_n = \{p \mid p \in P \wedge p \le n/2\} .$$

Step 2.

Determine the set

$$P_2 = \{p \mid p \in I_n \wedge \beta(p) \le 1\}$$

where

$$\beta(p) = \min_{o \le v \le p} \text{card } \{i \mid w_i \equiv v \mod p\}.$$

Then P_2 contains all primes $\le n/2$ such that at least one residue v mod p occurs at most once among the residues w_i mod p.

Step 3.

Determine $P_1 = I_n - P_2$ and put

$$D = 1 \text{ if } P_1 = \emptyset, \quad D = \prod_{p \in P_1} p \quad \text{, otherwise.}$$

Step 4.

Determine for each $p \in P_2$ the set

$$M(p) = \{-Dv \mod p \mid o \le v < p \wedge \text{card } \{i \mid w_i \equiv v \mod p\} \le 1\} .$$

M(p) is not empty for all these p.

Step 5.

Examine all integers E for which

$$(E \mod p) \in M(p) \quad \text{for } p \in P_2 \quad \text{and}$$

$$(E \mod p) \ne o \quad \text{for } p \in P_1 ,$$

whether the $Dw_i + E$ are pairwise relatively prime or not. The algorithm terminates successfully before E has reached the upper bound $b = \prod_{p \in T} p$ where $T = I_n \cup \{p \mid \Delta \equiv o \mod p\}$ and $\Delta = \prod_{i>j} (w_i - w_j)$.

Remark:

The algorithm C can also be used to construct universal classes of hash functions of reciprocal type. Let A,B,C be the following sets

A = {31,37,41,43,47,53,59,61,67,71,73,79,83,89,97}

B = {o,1,2,3,4,5,6,7,8,9}

C = {248213,388752,4o5363,4168o9,757212,817594,857956,
912373,93o548,93o993} .

If $Q = \{h_1, h_2, \dots h_{10}\}$ with $h_i(x) = [C_i/x] \mod 1o$ for $i = 1, \dots 1o$, $C = \{C_1, C_2, \dots C_{10}\}$, then Q is such a universal class.

References

/1/ Brent,R.P. Reducing the Retrieval Time of Scatter Storage Techniques, CACM 16,2, Feb 1973,pp.1o5-1o9

/2/ Lyon,G. Packed Scatter Tables, CACM 21,1o, Oct 1978, pp.857-865

/3/ Rivest,R.L.(Optimal Arrangement of Keys in a Hash Table, JACM 25,2, April 1978, pp.2oo-2o9

/4/ Sprugnoli,R. Perfect Hashing Functions A Single Probe Retrieving Method for Static Sets, CACM 2o,11, Nov 1977, pp.841-85o

/5/ Cichelli,R.J. Minimal Perfect Hash Functions Made Simple, CACM 23,1, Jan 198o, pp.17-19

/6/ Jaeschke,G. Minimal Perfect Hashing, TR 8o.o2.oo3, IBM Scientific Center, Heidelberg

/7/ Knuth,D.E. The Art of Computer Programming, 1968 vol.1-3, Addison-Wesley,Reading Mass., 1968-1973

/8/ Carter,J.L. and Wegman,M.N. Universal Classes of Hash Functions, Journal of Computer and Systems Sciences vol.18,2, April 1979, pp.143-154

DAS KARLSRUHER BEWEISSYSTEM

N. Eisinger, J. Siekmann, G. Smolka
E. Unvericht, Chr. Walther

Institut für Informatik I
Universität Karlsruhe
D-7500 Karlsruhe 1
Postfach 6380
West Germany

Zusammenfassung

Wir beschreiben den gegenwärtigen Stand eines Automatischen Beweissystems (ABS), das seit 1977 an der Karlsruher Universität entwickelt wird [DS77, DS79]. Bis zur endgültigen Fertigstellung des Systems sind weitere drei Jahre geplant.

Der Beitrag, den das Projekt zu dem Gebiet des Automatischen Beweisens leisten soll, läßt sich in den folgenden drei Thesen zusammenfassen:

Es ist möglich, ein Automatisches Beweissystem zu entwickeln, das - unterstützt durch geeignete Heuristiken und fachspezifisches Wissen -

(i) ein "aktives" und zielgerichtetes Verhalten bei der Suche nach einem Beweis zeigt, im Gegensatz zu dem charakteristischen Verhalten der traditionellen Beweissysteme, die "passiv", d. h. rein kombinatorisch, sehr große Suchräume verarbeiten;

(ii) nicht mehr einen Suchraum aus tausenden von Klauseln erzeugen muß, sondern in der Lage ist, mit vergleichsweise wenigen redundanten Schritten einen Beweis zu finden.

(iii) Ein solches ABS wird bezüglich seiner Leistungsfähigkeit traditionelle Beweiser bei weitem übertreffen. Ein Maß für die Leistungsfähigkeit ist der Schwierigkeitsgrad der Sätze, die das ABS in der Lage ist, zu beweisen.

Die Erfahrungen, die bis jetzt mit dem System gemacht wurden, belegen die ersten beiden Thesen.

O. EINLEITUNG

Die dem Projekt zugrunde liegende Arbeitshypothese, zuerst 1975 formuliert, reflektiert die damals dominierende Desillusionierung bezüglich der traditionellen Forschung auf dem Gebiet des Automatischen Beweisens:

Automatische Beweissysteme haben eine gewisse Leistungsfähigkeit erreicht, die nicht mehr entscheidend verbessert werden kann, indem

(i) immer kompliziertere Refinementstrategien [LO78] (wie unit preference, linear resolution, TOSS, MTOSS, ...) entwickelt werden,

(ii) andere Logiken (wie natural deduction logics, sequence logics, matrix reduction methods usw.) verwendet werden.

Die Schwäche Automatischer Beweissysteme, im Vergleich zur Leistungsfähigkeit des Menschen, ist erklärbar dadurch, daß fachspezifisches und sonstiges Wissen, das dem

Mathematiker zur Verfügung steht, nicht genutzt wird. Das zumeist implizite Wissen eines bestimmten mathematischen Gebietes explizit zu machen und Techniken zu entwikkeln, dieses Wissen zu repräsentieren und zu nutzen, ist Forschungsgegenstand des Projektes.

Als Testfall wurde das Gebiet der Automatentheorie gewählt, und zur Demonstration des Erfolges (bzw. Mißerfolges) des gewählten Ansatzes sollen die Sätze eines Standardlehrbuches auf diesem Gebiet [DE71] bewiesen werden. Im ersten Abschnitt dieses Berichtes geben wir einen Überblick über das System, einschließlich der Komponenten, die noch nicht betriebsbereit sind. Die Teile des Systems, deren Implementierung abgeschlossen und evaluiert worden ist, werden im zweiten Abschnitt beschrieben, dabei kann aus Platzmangel nur auf einige Komponenten des Systems eingegangen werden. Im dritten Abschnitt werden einige Resultate vorgestellt und im letzten Abschnitt die bis jetzt gewonnenen Ergebnisse ausgewertet.

In der Darstellung gehen wir davon aus, daß der Leser mit den wesentlichen Techniken und Begriffen des Automatischen Beweisens vertraut ist.

1. EINE ÜBERSICHT

Das System aus der Vogelperspektive

Das Beweisen eines mathematischen Satzes hat zwei grundsätzlich verschiedene Aspekte: erstens den *kreativen Aspekt*, einen Beweis zu finden. Dies wird im allgemeinen als ein Problem der *Psychologie* angesehen und unterliegt gänzlich anderen Fragestellungen und Methoden als der zweite, der *logische Aspekt*. Dieser Aspekt ergibt sich aus der Fragestellung, was ein Beweis ist und wie man ihn aufschreibt und ist ein Problem der *Beweistheorie*. Natürlich sind diese beiden Aspekte nicht völlig losgelöst voneinander (siehe z. B. [SZ69]), jedoch erschien uns diese Unterscheidung wesentlich genug, um den globalen Entwurf des Systems danach auszurichten:

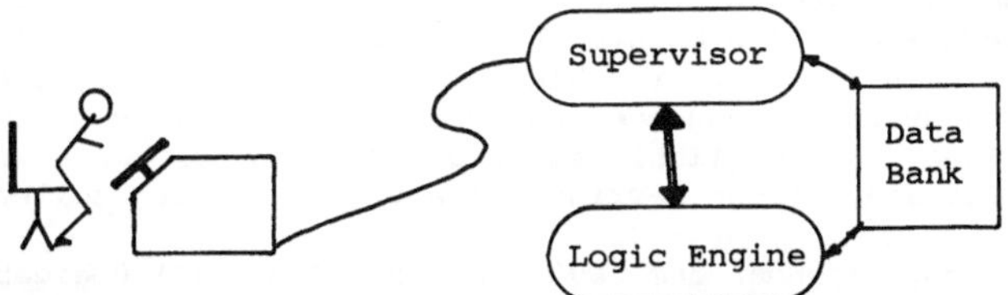

Diagramm 1

Der Supervisor besteht aus mehreren unabhängigen Moduln, die die Aufgabe haben, zu einem vorgelegten Satz eine oder mehrere Beweisideen zu erzeugen und das Wissen, das zum Auffinden eines Beweises hilfreich sein kann, bereitzustellen. Mit diesen Informationen steuert der Supervisor die *Logik-Maschine*, die im Kern als ein traditioneller Automatischer Beweiser, basierend auf Kowalskys "Connection Graph Proof Procedure" [KO75], konzipiert wurde.

Die *Datenbank* enthält das faktische Wissen eines bestimmten mathematischen Gebietes, wie z. B. Definitionen, Axiome, bereits bewiesene Sätze und Lemmata, die so weit wie möglich mit Informationen über ihren potentiellen Gebrauch versehen sind.

Ein Blick aus geringer Höhe

Diagramm 2 gibt eine etwas detailliertere Darstellung als Diagramm 1 und soll ein Gefühl für die Arbeitsweise des Systems vermitteln:

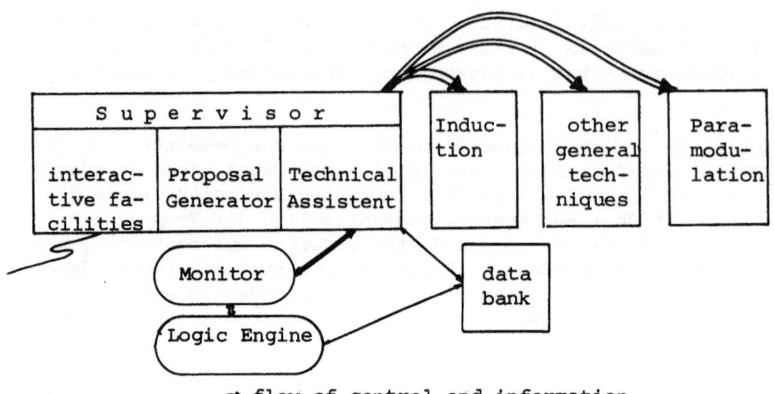

Diagramm 2

Der Benutzer gibt den zu beweisenden Satz ein und kann noch zusätzliche Informationen und Tips, wie der Beweis gefunden werden könnte, hinzufügen. Aufgrund dieser Informationen entscheidet der *Proposal Generator* (PG) zunächst, ob der Satz am besten mit einer bestimmten allgemeinen Technik, z. B. durch Induktion, bewiesen werden sollte. In diesem Fall übergibt der Supervisor die Steuerung an den entsprechenden Modul, also an den *Induktionsmodul* [CW79]. Eine andere Alternative wäre die folgende: Der PG erkennt, ob Gleichheitsliterale in der initialen Formelmenge vorkommen und veranlaßt in diesem Falle, daß die Klauselmenge in eine zweckmäßigere Form transformiert wird und übergibt die Kontrolle an den *Equality-Reasoning-Modul* [SI79], [SW80].

Wenn keine der allgemeinen Techniken anwendbar ist, generiert der PG einen *Vorschlag (proposal)* (oder mehrere Vorschläge), der lokale Informationen darüber enthält, wie der Satz am besten bewiesen werden könnte. Er enthält zum Beispiel Definitionen und Lemmata, die relevant sein könnten, er schlägt Beweistechniken vor, die geeignet erscheinen oder rät, welche Behauptung oder welches Unterproblem am besten zuerst bewiesen wird. Er versucht (wenn möglich), einen *Generalplan* für den Beweis zu finden und entscheidet schließlich, welche Heuristiken aktiviert werden sollen.

Die Vorschläge werden nacheinander dem *Technical Assistent* (TA) übergeben, dessen Aufgabe darin besteht, den Vorschlag, der bis zu diesem Zeitpunkt für den Benutzer lesbar ist, in entsprechende technische Anweisungen und Programme zu transformieren. Diese sollen dann das Verhalten der Logik-Maschine global steuern und werden daher an den Monitor übergeben.

Der *Monitor determiniert* und *kontrolliert* das globale Verhalten der Logik-Maschine: Unmittelbar nach seiner Aktivierung versucht er durch reine Simplifikation den Satz zu beweisen. Falls dies nicht gelingt, versucht er mit Hilfe der Terminator-Heuristik (siehe Abschnitt 2) einen einfachen Beweis zu finden. Erst wenn dies fehlschlägt, wird die gesamte Logik-Maschine aktiviert. Typische *Kontrollaufgaben* des Monitors sind z. B. die wiederholte Verwendung eines Lemmas, die zyklische Entwicklung des Suchraums oder die Verwendung bestimmter 'gefährlicher' Klauseln (wie z. B. die selfresolving clauses) zu kontrollieren. Ein weiteres Beispiel dafür, wie der Monitor das globale Verhalten des Systems kontrolliert, ist die Verhinderung des unstetigen Verhaltens des Systems: Die Auswahl-Heuristiken schlagen beständig "interessante" Schritte vor, die dazu führen, daß das System laufend zwischen verschiedenen Teilen des Suchraums hin- und her springt - ganz im Unterschied zum Verhalten von Menschen, die eine bestimmte Idee solange verfolgen, bis sich der Erfolg einstellt oder sie mehr oder weniger überzeugt sind, daß der eingeschlagene Weg eine Sackgasse ist.

Die Entscheidungen und Aktivitäten des PG und des TA sind im wesentlichen durch die Semantik der untersuchten Theorie und durch das Wissen über Beweistechniken, die für diese Theorie typisch sein können, bestimmt. Das Hauptziel (maingoal) dieser Aktivität ist, das System zu unterstützen, *einen Beweis zu finden*. Wenn dies abgeschlossen ist, wird das Hauptziel des Beweisers, *einen Widerspruch* (d. h. die leere Klausel) *abzuleiten* und obwohl dies natürlich mit dem ursprünglichen Ziel identisch ist, wird durch die unterschiedliche Formulierung impliziert, daß ganz verschiedene Informationen zu einem *zielgerichteten Verhalten* beitragen können: im ersteren Fall die Semantik und Pragmatik des jeweiligen Gebietes und im zweiten Fall zusätzliche Informationen, basierend auf der Syntax der jeweiligen Formelmenge (hier des Connectiongraphen). Diese letztere Information wird in den im folgenden Abschnitt beschriebenen Selektionsheuristiken genutzt.

Sowohl der Monitor, als auch der PG und der TA befinden sich noch im Entwicklungsstadium.

2. DIE LOGIK-MASCHINE

Eine wesentliche Erfahrung, die wir in der bisherigen Entwicklung des Systems gemacht haben, läßt sich in der These zusammenfassen, daß mathematische Intelligenz, wie sie zu der Suche nach einem Beweis benötigt wird, sich nicht durch eine einzige Methode (eine einzige Ableitungsstrategie) auf dem Computer simulieren läßt. *Vielmehr beruht die Leistungsfähigkeit eines mechanischen Beweissystems auf einer grossen Vielzahl an Methoden und globalen wie lokalen Heuristiken, deren Entwicklung und Integration in eine angemessene Systemarchitektur mehr ingenieurmäßigen als logischen Charakter hat.*

Die Logik-Maschine basiert auf Kowalskis "Connection Graph Proof Procedure" [KO75], deren Vorteile gegenüber anderen, auf dem Resolutionsverfahren aufbauenden Beweisprozeduren für den von uns intendierten Ansatz ausschlaggebend waren: Es gibt - außer beim Aufbau des Graphen - keine Suche nach unifizierbaren Literalen, jeder Resolutionsschritt wird höchstens einmal ausgeführt und das Löschen von Links und Klauseln, wovon der Deletion-Modul in großem Maße Gebrauch macht, führt zu einer bemerkenswerten Einschränkung des Suchraumes. Entscheidend für unser Vorgehen ist die Beobachtung, daß die Auswahl einer geeigneten Folge von Links zu einem *aktiven* und *zielgerichteten* Verhalten des Systems führen kann. Dies steht im Gegensatz zu den traditionellen, "passiven" Beweisstrategien, deren wesentliches Charakteristikum, bestimmte mögliche Schritte im Suchraum zu verbieten, zwar den Suchraum enorm einschränken kann, in dem verbleibenden Teil führen sie jedoch eine blinde, rein kombinatorische Suche aus.

Ein- und Ausgabe, Simplifikation und Evaluation

Die *interaktiven Möglichkeiten* des Systems sind zu umfangreich, um hier beschrieben zu werden und sollen statt dessen durch das Protokoll einer typischen Sitzung auf der Konferenz präsentiert werden. Es ist dabei zu bemerken, daß diese interaktiven Möglichkeiten eine gewisse Ausbauphase charakterisieren und nun zu einem immer grösseren Teil von dem Supervisor selbst entschieden werden, so daß sich die Schnittstelle nach "außen" verschiebt und nur zwei Befehlssätze übrigbleiben: Der *INPUT-Modul* erzeugt und liest die Datenbank, deren Syntax an dieser Stelle auf den Benutzer zugeschnitten wurde. Dieser Modul führt auch zahlreiche syntaktische und semantische Fehleranalysen aus, um die Konsistenz und Korrektheit der Datenbank, die am Ende mindestens ein ganzes mathematisches Textbuch umfassen wird, soweit wie möglich sicherzustellen. Der zweite Befehlssatz wird von dem *PROTOCOL-Modul* verarbeitet, der es ermöglicht, das Verhalten des Systems auf verschiedenen Abstraktionsstufen zu verfolgen und entsprechende Protokolle zu erstellen.

Sobald sich die Logik-Maschine im "Beweis-Modus" befindet, formt der *CSS-Modul* den *aktivierten* Teil der Datenbank in skolemisierte Klauselnormalform um und führt verschiedene Splittingregeln und logische Reduktionsregeln aus [WB71]. Aus der so generierten Klauselmenge erzeugt der *CG-Modul* den Connection-Graphen, wobei mit Hilfe des *ERS-Moduls* Terme symbolisch ausgewertet, reduziert und algebraisch vereinfacht werden. Das Resultat dieser Umformungen ist der *initiale Connection Graph*, in dem nun die Suche nach einem Beweis, lokal gesteuert durch den *CONTROL-Modul*, beginnt.

Der CONTROL-Modul selektriert jeweils einen Link für den nächsten Resolutionsschritt, wobei die Entscheidung lokal aufgrund von Informationen aus dem HEURISTIC-Modul, dem REFINEMENT-Modul, dem DELETION-Modul und möglicherweise dem EQUALITY-REASONING-Modul vorgenommen wird. Die jeweilige lokale Entscheidung wird jedoch durch globale Informationen, die vom Supervisor gegeben wurden, überlagert.

Statt die Darstellung der eigentlichen Suche fortzusetzen, werden wir zunächst die heuristischen Bewertungsfunktionen, die in dem HEURISTIC-Modul codiert sind, beschreiben.

Die heuristischen Bewertungsfunktionen

Im Gegensatz zu den globalen Suchstrategien und Heuristiken basieren die heuristischen Bewertungsfunktionen des HEURISTIC-Moduls auf *lokaler syntaktischer* Information über den Graphen bzw. über die Resolvente. Kriterien für solche heuristischen Bewertungsfunktionen wurden durch folgende zwei Typen von Experimenten gewonnen: Im ersten führt eine Testperson einen Resolutionsbeweis für eine vorgegebene Formelmenge aus, ohne die Bedeutung der darin vorkommenden Prädikats- und Funktionssymbole zu kennen. Die Kriterien, nach denen sie jeden einzelnen Schritt auswählt, werden untersucht und daraus Ideen für neue Heuristiken gewonnen.
In dem anderen Experiment läßt man das System zunächst eine Formelmenge beweisen. Das Protokoll, in dem jeder für den Beweis notwendige Schritt markiert ist, gibt Aufschluß darüber, warum bestimmte unnötige Schritte gewählt wurden. Daraus lassen sich sehr erfolgreich Ideen zur Verbesserung der Selektionsfunktionen bzw. deren relativer Gewichtung gewinnen. In den letzten zwei Jahren wurden einige hundert solcher Protokolle ausgewertet.

Ursprünglich wurde mit 19 verschiedenen *heuristischen Features* experimentiert, wobei jedes *Feature* einem Link k in G_i einen gewissen Wert zuordnet. Dabei ist G_i der augenblickliche Graph, G_{i+1} ist der Graph, der aus dem Resolutionsschritt auf Link k resultiert und Res ist die resultierende Resolvente:

- (i) Summe der Literale in G_{i+1}
- (ii) Summe der Klauseln in G_{i+1}
- (iii) Summe der Links in G_{i+1}
- (iv) Durchschnittliche Länge der Klauseln in G_{i+1}
- (v) Durchschnittliche Anzahl von Links an Literalen in G_{i+1}
- (vi) Summe (bzw. durchschnittliche Summe) von Konstantensymbolen in G_{i+1}
- (vii) Anzahl verschiedener Prädikatensymbole in G_{i+1}
- (viii) Anzahl verschiedener Variablensymbole in G_{i+1}
- (ix) Summe der Literale in Res
- (x) Summe der Links in Res
- (xi) Anzahl verschiedener Konstantensymbole in Res
- (xii) Anzahl verschiedener Variablensymbole in Res
- (xiii) Anzahl verschiedener Prädikatensymbole in Res
- (xiv) Termkomplexität von Res
- (xv) Minimale Anzahl von Links an Literalen in Res
- (xvi) Komplexität des Unifikators σ_k von Link k
- (xvii) Alter von Res
- (xviii) Isolationsfaktor von Res
- (xix) Isolationsfaktor der Eltern von Res

Die Wahl der zu berechnenden Features wird durch die Komplexität ihrer Berechnung bzw. Abschätzung wesentlich eingeschränkt, denn, obwohl jedes Feature einen gewissen Wert hat, können die Kosten der Berechnung diesen möglichen Nutzen hinfällig werden lassen. Außerdem sind die angegebenen Features nicht unabhängig: z. B. schätzen sowohl (xi) wie (xii) ab, inwieweit die Resolvente instantiiert wurde. Oft sind auch die Werte für die Resolventenkomplexität direkt von dem Wert der Graphenkomplexität abhängig (z. B. (xiii) und (vii)).

Ferner ist für jedes Feature eine Metrik zu finden und der *relative Wert* eines bestimmten Features ist im Konfliktfall mit anderen Features festzulegen.

Die Information, die in den Features enthalten ist, wird unterschiedlich verarbeitet: gewisse Tatsachen (z. B. abnehmende Größe des Connectiongraphen) haben *absolute Priorität* und unterdrücken alle anderen Informationen (s. auch [DA78]). Die Information in den meisten anderen Features wird durch eine reelle Zahl im Bereich [0,1] ausgedrückt, wobei diese Zahl durch verschiedene empirisch gefundene Metriken bestimmt wird. Diese Zahl ist dann Argument eines gewichteten Polynoms und die resultierende reelle Zahl - der Prioritätswert (priority value) - drückt den *relativen Wert* eines bestimmten Links aus und wird diesem zugeordnet; im allgemeinen selektiert der CONTROL-Modul dann den Link mit der höchsten Priorität (falls keine gegenteilige Information vorliegt). Andere Informationen werden mit einer 'Fenstertechnik' verarbeitet: von den Links, deren Prioritätswert in einem gewissen Intervall (dem Fenster) liegt, wird derjenige Link ausgewählt, der gewisse andere Features minimiert.
Die Größe des Fensters sowie die relativen Gewichte wurden experimentell bestimmt und können vom Benutzer verändert werden. Das System wurde so entwickelt, daß die heuristischen Features leicht ausgewechselt werden können, jedoch nach zwei Jahren Experimentierzeit hat sich folgende Lösung als stabil erwiesen (stabil in dem Sinne, daß weder ein Hinzufügen weiterer Features von der obigen Liste noch ein Verwenden anderer Metriken zu einem signifikant verbesserten Verhalten des Systems führen würde).

1. Graphenkomplexität
   - 1.1 FCLSUM = (Σ der Klauseln in G_{i+1}) - (Σ der Klauseln in G_i)
   - 1.2 FLINKSUM = (Σ der Links in G_{i+1}) - (Σ der Links in G_i)
   - 1.3 FCANCEL = Σ der verschiedenen Prädikatensymbole in G_{i+1}
   - 1.4 FTERMINATE (s. unten)

2. Resolventenkomplexität
   - 2.1 FAGE = Alter der Resolvente
   - 2.2 FLITSUM = Summe der Literale in Res
   - 2.3 FTERM = Termkomplexität von Res
   - 2.4 FRESISO = Isolationsgrad von Res

3. Komplexität der Eltern einer Resolvente
   - 3.1 FPARISO = Isolationsgrad der Eltern

Diese Features werden wie folgt verarbeitet: alle Schritte, die zu einem echten "Kleinerwerden" des Graphen führen, erhalten *absolute Priorität* und werden sofort ausgeführt; d. h. jeder Link, der zu einem Graphen mit weniger Klauseln oder Links führt, wird in eine spezielle Klasse eingetragen, die sofort vor jeder weiteren Evaluierung abgearbeitet wird. Die Entscheidung darüber, ob ein Link zu einer Reduktion des Graphen führt, basiert auf Informationen, die von dem DELETION-Modul berechnet werden und zwar optional nur für die aktiven Links bzw. für alle Links. Dabei ist zu beachten, daß die Reduktion des Graphen zu einem weiteren Löschen von Klauseln führen kann, also potentiell zu einem Schneeballeffekt. Das sofortige Erkennen und Ausführen solcher Reduktionen ist eine der Ursachen für den Erfolg des Systems.

Alle anderen Features haben eine *relative Priorität* und werden als situationsabhängig bzw. situationsunabhängig klassifiziert; diese Klassifizierung trägt der Tatsache Rechnung, daß die Kosten der Berechnung und des späteren 'updating' der Features enorm schwanken [SS80].

Eine erfolgreiche Verwendung der relativen Prioritäten hängt nicht zuletzt von der

Wahl einer entsprechenden Metrik ab, die den geschätzten heuristischen Wert des Features mißt. Eine eingehende Diskussion der folgenden Metriken ist aus Platzgründen nicht möglich [siehe SS80], der wesentliche Punkt ist jedoch, daß jede Metrik eine bestimmte Charakteristik über ihrem Definitionsbereich zeigt (z. B. linear oder nicht linear usw.), die für das zugehörige Feature wesentlich ist.

$$\text{FAGE} := 1 - \left(\frac{\text{Age}}{D_{max}}\right)^{3/2}$$

Age: max{Age Parent 1, Age Parent 2}+1

D_{max}: Benutzerdefinierte maximal erlaubte Ableitungstiefe

Charakteristik: FAGE
(für D_{max} = S)

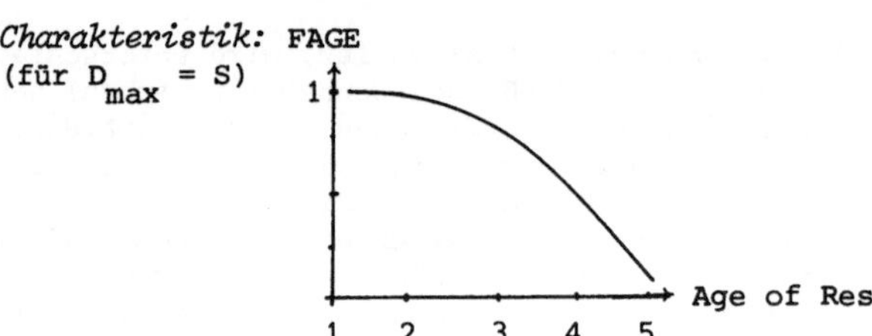

Dieses Feature wird im wesentlichen benutzt, um "unendliche Löcher" im Suchraum zu vermeiden.

$$\text{FLITSUM} := \frac{1}{\Sigma \text{ Literale in Res}}$$

Charakteristik: FLITSUM

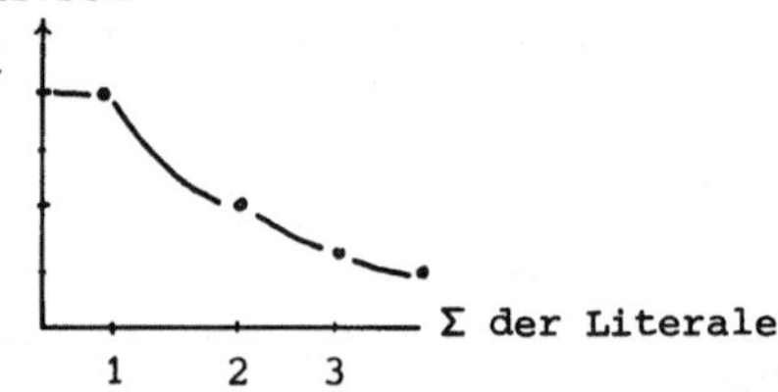

Dieses Feature gibt dem System ein starkes "unit-preference-Verhalten".

$$\text{FTERM} := \begin{cases} 1 & \text{falls keine Terme oder keine geschachtelten Terme in Res} \\ \frac{1}{2} \cdot \left(1 - \frac{\frac{1}{n} \sum_{i=1}^{n} \left(s_i\right)^{3/2}}{\left(s_{max}\right)^{3/2}} \right) & \text{sonst} \end{cases}$$

wobei: s_i: maximale Schachtelungstiefe des i-ten Terms in Res

s_{max}: Benutzerdefinierte maximal zulässige Schachtelungstiefe

n: Anzahl an (top-level) Termen in Res.

$$\text{FCANCEL} := \text{LIT}(G_i) - \text{LIT}(G_{i+1})$$

wobei $\text{LIT}(G_i) = \#\{P \mid P \text{ ist Prädikatensymbol in } G_i\}$

Der Wert ist entweder 0 oder 1, und dieses Feature ist nützlich, um Colmerauers Cancellationstrategie [KO75] zu simulieren.

FLINKSUM: Dieses Feature hat entweder absolute Priorität, falls der Wert abnimmt, oder der Wert des Features wird dem CONTROL-Modul mit Hilfe der "Fenster-Technik" übergeben.

FRESISO: hat entweder absolute Priorität, falls Res isoliert ist [(i)] oder

$$\text{FRESISO} = \begin{cases} 0 & \text{jedes Literal in Res hat min. 3 Links} \\ 1/3 & \text{es gibt ein Literal in Res mit 2 Links} \\ 1 & \text{es gibt ein Literal in Res mit 1 Link} \end{cases}$$

FPARISO: hat entweder absolute Priorität, falls beide Eltern isoliert werden oder ein Elternteil isoliert wird und zusätzlich Schneeballeffekt auftritt, sonst:

$$\text{FPARISO} = \begin{cases} 0 & \text{jedes Literal in beiden Eltern hat min. 3 Links} \\ 1/3 & \text{es gibt ein Literal mit 2 Links} \\ 1 & \text{es gibt ein Literal mit 1 Link} \end{cases}$$

Die Nützlichkeit von FRESISO und FPARISO liegt darin, daß sie den CONTROL-Modul mit der Information versehen, daß nach einem weiteren Schritt (bzw. nach zwei weiteren Schritten) ein erneutes Löschen von Klauseln möglich ist, das potentiell zu einem weiteren Schneeballeffekt führen kann.

Die wesentliche Randbedingung für die Auswahl solcher Heuristiken ist die, daß die nach jedem Schritt notwendige Änderung (updating) der Werte weniger aufwendig ist, als das Ausführen aller möglichen Resolventenschritte. Unter anderem werden darum die Argumente der Metriken auch nicht in jedem Fall exakt berechnet, sondern durch heuristische Schätzfunktionen ermittelt.

Ferner haben diese Heuristiken den Nachteil, daß sie nur einen einzigen Schritt vorausberechnen, dagegen die Berechnung eines echten "n-level-look-ahead" für n≥2 zu aufwendig wäre. Darum haben wir zusätzlich eine Terminatorheuristik implementiert, die mit vertretbaren Kosten berechnet, ob ein Beweis innerhalb eines gewissen Komplexitätsbereiches möglich ist. Diese Heuristik FTERMINATE ist der Schleifenheuristik von [SI76, p. 832] und der n-level-look-ahead-Heuristik in [KO75, p. 593] verwandt und ist eine weitere Ursache für die Stärke des Systems. Der wesentliche Gedanke läßt sich aus folgendem Diagramm ersehen:

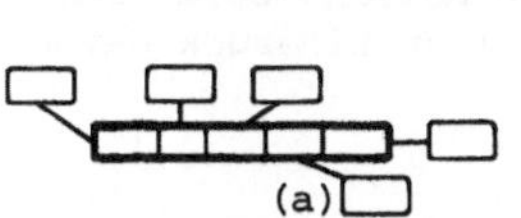

(b)

Diagramm 3

Jeder Kasten in dem obigen Diagramm repräsentiert ein Literal, zusammenhängende Kästen stellen eine Klausel dar und komplementäre Literale (Kästen) sind durch einen Link verbunden. Die stark umrandete Klausel ist der Kern der Terminatorsituation. Falls im Diagramm 3a alle dem jeweiligen Link zugeordneten Unifikatoren kompatibel sind, so stellt die Konfiguration einen Ein-Level-Terminator dar, da die leere Klausel sofort ableitbar ist. Im gleichen Sinne stellt Diagramm 3b einen Zwei-Level-Terminator dar, falls alle Unifikatoren kompatibel sind: der Kern ist nur mit EIN-Level-Terminatoren verbunden (siehe [SS80] für eine detailliertere Darstellung).

Abarbeiten des Suchraumes

Wir kehren nun zur Beschreibung der Suche nach einem Beweis zurück: der CONTROL-Modul selektiert einen Link für den nächsten Resolutionsschritt. Die Selektion basiert je-

(i) Eine Klausel ist isoliert, wenn mindestens ein Literal nicht mehr durch einen Link verbunden ist. Die Klausel kann dann gelöscht werden.

doch nur zum Teil auf Informationen, die von dem HEURISTIC-Modul, wie im vorigen Abschnitt beschrieben, geliefert werden. Weitere Information wird von dem DELETION-Modul geliefert, der gewisse Klauseln zum Löschen markiert. Damit wird die wichtigste Eigenschaft der Beweisprozedur [KO75], die sie von anderen Graph-Verfahren unterscheidet [SH76], [SI76] - nämlich die Tatsache, daß das Löschen von Links und Klauseln ein weiteres Löschen auslösen kann, soweit wie möglich ausgenutzt. Wegen dieses Effektes ist es lohnend, hier einen hohen Aufwand zu treiben und so viele Kriterien wie möglich zu finden und zu berechnen, die ein potentielles Löschen anzeigen. Im Augenblick wird eine Klausel zum Löschen markiert, wenn:

(i) ein Literal in der Klausel isoliert wird
(ii) wenn die Klausel eine Tautologie ist
(iii) wenn sie von einer anderen Klausel subsumiert wird [EI80].

Ferner ist geplant, modelltheoretische Kriterien zum Löschen von Klauseln zu implementieren, Kriterien zum Löschen zu entwickeln, die auf bestimmten Konfigurationen von Links basieren (z. B. Zirkulare Links etc.) und das Löschen aufgrund der Evaluation von Prädikaten (Literalen) zu ermöglichen.

Im allgemeinen wird nur ein kleiner Teil der Links im Graphen als *aktiv* deklariert. Die Entscheidung, welche Links aktiviert werden, wird von dem *REFINEMENT-Modul* gefällt, der gewisse Standard-Refinements [LO78] simuliert:
Werden z. B. nur diejenigen Links im initialen Graphen als "aktiv" erklärt, die von Klauseln des negierten Theorems ausgehen, und werden weiterhin die Links jeder Resolvente als "aktiv" und die vorherigen als "passiv" gekennzeichnet, so ergibt sich eine *lineare* Ableitung, wenn nur auf "aktiven" Links resolviert wird. Dies stellte sich als vorteilhaft heraus, weil die Anzahl der "aktiven" Links und damit der Aufwand der Berechnung der heuristischen Bewertungsfunktion beträchtlich verringert wird. Außerdem führt es zu einem ausgeglicheneren Verhalten des Systems und die erfolgreichsten Testläufe wurden mit diesem "mixed approach" durchgeführt. Die Auswahl eines bestimmten refinements erfolgt durch den Monitor auf der Basis einiger allgemeiner Heuristiken.

Allerdings ist die gesamte Ableitung durch die komplexe Interaktion der verschiedenen Moduln, die auch noch durch Informationen von dem Supervisor überlagert werden, nicht notwendig linear oder in irgend einem Sinne 'standard' und die entsprechenden Vollständigkeitsresultate sind nicht übertragbar.

Die potentielle Explosion der Anzahl der Links ist der eigentliche Engpaß in Kowalskis Beweisprozedur. Das folgende Beispiel, von P. Andrews, Carnegie Mellon, beim Deduction Workshop 1979 als "Herausforderung" vorgeschlagen, vermittelt einen Eindruck davon:

$$(\exists x\ Qx \equiv \forall y\ Qy) \equiv (\exists x\ \forall y\ Qx \equiv Qy).$$

Der initiale Graph für diese Formel enthält fast 10.000 Links, und bei jedem Resolutionsschritt kommen einige Hundert neue Links hinzu. Wenn alle diese Links als "aktiv" gekennzeichnet würden, wäre die Berechnung der heuristischen Selektionsfunktion, die eine aufwendige Untersuchung des potentiellen Ergebnisses für *jeden* Link durchführt, nicht mehr praktikabel. Andererseits ist das Beispiel nicht übermäßig schwierig und wird erst durch die Transformation in die Klauselnormalform zu einem Problem.

In unserem System wird das Beispiel gesplittet [WB 71], reduziert und schrittweise zu einem Graphen verkleinert, der nie mehr als 50 Links enthält und in wenigen Schritten bewiesen wird. Auch bei "natürlicheren" Beispielen beträgt der Anteil der Deletion-Schritte an der Gesamtzahl von Schritten etwa ein Drittel und oft mehr als die Hälfte.

Technische Daten zum Projekt

Das Projekt wird von der Deutschen Forschungsgemeinschaft (DFG) Bonn gefördert (De 238/1, De 238/2).
Name des Projekts: Untersuchung zur Einbeziehung mathematischen Wissens beim Automatischen Beweisen am Beispiel der Automatentheorie
Zeitraum: 1976 - 1982 (6 Jahre)

Rechenanlage:	SIEMENS 7.760
erforderlicher Speicherplatz:	5000 K (virtueller Speicher)
Programmiersprachen:	SIEMENS-INTERLISP[EP75]/(CSSA [RA79])
derzeitige Größe des Systems:	> 600 K an Source Code
bisheriger Programmieraufwand:	> 10 Mannjahre

Mit derzeit über 600 K an Quellcode und weiterhin ca. 400 K an geplanter Softwareentwicklung für die nächsten zwei Jahre ist unser Beweiser von der Software her das aufwendigste Projekt auf dem Gebiet des Automatischen Beweisens und neben den anderen "Mammut-Systemen" [BM78], [MOW76] ein Indikator für den sich wandelnden Forschungsstil auf diesem Gebiet.

3. LEISTUNGS-STATISTIKEN

Um die Leistungsfähigkeit des Systems zu testen und insbesondere um die Einseitigkeit statistischer Daten durch einseitige Auswahl von Beispielen zu vermeiden, wurde das System an allen in der Literatur bekannten Beispielen [WM76], [MOW76], [RRYKU72] getestet. Die vorläufigen Ergebnisse zeigen dabei, daß bereits jetzt das Verhältnis der insgesamt ausgeführten Ableitungsschritte zu den für den Beweis tatsächlich notwendigen Schritten bei unserem Beweiser stets wesentlich günstiger ist, als bei anderen Systemen. Um ein Gefühl für die enorme Leistungsverbesserung zu vermitteln, sind in der folgenden Tabelle einige typische Beispiele zusammengefaßt, die einer Studie entnommen sind, die an der University of Maryland [WM76] durchgeführt wurde und in der insgesamt 152 Beispiele mit 8 verschiedenen Beweisprozeduren getestet wurden.

Die Tabelle ist wie folgt zu interpretieren: In der ersten Spalte steht der Name der Axiomenmenge nach [WM76], z. B. LS-35 in Zeile 9. Die nächsten 3 Spalten geben die statistischen Werte für den Maryland-Beweiser an, wobei die Zahlen in Klammern den ungünstigsten Wert, die anderen Zahlen den besten Wert für die 8 getesteten Beweisprozeduren angeben. (i) Die letzten 3 Spalten enthalten die entsprechenden Werte für den Karlsruher Beweiser. Um z. B. die Axiomenmenge LS-35 (Zeile 9) zu beweisen, generierte die beste Beweisprozedur von [WM76] 335 Klauseln, die schlechteste Prozedur 1.521 Klauseln, obwohl in dem dort gefundenen Beweis nur 14 Klauseln auftreten. Unser System dagegen fand einen Beweis, der nur aus 8 Klauseln bestand und generierte insgesamt 9 Klauseln (!). Die in der Tabelle zusammengefaßten Beispiele sind typisch (und 'worst case'), die Ergebnisse fallen zum Teil noch günstiger für alle anderen Beispiele aus, und sie sind damit der statistische Beleg und die Rechtfertigung für die ersten beiden Thesen der Zusammenfassung.

Beispiel	Maryland Refutation Procedure			Markgraf Karl Refutation Procedure		
	NOC-P	NOC-G	G-P	NOC-P	NOC-G	G-P
Ances	19 (18)	62 (943)	0,306 (0,019)	7	7	1
Ew 33	19 (21)	63 (2585)	0,302 (0,008)	8	16	0,5
Prim	21 (20)	89 (221)	0,236 (0,09)	12	12	1
Wos 3	7 (7)	17 (154)	0,412 (0,045)	3	3	1
Wos 7	13 (12)	241 (244)	0,054 (0,049)	9	10	0,9
Wos 8	12 (12)	210 (360)	0,057 (0,033)	6	9	0,667
LS-17	20 (14)	98 (1273)	0,204 (0,011)	4	7	0,571
LS-21	12 (12)	252 (684)	0,048 (0,018)	7	12	0,583
LS-35	14 (14)	335 (1521)	0,042 (0,009)	8	9	0,889
LS-115	13 (13)	20 (227)	0,65 (0,057)	7	11	0,636
LS-121	31	536	0,058	12	30	0,4

NOC-P = Number of Clauses in the Proof
NOC-G = Number of Clauses generated
G-P = G-Penetrance

$$G\text{-}P = \frac{NOC\text{-}P}{NOC\text{-}G}$$

Diagramm 4

(i) Dabei ist keine der 8 Beweisprozeduren uniform die 'beste' für alle angegebenen Beispiele, während unsere Resultate uniform gelten.

5. SCHLUSSBETRACHTUNG

Einfluß anderer Deduktionssysteme

Die Forschungsberichte der Gruppe um W. Bledsoe, University of Texas [BT75], [BB75], [BBH72], [WB71], [WB77] haben die Entwicklung unseres Systems sehr beeinflusst. Im Gegensatz zu [BT75] versuchen wir jedoch, die *Logik*, in der die Beweise ausgeführt werden, soweit wie möglich von den *Heuristiken* zu trennen, die in der Suche nach einem Beweis hilfreich sein können.

Das erfolgreichste Beweissystem auf Resolutionsbasis ist zur Zeit [MOW76],und wir haben deren Beispiele ebenfalls gerechnet. Die in [MOW76] zitierten Resultate zeigen im Vergleich zu den von uns gefundenen Werten die gleiche Tendenz: wenn das Karlsruher System einen Beweis findet, ist es in einem Maße überlegen, wie es auch die vorhergehende Tabelle für [WM76] zeigt. Allerdings gibt es eine Reihe schwieriger Theoreme in [MOW76], die unser Beweissystem zur Zeit nicht lösen kann. Das liegt im wesentlichen daran, daß die Stärke des Systems von [MOW76] auf einer erfolgreichen Behandlung des Gleichheitsprädikates beruht. Zur Zeit ist der Equality-Reasoning-Modul, der für Beweise dieser Art zuständig ist, noch nicht völlig fertiggestellt und daher ist ein echter Vergleich für diese Beispiele noch nicht möglich.

Ferner gehört das Beweissystem von Boyer/Moore [BM78] zu den Systemen, die derzeit in der Forschung dominieren. Die Stärke dieses Systems beruht auf einem eigenen Ansatz zur Behandlung von Induktionsbeweisen und solange unser Induktionsmodul nicht fertiggestellt ist, muß ein Vergleich ebenfalls zu unseren Ungunsten ausfallen.

Ein Automatischer Beweiser, der ähnliche Heuristiken verwendete, wurde von Slagle und Mitarbeitern [SF71] entwickelt; es scheint jedoch, daß sich heuristische Schätzfunktionen bezüglich des möglichen Wertes einer Resolvente nicht erfolgreich in einem traditionellen Resolutionsbeweiser verwenden lassen.

Zusammenfassung

Zum jetzigen Zeitpunkt ist unser System den meisten in der Literatur zitierten Automatischen Beweissystemen wesentlich überlegen, es gibt jedoch bestimmte Klassen von Beispielen - solche z. B. die Induktion oder die Behandlung von Gleichheitsaxiomen benötigen - bei denen ein Vergleich zu Ungunsten unseres Systems ausfällt. Aber zweifellos spiegeln diese Unzulänglichkeiten den momentanen Entwicklungsstand wider; sobald die noch fehlenden Komponenten fertiggestellt sind, werden traditionelle Beweiser nicht mehr konkurrenzfähig sein.

Diese Behauptung ist weniger ermutigend als es den Anschein hat: Der Vergleich nimmt das Verhältnis von generierten Klauseln zu notwendigen Klauseln zum Maßstab und vernachlässigt völlig den enormen Aufwand der getrieben werden muß, um ein Beweisverhalten, wie es hier beschrieben wird, zu erreichen. Auf diese Weise könnte man leicht eine "perfekte" Beweisprozedur entwerfen: der Supervisor und die Prozeduren mit Vorausschau würden den Beweis finden und dann das System ohne irgendeinen unnötigen Schritt durch den Suchraum führen. Unser System stellt in gewisser Weise einen Kompromiß zwischen den beiden Extremen des traditionellen Beweisers einerseits und dieser "perfekten" Prozedur andererseits dar.

Zweifellos muß in Zukunft zur Beurteilung eines Beweissystems der gesamte Aufwand, d. h. sowohl der Aufwand an Berechnungen einschließlich der Heuristiken, ebenso wie die Anzahl an Klauseln, die zum Finden eines bestimmten Beweises notwendig sind, berücksichtigt werden.

Aber welches System wird dann mit diesem verbesserten Aufwandsmaß für das bessere gehalten? Wird es das komplexe System A sein, das selbst bei relativ einfachen Theoremen einen enormen Aufwand treibt, dafür aber schwierige Theoreme beweisen kann, oder wird es das scheinbar bessere System B sein, das mit weniger Aufwand einen Beweis findet, aber nicht in der Lage ist, einen Satz zu beweisen, der auch nur knapp über dem durchschnittlichen Fähigkeitsgrad der Beweismaschinen seiner Zeit liegt? Andererseits ist die Tatsache, daß das System A einen Beweis findet, an dem B gescheitert ist, ebenfalls kein Maß für die Leistungsfähigkeit eines Systems, solange es kein objektives Maß für den Schwierigkeitsgrad eines Beweises gibt. Wird jedoch die Schwierigkeit eines Theorems anhand des Aufwandes, der nötig ist, es zu beweisen, gemessen, schließt sich der circulus vitiosus und es wird deutlich, daß der "objektive" Vergleich von Systemen den gleichen Problemen unterliegt wie die Versuche, menschliche Intelligenz zu "objektivieren" und zu "messen": *man mißt gewisse Aspekte und ignoriert andere.*

Zusammenfassend läßt sich sagen, daß es zwar eine Reihe grundsätzlicher Argumente für die These gibt, die Zukunft gehöre den Automatischen Beweisssystemen mit "eingebautem Wissen" von der hier vorgeschlagenen Art, daß es bisher jedoch keine experimentelle Evidenz dafür gibt, daß ein traditioneller Beweiser, mit der Fähigkeit, tausende von Klauseln mit relativ geringem Aufwand zu erzeugen, nicht ebenso leistungsfähig ist. Die Situation erinnert stark an die der gegenwärtigen Schachprogramme, wo die Programme, die anspruchsvollere Konzepte enthalten, auch nicht leistungsfähiger sind als die, deren Fähigkeiten hauptsächlich auf einer perfekten Hardware und entsprechend riesigen Suchräumen beruhen.

Literaturverzeichnis

[AH72] B. Anderson, P. Hayes, An Arraignment of theorem proving or the logicians folly, Comp. Logic memo 54, University of Edinburgh

[BB75] M. Ballantyne, W. Bledsoe, Autom. Proofs and Theorems in Analysis using nonstandard Techniques, ATP-23, 1975, University of Texas, Austin

[BBH72] W. Bledsoe, B. Boyer, Hemmeman, Computer Proofs of Limit Theorems, J. Art. Intellig. vol 3, 1972

[BM78] R. S. Boyer, J.S. Moore, A Computational Logic, SRI International, Comp. Sci. Lab., 1978

[BT75] W. Bledsoe, M. Tyson, The UT Interactive Prover, University of Texas, Austin, ATP-7, 1975

[DE71] P. Deussen, Halbgruppen und Automaten, Springer, 1971

[DS77] P. Deussen, J. Siekmann, Neuantrag zum Forschungsvorhaben 'Untersuchung zur Einbeziehung mathematischen Wissens beim Automatischen Beweisen am Beispiel der Automatentheorie', DFG-Forschungsprojekt, Aktenzeichen De 238/1, 1977

[DS79] P. Deussen, J. Siekmann, Zusatzantrag zum Forschungsvorhaben 'Untersuchung zur Einbeziehung mathematischen Wissens beim Automatischen Beweisen am Beispiel der Automatentheorie, DFG-Projekt De 238/1, 1979

[EP75] B. Epp, INTERLISP Programmierhandbuch, Institut für Deutsche Sprache, Mannheim

[HE72] C. Hewitt, Description and Theoretical Analysis of PLANNER, AI-TR-258, MIT

[KO75] R. Kowalski, A Proof Procedure based on Connection Graphs, JACM, vol 22, no. 4, 1975

[LO78] D. Loveland, Automated Theorem Proving, North Holland, 1978

[MOW76] J.McCharen, R. Overbeck, L. Wos, Problems and Experiments for and with Automated Theorem Proving Programs, IEEE Transac. on Computers, vol-C-25, no. 6, 1976

[RA79] G. Fischer, P. Raulefs, CSSA Primer, Universität Bonn, Programming manual

[RRYKV72] Reboh, Raphael, Yates, Kling, Velarde, Study of Automatic Theorem Proving Programs, 1972, Stanford Research Institute, SRI-TN-75

[SF71] J.R. Slagle, C.D. Farrell, Experiments in Automatic Learning for a Multipurpose Heuristic Program, CACM, vol 14, 1971

[SG65] A.I. Schulze-Gauss, Resolution considered harmless, Acta Theoria, vol 2, 1965

[SH76] R.F. Shostak, Refutation Graphs, J. of Art. Intelligence, vol 7, no. 1, 1976

[SI76] Sickel, Interconnectivity Graphs, IEEE Trans. on Computers, vol C-25, no. 6, 1976

[SI79] J. Siekmann, Forschungsvorhaben zur Behandlung des Gleichheitsprädikates beim Automatischen Beweisen

[SS80] J. Siekmann, G. Smolka, Selection Heuristics, Deletion Strategies and N-Level-Terminator Situations in Connection Graphs, Universität Karlsruhe, Interner Bericht, 1980

[SW80] J. Siekmann, G. Wrightson, Paramodulated Connection Graphs, Acta Informatica, 13, 1980

[SZ69] P. Szabó, The collected papers of G. Gentzen, North Holland, 1969

[WB71] W. Bledsoe, Splitting and Reduction Heuristics in ATP, J. Art. Int., vol 2, 1971

[WB77] W. Bledsoe, A maximal method for set variables in ATP, ATP-33, University of Texas, Austin, 1977

[WM76] G. Wilson, J. Minker, Resolution, Refinements and Search Strategies; A Comparative Study, IEEE Transac. on Comp., vol C-25, no. 6, 1976

[CW79] Chr. Walther, Forschungsvorhaben zur Automatisierung von Induktionsbeweisen, Universität Karlsruhe, 1979

EIN ENTWURF ZUR MASCHINELLEN UNTERSTÜTZUNG VON KORREKTHEITSBEWEISEN BEI SIMULATIONEN

Wolfram-Manfred Lippe Franz Wagner
Institut für Informatik und Praktische Mathematik
Christian-Albrechts-Universität Kiel
Olshausenstr. 40-60, D-2300 Kiel 1

I. Einleitung

Bei einer Beweisführung kann man zwei Phasen unterscheiden: das Finden einer Beweisidee (Beweismuster) und die Durchführung des Beweises gemäß dieses Musters. Bei dieser Durchführung wiederholen sich häufig gleichartige Folgen von Beweisschritten (z.B. bei Fallunterscheidungen). Es ist daher sinnvoll, Programme zu entwickeln, die derartige Folgen von Beweisschritten maschinell durchführen können. Für eine solche Beweisunterstützung eignen sich vor allem Simulationen, da bei ihnen in der Regel eine große Anzahl ähnlich gearteter Fälle auftreten.

In Kapitel II wird das Wesen einer Simulation genauer untersucht und die theoretischen Grundlagen eingeführt. Wir definieren zunächst den Begriff "System" und sodann die "Systemsimulation". Ein System ist im wesentlichen eine Menge, deren Elemente Konfigurationen genannt werden, welche sich nach gewissen Regeln verändern. Ein System simuliert ein anderes System genau dann, wenn diese Simulation "korrekt" und "vollständig" ist.

Wir skizzieren sodann einen Algorithmus zur maschinellen Überprüfung der Korrektheit und Vollständigkeit einer Simulation. Dieser Algorithmus benötigt als Eingabe das Simulationsmuster in Form einer Beschreibung des simulierten und des simulierenden Systems und eine Beziehung zwischen diesen beiden Systemen. Im Fehlerfall liefert das Programm dem Benutzer eine genaue Beschreibung der Fehlersituation, die es dem Benutzer erlaubt, sein Simulationsmuster gezielt zu korrigieren und sodann das Programm neu zu starten.

In Kapitel II zeigen wir zunächst, daß dieses Konzept bei vielen Simulationen aus dem Gebiet der Automatentheorie anwendbar ist. Sodann wird das Verfahren auf eine Simulation aus dem Gebiet der Betriebssysteme angewandt. Zur Steuerung von konkurrierenden Prozessen wurde von Dijkstra [Dij 68] das Semaphorkonzept entwickelt. Bekanntlich lassen sich allgemeine Semaphore durch binäre Semaphore simulieren [Jü 73]. Es wird gezeigt, daß sich allgemeine und binäre Semaphore als Systeme in unserem Sinne darstellen lassen und daß sich mit dem Algorithmus die Korrektheit und Vollständigkeit der o.g. Simulation zeigen läßt. In einem weiteren Beispiel befassen wir uns mit einem Problem aus dem Gebiet der Programmiersprachen. In [Li 75] wurde das Verhalten von speziellen monadischen Programmen bezüglich der in ihnen auftretenden Prozeduren durch Baumsysteme simuliert. Die Anwendung unseres Algorithmus auf diese Simulation zeigt, wie man durch geeignetes Ausnutzen von Eigenschaften der Simulation (z.B. jedem Schritt des simulierten Systems entspricht genau ein Schritt des simulierenden Systems) den Aufwand des Verfahrens erheblich verringern kann.

Die aufgeführten Beispiele zeigen, daß das hier vorgestellte Lösungskonzept für Simulationen bei ganz unterschiedlichen Systemen anwendbar ist. Ansatzpunkte für Verbesserungen sind genauere Aussagen über die Beschreibungssituation, da die "Beschreibung" (eine Simulation muß für den Algorithmus in geeigneter Weise beschrieben werden) doch eine große Einschränkung darstellt. Ebenso erfolgversprechend dürften Untersuchungen über den Einfluß von Beziehungen zwischen den Regelmengen bei Simulationen sein (bei Beispiel 3 werden solche Beziehungen ausgenutzt). Gerade dieser Punkt dürfte den Aufwand des Verfahrens erheblich mindern (siehe [Pe 78]).

II. Basisdefinitionen und Lösungskonzept

Unter einem System verstehen wir folgendes:

Definition 2.1:

Ein System S ist ein Paar (Σ, R), wobei Σ eine beliebige Menge (Konfigurationsmenge) und R eine endliche Menge (Regelmenge) von Abbildungen von Σ in die Menge der Teilmengen von Σ ist.

$R = \{r \mid r: \Sigma \longrightarrow 2^{\Sigma}\}$.

Schreibweisen:

Seien $a, b \varepsilon \Sigma$; $A \subseteq \Sigma$; $r, r_1, \ldots, r_n \varepsilon R$ und $w = r_1 \ldots r_n \varepsilon R$.

Dann

i) $a \vdash b \;:\Leftrightarrow \exists r \varepsilon R: b \varepsilon r(a)$,

$a \overset{r}{\vdash} b \;:\Leftrightarrow b \varepsilon r(a)$,

ii) $a \overset{w}{\vdash} b \;:\Leftrightarrow \exists a_0, \ldots, a_n \varepsilon \Sigma : a = a_0 \overset{r_1}{\vdash} a_1 \ldots \overset{r_n}{\vdash} a_n = b$,

$a \overset{*}{\vdash} b \;:\Leftrightarrow \exists w \varepsilon R : a \overset{w}{\vdash} b$,

iii) $a \overset{w}{\underset{A}{\vdash}} b \;:\Leftrightarrow \exists a_1, \ldots, a_{n-1} \varepsilon A: a \overset{r_1}{\vdash} a_1 \ldots a_{n-1} \overset{r_n}{\vdash} b$,

$a \overset{*}{\underset{A}{\vdash}} b \;:\Leftrightarrow \exists w \varepsilon R : a \overset{w}{\underset{A}{\vdash}} b$.

Wenn für alle $r \in R$ und für alle $a \in \Sigma$, $|r(a)| \leq 1$ ist, dann heißt S ein deterministisches System. Statt $\{b\} = r(a)$ schreiben wir dann auch $r(a)=b$.

Unter Σ werden z.B. Speicherzelleninhalte oder Zustände und unter R die Vorschriften, nach denen sich die Konfigurationen ändern können, verstanden. Es wird dabei nicht verlangt, daß immer eine Folgekonfiguration existiert, und daß, wenn sie existiert, sie sich deterministisch ergibt.

Bei einem Systemverhalten interessieren oft nur die von einer konkreten Anfangskonfiguration aus "erreichbaren" Konfigurationen.

<u>Definition 2.2:</u>

Sei $S = (\Sigma,R)$ ein System und $I \in \Sigma$.

Dann heißt $\Sigma_I = \{K \mid I \vdash^{*} K\}$ die von I aus <u>erreichbare</u> Konfigurationsmenge.

Diese Definition läßt sich noch verallgemeinern, indem wir anstelle einer einzelnen Konfiguration I eine Menge von Konfigurationen zulassen.

Unter einer Simulation eines Systems durch ein anderes System soll das Folgende zu verstehen sein:

i) ein Übergang von Konfigurationen im simulierenden System impliziert einen Übergang von "entsprechenden" Konfigurationen im simulierten System,

ii) ein Konfigurationsübergang im simulierenden System an "entsprechenden" Konfigurationen soll dann vorliegen, wenn dies durch das simulierte System gefordert wird.

Bei der Definition von Systemsimulation wird die "entsprechende" Konfiguration durch eine Abbildung h näher spezifiziert.

<u>Definition 2.3:</u>

Seien $S1 = (\Sigma 1,R1)$ und $S2 = (\Sigma 2,R2)$ zwei Systeme. Sei weiterhin $A1 \subseteq \Sigma 1$, $A2 \subseteq \Sigma 2$ und h eine partielle Abbildung $h: A1 \longrightarrow A2$.

Dann

wird die Konfigurationsmenge A2 in $\Sigma 2$ durch die Konfigurationsmenge A1 in $\Sigma 1$ mittels der Abbildung h simuliert [$S1(A1) \succ S2(A2)$ mittels h]:

✱ D1) $\forall K1, K1' \in A1$ gilt:

$$\begin{array}{ccc} K1 \vdash^{*} K1' & & \exists K2' \in A2 \text{ mit: } K1 \vdash^{*} K1' \\ \downarrow h & \Rightarrow & \downarrow h \quad \downarrow h \\ K2 & & K2 \models^{*} K2' \end{array}$$

(simulierendes System) / (simuliertes System)

(<u>Korrektheit</u> der Simulation)

und

D2) $\forall K2, K2' \in A2$ gilt:

$$\begin{array}{ccc} K1 & & \exists K1' \in A1 \text{ mit: } K1 \vdash^{*} K1' \\ \downarrow h & \Rightarrow & \downarrow h \quad \downarrow h \\ K2 \models^{*} K2' & & K2 \models^{*} K2' \text{ gilt.} \end{array}$$

(<u>Vollständigkeit</u> der Simulation)

Bei D1) ist die Konfiguration K2', deren Existenz verlangt wird, durch die Abbildung h eindeutig bestimmt; wohingegen die Konfiguration K1' bei D2) i.a. nicht eindeutig bestimmt ist.

Die Eigenschaft D1 wird als Korrektheit der Simulation und die Eigenschaft D2 als Vollständigkeit bezeichnet. Seien K2 und K2' ε A2 gegeben, und es soll festgestellt werden, ob K2 $\overset{*}{\models}$ K2' gilt, dazu kann man wie folgt vorgehen:

i) zu K2 wähle irgendeine Konfiguration K1 $\varepsilon\, h^{-1}$(K2),

ii) stelle fest, ob ein K1' $\varepsilon\, h^{-1}$(K2') existiert, so daß K1 $\overset{*}{\vdash}$ K1' gilt,

iii) falls die Antwort hier ja heißt, gilt K2 $\overset{*}{\models}$ K2' und ansonsten gilt K2 $\overset{*}{\models}$ K2' nicht.

Wenn $\overset{*}{\vdash}$ in dem simulierenden System S1 entscheidbar und h genügend einfach ist, so liefert dieses Vorgehen einen Algorithmus zur Entscheidung von $\overset{*}{\models}$.

Bei einer Simulation brauchen nicht alle Ausgangssituationen D1 und D2 gemäß der Definition einer Simulation überprüft zu werden, wie das folgende Lemma zeigt.

Lemma 2.4:

Seien S1 = (Σ1,R1) und S2 = (Σ2,R2) zwei Systeme. Sei A1 $\subseteq \Sigma$1, A2 $\subseteq \Sigma$2 und h: A1 $\rightarrow$ A2 eine partielle Abbildung.

Dann gilt S1(A1) $\succ$ S2(A2) mittels h $\Leftrightarrow$ es gilt:

D1') $\forall$ K1,K1' ε A1 gilt:

$$\begin{array}{ccc} K1 & \overset{*}{\underset{C(A1)}{\vdash}} & K1' \\ \downarrow h & & \\ K2 & & \end{array} \quad\Longrightarrow\quad \exists K2' \,\varepsilon\, A2 \text{ mit: } \begin{array}{ccc} K1 & \overset{*}{\underset{C(A1)}{\vdash}} & K1' \\ \downarrow h & & \downarrow h \\ K2 & \overset{*}{\models} & K2' \end{array}$$

und

D2') $\forall$ K2,K2' ε A2 gilt:

$$\begin{array}{ccc} K1 & & \\ \downarrow h & & \\ K2 & \overset{*}{\underset{C(A2)}{\models}} & K2' \end{array} \quad\Longrightarrow\quad \exists K1' \,\varepsilon\, A1 \text{ mit: } \begin{array}{ccc} K1 & \overset{*}{\vdash} & K1' \\ \downarrow h & & \downarrow h \\ K2 & \overset{*}{\underset{C(A2)}{\models}} & K2' \end{array} \text{ gilt.}$$

Mit C(A1) (bzw. C(A2)) bezeichnen wir hier das Komplement von A1 (bzw. A2) in der Grundmenge Σ1 (bzw. Σ2).

Der Beweis ergibt sich durch Induktion über die Anzahl der Zwischenkonfigurationen bei K1 $\overset{*}{\vdash}$ K1' (bzw. K2 $\overset{*}{\models}$ K2'), die Elemente aus A1 (bzw. A2) sind. Als Korollar von Lemma 2.4 erhält man für erreichbare Konfigurationen folgendes:

Korollar 2.5:

Seien S1 = (Σ1,R1) und S2 = (Σ2,R2) zwei Systeme. Sei A1 = Σ_{I1} mit einem I1 $\varepsilon\, \Sigma$1, und sei A2 = Σ_{I2} mit einem I2 $\varepsilon\, \Sigma$2. Sei h eine partielle Abbildung h: A1 $\rightarrow$ A2.

Dann gilt $S1(A1) \succ S2(A2)$ mittels h $\Leftrightarrow$ es gilt:

D1'') $\forall K1, K1' \varepsilon A1$ gilt:

$$\begin{array}{ccc} K1 & \vdash & K1' \\ \downarrow h & & \\ K2 & & \end{array} \quad \Longrightarrow \quad \exists K2' \varepsilon A2 \text{ mit: } \begin{array}{ccc} K1 & \vdash & K1' \\ \downarrow h & & \downarrow h \\ K2 & \overset{*}{\models} & K2' \end{array}$$

und

D2'') $\forall K2, K2' \varepsilon A2$ gilt:

$$\begin{array}{ccc} K1 & & \\ \downarrow h & & \\ K2 & \models & K2' \end{array} \quad \Longrightarrow \quad \exists K1' \varepsilon A1 \text{ mit: } \begin{array}{ccc} K1 & \overset{*}{\vdash} & K1' \\ \downarrow h & & \downarrow h \\ K2 & \models & K2' \end{array} \text{ gilt.}$$

Um durch ein Programm eine Simulation bei gegebenem h zu beweisen, muß eine endliche Beschreibung des Problems vorliegen. Hier wird davon ausgegangen, daß bei der Simulationsüberprüfung i.a. eine große Anzahl von Fällen ($K \overset{*}{\vdash} K'$) zu untersuchen ist.

Ein erster Versuch ist, die Konfigurationsmenge in Klassen einzuteilen, auf denen Regeln gemäß den ursprünglichen Regeln definiert sind:

$a \vdash b \Longrightarrow k(a) \models k(b)$, wobei k eine Abbildung ist, die einer Konfiguration ihre Klasse zuordnet.

Wenn nun zwei Systeme S1 und S2 gegeben sind, und es soll überprüft werden, ob S1 das System S2 mittels einer vorliegenden Abbildung h simuliert, dann soll dies an den (endlichen) Beschreibungen (Klasseneinteilung) der Systeme S1 und S2 für eine Abbildung hb zwischen den Klasseneinteilungen überprüft werden.

<u>Skizze 1:</u> Beschreibung SB1 Beschreibung SB2

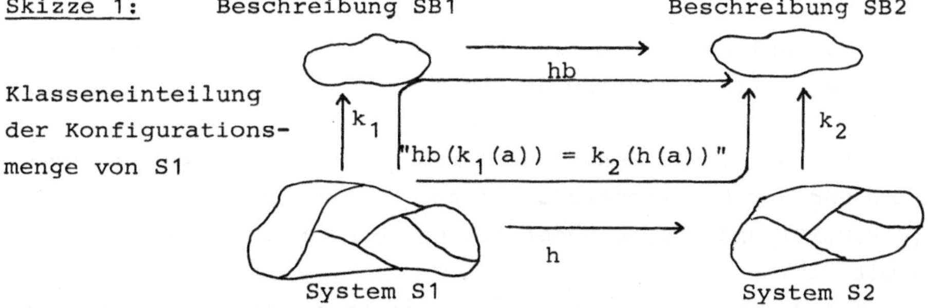

Daß die Beschreibungen durch k_1 und k_2 zueinander "passen", soll durch die Kommutativität $hb(k_1(a)) = k_2(h(a))$ ausgedrückt werden.

Dieser erste Versuch gelingt jedoch nicht (d.h. wir können bei den Beschreibungen eine Simulation bezüglich hb feststellen, ohne daß eine Simulation bezüglich h vorliegt), wie das folgende Beispiel zeigt.

<u>Beispiel:</u> Sei $S1 = (\mathbb{N}, \{r_1\})$, wobei $r_1(n) = n+1$ ist für alle $n \varepsilon \mathbb{N}$, und $S2 = (\mathbb{N}, \{r_2\})$, wobei $r_2(n) = n+2$ ist für alle $n \varepsilon \mathbb{N}$. Sei $h: \mathbb{N} \rightarrow \mathbb{N}$ mit $h(n) = n$. Sei $SB1 = (\,\mathbb{N}\,, \{r\}) = SB2$ mit $r(\mathbb{N}) = \mathbb{N}$. Sei $hb(\mathbb{N}) = \mathbb{N}$.

Wir haben also jeweils die triviale Klasseneinteilung (die gesamte

Menge als einzige Klasse) als Beschreibung.

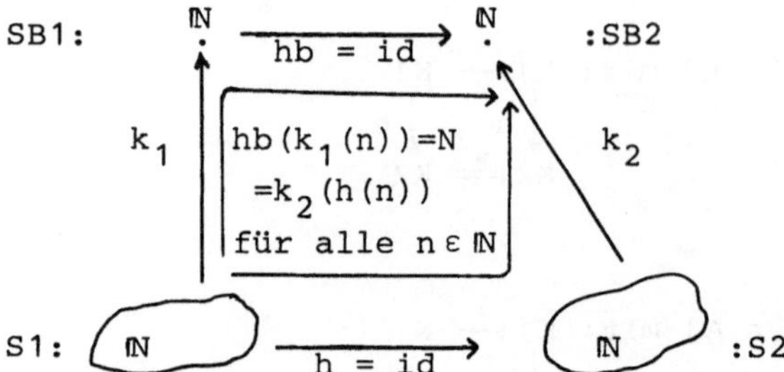

Nun gilt sicherlich, daß SB1 das System SB2 mittels hb simuliert. Andererseits liegt keine Simulation von S2 durch S1 mittels h vor, es gilt nämlich $1 \vdash^{r_1} 2$, aber es gilt nicht $h(1)=1 \vdash^{r_2} 2=h(2)$.

Im Beispiel wurden zu viele Konfigurationen zu einer Klasse zusammengefaßt; es wurden mehr als nur "gleichartige" zusammengefaßt. Daher beschränken wir uns auf Systeme, deren Konfigurationen Tupel sind.

<u>Definition 2.6:</u>

Seien $B_1,\ldots,B_n$ Mengen.

Dann

heißt (Σ,R) ein <u>Tn-System über $B_1,\ldots,B_n$</u>: $\Leftrightarrow$ (Σ,R) ein System ist und $\Sigma \subseteq B_1 \times \ldots \times B_n$ ist.

Ein <u>DTn-System</u> ist ein deterministisches Tn-System.

Das Hilfsmittel, mit dem es gelingt das "Gleichartige" von Konfigurationen zu fassen, ist die Substitution.

<u>Definition 2.7:</u>

Sei VAR eine Variablenmenge, B eine Konstantenmenge und FU eine Funktionszeichenmenge, die paarweise disjunkt sind.

Dann wird mit

$\theta(VAR,B,FU)$ die Menge der Terme über der Argumentzeichenmenge $VAR \cup B$ und der Funktionszeichenmenge FU bezeichnet.

Sei $a \in \theta(VAR,B,FU)$ und σ eine Substitution (d.h. $\sigma: VAR \longrightarrow B$).

Dann wird mit

$\sigma(a)$ der Term aus $\theta(\emptyset,B,FU)$ bezeichnet, der aus a durch die Variablensubstitution σ entsteht.

Falls der Term $\sigma(a)$ einen Wert aus B darstellt (gemäß einer Standardinterpretation), so soll nicht zwischen $\sigma(a)$ und dem Wert unterschieden werden.

Falls $A = (a_1,\ldots,a_n)$ ist mit $a_i \in \theta(VAR,B,FU)$ für $i=1,..,n$, so verstehen wir unter $\sigma(A)$ das Tupel $(\sigma(a_1),\ldots,\sigma(a_n))$.

<u>Beispiel:</u> $B = \mathbb{N}$, $VAR = \{x\}$, $FU = \{+,-\}$

$a = x+3$ und $\sigma(x) = 2 \implies \sigma(a) = 2+3 = 5$.

Mit Hilfe der Substitution definieren wir nun die "Beschreibung" eines DTn-Systems.

Definition 2.8:

Sei (Σ,R) ein DTn-Sytem über $B_1,\ldots,B_n$ und sei $A \subseteq \Sigma$ und $B = \bigcup_i B_i$.
Sei VAR eine Variablenmenge und FU eine Funktionszeichenmenge, so daß VAR, FU und B paarweise disjunkt sind.
Dann heißt

$(\Sigma B,RB)$ eine (f,VAR,FU)-Beschreibung von A in (Σ,R) durch AB:

i) $AB \subseteq \Sigma B \subseteq \{(a_1,\ldots,a_n) \mid a_i \in B_i$ oder $a_i \in \theta(VAR,B_i,FU)$ für $i=1,..,n\}$ ist und $f: R \xrightarrow[\text{total}]{\text{auf}} RB$ eine totale und surjektive Abbildung ist,

ii) $\forall a,b \in A$ gilt:
$a \vdash^{r_1\ldots r_m}_{C(A)} b \implies \exists a_o,b_o \in AB$ und $\exists \sigma: VAR \longrightarrow B$, so daß $a_o \vdash^{f(r_1)\ldots f(r_m)} b_o$ gilt und $\sigma(a_o)=a$ ist und $\sigma(b_o)=b$ ist

und

iii) $\forall a_o,b_o \in \Sigma B$, $\forall r_o \in RB$ und $\forall$ Substitutionen σ gilt:
$a_o \vdash^{r_o} b_o$ mit $\sigma(a_o) = a \in \Sigma \implies \exists r \in f^{-1}(r_o)$, so daß $r(a) \neq \emptyset$ ist und $r(a)=\sigma(b_o)$ ist

gilt.

Eine Beschreibung heißt endlich, genau dann, wenn $|\Sigma B|<\infty$ ist.

Skizze 2:

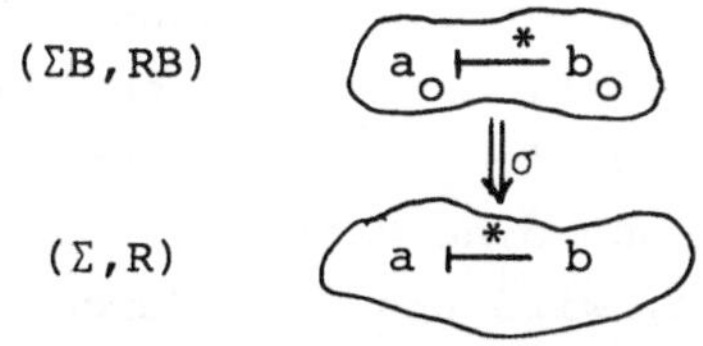

$(\Sigma B,RB)$ $\quad a_o \vdash^{*} b_o$

$\Downarrow \sigma$

(Σ,R) $\quad a \vdash^{*} b$

Unter einer Beschreibung ist also ein Zusammenfassen von Konfigurationen zu verstehen, wobei das Zusammenfassen die Regelanwendungen (siehe ii und iii von Definition 2.8) berücksichtigt. Da bei Definition 2.8 gefordert wird, daß man von einer Konfigurationsbeschreibung mittels Substitutionen zu den beschriebenen Konfigurationen zurückkommt, haben wir damit in unserem Sinne die "Gleichartigkeit" ausgedrückt.

Wird nun das ganze Simulationsverhalten (es sind also zwei Systeme beteiligt) beschrieben, so muß nicht nur das Zusammenfassen von Konfigurationen innerhalb eines Systems konsistent bezüglich der Regeln sein, sondern es muß auch die neu zu definierende Abbildung hb für die Simulation der beschriebenen Systeme zu der gegebenen Abbildung h "konsistent" sein.

<u>Definition 2.9:</u>

Sei S1 = (Σ1,R1) ein DTn-System über $A_1,\dots,A_n$.
Sei S2 = (Σ2,R2) ein DTm-System über $B_1,\dots,B_m$.
Sei A1 ⊆ Σ1 und A2 ⊆ Σ2.
Sei SB1 = (ΣB1,RB1) eine $(f_1$,VAR,FU)-Beschreibung von A1 in S1 durch AB1 und SB2 = (ΣB2,RB2) eine $(f_2$,VAR,FU)-Beschreibung von A2 in S2 durch AB2.
Seien h: A1 $\xrightarrow[\text{total}]{}$ A2 und hb: ΣB1 $\xrightarrow[\text{partiell}]{}$ ΣB2 Abbildungen, wobei AB2 ⊆ hb(ΣB1) ist und AB1 ⊆ hb^{-1}(ΣB2) ist.
Dann heißt

(SB1,AB1,hb,SB2,AB2) eine <u>konsistente</u> Beschreibung von (S1,A1,h,S2,A2) mittels $(f_1,f_2$,VAR,FU):

$\Leftrightarrow$ $\forall a_o \varepsilon$ ΣB1 und ∀ Substitutionen σ mit $\sigma(a_o)\varepsilon\Sigma1$ gilt:

i) $\sigma(hb(a_o))$ existiert

$\Leftrightarrow$

$h(\sigma(a_o))$ existiert

und

ii) $\sigma(hb(a_o)) = h(\sigma(a_o))$ gilt.

(SB1,AB1,hb,SB2,AB2) heißt eine <u>endliche</u> konsistente Beschreibung von (S1,A1,h,S2,A2) mittels $(f_1,f_2$,VAR,FU) genau dann, wenn $|\Sigma B1| < \infty$ und $|\Sigma B2| < \infty$ ist.

Durch eine Beschreibung (siehe Definition 2.8 ii) sind einer Konfiguration möglicherweise mehrere "Konfigurationstypen" zugeordnet. Die Beschreibung impliziert i.a. also eine Überdeckung der Konfigurationsmenge A. Im Spezialfall kann diese Überdeckung eine Partition sein wie im Beispiel 3. Wie diese Bemerkungen zeigen, wird uns also durch eine Beschreibung eine Fallunterscheidung für den Simulationsbeweis vorgegeben.

Der folgende Satz zeigt nun, daß eine Simulation an dazugehörigen Beschreibungen (siehe Definition 2.8 und 2.9) überprüft werden kann.

<u>Satz 2.10:</u>

Seien die Voraussetzungen wie in Definition 2.9 gegeben, und sei weiterhin (SB1,AB1,hb,SB2,AB2) eine konsistente Beschreibung von (S1,A1,h,S2,A2) mittels $(f_1,f_2$,VAR,FU).
Sei die Konfigurationsmenge AB2 in ΣB2 durch die Konfigurationsmenge AB2 in ΣB2 mittels der Abbildung hb simuliert
[SB1(AB1) $\succ$ SB2(AB2) mittels hb].
Dann gilt

S1(A1) $\succ$ S2(A2) mittels h.

Skizze 3:

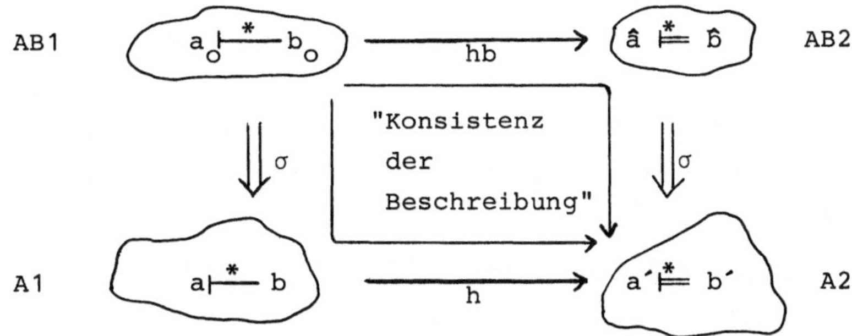

Beweisskizze zu Satz 2.10 (Korrektheit der Simulation mittels h):

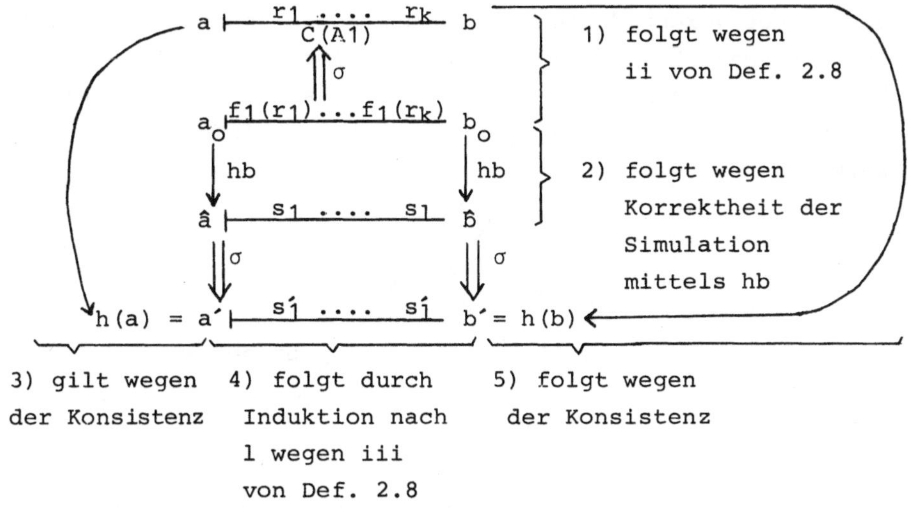

, wobei $s_i' \varepsilon f_2^{-1}(s_i)$ ist für $i = 1,\dots,l$.

Die einzelnen Beweisschritte sind von 1) - 5) durchnummeriert.

Bei obiger Beweisskizze erkennt man, daß zum Beweis der Korrektheit der Simulation mittels h lediglich die Korrektheit der Simulation mittels hb erforderlich ist. Der Beweis der Vollständigkeit geht analog vor sich und benötigt nur die Vollständigkeit der Simulation bezüglich hb.

Durch die Beschreibungen von A1 und A2 werden Überdeckungen induziert. Die Überdeckungselemente (Mengen) sind als die relevanten Fälle zu betrachten, die beim Prüfen der Simulation zu untersuchen sind. Durch die Beschreibungen sollen die zu betrachtenden Situationen (Fälle) auf eine endliche Anzahl reduziert werden, so daß dann für eine gegebene Abbildung hb die Simulation (bezüglich der Fallunterscheidung) überprüft werden kann. Bei einem positiven Ausgang der Prüfung liegt dann (siehe Satz 2.10) auch die Simulation mittels h vor.

Das Ziel bei vorliegendem Simulationsproblem ist also, zu einer endlichen Beschreibung des Problems (im Sinne von Definition 2.8 und 2.9) zu kommen, so daß das Verfahren A angewendet werden kann.

Algorithmus A:

Seien die Systeme $S1 = (\Sigma 1, R1)$ und $S2 = (\Sigma 2, R2)$ gegeben, und sei $B1 \subseteq \Sigma 1$, $B2 \subseteq \Sigma 2$ mit $|B1| = k_1$ und $|B2| = k_2$. Weiterhin liege die Abbildung $hb: B1 \longrightarrow B2$ vor.

1. Prüfung der Korrektheit von $S1(B1) \succ S2(B2)$ mittels hb:

Sei $b \in B1$.

i) Zu $b \in B1$ wird $\{b' \mid b \overset{*}{\vdash} b'\} = AB_b$ gebildet. Wegen $|B1| = k_1$ genügt es, die maximale Zahl von Regeln aus R1, die hintereinander auf b angewendet werden, durch k_1 zu beschränken, dabei kann ein dabei entstehender Ableitungspfad schon abgebrochen werden, wenn eine Konfiguration erreicht wird, die zuvor schon auf demselben Pfad erschien. Bei der Bildung von AB_b entsteht folgender Ableitungsbaum:

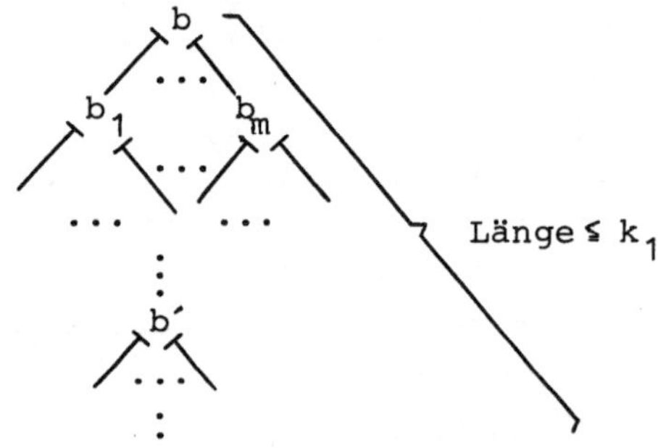

ii) Dann wird, analog dazu im System S2 (Anwendung der Regeln aus R2) der Ableitungsbaum $AB'_b = \{c \mid hb(b) \overset{*}{\models} c\}$ gebildet.

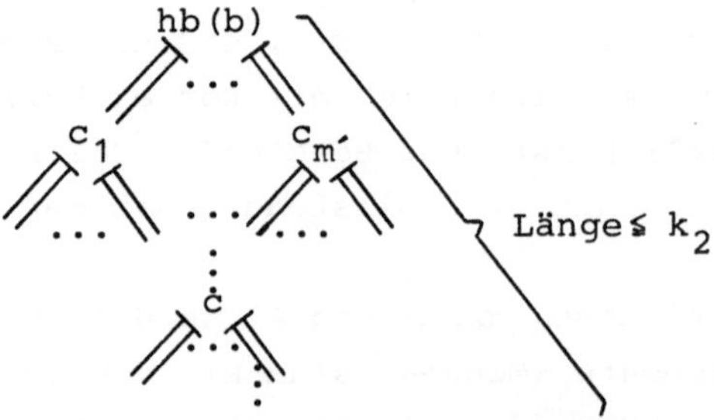

iii) Testen aller Ausgangssituationen des Diagramms D1 (siehe Definition 2.3):

Für alle $b' \in AB_b$ wird $hb(b')$ konstruiert, und es wird getestet, ob $hb(b') \in AB'_b$ ist. Ist dies der Fall, so wird das nächste $b \in B1$ gewählt, und man beginne wieder bei i) (erneuter Schleifendurchlauf), ansonsten $(hb(b') \notin AB'_b)$ liegt keine Korrektheit vor, und man beende die Prüfung. Ist das Testen für alle $b \varepsilon$ B1 erfolgreich gewesen, so liegt Korrektheit vor.

2. Prüfung der Vollständigkeit von S1(B1) $\succ$ S2(B2) mittels hb:

Sei $c \varepsilon$ B2.

i) Bildung des Ableitungsbaumes $\overline{AB}_c = \{ c' \mid c \models\!\!\overset{*}{=} c' \}$.

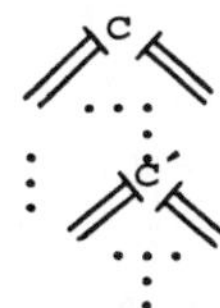

ii) Im System S1 wird dazu jetzt eine Menge von Ableitungsbäumen $\overline{AB}'_b = \{ b' \mid b \overset{*}{\models} b' \}$ gebildet; zu jedem $b \varepsilon hb^{-1}(c)$ ein Baum.

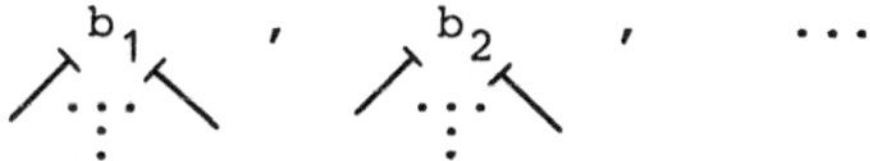

iii) Testen aller Ausgangssituationen (siehe D2 von Definition 2.3): Dies geschieht wie beim Testen der Korrektheit, nur muß hier noch gemäß der Definition von Vollständigkeit ii) (Menge von Ableitungsbäumen) berücksichtigt werden. Dann wird bei erfolgreichem Testen mit dem nächsten $c \varepsilon$ B2 bei i) fortgefahren, bis (bei vorliegender Vollständigkeit) mit allen c die Schleife durchlaufen wurde.

Optimierungen dieses Verfahrens sind möglich beim Erzeugen der Ableitungsbäume, da sie nicht für jeden Schleifendurchlauf völlig neu erzeugt werden müssen. Bei 2.ii) und iii) kann der Aufwand gesenkt werden, indem bei ii) nur ein Baum $\overline{AB}'_b$ erzeugt wird, dann durch iii) getestet wird und bei erfolglosem Test bei ii) der nächste Ableitungsbaum erzeugt wird. Bei dieser Änderung brauchen i.a. nicht alle Bäume $\overline{AB}'_b$ konstruiert zu werden (siehe D2). Für konkrete Beispiele, bei denen auch noch eine Beziehung (neben der Entsprechung von Konfigurationen) zwischen den Regelmengen R1 und R2 besteht, kann das Erzeugen der Bäume noch weiter optimiert werden. Weitere Einschränkungen im Aufwand sind möglich, wenn bei der Definition 2.3 der $*$- Operator bei $\overset{*}{\vdash}$ bzw. $\overset{*}{\models}$ durch feste Zahlen oder Schranken ersetzt würde (siehe dazu auch Korollar 2.5).

Auch wenn beim Verfahren A eine Korrektheit bzw. Vollständigkeit der Simulation nicht bestätigt werden kann, so lassen sich die Ergebnisse der Überprüfung evtl. nutzen, um weitere Einsichten in die Gestalt der Simulation zu gewinnen. Dies ist beispielsweise so vorstellbar, daß das programmierte Verfahren A den Fall mitteilt, bei dem die Überprüfung scheiterte, und der Benutzer auf diese Weise einen Hinweis auf die Stelle erhält,an welcher er beim weiteren Beweisen ansetzen muß.

III. Beispiele

Beispiel 1: Simulation von Automaten [HS 66]

Simulationen von Automaten (siehe [HS 66]) sind in diesem Sinne ein Spezialfall der Korrektheit einer Simulation, wenn die Ausgabe vernachlässigt wird (Halbautomat). Durch die Abbildung zwischen den Alphabeten der Automaten wird zusätzlich eine Beziehung zwischen den Regelmengen hergestellt. Die Zustände der Automaten stellen die Konfigurationen dar, und die Übergangsfunktion δ_x ($x \varepsilon$ Eingabealphabet) sind die Regeln.

Bei der Automat B wird durch den Automaten A simuliert liegt folgende Situation vor:

$$\begin{array}{llcl} A: & z' \vdash z'' & \Longrightarrow & z'' \\ & \downarrow \alpha & & \downarrow \alpha \\ B: & z & & z \models \bar{z} \end{array}$$

, wobei α eine Abbildung zwischen den Zustandsmengen der Automaten ist und $\vdash$ bzw. $\models$ die einmalige Anwendung einer Übergangsfunktion bzw. Regel bedeuten.

Auf analoge Weise ist die Realisierung von Halbautomaten [HS 66] ein Spezialfall der Korrektheit einer Simulation. Bei der Realisierung des Zustandsverhaltens von Automaten [HS 66] liegt auch noch die Vollständigkeit der Simulation als Spezialfall vor.

Beispiel 2: Simulation von allgemeinen Semaphoren durch binäre Semaphore [Jü 73]

In [Jü 73] ist folgende Simulation eines allgemeinen Semaphors s angegeben, wegen der Beschreibung durch ein DTm-System wurden hier noch "Prozeßzähler" hinzugefügt.

allgemeiner Semaphor s:

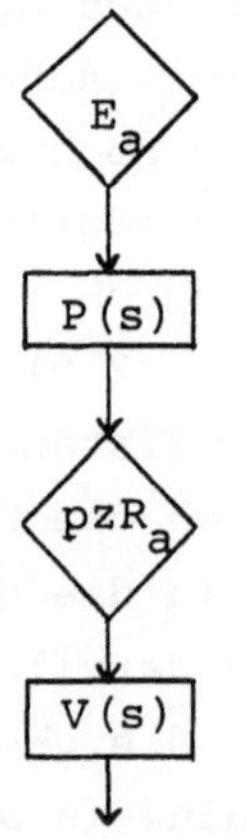

Initialisierung:

$E_a = n \varepsilon \mathbb{N}_0$,
$s = n_0 \varepsilon \mathbb{N}$ (festgelegt),
$pzR_a = 0$.

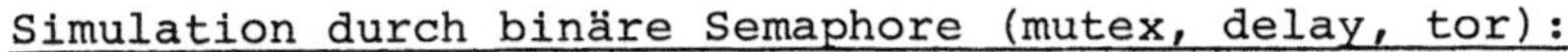

Simulation durch binäre Semaphore (mutex, delay, tor):

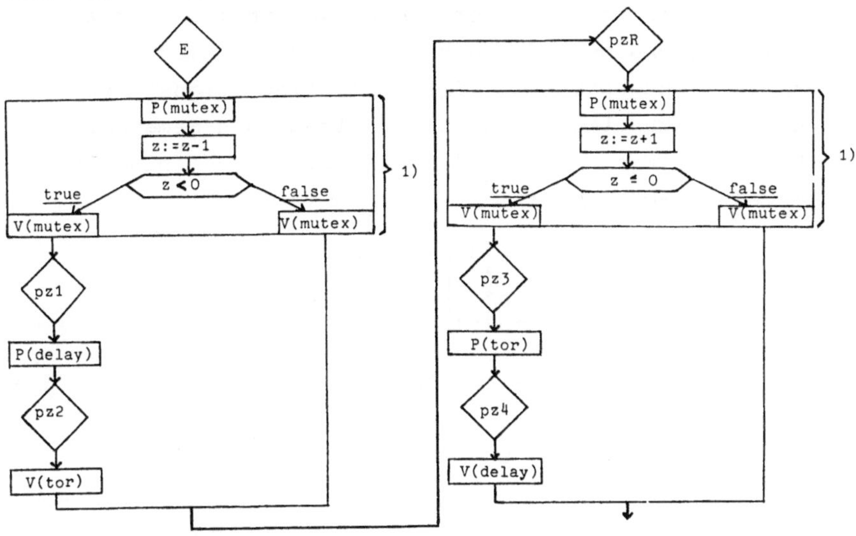

Initialisierung: $E = n \in \mathbb{N}_o$, $z = n_o \in \mathbb{N}$ (festgelegt), mutex = tor = 1,
delay = 0, sonstige Prozeßzähler alle auf 0.

Durch ▭ sind jeweils "unteilbare" Operationen und durch ◇ Prozeßzähler (d.h. es werden die Prozesse gezählt, die sich gerade an dieser Stelle im System befinden) gekennzeichnet.

Als Konfigurationen werden für beide Systeme die Tupel, deren Komponenten die Variablen- bzw. Semaphorinhalte und die Prozeßzählerstände sind, genommen. Die Regeln lassen sich direkt aus den "Flußdiagrammen" ablesen, dabei ist insbesondere auf die Prozeßzähler (Prozesse fahren fort) zu achten. Bei E und E_a werden die anstehenden und evtl. "blockierten" Prozesse gezählt. Blockiert heißt, daß keine Regel anwendbar ist.

Die erreichbare Konfigurationsmenge beim System der binären Semaphore, welche auch die simulierende Konfigurationsmenge A1 ist, ist durch die Angaben a) - d) bestimmt:

a) $z = n_o-(pz1+pz2+pzR)$,

b) $z \geq 0 \Rightarrow pz1 = pz3+pz4+delay$,

c) $z \leq 0 \Rightarrow z+pz1 = pz3+pz4+delay$,

d)

	pz2	pz4	tor	delay
	0	0	1	0
oder				
	0	1	0	0
oder				
	0	0	0	1
oder				
	1	0	0	0 .

Zur Beschreibung der erreichbaren Zählerstände von E, pz1, pzR und pz3 führen wir die Variablen (über $\mathbb{N}_o$) n, n1, nR und n3 ein. Für z werden

1) Dieser gesamte Teil kann wegen des wechselweisen Ausschlusses als unteilbare Operation angesehen werden.

z_1 (über $\mathbb{N}$) und z_2 (über $\mathbb{Z}\setminus\mathbb{N}_0$) als Variablen eingeführt. Die Regeln werden für die Beschreibung entsprechend übernommen. So erhalten wir z.B. als Terme bei der Beschreibung n-1 oder auch z_2+1 u.s.w. gemäß den Regelanwendungen. Wir erhalten insgesamt 40 "Fälle" (Konfigurationstypen).

Die zu simulierende Konfigurationsmenge beim allgemeinen Semaphorsystem ist $A2 = \{(E_A, pzR_a) \mid E_a \varepsilon \mathbb{N}_0,\ pzR_a = n_0 - s\}$, die durch folgende Konfigurationstypen beschrieben wird:

E_a	pzR_a
n+n1	nR+n3
n+n1+1	nR+n3
n+n1	nR+n3+1
n+n1-1	nR+n3+1

und

E_a	pzR_a
n+n1	nR+n3-1
n+n1+1	nR+n3-1
n+n1-1	nR+n3+2

.

Bei diesen "Typen" spiegelt sich die Abbildung h: A1 $\longrightarrow$ A2 wieder, die wie folgt definiert ist:

$$h(a) = a' : \Leftrightarrow E+pz1+pz2 = E_a \text{ und } pzR+pz3+pz4 = pzR_a .$$

Die Abbildung hb "bei den Beschreibungen" erhalten wir, indem h für die Terme auf den Komponentenstellen bei den Beschreibungen "umgeschrieben" wird, wodurch sich auch die Konfigurationstypen des allgemeinen Semaphorsystems erklären.

Die Konsistenz (Definition 2.9) ergibt sich hier wegen dieser Definition von hb sofort. Nun kann man durch ein Programm (Verfahren A) die Korrektheit und Vollständigkeit dieser Simulation überprüfen, wobei durch Berücksichtigung der Ergebnisse von Korollar 2.5 der Aufwand des Verfahrens verringert werden kann.

<u>Beispiel 3:</u> Simulation von monadischen Programmen mit maximaler Prozedurschachtelungstiefe 2 durch Baumgrammatiken [Li 75, Pe 78]

Ein monadisches ALGOL 60-P Programm wird zunächst in ein formal äquivalentes ALGOL 60-PG Programm transformiert [Lan 73]. Ein ALGOL 60-PG Programm π kann als ein DTn-System A_π aufgefaßt werden, wobei die Konfigurationen die gemäß der ALGOL 60 - Kopierregel erzeugten Programme sind. Die Regeln sind die Prozeduranweisungen des Hauptprogramms von π bzw. die Prozeduranweisungen in den Hauptteilen der Prozeduren. Die Anwendung der Regeln erfogt gemäß der Kopierregel.

Das System A_π soll nun durch ein Baumsystem B_π simuliert werden, und zwar soll ein Schritt $a \overset{r}{\models} a'$ in A_π durch einen Schritt $b \overset{s}{\vdash} b'$ in B_π simuliert werden, wobei r funktionell abhängig von s sein soll. Sowohl A_π als auch B_π lassen sich durch zwei endliche DT-Systeme und einer Abbildung hb zwischen den Konfigurationsmengen dieser Systeme beschreiben. In [Li 75] wurde nämlich gezeigt, daß sowohl bei A_π als auch bei B_π nur

32 Konfigurationsarten und 84 Regelarten existieren können. Dabei liefern hier die Beschreibungen A und B Partitionen der Konfigurationsmengen von A_π und B_π. Für die Simulation mittels hb fordern wir hier zusätzlich die Berücksichtigung einer Abbildung fb zwischen den Regelarten, da Schritt für Schritt simuliert werden soll, wobei die beim System A benutzte Regel funktionell abhängig von der bei B benutzten Regel sein soll.

Da hb und fb Bijektionen sind, gestaltet sich das Überprüfen durch das programmierte Verfahren A besonders einfach. Diese Überprüfungen müssen sowohl beim System B als auch bei A die 32 Konfigurationen und 84 Regeln berücksichtigen, so daß der Einsatz eines beweisunterstützenden Programms durchaus gerechtfertigt ist. Der Aufwand beim Aufbau der Ableitungsbäume ist gering, da eine Regelanwendund im System A_π (bzw. A) genau einer Regelanwendung im System B_π (bzw. B) entspricht (d.h. anstelle von $\vdash^{*}$ braucht nur $\vdash^{1}$ überprüft zu werden).

Literatur:

[Dij 68] Dijkstra, E. W.: Co-operating Sequential Processes. in: Programming Languages (Ed. F. Genuys), Academic Press, London, 1968, S. 43 - 112

[HS 66] Hartmanis, J., Stearns, R. E.: Algebraic Structure Theory of Sequential Machines. Prentice Hall, Englewood - Cliffs, 1966

[Jü 73] Jürgens, J.: Synchronisation paralleler Prozesse anhand von Zuständen. Diss., München, 1973

[Lam 77] Lamport, L.: Proving the Correctness of Multiprocess Programs. IEEE Transactions on Software Engineering, Vol. SE3, No. 2, 1977, S. 125 - 143

[Lan 73] Langmaack, H.: On Procedures as open Subroutines I, II. Acta Informatica Vol. 2, 1977, S. 311 - 333, Vol. 3, 1974 S. 227 - 241

[LLW 79] Langmaack, H., Lippe, W.-M., Wagner, F.: The Formal Termination Problem for Programs with Finite ALGOL 68-Modes. Information Processing Letters, Vol. 9, No. 3, 1979, S. 155 - 159

[Li 75] Lippe, W.-M.: Über die Entscheidbarkeit der formalen Erreichbarkeit von Prozeduren bei monadischen Programmen. Diss. Saarbrücken, 1975

[Pe 78] Petzhold, E.-G.: Zur Simulation von monadischen Programmen mit maximaler Prozedurschachtelungstiefe 2 durch Baumgrammatiken. Diplomarbeit, Kiel, 1978

[Pre 75] Presser, L.: Multiprogramming Coordination. ACM, Computing Surveys, Vol. 7, No. 1, 1975, S. 21 - 44

[Zi 76] Zima, H.: Betriebssysteme. Reihe Informatik/20, BI-Verlag, Zürich, 1976

On the Treatment of Equivalence Connectives in Automated Theorem Proving

Graham Wrightson, Fakultät für Informatik I
Universität Karlsruhe, Germany

For automated theorem proving it is shown in [1] how formulas containing equivalence connectives can be treated so as to avoid excessive storage space explosion during runtime. The approach is logically based and is not an implementation technique. In [1] the approach is first restricted to the class of propositional formulas in which, apart from negation, only the equivalence and non-equivalence connectives appaer. For example take $((A \Leftrightarrow B) \not\Leftrightarrow C) \Leftrightarrow (D \not\Leftrightarrow E)$, where A,B,C,D,E are literals. Although computing time is not reduced the storage space required to prove this formula not valid is no more than the formula itself. First, in one pass, the literals are found and the proof can be carried out simply by placing negation connectives in front of the literals (i.e. the literals are 'weighted' with negations depending upon the number of $\Leftrightarrow$'s and $\not\Leftrightarrow$'s). Then the weighted literals are treated as a conjunction. If this conjunction does not contain a contradiction then the procedure stops.Otherwise the weighting and testing of the resulting conjunction for a contradiction is done 2^{n-1} times, where n is the number of literals.If conjuncions are found each time then the negation of the given formula is valid. The main theorem in [1], based on combinatorial considerations, shows how the literals are to be weighted according to a simple formula. For formulas of the above class no recursion or splitting is needed and it can easily be shown that the space complexity is reduced from $O(2^{n-1})$ to $O(n)$. If literals are replaced by non-atomic formulae not containing $\Leftrightarrow$'s or $\not\Leftrightarrow$'s then recursion is still not required. The approach can be carried over to propositional logic in general [2] and first-order logic [3].It can also be built into resolution, tableau, matrix reduction and path-finding theorem provers. The exclusive or connective can be treated in a similar manner.

Acknowledgement: Wolfgang Bibel and Karl Dürre gave much helpful advice and suggestions. This research was carried out under the auspices of Prof. Alfred Schmitt.

[1] Wrightson,G.: On the Treatment of Equivalence Connectives in Automated Theorem Proving. Interner Bericht Nr.18/79, Institut für Informatik, Uni.Karlsruhe 1979.

[2] Wrightson,G.: Avoiding Equivalence Explosions in Automated Theorem Proving - Propositional Logic. Proceedings AISB Conference on Artificial Intelligence, Amsterdam, July 198o.

[3] Wrightson,G: Avoiding Equivalence Explosions in Automated Theorem Proving - First-Order Logic. Interner Bericht. Institut für Informatik, Uni.Karlsruhe (forthcoming).

KNOWLEDGE-BASED THEOREM PROVING

Dominique Pastre *

After having observed how mathematicians work, we were convinced that, in order to prove rather difficult theorems, a program must require a lot of knowledge. As it has already been done, and successfully, in other areas of Artificial Intelligence, items of knowledge (known theorems, rules, types of proofs, heuristics, examples, ...) should be given to the program, as data, in a suitable language. We are writing such a program.

The principles are of general value, but are applied to the following domain as a concrete support : Topological Linear Spaces and Convex Sets.

The "prover" and the "analyser" are the two different parts of this program. The prover, written in an usual programming language, uses classical and universal programmed methods and interprets items of knowledge. These items form the analyser and constitute data for the prover. The analyser, written in a suitable language, concerns a precise domain. It defines objects and describes all that a mathematician knows before studying this domain. One must be able to write another analyser for another domain only by studying the mathematical content of the new subject.

Mathematical objects are classified in different types. Some are universal (element, set, subset, family of sets, mapping, ...) or almost universal (real, set of reals, real interval, ...). Others are particular to a domain and correspond to fundamental notions for this domain (segment, relation, ...). So, time is gained by knowing what sort of object is handled, ambiguous notations may be used, and the notion corresponding to a type does not need to be explicitly defined (but its properties are given and are more important that its definition).

Concepts are predicates corresponding to important notions for the domain. They are linked one to another, and also to rules, methods, known theorems, hypothesis and conclusion of the theorem to prove. They are obtained from definitions, theorems, or properties characterizing the domain. Their interest is to select what can be applied, and valuations help to guide proofs.

Tools are useful objects which help to give methods of deduction. For example, contractions (similarities) can avoid formal calculus which would be difficult to do.

As far as we know, this approach has not yet been experimented in Automatic Theorem Proving. It is based on the idea that simple deduction methods, not using a complex network of knowledge and specific methods, although theoretically powerfull, cannot in practice be efficient.

*UER de Mathématiques de l'Université Paris VII et GR22 du CNRS (Université Paris VI)

EDINBURGH LCF supporting FP systems

Jacek Leszczylowski
Institute of Computer Science
Polish Academy of Sciences
P.O.Box 22
00-901 Warszawa PKiN
POLAND

J.Backus, in CACM 21/8, defined a class of applicative programming systems called FP (functional programming) systems in which users have: (1) objects built recursively from atoms, $\perp$ (an undefined element) and objects by a $\perp$-preserving "list" operator, (2) elementary functions over objects, (3) tools for building functions out of already existing functions. It is an important feature of FP systems that these tools use no variables in the sense of programming languages. In fact Backus also avoided the use of variables while building the algebra of FP systems which is supposed to be a calculus to express and prove facts about the defined functions in the system.

We generalized Backus' ideas in the following way. The new FP systems consist of two parts: the kernel (the same for all of them) and user's extensions. The kernel itself is a system with no assumptions about the set of atoms (except that the truth values are atoms; Backus also proposed to have "numbers" as atoms) , with a "list" operator (no longer strict - following a suggestion of Backus himself) for constructing other objects, and with elementary functionals for defining functions. The user can extend the kernel by: defining new types (the mechanisms for doing this are those for defining type operators in EDINBURGH LCF) and defining functions over the types. We also found it unnatural to exclude variables from the algebra, so it is now possible to use them while formulating theorems concerning the defined functions.

One can think of a machine support while working in the FP systems and proving facts about the functions being defined. The choice of EDINBURGH LCF is rather natural because it is an interactive computer system (implemented in LISP) for reasoning about functions. It consists of two parts. The first part is a family of calculi each of which is characterized by four factors: (1) type operators (representing domains in the sense of Scott's theory) , (2) constants (representing continuous functions) , (3) axioms , (4) inference rules. One of them, PPLAMBDA, is given as the "initial" calculus, and other calculi may be built by users as extensions of previously defined calculi. The second part is a high level programming language ML which is fully higher order and is strongly typed. Its polymorphic types make it as convenient as typeless languages.

PPLAMBDA also has a polymorphic type descipline, which can also be used to structure the information given to the system. Thus defining the kernel of the generalized FP systems in EDINBURGH LCF can be done in steps consisting in creating seperate calculi. We devided all notions and the laws of the algebra formulated by Backus into three calculi: (1) general purpose notions like function composition, identity function, etc., (2) notions connected with the type "list" like the definition of the type itself and the primitive functions CONS,TAIL,etc., (3) other notions combining the two previously defined calculi.

The generalization of FP systems allows one to formulate the theorems in stronger form than it was done by Backus. EDINBURGH LCF allowed us to prove them in a natural way; this is because the style of proving adopted in the system involves subgoaling methods. These methods are called tactics and can be programmed in ML by users; they can be combined by means of functionals (called tacticals) which in turn can also be programmed. It should be emphasized that the tactics used to prove the theorems are of a general nature and have been used in different applications.

AN EXPERT SYSTEM FOR AUTOMATIC CODING OF ABSTRACT DATA TYPE SPECIFICATIONS

H. Eigemeier, Ch. Knabe, P. Raulefs, K. Tramer

SEKI - PROJEKT
Institut für Informatik III
Universität Bonn
Postfach 2220
D-5300 Bonn 1, West Germany

Abstract

The system ADTCOMP constructs working programs from algebraic specifications of abstract data types. It is an experimental system devised to develop methods for codifying a rather broad extent of programming knowledge necessary to generate programs from axiomatizations constituting the most abstract form of specifying data types.

ADTCOMP codifies programming knowledge in terms of five separate production systems which are successively applied to an algebraic specification and intermediate results. So far, the system is restricted to specifications of data types with objects being inductively constructed from elementary objects. ADTCOMP admits hidden operations and successively generates code for all specifications we could get hold of. ADTCOMP compiles LISP-programs representing data objects as singly/doubly linked lists, association lists, and arrays.

Keywords and phrases.

Abstract data types, automatic programming, codification of programming knowledge, expert systems, knowledge representation, production systems.

1. Introduction

A standard paradigm of software design is to start with abstract specifications, and to gradually expand, refine, and transform them to an appropriate level to obtain efficient implementations. This approach factors software design into the construction of abstract specifications, and the development of more concrete representations. Such a factorization entails a corresponding structuring of design, validation, adaption, and maintenance of software systems.

Algebraic specifications [ADJ 76, HR 80] of abstract data types (ADTs) allow to specify data types by characterizing the behavior of data objects under characteristic operations without resorting to particular representations. Hence, developing algorithms at the level of manipulating objects of algebraically specified ADTs provides an optimum of freedom from specific specifications, facilitates the manipulation of algorithms (program transformations), and allows proving properties of algorithms independent of representation details. The remaining task consists in implementing such *abstract algorithms* in terms of appropriate representations supported at the machine level.

Implementing an ADT-specification requires
- to design *concrete representations* for encoding abstract data objects in them.
- to design algorithms implementing abstract operations on concrete representations.

For an ADT-specification, (1) a concrete representation and (2) algorithms implementing all abstract operations on concrete representations together form a *concrete implementation* of ADT-specifications. To be run on computers, concrete representations must be expressed in terms of an executable programming language. Hence, concrete representations must must be designed in terms of the data structures supported by the programming language.

Given a programming language, developing a concrete implementation from an abstract algorithm usually consists of a multitude of only partially interrelated design decisions based on insight, experience, and training. Many such decisions are isolated in that they are taken from different domains of knowledge, i.e. there are no well-structured transformation algorithms.

We call knowledge contributing to develop concrete implementations from abstract algorithms *programming knowledge*. The nature of programming knowledge suggests to encode it in terms of *production systems* [DK 77]. A *production rule* encodes an isolated piece of knowledge. A production system consists of a *production base* containing production rules, and a *production control* for sequencing the application of production rules. Single as well as systems of production systems are an appropriate tool for both encoding and utilizing loosely interrelated pieces of knowledge.

Production systems are particularly well suited for being developed experimentally: Start with an initial set of productions, and try to apply them to typical examples. If the initial production system does not work, analyze what goes wrong, and add resp. change production rules, or adjust the production control. A resulting production system may then incorporate all domain-specific knowledge of those who have developed it.

Among other approaches to automatic programming, two systems have been developed along a similar paradigm:

(1) DAEDALUS [MW 79] is a rule-based system for deriving programs from descriptions of input/output-relations, giving no informations about algorithms to be employed. The main contribution of DAEDALUS are formation-rules for control-structures (conditional-, recursion-, procedure-formation), and a generalization rule (for related results, see [BI 79]).

(2) PECOS [BA 78a,b], the coding expert of the Ψ-system [GR 76], generates Lisp-programs from algorithms given as programs in a high-level language admitting some reasonably "abstract" data structures (such as sets). In the Ψ-system, PECOS is meant to be supported by an efficiency expert [KA 79] embodying knowledge about the efficiency of various representations of data structures.

The problem of generating concrete code from algebraic ADT-specifications has not been attacked before. Compared with what is achieved by PECOS, this is a much more challenging task as we start from the most abstract level of data type specification. However, ADTCOMP is not yet capable of automatically coding abstract algorithms. We plan to incorporate ADTCOMP in an automatic programming system in future work.

Section 2 introduces abstract data type specifications. The way production systems work is described in section 3. Section 4 gives a survey of the structure of ADTCOMP, illustrated by a detailed walk through the implementation of a familiar simple data type in Section 5. More details on ADTCOMP are given in a companion paper [EKRT 80].

ADTCOMP is implemented and fully operational in both Siemens-Interlisp and Lisp-F3. The system as well as a detailed reference manual are available from the third author.

2. Specification of Abstract Data Types

We briefly review some basic concepts of algebraic da a type specifications.

An abstract data type is specified by a *signature* (S,Σ) and a set E of *equations*. A signature (S,Σ) determins a syntax for denoting objects of the data type, and consists of

- a set S of *sorts*. Sorts are names for sets of objects belonging to the data type.
  Example: S={atom,stack} is a set of two sorts for the unbounded stack abstraction. stack is a name for the set of all stacks, and atom a name for the set of all objects that may be pushed on to stacks.
- a set Σ of *operation symbols*. Taking each sort $s\in S$ to be a name of a set D_s of data objects, an operation symbol in Σ is the name of a function among appropriate sets of data objects. To specify domain and range for each operation symbol $f\in\Sigma$, an *arity* is ascribed to f:

  arity (f) = $(s_1 \ldots s_n, s)$ for sorts $s_1,\ldots s_n, s\in S$ iff f denotes a function

  f_D: $D_{s_1} x \ldots x D_{s_n} \to D_s$. This is denoted by $f:(s_1 \ldots s_n, s)$, and $\Sigma_{(s \ldots s_n, s)}$ is the set of all operation symbols with this arity. An operation symbol $c:(\varepsilon,s)$ denotes a value in D_s.

  Example: Σ={empty:stack, undef:atom, push: (stack atom, stack), pop: (stack, stack), top: (stack, atom)} is a set of operation symbols for the unbounded stack abstraction.

Given a signature (S,Σ), we consider for each sort $s\in S$ to have an infinite set X_s of variable symbols s.t. for different sorts $s_1,s_2\in S$, X_{s_1} and X_{s_2} are disjoint. From operation and variable symbols we can construct (S,Σ)-*terms* by observing arities: The set T_Σ of all (S,Σ)-terms is defined to be the least family $T_\Sigma=(T_{\Sigma,s}|s\in S)$ s.t.

(1) $\forall s \in S.\ X_s \cup \Sigma_s \subseteq T_{\Sigma,s}$ $\{\Sigma_s$ stands for $\Sigma_{(\epsilon,s)}\}$

(2) $\forall n \in \omega.\ \forall s_1,\ldots,s_n,s \in S.\ \forall t_1 \in T_{\Sigma,s_1},\ldots,t_n \in T_{\Sigma,s_n}.$

$\forall f:(s_1 \ldots s_n,s) \in \Sigma.\ \ f(t_1,\ldots,t_n) \in T_{\Sigma,s}.$

A (S,Σ)-*equation* p=q is a pair of (S,Σ)-terms of same sort. *if* p=p' *then* q *else* r *fi* is a *conditional* (S,Σ)-*equation* consisting of a condition p=p' and alternatives q and r s.t. p,p' and q,r are terms of same sorts, respectively

Example: E={ pop(empty) = empty, top (empty) = undef,
pop (push (s,a)) = s, top (push (s,a)) = a }
with $s \in X_{stack}$, $a \in X_{atom}$ is a set of equations of the unbounded stack abstraction.

A set E of (S,Σ)-equations induces a congruence relation $\equiv_E$ on T_Σ s.t. for two terms p and q, $p \equiv_E q$ holds iff the equality of p and q is deducible from E. Taking the quotient $T_\Sigma/_{\equiv_E}$ results in a (S,Σ)-algebra $T_{\Sigma,E}$. The isomorphism class of $T_{\Sigma,E}$ is the (*initial*) *abstract data type* specified by the *specification* (S,Σ,E).

3. Production Systems

A *production system* consists of

- a *production base* containing *production rules*
- a *production control* guiding the selection of production rules.
- a *data base* to which production rules are applied.

Production rules operate on the data base. A production rule is of the form <test> => <action>.
<test> is evaluated to a predicate which is satisfied or not by the data base. If the <test> is satisfied by the data base, the rule is *applied* by executing <action> on the data base. The effect of <action> is to possibly alter the data base. In many production systems, production rules may also change the production base.(e.g. by adding/deleting production rules), or the production control. In ADTCOMP, however, production rules only affect the data base.

The production control selects production rules to be checked for applicability and subsequent application. In the simplest form of a production system, the production base is just a list of production rules, and the production control moves through the list from one rule to the next. Initially, our production control used *agendas*. An agenda is a control program for sequencing the order of considering production rules, e.g. a regular expression of names of production rules and intermediate tests for branching. In the evolution of our system, however, more and more "control knowledge" in agendas was transferred to the organization of production bases, and our present system uses no agendas at all any more.

4. System Structure

Upon encountering an input instruction, ADTCOMP works through seven phases that successively construct a LISP-implementation of the data type. Except for the first and last one, each phase incorporates spezialized programming knowledge and refines the intermediate constructions obtained from the previous phase.
These seven phases are:

(1) *Initialization (I-) Phase*. The I-phase converts the *input specification* into a LISP-representation.

(2) *Functionality (→-) Phase*. The →-phase considers the *signature* of the input specification only. Conclusions from the operations' functionalities are drawn, and the structure of LISP-functions implementing these operations is established.

(3) *Axiom (=-) Phase*. The =-phase considers the *axioms* of the input specification only, and make inferences from observations on the axioms.
After the =-phase, the input specification is no longer considered.

(4) *Representation (R-) Phase*. The R-phase combines conclusions of the previous phases to determine the data structure in which D-objects are represented.

(5) *Compile (C-) Phase*. Using all information obtained so far, the C-phase constructs actual LISP-code to make optimizations and improvements.
(6) *Cleanup Phase*. The Cleanup-phase refines and/or rearranges the LISP-code obtained from the C-phase to make optimizations and improvements.
(7) *LISP-Phase*. The LISP-phase constructs the final LISP-code. As LISP does not support a module-construct such as SIMULA-class or ALPHARD-form, a corresponding mechanism is built up in the LISP-phase.

Phases (2)-(6), which actually apply programming knowledge, are production systems. Applications of production rules is controlled by meta-rules and attention focussing. These mechanisms, dependency-directed backtracking, and pattern matching are not discussed in this paper.

5. A Walk Through the Automatic Implementation of an Abstract Data Type Specification

To explain how ADTCOMP works, we present a walk through the implementation of the algebraic specification for unbounded queues:

```
DATATYPE      : QUEUE D.
COMPONENTSORT: X.
OPERATIONS    : ENQUEUE : D X → D.
                DEQUEUE : D   → D..
                READ    : D   → X.
AXIOMS:  [Q1] (DEQUEUE DO) = UNDEF.
         [Q2] (DEQUEUE (ENQUEUE D2 X2).
                 = if (EQ D2 DO) then D2
                                 else (ENQUEUE (DEQUEUE D2)X2).
         [Q3] (READ DO) = UNDEF
         [Q4] (READ (ENQUEUE D2 X2))
                 = if (EQ D2 DO) then X2
                                 else (READ D2).
```

Remarks.
1. The above specification is an example for how input to ADTCOMP looks like.
2. So far, ADTCOMP is restricted to specifications of data types D s.t. all D-objects can be inductively generated from a basic D-object DO which is the empty queue in our example. For all sorts, UNDEF is the error element of the respective sort.
3. For any sort identifier S, the integer i in the variable identifier Si occurring in a term stands for the nesting depth of the occurrence of Si in the term. Starting with depth 1, e.g. D2 and X2 occur at depth 2 in (DEQUEUE (ENQUEUE D2 X2)). An exception is SD *always* denoting the basic object of sort S.

Initialization (I-) Phase. The input specification is converted into an internal Lisp-representation, and the Lisp-atoms D,X,ENQUEUE,DEQUEUE, and READ are associated with the following properties:

D	NAME	QUEUE	NAME-property of D has value QUEUE
X	COMPSORT		COMPSORT-*property of* X *has value* TRUE *(omitted)*
ENQUEUE	OP	(IMPLEM)	
			these operations are to be IMPLEMented, *i.e. they*
DEQUEUE	OP	(IMPLEM)	
			are no hidden operations.
READ	OP	(IMPLEM)	

Functionality (→ -) *Phase*. →-rules check functionalities of operations to make useful operations. In our case, the three rules →01, →02A, and →08 apply:

```
→01.  *OP1: D <1 *Y> ... → D, <1 *Y NOTEQUAL D>
        =>*OP1 CONTINUABLE SINGLE
```
if *OP1 maps a D-object and possibly a *Y-object to a D-object *and* *Y is not D *then* *OP1 is a singly continuable operation

Note. (1) An operation op is *n-fold continuable* iff op constructs from n D-objects another D-object.
(2) The first clause of the above rule is matched against the OPERATIONS-part of the specification. * prefixes match-variables. In '<1 *Y>', 1 is a

LISP-atom bound to TRUE iff *Y is matched to something. 1 serves as a condition for the test '<1 *Y NOTEQUAL D>' which is evaluated only if 1 is bound to TRUE. We call such a test a *conditioned test*.

```
→01:Result. ENQUEUE CONTINUABLE SINGLE
            DEQUEUE CONTINUABLE SINGLE

→02A.  *OP1: D ...  → X  =>  *OP1 READS
    if *OP1 maps D-objects and possibly more arguments to component sort X
  then *OP1 reads some contents from D-objects.

  →2A only fires for operation READ and results in

  →02A:Result. READ READS
```

The third applicable rule sets up the structure of the LISP-functions that will implement the operations:

```
→08. *OP1 OP IMPLEM,                    | if *OP1 is to be implemented, and
     NOT *OP1 CONTINUABLE DOUBLE,       |   *OP1 is not doubly continuable, and
     LET *LIST BE LIST,                 |   the variable *LIST is declared to be
     <1 *NA MEMORY 1>,                  |      bound to list structures, and
     <2 *NB MEMORY 2>,                  |   (these conditiones don't apply here), and
     LET 3 BE NOT 1, 4 BE NOT 2,        |   3,4 are bound to TRUE (as 1,2 are NIL),and
     <7 *OP1 CONTINUABLE>,              |   7 is TRUE if *OP1 is continuable, and
     <8 *OP1 SETS>                      |   (doesn't apply here, i.e. 8 is NIL), and
     *OP1:<D><5 *NA> <6 *NB> *LIST →    |   the functionality of *OP1 matches this
                                        |   pattern;*LIST is the list of all sorts
  => *OP1 FUNCT                      then       following the 3rd argument
   (λD<1 *NA><2 *NB><3<5 *NA>><4<6 *NB>> *LIST)
     FORM <1<7 S>> <8 S> <3<7 D>>,      |   this is the structure of the LISP-function
     *OP1 PARAMS <1 *NA><2 *NB>         |   implementing  OP1, entered under property
               <3<5 *NA>><<4<6 *NB>> *LIST)                 FUNCT OF *OP1,
                                        |   the property PARAMS of  OP1 records all
                                        |   parameters except for the first (for
D-objects); the PARAMS-property is used in recursive calls.

 08:Result. ENQUEUE FUNCT  ((LAMBDA (D X) FORM D))
            ENQUEUE PARAMS  (X)
            DEQUEUE FUNCT  ((LAMBDA (D)   FORM D))
            DEQUEUE PARAMS
            READ    FUNCT  ((LAMBDA (D)   FORM))
            READ    PARAMS
```

Axiom (=-)Phase. =-rules analyse the axioms of specification.

The first rule detects the elementary construction operator and determines which operations extract constituents of terms built up with the elementary construction operator.

```
=01.  *OP1 READS TRUE, /(*OP1 (*OP2 ... X2 ...)...) = X2 <1 IF *COND>/
   =>*OP1 READS <1 IF *COND>, *OP2 WRITES  ELEM, *E DENOTES *OP2

  if  *OP1 is a read-operation extracting information from a term as described by
      the axiom-pattern in slashes (possibly qualified by a condition *COND)
then  *OP1 is a read-operation (possibly under *COND), and *OP2 writes elementary
      objects into objects *OP1 reads from, and *E is a pseudo-property (=variable)
      permanently bound to *OP2.
```

Note. Including an axiom in slashes results in omitting the respective axiom from any further consideration after the respective rule has been applied successfully. The conditioned test <1 IF *COND> is checked in the consequence-part of the rule if the test has been *established* in the precondition, i.e. the axiom which matches is a conditional axiom.

```
=01:Result.   READ READS  (IF (EQ D2 DO))    READ reads from D-objects.
              ENQUEUE WRITES (ELEM)          ENQUEUE writes elementary objects into
              *E DENOTES (ENQUEUE)                D-objects to construct new D-
                                                  objects.
                                             *E is a variable bound to ENQUEUE
                                             axiom [Q4] will no longer be considered.

=03.  LET *EXPR BE EXPR, /(*OP1 *EXPR ...) = UNDEF <1 IF *COND>/,
      <2  *EXPR EQUAL DØ>
  => *OP1 UNDEF     IF <1<2(AND>> <2(EQ D DØ)> <1 *COND> <1 2)>>.

   if *OP1 applied to some expression *EXPR yields UNDEFined, possibly under
      conditions (a) *COND, and (b) *EXPR can be shown to be EQUAL DØ
 then applying *OP1 returns UNDEFined under the conditions established in the
      precondition of this rule. The axiom involved in a successful application
      of the rule  is deleted.
```

Note. A meta-rule makes sure this rule is never applied when neither condition (a) nor (b) holds.

=03 applies to axioms [Q1] and [Q3] and results in:

```
=03:Result.  DEQUEUE  UNDEF  (IF (EQ D DO))
             READ     UNDEF  (IF (EQ D DO))
```

Both DEQUEUE and READ work recursively through queues until encountering an empty queue. This is detected by rule =04:

```
=04. *E CONTINUABLE SINGLE,         if the elementary construction operation is
     (*OP1 (*E D2 ...)...) =           singly continuable, and *OP1 moves inside
       <1(*E>...(*OP1 D2...)<1...)>    *E-terms, possibly under condition  COND,
       <2 IF *COND>,
     *OP1 NOTEQUAL *E                  and *OP1 is not the elem. constr. operation
 =>  *OP1 WORKSTHRU <2 IF *COND>   then*OP1 works recursively thru D-objects,
                                       possibly under condition *COND.

=04:Result.  DEQUEUE  WORKSTHRU  (IF (NOT (EQ D2 DO)))
             READ     WORKSTHRU  (IF (NOT (EQ D2 DO)))

=06C. *OP1 CONTINUABLE, *E CONTINUABLE SINGLE, NOT *OP1 WRITES,
      (*OP1 (*E ... D2 ...) ...) = <1(*OP1>...D2<1...)> <2 IF *COND>
  => *OP1 DELETES <2 IF *COND>

   if *OP1 is a continuable operation extracting a D-object from an object built
      up by the elementary construction operation E, possibly under condition
      *COND
 then *OP1 is a deletion operation whenever *COND holds (if *COND is established).

=06C only applies to axiom [Q2] yielding

=06C:Result.  DEQUEUE  DELETES  (IF (EQ D2 DO))
```

Representation (R-) Phase. There is a wealth of conclusions which can be drawn from the results of the previous phase. First, rule R01 decides to implement data types as lists if their elements are constructed by a singly continuable construction operation.

```
R01. *E CONTINUABLE SINGLE  => D  LIST
R01:Result.   D  LIST
```

For operations which read or delete, and work thru D-objects until the end, our next rule concludes that their action affects the OLDEST element which had been added by the elementary construction operation:

```
R05. D LIST,
     LET *ACTION BE !READS DELETES!, {!...! encloses alternatives ( ORing)}
     *OP1 /WORKSTHRU IF <1 (AND> (NOT (EQ D2 DO)) <1 *COND)>/,
     *OP1 *ACTION /IF <1 (AND> (EQ D2 DO) <1 *COND)>/
 => *ACTION OLDEST <1 IF *COND>
```

```
   if   D-objects are represented by lists, and
        *OP1 works recursively thru lists representing non-empty D-objects,
          possibly under condition  *COND, and
        *OP1 READs or DELETEs, possibly under condition *COND
 then   READing (DELETing) of *OP1 affects the OLDEST element in the list (under
                                                                    *COND)

R05:Result.  DEQUEUE  DELETES  (OLDEST)
             READ     READS    (OLDEST)
```

Although R01 has decided that stacks should be implemented as lists, it is still open what particular kind of list structure -such as singly or doubly linked lists- should be chosen. E.g., the doubly linked list structure is selected when reading is done at one end, and a counting operation recursively works through the list from the other end. To prepare this decision, we have to find out about whether operations work at the front resp. back end.

```
R11A.  D LIST, NOT D DIRECTED, *OP1 OP IMPLEM,
       LET *PLACE BE !NEWEST OLDEST! OP1 DELETES  PLACE<1 IF *COND>
   =>  D DIRECTED, *OP1 DELETES FRONT  <1 IF *COND>

    if D is to be implemented as a list, but no direction has been established yet,
       and *OP1 is an operation to be implemented,
       and *OP1 deletes the NEWEST (resp. OLDEST) elements from D-objects,
            possibly under some condition *COND
  then *OP1 deletes at the front end of D-objects under condition *COND (if estab-
       lished), and the lists representing D-objects are directed now.
```

R11A applies to DEQUEUE:

```
R11A:Result.  DEQUEUE  DELETES  (FRONT)
```

Remark. After having applied R11A to some operation, this rule is no longer applicable for any other operation, as D is tagged DIRECTED now. This is important because operations may work on opposite ends s.t. choosing one operation to work at the front end implies the other operation works at the back end.

With rule R11A, we have now established what is taken to be front resp. back end of lists representing D-objects w.r.t. operation DEQUEUE. The next two rules determine at which end the other operation work.

```
R14A. D LIST, *OP1 DELETES FRONT, *OP1 DELETES /OLDEST
   => *E WRITES BACK

   if the data type is represented by lists, and *OP1 DELETEs the OLDEST element
      of D-objects, and the oldest element is in the FRONT position of the list
 then the elementary construction operation *E WRITES into the back position, and
      the NEWEST value under property DELETES of *OP1 is deleted.

R14A:Result.  ENQUEUE  WRITES  (BACK)
```

The elementary construction operation determines at which position of lists all other operations work if it is known whether they affect the NEWEST or OLDEST element:

```
R18A. D LIST, *E WRITES BACK, LET *ACTION BE !WRITES READS DELETES!,
      *OP1 *ACTION /OLDEST <1 IF *COND>/
   => *OP1 *ACTION FRONT

R18A:Result.  READ  READS  (FRONT)
```

We have now collected all information which makes the next rule choose the singly linked list structure to represent D-objects:

```
R21.   D LIST, EXISTS NO *OP: *OP DELETES BACK AND *OP OP IMPLEM
               EXISTS NO *OP: *OP COUNTS BACK  AND *OP OP IMPLEM
  =>   D LIST SL

   if  D-objects are represented as lists, and there is no operation to be imple-
       mented which deletes or counts at the back ends of lists
 then  D-objects are represented as singly linked lists.
```

Note. The value IMPLEM of property OP of *OP rules out that *OP is a *hidden operation.*

```
R21:Result.  D  LIST  SL
```

Finally, R29 establishes the LISP-representation of the basic D-object DØ (empty queue):

```
R29.  D  LIST  SL
   => DØ FUNCT (NLAMBDA (FRONT) (SETQ FRONT (CONS)) (RPLACA FRONT FRONT))

   if D-objects are represented as singly linked lists
 then implement the basic D-element DØ by the above LISP-function.

R29:Result.  DO FUNCT (NLAMBDA (FRONT) (SETQ FRONT (CONS))(RPLACA FRONT FRONT))
```

Compile (C-) Phase. C-rules work on the FUNCT-property of operation names which is a pattern of the LISP-function to implement the respective operation. All strings in such a FUNCT-pattern that are not LISP-atoms are regarded as keywords to be *expanded* to LISP-code by C-rules. C-rules work from front to back ends of FUNCT-patterns. A C-rule inspects the next keyword after the current position. The §-sign indicates the current position pointer.

First, we work on operation ENQUEUE

```
C01.  D LIST,
      LET *ACTION BE !READS DELETES WRITES!, LET *POSITION BE !FRONT BACK!,
      *OP1 *ACTION *POSITION, *OP1 FUNCT: /FORM/
   => (COND UNDETERMINED (T *ACTION *POSITION)).

   if D is a list, and *OP1 does *ACTION∈{READS, DELETES, WRITES} at the
      *POSITION∈{FRONT, BACK}  end
 then in the FUNCT-pattern of *OP1, FORM is replaced with
      (COND UNDETERMINED (T  ACTION  POSITION))
```

Note. C-rules differ from all previous rules in that /FORM/ occurring in the precondition is replaced with the value of the consequence of the rule (shorthand notation).

```
C01:Result.  ENQUEUE FUNCT ((LAMBDA (D X) § (COND UNDETERMINED (T WRITES BACK)) D))
```

The next keyword after § is UNDETERMINED; it is simply deleted by rule C10B:

```
C10B. NOT *OP1 UNDEF          IF *COND, *OP1 FUNCT:/UNDETERMINED/  => .
C10B:Result.  ENQUEUE FUNCT ((LAMBDA (D X) (COND § (T WRITES BACK)) D ))
```

C18 generates LISP-code from the observation "WRITES BACK":

```
C18.  D LIST SL, *OP1 FUNCT:/WRITES BACK/
   => (REPLACE BACK (CDR (RPLACD BACK (CONS X) ))))) D ))
C18:Result.  ENQUEUE FUNCT ((LAMBDA (D X)
             (COND (T §(REPLACE BACK (CDR (RPLACD BACK (CONS X) ))))) D ))
```

We omit further expansions and show the final result of compiling all operations.

```
C-Phase:Result.
ENQUEUE FUNCT  ((LAMBDA (D X)
        (COND (T (REPLACE (CAR D)(CDR (RPLACD (CAR D)(CONS X)))))) D ))

DEQUEUE FUNCT  ((LAMBDA (D)
        (COND ((NULL (CDR D))(RETURN (QUOTE UNDEF)))
              (T (AND (EQ (CAR URD) (CDR D))(RPLACA URD D))
                     (REPLACE (CDR D)(CDR (CDR D))))) D)

READ    FUNCT  ((LAMBDA (D)
        (COND (NULL (CDR D))(RETURN QUOTE UNDEF)))
              (T (CAR (CDR D))))))
```

Cleanup (CLEAN-) Phase. The Cleanup phase again works through the FUNCT-property of operation names, and makes optimizations and final expansions. In our example, the following rules apply:

```
CLEAN04.  LET *VAR1 BE LIST, *OP1 FUNCT:/(COND (T *VAR1))/ =>  *VAR1.
          any COND-form having only a T-branch is replaced with the T-branch.
```

The following rules replace REPLACE applied to a CAR- resp. CDR-form with RPLACA resp. RPLACD:

```
CLEAN01. LET *VAR BE EXPR, *OP1 FUNCT:/REPLACE (CAR *VAR)/ =>  RPLACA *VAR!
CLEAN02! LET *VAR BE EXPR, *OP1 FUNCT:/REPLACE (CDR *VAR)/ =>  RPLACD *VAR.
```

LISP Phase. Simulating a construct for operation-clusters in Lisp, the Lisp-Phase returns the following Lisp-code:

```
(PRINT 'QUEUE)
 <DEFINEQ
 <QUEUE
 <NLAMBDA  (OP DLIST)
           (SETQ DLIST (EVLIS DLIST))
           (PROG (CURD (CAR DLIST)))
                 (RETURN (NEVALA (APPLY (EVAL OP) DLIST) QUEUE>)
 >
 <SETQQ QUEUE
        (<READ LAMBDA (D)
               (COND (CNULL (CDR D)) (RETURN 'UNDEF))
                     (T (CAR (CDR D>
         (DEQUEUE LAMBDA (D)
                  <COND ((NULL (CDR D))(RETURN 'UNDEF))
                         (T (AND (EQ (CAR URD) (CDR D))
                                 (RPLACA URD D))
                            (RPLACD D (CDR (CDRD> D)
         (ENQUEUE LAMBDA (D X)
                 <RPLACA D (CDR (RPLACD (CAR D) (CONS X> D)
         (DO NLAMBDA (FRONT)
                     (SETQ FRONT (CONS)) (RPLACA FRONT FRONT>
```

As an example, the empty queue is generated by
(SETQ Q (QUEUE QO)).
ENQUEUing 13 into the empty queue is done by
(QUEUE ENQUEUE Q 13), and (QUEUE ENQUEUE 15) inserts 15 into Q, and we obtain by (QUEUE READ Q) the value 13, and (QUEUE DEQUEUE Q) followed by (QUEUE READ Q) yields 15. DEQUEUEing Q twice yields UNDEF.

6. Final Remarks and Conclusions

6.1. *Interactive System Development and Theory Formation*. The development of ADTCOMP has been evolutionary, driven by considering more and more examples, and feeding the programming knowledge necessary to implement the examples into the production bases. To support codifying and incorporating programming knowledge, ADTCOMP has an extensive interactive user interface. This interface helps a user to find out why ADTCOMP failed, coding new rules and experimenting with them, and finally changing meta-rules and the production control unit after inserting new rules into the production bases. The userinterface is extremly important for *upgrading* the production bases: whenever a new portion of programming knowledge has been fed to ADTCOMP, it is usually in order to condense rules into fewer and more general rules. *Rule condensation* actually contributes to the formation of a *theory of programming*, and we expect such a theory to eventually evolve from our investigation.

6.2. *Accomplishments*. Previous systems start at a much more concrete level of data structures such as sets, collections, etc., and implement them at the somewhat more "concrete" level of lists, arrays, etc. ADTCOMP generates code from representation-free *axiomatizations* of all structures previous systems could implement, and in addition succeeded for about 60 other axiomatizations. ADTCOMP generates clusters of routines which may be mutually recursive. Previous systems could not introduce recursions.

6.3. *Automatic Programming Environment*. ADTCOMP is part of the automatic programming environment PEN currently under development. In PEN, a user specifies structures in terms of equations about the behavior of data objects under operations intended to manipulate them. The system analyses such specifications, and guides the user to make them consistent and complete. The user then develops algorithms in terms of self-defined or library-supplied data abstractions, obtaining abstract algorithms to be compiled into efficient and machine-executable code by ADTCOMP.

6.4. *Current Work.* ADTCOMP is currently being extended in three directions: (1) Generating code in other target languages; (2) an extension to generate code from parameterized ADT-specifications; (3) compiling abstract algorithms.

7. References

[ADJ 76] Goguen, J.A., J.W. Thatcher, E.G. Wagner. An Initial Algebra Approach to the Specification, Correctness and Implementation of Abstract Data Types. IBM Research Rept. RC-6487 (1976).

[ADJ 79] Thatcher, J.W., E.G. Wagner, J.B. Wright. Data Type Specification: Parametrization and the Power of Specification Techniques (Revised). IBM Res. Rept. (1979).

[BAR 78a] Barstow, D.R. Automatic construction of algorithms and data structures using a knowledge base of programming rules. Rept. STAN-CS-77-641(77), Stanford U.

[BAR 78b] Barstow, D.R. Experience with a refinement paradigm in a knowledge-based automatic programming system. Proc. AISB/GI-Conference on Artificial intelligence 1978.

[BI 79] Bibel, W. Syntax-directed, semantics-supported program synthesis. Proc. 4th Workshop on Automatic Deduction (Austin, Texas), 1979.

[DK 77] Davis, R., I.King. An overview of production systems in Elcock, Michie (Eds.) *Machine Representation of Knowledge*. Horwood & Wylie, 1977.

[EKRT 80] Eigemeier, H., Ch.Knabe, P.Raulefs, K.Tramer. Automatic implemen ion of algebraic specifications of abstract data types. Memo SEKI-BN-79- (Nov. 79), Univ. Bonn, Inst. f. Informatik III *and* Proc. AISB-80 Conf. on Artificial Intelligence (in press).

[GR 76] Green, C.C. The design of the PSI program synthesis system. Proc. 2nd Inf. Conf. on Software Engineering (San Francisco, CA), 1976.

[HR 80] Hornung, G., P.Raulefs. Terminal algebra semantics and retractions for abstract data types. Proc. 7th ICALP, 1980. Springer LNCS (in press).

[KA 79] Kant, E. Efficiency considerations in programming synthesis: a knowledge-based approach. Tech. Rept. STAN-CS-79-755, Comp. Sci. Dept, Stanford Univ.

[MW 79] Manna, Z., R.Waldinger. Synthesis: Dreams => Programs. IEEE-TSE:5(1979)294-327.

INDUCING NON-TRIVIAL PROGRAMS FROM EXAMPLES

Eric PAPON

UNIVERSITE DE PARIS-SUD
LABORATOIRE DE RECHERCHE EN INFORMATIQUE
BATIMENT 490
91405 ORSAY CEDEX (FRANCE)

Abstract : This paper describes the synthesis of functions from input-output examples. The synthesis is achieved by transforming the examples into computation traces and finding recurrent relations between these traces.
The algorithm can also transform a recursive program into an iterative one, when the recursive program is used to obtain computation traces.
In order to obtain the recurrent relations, the algorithm uses pattern-matching, generalization, and the composition of functions. From these relations, we construct a program by using powerful synthesis theorems.
The programs we can synthesize are defined on a totally ordered domain, and have traces of polynomially or exponentially increasing length.

1. INTRODUCTION.

The synthesis of functions from input-output examples often relies on the construction of traces from the examples and then on finding relations between these traces in order to generate a program [2,5,6,7,8,9,15].

We present a methodology, based on this model, which follows of a system, BMWK [8,9], and which extends it in order to reach a greater class of programs, particulary a subset of the functions which have an exponential growth.

The tools we used are now well-known : pattern-matching [13], generalization [12], and composition of functions. We also used synthesis theorems, which are powerful extensions of the "basic synthesis theorem" of Summers [15], and which give us the possibility to synthesize more complicated functions.

A restriction of the algorithm can be also used to transform recursive programs into terminal recursive procedures. The transformation of a terminal recursive program into an iterative one is then easy and well-known [4,11]. These two topics can look quite different but we shall further see that we work on computations traces that can be obtained from examples or from the symbolic execution of a recursive program.

2. BUILDING THE TRACES.

The traces upon which we work can come either from a program or from input-output examples. These traces are of two kinds, called thereafter predicates and fragments. The predicates describe the domain of definition of the function and the fragments the computations made by the function.

2.1. Traces issued from a program.

Let be F the name of a program we want to transform. We suppose that F contains recursive symbols and that its domain of definition is totally ordered so that it can be described by a sequence $\{P_i(x)\}_{i\in\mathbb{N}}$ of predicates which verify :
$P_{i+k}(x)=P_i(a(x))$. The fragments are obtained by evaluating the recursive calls only (i.e. the computation of the auxiliary functions is suspended).

For example consider the function F (given in LISP) :

```
(DE F (X Y) (COND ((P Y) (C X))
                  (T(G X Y (F (B X) (A Y)))) ))
```

where C,G and B are any functions.

Its sequence of predicates is $\{(P(A^i\ X))\}_{i\in\mathbb{N}}$ and verifies $(P_{i+1}\ Y)=(P_i(A\ Y))$, and the sequence of fragments is :

(C X) ; (G X Y (C (B X))) ; (G X Y (G (B X) (A Y) (C (B^2 X)))) ; ...

This sequence of fragments can be easily obtained by transforming the initial program F into :

```
(DE FT (X Y) (FTT Y 'X 'Y))
(DE FTT (Y1 X Y) (COND((P Y1) (LIST 'C X))
                 (T (LIST 'G X Y (FTT (A Y1)(LIST 'B X)(LIST 'A Y))))))
```

and by applying this program to entries Y1,Y2,Y3, ... which verify (P Y1), (P(A Y2)), (P(A^2 Y3)), ...

2.2. Traces issued of examples.

The way to obtain traces from input-output examples has been often described [7,8,15], we recall it rapidly.

We start from a finite sequence of examples : $\{x_i\rightarrow y_i\}_{1\le i\le n}$ where x_i and y_i are lists.

We suppose that the sequence $\{x_i\}_{1\le i\le n}$ is totally ordered ; we compute a sequence $\{P_i(x)\}_{1\le i\le n-1}$ which verifies : $P_i(x)$=TRUE if $x=x_i$ and FALSE if $x<x_i$. We restrict ourselves to the case where there exists a function a and an integer k such that : $P_{i+k}(x)=P_i(a(x))$.

The functionnal expression of an atom A in a list x is the unique composition of CAR and CDR, b, such that b(x)=A. The fragments are made by building the CONS-tree of y_i and by substituing the atoms of x_i which appear in y_i by their functionnal expression in x_i.

For example consider the sequence :

(A)→ (A A (A))

(A B C) →(C A B C (C))

(A B C D E) →(E A D C B C (E)) ...

We obtain the sequence of predicates (ATOM(CDR X)), (ATOM(CD^3R X)), ... such that((P_{i+k} X)=(P_i (CD^2R X)), and the sequence of fragments (written as trees, each node of which is a CONS) :

(f_1 X) = (CAR X) (CAR X) (CAR X) NIL NIL ;

(f_2 X) = (CAD^2R X) (CAR X) (CADR X) (CAD^2R X) (CAD^2R X) NIL NIL ;

(f_3 X) = (CAD^4R X) (CAR X) (CAD^3R X) (CAD^2R X) (CADR X) (CAD^2R X) (CAD^4R X) NIL NIL ; ...

3. SYNTHESIS THEOREMS.

Let be $\{p_n(y)\}_{n\in\mathbb{N}}$ a sequence of predicates, $\{f_n(\vec{x})\}_{n\in\mathbb{N}}$ a sequence of functions where $\vec{x}$ is the vector of variables (x_1 x_2...x_p). All the functions used without definition are supposed to be monotonic [10] .

We define F_n :

$F_n(\vec{x},y)$=If $p_1(y)$ then $f_1(\vec{x})$ else ... If $p_n(y)$ then $f_n(\vec{x})$ else Ω

where Ω is the function everywhere undefined.

The functions F_n are approximations of the program we are seeking.

3.1. SUMMERS's basic synthesis theorem [15] .

Suppose that there exists a substitution σ and a number k :

$\sigma = (y/b(y))(x_1/a_1(\vec{x}))(x_2/a_2(\vec{x})) \ldots (x_p/a_p(\vec{x}))$ such that

$\forall\ i\geq 1\ \ f_{i+k}(x)=f_i\ (a_1(x),\ \ldots,a_p(x))$ and $p_{i+k}(y)=p_i(b(y))$
then the limit of F_n when n tends towards infinity is given by :

$$F(\vec{x},y) = \underline{\text{If}}\ p_1(y)\ \underline{\text{then}}\ f_1(\vec{x})\ \underline{\text{else}}\ \ldots\ \underline{\text{If}}\ p_k(y)\ \underline{\text{then}}\ f_k(\vec{x})\ \underline{\text{else}}\ F(a_1(\vec{x}),\ldots,a_p(\vec{x}),b(y)).$$

Proof : see [15].

3.2. Extension to composition.

We suppose that f_i verifies : $\forall\ i\geq 1\ f_i(\vec{x})=g_i(\vec{x},h_i(\vec{x}))$ then the limit of F_n when n tends towards infinity is given by :

$$F(\vec{x},y) = G(\vec{x},y,H(\vec{x},y))$$

where G and H are the limits of the functions G_n and H_n defined as F_n, by the sequences $\{p_n(y),g_n(\vec{x},z)\}_{n\in\mathbf{N}}$ and $\{p_n(y),h_n(\vec{x})\}_{n\in\ \mathbf{N}}$.
Proof : see [8].

3.3. Embedded recursions.

As before we suppose that the sequence of predicates verifies $p_{i+k}(y)=p_i(b(y))$, and we suppose that there exists a q+1-ary function h and q substitutions :

$\sigma_j= (x_1/a_1^j(\vec{x}))\ldots(x_p/a_p^j(\vec{x}))\quad 1\leq j\leq q$ such that :

$\forall\ i\geq 1\ f_{i+k}(\vec{x})=h(\vec{x},f_i(a_1^1(\vec{x}),\ \ldots,a_p^1(\vec{x})),\ldots f_i(a_1^q(\vec{x}),\ldots,a_p^q(\vec{x})))$

then the limit of F_n when n tends towards infinity is :

$$F(\vec{x},y) = \underline{\text{If}}\ p_1(y)\ \underline{\text{then}}\ f_1(\vec{x})\ \underline{\text{else}}\ \ldots\ \underline{\text{If}}\ p_k(y)\ \underline{\text{then}}\ f_k(\vec{x})\ \underline{\text{else}}\ h(\vec{x},F(a_1^1(\vec{x}),\ \ldots,a_p^1\ (\vec{x}),b(y)),\ldots,F(a_p^q(\vec{x}),\ldots,a_p^q(\vec{x}),b(y))).$$

(We suppose that h is strict).

Proof : For simplicity we take k=1. The functions F_n define a functionnal $\mathcal{T}_1$ by $\mathcal{T}_1^n\ [\Omega]\ (\vec{x},y)=F_n(\vec{x},y)$ and F defines a functionnal $\mathcal{T}_2$.

The proof is made by induction using SCOTT's methodology [14] : we know that F is the least fixed point of $\mathcal{T}_2$, and we also know that the least fixed point of a functionnal is given by the limit of $\mathcal{T}^n\ [\Omega\ ]\ (\vec{x},y)$ when n tends towards infinity. So we show that $\mathcal{T}_1^n[\Omega](\vec{x},\ y) = \mathcal{T}_2^n\ [\Omega\ ](\vec{x},y)$.

The property is trivial for n=0. Suppose that it is true for n, we have $\mathcal{T}_2^{n+1}[\Omega\ ](\vec{x},y)=\mathcal{T}_2[\mathcal{T}_2^n[\Omega]]\ (x,y)=\mathcal{T}_2[\mathcal{T}_1^n[\Omega]\ ](\vec{x},y)$ using induction hypothesis.
So that we have :

$$\mathcal{T}_2^{n+1}[\Omega\ ](\vec{x},y)=\underline{\text{If}}\ p_1(y)\ \underline{\text{then}}\ f_1(\vec{x})\ \underline{\text{else}}\ h\left(\vec{x},\ \begin{pmatrix}\underline{\text{if}}\ p_1(y)\ \underline{\text{then}}\ f_1(a_1^1(\vec{x}),\ldots,a_p^1(\vec{x}))\underline{\text{else}}\\ \ldots\\ \underline{\text{if}}\ p_n(y)\ \underline{\text{then}}\ f_n(a_1^1(\vec{x}),\ldots,a_p^1(\vec{x}))\underline{\text{else}}\ \Omega\end{pmatrix},\ldots\right)$$

which is :

$$= \underline{\text{If}}\ p_1(y)\ \underline{\text{then}}\ \ f_1(\vec{x})\ \underline{\text{else}}$$

$\underline{If}\ p_1(b(y))\ \underline{then}\ \ h(\vec{x},f_1(a_1^1(\vec{x}),\ldots,a_p^1(\vec{x})),\ldots,f_1(a_1^q(\vec{x}),\ldots,a_q^q(\vec{x})))\underline{else}\ldots$
$\underline{If}\ p_n(b(y))\ \underline{then}\ \ h(\vec{x},f_n(a_1^1(\vec{x}),\ldots,a_p^1(\vec{x})),\ldots,f_n(a_1^q(\vec{x}),\ldots,a_q^q(\vec{x})))\underline{else}$
Ω (h is strict)

and with the relations that link p_i and p_{i+1}, f_i and f_{i+1} we finally obtain that $\mathcal{T}_2^{n+1}[\Omega]\ (\vec{x},y)=\mathcal{T}_1^{n+1}[\Omega]\,(\vec{x},y)$.

3.4. Exponential type relations.

The sequence $p_n(y)_{n\in\mathbb{N}}$ is as before, and we suppose that there exists two substitutions σ_1 and σ_2:

$\sigma_1=(x_1/a_1(\vec{x}))\ldots(x_{p-1}/a_{p-1}(\vec{x}))\ ;\sigma_2=(x_1/b_1(\vec{x}))\ldots(x_p/b_p(\vec{x}))$ such that

$\forall\ i\geq 1\ f_{i+k}(\vec{x})=f_i(a_1(\vec{x}),\ldots,a_{p-1}(\vec{x}),f_i(b_1(\vec{x}),\ldots,b_p(\vec{x})))$

then the limit of F_n when n tends towards infinity is :

$F(\vec{x},y)=\underline{If}\ p_1(y)\ \underline{then}\ f_1(\vec{x})\ \underline{else}\ \ldots\ \underline{If}\ p_k(y)\ \underline{then}\ f_k(\vec{x})\ \underline{else}$
$\quad F(a_1(\vec{x}),\ldots,a_{p-1}(\vec{x}),G(\vec{x},y),b(y))$

$G(\vec{x},y)=F(b_1(\vec{x}),\ldots,b_p(\vec{x}),b(y))$

Proof : Similar to the proof of 3.3.

3.5. Remarks.

In the following we will suppose that k=1 for simplicity. These theorems are combined together to obtain a program from traces, but the two last theorems will not be used in program transformation for they do not lead to terminal recursive functions.

4. THE ALGORITHM.

We describe the complete methodology which is used to obtain programs from examples. The transformation programs aspect of our work is obtained by a restriction of the algorithm : we eliminate the parts that could lead to non-terminal recursive programs.

The way we operate can be summarized by :

1.) Consider a problem given by its sequence of fragments $f_1,f_2,\ldots,f_n$.

2.) Match h_i with f_i, if h_i is a fragment of a previously solved problem. If the matching succeeds for all i then synthesize a function by the use of theorem 3.4. and corollaries. (see 4.4)

3.) If 2.) fails, then match f_i and f_{i+1}, if it succeeds for $1\leq i\leq n$, then synthesize a program with theorem 3.1 (see 4.2).

4.) If the matching of f_i and f_{i+1} fails for $1\leq i\leq q<n-1$, then the first q-1 fragments are considered as particular cases and we write the function F we are

seeking as :

(DE F (X) (COND((p_1 X)(f_1 X)) ... ((p_{q-1} X))(T(F1 X))))

where F1 has $f_q,\ldots,f_n$ for fragments (and $p_q,\ldots,p_n$ for predicates if F has $p_1,\ldots,$ p_n for predicates).

In the following we will have to face again this particular case phenomenon. It will be treated in the same way and will be considered as trivial.

5.) If the matching of f_i and f_{i+1} fails for $1\le i\le n-1$, then we try to write the function as a composition. If this is not possible, we compute g_i=least generalization of f_i and f_{i+1} $1\le i\le n-1$, and the function F is defined as a particulization of a more general function G with fragments $g_1, \ldots, g_n$.(see 4.3).

6.) We look to the least generalizations $g_1,\ldots,g_n$ to see if the number of variables in g_i is constant. If the answer is positive, the algorithm is run again with $g_1,\ldots,$ g_n. (see 4.1).

7.) If not, we try to match f_i with sub-trees of f_{i+1} in order to apply theorem 3.3 (this could also lead to generalizations, see 4.5).

Parts 2.) and 7.) are not used in the case of programs transformation.

All these points will now be explained in details. Beware that these details are not given in the same order as above for the sake of a better readibility.

4.1. Generalization.

4.1.a. Looking for composition.

When the matching of f_i and f_{i+1} fails, we attempt to generalize but this operation actually consists in taking a new variable, say xx, and replace the illegal substitution (t_1/t_2) by (xx/t_2). This can be part of an infinite process only if the size of t_1 is "less" than the size of t_2. This brings us to define :

A term t_1 is less complex than a term t_2 if :

1) The number of functions of arity greater than 1 is less in t_1 than in t_2.

2) If these numbers are equal then the number of unary functions is less in t_1 than in t_2.

Suppose that we have to generalize on the "substitution" (t_1/t_2) where t_2 is less complex than t_1. The repetition of this action would lead to the loss of the right term t_2. In this case we would write the function as a composed function (4.3).

4.1.b. Generalization.

If the preceding phenomenon does not appear, we compute the least generalization of f_i and f_{i+1}, $1\le i\le n-1$. Let be $g_1,\ldots,g_{n-1}$ those least generalizations. Again we match g_i and g_{i+1} and repeat this procedure until the matching succeeds.

For example consider the function F given in 2.2.

(A)→ (A A (A)) ; (A B C)→ (C A B C (C)) ; (A B C D E)→ (E A D C B C (E));

The matching of f_i and f_{i+1} fails, we thus compute the least generalization of f_i and f_{i+1} :

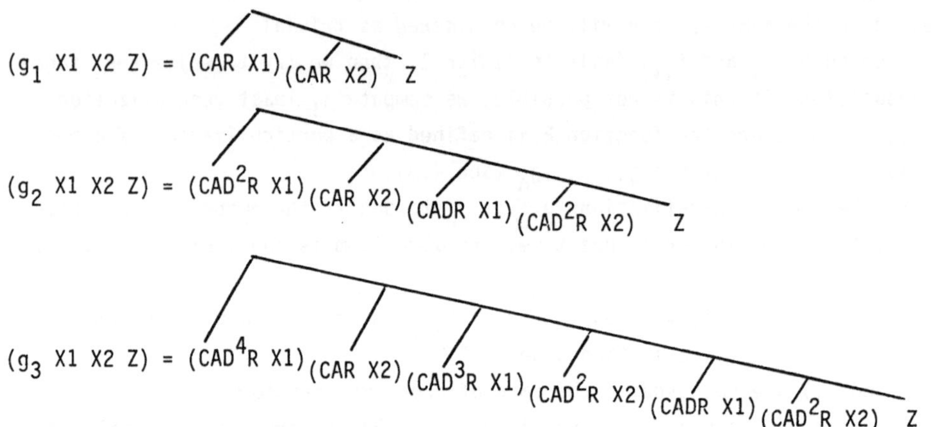

...

and now the matchings succeed and lead to the constant substitution :

σ = (X1/ (CD²R X1)) (X2/X2) (Z/(CONS(CADR X1) (CONS(CAD²R X2) Z)))

so that G is given by (with theorem 3.1) :

```
(DE G (X1 X2 Z) (COND ((ATOM(CDR X1)) (CONS(CAR X1) (CONS(CAR X2) Z)))
                      (T (G(CD²R X1) X2(CONS(CADR X1)(CONS(CAD²R X2) Z)))) ))
```

4.1.c. <u>Initialization</u>.

The next step is to give initial values to the new variables introduced by generalization. We match g_i with f_i (the matching always succeeds by the definition of the least generalization of two terms) and that gives us the initialization which enable us to pass from g_i to f_i. In the preceding example :

τ_1 = matching of g_1 and f_1 = (X1/X) (X2/X) (Z/ ((CAR X) NIL) NIL)

τ_2= (X1/X) (X2/X) (Z/ ((CAD²R X) NIL) NIL)

τ_3= (X1/X) (X2/X) (Z/ ((CAD⁴R X) NIL) NIL) ...

We transform $\{\tau_i\}$ into a constant substitution τ by taking first the constant couples of $\tau_1,\tau_2,\ldots$ (in the example : (X1/X) (X2/X)) . The non-constant substitutions introduce new subproblems : if we have (Z/ (H1 X Z)) in τ_1, (Z/(H2 X Z)) in τ_2,... we put (Z/(H X Z)) in τ and H has H1,H2,... for fragments, $p_1,p_2,\ldots$ for predicates.

In the example τ is (X1/X) (X2/X) (Z/ (H X Z)) with H defined by the fragments :

(H1 X Z) = (CAR X) NIL NIL ; (H2 X Z) = (CAD^{2}R X) NIL NIL ; (H3 X Z) = (CAD^{4}R X) NIL NIL

The matching of Hi and Hi+1 succeeds leading to the constant substitutions: (X/(CD^{2}R X)). We finally have F as :

```
(DE F (X) (G X X(H X))
(DE H (X) (COND((ATOM(CDR X)) (CONS(CONS (CAR X) NIL) NIL))
              (T (H (CD²R X))) ))
(DE G (X1 X2 Z) (COND((ATOM(CDR X1)) (CONS(CAR X1)(CONS(CAR X2) Z)))
                     (T (G (CD²R X1) X2 (CONS(CADR X1) (CONS(CAD²R X2) Z)))) ))
```

4.2. The matching succeeds.

4.2.a. Lethal successes.

The matching of f_i and f_{i+1} might succeed in a way which is not suitable for Summers's theorem. Suppose that we start with n traces and that because of the generalizations and the particular cases, we have only two terms left. This is not enough in order to verify that we have recurrent relations. We conclude that it was a mistake to look for relations between f_i and f_{i+1} and start again by seeking relations between f_i and f_{i+2},...

Three other cases of lethal successes are possible :

1.) X_i is rewritten as $\lambda(X_j)$ at the kth step and we find at the $(k+q)^{th}$ step that X_j is rewritten as $\mu(X_i)$. This means that we have to look for recursion relations between f_i and f_{i+q}.

2.) X_i is rewritten as $\lambda(X_j)$ and there is no step where X_j is rewritten in terms of X_i. This means that we would need an infinite number of variables, or, otherwise stated, that the algorithm does not stop. We attempt then to write f_i as a composition.

3.) The domain is characterized by a recurrence (X/b(X)) and we find substitutions of the type $(X_i/b_i(X_i))$. If there is no d_i such that $b_i \circ d_i = b$; the obtained function would not be everywhere defined. We attempt then also to write f_i as a composition.

Example of the case 2.) : (A) → (A) ; (A B) → (B B A) ; (A B C) → (B C C B A) ; (A B C D) → (B C D D C B A) ; ... and of case 3.) : (A B C) → A ; (A B C D) → C; (A B C D E) → E.

4.2.b. Building a constant substitution.

Suppose that Matching (f_i, f_{i+1}) = Matching(f_j, f_{j+1}) for all i and j then

Summers's theorem can be applied. If it is not the case we build a constant substitution σ as in 4.2.c. : we put in σthe constant couples and introduce new subproblems.

For example consider the program given in 2.1. :

The first fragment is a particular case (all variables are not present). The other fragments require a generalization since the matchings fail and we have the least generalizations as :

```
                    G                                  G
(g1 X Y Z) =       /|\      ; (g2 X Y Z) =   X ------- | ----------- G
                  X Y Z                                Y            /|\
                                                             (B X) (A Y) Z

                          G
(g3 X Y Z) =  X --------- | ----------- G
                          Y            /|\
                                 (B X) (A Y) \
                                              G
                                             /|\
                                   (B^2 X) (A^2 Y) Z
```

The matchings of the g_i give :

```
                           G                                     G
σ1 = (X/X) (Y/Y) (Z/     / | \      ) ;  σ2 = (X/X) (Y/Y) (Z/    / | \        );...
                    (B X) (A Y) Z                         (B^2 X) (A2 Y) Z
```

We write :

σ = (X/X) (Y/Y) (Z/ (F_3 X Y Z))

F_3 is given by the right parts of the substitutions on Z and has $p_3, p_4, \ldots$ as predicates.

Here the domain subtitution is (Y/ (A Y)) so in fact we have to introduce a new variable Y1 for the domain.

We again apply the same methodology and finally obtain that

```
(DE F (X Y) (COND((P Y) (C X))
                 (T (G X Y (F (B X) (A Y)))) ))
```

is equivalent to :

```
(DE F (X Y) (COND((P Y) (C X))
                 (T (F1 X Y Y (F2 X Y))) ))
(DE F2 (X Y) (COND((P(A Y)) (C (B X)))
                  (T (F2 (B X) (A Y))) ))
(DE F1 (X Y Y1 Z)(COND((P(A Y1)) (G X Y Z))
                      (T (F1 X Y (A Y1) (F3 X Y Y1 Z))) ))
(DE F3 (X Y Y1 Z)(COND((P(A^2 Y1)) (G (B X) (A Y) Z))
                      (T (F3 (B X) (A Y) (A Y1) Z)) ))
```

Remark.

Let n be the length of Y (i.e. the number of time A has to be applied to Y in order to reach (P (A^n Y)) = TRUE), then the recursive expression has a complexity of n while the tail recursive one has a complexity of n^2 (see above). At first sight one may question the interest of this transformation. There are two answers. First, it happens in other cases (see further) that the tail recursive expression is of less complexity than the recursive one. Second, even in the above example, the recursive expression uses a stack of size n while the iterative one uses a constant place. It follows that for some n, for a given amount of available memory the tail recursive expression may be runnable while the recursive one cannot be computed.

4.3. Composition.

In 4.1.a. and 4.2.a., we knew that something was wrong with a substitution of t_1 by t_2. We then cut the function into two parts. f_i is written :
$f_i(X) = g_i(X,h_i(X))$ where $h_i(X)$ contains the sons of the first function of arity greater than one which is the father of the place where the lethal success occurs and where $g_i(X,Z)$ contains their context in f_i.

For example consider the function :

```
(DE F (X) (G X X C))
(DE G (X Y Z) (COND((P(B Y)) (H (B X) (H (B Y) Z) C)))
                   (T (S X Y (G X (B Y) (H (B Y) Z)))) ))
(DE S(X Y Z) (COND((P(B² Y)) (H (B² X) Z))
                   (T (S (B X) (B Y) Z)) ))
```

which leads to the fragments (when S is also symbolically evaluated) :

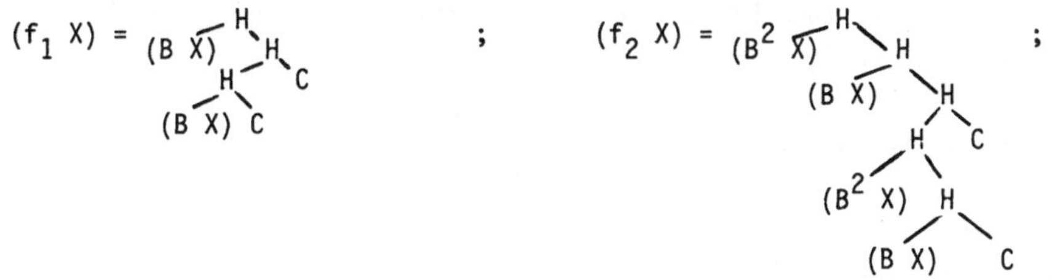

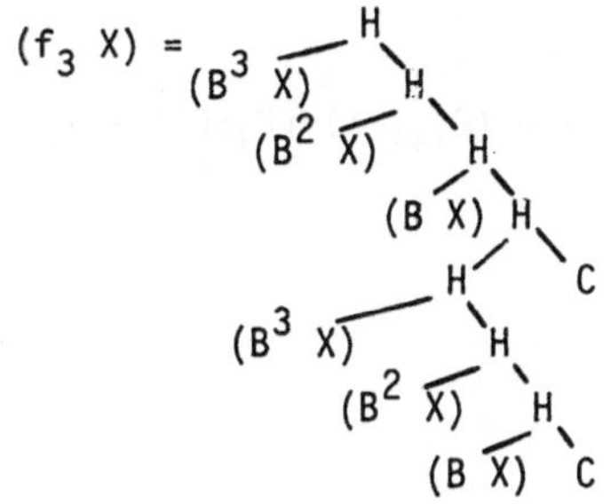

```
(f1 X) =      H                    ;   (f2 X) =      H                ;
       (B X)    H                             (B² X)    H
              H   C                             (B X)     H
         (B X) C                                        H   C
                                                   (B² X) H
                                                     (B X)   C

(f3 X) =        H
       (B³ X)     H
          (B² X)   H
             (B X) H
                 H    C
       (B³ X)      H
          (B² X)    H
              (B X)  C
```

The matching of f_1 and f_2 needs the substitution ((B X)-H-C/ (B X)). The matching of f_2 and f_3 is similar. We have seen in 4.1.a. that we have to write
$(f_i\ X) = (g_i\ X\ (s_i\ X))$ with :

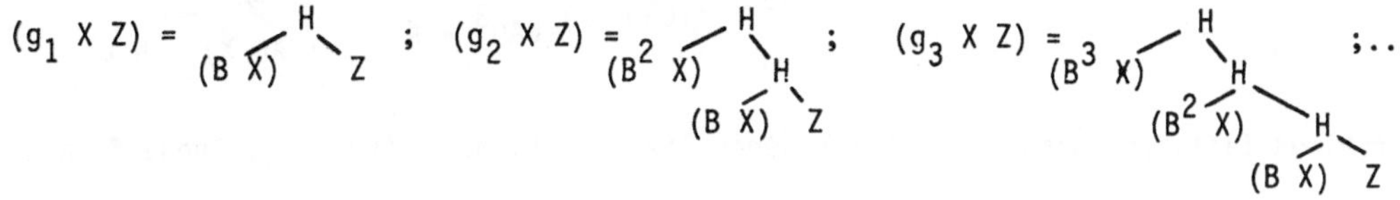

```
(g1 X Z) =      H        ;  (g2 X Z) =       H     ;   (g3 X Z) =        H          ;...
           (B X)  Z                   (B² X)   H               (B³ X)     H
                                          (B X)  Z                  (B² X)   H
                                                                         (B X) Z
```

and :

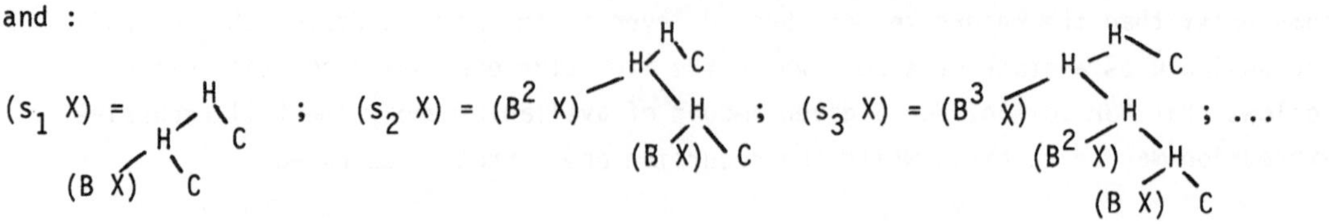

$(s_1\ X) =$ (B X) H H C C ; $(s_2\ X) = (B^2\ X)$ H H C (B X) H C ; $(s_3\ X) = (B^3\ X)$ H H C $(B^2\ X)$ H (B X) H C ; ...

We apply the methodology to the g_i and s_i and finally find that F is equivalent to :

```
(DE F (X) (G X (S X C))
(DE G (X Z) (COND ((P(B X)) (H (B X) Z))
                  (T (G (B X) (H (B X) Z))) ))
(DE S (X Z) (COND ((P(B X)) (H (H (B X) Z) C))
                  (T (S (B X) (H (B X) Z))) ))
```

In this example, we reach a new program the complexity of which is 2n instead of $\frac{n(n-1)}{2}$ for the initial one. We therefore win in time as in place.

4.4. Comparisons.

If we find that the fragments we are studying match with the fragments h_i of a previously solved problem H, we then build a constant substitution σ as was done in 4.1.c. and 4.2.b. and we synthesize F as :

$$F(\vec{x}) = H(\sigma(\vec{x}))$$

For example consider the function F given by :

(A) → (A)

(A B C) → (B B C A)

(A B C D E) → (C C D B B D D E C A)

(A B C D E F G) → (D D E C C E E F D B B E E F D D F F G E C A)

The predicates are $(P_i\ X)$: (ATOM $(CD^{2i+1}$ R X)) and we have $(P_{i+1}\ X)=(P_i(CD^2\ R\ X))$

The fragments are :

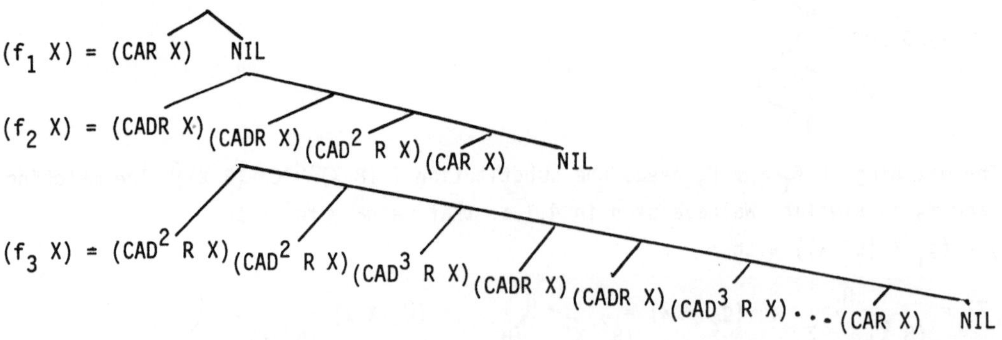

$(f_1\ X) =$ (CAR X) NIL

$(f_2\ X) =$ (CADR X) (CADR X) $(CAD^2\ R\ X)$ (CAR X) NIL

$(f_3\ X) =$ $(CAD^2\ R\ X)$ $(CAD^2\ R\ X)$ $(CAD^3\ R\ X)$ (CADR X) (CADR X) $(CAD^3\ R\ X)$ ... (CAR X) NIL

...

The matchings fail, we compute the least generalization f'_i of f_i and f_{i+1}. These f'_i are simply equal to f_i except that the NIL in f_i is replaced by a variable Z in f_i'.

The matchings succeed and give :

σ_i= (X/ (CDR X)) (Z/ (h_i X Z))

with

(h_1 X Z) = (CADR X) (CAD^2R X) (CAR X) Z

(h_2 X Z) = (CADR X) (CAD^3R X) (CAD^3R X) (CAD^4R X) (CAD^2R X) (CAR X) Z

(h_3 X Z) = (CADR X) (CAD^4R X) (CAD^4R X) (CAD^5R X) (CAD^3R X) (CAD^3R X) (CAD^3R X)...(CAR X) Z

The matching of h_i and h_{i+1} also fails since it leads to a substitution (X/ (CD^2R X)) (in fact (X_1/(CD^2R X_2))) which is a case of lethal success (see 4.2.a:2)), and force us to introduce a composition. Furthermore, other contradictions appear : (X / X) contradicts (X / (CDR X)) and force us to introduce two variables initiated by X. It follows that we write (h_i X Z)=(g_i X X (1_iX Z)) where :

(1_i X Z) = (CONS (CAR X) Z).

1_i is a constant function and we can write :

(h_i X Z) = (g_i X X (CONS (CAR X) Z))

The values of g_i are :

(g_1 X1 X2 Z) = (CADR X1) (CAD^2R X2) Z

(g_2 X1 X2 Z) = (CADR X1) (CAD^3R X2) (CAD^3R X2) (CAD^4R X2) (CAD^2R X2) Z

(g_3 X1 X2 Z) = (CADR X1) (CAD^4R X2) (CAD^4R X2) (CAD^5R X2) (CAD^3R X2) ...(CAD^2R X2) Z

Matching of g_i and g_{i+1} is a success which give :

μ_i = (X1/X1) (X2/ (CDR X2)) (Z/ (m_i X2 Z))

with

(m_1 X2 Z) = (CAD^3R X2) (CAD^4R X2) (CAD^2R X2) Z

(m_2 X2 Z) = (CAD^3R X2) (CAD^5R X2) (CAD^5R X2) (CAD^6R X2) (CAD^4R X2) (CAD^2R X2) Z

$(m_3\ X2\ Z)$ = (CAD^{3}R X2) (CAD^{6}R X2) (CAD^{6}R X2) (CAD^{7}R X2) (CAD^{6}R X2) ... (CAD^{2}R X2) Z

The matching of h_i with m_i succeeds with the constant substitution :
ν = (X/ (CD^{2}R X2)) (Z/Z)
We finally obtain F as :

```
(DE F (X) (F' X X NIL))
(DE F' (X Y Z)(COND ((ATOM(CDR Y)) (CONS(CAR X) Z))
                   (T (F' (CDR X) (CD2 R Y) (H X Y Z))) ))
(DE H (X Y Z) (G X X Y (CONS (CAR X) Z)))
(DE G (X1 X2 Y Z)(COND((ATOM(CD3R Y)) (CONS(CADR X1)(CONS(CAD2R X2) Z)))
                        (T (G X1 (CDR X2) (CD2R Y) (M X2 Y Z))) ))
(DE M (X2 Y Z) (H (CD2R X2) (CD2R Y) Z))
```

4.5. Embedded recursion.

If all the preceding methods fail we then try to match f_i with sub-trees of f_{i+1} in order to apply theorem 3.3.

For example consider the sequence of input-output :

(A) →(A)
(A B C) → ((B A) C B)
(A B C D E) → (((C B A) D C A)(D C B) E D B)
(A B C D E F G) → ((((D C B A) E D B A)(E D C A) F E C A)((E D C B) F E C B) (F E D B) G F D B)
...

The fragments are :

$(f_1\ X)$ = (CAR X) NIL

$(f_2\ X)$ = (CADR X) (CAR X) NIL (CAD^{2}R X) (CADR X) NIL

$(f_3\ X)$ = (CAD^{3}R X) (CAD^{2}R X) (CAR X) NIL (CAD^{4}R X) (CAD^{3}R X) (CADR X) NIL
(CAD^{2}R X) (CADR X) (CAR X) NIL (CAD^{3}R X) (CAD^{2}R X) (CADR X) NIL

...

Matching f_i and f_{i+1} requires a generalization which introduces a number of variables depending on i, one thus has to attempt a matching between f_i and sub-trees of f_{i+1}. During this process, NIL has to be replaced by a variable Z and we find :
(f_{i+1} X Z) =(CONS (f_i (CDR X) (CONS(CAR X) Z)) (f_i (CD^2R X) (CONS (CADR X) Z)))

So F is given by :

```
(DE F (X) (FF X X NIL))
(DE FF (X Y Z) (COND
    ((ATOM(CDR Y)) (CONS (CAR X) Z))
    (T (CONS (FF (CDR X) (CDDR Y) (CONS (CAR X) Z))
             (FF (CD²R X) (CDDR Y) (CONS (CADR X) Z)))) ))
```

5. CONCLUSION.

This work describes an extension of previously obtained results [2,5,6,7,8,9,15] As a main result we reach a much greater class of functions. Our goal was reached by the use of theorems about composition, embedding, self-embedding.

These methods also give us a way to transform recursive functions into iterative ones, which complete existing program transformation systems [1,3] .

A great asset to our methodology follows from the facts that it avoids combinatorial explosion and that it has been implemented (in the Reduce LISP of an UNIVAC-1110). On the contrary, the strong restrictions put on the function domain are clearly its main drawback.

References.

1. ARSAC J., KODRATOFF Y., "Some methods for transformation of recursive procedures into iterative ones", *W.G.3 meeting Zakopane (1979) and Pub. LITP 79-2.*

2. BIERMAN A.W., SMITH D.R., "The hierarchical synthesis of LISP programs", *Information Processing 77 (1977) pp 41-45.*

3. BURSTALL R.M., DARLINGTON J., "A transformation system for developping recursive programs", *J. ACM 24 (1977) pp 44-67.*

4. GREUSSAY P., *Thesis Publication LITP (1978).*

5. JOUANNAUD J.P., GUIHO G., "Inference of functions with an interactive system", *Machine Intelligence 9, D. Michie ed. (1979), pp 227-250.*

6. JOUANNAUD J.P., KODRATOFF Y., "Characterization of a class of functions synthesized from examples by a SUMMERS like method using a BMW matching technique", *Proc IJCAI-79, pp 440-446.*

7. KODRATOFF Y., "A class of functions synthesized from a finite number of examples and a LISP program scheme", *Int. J. of Comp. and Sci., Vol 8 n°6 (1979), pp489-521.*

8. KODRATOFF Y., "Un algorithme pour l'obtention de formes terminales récursive à partir de traces de calcul", *Actes des journées francophones : production assistée de logiciel, Genève, Janvier 1980, pp 36-63.*

9. KODRATOFF Y., PAPON E., "A system for program synthesis and program optimization", *Proc. AISB meeting, Amsterdam, 1980.*

10. MANNA Z., NESS S., VUILLEMIN J., "Inductive methods for proving properties of programs", *C. ACM* 16 *(1973), pp 491-502.*

11. MC. CARTHY J., "Towards a mathematical science of computation", *Proc IFIP, 1962, pp 21-28.*

12. PLOTKIN G.D., "A note on inductive generalization", *M. Int. 5, 1969, pp 153-163.*

13. ROBINSON J.A., "A machine oriented logic based on the resolution principle", *J.ACM, 1965, pp 23-41.*

14. SCOTT D., "Outline of mathematical theory of computation", *4th An. Princeton Conf. Inf. Sci. & Syst. (1970), pp 169-176.*

15. SUMMERS P.D., "A methodology for LISP program construction from examples", *J.ACM* 24 *(1977), pp 161-175.*

A METHOD FOR DESCRIBING CONCURRENT PROBLEMS BASED ON LOGIC

by

Georg Winterstein
Manfred Dausmann
Guido Persch

Institut für Informatik II, Universität Karlsruhe,
Postfach 6380, D-7500 Karlsruhe 1, Fed. Rep. of Germany

SUMMARY

In this talk we investigate the usefulness of logic programming for the description of concurrent problems. A logic program consists of an axiomatization of the problem domain together with the specification of a certain control. To describe the axiomatization only a restricted form of predicate logic is used which is known as Horn clauses. For this class a "procedural interpretation" can be given. The control specification determines in which way procedure invocations should be executed. Synchronization of processes can be obtained with the help of a data structure the processes have in common.

Synchronization through data structures gives an implicit description of concurrent problems. To make it explicit we extend the concept of logic programming by introducing "message predicates". Processes which are in the same message area can send or ask for messages. Sending a message does not affect the execution of a process while asking for a message delays a process until an appropriate message is received. The way in which information is passed between different processes through message predicates is the same as for the invocation of a procedure by a procedure call, i. e. unification. Therefore we have to demand that unification is an undivisible operation.

We give several examples for the capability of our method.

Abstract

Das Saarbrücker Übersetzungssystem SUSY

Heinz Dieter Maas

Im Sonderforschungsbereich "Elektronische Sprachforschung" wurde in den vergangenen Jahren ein System zur automatischen Sprachübersetzung geschaffen, das durch die Einteilung in eine quellsprachliche Analyse, einen sprachpaarbezogenen Transfer und eine zielsprachenabhängige Synthese charakterisiert ist.

Die Analyse gliedert sich - ebenso wie die Synthese - in Morphologie, Syntax und Semantik. In der morphologischen Analysephase werden allen Textwörtern die für die nachfolgende Syntaxanalyse benötigten Informationen unter Verwendung eines morphosyntaktischen Lexikons zugeordnet. Mehrdeutigkeiten werden z.T. durch Anwendung von Grammatikregeln, z.T. durch eine mit Gewichtungen arbeitende Netzwerkanalyse ausgefiltert. Der syntaktische Analyseteil besteht in der Zerlegung von Sätzen in Teilsätze, in der Erkennung von Nominal- und Verbalgruppen, sowie in der Zuordnung der komplemente zu den praedikaten. Hieran schließt sich die semantische Disambiguierung an, deren Grundlage das Vorhandensein einer syntaktischen Struktur (in Baumformat) sowie die Klassifizierung und Beschreibung von Nomina, Verben und Präpositionen ist. In dieser Phase können zu den im Satz vorliegenden Strukturen synonyme Konstruktionen erzeugt werden, die im Übersetzungsprozeß u.U. verwendet werden. Für die semantische Disambiguierung wird ein spezielles Lexikon verwendet.

Der Transfer beschränkt sich zum großen Teil auf die Wortübersetzung und läßt den Analysebaum invariant.

Auf der Grundlage des Transferergebnisses arbeitet der Synthesealgorithmus, der die Baumstruktur durch zielsprachlich bedingte Transformationen modifiziert und dann die Erzeugungsoperationen durchführt, die zunächst für jeden Satz jeweils eine Kette von präterminalen Symbolen liefern. In einem letzten Schritt werden diese durch flektierte Wortformen ersetzt.

Die wichtigsten von SUSY verarbeiteten Sprachen sind Deutsch, Englisch, Französisch und Russisch, daneben auch Esperanto und Dänisch.

THE NATURAL LANGUAGE SYSTEM HAM-RPM AS A HOTEL MANAGER: SOME REPRESENTATIONAL PREREQUISITES

Anthony Jameson, Wolfgang Hoeppner, Wolfgang Wahlster

Research Group 'Simulation of Language Understanding'
Universitaet Hamburg
Germanisches Seminar
Von-Melle-Park 6
D-2000 Hamburg 13
Federal Republic of Germany

ABSTRACT. The dialogue system HAM-RPM simulates a person conversing about one of several interchangeable scenes in colloquial German. Attention is currently being focused on a hotel reservation situation in which the system is required to construct and make use of a model of its dialogue partner's goals and beliefs. This situation calls for a semantic representation language which is declarative and which permits the representation, among other things, of various numerical and natural language quantifiers, conjoined noun phrases and belief modifiers. This paper describes this this language and sketches the processes in the course of which expressions of the language are analysed, constructed, transformed, or evaluated. The system's behavior is described in detail to illustrate the relationships among these processes.

1. Introduction

Research on the natural language dialogue system HAM-RPM (Hamburg Dialogue Partner Model) is guided by the principle that many basic phenomena which have traditionally been subjected to purely linguistic or philosophical analysis can be fully understood only if investigated within a larger context which includes, among other things, the beliefs the dialogue partners have about their domain of discourse and about each other, the goals which motivate their participation in the dialogue, and the algorithms and heuristics they employ in attempting to attain these goals (cf. WINOGRAD 1976, BOBROW et al. 1977). The design of a system which simulates a natural dialogue partner is a useful way of approaching such phenomena in that it makes it both necessary and possible to do justice systematically to the roles played by these factors and to their interactions with one another.

One of the relevant factors, the knowledge relevant to the domain about which the dialogue partners converse, has been represented in HAM-RPM to date for three different scenes: two living-room interiors and a traffic scene (cf. v.HAHN et al. 1980). This knowledge is represented in two semantic networks: The referential semantic network contains extensional information concerning the scene being discussed, while the conceptual semantic network contains relevant intensional information. Both of these networks are implemented with the help of FUZZY's assertional data base (LEFAIVRE 1977). On the whole, however, HAM-RPM's knowledge base is heterogeneous, integrating several procedural and declarative representation languages, including production rules, semantic nets, ATN grammars, FUZZY 'Deduce Procedures' and a logic-oriented representation language. The system's knowledge base is distributed over nine files, which contain: a word lexicon, an idiom lexicon, a set of morphological rules, an ATN grammar for syntactic analysis, a coordinate-system representation of spatial data, a set of inference rules, an ATN grammar for generation and the referential and conceptual semantic networks. In addition, the following internal knowledge sources are built up during the dialogue: a record of references to objects, a syntactic and a semantic dialogue memory, an inference memory, and a partner model.

The following excerpt from a dialogue concerning the traffic scene may provide an impression of the behavior of the system.(The system's utterances are typed in capital letters.)

(1) Wo befindet sich das gelbe Auto?
(Where is the yellow car?)

WELCHES GELBE AUTO MEINST DU? Wieso fragst Du mich das?
(Which yellow car do you mean?) *(Why do you ask?)*

WEIL ES HIER DREI GELBE AUTOS GIBT.
(Because there are three yellow cars.)

WELCHES GELBE AUTO MEINTEST DU? Das, das in etwa neben dem Kombi parkt.
(Which yellow car did you mean?) *(The one parked more or less next to the station wagon.)*

VOR DEM FACHBEREICH FÜR INFORMATIK.
(In front of the department of computer science.)

(2) Ist dieses Gebäude groß?
(Is this building large?)

JA. *(Yes.)*

(3) Kannst du bitte ausführlicher antworten! Was steht neben der Ampel, die rot ist?
(Could you please give more detailed answers! What's next to the traffic light which is red?)

DAS GRÜNE AUTO UND DER GROSSE BAUM.
(The green car and the yellow tree.)

The three domains of discourse mentioned above have permitted the investigation of a variety of interesting phenomena, but they have the disadvantage that it is unclear what motivation the user might have for asking questions about such a domain; this means that the system in turn can have no other overall goal than the usual goal of question-answering systems, namely that of providing accurate information in an easily understandable form. But participants in natural dialogues often have goals of a quite different sort, and their behavior is determined to a large degree both by their own goals and by the perceived goals of their partner. So that these factors could be studied in a natural manner within HAM-RPM, a fourth domain of discourse has been introduced: The system takes the role of a hotel manager who is talking on the telephone with a caller who is interested in renting a room. The caller is assumed to have the overall goal of determining whether the room offered meets his requirements, which are not known to the manager in advance and which may be quite vague. The hotel manager is assumed to want to present the room in question in a particularly favorable light without saying anything which might later be revealed to be an outright untruth. The system must thus attempt to recognize the caller's specific desires concerning the room, as they are revealed -- usually indirectly -- in his utterances; to recognize when a specific question is asked, what desire of the caller's underlies it; and to make use of the various devices offered by the natural language which permit a particular state of affairs to be presented in a way which appears favorable with respect to a particular desired state of affairs.

The core of the dialogues simulated in this hotel domain consists of exchanges in which the caller expresses, directly or indirectly, some desire concerning the hotel room and the manager attempts to convince him that this wish would in fact be fulfilled. The beginning and the end of the telephone call deviate from this pattern, consisting largely of standard phrases and amenities. These parts of the dialogue are to be handled by an analysis based on a relatively simple dialogue grammar, though even here some important information about the caller may be obtained, for example if he introduces himself as a senior manager.

The dialogue situation described requires that the semantic representation language used by the system be declarative in nature, since it is not only questions which must be represented (other semantic representation languages for German are KS in PLIDIS (cf. ZIFONUN 1979) and MSRL in BACON (cf. HABEL et al. 1978)). For example, the system must generate more complex answers if it is to attempt to *sell* the hotel room than it would have to if it merely attempted to provide adequate factual answers (cf. COHEN 1978). Such answers cannot be generated directly in natural language, but must first be represented in an internal language. A declarative semantic representation language is also required for the model of the beliefs and desires of the caller which the system builds up in the course of the dialogue (cf. RICH 1979).

In addition to requiring a declarative semantic representation language the hotel situation poses several more specific problems for the representation language and the associated processes, problems which are not faced by more typical question-answering systems:

Numerical quantifiers (cf. SHAPIRO 1979) and other *natural language quantifiers* occur frequently in such dialogues, as do utterances expressing the *goodness of fit* between a quantifier and a given state of affairs, e.g.:

(4) *Caller:* Are all of the pictures oil-paintings?
Manager: Well, not quite, but most of them are.
One or two are etchings.

The main challenge here lies in the fact that the differences in the ways in which such quantifiers are used are often subtle and difficult to express within a single general schema. For example, consider the conditions under which it might be appropriate to give an unqualified affirmative answer to each of the following questions:

(5) *Caller:* Are all of the pictures framed?

(6) *Caller:* Is each of the pictures framed?

In (5) the number of pictures in the room would have to be at least three, since in colloquial English 'all' is not normally applied to sets consisting of two or fewer objects. In (6) the manager would have to have specific knowledge concerning each of the pictures, and not, e.g., merely general knowledge of the policy of the hotel concerning pictures.

Conjunctions of noun phrases are often called for in answers to questions about the room, as in example (7). The fact that such conjunctions are seldom used in questions themselves may incidentally explain why they have received little attention in the AI systems developed to date.

(7) *Manager:* One of the tables and all of the chairs are antiques.

A general treatment of such noun phrases is complicated by the fact that, as this example shows, the conjoined noun phrases may contain different quantifiers.

Particles which reveal the *beliefs* and *desires* of the speaker concerning the room represent for the hotel manager a valuable means of recognizing and influencing the caller's beliefs concerning the room (cf. example (8)).

(8) *Caller:* Does the room <u>by any chance</u> have a colour TV?
Manager: Yes, <u>of course</u> it does.

Since such phenomena as these could not be handled in a general way by the representation language used in connection with HAM-RPM's first three domains of discourse -- and in fact have attracted little attention within other natural language systems -- a new language has been developed, together with procedures for constructing, analysing, transforming, and evaluating expressions in it. The main purpose of the present paper is to describe the distinguishing features of this language and to sketch the associated processes (section 2). The relationships among these processes and their role within the system as a whole will be illustrated in section 3 with a detailed desription of one example of the system's behavior.

2. Semantic Representation Language: Definition and Interpretation

2.1 Syntactic Definition

The definition of the new semantic representation language in extended BNF notation is given in Fig. 1, in which the nonterminals of the language are listed in alphabetical order. The periods and the one-word comments preceded by a semicolon are not part of the syntactic definition, but are used internally by the system to make the manipulations of language structures more abstract and efficient. Capitalized symbols without the semicolon are terminal elements of the language. Where the right-hand side of an

```
<arc>            ::=  <arc2>
                 ::=  <arc3>
<arc2>           ::=  ISA | REF | MODUS | RELATOR | AGENS | OBJEKTIV | INSTRUMENTAL | BENEFAKTIV | PROFORM
<arc3>           ::=  ZEIT | RAEUMLICH
<atomic-formula> ::=  (<arc2> <term>. ;TERM1 <term>. ;TERM2)                              ;Arc2
                 ::=  (<arc3> <term>. ;TERM1 <term>. ;TERM2 <term>. ;TERM3)               ;Arc3
                 ::=  (<arc>  <term>.2-3 ;TERMS)                                          ;Arc
                 ::=  (<d-arc> <term>. <description>.)                                    ;D-Arc
                 ::=  (<f-arc> <term>. <formula>.)                                        ;F-Arc
<constant>       ::=  (*R ?C (ATOM !C))
<d-arc>          ::=  IS
<description>    ::=  (D: <operator2><description>. ;DESCRIPTION1  <description>. ;DESCRIPTION2)   ;Operator2
                 ::=  (D: <operator1> <description>.)                                     ;Operator1
                 ::=  (D: <operator> <description>.1-2 ;DESCRIPTIONS)                     ;Operator
                 ::=  (LAMBDA: <variable>. <formula>.)                                    ;Lambda:
<f-arc>          ::=  SAG | GLAUB | HOFF
<formula>        ::=  (F: <term> <formula>. ;PREDICATE)                                   ;Deep
                 ::=  (F: <operator1> <formula>.)                                         ;Operator1
                 ::=  (F: <operator2> <formula>. ;FORMULA1  <formula>. ;FORMULA2)         ;Operator2
                 ::=  (F: <operator> <formula>.1-2 ;FORMULAS)                             ;Operator
                 ::=  <atomic-formula>                                                    ;Atomic
                 ::=  T                                                                   ;True
<hedge>          ::=  ETWA | GENAU | FAST | UNGEFAEHR | DIREKT | IN/ ETWA | EINIGERMASSEN
<number>         ::=  (*R ?N (NUMBERP !N))                                                ;Finite
                 ::=  T                                                                   ;Infinite
<number-word>    ::=  <number>
                 ::=  VIEL | EINIG | MEHRER | ETLICH | WENIG | E- | KEIN
<operator>       ::=  <operator1>
                 ::=  <operator2>
<operator1>      ::=  NOT | LEIDER | SELBSTVERSTAENDLICH | MOEGLICH | WUENSCHENSWERT
<operator2>      ::=  AND | OR
<quantifier>     ::=  (FOR: <quantifier-operator>.<variable>.)                            ;Deep
<quantifier-operator>
                 ::=  (Q: <quantifier-word>)
                 ::=  (Q: <quantifier-word> <quantity>. ;PRESUPPOSITION?)                 ;Presupposition?
                 ::=  (Q: <quantity>)                                                     ;Quantity
                 ::=  (Q: <constant>)                                                     ;Constant
<quantifier-word>::=  (<hedge> <quantifier-word>)                                         ;Hedge
                 ::=  ALL | MEIST | WELCH | WIEVIEL | D- | JED | DIES | JEN | BEID
<quantity>       ::=  (<hedge> <number-word>)                                             ;Hedge
                 ::=  <number-word>
                 ::=  <range>
<range>          ::=  (<number-word> ;FROM <number-word> ;TO)
<term>           ::=  <constant>
                 ::=  <variable>
                 ::=  (T: <quantifier-operator> <description>.)                           ;Surface
                 ::=  (T: <quantifier> <formula>.)                                        ;Quantifier
                 ::=  (NT: <term>. ;TERM1 <term>. ;TERM2)                                 ;Nested
                 ::=  (T: <hedge> <term>.)                                                ;Hedge
                 ::=  (T: <operator1><term>.)                                             ;Operator1
                 ::=  (T: <operator2><term>. ;TERM1  <term> ;TERM2)                       ;Operator2
                 ::=  (T: <operator><term>.1-2 ;TERMS)                                    ;Operator
<variable>       ::=  (*R ?ATOM  (AND  (ATOM !ATOM) (EQ (NTHCHAR !ATOM 1) 'X)))
```

Fig. 1

expansion contains only terminal elements, the list of symbols is subject to extension. The two most important elements are the top-level 'FORMULA', onto which, roughly speaking, sentences and clauses are mapped, and 'TERM', onto which both noun phrases and predicates are mapped.

2.2 The Sublanguages SURF and DEEP

It is helpful, when describing the use of the language in HAM-RPM, to speak of two sublanguages, SURF and DEEP. Most of the productions in Fig. 1 are common to both sublanguages, but the element 'DESCRIPTION' occurs only in SURF, and the productions bearing the labels ;SURFACE and ;DEEP are possible only in the respective sublanguage.

SURF is used as a target and source language by the two ATN grammars which analyse and generate natural language utterances, respectively. It is well suited for this purpose in that its expressions are roughly parallel to those of natural language. For example, the scope of quantifiers is not expressed explicitly. Example (10) is the SURF representation of sentence (9).

(9) Mehrere Blumen stehen auf jedem Tisch.
(Several flowers are on each table.)

```
(10)  (IS (T: (Q: MEHRER) (LAMBDA: X71 (ISA X71 BLUME)))
          (LAMBDA: X72 (RAEUMLICH AUF X72
                            (T: (Q: JED) (LAMBDA: X74 (ISA X74 TISCH))))))
```

DEEP, on the other hand, is better suited for the analysis and construction of expressions by the internal processes which draw inferences on the basis of the partner's utterances, update the partner model accordingly, and derive answers to the partner's explicit or implicit questions. Example (11) is the DEEP representation corresponding to the SURF expression in example (10).

```
(11)  (F: ((FOR: (Q: JED) X76) (ISA X76 TISCH))
        (F: ((FOR:(Q:MEHRER) X75)(ISA X75 BLUME)) (RAEUMLICH AUF X75 X76)))
```

Although lexical and syntactic ambiguities in the input utterance are resolved when the corresponding SURF representation is constructed, the SURF expression itself may still be ambiguous. Referential or semantic ambiguities, e.g., in connection with the resolution of noun phrases, are not removed until the DEEP representation is generated. Even the DEEP expression, of course, may contain certain ambiguities concerning its interpretation as a speech act.

Vagueness, which, unlike ambiguity, is a typical feature of colloquial language, also differs from ambiguity in that it cannot be removed during the translation process, but must be reflected directly in the DEEP constructions. This is why DEEP provides for vague and explicitly hedged quantifiers as well as for hedged predications (see Fig. 1).

The way in which syntactic or lexical ambiguities are removed during the construction of SURF expressions becomes evident when the SURF expression corresponding to an ambiguous utterance is verbalized by HAM-RPM's ATN-based language generator via the procedure PARAPHRASE. For example, the input (12) would be paraphrased as (13). This

(12) Is the razor socket above the mirror in the bathroom?

(13) Is the razor socket above the mirror which is located in the bathroom?

paraphrase capability is used on the one hand in clarification dialogues (cf. v.HAHN et al. 1980) to check a given interpretation when an ambiguity is not easily resolvable on the basis of context information. On the other hand, it enables the system to give helpful answers to follow-up questions such as *'Did I ask you that?'*, which the user may ask when he is puzzled by the system's answer. Incidentally, it is the SURF representation, not the surface string, which is stored in the system's dialogue memory, so that in general the verbalization of a question as it is recalled is not identical to the original verbal input.

The translation from SURF to DEEP is performed by the procedure NORMALIZE. This procedure works top-down and recursive, and can be passed any well-formed structure as an argument. It first normalizes the structure's immediate constituents and then transforms it in a way which varies from one type of structure to another. For example, when passed an 'ATOMIC-FORMULA' of type ;ARC2, it first normalizes each of the two 'TERMS' and then extracts any quantifiers they may contain in the appropriate order.

As a comparison of the last two examples will show, one of the main tasks of NORMALIZE is the determination of the scope of quantifiers. The algorithm used for this purpose is modeled after the one described by Hendrix (cf. HENDRIX 1976); it takes into account the intrinsic strenghts of the various natural language quantifier expressions and their relative positions within the SURFACE structure. A more sophisticated algorithm would, of course, take into account other factors.

The translation from DEEP to SURF is performed by the inverse procedure NORMALIZE-1 whose basic control structure is similar to that of NORMALIZE. Fig. 2 sketches the translations which occur when an input utterance is analysed and evaluated and leads to the generation of a natural language response.

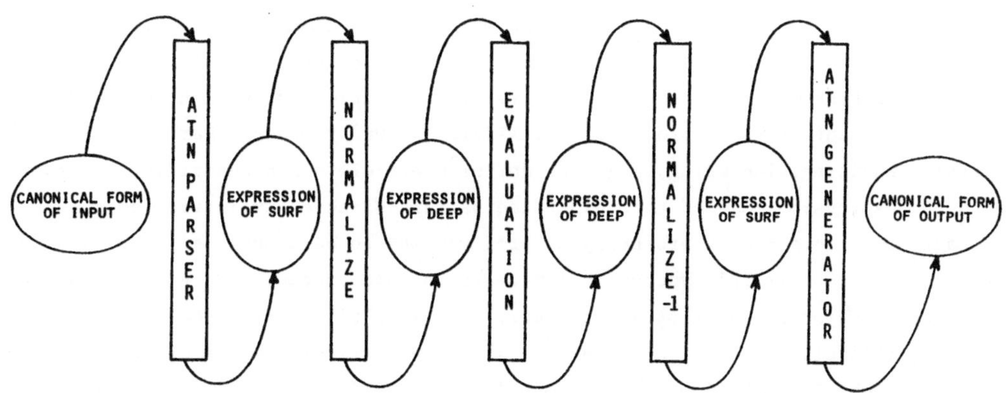

Fig. 2

Although Fig. 2 represents normalization as a separate pass, the fact that NORMALIZE can be applied to any well-formed structure of the language makes it possible to integrate this translation with the parsing of the natural language input: Substructures can be normalized as soon as they have been constructed by the parser, so that they can be further processed before the parsing proceeds further. This possibility is particular important in those cases in which it is useful to resolve a pronoun or definite noun phrase during the course of parsing.

2.3 The Evaluation Component

The evaluation component in HAM-RPM is, among other things, the procedural counterpart of what in logic is called the 'interpretation function'. Its tasks include the determination of the truth value of a given expression within a given context and the derivation of specific conclusions from an expression.

Evaluation is pattern-directed, being performed by two 'teams' of FUZZY 'Deduce procedures' called TEST-PROCs and GEN-PROCs. Each procedure has a characteristic pattern which matches some specified class of 'FORMULAS', though the patterns differ in their degree of specificity. GEN-PROCs generate constants which, when subsituted for a given variable, make a given formula true; TEST-PROCs determine the truth value of a given formula when a given variable is assigned a given value. For example, one GEN-PROC specializes in generating constants which fulfill a given conjunction of formulas, and one TEST-PROC checks the truth of assertions concerning spatial relations. The two teams call each other recursively, processing the input expression in a top-down manner.

The major advantage of this control structure for evaluation is that it relieves the designer of the temptation to handle syntactically similar structures according to a uniform scheme even when they in fact exhibit differences worth taking into account: Structures with special properties can be handled by separate specialized procedures (cf. section 2.4).

2.4 Selected Problems of Representation

We are now in a position to examine the way in which HAM-RPM deals with the representational problems mentioned in section 1. Inspection of the definition of the element 'QUANTIFIER-OPERATOR' shows that a relatively large and in fact open-ended-repertoire of quantifiers is provided. 'QUANTIFIER-WORDS' represent variants of the universal quantifier, including, e.g. the definite article and a quantifier corresponding to the expression *most of the*. Since the pattern-directed evaluation component just described allows nearly arbitrary control regimes to be associated with each of these quantifiers their idiosyncrasies can be taken into account in a natural manner.

The other major category of quantifiers, 'QUANTITIES', generalises the existential quantifier; it includes numerical quantifiers and in particular vague expressions such as *several* which, like the 'QUANTIFIER-WORDS', have special definitions associated with them.

The necessity of representing conjoined noun phrases which may have different quantifiers is responsible for the unusual first production in the definition of the element 'FORMULA': The quantifiers do not occupy the first position in the formula, as is usual in logic-based formalisms, but rather are contained within the first 'TERM', and not even on the top level, as can be seen from the definition of 'TERM'. Several specialized TEST-PROCs are required to locate quantifiers during the evaluation and to supervise their interpretation. Incidentally, conjoined noun phrases present some interesting problems in connection with normalization, as their quantifiers must have the same scope

Modifiers such as *of course* and *unfortunately* have the same syntactic role as the unary 'OPERATOR1' NOT, i.e., they can modify 'FORMULAs', 'TERMs', or 'DESCRIPTIONs'. Leaving the interpretation of the particles to the corresponding GEN-PROCs and TEST-PROCs has the advantage of leaving open the exact use to which they will be put during evaluation. This is important because such particles do not always serve to express information about the speaker's beliefs or desires but may instead simply help to disambiguate referring expressions, as in (14) when the two possible antecedents for *it* are *the bathtub* and *the hole in the wall*.

(14) *Manager:* Unfortunately, it is rather large.

3. The Processing of an Example Dialogue Segment

All of the processing phases which can occur when HAM-RPM responds to an utterance of the user's are presented in linear order in Fig. 3. The actual flow of control in any particular case is in general quite different, involving the repetition or omission of various processing phases. This is the case in particular when clarification dialogues occur.

In the remainder of this section a possible response of the system to the question (15) in the hotel situation will be traced. An example was chosen in which the representational problems discussed above and the system's construction and use of a partner model play a relatively minor role, as work on some aspects of these problems has not yet been completed.

(15) Was fuer Sitzgelegenheiten, die einigermassen bequem sind, befinden sich in diesem Zimmer?
(What chairs that are reasonably comfortable are there in this room?)

The following discussion can best be understood if continual reference is made to Fig.3.

The task of the component *Lexical Analysis* is to create a canonical representation of the input string. This requires a nontrivial control structure, as the results of one process may in turn establish preconditions for other processes (cf. HOEPPNER/ JAMESON 1979). A first set of processes tries to find the canonical form of each word in the input utterance using declarative and procedural lexical knowledge. In the example inflectional suffixes and punctuation marks are separated from the words to which they are appended. A second set of processes identifies and transforms special syntagmatic groups of words. The reflexive verb *sich befinden*, whose two words in general needn't even be adjacent within the sentence, is replaced by the nonreflexive verb *stehen* (to stand). The construction *was fuer* is replaced by the synonymous word *welch* (which). The final string which leaves *Lexical Analysis* is:

(16) WELCH SITZGELEGENHEIT /, D- EINIGERMASSEN BEQUEM SEIN /,
STEH IN DIES ZIMMER /?

In the system's lexicon each canonical word form is associated with its part of speech (or parts of speech, if it is lexically ambiguous) and other syntactic markers such as gender or article type. The preterminal string generated by the next component

INPUT UTTERANCE OF HUMAN PARTNER

LEXICAL ANALYSIS

OPERATIONS ON SINGLE WORDS
- Correction of simple spelling errors
- Identification of inflectional suffixes
- Replacement of words by canonical stems
- Transformation of derivatives
- Recognition of synonyms
- Treatment of punctuation marks
- Clarification dialogues

OPERATIONS ON SYNTAGMATIC UNITS
- Reduction of multipla-word phrases and discontinuous constituents
- Recognition of idiomatic expressions
- Segmentation of utterances consisting of more than one sentence
- Response to metacommunicative utterances

GENERATION OF PRETERMINAL STRING
- Association of parts of speech with canonical word forms

FOLLOW UP-QUESTIONS
- Why-questions
- Requests for detailed answers

PRONOUN RESOLUTION
- Grammatical gender
- Potential referents
- Clarification dialogues

HANDLING OF ELLIPSIS
- Reconstruction of complete semantic representation

ATN PARSER
- Case frames
- Recognition of ambiguous syntactic constructions
- Recognition of ellipsis
- Updating of dialogue memories
- Generation of SURF structures

NP-RESOLUTION
- Evaluation of normalized NP representation
- Discrimination between definite/indefinite and generic use of articles
- Restrictive attributes and relative clauses
- Treatment of presuppositions
- Thinking aloud
- Clarification dialogues
- Analysis of hedges
- Explicit focus on objects
- Checking of spatial relations

NORMALIZE
- Determination of range of quantifiers
- Construction of DEEP representations

META-LEVEL INFERENCES CONCERNING USER MODEL
- Interpretation of particles revealing user's beliefs and desires
- Performing assumed inferences of the user
- Hypotheses about user's intentions and expectations

EVALUATION
- Recursive analysis of DEEP expressions
- Generate-and-test cycles

GENERATION OF RESPONSE IN DEEP
- Vague inferences
- Network search
- Selectional restrictions
- Construction of inference memory

SIMULATION OF VISUAL SEARCH
- Checking of spatial relations
- Search for possible referents
- Rating of referents
- Consideration of dialogue focus

Fig. 3

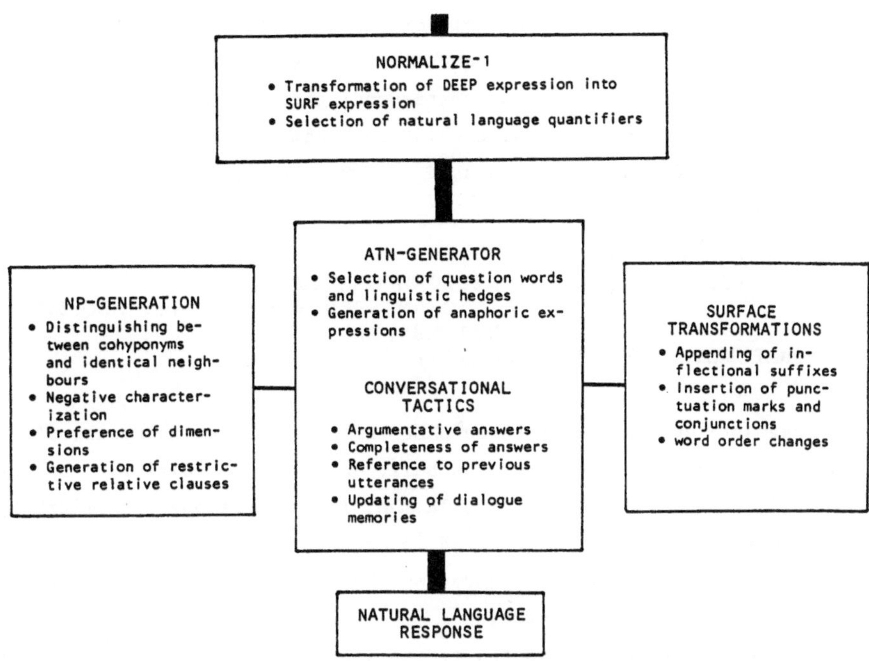

Fig. 3 (cont'd)

consists of the word forms and their parts of speech:

```
(17)  ((WELCH IPRN) (SITZGELEGENHEITEN NOM) (/, SATZZ) (D- DET RELPRN)
      (EINIGERMASSEN ADV) (BEQUEM ADV) (SEIN VRB) (/, SATZZ) (STEH VRB)
      (IN PRP) (DIES DEM PRN) (ZIMMER NOM) (/? SATZZ))
```

This preterminal string forms the input to the ATN parser (cf. FININ 1977), a component which on the one hand generates the SURF structure of the utterance and on the other hand activates complex semantic-pragmatic processing phases. (18) is the SURF expression for the preterminal string (17). This SURF representation contains only one struc-

```
(18) (IS (T: (Q: WELCH)
             (D: AND (LAMBDA: X1 (ISA X1 SITZGELEGENHEIT))
                     (LAMBDA: X2 (REF X2 (T: EINIGERMASSEN BEQUEM)))))
         (LAMBDA: X3 (RAEUMLICH IN X3
                      (T: (Q DIES) (LAMBDA: X4 (ISA X4 ZIMMER))))))
```

ture -- the embedded term for the noun phrase *dies Zimmer* -- which causes the activation of a reference-semantic processing component. SURF structures which represent noun phrases with the definite article are, when appropriate, NORMALIZEd, in this case yielding the DEEP 'TERM' (19), and passed to the NP-resolution component. In such cases

```
(19)   (T: (FOR: (Q: DIES) X40) (ISA X40 ZIMMER))
```

this component looks for a unique referent in the domain of discourse. The system refers to the knowledge base, in particular to the conceptual and referential semantic networks and the dialogue memories, to try to identify the internal name of the object the NP was intended to refer to. The analyis of the noun phrase in the example described here is particularly simple: The room in question is assumed to be the one the hotel manager has offered. The SURF expression corresponding to the noun phrase in now replaced in (18) by the constant ZIMMER4, the internal name of the room. The resulting structure, an 'ATOMIC-FORMULA', is now passed to NORMALIZE, which transforms it into a 'FORMULA' of the type ;DEEP:

```
(20)(F: (T: (FOR: (Q WELCH) X31)
            (F: AND (ISA X31 SITZGELEGENHEIT)
                    (F: (T: EINIGERMASSEN (T:(FOR: (Q: BEQUEM) X33) T))
                         (REF X31 X33)))))
          (RAEUMLICH IN X31 ZIMMER4))
```

The semantic-pragmatic evaluation of these DEEP structures makes heavy use of the model of the caller that the hotel manager has built up during the dialogue. Let us assume that he believes the caller to be a salesman. The present question might then lead to the assumption that he is interested in meeting with customers in his hotel room. This new hypothesis will then be added to the system's user model so that it can be referenced again during the dialogue.

This structure is then passed to the evaluation component so that an answer can be determined. The evaluation begins with an application of the team TEST-PROCs, just as if the structure represented a yes-no-question, because *WELCH* is defined as a quantifier which causes a description of a set of objects to be returned (instead of a truth value).

A uniform evaluation procedure might begin by generating arbitrary chairs from the system's knowledge base -- i.e. chairs in all rooms of the hotel with which the manager is familiar -- testing to see if they are *'reasonably comfortable'*, and finally checking whether they are located in the room in question. It is obviously more efficient and psychologically more realistic if the system immediately takes the spatial restriction into account by restricting its attention to the room in question. This is easily accomplished within the general control structure outlined in section 2.3: A TEST-PROC is defined which, when recognizing certain sorts of spatial restrictions in certain parts of a 'FORMULA', simply switches to the corresponding CONTEXT of FUZZY's data base and applies TEST-PROCs to the rest of the structure.

The following procedures are activated during the remainder of the evaluation: a TEST-PROC capable of handling the quantifier WELCH; a GEN-PROC specialized in conjunctions; a GEN-PROC which generates names of objects corresponding to a general concept (*SITZGELEGENHEIT* applies to all kinds of chairs, as well as couches, stools, etc.); a TEST-PROC specialized in hedges such as *EINIGERMASSEN* and a TEST-PROC which can determine how *'comfortable'* a given object is, using, if necessary, general knowledge about the properties of various types of furniture. The TEST-PROC responsible for WELCH collects the internal names of the objects which fulfill the stated conditions, eventually outputting the DEEP expression (21) which represents their conjunction.

```
(21)  (T: AND (T: (FOR: (Q: SOFA3) X31) T)
              (T: AND (T: (FOR: (Q: SESSEL1) X31) T)
                      (T: (FOR: (Q: SESSEL5) X31) T)))
```

If the system had any reason to generate a syntactically complete answer, it would substitute (21) for the corresponding structure in (20) and verbalize the entire structure, but we will assume that it simply passes (21) to NORMALIZE-1, which returns the SURF structure (22), and then calls the ATN-based generator to verbalize this

```
(22)  (T: AND SOFA3 (T: AND SESSEL1 SESSEL5))
```

structure. The generator calls the NP-generation component as a subroutine when it encounters the internal names of the three objects.

If any of the three objects has already been mentioned during the dialogue, it will be described with a definite noun phrase; we will assume this not to be the case, so that indefinite descriptions are appropriate. Noticing that two of the descriptions returned by the NP-generator are identical (*'E- SESSEL'*), the ATN-based generator combines them before outputting the canonical string (23).

```
(23)  (E- SOFA 2 SESSEL)
```

The last component in the generation process is the *Surface Transformations*, the complement to *Lexical Analysis*. Here inflectional suffixes which mark case and number are appended, punctuation marks and conjunctions are inserted, and numbers are replaced by words. The natural language response to (15) is therefore:

(24) EIN SOFA UND ZWEI SESSEL.

Before HAM-RPM will be able to respond appropriately in cases where the user's utterance is less transparent and a straightforward response would be less encouraging, much work must be devoted to enabling it to construct and make use of an explicit model of its dialogue partner. But we believe that the representation language and associated processes described here have sufficient expressive power and generality to serve as an adequate foundation for these further developments. (See v.HAHN et al. 1980 for a detailed description of HAM-RPM's processing phases, including those which were not involved in this example, e.g., the handling of pronouns, ellipsis and follow-up questions.)

4. Technical Data

A noncompiled version of HAM-RPM is running under the TOPS10 Operating system on the DECsystem 1070 (PDP-10) of the Fachbereich für Informatik at the University of Hamburg. Compromising approximately 600 LISP/FUZZY procedures, the current version requires from one to fifteen seconds for a response. The ATTACH package (Jameson 1980) was developed as a piece of auxiliary system software for HAM-RPM to allow direct access to programs and data on secondary storage. The complete system, which occupies at present 150k of 36-bit words thus only needs to be loaded when all components are being used and speed is important. The system of demand fetching provided by the

ATTACH package makes it possible for records in the assertional data base, the lexica, and the ATN grammars to be loaded into core only when required. ATTACH permits to interface HAM-RPM to large data bases which are written in nearly arbitrary formats, which needn't conform to LISP syntax. An important prerequisite for the application of a version of HAM-RPM as an intelligent natural language interface to nonlinguistic AI systems and to documentation or information systems is thus fulfilled.

Acknowledgement

This research is currently being supported by the Deutsche Forschungsgemeinschaft (DFG) under contract Ha1026/2.

References

BOBROW, D.G., KAPLAN, R.M., KAY, M., NORMAN, D.A., THOMPSON, H., WINOGRAD, T. (1977): GUS - A frame-driven dialog system. In: Artificial Intelligence, 8, 1, 155-173

COHEN, P.R. (1978): On knowing what to say: Planning speech acts. Univ. of Toronto, Department of Computer Science, Technical Report No. 118

FININ, T.W. (1977): An interpreter and compiler for augmented transition networks. Thesis, Univ. of Illinois, Department of Computer Science

HABEL, CH., ROLLINGER, C-R., SCHMIDT, A. (1978): Eine semantische Repräsentationssprache zur Darstellung modaler Konzepte. Univ. Berlin, Fachbereich für Informatik, Technical Report SNR 6/78

v.HAHN, W., HOEPPNER, W., JAMESON, A., WAHLSTER, W. (1978): HAM-RPM: Natural Dialogues with an artificial partner. In: Proceedings of the AISB/GI Conference on Artificial Intelligence. Hamburg, 122-131

v.HAHN, W., HOEPPNER, W., JAMESON, A., WAHLSTER, W. (1980): The anatomy of the natural language dialogue system HAM-RPM. In: Bolc, L. (ed.): Natural language based computer systems. Munich: Hanser/Macmillan, 119-253

HENDRIX, G.G. (1976): Semantic aspects of translation. In: Walker, D.E. (ed.): Speech understanding research. Final technical Report, SRI, Menlo Park

HOEPPNER, W., JAMESON, A. (1979): Kooperatives Dialogverhalten im Simulationssystem HAM-RPM. In: Proceedings of the 4th Workshop on Artificial Intelligence. Bad Honnef, 21-31

JAMESON, A. (1980): ATTACH: A package for accessing LISP programs and data from disc. HAM-RPM Memo 12

LEFAIVRE, R.A. (1977): FUZZY reference manual. Rutgers University, Computer Science Department

RICH, E. (1979): Building and exploiting user models. Carnegie Mellon University, Computer Science Department, CMU-CS-79-119

SHAPIRO, S.C. (1979): Numerical quantifiers and their use in reasoning with negative information. In: Proceedings of the 6th International Joint Conference on Artificial Intelligence, Tokyo, 791-796

WAHLSTER, W., JAMESON, A., HOEPPNER, W. (1978): Glancing, referring and explaining in the dialogue system HAM-RPM. In: American Journal of Computational Linguistics, Microfiche 77, 53-67

WINOGRAD, T. (1976): Towards a procedural understanding of semantics. Stanford Artificial Intelligence Laboratory, Memo AIM 292

ZIFONUN, G. (1979): Formale Repräsentation natürlichsprachlicher Äußerungen. In: Kolvenbach, M., Lötscher, A., Lutz, H.D. (eds.): Künstliche Intelligenz und natürliche Sprache. Sprachverstehen und Problemlösen mit dem Computer. Tübingen: Narr, 93-134

A NATURAL LANGUAGE PROCESSING MODEL

by J-H. JAYEZ, P. LEVASSEUR, M. LISCOUET
(LIANA - Université de Nantes - FRANCE)

Our team is presently working on a Natural Language Processing (N.L.P.) System ; our objective is to achieve an automatic analysis of certain classes of phrases of the natural language ; we are concerned, then, with the noun phrases which are to be found in most languages ; our study will bear on the French language although the model we are submitting here could be applied to most natural languages.

The main idea of this research work is that, in order to set up an NLP system, one should start from the basic assumptions provided by today's linguists, in particular those of the transformationalist school of Z.S. Harris. According to that school, any sentence of the language should be analysed as a network of elementary sentences of the "subject - verb - complement" type, linked together by coreference.

Then, the system includes, besides a glossary of words :

- A collection of about 80 automatic analysis procedures combined with the body of noun phrase structures as may be observed in reality.
- A semantic data base whose task is to record all the meaningful elementary sentences within the context to be considered.

This system has been tested upon the nouns of the data used for invoicing by some 50 French firms located in one large region of the country.

The result of this study is that, if traditional syntax is unable, by itself, to grasp a natural language, semantics, as can be presently observed in a number of NLP models, is unable to achieve this goal either.

What our model proposes is to blend syntax and meaning at the deepest level one can possibly reach, i.e. at the most elementary level of the analysis.

Such is the conclusion that can be drawn from the findings of modern linguistics and it applies quite well to N.L.P. concrete cases as out experience shows.

We are currently trying to extend this method to the whole body of complex noun phrase structures, as may be found in the titles of scientific works (automatic documentation), in the requests to a data base, in scientific documents (automatic translation), etc...

In our view, an automatic language analysis is likely to succeed, considering those complex phrases, sentences or texts, only if a very deep and systematic linguistic study is carried out.

The programs we devised using the assembler language are available from the IBM 370/135 computer of the "Université de Nantes".

REFERENCE WORKS :

- GROSS M. "Sur quelques problèmes posés par les représentations formalisées de textes" in BORILLO M., VIRBEL J. (eds) "Analyse et validation dans l'étude des données textuelles". CNRS-Paris-1977- pp. 65-82.
- JAYEZ J-H. "Une approche de la compréhension par machine du langage naturel". Thèse d'Etat - Paris VII - 1979.
- JAYEZ J-H., LISCOUET M. "Un logiciel conversationnel de compréhension d'un sous-langage naturel" Proc. Cong. AFCET. Gif/Yvette - Nov. 1978 - pp. 385-395.
- SAGER N. "Natural Language Information Processing : the Automatic Conversion of Texts to a Structural Data Base". Adv. in Comp. 1978. Vol. 17 pp. 89-162.
- SALKOFF M. "Les principes d'un analyseur syntaxique du français". In Linguisticae Investigationes. Vol. 1 - 1977 - pp. 235-257.

Computergestützte Informationssysteme in der Materialwirtschaft

Joachim Griese, Universität Dortmund

Kurzfassung[1)]

In einer Übersicht wird über den derzeitigen Stand der konzeptionellen Möglichkeiten und des Einsatzes von computergestützten Informationssystemen für administrative, dispositive und planerische Entscheidungen in der Materialwirtschaft berichtet; hierbei wird auch die Verbindung zur Lagerorganisation einbezogen.

---

1) Die Langfassung erscheint in der Zeitschrift Informatik-Spektrum.

Den Hörern wird die schriftliche Fassung ausgehändigt.

ONLINE-SYSTEME IM FINANZ- UND RECHNUNGSWESEN

- Stand und Ergebnisse eines Anwendergesprächs -

Peter Stahlknecht, Berlin

1. Einleitung und Begriffsdefinitionen

Das Adjektiv "online" bezeichnet üblicherweise "Funktionseinheiten oder Prozesse, die in Verbindung mit einem DV-System stehen" (siehe etwa /18/). Eine RJE-Station arbeitet also auch "online", bekanntlich aber im Stapelbetrieb. Somit ist der Begriff "online" denkbar ungeeignet, die gegenwärtige Entwicklung bei den DV-Anwendungssystemen für das Finanz- und Rechnungswesen zu beschreiben, wenngleich er dort häufig und deswegen auch im Titel des vorliegenden Aufsatzes benutzt wird. Auf diesem Gebiet vollzieht sich nämlich

- entweder (bei schon vorhandenem DV-Einsatz, vorwiegend also in großen und mittleren Unternehmen) die Umstellung vom Stapel- auf den D i a l o g b e t r i e b
- oder (bei bisheriger manueller oder halbautomatischer Bearbeitung, vorwiegend also in kleinen Unternehmen) die direkte Einführung des Dialogbetriebs in Verbindung mit dem erstmaligen DV-Einsatz.

Dabei bedeutet Dialogbetrieb nach DIN 44300 /5/ den "Betrieb eines Rechensystems, bei dem zur Abwicklung einer Aufgabe Wechsel zwischen dem Stellen von Teilaufgaben und den Antworten darauf stattfinden können". Einfacher und verständlicher formuliert: Dialogbetrieb ist die ständige Kommunikation zwischen Mensch und Maschine.

Die Entwicklung zum Dialogbetrieb hat im Finanz- und Rechnungswesen vor vier bis fünf Jahren begonnen. Nicht dialogfähige Online-Systeme werden dagegen schon seit über zehn Jahren eingesetzt. Abbildung 1 zeigt am Beispiel "Buchung von Geschäftsvorfällen" die verschiedenen Betriebsarten und ihre Mischformen, die heute in der Praxis benutzt werden, beispielsweise

- Eingabe, Prüfung und Erstellung eines Fehlerprotokolls im Stapel, anschließend Korrektur (anhand des Protokolls) und Verarbeitung im Dialog oder
- Eingabe, Prüfung und Kontrolle im Dialog ("Dialogerfassung" /8/),

Verarbeitung aber (unter Verwendung einer Zwischendatei) anschließend im Stapel.

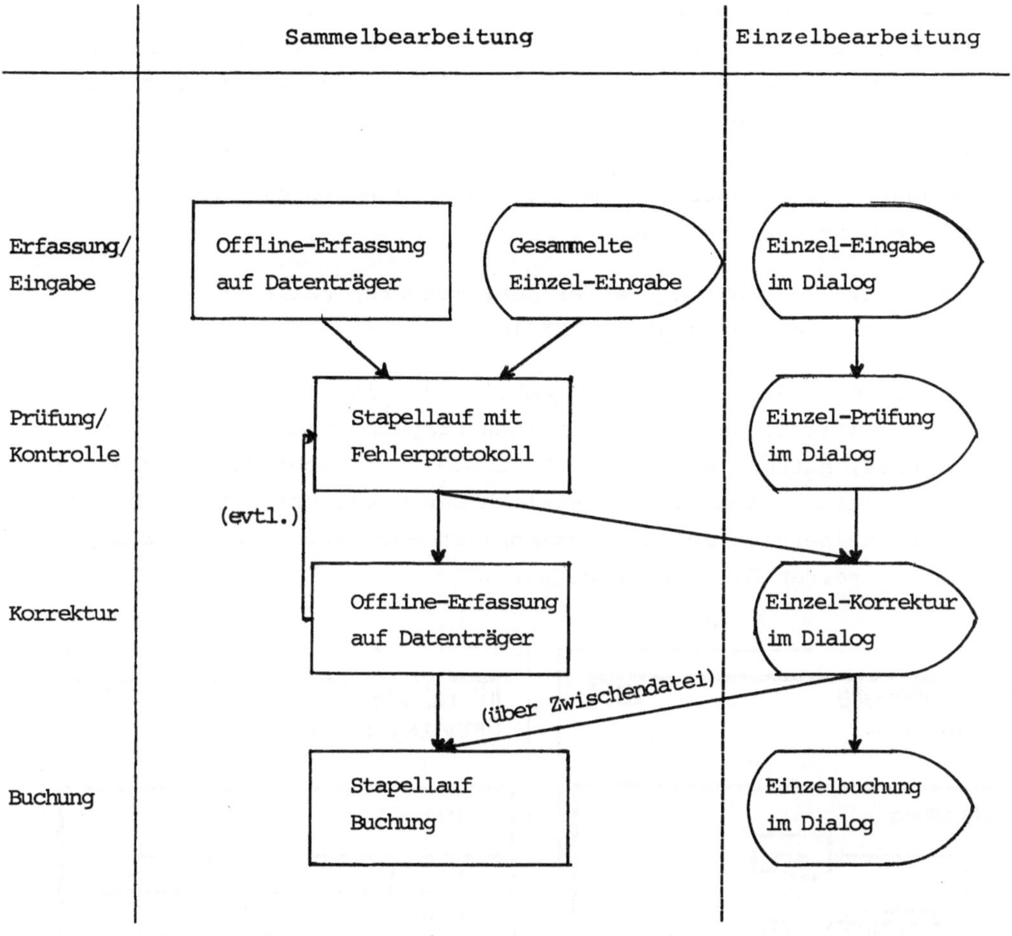

Abb. 1: Alternativen der Erfassung und Buchung von Geschäftsvorfällen im Bereich der Finanzbuchhaltung

Die von links nach rechts verlaufende Querverbindung in Abbildung 1 läßt sich wie folgt beschreiben /38/: Der Buchungsstoß wird im Stapelbetrieb über eine sequentielle Eingabe erfaßt. Fehlerhafte Sätze werden in Fehlerprotokollen ausgewiesen und in einer Datei zwischengespeichert. Zur Buchung gelangen die fehlerfreien Daten. Die falschen Daten können nachträglich im Dialogbetrieb korrigiert und dann verbucht werden.

Konsequenterweise müßte man im betrachteten Beispiel "Buchung von Geschäftsvorfällen" zwischen

- der "Sammelbearbeitung" aller oder mehrerer Fälle und
- der "Einzelbearbeitung" der Fälle

unterscheiden. Hält man sich in Abbildung 1 in allen Stufen so weit links wie möglich, hat man den reinen Stapelbetrieb, bleibt man immer ganz rechts, hat man den reinen Dialogbetrieb. Abbildung 2 und Abbildung 3 zeigen noch einmal deutlich den Unterschied zwischen dem reinen Stapelbetrieb der konventionellen Buchhaltung und der Buchhaltung im reinen Dialogbetrieb /12/.

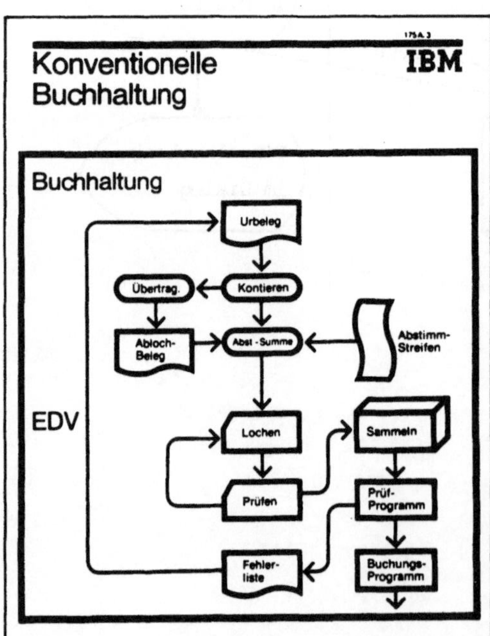

Abb.2: Erfassen und Buchen im Stapel /12/

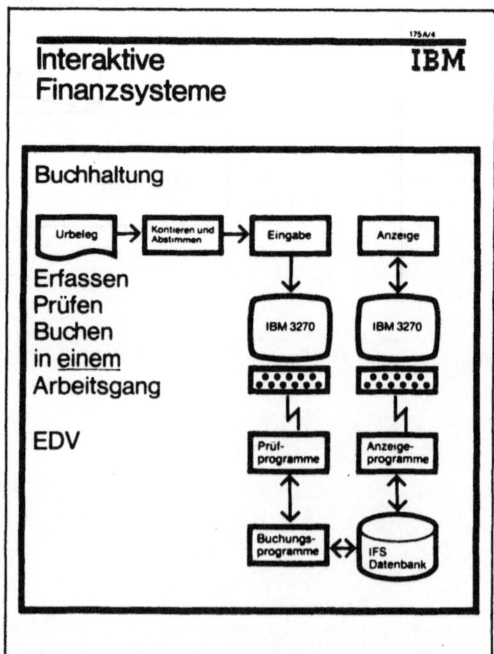

Abb.3: Erfassen und Buchen im Dialog /12/

Empirische Untersuchungen bei Anwendern von Finanzbuchhaltungssystemen haben ergeben, daß die Dialogbuchung der arbeitsteiligen Abwicklung Dialogerfassung und Stapelbuchung vorgezogen wird /9/.

Betrachtet man den Gesamtkomplex der Arbeitsabläufe des Finanz- und Rechnungswesens, so wird man in der Praxis immer eine wirtschaftliche Kombination aus Stapel- und Dialogbetrieb anstreben. Stapelbetrieb ist beispielsweise erforderlich

- für die Eingabe von Daten, die als Ergebnis einer vorangehenden Bearbeitung (z.B. Fakturierung) oder im Rahmen eines Datenaustauschs auf Datenträgern vorliegen (siehe Abbildung 4),
- für umfangreiche Auswertungen in Listenform, wie z.B. Buchungsjournale, Banküberischten usw. oder
- generell für die Erstellung von Monats- und Jahresabschlüssen sowie bei Nebenbuchhaltungen wie etwa der Anlagenrechnung.

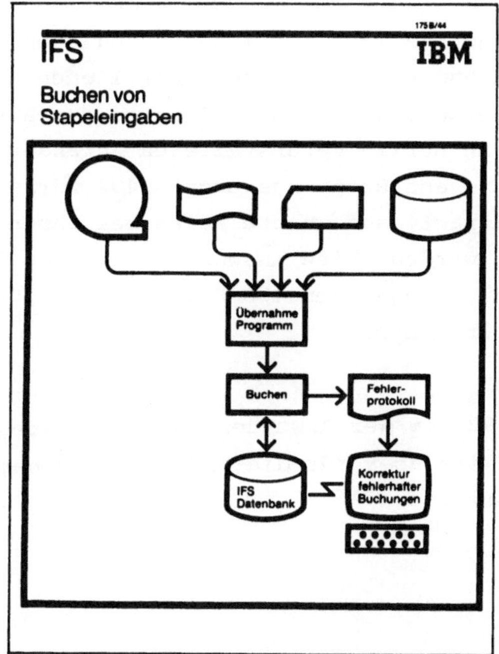

Abb.4: Eingabe im Stapel,
Verarbeitung im Dialog /12/

Bei der klassischen Offline-Erfassung auf Datenträger werden alle bekannten Varianten benutzt, beispielsweise

- bei der Eingabe die Datenfernübertragung mit Hilfe von Stapelstationen oder
- bei der Prüfung die Verlagerung von Rechenvorgängen auf das Datenerfassungsgerät bzw. auf das Datensammelsystem.

Ein Beispiel für einen Arbeitsablauf, in dem sich Stapel- und Dialogbetrieb sinnvoll ergänzen, ist die Rechnungsregulierung: Durch ein Stapelverarbeitungsprogramm werden Zahlungsvorschläge erstellt. Der Feinabgleich erfolgt im Dialog durch die Bearbeitung dieser Vorschläge. Nach der Freigabe der Zahlungsvorschläge führt ein weiteres Stapelverarbeitungsprogramm die notwendigen Buchungen durch und druckt die Zahlungsträger aus /3/. Für den Dialogbetrieb sind im Prinzip nur diejenigen Arbeitsschritte vorzusehen, bei denen eine sofortige Auskunftsbereitschaft notwendig ist /25/.

2. Zahlen zum heutigen Stand

Bei dem vom Fachausschuß 12 (Betriebliche Anwendungen) der Gesellschaft für Informatik und von der Wissenschaftlichen Kommission Betriebsinformatik im Verband der Hochschullehrer für Betriebswirtschaft im April 1980 in Berlin veranstalteten Anwendergespräch "Online-Systeme im Finanz- und Rechnungswesen" /40/ wurden die Teilnehmer schriftlich befragt, auf welche Weise bei ihnen die Daten erfaßt und eingegeben werden. Eine Auswertung der von den Teilnehmern aus der Industrie abgegebenen 150 Fragebogen zeigt das in Tabelle 1 dargestellte Ergebnis.

Danach wird also bei 92,0 % der Anwender noch mit Datenträgern gearbeitet, bei 44,7 % wird aber für die Dateneingabe bereits der Dialogbetrieb eingesetzt.

Verfahren	Anzahl	Prozent
Datenerfassung		
- über Buchungsautomat	8	5,3
- auf Lochkarte	38	25,3
- auf Magnetband	73	48,7
- auf Diskette	19	12,7
- über Datenträger insgesamt	138	92,0
Dateneingabe am Bildschirm		
- ohne Dialog	51	34,0
- im Dialog	67	44,7
- Online gesamt	118	78,7

Tabelle 1: Verteilung der Verfahren zur Datenerfassung und -eingabe (Mehrfachnennungen möglich)

Der ISIS-Software-Katalog I/80 / 27, S. 2002-2102/ enthält 278 Programme zur Finanzbuchhaltung (einschließlich Kontokorrent, Anlagenbuchhaltung und sonstige Nebenbuchhaltungen) und zur Unterstützung der Bilanzierung und Finanzplanung. Nach der dort vorgenommenen groben Unterscheidung in die Verarbeitungsformen

- Stapel,
- Dialog,
- Stapel/Dialog

beschränken sich 31 % der Programme auf reine Stapelverarbeitung, hingegen gestatten 64 % die Dialogverarbeitung (bei 5 % der Programme sind keine Angaben gemacht). Größer, nämlich über 73 %, ist der Anteil der dialogfähigen Programme, wenn man nur die 175 Programme der Finanzbuchhaltung mit Sachkonten, Debitoren und Kreditoren betrachtet (siehe Tabelle 2). Dieser Anteil läge noch höher, wenn im Katalog die entsprechenden Module aus den Programmsystemen zur Basisdatenverarbeitung von IBM (MAS), SIEMENS (SIMAS) und von anderen Hardware-Herstellern aufgeführt wären.

	Stapel	Dialog	Stapel/ Dialog	keine Angabe	gesamt
Gesamtbereich Finanzbuchhaltung	21	44	48	5	118
nur Sachkonten	3	6	9	-	18
nur Debitoren	8	2	8	3	21
nur Kreditoren	6	3	8	1	18
Finanzbuchhaltung	38	55	73	9	175
- in Prozent	21,7	31,4	41,7	5,2	100

Tabelle 2: Verarbeitungsformen der Programme zur Finanzbuchhaltung lt. ISIS-Katalog I/80 /27/

Zieht man zusätzlich die angegebenen Installationszahlen heran, so werden die Programme der Tabelle 2 insgesamt 6.917-mal eingesetzt, davon diejenigen mit ausschließlicher Stapelverarbeitung aber nur 720-mal; also in nur 10,4 % der Fälle.

Betrachtet man dagegen die Auswertung der schon erwähnten Befragung, so ergibt sich - wie Tabelle 3 zeigt - ein anderes Bild:

	Manuell	Buchungs-Automat	MDT	Stapel	Online	gesamt
Kontokorrent	0,6	8,2	4,7	55,5	31,0	100,0
Sachkonten	0,6	15,0	5,6	57,2	21,6	100,0
Kostenrechnung	1,9	1,9	1,9	86,5	7,8	100,0
Statistik	4,6	0,8	1,5	87,7	5,4	100,0
Planungsrechnung	9,4	0,9	2,8	81,2	5,7	100,0

Tabelle 3: DV-Verarbeitungsformen im Finanz- und Rechnungswesen (alle Angaben in %)

Demnach überwiegt noch deutlich die Stapelverarbeitung, auch in der Finanzbuchhaltung, und zwar beim Kontokorrent mit 55,5 %, bei den Sachkonten mit 57,2 %. Der Durchbruch zur Online-Verarbeitung bahnt sich mit deutlichem Vorsprung (31,0 %) bei den Personenkonten an.

Ein Widerspruch zu den Werten von Tabelle 2 besteht nicht, weil viele Anwender im Stapelbetrieb mit Anwendungsprogrammen arbeiten, die nicht mehr oder - als eigenständige Entwicklungen - überhaupt nicht im ISIS-Katalog stehen. Auch dort, wo bereits Online-Lösungen realisiert sind, arbeiten - nach einem weiteren Ergebnis der Befragung - 44,8 % mit selbst oder im Fremdauftrag erstellter Software, dagegen nur 16,0 % mit gekaufter Software. Allerdings konnten 39,2 % hierzu keine Angaben machen, wohl vorwiegend deswegen, weil nur 55,3 % der Beantworter aus den Bereichen Organisation und Datenverarbeitung kamen, jedoch 44,7 % (mit möglicherweise geringeren DV-Kenntnissen) aus dem Finanz- und Rechnungswesen oder aus anderen Fachabteilungen. Eine Auswertung nach der Unternehmensgröße ließen die Ergebnisse der Befragung leider nicht zu.

3. Einsatzziele

Bei den Einsatzzielen von Online-Systemen im Finanz- und Rechnungswesen kann man grob zwischen

- operativen Zielen und
- informativen Zielen

unterscheiden /41/. Operative Ziele bezwecken, den Ablauf der organisatorischen Funktionen

- Erfassung,
- Prüfung/Kontrolle und
- Verarbeitung

zu verbessern. Informative Ziele dienen der Informationsverbesserung, im wesentlichen durch Unterstützung der betriebswirtschaftlichen Funktionen

- Planung,
- Steuerung und
- Überwachung.

Bei der reinen Dialogverarbeitung werden diese Ziele wie folgt realisiert /28/, /38/:

- Beim Buchen finden sofort alle Prüfungen statt.
- Fehler werden direkt angezeigt und können sofort korrigiert werden. Jeder Buchungsvorgang ist daher nach Eingabe des Belegs endgültig abgeschlossen.

- Transportwege und -zeiten für Buchungsbelege und Datenträger zwischen Buchhaltung, Datenerfassung und Datenverarbeitung sowie zeitaufwendiges Suchen in Listen entfallen.

- Der gesamte Buchungsstoff befindet sich somit immer auf einem aktuellen Stand.

Man kann sie kurz wie folgt zusammenfassen /21/:

- Fehlerfreie Datenerfassung,
- Sofortverarbeitung,
- permanente Auskunftsbereitschaft.

Ob der Anwender diese Ziele überhaupt anstrebt, kann er sich mit Hilfe einiger grundlegenden Fragen selbst beantworten /45/:

- Wollen Sie die Zeitspanne zwischen Beleganfall und effektiver Verbuchung verkürzen ?

- Wollen Sie, daß ein Geschäftsvorgang einmal und nicht mehrfach bearbeitet wird ?

- Wollen Sie, daß an die Stelle von Fehlerprotokollen Möglichkeiten der Sofortkorrektur treten ?

- Wollen Sie die Soll-/Haben-Gleichheitsprüfung je Beleg und/oder je Abstimmkreis ?

- Wollen Sie eine absolute Belegfertigkeit ?

- Wollen Sie, daß Konten so aktuell sind, wie gerade gebucht wird ?

- Wollen Sie über Möglichkeiten verfügen, Ihr Buchwerk in Form strukturierter Berichte auszuwerten ?

Die Realisierung der operativen Ziele läßt sich häufig direkt als Rationalisierungserfolg messen, beispielsweise durch die Einsparung von Datenerfassungsplätzen und -geräten oder durch den Wegfall von Transportzeiten. REBLIN /32/, /33/ sieht darin überhaupt den Vorteil von Dialogsystemen und weist nach, daß sich der Arbeitsablauf von 19 Schritten bei der Stapelverarbeitung auf 5 Schritte bei der Dialogverarbeitung reduziert.

Schwieriger ist es, das Erreichen der informativen Ziele in Zahlen auszudrücken. Erhöhte Aktualität als eines der informativen Ziele ließe sich beispielsweise wie folgt quantifizieren /41/:

- Abbau von Forderungen durch zügigeres Buchen und ein strafferes Mahnwesen,
- Verhinderung von Verkaufsabschlüssen mit dubiosen Kunden durch schnellere Informationen über Zahlungsobligo, Limitüberschreitung usw. an den Vertrieb,
- bessere Ausnutzung von Skonti bei Lieferantenrechnungen.

Die Meinungen gehen auseinander, ob Aktualität und jederzeitige Auskunftsbereitschaft im Finanz- und Rechnungswesen - im Gegensatz etwa zur Fertigungssteuerung, Materialdisposition und Auftragsabwicklung - überhaupt die ausschlaggebenden Kriterien sind. Als Gegenargumente werden beispielsweise angeführt /33/:

- Lieferantenrechnungen, die tagelang durch den Betrieb wandern, bevor sie auf den Tisch des Buchhalters kommen,
- Lohnbelege, welche die Arbeiter zurückbehalten, um einen Akkordausgleich zu erzielen,
- Buchungsdaten aus Arbeitsgebieten wie Lohn-, Gehalts- und Provisionsabrechnung, die ohnehin erst im Folgemonat abgeschlossen werden können,
- die nur monatliche und damit meistens völlig ausreichende Berichterstattung.

Die Befragung der Teilnehmer des Anwendergesprächs zeigt aber in diesem Punkt ein anderes Bild (Tabelle 4):

Ziel	Relative Anzahl der Nennungen
Aktualität der Daten	95,3 %
Straffung von Arbeitsabläufen	86,0 %
Kosteneinsparung	78,0 %
Dezentralisierung der Verantwortung	58,7 %
Besserer Kundenservice	58,0 %
Humanisierung der Arbeitsplätze	50,0 %

Tabelle 4: Ziele von Online-Systemen aus Anwendersicht

Auf die Frage nach dem oberstenZiel steht die Aktualität der Daten ebenfalls an erster Stelle (Tabelle 5).

Ziel	Aufteilung der Nennungen für das oberste Ziel
Aktualität der Daten	40,1 %
Kosteneinsparung	36,7 %
Straffung von Arbeitsabläufen	17,4 %
Besserer Kundenservice	2,4 %
Dezentralisierung der Verantwortung	2,4 %
Humanisierung der Arbeitsplätze	0,5 %

Tabelle 5: Oberstes Ziel aus Anwendersicht

Bei einer Befragung von 17 Anwendern des Online-Finanzbuchhaltungssystems PHIDAS /30/ wurde bei der Frage nach geplanten Rationalisierungserfolgen die Aktualität der Daten ebenfalls mehrheitlich an erster Stelle genannt /9/.

Aus den divergierenden Ansichten ergibt sich für den DV-Organisator die Konsequenz, vor der Erarbeitung eines Soll-Vorschlags genau festzustellen, w e l c h e Daten aktuell sein sollen. Schon zwischen dem Kontokorrent und den Sachkonten und erst recht zwischen Finanzbuchhaltung und Betriebsabrechnung bestehen gravierende Unterschiede in den Anforderungen. Das haben schon die Mehrfachnennungen in Tabelle 1 gezeigt.

4. Einsatzgebiete

4.1. Finanzwesen

Das Angebot der heute verfügbaren Online-Systeme deckt praktisch den Aufgabenumfang des gesamten Finanz- und Rechnungswesens ab, wobei das Schwergewicht auf dem Gebiet der Finanzbuchhaltung liegt, weil dort - im Gegensatz zur Betriebsbuchhaltung -

- die Aufgaben weitgehend branchen- und firmenunabhängig zu formulieren sind und
- durch HGB, AO, EStR, Aktiengesetz, Kontenrahmen usw. von außen eine gewisse Standardisierung vorgegeben ist.

Will man den gesamten Anwendungsbereich der Finanzbuchhaltung strukturieren, so kann man

- entweder - wie in den meisten Programmbeschreibungen (siehe z.B. /14/ - von den buchhalterischen Arbeitsgebieten wie Debitoren-, Kreditoren-, Sachbuchhaltung ausgehen und ihnen die verarbeitungstechnischen Funktionen Buchen, Auskunft, Verarbeitung usw. zuordnen
- oder "Verarbeitungsgruppen" wie Erfassen, Prüfen, Verarbeiten, Ausgeben, Transfer, Löschen definieren und diesen betriebswirtschaftliche Funktionen zuweisen /36/.

Als sinnvolle Kombination beider Ansätze erweist sich - ausgehend von /21/ - folgende Gliederung:

(1) Buchen

- Zahlungseingänge,
- Retouren/Gutschriften,
- Ausgangsrechnungen,
- Eingangsrechnungen,
- Dauerbuchungen,
- Lastschriften,
- Buchungsdaten Sachkonten

(2) Bildschirmauskünfte

- Konten,
- offene Posten,
- Abstimmsummen,
- Skontobedingungen
- Fälligkeitsdatum,
- Tagesstatus,
- Finanzstatus

(3) Periodische Arbeiten

- Journale,
- Kontoauszüge,
- OP-Listen,
- Saldobestätigungen,
- Saldenlisten
- Umsatzsteuer-Voranmeldung,
- Außenstands-Listen,
- Verbindlichkeits-Listen

(4) Abschlußarbeiten

- Hauptabschlußübersicht,
- kurzfristige Erfolgsrechnung,
- Jahresabschluß,
- Bilanz,
- Gewinn- und Verlust-Rechnung

(5) Betriebswirtschaftliche Auswertungen

- Umsatzanalysen,
- OP-Analysen,
- Erfolgsanalysen,
- Soll/Ist-Vergleiche,
- Perioden-/Vorjahresvergleiche,
- Kennziffernrechnungen
- Liquiditätsbericht,
- Finanzstatus.

Hinzu kommen wahlweise weitere buchhalterische Funktionen wie

- automatisches Mahnwesen,
- automatischer Zahlungsverkehr.

Notwendige Voraussetzung ist die Stammdatenverwaltung, und zwar für

- Personen- und Sachkonten,
- Anschriften,
- Match-Codes,
- Bankverbindungen,
- Zahlungskonditionen,
- Buchungsarten,
- Texte,
- Fremdwährungen u.a.

Die hier aufgezählten Funktionen werden bei den angebotenen Softwaresystemen selbstverständlich nicht in einem einzigen Programm realisiert. Es gibt Aufteilungen

- in separate "Softwareprodukte" mit Schnittstellen zu vor- und nachgelagerten Arbeitsgebieten /38/,

- in "Anwendungen" wie Debitoren-, Kreditoren- und Sachbuchhaltung oder Statistik/Erfolgsanalyse /13/,

- in ein "Basispaket" und "Ergänzungsmodule" /30/,

- in ein "Basismodul" und "Erweiterungen" /21/ oder

- in eine "Grundausstattung" und eine "Zusatzausstattung" /37/.

Eine wichtige Frage ist immer:

- Wie wird die Verbindung zu vor- und nachgeschalteten bzw. benachbarten Arbeitsgebieten wie Auftragsbearbeitung, Fakturierung, Lohn-/Gehaltsabrechnung, Materialwirtschaft, Fertigungssteuerung usw. realisiert ?

Beispielsweise bei der Fakturierung:
Direktes Buchen auf Debitorenkonten oder Zwischenspeicherung über Datenträger ?

Aus der Vielzahl weiterer Fragen, die sich vor der Programmentwicklung oder -anschaffung stellen können, seien noch folgende erwähnt:

- Sind die Programme mandantenfähig, d.h. bieten sie die Möglichkeit, mehrere Buchhaltungen gleichzeitig nebeneinander zu führen ?

- Gibt es individuelle Branchenlösungen ?

  Der ISIS-Katalog enthält individuelle Programmpakete für Branchen wie Buch- und Zeitschriftenverlage, Bauwirtschaft, Wohnungswirtschaft, Architekturbüros, Getränkehandlungen, Dentallabors u.a.

- Sind die Programmpakete auch für ausländische Buchhaltungen verwendbar ?

  Diese Frage kann bei multinationalen Unternehmen eine wichtige Rolle spielen. Nach Angaben von Quantum Science /31/ sollen sich bei Kleincomputern im kommerziellen Bereich ("Small Business Systems") multinationale Anwendungspakete bisher nicht als erfolgreich erwiesen haben, ausgenommen COMET (Nixdorf) und MAS (IBM).

Als selbstverständlich sollte gelten, daß /23/

- die Ordnungsmäßigkeit der Buchführung gewährleistet ist,

- die Arbeit der Innenrevision unterstützt und erleichtert wird und

- ständige Ausdruckbereitschaft im Sinne des § 43 Abs. 4 HGB vorhanden ist.

Die durchschnittliche Anzahl von Installationen beträgt bei den im ISIS-Katalog genannten Programmprodukten

- zur Finanzbuchhaltung 39,5 Installationen/Paket,
- zur Unterstützung der <u>Bilanz- und Finanzplanung</u> dagegen nur 18,2 Installationen/Paket.

Wenn überhaupt eine computergestützte Bilanz- oder Finanzplanung durchgeführt wird, bevorzugen die Unternehmen offensichtlich individuelle Programmentwicklungen. Eine Veränderung ist denkbar, sobald das Dialogmodell "PLAN" zur integrierten Finanz-, Ergebnis- und Steuerplanung, das die DATEV seit 1979 allen ihr angeschlossenen Steuerberatern anbietet, in kleinen und mittleren Unternehmen stärkeren Eingang findet. Ein Pretest bei Steuerberatern hat bereits gezeigt, daß der Bearbeitungsaufwand bei Einsatz dieses Dialogmodells im Verhältnis zur manuellen Bearbeitung im Verhältnis 1 : 8 zurückgeht /43/.

4.2. Rechnungswesen

Im ISIS-Katalog I/80 /27, S. 2146-2186/ werden 109 Programme zur Kostenrechnung angeboten. Die Verarbeitungsformen sind in Tabelle 6 zusammengestellt.

	Anzahl	Anteil (%)
Stapel	66	60,6
Dialog	13	11,9
Stapel/Dialog	18	16,5
keine Angabe	12	11,0
Gesamt	109	100,0

Tabelle 6: Verarbeitungsformen der Programme zur Kostenrechnung lt. ISIS-Katalog I/80 /27/

Bei 8 Stapelverarbeitungsprogrammen ist die Aufnahme der Dialogverarbeitung geplant. Man kann unterstellen, daß die Programme, bei denen keine Angabe gemacht ist, nur die Stapelverarbeitung zulassen. Demnach sind 71,6 % aller Programme reine Stapelverarbeitungsprogramme. Nur 28,4 % sind dialogfähig. Davon sind mehrere Pakete noch gar nicht installiert. Diese Aussagen sind konform zu den Angaben in Tabelle 3, wonach bei computergestützter Kostenrechnung in 87,7 % der Fälle reine Stapelverarbeitung eingesetzt wird.

Vom praktischen Standpunkt her ist es fraglich, ob der Dialogfähigkeit bei der Kostenrechnung überhaupt die Bedeutung zukommt wie bei der Finanzbuchhaltung. Im Normalfall wird die Kostenrechnung auf der Basis von Ist-Kosten durchgeführt /30/. Die entsprechenden Daten sind aber bereits einmal - bei der Sachkontenführung, der Anlagenbuchführung oder der Lohn- und Gehaltsabrechnung - erfaßt und eingegeben worden. Sie stehen dann also schon in separaten Dateien bereit. Somit ist die Eingabe im Dialog die Ausnahme, aber nicht die Regel.

Die verschiedenen Teilgebiete der Kostenrechnung wie

- Kostenartenrechnung,
- Kostenstellenrechnung,
- Kostenträgerrechnung,

und die Methoden wie

- Vollkostenrechnung,
- Teilkostenrechnungen,
- Deckungsbeitragsrechnung usw.

haben das Ziel, Kosten nach verschiedenen Gesichtspunkten zuzuordnen, aufzuteilen und zu vergleichen. Solche Vergleiche sind häufig nur für den Monat als kleinste Zeiteinheit sinnvoll, zu ihrer Darstellung reichen im Stapel erstellte Listen aus. Somit ist in vielen Fällen ständige Auskunftsbereitschaft am Bildschirm nicht erforderlich. Es bleibt abzuwarten, wie ein hinsichtlich der Kostenrechnung universell angelegtes dialogfähiges Anwendungssystem wie SIMAS /37/ in der Praxis akzeptiert wird. In den Anwendungssystemen MAS /13/ und MAS II /15/ ist die Kostenrechnung überhaupt nicht enthalten.

Von Bedeutung können Aktualität der Daten und ständige Auskunftsbereitschaft bei der Vorkalkulation von Kostenträgern sein, insbesondere

- wenn kurzfristig neue Erzeugnisse zu fertigen sind oder bei Typen des Standardsortiments erhebliche Veränderungen auftreten /35/, und

- wenn die Rohstoffpreise starken Schwankungen unterliegen /24/.

Standard-Software ist für solche Anwendungen in den seltensten Fällen verwendbar, wohl aber systemnahe Software wie Datenbankverwaltungssysteme /35/ oder Matrizen-Bearbeitungs-Systeme /29/.

5. Realisierung

5.1. Softwareerstellung oder -auswahl

Bei der Frage nach der Anwendungssoftware für Online-Systeme im Finanz- und Rechnungswesen muß man klar zwischen Großunternehmen auf der einen sowie kleinen und mittleren Unternehmen auf der anderen Seite unterscheiden. Großunternehmen, die über langjährige DV-Erfahrungen im eigenen Hause verfügen, können zwischen

- der Individuallösung durch eigene Mitarbeiter oder Softwarehäuser,

- der Anmietung von Lizenzprogrammen des Herstellers der eigenen DV-Anlage und

- der Anschaffung von Markt-Software

wählen. Für die Auswahl von Markt-Software gelten die bekannten Kriterien /6/, /22/. Kleine und mittlere Unternehmen stehen dagegen vor dem Problem der Simultanauswahl von Hardware und Software /42/. Erschwerend ist für sie das fehlende "know how" in Datenverarbeitung.

Zur Beurteilung der Anwendungssoftware genügt es nicht, allein den in den vorangegangenen Abschnitten besprochenen betriebswirtschaftliche Leistungsumfang zu betrachten. Hierzu gehört auch eine Reihe DV-technischer Kriterien hinsichtlich Benutzerfreundlichkeit und Wartbarkeit der Programme. Als Beispiele seien stichwortartig erwähnt:

- Bildschirmroutinen (Maskensprachen),
- Dateiverwaltungsroutinen bzw. Datenbankprozessoren,
- Zugriff über Match-Codes,
- Prüf- und Kontrollverfahren,
- Fehlerbehandlungsroutinen,
- Restart (Wiederanlauf)-Verfahren
- Verwaltungsprogramme für Benutzertabellen,
- Auswertungsprozeduren,
- Berichtsgeneratoren.

Wird Standardsoftware angeschafft, ist für den Benutzer bei garantierter Softwarepflege durch den Anbieter die Programmiersprache von sekundärer Bedeutung. Im Bereich der Kleincomputer bzw. Basisdatenverarbeitungssysteme werden unter anderem verwendet:

- BASIC bei COMET (Nixdorf),
- RPG bei MAS (IBM),
- COBOL (mit Assembler-Unterprogrammen) bei SIMAS (SIEMENS).

Die Verwendung von maschinenorientierten Sprachen gilt als problematisch /20/.

Bei der Programmbeurteilung dürfen die Vorkehrungen zum Datenschutz nicht außer acht gelassen werden. Hierzu gehören gestaffelte Berechtigungscodes /44/, u.a.

- zur Anzeige bestimmter Konten,
- zur Bebuchung bestimmter Konten,
- zum Anlegen/Ändern bestimmter Konten,
- zur Benutzung bestimmter Programmfunktionen.

Versieht man alle eingegebenen Vorgänge mit dem Namen des Autors, Datum und Uhrzeit und speichert die Änderungen von Stammsätzen in Änderungsbelegen, die mit dem Stammsatz verknüpft sind /38/, erhält man eine Protokollierung im Sinne von Ziffer 7 der Anlage zu § 6, Abs. 1 BDSG.

5.2. Implementierung

Für die Implementierung von Online-Systemen im Finanz- und Rechnungswesen stehen verschiedene Typen von Checklisten zur Verfügung. Man kann unterscheiden zwischen Checklisten

- zur Grundsatzentscheidung zwischen Stapel- und Dialogverarbeitung,
- zur Beschreibung des Mengengerüsts und
- zur Programmdefinition und -generierung.

Checklisten zur Grundsatzentscheidung /45/ beinhalten im wesentlichen die schon in Abschnitt 3 aufgeführten Fragen. Ein Muster für eine Checkliste zur Ermittlung des Mengengerüsts zeigt Abbildung 5.

Die Eintragungen bilden die Basis für eine computergestützte Kapazitätsanalyse über die erforderliche Hardware.

Komfortable Checklistensysteme wie die "Auswahlbögen" zum System MAS /10/,/16/, /17/, das Implementierungs-Werkzeug CHICO zum System

1.0 Debitorenbereich

1.1 Anzahl Debitoren ....

1.2 Anzahl Ausgangsrechnungen pro Tag/ oder Fakturierlauf ....

1.3 Wenn Fakturierlauf nicht täglich, welcher Rhythmus ....

1.4 Ist/wird die Buchhaltung mit der Fakturierung integriert ....

1.5 Wieviel Erlöskonten (Gegenbuchungen) bei Rechnungsausgang ....

1.6 Um wieviel Sektoren muß der Debitoren-Stammsatz erweitert werden (Standard 2 Sektoren) ....

1.7 Anzahl der Eingangszahlungen Tag/Monat ....

1.8 Nach wieviel Tagen werden die Rechnungen durchschnittlich ausgeglichen ....

1.9 Wieviele Zahlungen werden durchschnittlich pro Rechnung geleistet (Abschlagszahlungen) ....

1.10 Sollen für Debitoren Einzelposten geführt werden (ausgeglichene OP's werden nicht gelöscht) ....

1.11 Wie groß ist der OP-Bestand ....

1.12 Mahnrhythmus nach Fälligkeit (in Tagen) ....

NICHTZUTREFFENDES STREICHEN!

Abbildung 5: Checkliste zur Beschreibung des Mengengerüsts /19/

COMET /1/, /26/ oder der SIMAS-Gesamtübersetzer /39/ dienen primär zur Festlegung der Programmbeschreibung, darüberhinaus bilden sie die Basis für die Programmgenerierung.

Solche Checklistensysteme werden wie folgt angewandt /10/:

- Zunächst werden die gewünschten Programmfunktionen anhand eines Fragebogens festgelegt (siehe Abbildung 6).
- Dann erfolgen maschinelle Prüfungen auf Logik und Hardware-Realisierbarkeit. Gegebenenfalls sind Korrekturen vorzunehmen.
- Abschließend wird das gesamte Programm maschinell generiert ("customized").

Die maschinelle Prüfung und Generierung erfolgt entweder auf dem für den späteren Einsatz vorgesehenen Computer selbst (CHICO) oder auf Großanlagen (MAS). Bei CHICO kann der Fragebogen auch am Bildschirm abgearbeitet werden.

Man kann die Checklisten zur Programmdefinition noch weiter spezifizieren /36/ in Checklisten

- für das Verarbeitungssystem,
- für das Dateiensystem,
- für die Projektabwicklung.

Ob damit der Anwender in Klein- und Mittelbetrieben, auf den diese Programmpakete zugeschnitten sind, noch etwas anzufangen weiß, ist anzuzweifeln.

5.3. Personelle Aspekte

Das Kriterium "Humanisierung der Arbeitsplätze" wurde von den Teilnehmern des Anwendergesprächs mehrheitlich erst

- an 4. Stelle (17,3 % der Nennungen),
- an 5. Stelle (28,0 % der Nennungen) oder
- an 6. Stelle (33,3 % der Nennungen)

eingestuft. Das liegt nicht daran, daß dieser Frage keine Bedeutung beigemessen wird, sondern in der vorherrschenden Einstellung, sie

Auswahlbogen für die Fertigungsindustrie Seite 15	2457

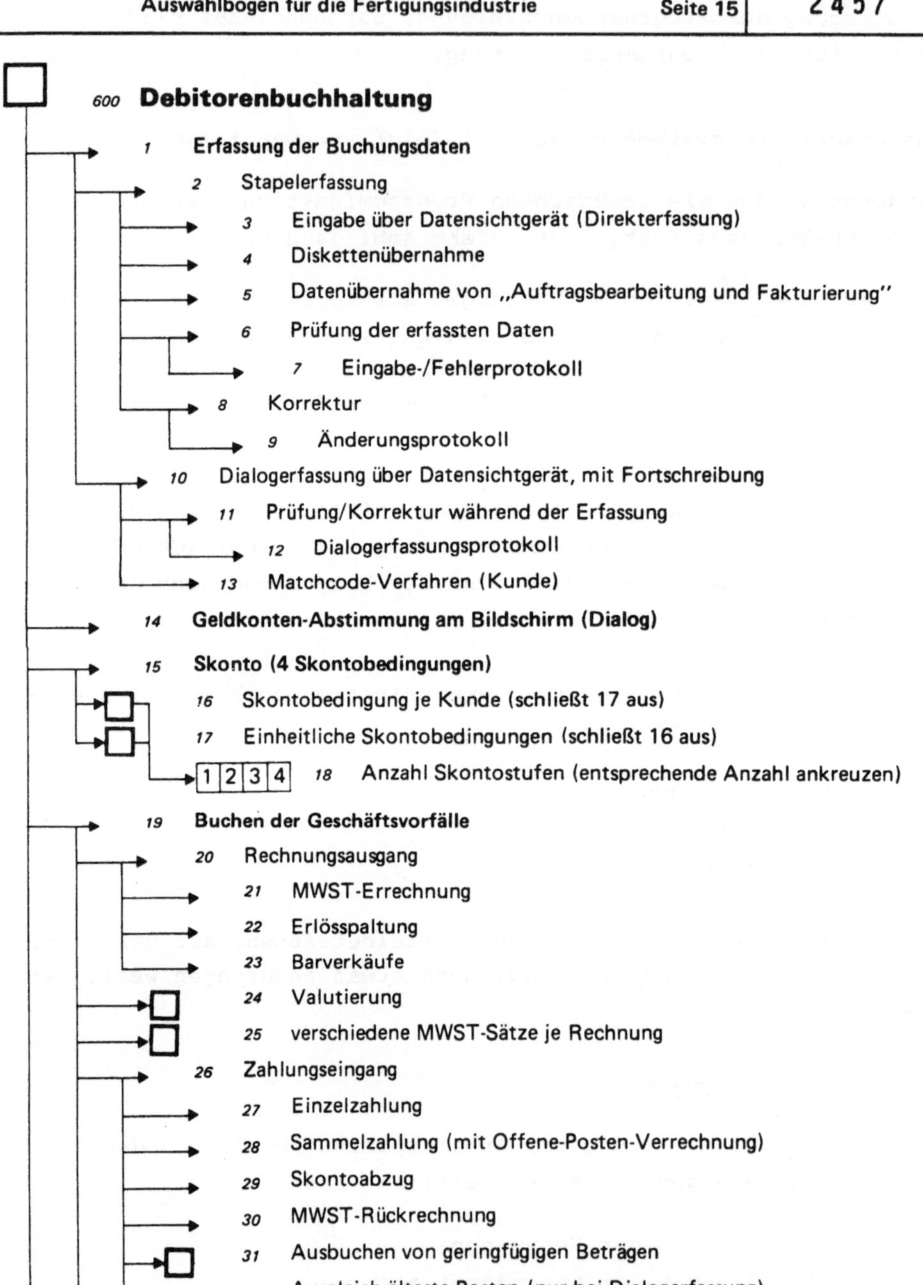

☐ Gewünschte Funktion hier ankreuzen

→ Bedeutet: Basisfunktion grundsätzlich Bestandteil bei Auswahl der jeweiligen Anwendung bzw. Funktion.

● Bedeutet: Überschrift für folgende Funktionen.

KA=F3401

Abbildung 6: Checkliste zur Programmdefinition /10/

nicht überzubewerten. Grundsätzlich wurde von den Anwendern betont, daß die Mitarbeiter im Finanz- und Rechnungswesen den Online-Anwendungen positiv gegenüberstehen und sich jetzt viel enger mit der Datenverarbeitung verbunden fühlen /35/. Im einzelnen wurde festgestellt:

- Der Bildschirm entspricht der früheren Kontokarte des Buchhalters, so daß Umstell- und Eingewöhnungsprobleme entfallen /7/.

- Die Mitarbeiter haben endlich wieder einen abgeschlossenen Arbeitsprozeß, die Einzelverarbeitung verschwindet nicht in der Anonymität /28/.

- Die Motivation der Mitarbeiter wird umso größer, je mehr Funktionen am Terminal beherrscht werden /2/.

- Es gibt keine Beschäftigten, die ausschließlich am Bildschirm arbeiten. Die Erfassung dauert selten länger als 2 bis 3 Stunden täglich. Der Abruf von Auskünften verteilt sich über den ganzen Arbeitstag /11/.

- An den Bildschirmen muß Fachpersonal eingesetzt werden. Die Arbeiten können nicht Datentypistinnen übertragen werden. Somit erfolgt keine Dequalifizierung von Arbeitsplätzen /34/.

- Durch die Fehlerkorrektur im Bildschirm-Dialog entfällt die Notwendigkeit, Fehlerlisten zu erstellen und damit möglicherweise Schwächen einzelner Mitarbeiter schriftlich zu dokumentieren /41/.

Über die Einführung von Online-Systemen im Finanz- und Rechnungswesen werden Mitbestimmungsrechte geltend gemacht. Die IG Metall faßt die Einführung eines Finanzbuchhaltungssystems wie SAFIR sogar als Betriebsänderung im Sinne des § 111 BetrVG (Ziffer 5: Einführung grundlegend neuer Arbeitsmethoden und Fertigungsverfahren) auf und verlangt eine entsprechende Mitbestimmung. Nach Ansicht der Landesvereinigung der industriellen Arbeitgeberverbände Nordrhein-Westfalen fehlt aber solchen Systemen jeder Bezug zur Mitbestimmung /4/.

Die Beurteilung der Antwortzeiten ist abhängig vom "Persönlichkeitsbild" des Mitarbeiters. Mehr als 10 Sekunden wurden als lästig und teilweise als "frustrierend" empfunden /11/.

6. Ausblick

Zu der Frage, ob die Einführung der Online-Verarbeitung im Finanz- und Rechnungswesen geplant sei, wurde in rd. 75 % der Antworten Stellung genommen. Davon gaben an:

- Umstellung in Vorbereitung 40,9 %
- Umstellung mittelfristig geplant 27,7 %
- Umstellung langfristig geplant 6,3 %

Diese Zahlen zeigen deutlich den Trend an und bedürfen keines Kommentars.

Selbstverständlich werden nicht nur Vorteile erwartet. Dazu äußerten sich 48,7 %. Nachteile werden gesehen

- in der Abhängigkeit vom Computer und in der technischen Anfälligkeit der Systeme (13,7 %),
- in den Kosten (7,7 %),
- für das Personal (5,3 %).

17,8 % geben ausdrücklich "keine Nachteile" an.

Zu Schwierigkeiten in der Umstellungsphase wurde von 54 % der Beantworter eine Meinung geäußert. Schwierigkeiten werden erwartet

- im personellen Bereich,
- mit der Hard- und Software,
- im organisatorischen Ablauf.

Wenngleich solche Aussagen mit Vorsicht zu behandeln sind, so läßt sich doch festhalten:

Die Entwicklung zu Online-Systemen im Finanz- und Rechnungswesen ist nicht aufzuhalten. Sie wird sich aber vorerst auf einen Einsatz im engeren Bereich der Finanzbuchhaltung konzentrieren.

7. Literatur

/1/ ADENA, K.: Einsatzmöglichkeiten und Wirtschaftlichkeit von checklistenorientierter Dialog-Software, dargestellt am Software-System Nixdorf COMET, in /40/, S. 72-82, 1980

/2/ BERNSHAUSEN, E.: Einsatz der Dialogbuchhaltung UNIREF/90 in der SIEMAG Rechenzentrum GmbH, in /40/, S. 507-524, 1980

/3/ BÖHM, E.: IBM Online-Buchhaltung IFS, in /40/, S. 83-106, 1980

/4/ DIEBOLD Deutschland: Szenen der Polarisierung, Diebold Management Report, S. 10-17, Februar/März 1980

/5/ DIN Deutsches Institut für Normung e.V. (Hrsg.): Informationsverarbeitung 1, 4. Auflage, Berlin/Köln 1978

/6/ FRANK, J.: Standard-Software, Köln-Braunsfeld 1977

/7/ GILLICH, E.: Buchhaltung im Dialog - eine Voraussetzung für mehr Wirtschaftlichkeit und Aktualität im Rechnungswesen, in /40/, S. 107-137, 1980

/8/ GRIESE, J.: Vergleich des Leistungsumfangs von Softwaresystemen zur Online-Finanzbuchhaltung, in /40/, S. 229-239, 1980

/9/ GRIESE, J., HÜTTENHAIN, T., WILMS, K.: Empirische Untersuchungen bei Anwendern von Finanzbuchhaltungssystemen, in /40/, S. 56-71, 1980

/10/ HASSELN, W. VON, Das "Modulare-Anwendungs-System" (MAS) - ein Konzept zur kostengünstigen Anwendungsprogrammierung, in Nagel, K. (Hrsg.): DV Aktuell 1980, S. 97-105, München/Wien 1980

/11/ HEISEL, W.: Online-orientiertes Grundsatzverfahren des Kienzle-Systems 9066 für das Finanz- und Rechnungswesen, in /40/, S. 138-154, 1980

/12/ IBM Deutschland: Interaktive Finanzsysteme - Anwendungsbeschreibung, Form GE 12-1408, 1976

/13/ IBM Deutschland: Modulares Anwendungs-System MAS, Anwendungen für die Fertigungsindustrie, Informationsbroschüre, Form P 12-3061, 1978

/14/ IBM Deutschland: Modulares-Anwendungs-System MAS, Finanzbuchhaltung, Form GE 12-1439, 1978

/15/ IBM Deutschland: IBM System /38, Modulares Anwendungssystem MAS II, Integriertes Buchhaltungssystem, Form GE12-3500, 1979

/16/ IBM Deutschland: Auswahlbogen für den Großhandel, Form ZX12-1417, 1978

/17/ IBM Deutschland: Auswahlbogen für die Fertigungsindustrie, Form ZX12-1418, 1978

/18/ IBM Deutschland (Hrsg.): Englisch/Deutsch, Fachausdrücke der Text- und Datenverarbeitung, Stuttgart 1978

/19/ ICL Deutschland: ICL System TEN, Standard-Finanzbuchhaltung SFB 010, 1977

/20/ IPSEN, F.: Praktischer Einsatz von Buchhaltungs- und Betriebsabrechnungssystemen im Dialogbetrieb für Klein- und Mittelbetriebe, in /40/, S. 155-169, 1980

/21/ KIENZLE Apparate: Finanzbuchhaltung CARAT 9055, DV 89 Programmbeschreibung, o.J.

/22/ KIRSCH, W., BÖRSIG, C., ENGLERT, G.: Standardisierte Anwendungssoftware in der Praxis, Berlin 1979

/23/ KRAUS, E.: Standardsoftware für das Rechnungswesen, Realzeitbuchhaltung mit SAFIR, Siemens Schriftenreihe "data praxis", Bestell-Nr. D 15/5747-01, o.J.

/24/ LANGER, H.: AKIS - Ein Kosteninformationssystem der HOECHST AG, in /40/, S. 416-430, 1980

/25/ NCR: Integriertes Finanzbuchhaltungs-Online-System NCR IFOS, 1978

/26/ NIXDORF Computer: Standard-Software Nixdorf COMET, Implementations-Werkzeuge M5, Bestell-Nr. 34052.00.6.93, 1979

/27/ NOMINA Information Services (Hrsg.): ISIS Software Report 11, Band 1.1, München 1980

/28/ OBERMÜLLER, H.: Erfahrungen beim Einsatz des Systems SAFIR bei der Südmilch AG, in /40/, S. 286-297, 1980

/29/ PEINZE, K.: Online-Vorkalkulation kaltgewalzter Bänder, in /40/, S. 442-456, 1980

/30/ PHILIPS DATA SYSTEMS: Programmpaket PHIDAS 400, o.J.

/31/ QUANTUM SCIENCE CORPORATION: MAPTEK Europe, Conference Report 1979, Volume IV, New York/London/Tokio 1979

/32/ REBLIN, E.: Batch- oder Dialogsysteme im Rechnungswesen, in HEILMANN, H. (Hrsg.): 6. Jahrbuch der EDV, S.191-206, Stuttgart/Wiesbaden 1977

/33/ REBLIN, E.: Stapel- oder Dialogverarbeitung im Rechnungswesen, in /40/, S. 43-55, 1980

/34/ SCHARF, H.: Das Rechnungswesen als Teil des Dialog Informations-Systems der Nürnberger Hercules Werke GmbH, in /40/, S. 320-328, 1980

/35/ SCHNEIDER, R.: Online-Kalkulation (Erzeugniskostenermittlung) und Kostenträgerrechnung bei SKF, in /40/, S. 392-405, 1980

/36/ SIEMENS: Basis-Datensystem 6.000, SIMAS-Datentechnik/SEVAG, Systembeschreibung, Bestell-Nr. D41/1204-01, o.J.

/37/ SIEMENS: Basis-Datensystem 6.000, SIMAS Systembaustein Rechnungswesen, Systembeschreibung, Bestell-Nr. D41/1159-01, o.J.

/38/ SIEMENS: Softwareprodukt SAFIR 2, Kurzbeschreibung, Bestell-Nr. D15/5992-01, 1980

/39/ SPLETTSTÖSSER, D., KREFFT, H.: Software-Paket SIMAS, data report 14, Heft 2, S. 30-35, 1979

/40/ STAHLKNECHT, P. (Hrsg.): Online-Systeme im Finanz- und Rechnungswesen, Informatik-Fachbericht Nr. 28, Berlin/Heidelberg/New York 1980

/41/ STAHLKNECHT, P.: Merkmale des Einsatzes von Online-Systemen im Finanz- und Rechnungswesen, in /40/, S. 32-42, 1980

/42/ STAHLKNECHT, P./NORDHAUSS, R.: Methodik der Hardware- und Software-Auswahl bei Einführung der EDV in einem Fachverlag, München/Wien 1980

/43/ SZYPERSKI, N./LUTHER, F.: FIESTA und PLAN - Dialogmodelle des BIFOA und der DATEV zur integrierten Finanz-, Ergebnis- und Steuerplanung kleiner Unternehmen, in /40/, S. 220-228, 1980

/44/ WINTER, A.: Computer am Arbeitsplatz Finanzbuchhaltung,in Nagel, K. (Hrsg.): DV Aktuell 1978, S. 95-102, München/ Wien 1978

/45/ WINTER, A.: Checkliste zur Einführung, zum Einsatz und laufenden Betrieb von Datensichtstationen für Zwecke der Finanzbuchhaltung,in Nagel, K. (Hrsg.): DV Aktuell 1978, S. 168-175, München/Wien 1978

RECHNERGESTÜTZTE INFORMATIONS- UND DISPOSITIONSSYSTEME FÜR DEN PERSONALBEREICH

Dietrich Seibt
Wilhelm Mülder
(Universität Essen)

1. Veränderungen des Informationsbedarfs und des Bedarfs an Informationsverarbeitungsleistungen im Personalbereich

2. Definitionen für Personalinformationssysteme (PIS), Personaldispositionssysteme(PDS) und Personalplanungssysteme(PPS)

3. Deduktiv abgeleitete Typen und Entwicklungsstufen von PIS, PDS und PPS

4. Ergebnisse empirischer Erhebungen zum aktuellen Stand der Rechner-Unterstützung im Personalbereich

5. Aktuelle Probleme der Praxis bei der Entwicklung von rechnergestützten PIS und PDS

6. Unterschiedliche Ausgangspositionen und Konzeptionen für den Aufbau von PIS und PDS

7. Software- Angebot und Software-Nachfrage

8. Entwicklungstendenzen in der Praxis

9. Literaturverzeichnis

(Der Beitrag wird aufgrund seines Umfangs separat veröffentlicht)

Den Hörern wird die schriftliche Fassung ausgehändigt.

VERTEILTE DATENVERARBEITUNG UND BILDSCHIRMTEXT

K. Wenke, M. Brinkmann AG, Bremen

Im Zusammenhang mit der stürmischen Weiterentwicklung von Computer- und Kommunikationstechnik ist jedes Unternehmen bestrebt, seinen Mitarbeitern Computerleistungen am Arbeitsplatz zur Verfügung zu stellen und ihnen darüber hinaus Kommunikationsmöglichkeiten mit anderen Sachbearbeitern zu bieten.

Es geht dabei um die systematische Verbesserung der informationstechnischen Infrastruktur eines Unternehmens und der Kommunikation mit seiner Umwelt.

Die Qualität der informationstechnischen Infrastruktur hängt von verschiedenen Faktoren ab. Bei einem hohen Anteil von Mitarbeitern mit leichtem Zugang zu dem Kommunikationssystem kann man von einer hohen Dichte des Kommunikationssystems sprechen. Wenn durch das Kommunikationssystem verschiedene Unternehmensteile an geografisch verschiedenen Orten miteinander verbunden werden, wenn gar mit Kunden oder mit anderen Firmen kommuniziert werden kann, sollte man von einer großen Reichweite des Kommunikationssystems sprechen. Das Übertragungsnetz ist Träger verschiedener Dienste wie bestimmter analytischer Auswertungs- oder Textverarbeitungsmöglichkeiten. Neben Dichte und Reichweite hängt die Qualität eines Kommunikationssystems also auch erheblich von den angebotenen Diensten ab.

Mindestens vier Faktoren bestimmen die Güte der informationstechnischen Infrastruktur eines Unternehmens

1. Die Dichte des Kommunikationssystems.
2. Die Reichweite des Kommunikationssystems.
3. Die Qualität der Dienste, die im Kommunikationssystem abgewickelt werden. (Prozesse)
4. Die Qualität der Informationsbasen. (Daten)

Eine große Rolle spielen auch die Daten, die zentral gehalten werden und dem Benutzer leicht zugänglich sind. Die Datenhaltung ist deshalb ebenfalls ein ausschlaggebender Faktor.

Die betriebsinternen Kommunikationsbedürfnisse eines Markenartikelbestellers ergeben sich aus der Beschäftigungsstruktur. Von den Beschäftigten üben etwa 20 % eine vorwiegend informationsbezogene Tätigkeit aus. Von diesem sicherlich nicht eindeutig abgrenzbaren Mitarbeiterkreis haben etwa 20 - 25 % schon direkten Zugang zu Datenendgeräten; sie sind gewissermaßen "Paßwortbesitzer".

Bei der organisatorischen Entwicklung wird in dem vorliegenden Fall das Ziel verfolgt, eine weitere Arbeitsteilung und Spezialisierung zu vermeiden, also keine reinen Bildschirmarbeitsplätze zu schaffen. Das Datenendgerät soll in der Regel dem Sachbearbeiter ähnlich wie das Telefon als ein vielseitiges Hilfsmittel seiner Tätigkeit dienen. Es ist das erklärte organisatorische Ziel, durch Integration von Teilaufgaben das Verständnis für die Zusammenhänge und das Verantwortungsbewußtsein des einzelnen Mitarbeiters zu stärken.

Als technische Hilfsmittel stehen vielfältige Geräte zur Verfügung wie Schreibmaschine, Datenendgeräte, eine Fernsprechnebenstellenanlage mit 1000 Anschlüssen.

Bemerkenswert ist, daß das Terminal dabei ist, die Schreibmaschine von ihrem Spitzenplatz als meistverbreitete Büromaschine zu verdrängen. Die dezentral aufgestellten Drucker übertreffen in ihrer Kapazität die zentrale Druckleistung. Es wird deshalb für möglich gehalten, in wenigen Jahren den zentralen Ausdruck im Rechenzentrum bis auf unbedeutende Reste abzubauen. Entsprechend ist die Datenerfassung weitgehend dezentralisiert. In die Planung des Kommunikationssystems muß auch das Telefonnetz einbezogen werden. Im vorliegenden Fall lösen modernste datentransparente Telefonvermittlungen noch in diesem Jahr die alten Systeme ab. Es wird immer fragwürdiger, bei den Übertragungssystemen zwischen Datenübertragung, Textübermittlung und Sprachkommunikation zu differenzieren. Die Unterschiede betreffen hauptsächlich die Endgeräte.

Eine einmal erreichte hohe Dichte des betriebsinternen Kommunikationsnetzes begünstigt die Installation weiterer Datenendgeräte, da jeder weitere Teilnehmer bereits viele Partner vorfindet, mit denen er Informationen austauschen kann. Aus einem Terminalanschluß an eine Rechenanlage wird ein Kommunikationssystem, wenn die Anzahl Teilnehmer genügend groß ist, um miteinander zu kommunizieren. Man darf davon ausgehen, daß ein Kommunikationssystem eine "kritische Masse von Teilnehmern" erfordert. Da die Kommunikation unter den Teilnehmern in der Regel nicht direkt sondern mittels einer dazwischen geschalteten Datenbank erfolgt, sind Umfang und Vielfalt der Datenbank von großer Bedeutung. Im vorliegenden Fall sind bereits 40 % aller Zugriffe auf Magnetplattenspeicher Datenbankzugriffe.

Bei einmal erreichter hoher Dichte des Kommunikationssystems ist man dann bestrebt, seine Qualität durch Erhöhung der Reichweite und eine Ausweitung der angebotenen Dienste zu verbessern. Aus dem Ortsverkehr wird Fernverkehr. Dabei kann man zunächst mit den Mitteln der klassischen Datenverarbeitung nur eine Verbindung mit größeren Betriebsstätten, Außenlägern und Verkaufsbüros herstellen.

Ein Markenartikelunternehmen muß einen besonders großen Wert auf die Kommunikation mit seinen Kunden und Verbrauchern legen. Die Nahtstelle zwischen betriebsinternen und unternehmensexternen Kommunikationsbedürfnissen sind die Mitarbeiter des Außendienstes, die als Mittler zwischen Unternehmer und Kundschaft fungieren. Eine typische Struktur kann folgendes

Aussehen haben.

Die unternehmensexternen Kommunikationsbedürfnisse entsprechen der Marktstruktur

400	Außendienstmitarbeiter
10.000	direkt beziehende Kunden
100.000	betreute Vertriebsstellen
15.000.000	Verbraucher

Typisch für die externen Kommunikationsbedürfnisse ist die mit der "Entfernung" vom Unternehmen zunehmende Anzahl der Teilnehmer. Daraus folgt, daß eine Ausweitung der Reichweite des Kommunkationssystems durch Einbeziehung der externen Kommunikationsbedürfnisse sehr große Anforderungen an die Wirtschaftlichkeit der Lösung stellt.

Die wichtigsten Kommunikationsvorgänge sind in der folgenden Übersicht schematisch dargestellt. Die Auslieferungsorganisation übermittelt den direkt beziehenden Kunden Bestellvorschläge und empfängt die Aufträge. Bestellvorschlag ist ein Angebot, das für einen speziellen Kunden und einen speziellen Zeitpunkt ausgearbeitet wurde. Im Gegenzug erhält der Kunde dann später die Rechnung.

Schematische Darstellung der wichtigsten Kommunikationsvorgänge

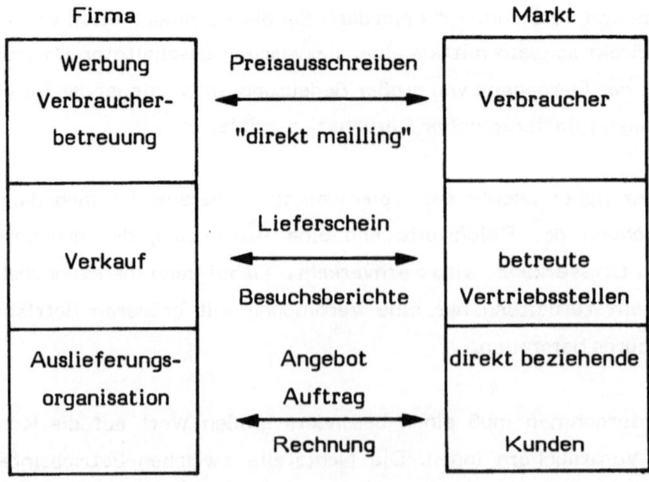

Die Vertreter, denen die Absatzförderung bei den betreuten Vertriebsstellen obliegt, liefern u. a. Besuchsberichte, die der Marktbeobachtung dienen. Sie führen verschiedene Aktionen aus, bei denen Lieferscheine anfallen können.

Die in Richtung Verbraucher wahrzunehmenden Aktivitäten bestehen in Werbemaßnahmen, Verbraucherinformationen, Wettbewerben und ähnlichem.

Das Volumen der Kommunikationsvorgänge mit dem Markt ist beachtlich

50.000	Lieferscheine	monatlich
60.000	Besuchsberichte	
55.000	Angebote	
100.000	Rechnungen	
	Telefongespräche	

Das Volumen der externen Kommunikationsvorgänge ist bezogen auf die tagsüber zur Verarbeitung zur Verfügung stehende Zeit in der Größenordnung von wenigen Stunden sehr erheblich. Das hängt damit zusammen, daß ein schneller Umschlag der Produkte eine wichtige Quelle guter Erträge ist. In der Vergangenheit standen für die Bewältigung dieser Kommunikationsvorgänge die klassischen Dienste der Post wie der Brief, das Telefongespräch oder der Besuch durch einen Firmenvertreter zur Verfügung.

Bei der Auswahl geeigneter neuer Medien zur Vergrößerung der Reichweite des bisherigen Kommunikationssystems spielen eine Reihe von Faktoren eine Rolle, von denen einige angesprochen werden sollen.

Bei den Medien, die für die Lösung zur Verfügung stehen, unterscheidet man zwischen exklusiven und öffentlichen Informationsformen. Werden individuelle Informationen unter möglichster Geheimhaltung zu wohl definierten Empfängern transportiert, dann heißen sie exklusiv. Das Telefongespräch und der Brief sind typische exklusive Kommunikationsformen. Werden gleiche Informationen zu einer potentiell unabgegrenzten Menge von Empfängern transportiert wie etwa Fernsehsendungen und Zeitungen, so heißen sie öffentlich. Für bestimmte Kommunikationsvorgänge wie z. B. die Rechnungsübermittlung kommen nur exklusive Kommunikationsformen in Frage, für andere wie z. B. die Verbraucher-Werbung sind öffentliche besser geeignet.

Bildschirmtext ist eine Form der visuellen Textkommunikation, die sich des Telefonnetzes zur Nachrichtenübertragung und des Fernsehers als Darstellungsmittel bedient. Bildschirmtext ist eine Kommunikationsform, die sowohl exklusiv als auch öffentlich eingesetzt werden kann. Damit hängen auch die Probleme des Gesetzgebers zuammen. Bildschirmtext setzt also voraus, daß die Teilnehmer über einen geeigneten Fernseher und einen Telefonanschluß verfügen.

Bildschirmtext wird ab Juni 1980 in Feldversuchen in Berlin und Düsseldorf/Neuß erprobt werden. Die endgültige Einführung ist für 1983 geplant. Es ist damit zu rechnen, daß die Ausbreitung zuerst im gewerblichen Bereich erfolgt. Es ist zu hoffen, daß die "kritische Masse" etwa 1985 erreicht sein wird.

Fernsehen + Fernsprechnetz = Bildschirmtext

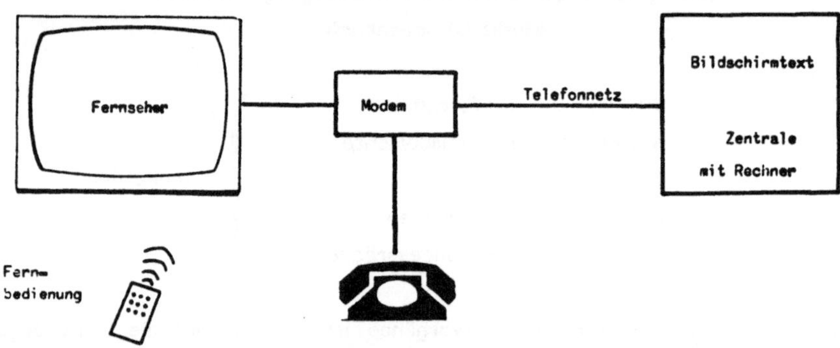

Es ist deshalb wichtig, zunächst nach der Verbreitung der zur Auswahl stehenden technischen Einrichtungen zu fragen.

Die Wahl der geeigneten Medien wird durch ihre Verbreitung beeinflußt

20 Mio.	Fernsehgenehmigungen	= 93 %	der Haushaltungen
23 Mio.	Fernsprechstellen	= 70 %	der Haushaltungen
23 Mio.	Tageszeitungen		
0,2 Mio.	Datensichtgeräte		
0,2 Mio.	Fernschreibteilnehmer		

Schon aus dieser Übersicht ist zu erkennen, daß die Bildschirmtext-Technik den Vorzug hat, auf technischen Voraussetzungen zu beruhen, die eine schnelle Ausbreitung begünstigen.

Der Medienkonsum und die Kosten einer Stunde Medienkonsum für den Benutzer sind andere interessante Größen.

Audiovisuelle Medien werden bevorzugt

Printmedien	23 %	der Gesamtzeit
Audiovisuelle Medien	72 %	
Telefon	5 %	

Die Medienbenutzung ist auch eine Frage der Kosten

Kosten einer Stunde Medienbenutzung pro Kopf in DM

Printmedien	0,50 DM
audiovisuelle Medien	0,20 DM
Telefon	2,10 DM

Es ist bemerkenswert, daß der Medienkonsum nicht mehr rapide steigt und deshalb mit einem Verdrängungswettbewerb gerechnet werden muß. Das ist auch die tiefere Ursache der medienpolitischen Diskussionen, die von der Furcht der Politiker genährt werden, daß der Politik Einfluß auf den Medienkonsum beschnitten werden könnte.

Die Wirtschaftlichkeit der verschiedenen Kommunikationsformen kann in diesem Zusammenhang nicht ausführlich behandelt werden. Man muß zwischen den Investitionskosten und den laufenden Kosten unterscheiden. Man muß auch zwischen den Kosten unterscheiden, die dem Informationsanbieter und dem Informationsbenutzer entstehen. Einige Angaben enthält die folgende Übersicht :

Ausgewählte Gebühren für die Medienbenutzung

Medien			
Exklusive		Öffentliche	
Standardbrief	0,60 DM	Monatsbezug Tageszeitung	12,67 DM
Ortsgespräch	0,23 DM	Fernsehgebühr	9,20 DM

H f D	abhängig von verschiedenen Einflußgrößen
Datex-L	
Datex-P	

Die elektronischen Medien zeichnen sich durch niedrigere Kosten aus. Verbreitung der Kommunikationsformen, Medienkonsum, Wirtschaftlichkeit und Schnelligkeit lassen die

Bildschirmtext-Technik als die Kommunikationsform der Wahl für die Ausdehnung der Reichweite eines Kommunikationssystems erscheinen.

Der Bildschirmtext ist die Kommunikationstechnik der Wahl

große Verbreitung
große Akzeptanz
geringe Kosten
exklusives und öffentliches Medium

Eine Anmerkung zum Bürofernschreiben oder korrekter zu Teletex :

Die dafür notwendigen Einrichtungen, zu denen man auch das Fernschreiben zählen darf, sind längst nicht so weit verbreitet wie Fernseher und Fernsprechanschlüsse. Diejenigen, die wegen des umfangreichen Briefverkehrs eine schnelle Ausbreitung des Bürofernschreibens erwarten, seien daran erinnert, daß der Briefinhalt oft ein Produkt der Datenverarbeitung ist. Die Verbindung des Fernschreibens mit den Datenverarbeitungsnetzen bereitet zur Zeit jedoch noch einige rechtliche Schwierigkeiten.

Anwendungstechnisch ist es mit Hilfe des Bildschirmtextes möglich, durch Besuchsvorschläge und Kundenstatistiken den Vertretereinsatz sehr flexibel zu unterstützen. Aufträge und Besuchsberichte, die aus dem Vertreterbesuch resultieren, können sehr schnell mit Bildschirmtext erfaßt und bearbeitet werden. (siehe Anlage A)

Den direkt beziehenden Kunden kann man Bestellvorschläge individuell übermitteln. Die Kunden können mit Bildschirmtext bequem Aufträge erteilen, die man postwendend bestätigen kann. Bildschirmtext übernimmt hier eine Datenerfassungs- und -sammelfunktion.

Den besonders betreuten Vertriebsstellen kann man im Rahmen von Absatzförderungsmaßnahmen Aktionsangebote unterbreiten.

Den Verbraucher kann man über Bildschirmtext mit Produktinformationen, werbewirksamen Wettbewerben und Spezialinformationen ansprechen.

Technische Voraussetzung dafür ist der Verbund des externen Bildschirmtext-Rechners mit dem betriebsinternen Computer. In Wirklichkeit handelt es sich dabei um die Verbindung zweier Rechnernetze, des betriebsinternen privaten mit dem unternehmensexternen öffentlichen. Die Kommunikation zwischen verschieden strukturierten Informationsbasen stellt eine Form der verteilten Datenbanken dar, über die bisher noch sehr wenig nachgedacht worden ist.

Nach Erreichen einer bestimmten Dichte des Kommunikationssystems und Ausdehnung der Reichweite insbesondere durch Einbeziehung der Bildschirmtext-Technik geht es weiter darum, das Kommunikationssystem als Träger weiterer Dienste zu nutzen.

Das Kommunikationssystem als Träger weiterer Dienste

Informationsbasen	Betriebsarten
Sprache	Teletex
Bildschirmtext für einfachen Abruf	Dialog mit speziellen Sprachen für Abfrage und Text
Texte	Teilhaberbetrieb
Klassische Datenbanken für Analysen	Stapelverarbeitung

Im Rahmen der Datenverarbeitung kann das Kommunikationssystem in bekannter Weise für die Datenerfassung am Ursprung der Daten, zum Ausdruck oder zur Anzeige der benötigten Informationen am Ort des Informationsbedürfnisses dienen. Das kann in recht unterschiedlichen Betriebsarten wie Stapel- und Dialogbetrieb erfolgen. Diese Form der Datenverarbeitung wird durch Datenbanken in Verbindung mit leistungsfähigen Abfragesprachen unterstützt, die flexible Analysen ermöglichen. Die Leistungsfähigkeit der Datenbank und der Abfragesprache tragen besonders dazu bei, schnell eine gewisse Dichte des Kommunikationssystems zu erreichen. Die Datenbasen sind gewissermaßen die Drehscheibe des Kommunikationssystems.

Datenbanken und analytischen Zwecken dienende Abfragesprachen können jedoch nur einen Teil der Kommunikationsbedürfnisse befriedigen. Ein wichtiges anderes Bedürfnis ist die zentrale Verwaltung von Texten in Verbindung mit Textbearbeitungsmöglichkeiten und Textkommunikation. Diese Textverarbeitung ist ein Dienst, der sich mit den vorhandenen Geräten weitgehend realisieren läßt. Es ist nicht einzusehen, warum man zwischen Texterfassung (Schreibdienst) und Datenerfassung unterscheidet. Das Angebot solcher Textverarbeitungsdienste in dem Kommunikationssystem ist eine wichtige Qualitätsverbesserung der nachrichtentechnischen Infrastruktur. Mit anderen Worten : Mit geringen Zusatzinvestitionen läßt sich ein großer Zusatznutzen erzielen.

Die Verwendung des Bildschirmtextes zur unternehmensexternen Kommunikation erfordert betriebsinterne Vorkehrungen und erweckt gleichzeitig das interne Bedürfnis, an den Möglichkeiten der unternehmensexternen Kommunikation teilzuhaben. Eine nähere Analyse des Informationsbedürfnisses ergibt, daß es eine große Menge von Daten gibt, die für den einfachen Abruf geeignet sind, ohne leistungsfähige Abfragesprachen zu erfordern. Beispiele sind Konten, Lagerbestände, Adressen, Bankleitzahlen usw. Ferner findet man, daß der Bildschirmtext auch innerhalb des Unternehmens wirtschaftlich ist, denn Bildschirmtext erfordert wegen des

Rückgriffs auf das vorhandene Telefonnetz keine zusätzlichen Leitungen. In Ausnahmefällen ist es möglich, auch von der Wohnung oder vom Hotel Informationen einzusehen, was für häufig reisende leitende Angestellte angenehmer sein dürfte als das Mitschleppen von Akten. Die Bedienung des Bildschirmtextes ist einfach. Man bedenke, daß bald jeder den Umgang damit aus dem privaten Bereich kennen wird.

Dies kann auch ein Schritt in Richtung auf einen speziellen "Datenbankrechner" sein, wenn man für die betriebsinterne Bildschirmtextdatei einen speziellen Rechner benutzt.

Dieser kurze Überblick zeigt, daß es für ein mittelgroßes Markenartikelunternehmen sehr interessant ist, die Bildschirmtext-Technologie für die Kommunikation in- und außerhalb des Unternehmens einzusetzen. Zu einem abschließenden Urteil kann man allerdings erst kommen, wenn man weiß, wie sich der Bildschirmtext in der Öffentlichkeit durchsetzen wird. Wichtig ist aber schon heute, daß man das Feld Bildschirmtext sowohl was die innerbetriebliche Planung der Kommunikationssysteme als auch die politischen Diskussionen anbelangt nicht alleine unter dem Gesichtspunkt Unterhaltung und Werbung behandeln darf. Es sind zunächst eine Fülle technischer Probleme zu lösen.

DIE REICHWEITE DES ELEKTRONISCHEN KOMMUNIKATIONSSYSTEMS

	Schalen	Medien	Nutzung
1	Betriebsinterne Benutzer am Ort des Rechenzentrums	klassische Datenverarbeitung mit HfD Datex-L Datex-P (für 1 und 2)	u.a. Rechnungswesen, Materialwirtschaft, Produktionssteuerung, Marketing, Vertriebssteuerung, Personalwesen
2	Betriebsinterne Benutzer an entfernten Betriebsstätten		
3	Außendienstmitarbeiter mit weit gestreuter geografischer Verteilung und begrenztem Informationsaufkommen	Bildschirmtext im Rechnerverbund mit Datex-P BSC-3270 Protokoll (für 3 bis 6)	Besuchsvorschläge, Besuchsberichte, Kundenspiegel, Lieferscheine
4	Kunden mit direkter Belieferung		Bestellvorschläge, Aufträge
5	Vertriebsstellen mit besonderer Betreuung		Aktionsangebote, Aufträge
6	Verbraucher		Verbraucherinformationen über Produkte, Wettbewerbe, Verbraucherservice

5 JAHRE BRIDGE

- Erfahrungen mit dem Vertriebsinformationssystem der IBM Deutschland GmbH

Stichworte und Abbildungen zu einem Referat von
D. Schmidtmann, IBM

GLIEDERUNG

1. AUSGANGSSITUATION

2. ANFORDERUNGEN

   - besondere Gegebenheiten
   - Anwendungen und Benutzer
   - Netzwerk

3. ERFAHRUNGEN

4. ZUKUNFT

1. AUSGANGSSITUATION

Die IBM Deutschland wickelte vor Einführung von BRIDGE die Auftragsverarbeitung mit einem System ab, dessen Teilsysteme/Verfahren in den Jahren 1963 - 1968 entwickelt wurden (Stapelverarbeitung).

Dieses historisch gewachsene System entsprach nicht mehr den veränderten und geforderten Ansprüchen an Informationsaktualität und -qualität.

Die IBM Deutschland entschied sich daher 1973 zur Entwicklung eines Vertriebsinformationssystems genannt "BRIDGE".

2. ANFORDERUNGEN

a) Datenqualität

- Durch Konsolidierung aller Auftrags- und Bestandsdaten in eine gemeinsame integrierte Datenbank.

- Logische Verknüpfungen dieser Daten und Sicherstellung einer zentralen Pflege dieser Datenbank durch das BRIDGE-System.

- Versorgung aller nachgelagerten Systeme mit Daten aus dieser Datenbank mit dem Ziel, daß überall gleiche Daten verwendet werden.

b) Endbenutzerkonzept

Durch die Realisierung als Echtzeitsystem wurde eine weitgehende Dezentralisierung der Verantwortung durchgeführt, da die Verarbeitung der Daten im direkten Dialog zwischen Endbenutzer und System geschieht.

Das System sollte den Benutzer im Dialogverkehr führen und unterstützen und ihn in die Lage versetzen, am Bildschirm alle Probleme und Aufgaben im Rahmen der entwickelten Anwendungen lösen zu können.

Dies führte zu bestimmten

- Dialogabläufen
- Bildschirmdesign
- Eingabetechnik
- Fehleranzeige und Bereinigung
- Hilfsfunktionen
- Schulungsmöglichkeiten
- Revisionsfähige Dokumentation der Eingabe.

c) Aktualität

- rationellere Aufgabenverteilung zwischen den Niederlassungen und Zentralstellen mittels Nutzung der Möglichkeiten einer Echtzeitverarbeitung (Realtime Systeme).

- Online Verarbeitung, Fehlerprüfung und Korrekturen dezentral.

- Beseitigung von Doppelfunktionen (Endbenutzerkonzept).

- Reduzierung der Durchlaufzeiten einschliesslich der Einsparung von Postwegen mit Hilfe der DFV. (Verbindung Endbenutzer → Fabrik).

- Reduzierung der Monatsabschlussarbeiten durch täglich aktuelle Datenbanken.

d) Einsatz als Planungssystem

- Angebotsunterstützung mit einem Angebotssystem und dem Zugriff auf alle hierfür notwendigen Daten.

- Planungssystem für den Auftragseingang und der geplanten Installationen und der Verbindung zum Zeitpunkt der Realisierung.

- Ermittlung des Vertriebsergebnisses und Soll/Ist Vergleich für alle Ebenen (z.B. Vertriebsbeauftragte, Geschäftsstelle, Distrikt, Gesamtergebnis IBM Deutschland).

e) Verwendung der IBM Standard Hard- und Software.

f) Berücksichtigung der besonderen Gegebenheiten

wie

- dezentralisierte Vertriebseinheiten
- umfangreiche Produktpalette
- Produktionsstätten in Europa und Übersee
- unterschiedliche, den Markterfordernissen entsprechende Verträge
- Dezentralisierte Vertragsverwaltung.

g) Netzwerk

h) Verfügbarkeit des Systems zwischen 8.00 Uhr und 17.00 Uhr täglich.

i) Antwortzeitverhalten

50 % < 6 Sekunden
75 % < 8 Sekunden
90 % < 12,5 Sekunden

3. ERFAHRUNGEN

- Verbesserung der Durchlaufzeiten zu
  - Kunden
  - Fabriken
  - Warenverteilungszentrum
  - Programmcenters
  - nachgelagerte Verfahren
  - Reduzierung des Monatsabschlusses auf 1 Tag für die BRIDGE-Anwendungen.

- Realisierung der Verfügbarkeit und Antwortzeitverhaltens.

- Verarbeitung des gesteigerten Verarbeitungsvolumens unter Einhaltung der vorgegebenen Ziele.

- Motivation der Aussendienstmitarbeiter durch Delegation der Verantwortung.

- Aktuelle Informationen des Managements.

4. ZUKUNFT

a) Massenverarbeitung

b) Konzeptionen über Rechnerverbund

c) Erweiterung der Angebotsunterstützung und Realisierung.

Ausgangssituation

- Auftragsabwicklung mit veralteten Batch-Systemen
  - Informationsaktualität
  - Kein Endbenutzerkonzept
  - Durchlaufzeiten
    - Kundenauftrag von Geschäftsstelle zur Fabrik bis zu 40 Tage
  - Vollständigkeit und Richtigkeit

A1

Anforderungen

- **Datenqualität**
  - Konsolidierung aller Auftrags- und Bestandsdaten in einer Vertriebsdatenbank
  - Datenpflege zentral
  - Versorgung aller Folgesysteme mit gleichen Daten
- **Endbenutzerkonzept**
  - Auftragsverantwortung
  - Führung und Unterstützung des Benutzers

A2

Anforderungen

- **Aktualität**
  - Durchlaufzeiten
  - Monatsabschluß
  - Beseitigung von Doppelfunktionen
- **Einsatz als Planungssystem**
  - Angebotsuntersützung
  - Ermittlung des Vertriebsergebnisses Soll/Ist
- **Verwendung IBM Standard Hard- und Software**

Besondere Gegebenheiten

→ Dezentralisierte Vertriebseinheiten

→ Umfangreiche Produktpalette

→ Produktionsstätten in Europa und Übersee

→ Unterschiedliche, den Markterfordernissen entsprechende Verträge

→ Dezentralisierte Vertragsverwaltung

Anwendungen und Benutzer

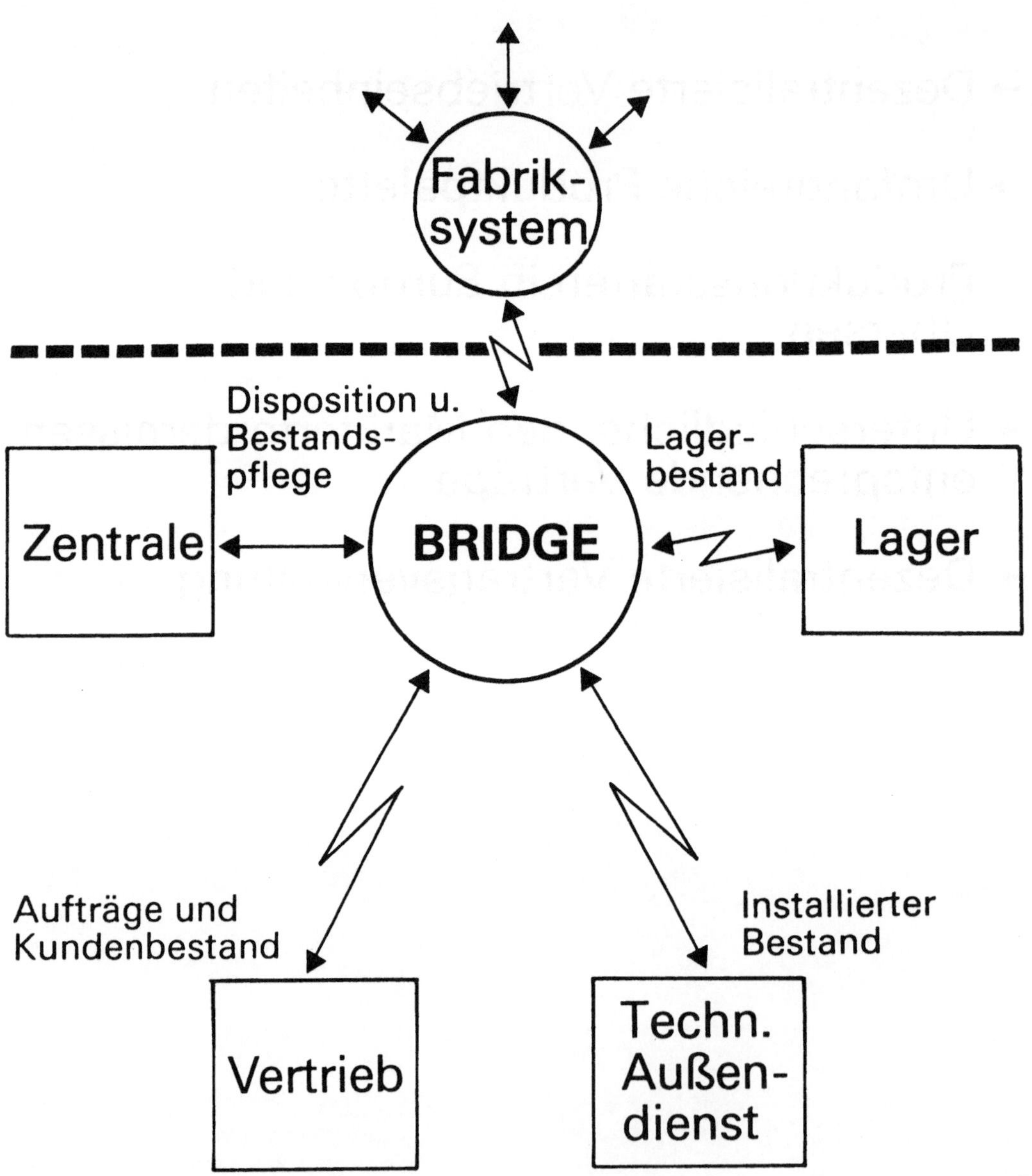

Anwendungsspektrum in BRIDGE

- Auftragsverarbeitungs- und Bestandsverwaltungs-System
  ↓
  - Auftragseingabe
  - Liefertermin-Verschiebungen
  - Installation/Abbauten
  - Bestands-umbuchungen
  - Kundenadreß-wesen
  - Verkaufshandbuch

- Informations-System
  ↓
  - Auftrags- und Bestands-Abfragen
  - Abfragen von Fabrik-informationen
  - Vertriebsergebnis Berichtswesen

- Planungs-System
  ↓
  - Auftragseingangs-Planung
    Eingabe
    Berichts-wesen
  - Integriertes Angebots-System

BRIDGE-Netzwerk

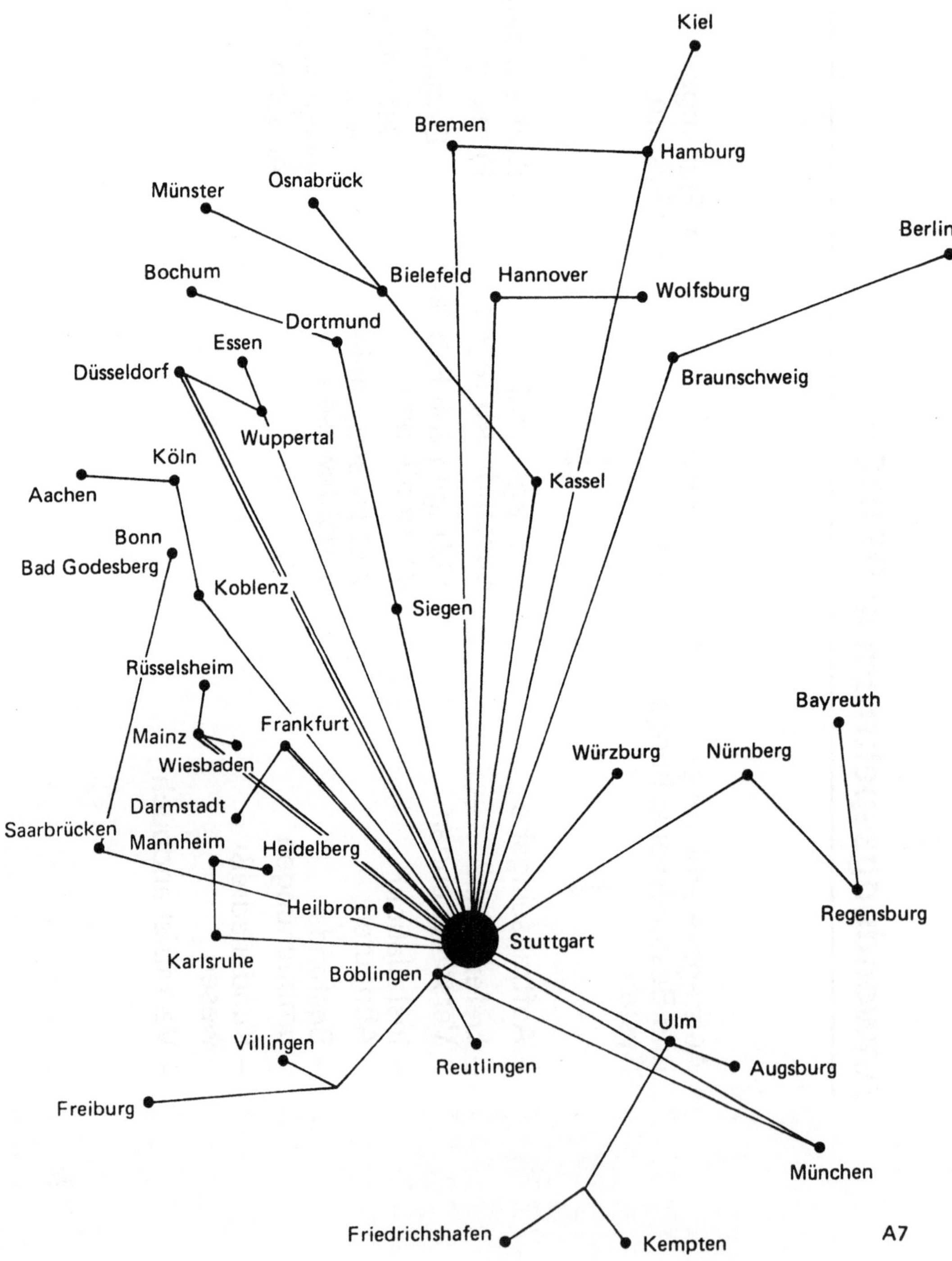

A7

BRIDGE — Umfang und Datenaustausch

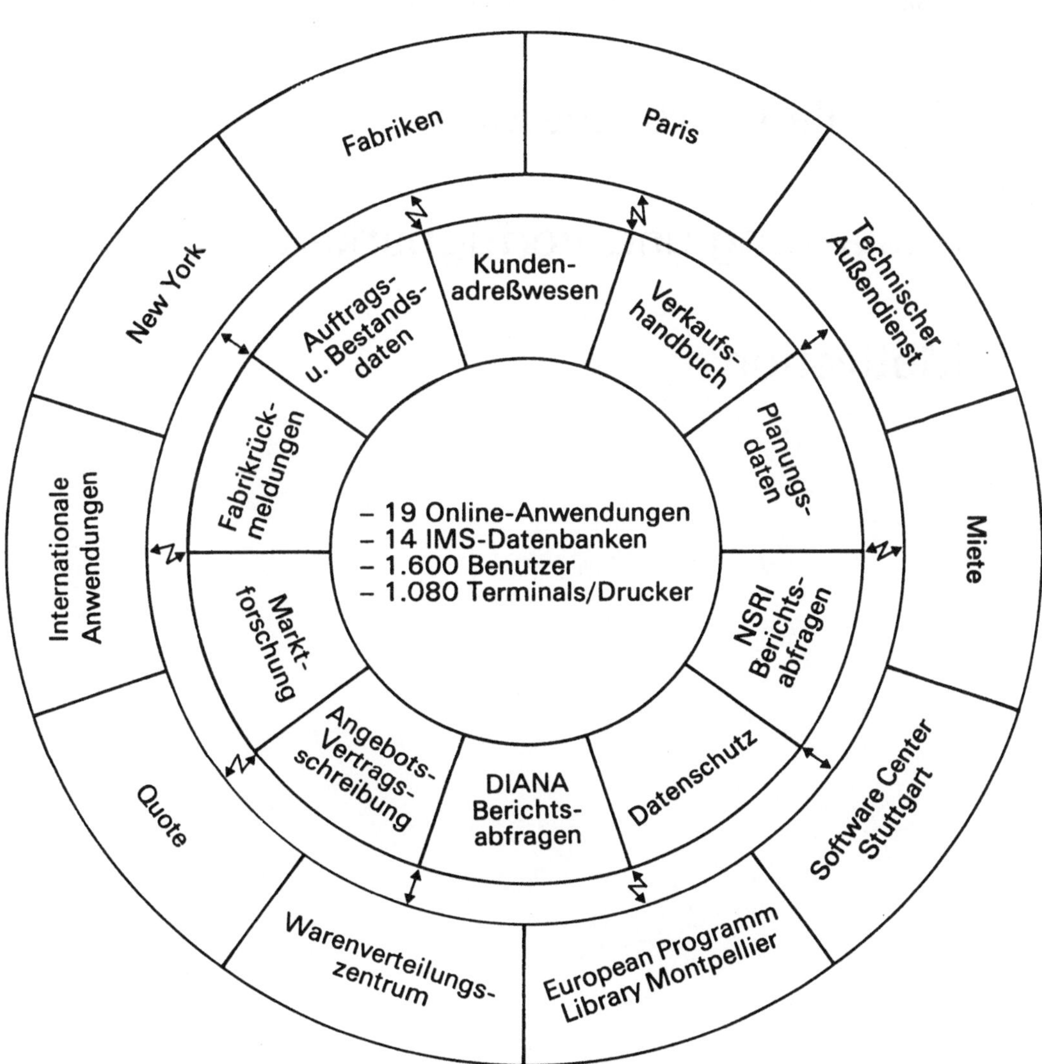

Erfahrungen

- **Produktivitätssteigerung**
  - Durchlaufverbesserung
  - Auslastung und Verfügbarkeit
  - Motivation

IBM

Entwicklung der Arbeitsvorgänge am Bildschirm (unterschiedliche Verwaltungs- und Anzeige-Transaktionen) in der Kundenauftragsbearbeitung der IBM Deutschland

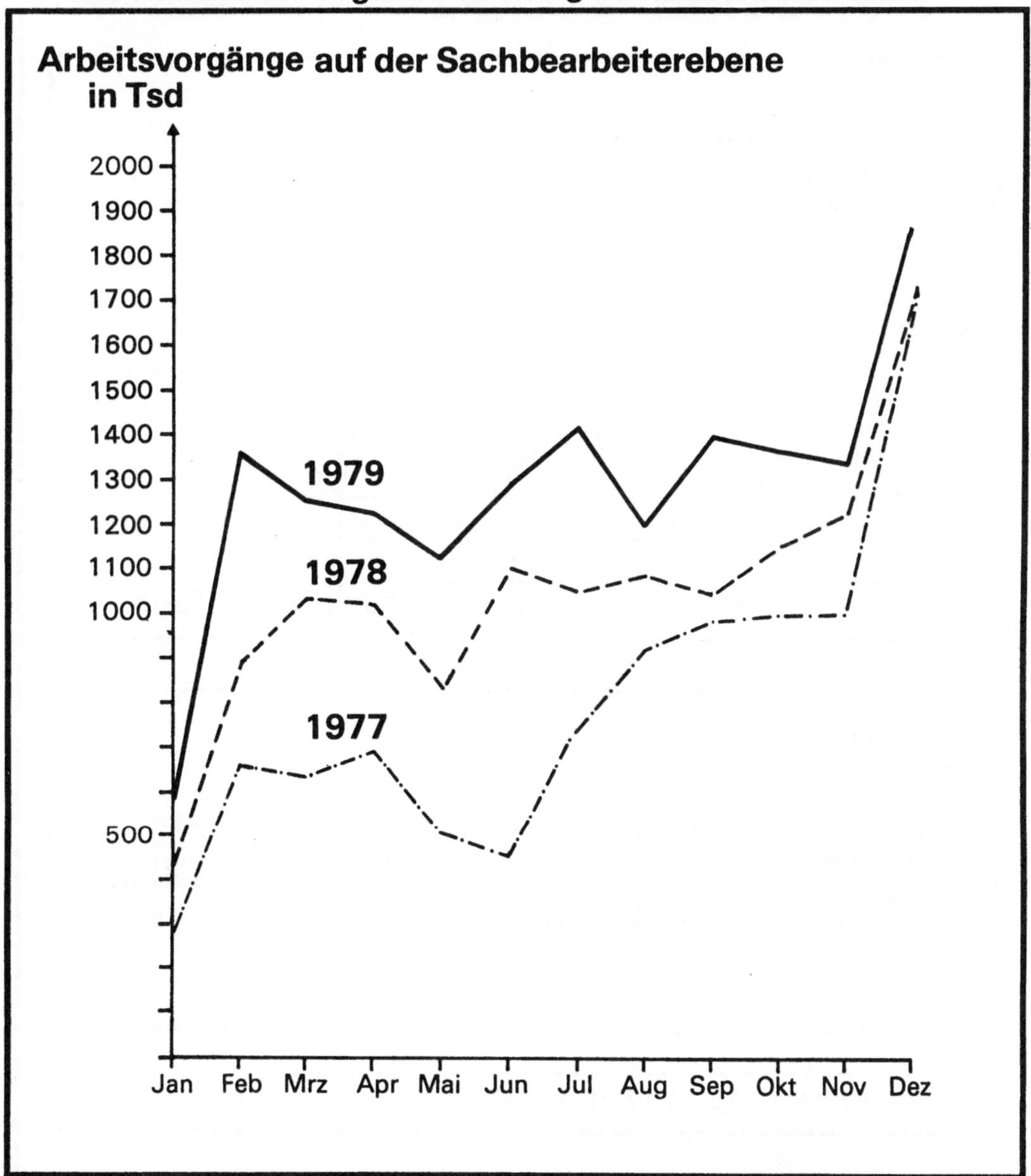

Geplantes und tatsächliches Antwortzeitverhalten
Monat: Januar '78

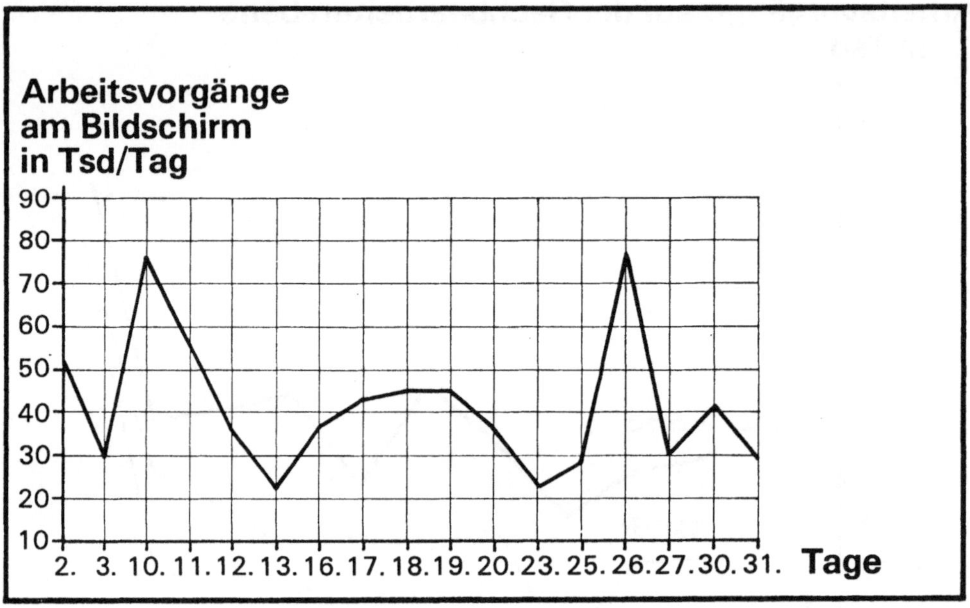

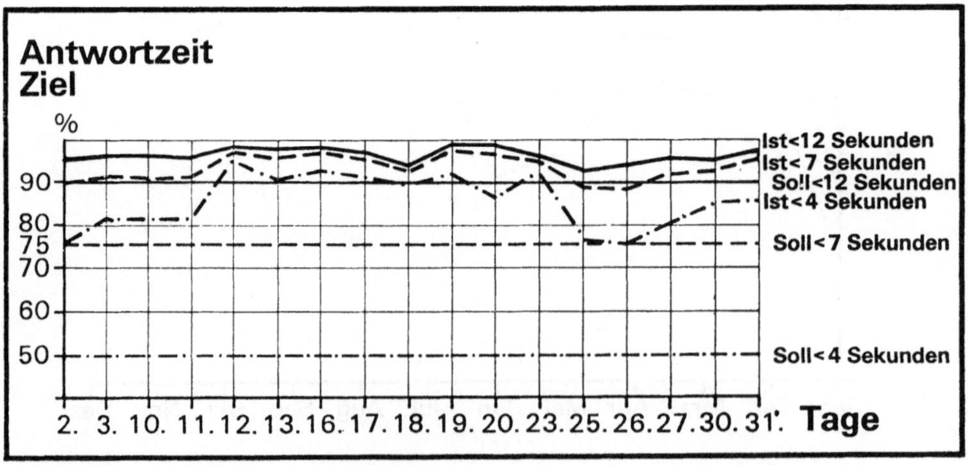

Arbeitsvorgänge am Bildschirm in Tsd/Tag

90
80
70
60
50
40
30
20
10

2. 3. 10. 11. 12. 13. 16. 17. 18. 19. 20. 23. 25. 26. 27. 30. 31. Tage

Antwortzeit Ziel

%

90
80
75
70
60
50

Ist<12 Sekunden
Ist< 7 Sekunden
Soll<12 Sekunden
Ist<4 Sekunden
Soll<7 Sekunden
Soll<4 Sekunden

2. 3. 10. 11. 12. 13. 16. 17. 18. 19. 20. 23. 25. 26. 27. 30. 31. Tage

Geplantes Antwortzeitverhalten (Planung auf der Basis von 6 Spitzentagen)

	Antwortzeit
50% aller Arbeitsvorgänge am Bildschirm	< 6 Sekunden
75% aller Arbeitsvorgänge am Bildschirm	< 8 Sekunden
90% aller Arbeitsvorgänge am Bildschirm	< 12,5 Sekunden

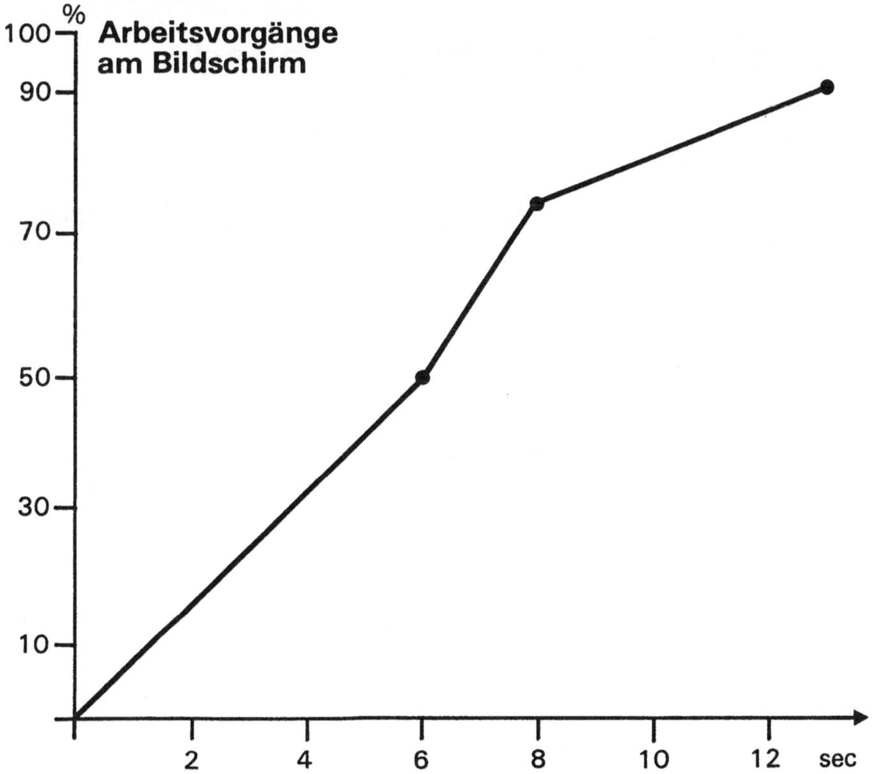

% Arbeitsvorgänge am Bildschirm

100
90
70
50
30
10

2 4 6 8 10 12 sec

Hinter den auf den ersten Blick relativ langen Antwortzeiten stehen umfangreiche Prüfungen und Rechenabläufe, beispielsweise die gesamte Konfigurationsüberprüfung.

Zukunft

- Massenverarbeitung
- Konzeption über Rechnerverbund
- Erweiterung der Angebotsunterstützung

ENTWICKLUNG UND BENUTZUNG INTERAKTIVER ANWENDUNGSSYSTEME MIT HILFE VON METHODEN- UND DATENBANKSYSTEMEN

G. Müller, L. Dumke
IBM Wiss. Zentrum Heidelberg

Diese Forschungsarbeit soll zeigen, daß mit allgemeinen interaktiven Daten- und Methodenbanksystemen (IDMS) Anwendungssysteme für den Problemlöser effizient entwickelt, vom Anwendungsexperten flexibel genutzt und veränderten Gegebenheiten leicht angepaßt werden können.
Zur Erreichung dieser Ziele ist am Wissenschaftlichen Zentrum der IBM in Heidelberg ein IDMS entwickelt und in verschiedenen Anwendungen praktisch erprobt worden. Aus diesen Anwendungen, die sowohl in der Medizin, im Ingenieurwesen und in der Wirtschaft angesiedelt sind, wird hier eine Anwendung zur Aktienanalyse vorgestellt, daraus die Anforderungen an ein IDMS allgemein abgeleitet und danach die Realisierung von Teilen der Anwendung beschrieben.
Forschungen über IDMS werden bisher im weitesten Sinne zu den Methoden des Software-Engineering gerechnet. Die Zielsetzung ist dabei die Steigerung der Produktivität von Anwendungsentwicklern. Dies wird entweder durch die Verfügbarkeit von Programmbibliotheken, die Anwendung von Programmierdisziplinen (z.B. strukturierte Programmierung), durch hohe aggregierte Programmiersprachen oder durch Softwaredokumentationssysteme versucht.
Das vorgestellte Interaktive Datenanalyse- und Managementsystem (abgek.: IDAMS), das in Heidelberg entwickelt wurde, verfolgt demgegenüber einen umfassenderen Ansatz. Anders als bei anderen IDMS soll die Benutzung, Entwicklung und Anpassung vieler Anwendungsklassen innerhalb nur eines Systems möglich sein.
Ein Bericht über die Erfahrungen beim Einsatz des Systems, deren Konsequenzen für die Architektur und die Anforderungen an die Systemkomponenten ist Gegenstand des Vortrages.

Literatur:

Erbe, R., Hartwig, R. Lehmann, H., Müller, G., Schauer, U.: Integrated Data Analysis and Management for the Problem Solving Environment. In: Information Systems, Vol. 5, No. 4, 1980.

"STAND DER ENTWICKLUNG VON BILDSCHIRMTEXT"

Jürgen C.W. Schröder
DATEL GmbH - danet
Ostend 29
6103 Griesheim

Das technische Konzept von BILDSCHIRMTEXT (BTXT) geht auf die britische PRESTEL-Entwicklung zurück. Es handelt sich hier um ein Minicomputer-System mit einer Datenbank, die vom Benutzer über ein einfaches Suchbaumverfahren abgefragt werden kann. Die Teilnehmereinrichtung besteht aus einem Standardfernsehempfänger mit Decoder, der an das öffentliche Fernsprechnetz mittels speziellem Modem angeschlossen wird. Der Aufbau von Datenbeständen erfolgt seitens des Informationslieferanten manuell über sogenannte Editierstationen.
Die Weiterentwicklung seitens der DBP hin zu BTXT beruht auf der Idee, den Informationslieferanten direkt mit seiner Datenbank über einen 'Rechnerverbund' an die BTXT-Zentrale anzuschließen. Als Transportsystem kommt DATEX-P (Datenpaketvermittlungstechnik) zum Einsatz. Mit diesem "Rechnerverbund" ergeben sich auf Seiten der BTXT-Zentrale und dem angeschlossenen Rechner als Informationslieferanten eine Reihe von softwaretechnisch zu lösenden Aufgaben, die näher erläutert werden.
Der im Feldversuch der DBP gewählte Lösungsweg mit Hilfe sog. Schnittstellen-Emulation bestehender, herstellerspezifischer Schnittstellen wird dargestellt. Je nach herstellerspezifischen Kommunikationsprotokollen müssen in der BTXT-Zentrale verschiedene "Datenübertragungsprozeduren" realisiert werden. In der Ebene oberhalb der Datentransportebene (Ebene 1 bis 4 des ISO-Referenzmodells) wird ein für BTXT spezifisches Benutzerprotokoll realisiert. Dieses BTXT-Protokoll muß auch im angeschlossenen HOST-Rechner implementiert werden. Der Beitrag diskutiert die heutigen Lösungsansätze auf der Basis vorhandener System- und Anwenderschnittstellen. Ein weiteres Problem besteht in der Abbildung bestehender Bildschirmformate auf die Formatstruktur des Standard-Fernsehempfängers.
Ein Ausblick hinsichtlich der zukünftigen Lösung mit Hilfe 'standardisierter' EDV-herstellerunabhängiger Kommunikationsprotokolle in Richtung eines offenen Rechnerverbundnetzes schließt den Beitrag ab.

Der Thesaurus als Datenbank

H. Werner
Projekt JUDO
Prof. Dr. H. Zimmermann
Universität Saarbrücken
D-6600 Saarbrücken

Kurzfassung

In Systemen zur automatischen Indexierung (Deskriptorerstellung) von Volltexten, an die höhere Qualitätsansprüche gestellt werden, werden - ebenso wie in Systemen zur automatischen Übersetzung - Thesauri mit verschiedenartigen linguistischen Informationen benötigt. Für deren Erstellung und Pflege wird ein gewisser intellektueller Aufwand benötigt, der durch eine geeignete Organisation des Thesaurus als Datenbank ebenso wie der technische Aufwand (Speicherbedarf, Rechenzeit) reduziert und effektiviert werden kann.

Die Ausführungen werden am Beispiel des Projekts JUDO (juristische Dokumentanalyse) erläutert.

Gliederung

Kurze Einführung in Gegenstand und Ergebnisse des Projekts JUDO: automatische Indexierung mit Verfahren der linguistischen Datenverarbeitung.

Die Funktionen des Thesaurus bei JUDO:
Anwendung bei Textanalyse und Recherche

Intellektueller Aufwand (hier: Aufwand zur Pflege des Thesaurus und zur Durchführung der Recherche) als Komplexitätsgröße (neben Speicher- und Zeitkomplexität)

Der Thesaurus als Datenbank (Optimierung hinsichtlich aller Komplexitätsgrößen)

Semantischer Inhalt des Thesaurus bei JUDO

Integritätsbedingungen

Modell des Thesaurus als Metadatenbank im Dokumentinformationssystem.

---

* Der Aufsatz erscheint in seiner Langform in Sprache & Datenverarbeitung 2/80

"EIN VERFAHREN ZUR AUFNAHME MEDIZINISCHER DIAGNOSEN IN EINE DATENBANK"

Michael Eulenstein
Universität des Saarlandes

Med. Diagnosen sind unverarbeitet zur Aufnahme in eine Datenbank nicht geeignet; Synonyme, Homonyme und sehr große Redundanz erschweren die sinnvolle Abspeicherung und verringern die Anfragemöglichkeiten.

Bisherige Lösungsansätze versuchten eine möglichst komplexe Analyse auf den Eingabedaten (Stichworte: Klartextanalyse, autom. Indexierung, Thesauruserstellung); diese Verfahren sind allerdings unvollkommen und lösen zudem nicht die Problematik der Bedeutungszuordnung, d.h. daß verschiedene befundende Ärzte ihren Diagnosen unterschiedliche Interpretationen zuordnen. Die Lösung dieses Problems schafft allerdings erst die Voraussetzung für eine Datenbank mit semantisch korrekten Daten; wenn die textlichen Diagnosen außerdem in einen umfassenden und präzisen Code übersetzt werden, werden zudem unnötige Redundanzen vermieden.

Das vorgeschlagene Verfahren verzichtet auf eine Wiederholung der bisherigen Ansätze zur Diagnosebehandlung. Vielmehr wird von den Ärzten die Formulierung der Diagnose gemäß einer (einfachen) Syntax verlangt; diese Forderung wurde von den Ärzten als keine große Belastung empfunden. Die so eingegebene Diagnose wird von einem Parser analysiert; syntaktisch korrekte Diagnosen werden einigen Umformungen unterworfen, um Ausgangsdaten für eine "Wörterbuch"-Suche zu erhalten. Dieses Wörterbuch ist analog zu dem verwendeten SNOP-Code (SNOP: "Systematized Nomenclature of Pathology") aufgebaut und enthält in Abhängigkeit von dem befundenden Arzt die Codierung (=sem. Interpretation) der eingegebenen Diagnoseteile; diese Interpretation muß von dem befundenden Arzt einmalig definiert werden. Die so erhaltenen Codierungen werden anschl. gemäß den in der SNOP geforderten Regeln zu sog. Statements zusammengesetzt, die als Ergebnis die vollständige Codierung der eingegebenen Diagnose darstellen.

Das Verfahren ermöglicht die einfache Vorbereitung von Diagnosen für die Aufnahme in eine Datenbank. Es gewährleistet, daß in der Datenbank nur sem. korrekte und eindeutig zurückübersetzbare Diagnosen enthalten sind. Zusätzlich erlaubt die Struktur des verwendeten Codes umfassende Anfragen nach Oberbegriffen bzw. Oberstrukturen und das befunderabhängig aufgebaute Wörterbuch interessante Untersuchungen über das Sprachverhalten der befundenden Ärzte. Das Verfahren soll als Teil der Datenbank PANIC am Pathologischen Institut der Universität des Saarlandes eingesetzt werden.

Einsatz von Hilfsmitteln der Netzplantechnik zur Planung und Steuerung des zeitlichen Ablaufes von Software-Projekten.

M.A. Ertel
Siemens AG München

Für ein erfolgreiches Arbeiten im Software-Bereich ist heute ein gutes DV-Fachwissen allein nicht mehr ausreichend. Genauso wichtig ist ein effektives Projektmanagement. In der Technik werden heute vielfältig Netzpläne als Hilfsmittel der Projektsteuerung eingesetzt. Ob manuell oder maschinell betreut, sind sie ein anschauliches Mittel, Projektverlauf, Abhängigkeiten von Randbedingungen, Verknüpfungen von Tätigkeiten und ihre Dauer darzustellen und auf diese Weise Informationen über Projektzusammenhänge auszutauschen.
Ein wichtiger Aspekt in der Softwarearbeit ist das Erstellen von Dv-Programmen oder Programm-Systemen durch zusammenarbeitende Teams. Hier sind eine Vielzahl von Aktivitäten erfolgreich zu organisieren. Erschwerend kommt hinzu, daß man zur Ausnützung von Spezialkenntnissen bestimmte Tätigkeiten auch nur bestimmten Mitarbeitern zuordnen kann. Will man hier Netzplantechnik in der üblichen Weise einsetzen, treten 2 Hindernisse auf. Entweder werden wegen des Auseinanderdriftens des geplanten und des wirklichen Geschehens die Netzpläne zum Managementberuhigungsinstrument und damit wertlos oder man wird durch die Umstände zum ständigen Ändern des Netzplanes gezwungen, wobei viel von dem Nutzen als Kommunikationsmittel eingebüßt wird.
Diese Schwierigkeiten werden umgangen, wenn man die Mitarbeiterzeiterfassung, die aus anderen Gründen sowieso erforderlich ist, mit der Netzplanung in geschickter Weise zusammen- und rückkoppelt. Die Mitarbeitertätigkeiten und ihre Dauer werden zunächst in Übereinstimmung mit dem Netzplan projektiert. Die Mitarbeiter erhalten diese Vorgaben in einem Rechnerausdruck und ergänzen ihn durch die tatsächlich erreichten Werte. Per Dv-Programm werden in 14-tägigem Rhythmus in einem Projektbericht Plan- und Istgeschehen gegenübergestellt. Dabei werden gleichzeitig die Abrechnungsdaten für die Weiterverarbeitung maschinell aufbereitet. Mit dieser rückgekoppelten Vorgehensweise wird die Selbstorganisation aller Beteiligten verbessert, die Netzpläne werden realistischer, die Mitarbeiter verlieren das Gefühl der Manipulation durch die Projektleitung und für die Projektfortschrittsgespräche existieren im Netzplan und Projektbericht aktuelle Kommunikationsmittel.

SYSTEMATISCHER ENTWURF VON MAKROPROZESSOREN

Michael Payer
Universität Dortmund, Informatik III
D-4600 Dortmund 50, Postfach 500 500

Der Prozeß der Makrogenerierung läßt sich im wesentlichen durch seinen Strukturbaum beschreiben. Die Blätter dieses Strukturbaums stellen den generierten String dar, die übrigen Teilbäume repräsentieren die Expansion der einzelnen Makros. Die Ähnlichkeit dieses Strukturbaum mit den aus der Syntaxanalyse bekannten Ableitungsbäumen legt es nahe, Makroprozessoren mit den üblichen Verfahren des Übersetzerbaus zu erstellen.

Bei der Beschreibung der Sprache, die ein Makroprozessor akzeptiert, wird zwischen einer Statischen und einer Dynamischen Syntax unterschieden. Die Statische Syntax definiert die Sprache, in der der Benutzer seine Eingabe für den Prozessor zu formulieren hat. Diese Syntax läßt sich - abgesehen von kontextsensitiven Eigenschaften - durch eine LL(1)-Grammatik beschreiben. Eine Eigenschaft der beschriebenen Makroprozessoren ist, daß sie bei der Interpretation von Makroprogrammen rekursiv neue Programme erzeugen, die dann bearbeitet werden wie das ursprüngliche Makroprogramm. Die Sprache, der diese dynamisch erzeugten Makroprogramme angehören, wird durch die Dynamische Syntax definiert. Diese Syntax läßt sich mit Hilfe einer zweischichtigen Grammatik beschreiben, die - abgesehen von ihren Hyperregeln - wieder die LL(1)-Eigenschaft hat.

Aufgrund dieser Definition der Dynamischen Syntax läßt sich systematisch ein Makroprozessor konstruieren, der die Makrogenerierung in einem Paß durchführt. Der gesamte Generierungsprozeß wird dabei vom Syntaxanalysemodul des Prozessors, der mittels Rekursiven Abstiegs realisiert wird, gesteuert. Die Werte von Makroparametern und -Variablen werden während der Semantischen Analyse berechnet. Die eigentliche Ersetzung von Makroaufrufen und -Parametern findet während der Lexikalanalyse statt.

Literatur: Payer, Michael: Erstellung eines Cross-Makroübersetzers für den IBM/7 Makroassembler auf der PDP 11-40; Diplomarbeit, Universität Heidelberg/Fachhochschule Heilbronn, 1978

PLÄDOYER FÜR DEN DATENTYP TREE

Klaus-Jürgen Engelberg
Sonderforschungsbereich 99
Universität Konstanz

Für die Erfordernisse in high-quality-Übersetzungssystemen dürfte ein bequemes Rechnen mit den in der Linguistik beliebten Phrasenstrukturbäumen unbedingt wünschenswert erscheinen. Denn bekanntlich sind die Fälle recht häufig, in denen die syntaktischen Strukturen von Ausgangs- und Zielsprachensatz grundsätzlich verschieden sind.

Das Papier stellt deshalb eine bestimmte Konzeption des rekursiven Datentyps TREE für funktionsorientierte Programmiersprachen vor. Diese geht von einer systematisch zunehmenden Verallgemeinerung der Nachfolgerrelation in den Algebren der natürlichen Zahlen, der Strings und der Bäume aus und versucht daher, diese Datentypen in einer gewissen formalen Parallelität im Rahmen einer universellen Programmiersprache zu behandeln.

Zu dem vorgesehenen Satz von elementaren Baummanipulationsoperationen gehören u.a. mehrstellige Baumnachfolgerfunktionen, Teilbaum-Selegierungen und -Ersetzungen sowie Knotenmanipulationen. Zur Identifizierung der Knoten wird hierbei eine von links nach rechts und von oben nach unten verlaufende kanonische Durchnumerierung im Baum benutzt. Diese ist auch nützlich für numerische Baumfunktionen, die die direkten Dominanz- und Links-Rechts-Beziehungen der Knoten im Baum zu ermitteln gestatten.

Sodann wird diese Konzeption verallgemeinert und TREE nicht mehr als Datentyp, sondern als mode creating device aufgefaßt (nach ALGOL 68-Terminologie), das die Deklaration beliebiger hierarchisch strukturierter Datenaggregate möglich macht, etwa im Gegensatz zu den bekannten linearen (mehrdimensionalen) arrays.

Zum Abschluß soll untersucht werden, inwieweit sich etwa (aus SNOBOL bekannte) Pattern-matching-Operationen über Strings auf Bäume übertragen lassen.

KURZVORTRAG: FLAECHENBEZOGENE DATENSTRUKTUREN

Andreas Meier, Institut für Informatik, ETH Zürich

Zusammenfassung
In verschiedenen Instituten der ETH und bei einigen öffentlichen Verwaltungen der Schweiz werden Daten bezüglich geographischer Flächen benötigt. Dafür existieren diverse flächenbezogene Datenmodelle und Anwendungen.

In einem Flächenmodellregister sind die wichtigsten flächenbezogenen Datensammlungen der Schweiz nach einheitlichen Kriterien erfasst worden. Alle flächenbezogenen Datenstrukturen werden im gleichen konzeptionellen Datenmodell dargestellt; sie zeigen im gewählten Entitätenblockdiagramm eine grosse Vielfalt: einerseits widerspiegeln sie das Anwendungsgebiet des Benutzers (z.B. Vermessungswesen, Kartographie, Raumplanung etc.), andrerseits veranschaulichen sie die verschiedenen Darstellungsformen flächenbezogener Daten (z.B. als Koordinatenraster, Punktmenge, Streckennetz etc.).
Jede betrachtete flächenbezogene Datensammlung enthält als Grunddaten geometrische Elemente wie Punkte, Linien und Flächen. Die Grundoperationen auf den Grunddaten (z.B. Vereinigung, Durchschnitt) sind oft rudimentär implementiert, metrische Eigenschaften (z.B. Distanz, Flächeninhalt) sind als selbständige Merkmale den Grunddaten hinzugeschlagen und topologische Betrachtungen (z.B. Zusammenhang, Nachbarschaft) sind andeutungsweise in wenigen Systemen verwirklicht. Die Datensammlungen auf dem Gebiet des Vermessungswesens erfüllen zusätzlich starke Bedingungen hinsichtlich Konsistenz.
Flächenbezogene Datensammlungen unterscheiden sich wesentlich von den herkömmlichen personen- und sachbezogenen Datensystemen, da sie sich auf den kontinuierlichen, meist 2-dimensionalen "Raum" beziehen. Die Forderung nach abstrakten Datentypen für die geometrischen Grundelemente Punkt, Linie, Fläche und ein Satz möglicher Basisoperationen scheint zweckmässig, weil dadurch der

Interpretation sprachorientierter Instruktionscodes in einem Timesharingsystem

Horst Kosanke
Technische Universität Berlin

PASCAL wird im allgemeinen in den Instruktionssatz einer Stackmaschine übersetzt (P-Code). Dies bringt Vorteile (Codegenerierung, Portabilität) und Nachteile (Laufzeit, Kommunikation mit anderen Programmen). Es gibt verschiedene Ansätze, diese Nachteile zu beseitigen. Hier wird versucht, auf einer Maschine (PDP 11/40) unter einem vorhandenen Timesharingsystem (UNIX) eine solche Stackmaschine (EM-1) zur Verfügung zu stellen. Dabei sollen die neuen Instruktionscodes parallel zu den bisherigen zur Verfügung stehen. Erreicht wird dies durch die Implementierung eines entsprechenden Interpreters im Microcode.

Es ergibt sich folgender Entwurf:

- Programme für die EM-1 werden von UNIX mit einer anderen Priorität verwaltet.
- Es gibt eine Instruktion, die von der Standardfirmware in den EM-1 Interpreter umschaltet.
- Der Interpreter seinerseits hat einen eigenen Fetch-Execute-Cycle.
- Er benutzt weder das Register 6 (Stack Pointer), noch Register 7 (Program Counter).

Die notwendigen Änderungen an UNIX bzw. dem Compiler sind gering.

λ-Kalkül Schemata als Kontrollstrukturen für LISP-Programme

N. Bauchrowitz, F. Simon
Institut für Informatik, Universität Kiel

Die Menge S der λ-Kalkül Schemata [Fi, Go] stellt eine abstrakte Beschreibung der Kontrollstrukturen dar, wie sie u.a. in Programmiersprachen des LISP-Typs auftreten. Für λ-Kalkül Schemata ist die Definition von denotationeller Semantik [Mi, Wa] wohl bekannt und darauf bezogene abstrakte Interpreter zur Definition einer äquivalenten operationalen Semantik [Fi] liegen vor. Durch eine Interpretation J(S) der Schemata, bei der die Menge E aller s-Ausdrücke als LISP-Daten eingeführt wird, so wie die Menge {car,cdr,cons,atom,eq} der LISP-Operationen, erhält man die Programmiersprache $LISP_\lambda$. Die operationelle Semantik $f_\pi : E^n \longrightarrow E$ eines Programms $\pi \in LISP_\lambda$ mit den Eingabedaten $a_1,...,a_n \in E$ ist gegeben durch $f_\pi(a_1,...,a_n) \triangleq ap_\lambda(\pi,(a_1,...,a_n))$, wobei sich die Funktion $ap_\lambda : LISP_\lambda \times (\bigcup_{n\geq 1} E^n) \longrightarrow E$ aus der Ein/Ausgabefunktion ap_S des abstrakten Interpreters für λ-Kalkül Schemata durch Anwendung von J ergibt.

Es ist zu klären, ob man bei diesem Vorgehen alle Programme der Sprache (pure) LISP im Sinne von McCarthy [Mc] erhält und in welcher Beziehung ap_λ zu der Ein/Ausgabefunktion apply des von McCarthy angegebenen Interpreters I [Mc p. 70/71] steht.

Die in LISP zulässige Benennung von λ-Ausdrücken mit Hilfe des LABEL-Konzeptes hat kein Analogon auf der Schemaseite; es gilt deshalb $LISP_\lambda \subset LISP$. Durch eine Programmtransformation lassen sich LABEL-Ausdrücke in geschlossene λ-Ausdrücke übersetzen. Da keine weiteren Unterschiede bestehen, wird der Sprachumfang von $LISP_\lambda$ als adäquat angesehen.

Für beliebige $LISP_\lambda$-Programme stimmen ap_λ und apply nicht überein. Man kann jedoch eine stark eingeschränkte Klasse $LISP_\lambda^o \subset LISP_\lambda$ von Programmen definieren [Ba] und zu jedem Programm $\pi \in LISP_\lambda^o$ eine gewisse Menge von Eingabedaten $E_\pi \subset E$, so daß für $e_1,...,e_n \in E_\pi$ gilt:

$$ap_\lambda(\pi,(e_1,...,e_n)) = apply(\pi,(e_1,...,e_n))$$

d.h. der Interpreter I ist korrekt für $LISP_\lambda^o$-Programme π mit Eingabedaten aus E_π.

Der Interpreter I läßt sich zu einem Interpreter I^* modifizieren, bei dem einige der $LISP_\lambda^o$ charakterisierenden Bedingungen abgeschwächt werden können und bei dem die Programmabhängigkeit der zulässigen Eingabedaten entfällt. Für die Restriktionen von ap_λ und der Ein/Ausgabefunktion $apply^*$ von I^* gilt:

$$ap_\lambda|LISP_\lambda^1 \times (\bigcup_{n\geq 1}\bar{E}^n) \equiv apply^*|LISP_\lambda^1 \times (\bigcup_{n\geq 1}\bar{E}^n)$$

Die Klasse $LISP_\lambda^1 \subset LISP_\lambda$ ist gegenüber $LISP_\lambda$ nur noch durch zwei triviale Bedingungen eingeschränkt, die den "Mißbrauch" von Standardidentifikatoren wie z.B. QUOTE oder COND ausschließen. Als Eingabedaten $\bar{E} \subset E$ sind nur solche s-Ausdrücke zulässig, in denen die Atome LAMBDA, CAR, CDR, CONS, ATOM und EQ nicht auftreten. Der Interpreter I^* ist für $LISP_\lambda^1$-Programme und Eingabedaten aus $\bar{E}$ korrekt bezüglich der Semantik für λ-Kalkül Schemata.

[Ba] Bauchrowitz, N.: Diplomarbeit, Kiel, 1980
[Mc] McCarthy, J. et. al.: LISP 1.5 Programmer's Manual. MIT Press, Cambridge, Mass., 1966
[Fi] Fischer, M.J.: Lambda Calculus Schemata. SIGPLAN Notices 7(1), 1972
[Go] Gordon, M.J.C.:Models of Pure LISP (a worked example in semantics). Dept. of Mach. Int. Univ. of Edinburgh, Rep. 31, 1973
[Mi] Milner, R.: Models of LCF. Memo AIM-186, Stanford University, 1973
[Wa] Wadsworth, C.: The Relational between Computational and Denotational Properties for Scotts D_∞-Models of the Lambda-calculus. SIAM J. Computing, Vol. 5, No. 3, 1976

THE CONTROL OF PARALLEL COMPUTATIONS BY LABELED PETRI NETS:

A STUDY IN TERMS OF MULTIPLE-FIRING AUTOMATA AND PARALLEL PROGRAM SCHEMATA

Eike Hagen Riedemann
Abteilung Informatik
Universität Dortmund
Postfach 50 05 00
D-4600 Dortmund 50

A generalized, labeled, simultaneously firing Petri net is considered as the control of parallel computations in the following way: Some of the transitions of the Petri net are labeled with signals, which initiate or terminate operations (instructions) on data.

Since some transitions may not be labeled, the following problem arises:
The firing of non-labeled transitions ("internal state changes") may lead to a state (i.e. marking) of the Petri net, where some of the previously enabled signals (transitions with corresponding label) become disabled or vice versa.

In addition we demand an "external" behaviour (where the firing or non-labeled transitions is neglected) of the Petri net which is described by a generalization of the concepts of parallel program schemata in the sense of Karp/Miller (1969) and Keller (1973). The generalization consists in allowing the control to process several signals simultaneously.

The concept of a multiple-firing automaton is introduced to deliver a common framework for the behaviour of generalized, labeled, simultaneously firing Petri nets and "multiple-firing" parallel program schemata.

Equivalent conditions for "consistent" internal state changes of the Petri net (i.e. all the state changes lead to "equivalent" states) and for an external behaviour, which is representable by a multiple-firing parallel program schemata, are presented. Since e.g. the decidability of "consistent internal state changes" implies the decidability of the reachability problem (an open problem) simpler but only sufficient conditions are presented.

For multiple-firing automata five sufficient conditions are presented, which are thus applicable to all sorts of "parallel" systems and not only Petri nets. Finally five sufficient conditions for the structure of generalized, labeled simultaneously firing Petri nets are presented, which imply that the Petri net is free-choice. Four of these conditions are decidable with a reasonable amount of effort (linear or at most $O(m^4)$, where m is the number of places, transitions and circuits in the graph of the Petri net), only one is only decidable with an exponential effort.

Automatisierte Parallelisierung von Programmen

Horst Niggemann
Eckhard Bartel
Universität Dortmund
Abt. Informatik I

Im Rahmen des vom BMFT und der Firma Nixdorf Computer AG geförderten Forschungsprojekts "Implementierung einer Beschreibungssprache für parallele Systeme mit Verifikations- und Parallelisierungsalgorithmen" wurden u.a. Algorithmen entwickelt und implementiert, die inhärente Parallelität in Programmen erkennen und explizit darstellen.
Diese Algorithmen operieren einerseits auf einem von einem Compiler generierten Transitionsnetz (CAP-Netz nach [RAM 78]), das den Programm-Kontrollfluß repräsentiert und andererseits auf einem mit diesem Netz assoziierten Datenflußgraphen.
Die Konzeption der Algorithmen basiert auf dem Grundsatz: Nur Daten- und Kontrollflußabhängigkeiten verhindern die parallele Ausführung von Programm-Anweisungen.

Die Datenflußabhängigkeiten werden durch eine Analyse der Datenkonflikte zwischen Anweisungen gefunden.
Anweisungen des Programms sind kontrollflußabhängig, falls die Ausführungsreihenfolge der Anweisungen durch Ergebnisse von Testoperationen bestimmt wird.

Aufbauend auf der Daten- und Kontrollflußanalyse wird ein maximal paralleles und dem sequentiellen Transitionsnetz berechnungsäquivalentes Transitionsnetz generiert.

Die in Pascal implementierte und ausgetestete Pilotversion der Algorithmen wird z.Zt. durch folgende Punkte erweitert und optimiert

- Vergröberung des Parallelitätsgrades
- Reduzierung der Komplexität des parallelisierten Transitionsnetzes

[RAM78] F.J. Rammig:
Überlegungen zur Kontrollstruktur einer Computer Hardware Beschreibungssprache
Forschungsbericht Nr. 62 d. Abt. Informatik d. Universität Dortmund

[RIE77] E.H..Riedemann:
Automatical Translation of Sequential Programs into Parallel Programs
Proceedings of the IMACS (AICA)-GI, Symposium, March 77, Munich

Semantik-Definition der Prozeß-Programmiersprache PEARL

Eberhard Wegner
Institut für Software-Technologie, GMD Birlinghoven
D-5205 Sankt Augustin 1

Für die Normvorlage DIN 66 253 (Programmiersprache PEARL) Teil 2 (Full PEARL), die 1980 als Norm-Entwurf erscheinen soll, wurde die Semantik der nichtsequentiellen Sprachmittel durch Petri-Netze beschrieben.

Soweit die Semantik eines Programms der Struktur des Syntaxbaums folgt, wird sie durch ein Produktionensystem für Netze beschrieben: Mit dem Startsymbol der attributierten Grammatik von PEARL (die unter der Leitung von U. Kastens entwickelt wurde) ist ein Petri-Netz verknüpft. Jeder Knoten in den Petri-Netzen, die die Semantik beschreiben, hat eine Inschrift; manche Inschrift ist ein Nonterminal der attributierten Grammatik. Wo bei der Produktion eines Programms aus dem Startsymbol ein Nonterminal durch ein Wort ersetzt wird, wird ein Knoten, der dieses Nonterminal als Inschrift enthält, durch ein Teilnetz ersetzt. Die Wahl der Alternative beim Ersetzen des Nonterminals bestimmt die Wahl des Teilnetzes zum Ersetzen des Knotens. (Insoweit ist das nicht neu: Lauer und Campbell, Acta Informatica 5 (1975) 297-332.)

Die Ersetzung von Knoten durch Teilnetze wird nicht nur durch die Wahl der Alternative in Produktionsregeln gesteuert, sondern zusätzlich durch den Wert der Attribute für das jeweilige Programm und gelegentlich durch Eigenschaften der Implementation (insbesondere Kapazitäten). Die Netze, die zu den nicht-terminalen Syntaxbäumen gehören, lassen sich durch ihre Knotennamen und Kommentare unmittelbar pragmatisch interpretieren. Bevor eine operationale Interpretation als Transitionsnetze möglich ist, muß noch derjenige Teil der Semantik berücksichtigt werden, der nicht der syntaktischen Struktur des Programms folgt.

Dazu gehört alles, was mit der Deklaration und Benutzung von Identifizierern zusammenhängt. Auf jede Deklaration können null oder mehr Benutzungen Bezug nehmen. Eine Benutzung im Text einer rekursiven Prozedur kann dynamisch auf verschiedene Deklarationen Bezug nehmen. Dies wird in der Normvorlage wie folgt modelliert: An jeder Deklaration (z.B. einer Variablen) hängen spezielle Knoten, sogenannte Konnektor-Definitionen, als Platzhalter für die Anschlüsse beliebig vieler Benutzungen. An jeder Benutzung hängen Konnektor-Applikationen als Platzhalter für den Anschluß zur dynamisch richtigen Deklaration. Nach Produktion des Netzes (Ersetzen von Knoten durch Teilnetze für alle berücksichtigten dynamischen Aufruf-Kombinationen) wird die Umgebung jeder Konnektor-Applikation mit der Umgebung der zugehörigen Konnektor-Definition verbunden und die Konnektoren werden vernichtet. Das so entstehende Netz kann als Transitionsnetz aufgefaßt werden, das die Semantik des Programms modelliert.

Umwandlung von EPOS-Spezifikationen in Petri-Netze

P. Göhner
Gesellschaft für Prozeßrechnerprogrammierung mbH
Balanstr. 136 - 138, 8000 München 90

EPOS (Entwurfsunterstützendes Prozeß - orientiertes Spezifikationssystem) ist ein Software-Werkzeug für Projektierung, Entwicklung, Inbetriebnahme, Wartung und Handhabung von Realzeitsystemen. Im Gegensatz zu anderen Spezifikations- und Entwurfssystemen, die lediglich bestimmte Phasen des Entwicklungsganges unterstützen, wurde bei der Konzipierung von EPOS großer Wert darauf gelegt, ein durchgängiges System von der Beschreibung der Aufgabenstellung im Pflichtenheft bis zur Programmierung bzw. bis zur Realisierung von Hardwareteilen bereitzustellen.

Entsprechend der Zielsetzung, die Entwicklung von Realzeitsystemen zu beschreiben, besitzt EPOS Ausdruckmittel für die Spezifikation von parallelen Rechenprozessen, für die Spezifikation von Resourcen und für die Spezifikation der erforderlichen Synchronisierung, wobei eine weitreichende Rechnerunterstützung sowohl hinsichtlich Analyse als auch hinsichtlich Dokumentation zur Verfügung steht.

Eine wesentliche Eigenschaft von EPOS-Spezifikation ist die rechnergestützte Umwandlung in Petri-Netze, wodurch einerseits die in der Petri-Netz-Theorie entwickelten Theoreme bei der Analyse benutzt werden können, andererseits das Zusammenwirken paralleler Rechenprozesse graphisch dargestellt werden kann.

Die Abbildung von EPOS-Spezifikationen in Petri-Netze ist auf zwei verschiedene Weisen möglich. Einerseits können die Rechenprozesse zusammen mit der aktionsorientierten Spezifikation der Synchronisierung in Petri-Netze umgewandelt werden, zum anderen können ausgehend von der Spezifikation der Resourcen und der erlaubten Zugriffe auf Resourcen Petri-Netze abgeleitet werden. Durch diese redundante Darstellung ist es möglich, bereits während des Entwurfs umfangreiche Prüfungen hinsichtlich der Konsistenz der Spezifikationen durchzuführen, indem die beiden Petri-Netzgraphen miteinander verglichen werden.

Da Petri-Netze auf jeder Entwurfsebene, d.h. mit beliebigem Feinheitsgrad generiert werden können, stellen sie ein wertvolles Hilfsmittel für die Dokumentation und für die Kommunikation dar. Zusätzlich können sie zusammen mit den Informationen in der EPOS-Datenbank als Basis für ein Simulationsmodell benützt werden, mit dem während des gesamten Entwurfs Analysen durchgeführt werden können.

Entwurfstechnologie auf der Grundlage von Petri-Netzen

W. K. Hackmann, E. Rudolph, H. Seidl
SIEMENS AG, D AP GE TKS, München

Softwaresysteme haben inzwischen Größenordnungen erreicht, bei denen nur durch konsequent ingenieursmäßigen Entwurf eine zuverlässige Planung gewährleistet werden kann. Es steht außer Frage, daß die überkommenen Planungs- und Entwurfsmethoden vielen heutigen Anforderungen nicht mehr gewachsen sind.

Petri-Netze gestatten es, eine Reihe von Entwurfsfehlern schon in der informationellen Ebene zu erkennen. Sie sind ein formales Mittel, mit dem man die "Kausalstruktur" eines Modells beschreiben kann. Außerdem sind sie benutzerfreundlich, da der Entwurf graphisch durchführbar ist.

Aus diesen und anderen Gründen wurde eine Entwurfstechnologie auf der Basis von Petri-Netzen entwickelt. Hierzu gehört ein Methodenpaket (PEM) und eine Rechnerunterstützung (PES).

Das Petri-Netz-Entwurfssystem PES dient vornehmlich der beim Entwurf komplexer Systeme der unterschiedlichsten Art auftretenden Massenprobleme.

PES besteht aus den Komponenten SYNTHESE, AKTIVIERUNG, ANALYSE und GRAFIK. Mit diesen lassen sich Netze aufbauen und manipulieren, Schaltvorgänge durchführen, kritische Eigenschaften ermitteln, andere Netzstrukturen ableiten sowie Protokolle und verschiedene graphische Darstellungen gewinnen. Ein Datenbankanschluß ist derzeit in Arbeit.

PES befindet sich kurz vor dem Abschluß der Erprobungsphase; für 1981 ist mit der Freigabe des Systems zu rechnen. Zur Demonstration des Leistungsumfangs werden einige Beispiele aus der praktischen Arbeit vorgestellt.

Modellieren und Simulieren mit dem Blockorientierten Interaktiven Simulationssystem BORIS

W. K. Hackmann, P. Theobald
SIEMENS AG, D AP GE TKS, München

Mit zunehmender Komplexität von Hard- und Softwaresystemen wird es immer häufiger erforderlich, vor der Realisierung Prognosen über das Verhalten der Systeme abzugeben. Dies kann mit der Erstellung von Simulationsmodellen und der Durchführung von Experimenten mit diesen Modellen erreicht werden.

Dazu wird ein Blockorientiertes Interaktives Simulationssystem (BORIS) entwickelt. Als Bestandteil einer sehr allgemein anwendbaren Entwurfstechnologie unterstützt es jede Phase des Modellierens und Simulierens.

Der Modellaufbau erfolgt aus Grundelementen, die zu Netzen zusammengefaßt werden können, welche dann ihrerseits Elemente einer höheren Repertoirestufe bilden. Die Repertoire-Bausteine sind als Prozeduren in jeder geeigneten Programmiersprache kodierbar.

Das derzeit noch in Entwicklung befindliche Simulationssystem BORIS wird unter software-technologischen Gesichtspunkten vorgestellt. Beschrieben werden die Struktur und die Funktionen des Definitions- und des Ablaufteils sowie die Eigenschaften der Anwenderschnittstelle. Besondere Erwähnung verdienen die Interaktionsmöglichkeiten.

Für immer wiederkehrende Fragestellungen und zur Entlastung von Routinearbeiten wird derzeit ein Repertoire vielseitig verwendbarer Bausteine entwickelt. Daneben entsteht ein Repertoire zur Simulation des Datenbanksystems UDS. Weitere Repertoires sind geplant.

Der Einsatz des Simulationssystems wird an einigen Beispielen demonstriert. Es wird angenommen, daß BORIS zum Jahreswechsel 198o/81 für erste Pilotanwendungen zur Verfügung stehen wird.

BEDIENUNGSSYSTEME MIT UNTERBRECHUNGEN

Bernd Meister

IBM Forschungslaboratorium Zürich
8803 Rüschlikon, Schweiz

Es wird das Warteschlangensystem mit einer Bedienungsstation untersucht, wobei diese Bedienungsstation ihre Arbeit für eine Pausenzeit von zufälliger Länge unterbrechen kann. Die Bedienungszeitverteilung ist beliebig, der Eingangsprozess ist Poisson oder ein zusammengesetzter Poissonprozess.

Es werden die Wartezeiten für verschiedene Verteilungen der Pausendauer verglichen. Dabei bestehen drei Möglichkeiten für den Beginn einer Pause: a) zu einem beliebigen Zeitpunkt (unterbrechende Pause), b) nach Beendigung der Verarbeitung einer Anforderung und c) nach Beendigung der Abarbeitung aller in der Warteschlange wartenden Anforderungen. In den Fällen a) und b) wird das betrachtete System auf ein Wartesystem mit zwei Warteschlangen zurückgeführt. Die zulässigen Pausenzeitverteilungen ergeben sich dann mit Hilfe des Satzes von Lagrange. Im Fall c) kann die Pausenzeitverteilung beliebig sein. Je nach dem untersuchten Fall hängt der Erwartungswert der Wartezeit nur vom Mittelwert oder auch von den ersten zwei Momenten der Pausenzeitverteilung ab.

Modelle dieser Art beschreiben die Unterbrechung durch äussere Ereignisse (interrupts), durch Anforderungen mit höheren Prioritäten oder durch notwendige Wartungs- oder Reparaturarbeiten.

ENTWURF UND IMPLEMENTIERUNG EINER SYSTEMUMGEBUNG FÜR ZEITDISKRETE SIMULATION IN PASCAL : PASIM

J.Reyes G.Roehmer
Institut für angewandte
elektronische Datenverarbeitung

Die Motivation für die Entwicklung von PASIM war, die Simulation von zeitdiskreten Systemen in Pascal zu ermöglichen. Dies erschien aufgrund der Verbreitung von Pascal auf Kleinrechnern sinnvoll. Von den bestehenden Simulationsmethoden haben wir uns für die prozeßorientierte entschieden, da sie die benutzerfreundlichste Eigenschaften aufweist. Bei dem Entwurf von PASIM wurde auf eine Modularstruktur geachtet, was unter anderem die Anforderung, ein portables Paket zu entwickeln, unterstützt. Die Realisierung dieses Vorhabens wird auf sprachlicher Ebene durchgeführt; dies impliziert, daß keine Änderungen im Compiler vorgenommen werden. Die zur Verfügung gestellten Sprachkonstrukte orientieren sich an den allgemein bekannten namens- und funktionsgleichen Begriffen anderer Sprachen : activate, hold und passivate.

Simula ähnliche Prozesse werden in PASIM mittels Prozeduren realisiert in deren Rumpf die Sprachkonstrukte process (name) und terminate appliziert werden.

Das Benutzermodell wird in die Prozedur MAINPROCESS eingebettet, in deren Rumpf sich sämtliche Prozessroutinen mittels init (process) identifizieren. Weiter kann der Benutzer hier die zur Verfügung gestellten Protokollroutinen aufrufen.

Die Prozeßkommunikation wird durch die Kernmodule Ereignis-, Prozeßliste und ein externes Modul, das das Koroutinenkonzept realisiert, sichergestellt.

Die Ereignisse werden in einer indexsequentiellen Liste verwaltet, wobei eine Reihe von Dummypointern diese Organisation unterstützt. In einer alphabetisch indizierten Liste werden die Namen der Benutzerprozesse eingeordnet und festgehalten. Beide Listen sind miteinander verkettet. Das Zusammenspiel beider Listen steuert das dynamische Verhalten des Modells.

Das Koroutinenkonzept läßt sich mit Hilfe zweier externer low-level Routinen realisieren. Beim Setzen eines Interaktionspunktes in einer Prozeßroutine wird der aktuelle Zustand des Prozeßes in der

Verwaltung zwecks späterer Reaktivierung festgehalten. Das geschieht durch die Manipulation des Verwaltungsteils von Prozeduren, ohne die Struktur der P4-Maschine zu verletzen. Dies genügt auch der Anforderung, den Compiler unberührt zu lassen. Diese Primitiven stellen den einzigen und eigentlichen maschinenabhängigen Teil des gesamten Pakets dar.

Ein weiteres Modul stellt Zufallszahlengeneratoren verschiedener Verteilungen zur Verfügung. Für ihre Periodenlänge empfiehlt es sich, die volle Wortlänge der jeweiligen Maschine auszunutzen, obwohl der Urgenerator auch auf sprachlicher Ebene zu formulieren gewesen wäre.

Durch die falsche Anwendung der Sprachkonstrukte werden neue Fehlermöglichkeiten kreiert. Eine hinreichende Fehlerbehandlung ist implementiert.

A Segment-Flow Model of Distributed Computing

H.J.Jeanrond, M.R. King, N. Shelness
University of Edinburgh
Computer Science Department

Summary: The aim of the project is to construct an operating system supporting the distribution of application programs over a number of (identical) computers, called "sites". The component parts of such a program, called "domains", communicate by sending "segments" to one another. Applications do not depend on the number of available sites: several domains can be held in one site (time sharing). A domain can run in any site unless it is tied to a resource that is itself tied to a site.

In slightly more detail the model of computation is as follows: Domains consist of a fixed number of segments marked by labels. (k-tuple of segments; labels mark slots in the k-tuple.)

Domains communicate by transfers of segments using the labels to specify the destinations. (Addressing of slots rather than domains as a whole.) For any transfer of a segment one may specify an effect: A segment may be retained (transfer a copy) or given up. Segments arriving at a slot are queued there in the order of their arrival. The labels, called "targets", are kept in special segments but otherwise are like any other data. This allows the "interconnection structure" of domains to change dynamically with segment transfers.

Execution Rule: A domain can only run if all its segments are present.

The hardware available to the project is a configuration of three interconnected Ferranti Argus 700 minicomputers, each consisting of an Argus 700 G as the main processor, 32 k (16 bit) words of store, and an additional Argus 700 F processor, working on the same memory, used as a "transfer-processor".

The language used is IMP 77 extended with transfer commands.

Experiments with the implementation are directed towards gaining insight into the following problems:

How critical are the size of segments and the bandwidth and topology of the interconnection medium? How resilient can the system be made with respect to partial failures, e.g. sites going down, partial communications breakdown? To what extent can we distribute single applications?

Statische Analyse des Echtzeitverhaltens von Softwaresystemen im DARTS-Entwurfssytem

Dipl.-Inform. Hans-H. Meyer
Dipl.-Math. Werner Tesch
GEI-Gesellschaft für elektronische Informationsverarbeitung mbH
Albert-Einstein-Str. 61
5100 Aachen

Im Rahmen der Entwicklung des rechnergestützten Entwurfssytems für Echtzeitsysteme - DARTS Design Aid for Real-Time Systems - (gefördert mit Mitteln des 3. DV-Programms der Bundesregierung) wird ein Verfahren entwickelt, das schon zum Entwurfszeitpunkt eine Analyse des zu erwartenden Echtzeitverhaltens ermöglicht.

Dabei wird der Systementwurf auf korrekte Synchronisation, Interruptverhalten, Deadlockfreiheit, Resourcenverwendung und isolierte Teile untersucht.

Das Verfahren beruht auf einer statischen Analyse des in der DARTS-Sprache beschriebenen Entwurfes. Zu diesem Zweck werden alle echtzeitrelevanten Sprachelemente aus dem Entwurf extrahiert und auf Activity-Vektoren abgebildet. Diese Activity-Vektoren repräsentieren die parallel ablauffähigen Teile des zu realisierenden Systems.

Im ersten Schritt der Analyse wird untersucht, welche Activity-Vektoren 'gleichzeitig' bearbeitet werden müssen, d.h. welche parallel ablauffähigen Teile des Systems aufgrund von Aktivierungen (intern oder per Interrupt) parallel ablaufen können. Diese Vektoren werden dann weiterverarbeitet bis sie entweder abgearbeitet sind, d.h. der durch einen Vektor dargestellte 'Prozeß' ist beendet, oder bis ein Wartezustand, hervorgerufen durch ein Synchronisationselement, erreicht wird. Sind alle betrachteten Vektoren soweit analysiert, wird im zweiten Schritt der Analyse eine Konfliktauflösung versucht, die u.a. Aufschluß darüber gibt, ob eine Synchronisation korrekt ist oder nicht.

Die Ergebnisse dieser Analysephase ergeben die Aussagen über das zu erwartende Echtzeitverhalten.

Die statische Analyse wird zur Zeit in das DARTS-Entwurfssystem implementiert.

Lokalitätsverhalten bei der Pufferung von Magnetplatten-Zugriffen

M. Blum, J. Höhne
Siemens AG
8000 München 70

Die hierarchische Gliederung aller in einer Datenverarbeitungsanlage benötigten Speichersysteme kann erhebliche Vorteile bei der Auslastung des Zentralprozessors bringen. Ein Schritt auf diesem Weg wäre das Einfügen einer weiteren Speicherebene zwischen Arbeits- und Magnetplattenspeicher; diese Pufferstufe (Arbeitsweise ähnlich dem Cache vor dem Hauptspeicher) soll die große Geschwindigkeitslücke zwischen den beiden Speichersystemen schließen.

Für die Arbeitsweise dieser Pufferstufe ist das Zugriffsverhalten zu den Plattengeräten von entscheidender Bedeutung. Für das Siemens-Betriebssystem BS2000 wurden mit Hilfe eines Software-Monitors I/O-Auftragsparameter aufgezeichnet und anschließend gerätespezifisch ausgewertet; die entsprechenden Geräteadressen wurden dabei bis auf Spurbasis aufgelöst.

Analysiert man einen vom Data-Management-System (DMS) verursachten Adresstrom in Hinblick auf die Ansprechhäufigkeit der einzelnen Plattenspuren, zeigen sich mehrere eindeutig begrenzte Bereiche mit hohen I/O-Aufkommen; die Ansprechhäufigkeit der einzelnen Spuren in einem bestimmten Bereich kann dabei recht unterschiedlich sein, wobei in manchen Fällen Erklärungen auf Grund der verwendeten Zugriffmethode geliefert werden können. Eine Auswertung der Spurdifferenz zweier aufeinander folgender Plattenzugriffe zeigt, daß mit großer Wahrscheinlichkeit sequentiell die Spur abgearbeitet und dann zu einer der beiden Nachbarspuren gewechselt wird. Größere Sprünge sind relativ selten und führen dann meistens zu einem Wechsel des Zugriffsbereichs. Dabei fällt auf, daß die Anzahl der Aussprünge etwa gleich der Zahl der Einsprünge in den Bereich ist; die Übergangswahrscheinlichkeit zwischen zwei Bereichen ist für beide Richtungen fast identisch.

Die Analyse des Adresstroms eines Paging-Bereiches zeigt dagegen eine fast gleichmäßige Zugriffshäufigkeit für alle erlaubten Spuren; die Auswertung der auftretenden Spurdifferenzen bietet das gesamte Spektrum erlaubter Sprünge mit leichter Bevorzugung kleiner Differenzen.

Die hohe Lokalitätsbildung der DMS-Zugriffe führt zu einer hohen Trefferrate in der Pufferstufe mit einem günstigen Verhältnis von Pufferspeicher- zu eröffneter Plattenspeicher- Kapazität, während der Paging-Algorithmus erst der geänderten Speicherstruktur angepaßt werden müßte.

Inzwischen sind die Einflüsse verschiedener Pufferparameter wie Speicherplatzverwaltung- und Datenersetzungsalgotithmen bekannt; in Zukunft sollen Rückwirkungen des Pufferstufeneinsatzes auf die Performance der Datenverarbeitungsanlage untersucht werden.

RECHNERSIMULATION UND LEISTUNGSMESSUNG IM RAHMEN DER KAPAZITÄTSPLANUNG VON RECHENZENTREN

Dipl.-Ing. J. Riedel
AEG-TELEFUNKEN, Z 3432
Theodor-Stern-Kai 1
6000 Frankfurt (Main)

Im Zuge der immer komplexer werdenden EDV-Anwendungen - besonders auf dem Online-Sektor - gewinnt die richtige Kapazitätsauslegung und das optimale Abstimmen aller Betriebsmittelkomponenten auf die Anwendungen zunehmend an Bedeutung. Eine Fehlanpassung bedeutet nicht nur Ärger (bei schleppender Verarbeitung), sondern auch Mehrkosten, die es zu vermeiden gilt.
Aus diesen Überlegungen heraus ist im Zentralrechenzentrum der AEG-TELEFUNKEN AG ein Programmpaket zur rechnergestützten Kapazitätsplanung von EDV-Anlagen entwickelt worden.
Kernstück dieses Programmpaketes ist ein Simulator, der das Betriebssystem der Anlage (HB 66/60-P unter GCOS) nachbildet. Auf diese Weise ist es möglich, zukünftige Konfigurationen und Anforderungen an den Rechner in ihren Auswirkungen vorherzusagen.
Der Simulator arbeitet mit GPSS-F (FORTRAN), das es gestattet, die Modelle nach dem Bausteinprinzip aufzubauen.
Die Eingabe in den Simulator ist zufallsgesteuert, d.h. es werden Jobs generiert, deren Betriebsmittelanforderung (Speicher, Processorzeit, I/O-Geräte, I/O-Zeit) von Zufallsgeneratoren erzeugt werden, wobei die Häufigkeitsverteilungen empirisch ermittelt werden. Dazu wurde ein Programm geschrieben, das das Job-Accounting auswertet und die Häufigkeitsverteilungen graphisch darstellt.
Zur Validierung des Simulators ist für die Anlage ein Software-Monitor geschrieben worden. Er führt die gleiche Leistungsmessung am Rechner durch, die auch der Simulator für sein "Modell" ausgibt, so daß ein Vergleich Simulator-Echtlauf möglich ist. Da beide übereinstimmen, kann der Simulator als validiert betrachtet werden. Die ersten Experimente mit vergrößerter Anforderung und mit veränderter Konfiguration haben gerade begonnen. Betrachtet man die bisherigen Ergebnisse mit "gesundem Menschenverstand", so erscheinen sie als plausibel, sie allerdings ohne Simulation voraussagen zu wollen, scheitert an der Komplexität sowohl der Anforderungen als auch der Abläufe in einer Rechenanlage.

Ein Compiler für die Register Transfer-Sprache KARL-2

R. Hartenstein, P. Liell
E. Schaaf, B. Weber
Universität Kaiserslautern

Die Register-Transfer-Sprache KARL-2 ist eine Weiterentwicklung der Sprache KARL. Sie stellt zur Entwicklung und Beschreibung von Hardware ähnliche strukturierte Hilfsmittel zur Verfügung wie bisher übliche Programmiersprachen (Anwendung veranschaulicht in /1/ und /2/).
An der Universität Kaiserslautern wurde eine Version implementiert, bei der Compiler und Simulator streng getrennt sind. Übergeben wird ein Zwischencode, RTC (Register-Transfer-Code).

Während KARL-2 an eine Sprache aus der ALGOL-Familie erinnert, ist RTC mit einer Assembler-Sprache zu vergleichen. Jede Zeile beschreibt genau ein Element eines bestimmten Typs, wie z.B. Register, Addierer u.s.w. mit Angabe des Formates und Verweisen auf die Zeilen, die die entsprechenden Eingangsvariablen enthalten. Somit können die im RTC erzeugten Tabellen nicht nur als Eingabe für den Simulator verwendet werden, sondern auch für künftige Erweiterungen des Programmiersystems, etwa zur Erzeugung einer graphischen Ausgabe auf dem Plotter oder zum Anschluß eines Layout-Programms.

Das System ist in PASCAL auf einer SIEMENS 7.738 implementiert. Die LALR (1) - Grammatik /3/,/4/ der Sprache KARL-2 sowie der Parser des Compilers wurden mit Hilfe eines Parser-Generator-Systems (PGS von P. Dencker /5/) entwickelt.

Literaturhinweise:

/1/ R.W. Hartenstein, "Fundamentals of Structured Hardware Design", North Holland Publ. Co., Amsterdam/New York, 1979.

/2/ R.W. Hartenstein, "KARL-Subset Used as a Hardware Design Algebra", Report, Univ. Kaiserslautern 1980, FB Informatik.

/3/ E. Schaaf, "Projektarbeit im Rahmen einer KARL-Implementierung in PASCAL", Univ. Kaiserslautern, FB Informatik, 1979.

/4/ R.W. Hartenstein, P. Liell, E. Schaaf, B. Weber, "The Grammar of KARL-2", Report, Univ. Kaiserslautern, 1980.

/5/ P. Dencker, "Ein neues LALR-System", Diplomarbeit, Univ. Karlsruhe, Institut für Informatik II, 1977.

SOME PROBLEMS IN PARALLEL IMAGE PROCESSOR DESIGN

Prof. G. STAMON - Université de Besançon - France
Dr. B. ZAVIDOVIQUE - Université de Technologie de Compiègne - France

I . We have designed and built a special purpose image acquisition and processing device, SATIR (Système Acquisition et Traitement d'Image pour la Robotique) [1]. This system is organized around a data-flow consisting of successive three-image-row-packs in a kind of pipe-line architecture. It is oriented towards edge-detection and shaping up. Considering its robotic context, the basic concept of the whole study was to be able to get from one given image, simply and in real time, several bilevel images which could be processed again in different ways. This led us to a two-step configuration - binarization and binary processing -

. binarization : based on local adding, absolute values of difference, histogram, thresholding ;

. binary processing : based solely on neighbourhood logic.

II . Such a device was simulated on classical computers (IBM 370-168, VAX 11-780, PDP 8E) and then built. In fact, it is intended to be the unitary processor in a more complicated image processing device. We choose not to associate one processing element to each pixel, which is the present tendency [2] [3] ; in our conception a set of such elements occurs in parallel on to the picture, as necessary. This is done, for instance, in the following ways :

a - processing several resulting transformed multi-or-bi-level images ;

b - processing several preselected images areas, or adaptively defined ones.

Simulation of such parallel processing with the help of a sequential computer brings many difficulties in achievement. It is even less realistic in case of interconnected parallel tasks. So we are now dealing with simultaneous process interaction ability. To this end :

1 . We have arranged several elementary processings into overlapping macroprocedures such as : + thresholding from histogram shape
+ grey scale compression keeping transitions
+ gradient grouping ...

Selection of such macroprocedures was set depending on their frequency in use of SATIR simulation and because they offer a large enough range of possible over-lapping. In addition these are useful for calibration runs which we are performing.

2 . We wrote a coding language for calling these procedures ; then interacting ability can be noticed in parameter transmission

3 . We have applied that to the following procedure : "simultaneous" multilevel processing on one image (equi-class level grouping, histogram level grouping, gradient for example) ; then parallel processing of the three obtained images, till contour following. In that phase, results concerning one obtained image provide some help and verification to the other.

REFERENCES

1. B. ZAVIDOVIQUE and G. STAMON, "SATIR - Image acquisition and Processing System for Robotics", 4th IJCPR, Kyoto, 1978

2. J.B. DUFF, "A user's look at parallel processing", 4th IJCPR, Kyoto, 1978

3. K. MORI and al., "TOSPICS", Toshiba Review, 1977

Overview of the device →

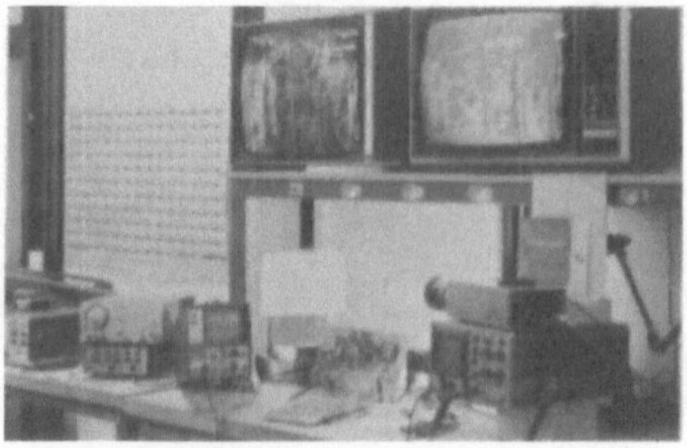

NETZE MIT ZEITVARIANTEN KOMPONENTENVERZÖGERUNGEN

Ipke Wachsmuth

Universität Osnabrück, Fachbereich Mathematik,
Albrechtstr. 28, D-4500 Osnabrück

Es kann gezeigt werden [1], daß sich das Synchronisationsproblem für Zellularautomaten, neben Ansätzen auf Kalkülebene, auch durch ein modifiziertes Automatenkonzept bewältigen läßt:
Durch ein dem Zellularautomaten unterlegtes Netz asynchroner paralleler Automaten wird eine Organisation der Verteilung von Taktsignalen herbeigeführt, die eine "lokal-synchrone" Arbeitsweise der (in der Ebene angeordneten) Zellen eines solchen Polyautomaten ergibt. Kurz gesagt arbeiten benachbarte Zellen im Takt, während weiter auseinander liegende Zellen durchaus im Mißtakt arbeiten können, bei gleichen Berechnungsresultaten wie in einem global-synchronen Automaten. Das für diesen Ansatz entwickelte Konzept des sog. T-Netzes ist hier Gegenstand der Betrachtung.

Um auf die Dauer von Teilprozessen in den Komponenten eines T-Netzes bezugnehmen zu können, wird ein lokales Zeitkonzept eingeführt. Das Verhalten bei der Verteilung von Taktsignalen wird dann unter der (physikalisch motivierten) Annahme untersucht, daß die in den Netzkomponenten dabei auftretenden Verzögerungen zeitlich variieren, wobei eine endliche Variationsbandbreite vorausgesetzt ist. Auf irgendeine Form von Rückmeldungen über die Abwicklung von zur Signalübermittlung führenden Teilprozessen wird dabei verzichtet.

In einem unbeschränkten T-Netz (anders gesagt: falls keine maximale Anzahl von Zellen a priori bekannt ist) kann unter diesen Voraussetzungen die nicht erwünschte Einholung aufeinanderfolgender Taktsignale eintreten. Es kann dann gezeigt werden, daß sich eine solche Einholung durch den Einsatz eines lokalen (keiner globalen Aufsicht unterstellten) Regelungsprozesses aus prinzipiellen Gründen nicht verhindern läßt (Negativresultat). Das bedeutet: Die aus der Annahme zeitvarianter Komponentenverzögerungen erhaltenen Konsequenzen lassen den unbegrenzten Einsatz eines solchen Organisationsschemas nicht zu.

Bei Kenntnis einer maximalen Anzahl von zum Einsatz gelangenden Zellen können Einholungen durch entsprechende Wahl der Taktfrequenz ausgeschlossen werden. Hier kann eine Erhöhung der Taktfrequenz nicht nur durch eine Verkleinerung der Komponentenverzögerungen erreicht werden, sondern - im Gegensatz zu globalen Synchronisationsschemata! - auch durch eine Verkleinerung der Variationsbandbreite, d.h. durch die Verwendung "exakterer" anstelle "schnellerer" physikalischer Bauteile.

[1] Wachsmuth, I.: Locally Synchronous Cellular Automata, preprint, Universität Osnabrück 1980.

INDUKTIVE INFERENZ UND MEHRWERTIGE LOGIK

Claudio Moraga

Abteilung Informatik
Universität Dortmund

Zusammenfassung:

Eine Methode zur Realisierung induktiver Inferenz wird eingeführt, die die Elemente der mehrwertigen Schaltwerktheorie benutzt. Grundannahmen sind: Es existiert irgendeine Anfangsinformation, damit man eine Hypothese konstruieren kann, und es existiert ein nicht immer verfügbares Orakel, das eine Hypothese billigen oder mißbilligen wird.

Als wesentliches Hilfsmittel wird der Begriff der Umgebung für induktive Inferenz eingeführt, welche aus Charakterisierungsparametern der zugrundelegenden Information besteht. Diese Umgebung wird in eine heterogenwertige Kartendarstellung umgestzt, womit man eine Hypothese als minimale Disjunktion von Produktionen lesen kann. Darüber hinaus ermöglichen topologische Merkmale, welche diese Darstellung veranschaulicht, wertvolle strukturelle Hinweise für neue Hypothesen.

Die vorliegende Methode scheint am besten für "langsame" Lernprozesse geeignet, wobei man eine Hypothese eine gewisse Zeit benutzen wird, und eine einfache Hypothesenbeschreibung ist sehr wünscheswert.

Literatur:

Moraga, C.: Inductive Inference using Multiple-valued Logic. Forschungsbericht 88, Abteilung Informatik, Universität Dortmund, (1979).

DEADLOCK PREDICTION USING PETRI NETS

Raymond Schneider
C.R.I.N. Centre de Recherche en Informatique
Laboratoire E.E.A., ENSEM, BP 850 - 54011 Nancy Cédex

Introduction

We are dealing with the deadlock problem resulting from distributed resource allocation in real-time systems having no central control over the different processes of the application. These processes are distributed among several machines, and need a set of common distributed resources to cooperate or to run concurrently. The resources are allocated by several controllers after request from the process. Each controller is able to avoid deadlock locally ; but the controllers are to be throught as new processes running concurrently and so may cause an allocation deadlock.

Petri Net Generation

The whole application is described in a high level language, where processes are completely specified as a set of interconnected modules. Synchronization is achieved by mean of the data flow between modules /THOMESSE 80/. This description is used to generate a Petri Net possessing the same behavior as the application. This is done by making a correspondance between modules and transitions, software or physical resources and places, data flow and flow relation /SCHNEIDER 80/.

Deadlock prediction

Allocations made by controllers are defined as injective applications from the set of places to the set of transitions. A set of transitions is said to be deadlockable if there is some allocation, where no transition of this set has all its input places allocated. We, now characterize, special subsets of transitions. Using the conflict situation, we define the relation "can be in conflict with" between two transitions having some common input place and deduce an equivalence relation from this relation. Special subsets called equivalence classes with body can be proved to be the only one causing allocation deadlocks.

Discussion

This result is useful in distributed systems where controllers achieve sharing of resources by controlling exclusive subsets of resources. Each request is then decomposed according to a fixed order and each subrequest is activated only if the preceding one have been satisfied. If a controller manages all the resources corresponding to input places of our conflict class with body, then ordering is not further necessary. Another helpfull result would occur, if the generated Petri Net would be without conflict classes with body. In such a case, no deadlock could occur between the different controllers.

References : /THOMESSE 80/ SYGARE : Une structuration pour la conception d'applications en temps réel et réparties. Thèse d'Etat, Nancy, mai 1980.

/SCHNEIDER 80/ Les réseaux de Pétri dans l'aide à la conception d'applications temps réel réparties. Congrès AFCET, Nancy, novembre 1980.